ENGINEERING PROBLEM SOLVING WITH C++

Third Edition

Delores M. Etter
Electrical Engineering Department
Southern Methodist University, Dallas, TX

Jeanine A. Ingber
Accurate Solutions in Applied Physics, LLC

Boston   Columbus   Indianapolis   New York   San Francisco   Upper Saddle River
Amsterdam   Cape Town   Dubai   London   Madrid   Milan   Munich   Paris   Montréal   Toronto
Delhi   Mexico City   São Paulo   Sydney   Hong Kong   Seoul   Singapore   Taipei   Tokyo

Vice President and Editorial Director, ECS: Marcia Horton

Editor-in-Chief: Michael Hirsch

Executive Editor: Tracy Dunkelberger

Editorial Assistant: Stephanie Sellinger

Vice President, Marketing: Patrice Jones

Marketing Manager: Yezan Alayan

Marketing Coordinator: Kathryn Ferranti

Marketing Assistant: Emma Snider

Vice President, Production: Vince O'Brien

Managing Editor: Jeff Holcomb

Production Project Manager: Kayla Smith-Tarbox

Senior Operations Supervisor: Alan Fischer

Manufacturing Buyer: Lisa McDowell

Art Director: Anthony Gemmellaro

Cover Designer: Anthony Gemmellaro

Manager, Visual Research: Karen Sanatar

Photo Researcher: Lily Ferguson, Bill Smith Group

Cover Art: Mars: U.S. Geological Survey/Photo Researchers, Inc. Arabia Dunes: NASA/JPL-Caltech/ASU

Media Editor: Daniel Sandin

Media Project Manager: John Cassar

Full-Service Project Management and Composition: Integra

Printer/Binder: Edwards Brothers

Cover Printer: Lehigh-Phoenix Color/Hagerstown

Text Font: 10/12, TimesNewRoman

Credits and acknowledgements borrowed from other sources and reproduced, with permission, are as follows: Chapter 1 opener NASA/Ames Research Center; Figure 1.1 © Adam Hart-Davis/Photo Researchers, Inc.; Figure 1.2 © Dr. Jeremy Burgess/Photo Researchers, Inc.; Figure 1.3 © Photo by Hulton Archive/Getty Images; Figure 1.4 © Science Source/Photo Researchers, Inc.; Figure 1.5 © AP Photo/Gautam Singh; Chapter 2 opener © yuyangc/Shutterstock.com; Chapter 3 opener © Mira.com/Howie Garber; Chapter 4 opener © Peter Calamai/Toronto Star/Toronto Star/Newscom; Chapter 5 opener © NASA/Science Source/Photo Researchers, Inc.; Chapter 6 opener © NASA/Science Source/Photo Researchers, Inc.; Chapter 7 opener © HO/AFP/Getty Images/Newscom; Chapter 8 opener © NASA/Jet Propulsion Laboratory; Chapter 9 opener © Warren Faidley/Photolibrary; Chapter 10 opener © Garry Gay/Alamy; Figure 10.1(a, b, and c) © NASA/JPL/Ames Research Center; Insert photo I.1 © NOAA/Science Photo Library; Insert photo I.2 and I.3 © Ilene MacDonald/Alamy; Insert photo I.4, I.5, I.6 © Mehau Kulyk/Photo Researchers, Inc.; Insert photo I.7 © NASA/Photo Researchers, Inc.; Insert photo I.8 and I.9 © NASA/Jet Propulsion Laboratory; Insert photo I.10 © Scott White/UIUC/Photo Researchers; Insert photo I.11 © Image generated by Robert F. Tomaro and Kenneth E. Wurtzler, Computational Sciences Branch, Air Vehicles Directorate, Air Force Research Laboratory.; Insert photo I.12 © Ramon Santos/Photo Researchers, Inc.; Screenshots pg. 69–76, 123–128 © Oracle Corporation; Screenshots pg. 170–174 © Microsoft Corporation.

Microsoft® and Windows® are registered trademarks of the Microsoft Corporation in the U.S.A. and other countries. Screen shots and icons reprinted with permission from the Microsoft Corporation. This book is not sponsored or endorsed by or affiliated with the Microsoft Corporation.

Copyright © 2012, 2008, 2003 Pearson Education, Inc., publishing as Prentice Hall 501 Boylston Street, Suite 900, Boston, MA 02116. All rights reserved. Printed in the United States of America. This publication is protected by Copyright, and permission should be obtained from the publisher prior to any prohibited reproduction, storage in a retrieval system, or transmission in any form or by any means, electronic, mechanical, photocopying, recording, or likewise. To obtain permission(s) to use material from this work, please submit a written request to Pearson Education, Inc., Permissions Department, One Lake Street, Upper Saddle River, New Jersey 07458, or you may fax your request to 201-236-3290.

Many of the designations by manufacturers and sellers to distinguish their products are claimed as trademarks. Where those designations appear in this book, and the publisher was aware of a trademark claim, the designations have been printed in initial caps or all caps.

Library of Congress Cataloging-in-Publication Data

Etter, D. M.

Engineering problem solving with C++ / Delores M. Etter, Jeanine A. Ingber.—3rd ed.

p. cm.

Includes bibliographical references and index.

ISBN 978-0-13-249265-2

1. C++ (Computer program language). 2. Engineering—Data processing.

I. Ingber, Jeanine A. II. Title.

QA76.73.C153E58 2012

620.00285 ' 5117—dc23

2011033021

10 9 8 7 6 5 4 3 2 1—EB—14 13 12 11

ISBN 10:   0-13-249265-2

ISBN 13: 978-0-13-249265-2

In loving memory of our fathers:

Murvin Lee Van Camp,
a loving and supportive father
—Delores

Robert William Huckell,
a generous and thoughtful man
—Jeanine

Contents

3 Control Structures: Selection   94

ENGINEERING CHALLENGE: Global Change

4 Control Structures: Repetition   138

ENGINEERING CHALLENGE: Data Collection

5 Working with Data Files 180

ENGINEERING CHALLENGE: Weather Prediction

6 Modular Programming with Functions 224

ENGINEERING CHALLENGE: Simulation

7   One-Dimensional Arrays   308

ENGINEERING CHALLENGE: Tsunami Warning Systems

Preface

The C++ programming language is derived from the C programming language, with added features to support object-oriented programming through the use of classes and programmer-defined types. The features of the C programming language that make it attractive for system-level operations and embedded programming are also supported by C++, making C++ one of the most powerful and versatile programming languages available—and a good choice for an introduction to computing course for scientists and engineers. This text was written to introduce engineering problem solving with C++ and also the object-oriented features of the C++ programming language. Our objectives are the following:

- to develop a consistent **methodology for solving engineering problems**
- to present the **object-oriented features of C++**, while focusing on the **fundamentals of programming and problem solving**
- to illustrate a problem-solving process with C++ through a variety of **engineering examples and applications**
- to provide an easy-to-understand, **integrated introduction to data types, functions, and container classes defined in the C++ Standard Template Library**

To accomplish these objectives, Chapter 1 presents a **five-step process** that is used consistently in the rest of the text for solving engineering problems. Chapter 2 introduces the **built-in data types** supported by C++ and provides an introduction to **classes**, **pre-defined objects**, and **member functions** that support **standard input and output**. Chapters 3–6 present the fundamental capabilities of C++ for solving engineering problems, including **control structures, data files, functions**, and **programmer-defined data types**. Chapters 7 and 8 present **arrays**, **vectors**, and the **string class**. Chapter 9 introduces the use of **pointers**, **dynamic memory allocation**, and **linked data structures**. Chapter 10 provides a more in-depth look at some advanced topics, including **function templates, class templates, recursive member functions, inheritance**, and **virtual functions**. Throughout all these chapters, we present a large number of examples from many different **engineering, science**, and **computer science disciplines**. The solutions to these examples are developed using the five-step process and Standard C++.

Features of the Third Edition

The third edition of our text:

- Introduces students to three integrated development environments (IDEs)
  - NetBeans
  - MS Visual Studio
- Includes new engineering applications using global positioning system (GPS) data and data used with tsunami warning systems.
- Includes coverage of bitwise operators.

- Has expanded coverage of control structures.

- Introduces classes and the development of programmer-defined data types early in the text as optional chapter sections, for flexibility.

- Integrates coverage of classes throughout the text and offers a comparison of standard and object-based solutions.

- Includes additional Statement Boxes, Program Traces and Memory Snapshots, and flowcharts.

Student Resources and an Instructor's Resource Center (IRC) are available online at www.pearsonhighered.com/etter.

Prerequisites

No prior experience with the computer is assumed. The mathematical prerequisites are **college algebra and trigonometry**. Of course, the initial material can be covered much faster if the student has used other computer languages or software tools.

Course Structure

The material in these chapters was selected to provide the basis for a one-term course in engineering and scientific computing. These chapters contain the essential topics of mathematical computations, character data, control structures, functions, arrays, classes, and pointers. Students with a background in another computer language should be able to complete this material in one semester. A minimal course that provides only an introduction to C++ can be designed using the nonoptional sections of the text. (Optional sections are indicated in the Contents with an asterisk.) Three ways to use the text, along with the recommended chapter sections, are

- **Introduction to C++** Many freshman introductory courses introduce the student to several computer tools in addition to language. For these courses, we recommend covering the nonoptional sections of Chapters 1–8. This material presents to students the fundamental capabilities of C++, and they will then be able to write substantial programs using mathematical computations, character data, control structures, programmer-defined data types, functions, and arrays.

- **Problem Solving with C++** In a semester course devoted specifically to teaching students to master the C++ language, we recommend covering all nonoptional sections of Chapters 1–10. This material covers all the fundamental concepts of the C++ language, including mathematical computations, character data, control structures, functions, arrays, classes, templates, and pointers.

- **Problem Solving with C++ and Numerical Techniques** Upper-level students or students who are already familiar with other high-level languages will be able to cover the material in this text very quickly. In addition, they will be able to apply the numerical-technique material to their other courses. Therefore, we recommend that these students cover all sections of Chapters 1–10, including the optional material.

The chapters in this text were designed to give the instructor flexibility in the ordering of topics. Coverage of programmer-defined types and classes is incorporated throughout the text, beginning with Chapter 2. However, coverage of classes is placed at the end of each chapter, in an optional section. A dependency chart is provided on the next page for illustration.

Dependency Chart

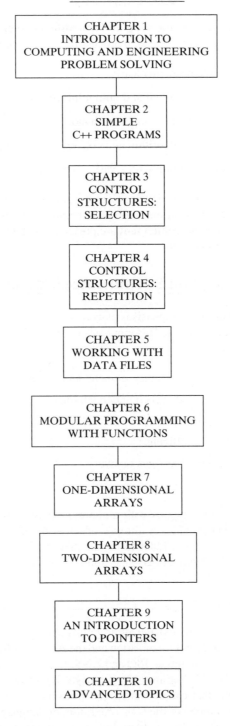

Problem-Solving Methodology

The **emphasis on engineering and scientific problem solving** is an integral part of the text. Chapter 1 introduces a five-step process for solving engineering problems using the computer:

1. State the problem clearly.

2. Describe the input and output information, and determine required data types.

3. Work a simple example by hand.

4. Develop an algorithm and convert it to a computer program.

5. Test the solution with a variety of data.

To reinforce the development of problem-solving skills, each of these five steps is clearly identified each time a complete engineering problem is solved. In addition, **top-down design** and **stepwise refinement** are presented with the use of **decomposition outlines**, **pseudocode**, and **flowcharts**.

Engineering and Scientific Applications

Throughout the text, emphasis is placed on incorporating real-world engineering and scientific examples and problems. This emphasis is centered around a theme of engineering challenges, which include

- prediction of weather, climate, and global change
- computerized speech understanding
- image processing
- artificial intelligence
- enhanced oil and gas recovery
- simulation

Each chapter begins with a photograph and a discussion of an aspect of one of these challenges that provides a glimpse of some of the exciting and interesting areas in which engineers might work. Later in the chapter, we solve a problem that not only relates to the introductory problem, but also has applications in other problem solutions.

Standard C++

The statements presented and all programs developed use C++ standards developed by the International Standards Organization and the American National Standards Institute (ISO/ANSI) C++ Standards committee. ISO and ANSI together have published the first international standard for the C++ programming language. By using Standard C++, students learn to write **portable** code that can be transferred from one computer platform to another. Many of the standard capabilities of the C++ programming language are discussed in the text. Additional components of the C++ standard library are discussed in Appendix A.

Software Engineering Concepts

Engineers and scientists are expected to develop and implement user-friendly and **reusable** computer solutions. Learning software engineering techniques is therefore crucial. **Readability** and **documentation** are stressed in the development of programs. Additional topics that relate to software engineering are discussed throughout the text and include issues such as **software life cycle**, **portability**, **maintenance**, **modularity**, **recursion**, **abstraction**, **reusability**, **structured programming**, **validation**, and **verification**.

Four Types of Problems

Learning any new skill requires practice at a number of different levels of difficulty. We have developed four types of exercises that are used throughout the text to develop problem-solving skills. The first set of exercises is **Practice!** problems. These are short-answer questions that relate to the section of material just presented. Most sections are immediately followed by a set of **Practice!** problems so that students can determine if they are ready to continue to the next section. Complete solutions to all the **Practice!** problems are included at the end of the text.

The **Modify!** problems are designed to provide hands-on experience with example programs and the programs developed in the **Problem Solving Applied** sections. In these sections, we develop a complete C++ program using the five-step process. The **Modify!** problems ask students to run the program with different sets of data, to test their understanding of how the program works and of the relationships among the engineering variables. These exercises also ask the students to make simple modifications to the program and then run the program to test their changes.

All chapters end with a set of **Exam Practice!** problems, and every chapter includes a set of **Programming Problems**. The **Exam Practice!** problems are short-answer questions that relate to the material covered in the chapter. These problems help students determine how well they understand the features of C++ presented in the chapter. The **Programming Problems** are new problems that relate to a variety of engineering applications, and the level of difficulty ranges from very straightforward to longer project assignments. Each programming problem requires that the student develop a complete C++ program or function. Engineering data sets for many of the problems are included within the Instructor's Resource Center to use in testing. Also provided within the IRC are solutions to all of the **Exam Practice!** problems and **Programming Problems**.

Study and Programming Aids

Statement Boxes, UML diagrams, and Program Traces provide easily accessible visual illustrations of important concepts. **Margin notes** are used to help the reader not only identify the important concepts, but also easily locate specific topics. In addition, margin notes are used to identify programming style guidelines and debugging information. **Style guidelines** show students how to write C++ programs that incorporate good software discipline; **debugging** sections help students recognize common errors so that they can avoid them. The programming style notes are indicated with the margin note **Style**, and the debugging notes with a **bug**

icon. Object-oriented features of C++ display an OOP icon to help students recognize these features early in the text. Each Chapter Summary contains a **summary of the style notes** and **debugging notes**, plus a list of the **Key Terms** from the chapter and a **C++ Statement Reference** of the new statements, to make the book easy to use as a reference.

Optional Numerical Techniques

Numerical techniques that are commonly used in solving engineering problems are also discussed in optional sections in the chapters, and include **interpolation**, **linear modeling (regression)**, **root finding**, **numerical integration**, and the **solution to simultaneous equations**. The concept of a **matrix** is also introduced and then illustrated using a number of examples. All of these topics are presented assuming only a trigonometry and college algebra background.

Appendices

To further enhance reference use, the appendices include a number of important topics. Appendix A contains a discussion of components in the C++ standard library. Appendix B presents the ASCII character codes. Appendix D contains a list of references used throughout the text. A MATLAB reference is also included as Appendix C, and solutions to Practice! problems make up Appendix E.

Additional Resources

All instructor and student resources can be accessed at www.pearsonhighered.com/etter. Here, students can access all source code for the book, and instructors can register for the password-protected Instructor's Resource Center. The IRC contains all the example programs used in the text, complete solutions to all the Programming Problems found at the end of each chapter, testbank questions, as well as data files to use with application problems and a complete set of Lecture PowerPoint slides.

Acknowledgments

We would like to thank our outstanding team of reviewers—Roman Tankelevich, Colorado School of Mines; John Sustersic, Penn State University; Tanya L. Crenshaw, University of Portland; Daniel McCracken, City College of New York; Deborah L. Pollio, Virginia Tech; Keith Hellman, Colorado School of Mines; Tammy VanDeGrift, University of Portland; Melanie Ford, Penn State University—Behrend Campus; Amar Raheja, California State Polytechnic University for their detailed and constructive comments and their valuable insights. We would also like to acknowledge and thank our excellent editorial staff, including Tracy Dunkelberger, Stephanie Sellinger, and Emma Snider, for their help in keeping everything on task. Finally, we would like to thank our outstanding production team, including Eric Arima, Kayla Smith-Tarbox, and Lily Ferguson, for their insight and attention to detail.

ENGINEERING PROBLEM SOLVING WITH C++

Third Edition

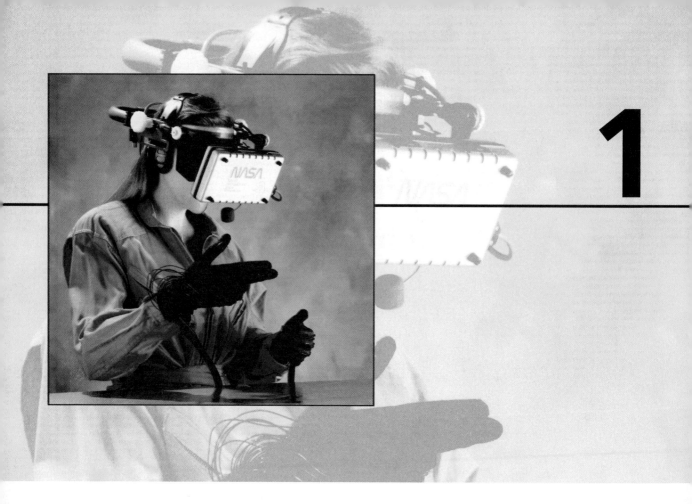

1

INTRODUCTION TO COMPUTING AND ENGINEERING PROBLEM SOLVING

CHAPTER OUTLINE

OBJECTIVES   *In this chapter we provide an introduction to computing and engineering problem solving, including:*

- a brief history of computing
- recent engineering achievements
- a discussion of hardware and software

- a discussion of number systems
- a five-step problem-solving methodology

1.1 Historical Perspective

In the early 1800s, Charles Babbage, an English mathematician, conceptualized a computer, which he called the **Analytical Engine**. Designed to process base ten numbers, the Analytical Engine had four parts: an input device, a "storehouse" or storage unit, a processing unit and an output device. The storage unit consisted of an indefinite number of columns of discs. Each disc was inscribed with the 10 decimal digits (0–9), and rotated about a column. The lowest disc on a column represented the one's position, the next disc the ten's position, the next the hundred's position, and so on up the column. By arranging the discs of one column, a decimal number could be displayed.

In 1842, the French engineer and mathematician, Luigi F. Menabrea, published a paper "Sketch of the Analytical Engine Invented by Charles Babbage, Esq. with notes by translator Ada Lovelace" In his paper, Menabrea described Babbage's vision of a machine capable of solving any problem using inputs, outputs and programs written on punch cards. As you will see in the following sections of this chapter, the Analytical Engine resembles the digital computers we use today in so far as they have input and output devices, storage units and processing units; however, digital computers represent data in base 2 rather than base ten. Although we no longer

3

Analytical Engine, Designed by Charles Babbage

Charles Babbage, 1792–1871

Augusta Ada Byron, 1815–1852

program our computers with punch cards, decks of punch cards were being used for computer programs as late as the 1980s.

Babbage was never able to acquire the financial backing to build his machine. As he realized, few people even understood his concept.

> *To describe . . . the Analytical Engine would require many volumes. I only propose here to indicate a few of its more important functions, and to give to those whose minds are duly prepared for it some information which will remove those vague notions of wonder, and even of its impossibility, with which it is surrounded in the minds of some of the most enlightened.*[1]

One mind that was duly prepared was that of Augusta Ada Byron. Ada Byron was the daughter of the nineteenth century poet Lord Byron and Anna Isabella Milbanke. Shortly after Ada was born, Milbanke left Lord Byron, believing that he was having an affair with his half-sister and that he was insane. Fearing that Ada would inherit her father's insanity, Milbanke, who was herself an amateur mathematician, prescribed for Ada a heavy dose of mathematics and science instruction. In 1842, Ada wrote the English translation of Menabrea's Sketch of the Analytical Engine from its original French text. Her translation included lengthy and extensive commentary and detailed instructions for numerical computations.

Ada Byron also envisioned the multidisciplinary potential of the Analytical Engine, as she expressed in the following commentary included in her translation:

---

[1]Charles Babbage, *Of The Analytical Engine*, 1864.

"Supposing, for instance, that the fundamental relations of pitched sounds in the science of harmony and of musical composition were susceptible of such expression and adaptations, the engine might compose elaborate and scientific pieces of music of any degree of complexity or extent."

According to Babbage,

"The notes of the Countess of Lovelace extend to about three times the length of the original memoir. Their author has entered fully into almost all the very difficult and abstract questions connected with the subject. These two memoirs taken together furnish, to those who are capable of understanding the reasoning, a complete demonstration–That the whole of the developments and operations of analysis are now capable of being executed by machinery."

The demonstrations written by Ada Byron are considered by many to be the first "computer program." The high-level programming language, **Ada**, developed for embedded systems, was named after Ada Byron Lovelace.

The first computing machine actually built that used the binary number system was developed at Iowa State University between 1939 and 1942 by Professor John Atanasoff and his graduate student Clifford Berry. The ABC (Atanasoff Berry Computer) weighted 700 pounds and could calculate about one instruction every 15 seconds. The onset of World War II prevented Atanasoff and Berry from completing their application for a patent, but their work was studied by many, and promoted for its potential in aiding the war effort. In 1943, the U.S. government sponsored a research team to develop a computing machine to calculate artillery-firing tables for weapons. The team was lead by John Mauchly and J. Presper Eckert.

Electronic Numerical Integrator and Calculator (ENIAC)

Their work resulted in the development of the ENIAC (Electronic Numerical Integrator and Calculator). The ENIAC weighed thirty tons and could calculate several hundred operations per second. It was used for research until 1955. Today, processors weigh ounces and are capable of processing trillions of operations per second.

Intel Pentium 4 Processor

1.2 Recent Engineering Achievements

The development of the digital computer has facilitated many significant engineering achievements over the past 5 decades. These achievements illustrate the multidisciplinary nature of engineering and demonstrate how engineering has improved our lives and expanded the possibilities for the future. We now briefly discuss a few of these major achievements.

moon landing

Several major achievements relate to the exploration of space. The **moon landing**, on July 21, 1969, was probably the most complex and ambitious engineering project ever attempted. Major breakthroughs were required in the design of the Apollo spacecraft, the lunar lander, and the three-stage Saturn V rocket. Even the design of the spacesuit was a major engineering project that resulted in a system that included a three-piece suit and backpack, which together weighed 190 pounds. The computer played a key role not only in the designs of the various systems, but it also played a critical role in the communications required during an individual moon flight; a single flight required the coordination of over 450 people in the launch control center and over 7,000 others on 9 ships, in 54 aircraft, and at stations located around the earth.

Mars Global Surveyor
Mars Orbiter Camera
High Gain Antenna

Exploration of space has motivated recent engineering achievements in the collection of scientific data. The **Mars Global Surveyor** was a spacecraft that was developed by NASA and launched in 1996 to collect scientific data while in orbit around the planet Mars. The Mars Global Surveyor carried state of the art science instruments including, the **Mars Orbiter Camera** for acquiring images and the **High Gain Antenna** for sending and receiving data at high rates of speed. The spacecraft made its last communication with earth on

November 2, 2006. You can view a gallery of images acquired by the Mars Orbiter Camera at **http://mars.jpl.nasa.gov/mgs/gallery/images.html**.

Mars
Reconnaissance
Orbiter

Some of the images collected by the Mars Global Surveyor suggest that liquid water has seeped onto the surface in the geologically recent past, leading NASA to develop and launch the **Mars Reconnaissance Orbiter** to begin a search for evidence that water persisted on the surface of the planet long enough to provide a habitat for life. The Mars Reconnaissance Orbiter uses a new spacecraft design provided by Lockheed Martin Space Systems. It is the first spacecraft designed from the ground up for aerobraking, a rigorous phase of the mission where the orbiter uses the friction of the martian atmosphere to slow down and settle into its final orbit around Mars. The Orbiter began its orbit around Mars on March 10, 2006. From March to November of 2006, the spacecraft shrunk its orbit by dipping more than 400 times into the top of the Martian atmosphere to reduce velocity and arrive at its final, nearly circular, orbit at altitudes of 155 to 196 miles.

CRISM

One of six science instruments aboard the Orbiter is the **Compact Reconnaissance Imaging Spectrometer for Mars (CRISM)**, designed and built by the Johns Hopkins University Applied Physics Laboratory in Laurel, Md. CRISM will read 544 colors in reflected sunlight to detect minerals in the surface. Its highest resolution is about 20 times sharper than any previous look at Mars. High-resolution images identify sites most likely to have contained water, and also determine the best potential landing sites for the **Mars Exploration Rovers**. The Mars Exploration Rovers are designed to move across the surface of the planet and examine the soil and rocks in fine detail.

Mars Exploration
Rovers

application
satellites

The space program also provided much of the impetus for the development of **application satellites** that are used to provide weather information, relay communication signals, map uncharted terrain, and provide environmental updates on the composition of the atmosphere. The **Global Positioning System (GPS)** originated as a constellation of 24 satellites that broadcasts position, velocity, and time information worldwide. GPS receivers measure the time it takes for signals to travel from the GPS satellite to the receiver. Using information received from four satellites, a microprocessor in the receiver can then determine very precise measurements of the receiver's location; the accuracy varies from a few meters to centimeters, depending on the computation techniques used.

GPS

advanced
composite materials

The aircraft industry was the first industry to develop and use **advanced composite materials** that consist of materials that can be bonded together in such a way that one material reinforces the fibers of the other material. Advanced composite materials were developed to provide lighter, stronger, and more temperature-resistant materials for aircraft and spacecraft. Additional markets for composites now exist in manufacturing and sporting goods. For example, downhill snow skis use layers of woven Kevlar fibers to increase their strength and reduce weight, and golf club shafts of graphite/epoxy are stronger and lighter than the steel in conventional shafts. Composite materials are also used in the design of prosthetics for artificial limbs.

computer
simulation

The development of advanced composite materials is aided by the use of **computer simulation**. Computer simulation of advanced composite materials allows for experimentation that may not be possible, due to size, speed, dangers to health and safety, or the economics of conducting the experiment. In simulations, mathematical models of physical phenomena are translated into computer software that specifies how calculations are performed. By repeatedly running the software using different data, an understanding of the phenomenon of interest emerges. We will write a program to simulate the design of a molten plastic material developed for insulating critical components in electronic assemblies from thermal and mechanical shock.

CAT scanner

The areas of medicine, bioengineering, and computer science were teamed for the development of the **computerized axial tomography (CAT)** scanner machine. This instrument can generate three-dimensional images or two-dimensional slices of an object using X-rays that are generated from different angles around the object. Each X-ray measures a density from its angle, and very complicated computer algorithms combine the information from all the X-rays to reconstruct a clear image of the inside of the object. CAT scans are routinely used to identify tumors, blood clots, and brain abnormalities. The U.S. Army continues to develop rugged, lightweight CAT scanners that can be transported to medical stations in combat zones.

Lasers

Lasers are light waves that have the same frequency and travel in a narrow beam that can be directed and focused. CO_2 lasers are used to drill holes in materials that range from ceramics to composite materials. Lasers are also used in medical procedures to weld detached retinas, seal leaky blood vessels, vaporize brain tumors, and perform delicate inner-ear surgery. Three-dimensional pictures called holograms are also generated with lasers.

global change

The **prediction of weather, climate, and global change** requires that we understand the coupled atmosphere and ocean biosphere system. This includes understanding CO_2 dynamics in the atmosphere and ocean, ozone depletion, and climatological changes due to the releases of chemicals or energy. This complex interaction also includes solar interactions. A major eruption from a solar storm near a "coronal hole" (a venting point for the solar wind) can eject vast amounts of hot gases from the sun's surface toward the earth's surface at speeds over a million miles per hour. This ejection of hot gases bombards the earth with X-rays, and can interfere with communication and cause power fluctuations in power lines. Learning to predict changes in weather, climate, and global change involves collecting large amounts of data for study and developing new mathematical models that can represent the interdependency of many variables. We will analyze the weather patterns at Denver International Airport over a 1-year period in later chapters. We will also develop a model for predicting ozone mixing ratios in the middle atmosphere using satellite data, and we analyze the altitude and velocity information for a helium-filled weather balloon.

Computerized
speech
understanding

Computerized speech understanding could revolutionize our communication systems, but many problems are involved. Software that teaches a computer to understand words from a rather small vocabulary set is currently in use. However, to develop systems that are speaker-independent and that understand words from large vocabularies and from different languages is very difficult. Subtle changes in one's voice, such as those caused by a cold or stress, can affect the performance of speech-recognition systems. Even assuming that the computer can recognize the words, it is not simple to determine their meaning. Many words are context-dependent, and thus cannot be analyzed separately. Intonation such as raising one's voice can change a statement into a question. Although there are still many difficult problems to address in automatic speech recognition and understanding, exciting applications are everywhere. Imagine a telephone system that determines the languages being spoken and translates the speech signals so that each person hears the conversation in his or her native language. We will analyze actual speech data to demonstrate some of the techniques used in word recognition.

Changing Engineering Environment

The engineer of the 21st century will work in an environment that requires many nontechnical skills and capabilities. Although the computer will be the primary computational tool of most engineers, the computer will also be useful in developing additional nontechnical abilities.

communication
skills

Engineers need strong **communication skills** for both oral presentations and for preparing written materials. Computers provide the software to assist in writing outlines and developing materials and graphs for presentations and technical reports. The problems at the end of this chapter include written and oral presentations to provide practice of these important skills.

design/process/
manufacture

The **design/process/manufacture** path, which consists of taking an idea from a concept to a product, is one that engineers must understand first-hand. Every step of this process uses computers in areas from design analysis, machine control, robotic assembly, quality assurance, and market analysis. Several problems in the text relate to these topics. For example, in Chapter 5, programs are developed to simulate the reliability of systems that use multiple components.

interdisciplinary
teams

Engineering teams of the future will be **interdisciplinary teams**, just as the engineering teams of today are interdisciplinary teams. The discussions of the engineering achievements of the last 50 years clearly show the interdisciplinary nature of those achievements. The teams that address, and will eventually solve, the challenges of the future will also be interdisciplinary teams. Learning to interact in teams and to develop organizational structures for effective team communication is an important skill for engineers. A good way to begin developing engineering team skills is to organize teams to study for exams. Assign specific topics to members of the team with the assignment that they then review these topics for the team, with examples and potential test questions.

world marketplace

The engineers of the 21st century need to understand the **world marketplace**. This involves understanding different cultures, political systems, and business environments. Courses in these topics and in foreign languages help provide some understanding, but exchange programs with international experiences provide invaluable knowledge in developing a broader world understanding.

analyzing
synthesizing

Engineers are problem solvers, but problems are not always formulated carefully. An engineer must be able to extract a problem statement from a problem discussion, and then determine the important issues related to the problem. This involves not only developing order, but also learning to correlate chaos. It means not only **analyzing** the data, but **synthesizing** a solution using many pieces of information. The integration of ideas can be as important as the decomposition of the problem into manageable pieces. A problem solution may involve not only abstract thinking about the problem, but also experimental learning from the problem environment.

societal context

ethical issues

Problem solutions must also be considered in their **societal context**. Environmental concerns should be addressed as alternative solutions to problems are being considered. Engineers must also be conscious of **ethical issues** in providing test results, quality verifications, and design limitations. Ethical issues are never easy to resolve, and some of the exciting new technological achievements will bring more ethical issues with them. For example, the mapping of the genome will potentially provide ethical, legal, and social implications. Should the gene therapy that allows doctors to combat diabetes also be used to enhance athletic ability? Should prospective parents be given detailed information related to the physical and mental characteristics of an unborn child? What kind of privacy should an individual have over his or her genetic code? Very complicated issues arise with any technological advancement because the same capabilities that can do a great deal of good can often be applied in ways that are harmful.

The material presented in this text is only one step in building the knowledge, confidence, and understanding needed by engineers of the 21st century. However, we enthusiastically begin the process with an introduction to the range of computing systems available to engineers and an introduction to a problem-solving methodology that will be used throughout this text as we use C++ to implement solutions to engineering problems.

1.3 Computing Systems

computing system
computer
software
hardware

Before we begin our presentation of C++, a brief discussion of computing systems will be useful. A **computing system** is a complete, working system. The system includes not only a computer, but also software and peripheral devices. A **computer** is a machine that is designed to perform operations that are specified with a set of instructions called **software**. Computer **hardware** refers to the physical parts of the system that have mass and can actually be touched. Hardware includes the computer and peripheral devices such as the keyboard, the mouse, the display, the hard disk, the printer, and even the ink.

Computer software refers to programs that reside and run electronically on the hardware such as compilers, operating systems, and application programs. Software provides a human computer interface (HCI) and defines the operations that a computer will perform.

Computer Hardware

control unit
ALU
accumulator

Recall Menabrea's description of Babbage's Analytical Engine as a machine capable of solving any problem using inputs, outputs, and programs written on punch cards. In 1946, John von Neumann proposed a computing model as shown in Figure 1.1 that is still used today in the design of most digital computers. In Von Neumann's model, we see an input device, an output device, a memory unit, and a machine that consists of a **control unit** and an **arithmetic logic unit (ALU)** with an **accumulator**. The memory unit stores data and the control unit controls the transfer and processing of data. The control unit retrieves and interprets instructions stored in memory, accepts data from an input device such as a keyboard or a mouse, sends data to a specified output device such as a printer or a display, and stores data in the memory unit.

CPU

Suppose that we wrote a program to instruct a computer to add two values and display the result. The control unit will interpret the executable instructions and send data to the ALU. The ALU will perform the addition and the control unit will send the result to the output divice. Together the control unit and the ALU are referred to as the **Central Processing Unit** or **CPU**. The accumulator in the ALU is a collection of high-speed registers for the temporary storage of values and results of arithmetic and logic operations. The time required to access the memory unit is large compared to the time required by the ALU to perform an arithmetic or logic operation. Thus, the use of registers within the ALU increases the overall speed of an

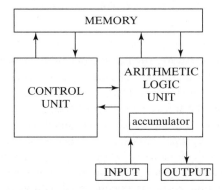

Figure 1.1 von Neumann computing model.

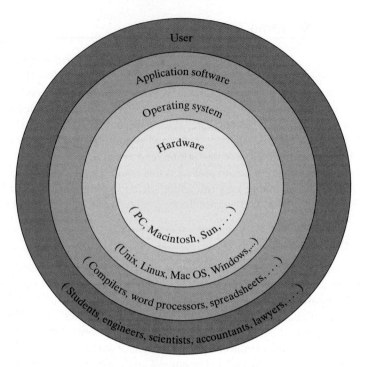

Figure 1.2 Software interface to the computer.

word size

bit

operation. The size of each register in the ALU corresponds to the **word size** of the computer. Common word sizes are 16 bits, 32 bits, and 64 bits, depending on the design of the processor. Note that a **bit** represents a binary digit, and the word size of a processor is a power of 2.

Computer Software

Computer software contains the instructions or commands that we want the computer to perform. There are several important categories of software, which include operating systems, software tools, and language compilers. Figure 1.2 illustrates the interaction between these categories of software and the computer hardware. We now discuss each of these software categories in more detail.

operating systems

Operating Systems.   Some software, such as the operating system, typically comes with the computer hardware when it is purchased. The operating system provides an interface between you (the user) and the hardware by providing a convenient and efficient environment in which you can select and execute the software on your system.

Operating systems also contain a group of programs called utilities that allow you to perform functions such as printing files, copying files, and listing the files that you have saved on file system. Whereas these utilities are common to most operating systems, the environment for executing commands vary from operating system to operating system. For example, to list your files with UNIX (a powerful operating system frequently used with workstations), or Linux (UNIX for PCs) from the command line is **ls**. Some operating systems simplify the interface

GUI

with the operating system by using icons and menus; examples of user-friendly **Graphical User Interface** (GUI) systems, are the Macintosh environment and the Windows environment.

Because C++ programs can be run on many different platforms or computer systems and because a specific computer can use different operating systems, it is not feasible to discuss the wide variety of operating systems that you might use while taking this course. We assume that your professor will provide the specific operating system information that you need to know to use the computers available at your university; this information is also contained in the operating system manuals, and provided via help menus.

word processors

text editors

spreadsheet
software

Application Software.   Numerous application programs are available to perform common operations. For example, **word processors** such as Word and Pages are application programs that have been written to help you create formatted documents such as resumes, newsletters and reports. Word processors have capabilities that allow you to enter mathematical equations and to check your spelling and grammar. Word processors also provide tools that facilitate the creation of charts and graphics with text and headlines. **Text editors**, such as **vi, NotePad**, and **WordPad**, are provided for the creation of text files such as C++ application programs and data files. More sophisticated text editors, such as **emacs**, include compilers and provide a user friendly environment for developing application programs. **Spreadsheet** programs are software tools that allow you to easily work with data that can be displayed in a grid of rows and columns. Spreadsheets were initially used for financial and accounting applications, but many science and engineering problems can be easily solved using spreadsheets. Most spreadsheet packages include plotting capabilities, so they can be especially useful in analyzing and displaying information. Lotus 1-2-3, OpenOffice, and Excel are popular spreadsheet packages.

database
management
software

Another popular group of software tools are **database management software**, such as **MySQL** and **Oracle**. These programs allow you to efficiently store and retrieve large amounts of data. Databases are used by many Web applications and search engines as well as organizations such as banks, hospitals, hotels, and airlines. Scientific databases are also used to analyze large amounts of data. Meteorology data is an example of scientific data that require large databases for storage and analysis.

computer-aided
design software

Computer-aided design software, such as **AutoCAD**, **Land Development Desktop**, **Civil 3D**, and **Architectural Desktop**, allow you to define objects and then manipulate them graphically. For example, you can define an object and then view it from different angles or observe a rotation of the object from one position to another.

mathematical
computation
software

There is also some very powerful **mathematical computation software** such as **MATLAB**, **Mathematica**, and **Maple**. Not only do these tools have very powerful mathematical commands, but they are also graphics tools that provide extensive capabilities for generating graphs. This combination of computational power and visualization power make them particularly useful tools for engineers. Appendix C contains a discussion on using **MATLAB** to plot data from a data file generated by a C++ program.

If an engineering problem can be solved using a software tool, it is usually more efficient to use the software tool than to write a program in a computer language to solve the problem. However, many problems cannot be solved using software tools, or a software tool may not be available on the computer system that must be used for solving the problem; thus, we also need to know how to write programs using computer languages. The distinction between a software tool and a computer language is becoming less clear as some of the more powerful tools such as MATLAB and Mathematica include a programming language in additional to specialized operations.

Computer Languages.   Computer languages can be described in terms of levels. Low-level languages or **machine languages** are the most primitive languages. Machine language is tied closely to the design of the computer hardware. Because computer designs are based on two-state technology (devices with two states such as open or closed circuits, on or off switches, positive or negative charges), machine language is written using two symbols, which are usually represented using the digits 0 and 1. Therefore, machine language is also a **binary** language, and the instructions are written as sequences of 0s and 1s called **binary strings**. Because machine language is closely tied to the design of the computer hardware, the machine language for a Sun computer, for example, is different from the machine language for a HP computer.

An **assembly language** is also unique to a specific computer design, but its instructions are written in symbolic statements instead of binary. Assembly languages usually do not have very many types of statements, and thus writing programs in assembly language can be tedious. In addition, to use an assembly language, you must also know information that relates to the specific computer hardware. Instrumentation that contains microprocessors often requires that the programs operate very fast, and thus the programs are called real-time programs. These **real-time programs** are usually written in assembly language to take advantage of the specific computer hardware in order to perform the steps faster. **High-level languages** are computer languages that have English-like commands and instructions and include languages such as C++, C, Fortran, Ada, Java, and Basic. Writing programs in high-level languages is certainly easier than writing programs in machine language or in assembly language. However, a high-level language contains a large number of commands and an extensive set of **syntax** (or grammar) rules for using the commands. To illustrate the syntax and punctuation required by both software tools and high-level languages, we compute the area of a circle with a specified diameter in Table 1.1 using several different languages and tools. Notice both the similarities and the differences in this simple computation.

machine languages

binary
binary strings

assembly language

real-time programs
high-level
languages

syntax

Executing a Computer Program.   A program written in a high-level language such as C++ must be translated into machine language before the instructions can be executed by the computer. A special program called a **compiler** is used to perform this translation. Thus, to be able to write and execute C++ programs on a computer, the computer's software must include

compiler

TABLE 1.1 Comparison of Software Statements	
Software	**Example Statement**
C++	area = 3.141593*(diameter/2)*(diameter/2);
C	area = 3.141593*(diameter/2)*(diameter/2);
MATLAB	area = pi*((diameter/2)∧ 2);
Fortran	area = 3.141593*(diameter/2.0)**2
Ada	area := 3.141593*(diameter/2)**2;
Java	area = Math.PI*Math.pow(diameter/2,2);
Basic	let a = 3.141593*(d/2)*(d/2)
Scheme	let area 3.141593*(d/2)*(d/2)

a C++ compiler. C++ compilers are available for the entire range of computer hardware, from supercomputers to laptops.

If any errors are detected by the compiler during compilation, corresponding error messages are printed. We must correct our program statements and then perform the compilation

syntax errors

step again. The errors identified during this stage are called **parse errors** or **syntax errors**. For example, if we want to divide the value stored in a variable called sum by 3, the correct expression in C++ is *sum*/3. If we incorrectly write the expression using the backslash, as in *sum*\3, we have a syntax error and an error message will be reported by the compiler when we attempt to compile our program. The process of compiling, correcting statements that have syntax errors, and recompiling must often be repeated several times before the program compiles without error. When there are no syntax errors, the compiler can successfully translate the program and generate a program in machine language that performs the steps specified by

source file
object file

the original C++ program. The C++ program is referred to as the **source file**, and the machine language version is called an **object file**. Thus, the source program and the object program specify the same steps, but the source program is specified in a high-level language and the object program is specified in machine language.

execution
linking
loading
logic errors
bugs

Once the program has compiled correctly, additional steps are necessary to prepare the object program for **execution**. This preparation involves **linking** other machine language statements to the object program and then **loading** the program into memory. After this linking/loading, the program steps are then executed by the computer. New errors called **execution errors, run-time errors**, or **logic errors** may be identified in this stage; these errors are also called **program bugs**. Execution errors often cause termination of a program. For example, the program statements may attempt to reference an invalid memory location, which may generate an execution error. Some execution errors do not stop the program from executing, but they cause incorrect results to be computed. These types of errors can be caused by programmer errors in determining the correct steps in the solutions and by errors in the data processed by the program. When execution errors occur due to errors in the program statements, we must correct the errors in the source program and then begin again with the compilation step. This process is

debugging

called **debugging** and can be quite time consuming. Even when a program appears to execute properly, we must check the answers carefully to be sure that they are correct. The computer will perform the steps precisely as we specify, and if we specify the wrong steps, the computer will execute these wrong (but syntactically legal) steps and thus present us with an answer that is incorrect. The processes of compilation, linking/loading, and execution are outlined in Figure 1.3.

A C++ compiler often has additional capabilities that provide a user-friendly environment for implementing and testing C++ programs. For example, some C++ environments such as Microsoft Visual C++ contain text processors so that program files can be generated, compiled, and executed in the same software package, as opposed to using a separate word processor

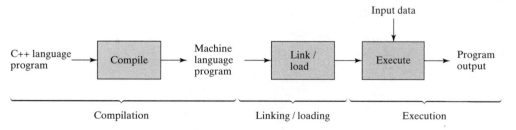

Figure 1.3 Program compilation/linking/execution.

that requires the use of operating system commands to transfer back and forth between the word processor and the compiler. Many C++ programming environments include debugger programs, which are useful in identifying errors in a program. Debugger programs allow us to see values stored in variables at different points in a program and to step through the program line by line.

As we present new statements in C++, we will also point out common errors associated with the statements or useful techniques for locating errors associated with the statements. The debugging aids will be summarized at the end of each chapter.

1.4 Data Representation and Storage

Recall that the design of the Analytical Engine's storage unit consisted of an indefinite number of columns of discs, each disc inscribed with the 10 decimal digits (0–9). By arranging the the discs of one column, a decimal number could be stored.

A modern digital computer follows a similar design except information is represented in base 2, or binary, rather than base 10. The base two number system has only two binary digits, 0 and 1, so a binary digit can be represented by one bit in a digital computer. The value of the bit at any given time can be either 0 or 1. In hardware terms, the bit is said to be off, or low, if it has a value of 0 and on, or high, if it has a value of 1.

word Binary numbers can be stored in memory as a sequence of bits, called a **word**. The right most bit of a word represents the one's position, the next bit represents the two's position, the next bit represents the four's position, and the left most bit represents the 2^{n-1} position where n is the number of bits. Each additional bit in a word increases the word size by a power of 2, and doubles the range of values that can be represented. The number of words available in

address space memory is referred to as the **memory space**, or **address space**.

Figure 1.4 provides a diagram of memory that has an address space of 8 (2^3) and a word size of 16 (2^4). The binary value stored at address 000 is $0000101011011101_2 = 2781_{10}$. It is important to note that the word size determines the range of values that can be stored in one word of memory and the address space determines the number of words that can be stored. The theoretical Analytical Engine has a word size defined by the number of discs on a column and a memory space defined by the number of columns.

The C++ programming language has built-in data types for representing integer values, floating point values, characters, and boolean values. Each built-in data type has a

bytes pre-determined size measured in **bytes**, where a byte is a sequence of 8 bits. **Type decla-**
type declaration **ration statements** are required to define **identifiers** and allocate memory. When an identifier
statements
identifiers

Address	Sixteen Bit Word
000	0000101011011101
001	0101100010010000
010	0001011010010100
011	0111011010011011
100	0000000000000000
101	0001000010010000
110	0111111111111111
111	0001011010010110

Figure 1.4 Memory Diagram: Address Space = 8, Word Size = 16

is defined, a data type is specified and the required number of bytes is allocated for storage. For example, the type declaration statement:

```
int iValue = 2781;
```

defines an identifier, iValue, that references the first byte of an integer value stored in memory. The initial value stored in memory is the binary representation of 2781_{10}. A memory diagram is given below:

iValue⟹ | 00000000 | 00000000 | 00001010 | 11011101 |

Before the development of compilers and high-level programming languages, programmers were required to load each memory location with instructions and data in binary form. Today, we have software (compilers, linkers and loaders) that perform these tasks for us. In Chapter 2 we begin our discussion of C++ statements and data types, but first we will provide a brief discussion of number systems and low-level data representation to allow for a better understanding of the operations that are performed when a program is executed.

Number Systems

The base 10 number system has 10 decimal digits, (0–9) and each digit in a decimal number multiplies a power of 10. Most of us have an easy time counting in base 10 and comprehending base 10 numbers. When we read the number 245_{10} for example, we read it as two hundred and fourtyfive. We understand that the 2 is in the hundreds position (10^2), the 4 in the tens position (10^1) and the 5 in the ones position (10^0). If we expand the number as follows:

$$2 * 10^2 + 4 * 10^1 + 5 * 10^0$$

we can add the terms $200 + 40 + 5$ to arrive at a value of 245_{10}. In the following sections, we will discuss three number systems, binary, octal and hexadecimal, that are useful when studying digital computer systems. We will also develop algorithms for converting numbers to different bases.

Binary Numbers.   Digital computers represent data in binary form. The base two number system has two binary digits, 0 and 1, and each digit multiplies a power of 2. If we examine the binary number, 0000101011011101_2, stored in memory location 000 in Figure 1.4, and we want to determine the equivalent decimal number, we can expand the number as follows, noting that the right most binary digit multiplies 2^0 and the left most digit multiplies 2^{15}.

$0000101011011101_2 =$

$$0 * 2^{15} + 0 * 2^{14} + 0 * 2^{13} + 0 * 2^{12} + 1 * 2^{11} + 0 * 2^{10} + 1 * 2^9 + 0 * 2^8 +$$
$$1 * 2^7 + 1 * 2^6 + 0 * 2^5 + 1 * 2^4 + 1 * 2^3 + 1 * 2^2 + 0 * 2^1 + 1 * 2^0 =$$

$$0 + 0 + 0 + 0 + 2048 + 0 + 512 + 0 + 128 + 64 + 0 + 16 + 8 + 4 + 0 + 1 =$$

$$2781_{10}$$

As we will see in the following sections, the above conversion algorithm can be applied to numbers represented in any base to obtain the equivalent base 10 value.

Suppose that we have a decimal number that we wish to represent in base 2. The equivalent binary number will be a sequence of binary digits. To generate these digits, we will use a conversion algorithm that repeatedly divides the decimal number by 2, and records the remainder of each division as a successive digit of the equivalent binary number.

least significant digit

most significant digit

We illustrate the use of the algorithm in the example below. Note that the remainder of the first division is recorded as the **least significant digit (LSD)** of the equivalent binary number, the remainder of the last division is recorded as the **most significant digit (MSD)**, and we divide until the quotient becomes zero.

Example

$245_{10} = ?_2$

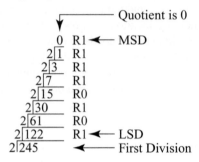

$$245_{10} = 11110101_2$$

The above conversion algorithm can be used to convert from base 10 to any other base. The base of the other number system defines the divisor, as we will see in the following sections.

Octal Numbers.   The octal, or base 8, number system has 8 octal digits, (0–7). Octal numbers are useful for understanding 8 bit character codes, and for setting permissions on files and directories on a linux/unix platform. For example, if we have a file that we want to be readable, writable, and executable by everyone, we can use the `chmod` command to set the permissions on the file as follows:

```
chmod 777 aFile
```

Permissions for `aFile` will be set to 7_8, or 111_2 for the owner, the group and the world. If we next do a long listing,

```
ls -l
```

we will see something like the following:

```
-rwxrwxrwx 1 jeaninei jeaninei 258 Jun 26 12:27 aFile.
```

The above indicates that (r)ead(w)rite(x)execute permission is granted to the owner, the group and the world. If we wish to grant only read status to the group and the world, we can change the permissions with the following command:

```
chmod 744 aFile
```

A long listing will now display the following:

```
-rwxr-r- 1 jeaninei jeaninei 258 Jun 26 12:27 aFile
```

indicating that the owner has `rwx` permission and the group and the world have read permission, but no write permission and no execute permission. The number $4_8 = 100_2$, thus a 1 grants permission and a 0 denies permission.

Each digit in an octal number multiplies a power of 8. To determine the equivalent decimal value of an octal number, we can apply the same conversion algorithm used to determine the decimal value of a binary number. Note that the base of the number being converted to decimal, 8 in this case, defines the base of the exponential terms.

Example

$217_8 = ?_{10}$

$$2 * 8^2 + 1 * 8^1 + 7 * 8^0 =$$
$$2 * 64 + 1 * 8 + 7 * 1 =$$

$$128 + 8 + 7 =$$

$$143_{10}$$

To illustrate the algorithm for converting from base 10 to any other base, we will convert 143_{10} back to base 8. We apply the algorithm using 8 as our divisor.

$143_{10} = ?_8$

```
      0   R2
   8⌐2   R1
  8⌐17   R7
 8⌐143
```

$143_{10} = 217_8$

We have thus far illustrated an algorithm for converting from base 10 to any other base and an algorithm for converting from any base to base 10, but now assume that we want to convert a base 8 number to base 2. One approach would be to first convert the base 8 number to base 10, and then convert the equivalent base 10 number to base 8. This approach is valid, but since 8 is a power of 2, $8 = 2^3$, and each of the eight octal digits can be represented in binary using three binary digits, we can use this relationship to quickly convert from binary to octal and octal to binary, as illustrated in the next two examples. Table 1.2 lists the binary representation of the 8 octal digits for your convenience.

TABLE 1.2   Binary Representation of Octal Digits

Octal Digit	Binary Representation
0	000
1	001
2	010
3	011
4	100
5	101
6	110
7	111

Example

$143_8 = ?_2$

$$
\begin{array}{ccc}
1 & 4 & 3 \\
\downarrow & \downarrow & \downarrow \\
001 & 100 & 011
\end{array}
$$

$143_8 = 001100011_2$

Example

$000101011011101_2 = ?_8$

$$
\begin{array}{ccccc}
\underbrace{000} & \underbrace{101} & \underbrace{011} & \underbrace{011} & \underbrace{101} \\
\downarrow & \downarrow & \downarrow & \downarrow & \downarrow \\
0 & 5 & 3 & 3 & 5
\end{array}
$$

$000101011011101_2 = 5335_8$

Practice!

Convert each of the following base 10 numbers to base 2.

1. $921_{10} = ?_2$

2. $8_{10} = ?_2$

3. $100_{10} = ?_2$

Convert each of the following base 8 numbers to base 10.

4. $100_8 = ?_{10}$

5. $247_8 = ?_{10}$

6. $16_8 = ?_{10}$

Convert each of the following numbers to the requested base.

7. $100_2 = ?_8$

8. $3716_8 = ?_2$

9. $110100111_2 = ?_{10}$

10. $221_6 = ?_8$

Hexadecimal Numbers.   The hexadecimal, or base 16, number system has 16 hexadecimal digits, (0–9,A–F), and each digit in a hexadecimal number multiplies a power of 16.

The decimal values of the hexadecimal digits represented by letters are (10,11,12,13,14,15) respectively.

The number $2BF_{16}$ is an example of a hexadecimal number. Applying the conversion algorithm for converting from any base to base 10, we can determine the equivalent decimal number, as illustrated below.

$2FB_{16} = ?_{10}$

$$2 * 16^2 + F * 16^1 + B * 16^0 =$$
$$2 * 256 + 15 * 16 + 11 * 1 =$$

$$512 + 240 + 11 =$$

$$763_{10}$$

To illustrate the algorithm for converting from base ten to any other base, we will convert 763_{10} back to base 16. The remainder of each division is a value between 0 and F.

$763_{10} = ?_{16}$

```
        0   R2
    16|2    R15(F)
    16|47   R11(B)
    16|763       ↑
                 └── Hex Digits
```

$$763_{10} = 2FB_{16}$$

Sixteen is a power of 2, $16 = 2^4$, and each of the hexadecimal digits can be represented in binary using four binary digits. This relationship can be used to quickly convert from binary to hexadecimal and hexadecimal to binary, as illustrated in the next two examples. Table 1.3 lists the binary representation of the hexadecimal digits for your convenience.

Example

$7BF_{16} = ?_2$

7	B	F
↓	↓	↓
0111	1011	1111

$$7BF_{16} = 011110111111_2$$

Example

$1010001101_2 = ?_{16}$

1010	000	1101
↓	↓	↓
A	0	D

$$101000001101_2 = A0D_{16}$$

TABLE 1.3   Binary Representation of Hexadecimal Digits

Hexadecimal Digit	Binary Representation
0	0000
1	0001
2	0010
3	0011
4	0100
5	0101
6	0110
7	0111
8	1000
9	1001
A	1010
B	1011
C	1100
D	1101
E	1110
F	1111

Practice!

Convert each of the following base 10 numbers to base 16.

1. $921_{10} = ?_{16}$

2. $8_{10} = ?_{16}$

3. $100_{10} = ?_{16}$

Convert each of the following base 16 numbers to base 10.

4. $1C0_{16} = ?_{10}$

5. $29E_{16} = ?_{10}$

6. $16_{16} = ?_{10}$

Convert each of the following numbers to the requested base.

7. $10010011_2 = ?_{16}$

8. $3A1B_{16} = ?_2$

9. $110100111_2 = ?_{10}$

10. $261_8 = ?_{16}$

Data Types and Storage

ANSI

When data is represented in memory, it is represented as a sequence of bits. The sequence of bits may represent an instruction, a numeric value, a character, a portion of an image or digital signal, or some other type of data. If we look at the bit sequence 01000110_2, for example, it has a decimal value of 70. It also is the **American National Standard Institute (ANSI)** character code for the character F.

Data representation is becoming an increasingly important and interesting field in engineering, math and computer science. The amount of data that can be generated and processed is increasing as computers become more powerful, and the use of computers in data intensive applications such as bio-computing, communications and signal processing present new challenges for defining and representing data. In this section, we will discuss the digital representation of two basic data types, **integer** and **floating point**.

Integer Data Type.   In the previous section, we used an algorithm to convert from base 10 to base 2. This algorithm works for any base 10 integer, so in theory we can represent, exactly, all base 10 integers in base 2. In practice, we may be limited by the word size of our computing system. Integer data is often stored in memory using 4 bytes, or 32 bits. The left most bit is reserved for the sign, leaving 31 bits for the magnitude of the number.

Consider the following example that uses a word size of 8 for simplicity. The largest signed integer that can be represented in 8 bits is $2^7 - 1$ or 127_{10}, as illustrated below.

0	1	1	1	1	1	1	1

2's complement form

The representation of data in a digital computer affects the efficiency of arithmetic and logic operations. Many computer systems store positive signed integers as illustrated above, and store negative signed integers in their **2's complement form**. Storing negative integers in their 2's complement form allows for efficient execution of arithmetic operations, without checking the sign bit. First, we illustrate how to form the 2's complement of a negative number, then we will illustrate how storing negative numbers in their 2's complement form can simplify arithmetic operations.

1's complement

The 2's complement of a binary number is formed by negating all of the bits and adding one. Negating a bit means switching the value, or state, of a bit from 1 to 0, or from 0 to 1. Negating all the bits of a binary number forms the **1's complement** of the number. Adding one to the 1's complement results in the 2's complement of the number. Using a word size of 8, the 2's complement of -127_{10} is computed in the following example.

Example   Compute the 2's complement representation for the value -127_{10}.

To form the 2's complement of a negative integer, we begin with the binary representation of the unsigned value.

$$127_{10} = 01111111_2.$$

Next, we negate the bits to form the 1's complements.

$$10000000_2.$$

Finally, we add $1_{10} = 00000001_2$ to form the 2's complement.

10000001.

Thus, the 2's complement representation for -127_{10} is 10000001.

Notice what happens when we add 127_{10} to the 2's complement of -127_{10}.

01111111_2	127_{10}
$+ \quad 10000001_2$	2's complement of -127_{10}
$= \quad 00000000_2$	result of addition is 0

The 2's complement form for representing signed integers has the property that adding a positive integer, n, to the 2's complement of n results in zero for all n. Another important property of 2's complement representation is that there is a unique representation for binary 0.

When performing addition on signed integers represented in 2's complement form, the result, if negative, will be in its 2's complement form, as shown in the following examples.

Example   Addition of 2 binary numbers, positive result.

11110110	-10_{10} represented in 2's complement
$+ \quad 00001101$	13_{10}
$= \quad 00000011$	3_{10}

Example   Addition of 2 binary numbers, negative result.

00001010	10_{10}
$+ \quad 11110011$	-13_{10} represented in 2's complement
$= \quad 11111101$	-3 represented in 2's complement

Practice!

Find the 2's complement of the following integers:

1. 11001111_2

2. -192_{10}

3. -45_8

Floating Point Data Type.   A floating point number, or real number, such as 12.25_{10} includes a decimal point. The digits to the left of the decimal point form the integral part of the number and the digits to the right of the decimal point form the fractional part of a number. The fractional part of a decimal number can be converted to binary by repeatedly multiplying the factional part by 2 and recording the **carry bits** until the factional part becomes zero. This algorithm is illustrated in the following example.

carry bits

Example   Convert 12.25_{10} to binary.

First, the integral part, 12_{10} is converted to binary:

```
      0  R1
    2|1  R1
    2|3   R0
    2|6    R0
  2|12
```

$12_{10} = 1100_2$

Next we will convert the fractional part, $.25_{10}$ to binary by repeatedly multiplying the fractional part by 2 and recording the carry bits:

$.25 * 2 = 0.5 \text{ C0}$
$.5 * 2 \ = 1.0 \text{ C1}$

$.25_{10} = .01_2$

The integral and fraction parts are now combined to form the equivalent binary value. Thus, the value $12.25_{10} = 1100.01_2$.

To convert the floating point binary number 1100.01_2 back to decimal, the binary digits to the right of the decimal point are multiplied by negative powers of 2, as shown below.

$1100.01_2 =$

$\quad 1 * 2^3 + 1 * 2^2 + 0 * 2^1 + 0 * 2^0 + 0 * 2^{-1} \ + 1 * 2^{-2} =$
$\quad 1 * 8 \ + 1 * 4 \ + 0 * 2 \ + 0 * 1 \ + 0 * (1/2) + 1 * (1/4) =$
$\quad 8 + 4 + 0 + 0 + 0 + 0.25 =$
$\quad 12.25$

$\quad 1100.01_2 = 12.25_{10}$

In the above example, we found an exact binary representation for the value 12.25_{10}. Unfortunately, many floating points decimal have only an approximate binary representation, as illustrated in the next example.

Example   Convert 12.6_{10} to binary.

The integral portion, 12_{10} has been shown to equal 1100_2. Converting the fractional portion, we repeatedly multiply by 2 and record the carry bits.

$.6 * 2 = 1.2 \text{ C1}$
$.2 * 2 = 0.4 \text{ C0}$
$.4 * 2 = 0.8 \text{ C0}$
$.8 * 2 = 1.6 \text{ C1}$
$.6 * 2 = 1.2 \text{ C1}$
$.2 * 2 = 0.4 \text{ C0}$
$.4 * 2 = 0.8 \text{ C0}$
$.8 * 2 = 1.6 \text{ C1}$

We can see that we are repeating the bit pattern of 1001 and will never arrive at a terminating value of zero. Thus, the best binary approximation of 0.6_{10} is the repeating binary number $0.100110011001\ldots_2$. Expanding this to 8 bits of precision, we have:

$$1 * 2^{-1} + 0 * 2^{-2} + 0 * 2^{-3} + 1 * 2^{-4} + 1 * 2^{-5} + 0 * 2^{-6} + 0 * 2^{-7} + 1 * 2^{-8} =$$
$$1 * \left(\frac{1}{2}\right) + 0 * \left(\frac{1}{4}\right) + 0 * \left(\frac{1}{8}\right) + 1 * \left(\frac{1}{16}\right) + 1 * \left(\frac{1}{32}\right) + 0 * \left(\frac{1}{64}\right) + 0 * \left(\frac{1}{128}\right) + 1 * \left(\frac{1}{256}\right) =$$
$$0.5 + 0 + 0 + 0.0625 + 0.03125 + 0 + 0 + 0.00390625 =$$
$$0.5976562$$

$$12.6_{10} \approx 1100.10011001_2$$

It is important to know that the binary representation of a floating point decimal is an approximation, not an equality. This affects the way we use and test floating point values in programs and it also affects the accuracy of numerical calculations.

1.5 An Engineering Problem-Solving Methodology

Problem solving is a key part of not only engineering courses, but also of courses in computer science, mathematics, physics, and chemistry. Therefore, it is important to have a consistent approach to solving problems. It is also helpful if the approach is general enough to work for all these different areas so that we do not have to learn one technique for mathematics problems, a different technique for physics problems, and so on. The problem-solving process that we present works for engineering problems and can be tailored to solve problems in other areas as well; however, it does assume that we are using the computer to help solve the problem.

The process or methodology for problem solving that we will use throughout this text has five steps:

1. State the problem clearly.

2. Describe the input and output information of the problem.

3. Work the problem by hand (or with a calculator) for a simple set of data.

4. Develop a solution and convert it to a computer program.

5. Test the solution with a variety of data.

We now discuss each of these steps using an example of computing the distance between two points in a plane.

1. PROBLEM STATEMENT

The first step is to state the problem clearly. It is extremely important to give a clear, concise problem statement to avoid any misunderstandings. For this example, the problem statement is the following:

Compute the straight-line distance between two points in a plane.

2. INPUT/OUTPUT DESCRIPTION

The second step is to describe the information, or data values, that are required to solve the problem and then identify the values that need to be computed for the final solution. Each of these values will be represented by an object in a C++ program. These objects represent the input and the output for the problem, and collectively can be called input/output, or I/O. For many problems, a diagram that shows the input and output is useful. At this point, the program is an "abstraction" because we are not defining the steps to determine the output; instead, we are only showing the information that is required to compute the desired output. The **I/O diagram** for this example follows.

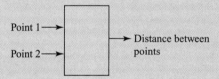

3. HAND EXAMPLE

The third step is to work the problem by hand or with a calculator, using a simple set of data. This is a very important step and should not be skipped even for simple problems. This is the step in which you work out the details of the problem solution. If you cannot take a simple set of numbers and compute the output (either by hand or with a calculator), then you are not ready to move on to the next step; you should reread the problem, and perhaps consult reference material. The solution by hand for this specific example follows:

Let the points p1 and p2 have the following coordinates:

$$p1 = (1, 5); p2 = (4, 7)$$

We want to compute the distance between the two points, which is the hypotenuse of a right triangle, as shown in Figure 1.5. Using the Pythagorean theorem, we can compute the distance with the following equation:

$$distance = \sqrt{(side_1)^2 + (side_2)^2}$$
$$= \sqrt{(4-1)^2 + (7-5)^2}$$
$$= \sqrt{13}$$
$$= 3.61$$

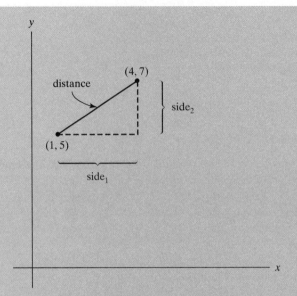

Figure 1.5 Straight-line distance between two points.

4. ALGORITHM DEVELOPMENT

Once you can work the problem for a simple set of data, you are then ready to develop an **algorithm**, or a step-by-step outline, of the problem solution. For simple problems such as this one, the algorithm can be listed as operations that are performed one after another. This outline of steps decomposes the problem into simpler steps, as shown by the following outline of the steps required to compute and print the distance between two points.

Decomposition Outline

1. *Give values to the two points.*

2. *Compute the lengths of the two sides of the right triangle generated by the two points.*

3. *Compute the distance between the two points, which is equal to the length of the hypotenuse of the triangle.*

4. *Print the distance between the two points.*

This **decomposition outline** is then converted to C++ commands so that we can use the computer to perform the computations. From the following solution, you can see that the commands are very similar to the steps used in the hand example. The details of these commands are explained in Chapter 2.

```
/*-------------------------------------------------------------*/
/*   Program chapter1_1                                    */
/*                                                         */
/*   This program computes the                             */
/*   distance between two points.                          */
```

```
#include<iostream>//Required for cout
#include<cmath>//Required for sqrt()

using namespace std;

int main()
{
   //   Declare and initialize objects.
   double x1=1, y1=5, x2=4, y2=7,
          side1, side2, distance;

   //   Compute sides of a right triangle.
   side1 = x2 - x1;
   side2 = y2 - y1;
   distance = sqrt(side1*side1 + side2*side2);

   //   Print distance.
   cout << "The distance between the two points is"
        << distance << endl;

   //   Exit program.
   return 0;
}
/*-----------------------------------------------------*/
```

5. TESTING

The final step in our problem-solving process is testing the solution. We should first test the solution with the data from the hand example because we have already computed the solution. When the C++ statements in this solution are executed, the computer displays the following output:

The distance between the points is 3.60555

This output matches the value that we calculated by hand. If the C++ solution did not match the hand solution, then we should review both solutions to find the error. Once the solution works for the hand example, we should also test it with additional sets of data to be sure that the solution works for other valid sets of data.

The set of steps demonstrated in this example are used in developing the programs in the Problem Solving Applied sections in the chapters that follow.

SUMMARY

A brief history of the development of the digital computer was provided, followed by a group of outstanding recent engineering achievements to demonstrate the diversity of engineering applications, and the impact of computers in engineering. We also discussed some of the non-technical skills required to be a successful engineer. Because the solutions to most engineering problems will be by computer, we presented a summary of the components of a computer system, from computer hardware to computer software and the importance of learning the new terminology. We also discussed number systems and data representation and introduced a five-step problem-solving methodology that we will use to develop a computer solution to a problem. These five steps are as follows:

1. State the problem clearly.

2. Describe the input and output information for the problem.

3. Work the problem by hand (or with a calculator) for a simple set of data.

4. Develop an algorithm and convert it to a computer program.

5. Test the solution with a variety of data.

This process will be used throughout the text as we develop solutions to problems.

Key Terms

algorithm	linking/loading
arithmetic logic unit (ALU)	logic error
assembler	machine language
assembly language	memory
binary	microprocessor
binary string	most significant digit
bug	number systems network
carry bit	object program
central processing unit (CPU)	objects
compiler	operating system
complement	parse error
computer	personal computer (PC)
database management	problem-solving process
debug	processor
debugger	program
decomposition outline	real-time program
electronic copy	software
execution	source program
graphics tool	spreadsheet
hardware	syntax
high-level language	word processor
I/O diagram	workstation
least significant digit	

Problems

Exam Practice!

True/False Problems

Indicate whether the following statements are true (T) or false (F).

1. A CPU consists of an ALU, memory, and a processor.
2. Linking and loading is the step that prepares the object program for execution.
3. An algorithm describes the problem solution step by step, while a computer program solves the problem in one step.
4. A computer program is the implementation of an algorithm.

Multiple-Choice Problems

Circle the letter for the best answer to complete each statement, or for the correct answer to each question.

5. Instructions and data are stored in
   (a) the arithmetic logic unit (ALU).
   (b) the control unit (processor).
   (c) the central processing unit (CPU).
   (d) the memory.
   (e) the keyboard.
6. An operating system is
   (a) the software that is designed by users.
   (b) a convenient and efficient interface between the user and the hardware.
   (c) the set of utilities that allow us to perform common operations.
   (d) a set of software tools.
7. Source code is
   (a) the result of compiler operations.
   (b) the process of getting information from the processor.
   (c) the set of instructions in a computer language that solve a specific problem.
   (d) the data stored in the computer memory.
   (e) the values entered through the keyboard.
8. An algorithm refers to
   (a) a step-by-step solution to solve a specific problem.
   (b) a collection of instructions that the computer can understand.
   (c) a code that allows us to type in text materials.
   (d) stepwise refinement.
   (e) a set of math equations to derive the problem solution.
9. Object code is
   (a) the result of compiler operations on the source code.
   (b) the process of obtaining information from the processor.
   (c) a computer program.
   (d) a process involving the listing of commands required to solve a specific problem.
   (e) the result of the linking and loading process.

10. Convert the following binary numbers to octal.
    (a) 110110101
    (b) 111101001101111
    (c) 1010111001
    (d) 1000000001
    (e) 111111111
11. Convert the following binary numbers to hexadecimal.
    (a) 100010101011
    (b) 1110011111110101
    (c) 1010111001
    (d) 1000000000000001
    (e) 11111111111
12. Convert the following decimal numbers to octal.
    (a) 1292
    (b) 607
    (c) 9350
    (d) 1000010
    (e) 1111111
13. Convert the following numbers to base 10.
    (a) 11010101_2
    (b) 4762_8
    (c) $30AF2_{16}$
    (d) 4103_5
    (e) 1111111_6

Additional Problems

The following problems combine an assignment in which you will learn more about one of the topics in this chapter with an opportunity to improve your written communication skills. (Perhaps your professor will even select some of the written reports for oral presentation in class.) Each report should include at least two references, so you will want to learn how to use library computers to locate reference information. Prepare your report using word-processor software. If you do not already know how to use a word processor, ask your professor for guidance or visit your university's Web site for links to resources on campus.

14. Write a short report on one of these outstanding engineering achievements:

    Analytical Engine
    Global Positioning Systems
    Composite materials
    Application satellites
    Mars Orbital Camera
    CAD/CAM
    Fiber optics
    CAT scans
    A good starting point for finding references is the World Wide Web and your local library.

Prediction of Weather, Climate, and Global Change

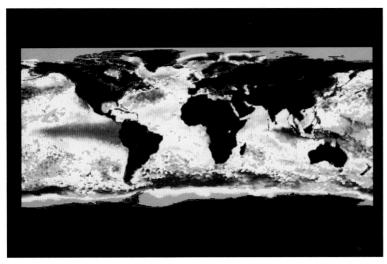

Courtesy of NOAA/Science Photo Library

◀ To predict weather, climate, and global change, we must understand the complex interactions of the atmosphere and the oceans. These interactions are influenced by many things, including temperature, wind, ocean currents, precipitation, soil moisture, snow cover, glaciers, polar sea ice, and the absorption of ultraviolet radiation by ozone in the earth's atmosphere. The satellite image of Earth, taken by an Advanced Very High Resolution Radiometer (AVHRR), shows an El Nino event in the east Pacific Ocean. El Nino is an oscillation of the ocean-atmosphere system that impacts weather around the world. The difference between normal sea temperatures and those during the El Nino are shown as colors from purple (furthest below normal) through blue and yellow to red (furthest above normal). Land masses are black and outlined in red. The El Nino is the red area moving eastward along the equator across the Pacific.

© *Ilene MacDonald/Alamy*

▲ Meteorologists monitor displays to provide weather forecasts, as illustrated in the photograph of a weather room in a television news station in Austin, Texas.

Courtesy of Mark & Audrey Gibson/The Stock Connection

◀ A computer image of a weather map of the northern hemisphere illustrates the use of technology to visually display satellite data for weather tracking.

Computerized Speech and Voice Recognition

Computerized speech recognition is the process of converting a speech signal to a sequence of words. Speech recognition is used successfully for voice dialing with cell phones and automated answering systems. Computerized voice recognition is the process of identifying the person who is speaking, as opposed to identifying what is being said. Voice recognition algorithms look at the acoustic features of speech. These acoustic features reflect both the physical size and shape of the mouth and throat of the speaker and learned speech patterns such as tone and pitch. Acoustical speech signals can be converted to electrical signals which can be analyzed, and visualized as illustrated in the computer generated image of several voice patterns. The voice patterns in this image are the jagged white waveforms. ▶

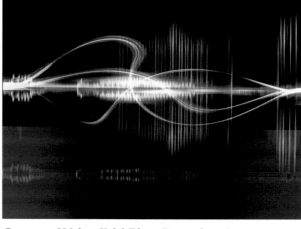

Courtesy of Mehau Kulyk/Photo Researchers, Inc.

◀ Voice recognition is classified as a behavioral biometric. Biometrics is the study of ways to identify individuals based upon one or more intrinsic physical or behavioral traits. Sophisticated algorithms convert voice patterns into a unique digital representation of an individual's voice, as suggested by the photo of a human ear and mouth on a background with a circuitry pattern.

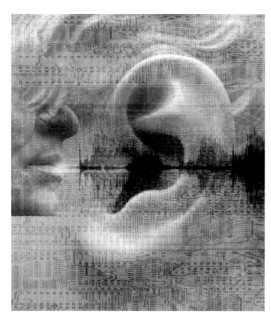

Courtesy of Mehau Kulyk/Photo Researchers, Inc.

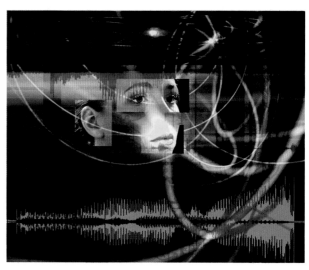

Computer generated image of an ear and mouth and multiple voice patterns represent the technology required for voice recognition and speech synthesis. ▶

Courtesy of Mehau Kulyk/Photo Researchers, Inc.

Space Exploration

The moon landing on July 21, 1969 was perhaps the most complex and ambitious engineering project in United States' history. Apollo XI was launched on July 16, 1969 and was the first manned lunar mission. Apollo XI astronaut Neil A. Armstrong took his first step on the moon on July 21, and his footprint, in the dust of the lunar surface, was photographed. ▶

Courtesy of.NASA/Photo Researchers, Inc.

◀ The exploration in space has motivated recent engineering achievements in the collection of scientific data. The Mars Exploration Rovers are designed to move across the surface of the planet and examine the soil and rocks in fine detail. The Mars Exploration Rover mission is part of NASA's Mars Exploration Program, a long-term effort of robotic exploration of the red planet. Primary among the mission's scientific goals is to search for and characterize a wide range of rocks and soils that hold clues to past water activity on Mars. The spacecraft are targeted to sites on opposite sides of Mars that appear to have been affected by liquid water in the past.

Courtesy of NASA/Jet Propulsion Laboratory

In the Payload Hazardous Servicing Facility, technicians reopen the lander petals of the Mars Exploration Rover 2 to allow access to one of the spacecraft's circuit boards. ▶

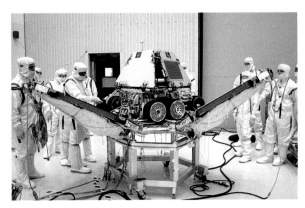

Courtesy of NASA/Jet Propulsion Laboratory

Computer Simulation

Computer simulation has become the third paradigm of science, advancing knowledge when physical experimentation is not feasible. The use of computer simulation in the design of advanced composite materials is an exciting application that benefits many areas of science and engineering, including manufacturing, structural mechanics, material science and medical science. Molten plastic materials can be engineered to have properties that are suitable for specific applications, as illustrated in the photo of a self-healing plastic. The red circles are microcapsules that are released from the self-healing plastic. Damage to the plastic ruptures the microcapsules, resulting in the release of a fluid that can repair the damage. This plastic was designed by a team at the University of Illinois and has applications in the design of materials for spacecraft and surgical implants. ▶

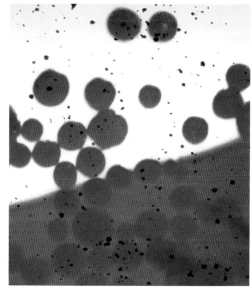

Courtesy of Scott White/UIUC/Photo Researchers, Inc.

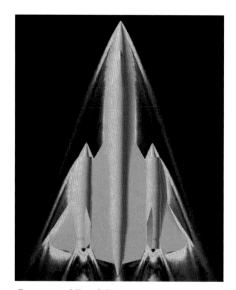

Courtesy of Frank Witzeman

◀ Computer simulation has had a major impact in the area of vehicle design and performance. Simulations can predict how a vehicle will respond under certain conditions, without the risk of damage to the vehicle, as illustrated in the simulation of shock-wave patterns of an SR-71 reconnaissance aircraft at a five degree angle of attack.

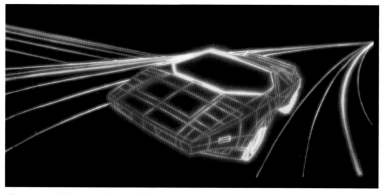

A wire-frame computer graphic of an aerodynamic sports car illustrates the use of computer simulation in vehicle design. ▶

Courtesy of Ramon Santos/Photo Researchers, Inc.

15. Write a short report on one of these engineering challenges:

    Predication of weather, climate, and global change
    Computerized speech understanding
    Mapping of the human genome
    Improved vehicle performance
    A good starting point for finding references is the NASA Web site: www.nasa.gov

16. Write a short report on an outstanding engineering achievement that is not included in the list given in this chapter. Past issues of *Scientific American* and the Web would provide some good ideas of recent achievements.

2

ENGINEERING CHALLENGE:
Vehicle Performance

Turboprop engines combine the power and reliability of jet engines with the efficiency of propellers. Turboprops use a gas turbine to turn a propeller. Their application has been limited to smaller aircraft because turboprop engines are most efficient at flight speeds under 500 mph. However, the engineering of new materials, blade shapes, and propellers continues to increase the speed and efficiency of the turboprop and the demand for the engine.

SIMPLE C++ PROGRAMS

CHAPTER OUTLINE

OBJECTIVES *In this chapter we develop problem solutions containing:*

- simple arithmetic computations
- user-supplied information from the keyboard
- information printed on the screen
- programmer-defined data types

2.1 Program Structure

In this section, we analyze the structure of a specific C++ program, and then we present the general structure of a C++ program. The program that follows was first introduced in Chapter 1; it computes and prints the distance between two points.

```
/*------------------------------------------------------*/
/*  Program chapter1_1                                  */
/*                                                      */
/*  This program computes the                           */
/*  distance between two points.                        */
```

```
#include <iostream>    //  Required for cout, endl.
#include <cmath>       //  Required for sqrt()

using namespace std;

int main()
{
   //  Declare and initialize objects.
   double x1(1), y1(5), x2(4), y2(7),
          side1, side2, distance;

   //  Compute sides of a right triangle.
   side1 = x2 - x1;
   side2 = y2 - y1;
   distance = sqrt(side1*side1 + side2*side2);

   //  Print distance.
   cout << "The distance between the two points is "
        << distance << endl;

   //  Exit program.
   return 0;
}
/*------------------------------------------------------------*/
```

We now briefly discuss the statements in this specific example; each of the statements is discussed in detail in later sections of this chapter.

comments

The first five lines of this program contain **comments** that give the program a name (chapter1_1) and that document its purpose:

```
/*---------------------------------------------------------------------*/
/*        Program chapter1_1                                           */
/*                                                                     */
/*        This program computes the                                    */
/*        distance between two points.                                 */
```

Comments may begin with the characters /* and end with the characters */ or, for single-line comments, may begin with the characters // and terminate at the end of the current line. A comment can be on a line by itself, or it can be on the same line as a command; a comment beginning with the characters /* can extend over several lines.

Each of the comment lines here is a separate comment because each line begins with /* and ends with */. Although comments are optional, good style requires that comments be used throughout a program to improve its readability and to document the computations. In the text programs, we always use initial comments to give a name to the program and to describe the general purpose of the program; additional explanation comments are also included throughout the program. C++ allows comments and statements to begin anywhere on a line.

preprocessor
directives

Preprocessor directives give instructions to the preprocessor that are performed before the program is compiled. The most common directive inserts additional statements in the program; it contains the characters *#include* followed by the name of the file containing the additional statements. This program contains the following two preprocessor directives:

```
#include <iostream>
#include <cmath>
```

iostream
cmath

These directives specify that statements in the files `iostream` and `cmath` should be included in place of these two statements before the program is compiled. The < and > characters around the file names indicate that the files are included with the Standard C++ library; this library is contained in the files that accompany an ANSI C++ compiler. The file `iostream` contains information related to the output statement used in this program, and the file `cmath` contains information related to the function used in this program to compute the square root of a value. Preprocessor directives are generally included after the initial comments describing the program's purpose. The next statement

```
using namespace std;
```

using directive

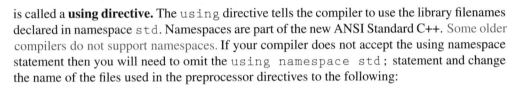

is called a **using directive.** The `using` directive tells the compiler to use the library filenames declared in namespace `std`. Namespaces are part of the new ANSI Standard C++. Some older compilers do not support namespaces. If your compiler does not accept the using namespace statement then you will need to omit the `using namespace std;` statement and change the name of the files used in the preprocessor directives to the following:

```
#include<iostream.h>
#include<math.h>
```

Older compiles use a *.h* extention for most of their header file names. You will see the file `math.h` included in C programs, as well as C++ programs because `math.h` is the C name of the C library header file. New compilers differentiate between C and C++ header file names. The C++ name for the `math.h` header file is `cmath`. In general, the C++ name for a C library header file is the same as the C name with the following changes: the `.h` is dropped and the letter `c` is added to the beginning of the file name. We will use the new ANSI Standard C++ names in this text.

block of code

Every C++ program contains exactly one function named `main`, defined by a **block of code**. In C++, a block of code is defined by a set of braces, { }. The keyword `int` indicates that the function returns an integer value to the operating system. The parentheses following `main` are required because `main` is a function. In order to easily identify the block of code that defines body of the function, we place the braces on lines by themselves. Thus, the two lines following the preprocessor directives specify the beginning of the `main` function:

```
int main()
{
```

declarations
statements

The main function contains two types of commands: **declarations** and **statements**. The declarations define identifiers and allocate memory and therefore must precede any statements that reference these identifiers. The declarations may or may not give initial values to be stored in the memory locations. A comment precedes the declaration statement in the following program:

```
// Declare and initialize objects.
double x1(1), y1(5), x2(4), y2(7),
       side1, side2, distance;
```

These declarations specify that the program will use seven objects named x1, y1, x2, y2, side1, side2, and distance. The term double indicates that the objects are of type double, one of the built-in C++ data types. Each object will store a double-precision floating-point value; these objects can store noninteger values such as 12.5 and −0.0005 with many digits of precision. In addition, this statement specifies that x1 should be **initialized** (given an initial value) to the value 1, y1 should be initialized to the value 5, x2 should be initialized to the value 4, and y2 should be initialized the value 7. The initial values of side1, side2, and distance are not specified and should not be assumed to be initialized to zero. Because the declaration was too long for one line, we split it over two lines; the indenting of the second line indicates that it is a continuation of the previous line. *The indenting is a matter of style and readability; it is not required.* The semicolon ends the declaration statement.

initialized

The statements that specify the operations to be performed in the example program are the following:

```
// Compute sides of a right triangle
side1 = x2 - x1;
side2 = y2 - y1;
distance = sqrt(side1*side1 + side2*side2);

//  Print distance
cout << "The distance between the two points is "
     << distance << endl;
```

These statements compute the lengths of the two sides of the right triangle formed by two points (see Figure 1.5, page 28) and then compute the length of the hypotenuse of the right triangle. The details of the syntax of these assignment statements are discussed later in the chapter. After the distance is computed, it is printed with the cout statement. This output statement is too long for a single line, so we separate the statement into two lines; the indenting of the second line again indicates that it is a continuation of the previous line. A semicolon ends the output statement. Additional comments were used to explain the computations and the output statement. Note that all C++ statements are required to end with a semicolon.

To end execution of the program and return control to the operating system, we use a return(0); statement.

```
//  Exit program
return (0);
```

This statement returns a value of zero to the operating system. A value of zero indicates a successful end of execution.

The body of the main function then ends with the right brace on a line by itself, and another comment line to delineate the end of the main function.

```
}
/*---------------------------------------------------------------*/
```

Style

Note that we have included blank lines (also called whitespace) in the program to separate different components. These blank lines make a program more readable and easier to modify. The statements within the main function were indented in order to show the structure of the program. This spacing provides a consistent style, and makes our programs easier to read.

Now that we have closely examined the C++ program from Chapter 1, we can compare its structure to the general form of a C++ program:

```
preprocessing directives
int main()
{
    declarations;
    statements;
}
```

This structure is evident in the programs developed in this chapter and in the chapters that follow.

Modify!

1. Create a file containing the sample program discussed in this section using either an editor that is part of your C++ compiler or using a word processor.* Then compile and execute the program. You should get this output:

   ```
   The distance between the two points is  3.61
   ```

2. Change the values given to the two points to the coordinates (−1, 6) and (2, 4). Run the program with these new values. Did the distance change? Explain.

3. Change the values given to the two points so that they represent the coordinates (1, 0) and (5, 7). Check the program's answer with your calculator.

4. Change the values given to the two points so that they represent the same coordinates (2, 4) and (2, 4). Does the program give the correct answer?

2.2 Constants and Variables

constants

variables
identifier

Constants and variables represent objects that we use in our programs. Literal **constants** are specific values such as 2, 3.1416, −1.5, 'a', or "hello" that we use to form C++ statements. The value of these objects cannot be changed. **Variables** are memory locations that are assigned a name or **identifier.** The identifier is used to reference the value stored in the memory location. A useful analogy for a memory location and its corresponding identifier is a mailbox that is associated with the name of an individual; the memory location (or mailbox) may contain an

---

*If you use a word processor to generate a source file, be sure to save it as a text file.

object. The following shows the variables, their identifiers, and their initial values after the following declaration statement from program `Chapter1_1`:

```
double x1(1), y1(5), x2(4), y2(7),
       side1, side2, distance;
```

| double x1 | 1.0 | | double y1 | 5.0 |

| double x2 | 4.0 | | double y2 | 7.0 |

double side1 `?`   double side2 `?`   double distance `?`

garbage

memory snapshot

The values of variables that were not given initial values are unspecified, and thus indicated with a question mark; sometimes these values are called **garbage** values because their values are unpredictable. A diagram such as this that shows an object along with its identifier, its value, and its data type is called a **memory snapshot.** A memory snapshot shows the contents of a memory location at a specified point in the execution of the program. The preceding memory snapshot shows the objects and their contents after execution of the declaration statement. The objects are declared to be of type `double` and will be represented in memory using the standard IEEE format. For simplicity we show only the value of the variable and its data type, but it is important to remember that the value of a floating point variable, even when initialized with an integer constant, will be represented in memory using the IEEE floating point representation of the integer value.

We frequently use memory snapshots to show the contents of objects both before and after a statement is executed in order to show its effect. The rules for selecting a valid identifier are as follows:

- an identifier must begin with an alphabetic character or the underscore character
- alphabetic characters in an identifier can be lowercase or uppercase letters
- an identifier can contain digits, but not as the first character
- an identifier can be of any length, but the first 31 characters of the identifier must be unique

case-sensitive

C++ is **case-sensitive,** which means uppercase letters are distinguished from lowercase letters; thus *Side*1, *SIDE*1 and *side*1 represent three different objects. C++ also includes keywords with special meaning to the C++ compiler that cannot be used for identifiers; a complete list of keywords is given in Table 2.1.

Examples of valid identifiers are *distance, x1, xSum, averageMeasurement,* and *initialTime.* Examples of invalid identifiers are 1*x* (begins with a digit), *switch* (a keyword), $*sum* (contains an invalid character $), and *rate%* (contains an invalid character %).

Style An identifier name should be carefully selected so that it reflects the contents of the object. *If possible, the name should also indicate the units of measurement.* For example, if an object represents a temperature measurement in degrees Fahrenheit, use an identifier such as *tempF* or *degreesF.* If an object represents an angle, name it *thetaRad* to indicate that the angle is measured in radians or *thetaDeg* to indicate that the angle is measured in degrees.

strongly typed

Declarations statements included in any block of code must include not only the identifiers of the objects that we plan to use in our program, but they must also specify the data type of the object. C++ is a **strongly typed** programming language. This means that every

TABLE 2.1   Keywords

asm	auto	bool	break
case	catch	char	class
const	const_cast	continue	default
delete	do	double	dynamic_cast
else	enum	explicit	export
extern	false	float	for
friend	goto	if	inline
int	long	mutable	namespace
new	operator	private	protected
public	register	reinterpret_cast	return
short	signed	sizeof	static
static_cast	struct	switch	template
this	throw	true	try
typedef	typeid	typename	union
unsigned	using	virtual	void
volatile	wchar_t	while	

identifier must be declared before it can be used in a statement. Data types are presented after a discussion on scientific notation.

Practice!

Determine which of the following names are valid identifiers. If a name is not a valid identifier, give the reason that it is not acceptable, and suggest a valid replacement.

1. density	2. area	3. Time
4. xsum	5. x_sum	6. tax-rate
7. perimeter	8. sec**2	9. degrees_C
10. break	11. #123	12. x$y
13. count	14. void	15. f(x)
16. f2	17. Final_Value	18. w1.1
19. reference1	20. reference_1	21. m/s

Scientific Notation

floating-point
scientific notation

A **floating-point** value is one that can represent both integer and non-integer values, such as 2.5, −0.004, and 15.0. A floating-point value expressed in **scientific notation** is rewritten as a mantissa times a power of 10, where the mantissa has an absolute value greater than or equal to 1.0 and less than 10.0. For example, in scientific notation, 25.6 is written as 2.56×10^1, −0.004 is written as $-4.0 \times 10^{(-3)}$, and 1.5 is written as 1.5×10^0. In **exponential notation**, the letter **e** is used to separate the mantissa from the exponent of the power of 10. Thus, in exponential notation, 25.6 is written as 2.56e1, −0.004 is written as −4.0e-3, and 1.5 is written as 1.5e0.

exponential
notation

precision

range

The number of digits allowed by the computer for the decimal portion of the mantissa determines the **precision**, and the number of digits allowed for the exponent determines the **range**. Thus, values with two digits of precision and an exponent range of -8 to 7 could include values such as 2.3×10^5 (230,000) and $5.9 \times 10^{(-8)}$ (0.000000059). This precision and exponent range would not be sufficient for many of the types of values that we use in engineering problem solutions. For example, the distance in mile from Mars to the Sun, with seven digits of precision, is 141,517,510, or 1.4151751×10^8; to represent this value, we would need at least seven digits of precision and an exponent range that included the integer 8.

Practice!

In problems 1 through 6, express the value in scientific notation. Specify the number of digits of precision needed to represent each value.

1. 35.004	2. 0.00042
3. $-50,000$	4 3.15723
5. -0.09997	6. $10,000,028$

In problems 7 through 12, express the value in floating-point notation.

7. 1.03e-5	8. -1.05e5
9. -3.552e6	10. 6.67e-4
11. 9.0e-2	12. -2.2e-2

Numeric Data Types

Numeric data types are used to specify the types of numbers that will be contained in objects. In C++, the built-in numeric types are either integers or floating-point values. The following diagram shows the built-in numeric data types and their specifiers that are discussed in the next few paragraphs:

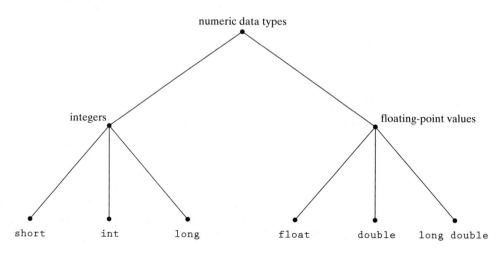

type specifiers

system dependent

The **type specifiers** for signed integers are `short`, `int`, and `long`, for short integer, integer, and long integer, respectively. The specific ranges of values are **system dependent**, which means that the ranges can vary from one system to another. In the last section of this chapter, we present a program that you can use to determine the ranges of the numeric data types on your system. On many systems, the short integer data type range from $-32,768$ to $32,767$, and the integer and long integer type often represents values from $-2,147,483,648$ to $2,147,483,647$. (The unusual limits such as $32,767$ and $2,147,483,647$ relate to conversions of binary values to decimal values.) C++ also allows an `unsigned` qualifier to be added to integer specifiers. An `unsigned` integer can represent only positive values. Signed and `unsigned` integers can represent the same number of values, but the ranges are different. For example, if an `unsigned short` has the range of values from 0 to $65,535$, then a `short` integer has the range of values from $-32,768$ to $32,767$; both data types can represent a total of $65,536$ values.

Declarations: A type declaration statement defines new identifers and allocates memory. An initial value may be assigned to the memory location at the time the identifier is defined. Modifiers may also be specified.

Syntax

```
[modifier] type specifier identifier [= initial value];
[modifier] type specifier identifier [(initial value)];
```

Examples

```
double x1, y1(0);
int counter=0;
const int MIN_SIZE=0;
bool error(false);
char comma(',');
```

The type specifiers for floating-point values are `float` (single precision), `double` (double precision), and `long double` (extended precision). The following statement from program `chapter1_1` thus defines seven objects that all contain double-precision floating-point values:

```
double x1(1), y1(5), x2(4), y2(7),
       side1, side2, distance;
```

The difference between the `float`, `double`, and `long double` types relates to the precision (or accuracy) and the range of the values represented. The precision and range are system dependent. Table 2.2 contains precision and range information for integers and floating-point values used by the Microsoft Visual C++ compiler. A program given in Section 2.9 allows you to obtain this information for your computer system. On most systems, a `double` data type stores about twice as many decimal digits of precision as are stored with a `float` data type. In addition, a `double` value will have a wider range of exponent values than a `float` value. The `long double` value may have more precision and a still wider exponent range, but this is again system dependent. A floating-point constant such as 2.3 is as-

TABLE 2.2   Example Data-Type Limits*

Integers	
short	Maximum = 32,767
int	Maximum = 2,147,483,647
long	Maximum = 2,147,483,647

Floating Point	
float	6 digits of precision Maximum exponent = 38 Maximum value = 3.402823e + 38
double	15 digits of precision Maximum exponent = 308 Maximum value = 1.797693e + 308
long double	15 digits of precision Maximum exponent = 308 Maximum value = 1.797693e + 308

*Microsoft Visual C++ 6.0 compiler.

sumed to be a `double` constant. To specify a `float` constant or a `long double` constant, the letter (or suffix) F or L must be appended to the constant. Thus, 2.3F and 2.3L represent a `float` constant and a `long double` constant, respectively.

Boolean Data Type

boolean data type

The **boolean data type,** named after the mathematician George Boole, can represent only two values: true and false. In C++, the value zero is interpreted as false and any nonzero value is considered to be true. There are two predefined boolean constants, `true` and `false`, that can also be used. Boolean objects can be defined using the type specifier `bool`. The following example illustrates the use of boolean objects and constants:

```
bool error(false), status(true);
cout << error << endl << status;
```

The output from this program is

```
0
1
```

Boolean objects are very useful in controlling the flow of a program and flagging error conditions.

Character Data Type

characters

Character data is easy to work with in C++, but to work with **characters** effectively, we need to understand more about their representation in the computer's memory. Recall that all information stored in a computer is represented internally as sequences of binary digits (0 and 1).

binary code

Each character corresponds to a **binary code** value. In the discussions that follow, we assume that American National Standards Institute (ANSI) code is used to represent characters.

TABLE 2.3   Examples of ANSI Codes

Character	ANSI Code	Integer Equivalent
newline, \n	0001010	10
%	0100101	37
3	0110011	51
A	1000001	65
a	1100001	97
b	1100010	98
c	1100011	99

Table 2.3 contains a few characters, their binary form in ANSI, and the integer values that correspond to the binary values. The character 'a' is represented by the binary value 1100001, which is equivalent to the integer value of 97. A total of 128 characters can be represented in the ANSI code. A complete ANSI code table is given in Appendix B.

A character constant is enclosed in single quotes, as in 'A', 'b', and '3'. The type specifier for character objects is `char`. Once a character is stored in memory as a binary value, the binary value can be interpreted as a character or as an integer, as illustrated in Table 2.3. However, it is important to note that the binary ANSI representation for a character digit is not equal to the binary representation for an integer digit.

From Table 2.3, we see that the ANSI binary representation for the character digit '3' is 0110011, which is equivalent to the binary representation of the integer value 51. Thus, performing a computation with the character representation of a digit does not yield the same result as performing the computation with the integer representation of the digit. The following program illustrates this feature of character data:

```
/*------------------------------------------------------------------*/
/* Program chapter2_1                                               */
/*                                                                  */
/* This program prints a char and an int                           */

#include<iostream> // Required for cout
using namespace std;

int main()
{
// Declare and initialize objects.
char ch ('3');
int i(3);

// Print both values.
cout << "value of ch: " << ch << " value of i: " << i << endl;

// Assign character to integer
i = ch;

// Print both values.
cout << "value of ch: " << ch << " value of i: " << i << endl;
```

```
//  Exit program
return( 0);
}
/*------------------------------------------------------------------*/
```

The output from this program is

```
value of ch: 3; value of i: 3
value of ch: 3; value of i: 51
```

String Data

string
C-style strings
string objects

A literal **string** constant is a sequence of characters enclosed within double quotes, as in "sensor", "F18", or "Jane Doe". String variables can be represented as **C-style strings** using arrays of type `char`, or as **string objects** using the `string` class. Both representations will be discussed in detail in Chapter 7. In this section, we give a brief introduction to the `string` class.

The C++ compiler does not have a built-in data type named `string`, but a `string` class definition is provided in the standard C++ library file `string`. To use the `string` class, a program must include the following preprocessor directive:

```
#include<string>
```

The following program illustrates the use of the predefined C++ `string` class:

```
/*------------------------------------------------------------*/
/* Program chapter2_2                                         */
/*                                                            */
/* This program prints a greeting                             */
/* using the string class.                                    */

#include <iostream>  // Required for cout
#include <string>    // Required for string
using namespace std;

int main()
{
// Declare and initialize two string objects.
string salutation("Hello"), name("Jane Doe");

// Output greeting.
cout << salutation << ' ' << name << '!' << endl;

// Exit program.
return(0);
}
```

The output from this program is

```
Hello Jane Doe!
```

A memory snapshot of program `chapter2_2` is provided below.

```
        string salutation("Hello"), name("Jane Doe");

        string salutation   | Hello |

        string name   | Jane Doe |
```

The `string` object `salutation` has a size, or length, of five. The `string` object `name` has a size of eight. The size of a `string` object may change during execution. For example, if the assignment statement

    salutation = "Goodbye";

were added to program `chapter2_2`, the memory snapshot would be modified and the size of salutation would change to seven.

    string salutation | Goodbye |

    string name | Jane Doe |

Symbolic Constants

symbolic constant

A **symbolic constant** is defined using the `const` modifier. Engineering constants such as π or the acceleration of gravity are good candidates for symbolic constants. For example, consider the following declaration statement to assign a value to the symbolic constant *PI*:

    const double PI = acos(-1.0);

The `acos` function, when evaluated at -1, will return an approximation for π that includes 15 digits of precision. Statements that need to use the value of π would then use the symbolic constant *PI* as illustrated in this statement:

    area = PI*radius*radius;

which computes the area of a circle.

Symbolic constants are usually defined with uppercase identifiers (as in PI instead of pi) to indicate that they are symbolic constants, and, of course, the identifiers should be selected so that they are easy to remember. Once an identifier has been declared and initialized using the `const` modifier, its value cannot be changed within the program.

Practice!

Give the declaration statements required to define symbolic constants for these constants:

1. Speed of light, $c = 2.99792 \times 10^8$ m/s

2. Charge of an electron, $e = 1.602177 \times 10^{-19}$ C

3. Avogadro's number, $N_A = 6.022 \times 10^{23} \, mol^{-1}$

4. Acceleration of gravity, $g = 9.8 \, m/s^2$

5. Acceleration of gravity, $g = 32 \, ft/s^2$

6. Mass of the Earth, $M_E = 5.98 \times 10^{24}$ kg

7. Radius of the Moon, $r = 1.74 \times 10^6$ m

8. Unit of length, UnitLength = 'm'

9. Unit of time, UnitTime = 's'

2.3 C++ Classes

programmer-defined data type

C++ supports the use of classes to define new data types, often referred to as **programmer-defined data types**. In the previous section, we looked at examples using built-in data types including `int`, `double`, and `char`, and we discussed the predefined data type `string` in program `chapter2_2`. Recall that predefined data types are included in the Standard C++ library and programs that want to use predefined types must include the appropriate compiler directive. Built-in data types do not require any include directives. A well-designed programmer-defined data type requires work to implement, but once defined a new data type can be used as easily as a predefined type. In this section, we will take our first look at building a programmer-defined data type.

As an introduction to building programmer-defined data types, we will define a new type that represents the concept of a point in a plane. A point in a plane is an object defined by a (x, y) coordinate. Coordinate values are often floating point values, as opposed to integer values, so we will use the built-in data type `double` to represent the coordinates in the implementation of our new data type. The definition of a programmer-defined data type usually consists of two parts: a **class declaration** and a **class implementation**. In general, the class declaration and the class implementation are written in separate files. The convention is to name the class declaration file with a .h extension and the class implementation file with a .cpp extension. Applications that want to use a programmer-defined type must include the class declaration file in their source code.

class declaration
class implementation

Class Declaration

A class declaration begins with the keyword `class` followed by an identifier that specifies the name of the new class. The body of the class declaration is a block of code, terminated with a semicolon. The declaration block includes declaration statements for the **data members** and declaration statements for the **class methods**. The keywords `public`, `private`, and `protected` are used to control access to the data members and class methods. Controlling access to data members and methods is a powerful feature of classes and will be discussed in more detail in later chapters. To illustrate the syntax of a class declaration, we will begin with the declaration of a class named `Point`.

data members
class methods

```
/*-------------------------------------------------------------*/
/* Point class chapter2_3                                     */
/* Filename: Point.h                                          */
class Point
{
// Type declaration statements
// Data members.
private:
double xCoord, yCoord; //Class attributes
public:
//Declaration statements for class methods
//Constructors for Point class
Point(); //default constructor
Point(double x, double  y); //parameterized constructor
};
/*-------------------------------------------------------------*/
```

Constructor

Note that a semicolon is required to terminate the declaration block.

Class methods define the operations that can be performed on class objects. A **constructor** is a special method that performs the operation of a type declaration statement. Recall that we can declare and initialize objects of type `double` with a type declaration statement as follows:

```
double xCoord, yCoord(0.0);
memory snapshot:
double xCoord  ?
double yCoord  0.0
```

The constructors declared in the `Point` class declaration provide type declaration statements for `Point` objects, as illustrated below.

```
Point p1, p2(1.0, 1.0);
memory snapshot:
Point p1 ->   ? double xCoord
              ? double yCoord
Point p2 ->  1.0 double xCoord
             1.0 double yCoord
```

Class Implementation

To complete the definition of our `Point` class, we need to write the class implementation file. The class implementation file must include a block of code for each of the methods declared in the class declaration. Each block of code must begin with a header that includes the name of the class, followed by the scope resolution operator (::) and the name of the method. The implementation file for our `Point` class is given below. Note that the implementation file includes the compiler directive `#include "Point.h"`. Because `Point.h` is not part of the C++ Standard Library, quotation marks are used to enclose the name of the declaration file.

```
/*------------------------------------------------------------*/
/* Class implementation for Point                             */
/* filename: Point.cpp                                        */
#include "Point.h"         //Required for Point
#include <iostream>        //Required for cout
using namespace std;

//Parameterized constructor
Point::Point(double x, double y)
```

```
{
  //input parameters x,y
  cout << " Constructing Point object, parameterized: \n" ;
  cout << " input parameters: "  << x << " ,"  << y << endl;
  xCoord = x;
  yCoord = y;
}
//Default constructor
Point::Point()
{
    cout << " Constructing Point object, default: \n" ;
    cout << " initializing to zero"  << endl;
    xCoord = 0.0;
    yCoord = 0.0;
}
```

The parameterized constructor begins with the header `Point::Point(double x, double y)`. Parameterized constructors provide parameters for specifying the initial values of the data members. The parameterized `Point` constructor provides two parameters, `x` and `y`, both of type `double`. Inside the statement block, the values of these parameters will be assigned to the data members. We begin our statement block with two `cout` statements for debugging and clarification. These statements will be removed once the `Point` class has been fully designed and implemented. Following the `cout` statements, the value of `x` is assigned to `xCoord` and the value of `y` is assigned to `yCoord`.

The default constructor begins with the header `Point::Point()`. Since no parameters are provided in the header, the statement block assigns the constant 0.0 to both `xCoord` and `yCoord`. Note that we could have chosen any constant as the initial value. The following program declares two objects of type `Point`.

```
/*------------------------------------------------------*/
/* Program chapter2_3                                   */
/*                                                      */
/* This program illustrates the use of the             */
/* programmer-defined data type Point                  */

#include <iostream>   //Required for cout
#include "Point.h"    //Required for Point
using namespace std;

int main()
{
  //Declare and initialize objects.
  cout << " In main, declare p1..."  << endl;
  Point p1;
  cout << " \nIn main, declare p2..."  << endl;
  Point p2(1.5, -4.7);
  cout << " \nIn main, declare ORIGIN..."  << endl;
  const Point ORIGIN(0.0, 0.0);
  return 0;
}
/*------------------------------------------------------*/
```

The output from this program is

```
In main, declare p1...
Constructing Point object, default:
initializing to zero

In main, declare p2...
Constructing Point object, parameterized:
input parameters: 1.5,-4.7

In main, declare ORIGIN...
Constructing Point object, parameterized:
input parameters: 0,0
```

We will continue to add functionality to the `Point` class as we learn new features of the C++ language.

Class Definition: The definition of a programmer-defined class consists of two parts: a class declaration and a class implementation.

Syntax: Class Declaration
//filename:className.h
 	
```class className```
`{`
  access modifier:
    declaration of attributes
  acccess modifier:
    declaration of methods
`};`
	Syntax: Class Implementation
	//filename: className.cpp
	
	`#include "className.h"`
	definitions of class methods

Example: class Declaration
//filename: Point.h
 	
```class Point```
`{`
  `private:`
    `double xCoord;`
    `double yCoord;`
 	
  `public:`
  `Point(double x, double y);`
`};`
	Example: class Implementation
	//filename: Point.cpp
	
	`#include "Point.h"`
	
	`Point::Point (double x, double y)`
	`{`
	  `xCoord = x;`
	  `YCoord = Y;`
	`}`

Usage:
```
#include "Point.h"
...
int main()
{
  Point p1(1.5, 2.7);
...
```

operators

To perform operations in a program, such as addition, multiplication, and comparison of objects, we use special **operators** that are defined for the built in data types supported by C++. In this section, we will look at several of these operators.

Assignment Operator

assignment
statement
assignment
operator

An **assignment statement** uses the **assignment operator,** = to store the result in the memory location named by the identifier. The general form of the assignment statement is

```
identifier = expression;
```

where an expression can be a constant, another object, or the result of an operation. Consider the following two sets of statements that declare and give values to the objects sum, x1, p1, and ch:

```
//Set One
double sum(10.5);
int x1(3);
Point p1(1.5, -4.7);
char ch('a');

//Set Two
double sum;
int x1;
Point p1, p2(1.5, -4.7);
char ch;

sum = 10.5;
x1 = 3;
p1 = p2;
ch = 'a';
```

After either set of statements is executed, the value of sum is 10.5, the value of x1 is 3, the value of p1 is (1.5, −4.7) and the value of ch is 'a', as shown in the following memory snapshot:

double sum $\boxed{10.5}$ int x1 $\boxed{3}$ Point p1 $\boxed{1.5}$ $\boxed{-4.7}$ char ch $\boxed{\text{'a'}}$

The statements in Set One declare and initialize the objects at the same time in the type declaration statement; the assignment statements in Set Two could be used at any point in the program and thus may be used to change (as opposed to initialize) the values of objects that have already been declared. Note that the compiler provides an assignment operator for the Point class. The assignment operator performs a bit-wise copy of the data members from the object on the right-hand side of the assignment operator to the corresponding data members of the object on the left-hand side of the assignment operator.

Multiple assignments are also allowed in C++, as in the following statement, which assigns a value of zero to each of the objects x, y, and z:

```
x = y = z = 0;
```

Multiple assignments are discussed further at the end of this section.

Assignment Statements: An assignment statement uses an assignment operator to store the value of an expression in the memory location named by the identifier. The expression can be a constant, a variable or an expression that evaluates to a type that is compatible with the data type of the identifier.

Syntax

```
identifier = expression;
```

Examples

```
x1 = y1;
counter = 0;
counter = counter + 1;
```

The assignment operator should not be confused with equality. Assignment statements should be read as *is assigned the value of*; thus, the statement `rate = stateTax` is read; *rate is read assigned the value of stateTax*. If `stateTax` contains the value 0.06, then `rate` also contains the value 0.06 after the statement is executed; the value in `stateTax` is not changed. The memory snapshots before and after this statement is executed are the following:

Before: `double rate` `?`   `double stateTax` `0.06`

After: `double rate` `0.06`   `double stateTax` `0.06`

If we assign a value to an object that has a different data type, then a conversion must occur during the execution of the statement. Sometimes the conversion can result in information being lost. For example, consider the following declaration and assignment statement:

```
int a;
 ...
a = 12.8;
```

Because `a` is declared to be an integer, it cannot store a value with a nonzero decimal portion. Therefore, in this case, the memory snapshot after executing the assignment statement is the following:

`int a` `12`

Note that the value 12.8 is truncated, not rounded.
    To determine whether a numeric conversion will work properly, we use the following order, which is from high to low:

```
high:    long double
         double
         float
         long integer
         integer
low:     short integer
```

If a value is moved to a data type that is higher in order, no information will be lost; if a value is moved to a data type that is lower in order, information may be lost. Thus, moving an integer to a double will work properly, but moving a float to an integer may result in the loss of some information or in an incorrect result. In general, use only assignments that do not cause potential conversion problems. Unsigned integers were not included in the list because errors can occur in both directions.

Arithmetic Operators

arithmetic operation

An assignment statement can be used to assign the result of an **arithmetic operation** to an object, as shown in this statement that computes the area of a square:

```
areaSquare = side*side;
```

Here the operator * is used to indicate multiplication. The operators + and - are used to indicate addition and subtraction, and the operator / is used for division. Thus, each of the following statements is a valid computation for the area of a triangle:

```
areaTriangle = 0.5*base*height;
```

```
areaTriangle = (base*height)/2.0;
```

The use of parentheses in the second statement is not required, but is used for readability.
Consider this assignment statement:

```
x = x + 1;
```

In algebra, this is invalid because a value cannot be equal to itself plus 1. However, this assignment statement should not be read as an equality; instead, it should be read as *x is assigned the value of x plus 1*. With this interpretation, the statement indicates that the value stored in the object x is incremented by 1. Thus, if the value of x is 5 before this statement is executed, then the value of x will be 6 after the statement is executed.

modulus operator

C++ also includes a **modulus operator %** that is used to compute the remainder in a division between two integers. For example, 5%2 is equal to 1, 6%3 is equal to 0, and 2%7 is equal to 2. (The quotient of 2/7 is zero with a remainder of 2.) If a and b are integers, then the expression a/b computes the integer quotient, whereas the expression a%b computes the integer remainder. Thus, if a is equal to 9 and b is equal to 4, the value of a/b is 2 and the value of a%b is 1. If the value of b is equal to zero in either a/b or a%b, or if either of the integer values in a and b is negative in a%b, the result is system-dependent.

The modulus operator is useful in determining whether an integer is a multiple of another number. For example, if a%2 is equal to zero, then a is even; otherwise, a is odd. If a%5 is equal to zero, then a is a multiple of 5. We will use the modulus operator frequently in the development of engineering solutions.

binary operators
unary operators

The five operators (+, −, *, /, %) discussed in the previous paragraphs are **binary operators**—operators that operate on two operands (values). C++ also includes **unary operators**—operators that operate on a single operand. For example, plus and minus signs can be unary operators when they are used in an expression such as −x.

The result of a binary operation with values of the same type is another value of the same type. For example, if a and b are double values, then the result of a/b is also a double

truncated
result

mixed
operation

value. Similarly, if a and b are integers, then the result of a/b is also an integer; however, an integer division can sometimes produce unexpected results because any decimal portion of the integer division is dropped; the result is a **truncated result,** not a rounded result. Thus, 5/3 evaluates to 1, and 3/6 evaluates to 0. Arithmetic operators for programmer-defined classes are not provided by the compiler, but can be defined by the programmer as class methods.

An operation between values with different types is a **mixed operation.** Before the operation is performed, the value with the lower type is converted or promoted to the higher type (as discussed in conversions within assignment statements), and thus the operation is performed with values of the same type. For example, if an operation is specified between an integer and a floating point, the integer will be promoted to a floating point before the operation is performed; the result will be a floating point.

Suppose that we want to compute the average of a set of integers. If the sum and the count of the integers have been stored in the integer objects sum and count, it would seem that the following statements should correctly compute the average:

```
int sum, count;
double average;
...
average = sum/count;
```

cast operator

However, the division between two integers gives an integer result that is then promoted to a double value. Thus, if sum is 18, and count is 5, then the value assigned to average is 3.0, not 3.6. To compute this average correctly, we use a **cast operator**—a unary operator that allows us to specify a type change in the value before the next computation. In this example, the cast (double) is applied to sum:

```
average = (double)sum/count;
```

The value of sum is promoted to a double value before the division is performed. The division is then a mixed operation between a double value and an integer, so the value of count is promoted to a double value; the result of the division is then a double value that is assigned to average. If the value of sum is 18, and the value of count is 5, the value of average is now correctly computed to be 3.6. The cast operator affects only the value used in the computation; it does not change the value stored in the object sum.

Practice!

Give the value computed by each of the following sets of statements, and draw a memory map. Use the Point class definition provided in section 2.3 to answer questions 5 and 6.

1. ```
   int a(27), b(6), c;
   ...
   c = b%a;
   ```

2. ```
   int a(27), b(6);
   double c;
   ...
   c = a/(double)b;
   ```

3. ```
   int a;
   double b(6), c(18.6);
   ...
   a = c/b;
   ```

4. ```
   int b(6);
   double a, c(18.6);
   ...
   a = (int) c/b;
   ```

5. ```
   Point p1, p2(-5.2, 0.0);
   ```

6. ```
   double x(2.0), y(4.3);
   Point p1(x,y);
   ```

TABLE 2.4	Precedence of Arithmetic Operators	
Precedence	**Operator**	**Associativity**
1	Parentheses: ( )	Innermost first
2	Unary operators: + − (type)	Right to left
3	Binary operators: * / %	Left to right
4	Binary operators: + −	Left to right

Precedence of Operators

precedence of arithmetic operators

In an expression that contains more than one arithmetic operator, we need to be concerned about the order in which the operations are performed. Table 2.4 contains the **precedence of** the **arithmetic operators,** which matches the standard algebraic precedence. Operations within parentheses are always evaluated first; if the parentheses are nested, the operations within the innermost parentheses are evaluated first. Unary operators are evaluated before the binary operations *, /, and %; binary addition and subtraction are evaluated last. If there are several operators of the same precedence level in an expression, the objects are grouped (or associated) with the operators in a specific order, as specified in Table 2.4. For example, consider the following expression:

```
a*b + b/c*d
```

Because multiplication and division have the same precedence level, and because the associativity (the order for grouping the operations) is from left to right, this expression will be evaluated as if it contained the following:

```
(a*b) + ((b/c)*d)
```

The precedence order does not specify whether a*b is evaluated before (b/c)*d; the order of evaluation of these terms is system dependent but does not affect the final value.

The spacing within an arithmetic expression is a style issue. Some people prefer to put spaces around each operator. We prefer to put spaces only around binary addition and subtraction, because they are evaluated last. *Choose the spacing style that you prefer, but then use it consistently.*

Assume that we want to compute the area of a trapezoid and that we have declared four objects of type double: base, height1, height2, and area. Assume further that the objects base, height1, and height2 already have values. A statement to correctly compute the area of the trapezoid is

```
area = 0.5*base*(height1 + height2);
```

Suppose that we omitted the parentheses in the expression

```
area = 0.5*base*height1 + height2;
```

The statement would be executed as if it were this statement:

```
area = ((0.5*base)*height1) + height2;
```

Although an incorrect answer has been computed, there is no error message to alert us to the error. Therefore, it is important to be very careful when converting arithmetic expressions into C++. In general, use parentheses to indicate the order of operations in a complicated expression to avoid confusion and to be sure that the expression is evaluated in the manner desired.

You may have noticed that there is no operator for exponentiation to compute values such as x^4. A special mathematical function to perform exponentiation will be discussed in the section on elementary math functions. Of course, exponentiations with integer exponents such as a^2 can be computed with repeated multiplications, as in a*a.

The evaluation of long expressions should be broken into several statements. For example, consider the following equation:

$$f = \frac{x^3 - 2x^2 + x - 6.3}{x^2 + 0.05005x - 3.14}.$$

If we try to evaluate the expression in one statement, it becomes too long to be read easily:

```
f = (x*x*x - 2*x*x + x - 6.3)/(x*x + 0.05005*x - 3.14);
```

We could break the statement into two lines:

```
f = (x*x*x - 2*x*x + x - 6.3)/
    (x*x + 0.05005*x - 3.14);
```

Another solution is to compute the numerator and denominator separately:

```
numerator = x*x*x - 2*x*x + x - 6.3;
denominator = x*x + 0.05005*x - 3.14;
f = numerator/denominator;
```

The objects x, numerator, denominator, and f must be floating-point objects in order to compute the correct value of f.

Practice!

In problems 1 through 3, give C++ statements to compute the indicated values. Assume that the identifiers in the expressions have been defined as objects of type double and have also been assigned appropriate values. Use the following constant: Acceleration of gravity: $g = 9.80665$ m/s^2

1. Distance traveled:

    $$\text{Distance} = x_0 + v_0 t + at^2.$$

2. Tension in a cord:

    $$\text{Tension} = \frac{2m_1 m_2}{m_1 + m_2} * g.$$

3. Fluid pressure at the end of a pipe:

    $$P_2 = P_1 + \frac{pv\left(A_2^2 - A_1^2\right)}{2A_1^2}.$$

In problems 4 through 6, give the mathematical equations computed by the C++ statements. Assume that the following symbolic constants have been defined, where the units of G are $m^3/(kg * s^2)$:

```
const double PI = acos(-1.0);
const double G = 6.67259e-11;
```

4. Centripetal acceleration:

```
centripetal = 4*PI*PI*r/(T*T);
```

5. Potential energy:

```
potential_energy = -G*M_E*m/r;
```

6. Change in potential energy:

```
change = G*M_E*m*(1/R_E - 1/(R_E + h));
```

Overflow and Underflow

The values stored in a memory have a wide range of allowed values. However, if the result of a computation exceeds the range of allowed values, an error occurs. For example, assume that the exponent range of a floating-point value is from -38 to 38. This range should accommodate most computations, but it is possible for the results of an expression to be outside of this range. For example, suppose that we execute the following commands:

```
x = 2.5e30;
y = 1.0e30;
z = x*y;
```

overflow

underflow

The values of x and y are within the allowable range. However, the value of z should be 2.5e60, but this value exceeds the range. This error is called exponent **overflow** because the exponent of the result of an arithmetic operation is too large to store in the memory assigned to the object. The action generated by an exponent overflow is system dependent.

Exponent **underflow** is a similar error caused by the exponent of the result of an arithmetic operation being too small to store in the memory assigned to the object. Using the same allowable range as in the previous example, we obtain an exponent underflow with the following commands:

```
x = 2.5e-30;
y = 1.0e30;
z = x/y;
```

Again, the values of x and y are within the allowable range, but the value of z should be 2.5e-60. Because the exponent is less than the minimum value allowed, we have caused an exponent underflow. Again, the action generated by an exponent underflow is system dependent; on some systems, the result of an operation with exponent underflow is set to zero.

Increment and Decrement Operators

increment operator
decrement operator
prefix
postfix

The C++ language contains unary operators for incrementing and decrementing objects; these operators cannot be used with constants or expressions. The **increment operator** $++$ and the **decrement operator** $--$ can be applied either in a **prefix** position (before the identifier), as in $++count$, or in a **postfix** position (after the identifier), as in $count++$. If an increment or decrement operator is used in a statement by itself, it is equivalent to an assignment statement that increments or decrements the object. Thus, the statement

```
y--;
```

is equivalent to the statement

```
y = y - 1;
```

If the increment or decrement operator is used in an expression, then the expression must be evaluated carefully. If the increment or decrement operator is in a prefix position, the identifier is modified, and then the new value is used in evaluating the rest of the expression. If the increment or decrement operator is in a postfix position, the old value of the identifier is used to evaluate the rest of the expression, and then the identifier is modified. Thus, the execution of

$$w = ++x - y; \qquad\qquad (2.1)$$

is equivalent to the execution of this pair of statements:

```
x = x + 1;
w = x - y;
```

Similarly, the statement

$$w = x++ - y; \qquad\qquad (2.2)$$

is equivalent to the pair of statements

```
w = x - y;
x = x + 1;
```

When executing either Equation (2.1) or Equation (2.2), if we assume that the value of x is equal to 5 and the value of y is equal to 3, then the value of x increases to 6. However, after executing Equation (2.1), the value of w is 3, but after executing Equation (2.2), the value of w is 2.

The increment and decrement operators have the same precedence as the other unary operators. If several unary operators are in an expression, they are associated from right to left. When using postfix notation, the value of the object will be incremented by the time the end of the statement is reached. Exactly when the increment occurs is system dependent. For this reason, the value of the object being modified is not definite from the point at which the postfix operator is applied to the end of the statement.

Abbreviated Assignment Operators

C++ allows simple assignment statements to be abbreviated. For example, each of the following pair of statements contains equivalent statements:

Abbreviated Operator	**Equivalent Statement**
x += 3;	x = x + 3;
sum += x;	sum = sum + x;
d /= 4.5;	d = d/4.5;
r %= 2;	r = r%2;

In fact, any statement of the form

```
identifier = identifier operator expression;
```

can be written in the form

```
identifier operator = expression;
```

multiple-assignment

Earlier in this section, we used the following **multiple-assignment** statement:

```
x = y = z = 0;
```

The interpretation of this statement is clear, but the interpretation of the following statement is not as evident:

```
a = b += c + d;
```

To evaluate this properly, we use Table 2.5, which indicates that the assignment operators are evaluated last, and their associativity is right to left. Thus, the statement is equivalent to the following:

```
a = (b += (c + d));
```

If we replace the abbreviated forms with the longer forms of the operations, we have

```
a = (b = b + (c + d));
```

TABLE 2.5 Precedence of Arithmetic and Assignment Operators

Precedence	Operator	Associativity
1	Parentheses: ( )	Innermost first
2	Unary operators: +- ++ - (type)	Right to left
3	Binary operators: * / %	Left to right
4	Binary operators: + -	Left to right
5	Assignment operators: = += -= *= /= %=	Right to left

or

```
b = b + (c + d);
a = b;
```

Evaluating this statement was good practice with the precedence and associativity table, but, in general, statements used in a program should be more readable. Therefore, using abbreviated assignment statements in a multiple-assignment statement is not recommended. *Also, note that the spacing convention that we use inserts spaces around abbreviated operators and multiple-assignment operators because these operators are evaluated after the arithmetic operators.*

 Style

Practice!

Give a memory snapshot after each statement is executed, assuming that *x* is equal to 2 and that *y* is equal to 4 before the statement is executed. Also, assume that all the objects are integers.

```
1. z = x++ * y;        2. z = ++x * y;
3. x += y;             4. y %= x;
```

2.5 Standard Input and Output

C++ uses the object `cin` (pronounced "see in") to perform standard input and the object `cout` (pronounced "see out") to perform standard output. These objects are defined in the Standard C++ library file `iostream`. To use either of these objects in a program, we must include the following preprocessor directive:

```
#include <iostream>
```

The `cout` Object

stream

output buffer

The `cout` object is defined to **stream** output to the standard output device. The word stream suggests a continual stream of characters that is generated by the program and sent to an **output buffer.** When the output buffer is filled, the contents are displayed on the standard output device. For our examples, we will assume that the standard output device is the screen.

> **Standard Output:** C++ uses the `ostream` object `cout` to stream the value of an expression to standard output. `cout` is defined in the header file `iostream`. To use `cout` a program must include the compiler directive `#include <iostream>`.
>
> Syntax
>   `cout << expression << expression;`
>
> Example
>   `cout << "The radius is "<< radius << " centimeters\n";`

The operator ≪ is used with `cout` to output a value to the screen. The following statement outputs three values to the screen:

```
cout << "The radius of the circle is "
     << radius << " centimeters\n";
```

Each value to be output must be preceded by the ≪ operator. In the foregoing example, the first value to be output is the literal string "The radius of the circle is ", the second value to be output is the value of the object `radius`, the third value to be output is the string " centimeters \n". The characters (\n) represent the **newline** character; the newline character causes an advance to a new line on the screen when printed. The following example illustrates the use of `cout`:

newline

```
double radius(10), area;
const double PI = acos(-1.0);
cout << "The radius of the circle is: " << radius
     << " centimeters\n"
     << "The area is " << PI*radius*radius
     << " square centimeters\n";
```

The output from these statements is:

```
The radius of the circle is: 10 centimeters
The area is 3.14159 square centimeters
```

Notice that no decimal point is displayed in the value of radius, even though radius is declared to be of type `double`. Although this is the default format for printing floating point values in C++, we can overide this format using stream functions and manipulators.

Stream Objects

member functions

The identifier `cout` is declared to be an object of type `ostream` and is defined by the compiler to stream data to standard output. The `ostream` class includes methods, also referred to as **member functions**. Member functions are defined within a class definition, and can be called only by objects of the same class type. Since `cout` is an object of type `ostream` the `cout` object can call member functions of the `ostream` class to set the state of the format flags associated with standard output. The format flags are data members of the ostream class. A special operator called the **dot operator (.)** is used when an object calls one of its member functions. The following program uses two member functions of the ostream class to set the desired format for streaming floating point values to standard output. The `setf()` member function is used to set the format for displaying a floating point value to fixed form, or decimal form. The member function `precision()` is used to set the number of significant digits that should be displayed to the right of the decimal point.

dot operator (.)

```
/*-------------------------------------------------------------------*/
/* Program chapter2_4                                                */
/*                                                                   */
/*     This program computes area of a circle.                      */
/*     Results are displayed with two digits                        */
/*     to the right of the decimal point.                           */
```

```
#include<iostream>  //Required for cout, setf() and precision().
#include<cmath>     //Required for acos().
using namespace std;

const double PI = acos(-1.0);

int main()
{
    //Declare and initialize objects.
    double radius(10), area;
    area = PI*radius*radius;

    //Call the setf member function using dot operator.
    cout.setf(ios::fixed); //Fixed form(xx.xx).

    //Call the precision member function using dot operator.
    cout.precision(2);   //Display 2 digits to right of decimal.

    cout << "The radius of the circle is: " << radius
         << " centimeters\nThe area is "
         << area << " square centimeters\n";

    //exit program
    return 0;
}
/*-------------------------------------------------------------------*/
```

The output from this program is

```
The radius of the circle is: 10.00 centimeters
The area is 314.16 square centimeters
```

When a format flag is set by a call to setf() the flag remains set until it is changed by another call to setf(), or is unset (reset to zero) by a call to the stream function unsetf(). Table 2.6 lists just a few of the format flags defined in the ios class. The value ios::showpoint, for example, refers to the identifier showpoint defined in the ios class. When cout calls setf() with a value of ios::showpoint, as in the statement

```
cout.setf(ios::showpoint);
```

TABLE 2.6 Common Format Flags	
Flag	**Meaning**
ios::showpoint	display the decimal point
ios::fixed	decimal notation
ios::scientific	scientific notation
ios::right	print right justified
ios::left	print left justified

the state of the showpoint flag associated with the `cout` object is set to true and all floating point values streamed to standard output will be displayed with a decimal point. The statement

```
cout.unsetf(ios::showpoint);
```

would result in setting the state of the showpoint flag back to false (or zero) and restoring the default formatting for displaying floating point values to standard output.

The member function `precision()` specifies the number of significant digits to be displayed for floating point values, and its behavior is dependent on the state of other format flags. For example, when `cout` calls `precision(2)` after setting the state of the format flag to fixed, the integer argument 2 specifies that two digits should be displayed to the right of the decimal point, as illustrated in program `chapter2_4`. If `cout` calls `precision(2)` after setting the state of the format flag to scientific, the integer argument 2 specifies that a total of two significant digits should be displayed.

Modify!

1. Create a file containing the program `chapter2_4` discussed in this section. Run the program

   ```
   The radius of the circle is: 10.00 centimeters
   The area is 314.16 square centimeters
   ```

2. Replace the setf() statement in program `chapter2_4` with the statement

   ```
   cout.setf(ios::scientific);
   ```

   Compile and run the modified program. How did the output change? Explain.

3. Replace the setf() statement in program `chapter2_4` with the statement

   ```
   cout.setf(ios::showpoint);
   ```

   Compile and run the modified program. How did the output change? Explain.

Manipulators

manipulators

In program `chapter2_4` we used stream functions to control the formatting of output printed to the screen. The formatting of output can also be controlled with the use of **manipulators**. A manipulator is a predefined object that can affect the state of an output stream. Program `chapter2_5` illustrates the use of manipulators instead of stream functions to control the formatting of the standard output stream. To use manipulators, a program must include the header file `<iomanip>`

```
/*--------------------------------------------------------------------*/
/* Program chapter2_5                                               */
/*                                                                   */
/*   This program computes area of a circle.                       */
```

```
/*    Results are diplayed with two digits                          */
/*    to the right of the decimal point.                            */

#include <iostream> //Required for cout, endl.
#include <iomanip>  //Required for setw() setprecision(), fixed.
#include <cmath>     //Required for acos().
using namespace std;

const double PI = acos(-1.0);

int main()
{
   //Declare and initialize objects,
     double radius(10),  area;
     area = PI*radius*radius;

     cout << fixed << setprecision(2);
     cout   << "The radius of the circle is: "
          << setw(10)   << radius <<  "  centimeters"  << endl;
     cout << "The area of the circle is:    " << setw(10)   << area
          << " square centimeters"  << endl;

     //exit program
     return 0;
}
/*--------------------------------------------------------------*/
```

The output from this program is:

```
The radius of the circle is:    10.00 centimeters
The area of the circle is:    314.16 square centimeters
```

The manipulator endl is defined in the header file <iostream>, and is used in program chapter2_5 to advance to the beginning of a new line. The endl manipulator sends a newline character ('\n') to standard output and it immediately flushes the output buffer, rather than waiting until the output buffer is full. When cout statements are used to print memory snapshots of a program for debugging, the endl manipulator should be used (in place of \n) to ensure that the output buffer is flushed and you see your output before the next statement is executed.

The manipulators fixed and setprecision() are used to set the form and precision for displaying floating point values. Notice that manipulators are not member functions and thus they are not called using the dot operator. However, they have the same affect on the state of the format flags as the stream functions used in program chapter2_4. The manipulator setw() is used to specify a width, or number of columns, to be used for displaying the next value sent to the output buffer. The setw() manipulator is useful when results need to be printed in a table format. Table 2.7 lists several of the commonly used manipulators defined in the header file iomanip. To use these manipulators, a program must #include the file <iomanip>.

TABLE 2.7 Common Manipulators

Manipulator	Meaning
showpoint	display the decimal point
fixed	decimal notation
scientific	scientific notation
setprecision(n)	set the number of significant digits to be printed to the integer value n
setw(n)	set the minimum number of columns for printing the next value to the integer value n
right	print right justified
left	print left justified

Practice!

Assume that the integer object `sum` contains the value 150 and that the double object `average` contains the value 12.368 and that the header files `iomanip` and `iostream` have been included. Show the output generated by the following code segments. Assume each is an independent code segment.

1. ```
cout << sum << " " << average;
```

2. ```
cout << sum;
cout << average;
```

3. ```
cout << sum << endl << average;
```

4. ```
cout.precision(2);
cout << sum << endl << average;
```

5. ```
cout.setf(ios::showpoint);
cout.precision(3);
cout << sum << ',' << average;
```

6. ```
cout.setf(ios::fixed);
cout.setf(ios::showpoint);
cout.precision(3);
cout << sum << ',' << average;
```

7. ```
cout << setprecision(2) << sum << endl << average;
```

8. ```
cout << fixed << setprecision(3)
     << setw(10) << average << endl << setw(10)
     << sum << endl;
```

The `cin` **Object**

The `cin` object is an object of type `istream` and is defined by the compiler to stream input from the standard input device. For our examples we will assume the standard input device is the keyboard.

Standard Input: C++ uses the `istream` object `cin` to stream data from standard input and store values in memory locations named by the identifiers. `cin` is defined in the header file `iostream`. To use `cin`, a program must include the compiler directive `#include <iostream>`.

Syntax

```
cin >> identifier >> identifier >> identifer;
```

Example

```
cin >> x >> y >> count;
```

The input operator `>>` is used with `cin` to input a value from the keyboard and assign the value to a variable. The `>>` operator uses whitespace (blanks, tabs, newlines) as delimiters, or separators, for values on the input stream and so the `>>` operator discards all whitespace. The following statement inputs three values from the keyboard.

```
cin >> var1 >> var2 >> var3;
```

In the statement above, the first value typed at the keyboard will be assigned to the variable `var1`, the second value to `var2` and the third value to `var3`. When a `cin` statement is executed, the program waits for input. A `cout` statement usually precedes a `cin` statement

prompt

to **prompt** the user to enter data. A prompt is text printed to the screen to describe to the user the order and data type of the values that are to be entered from the keyboard.

The data entered from the keyboard is stored in an input buffer and is not actually sent to the program until the < *Enter* > key is hit. This allows the user to backspace and make corrections while entering data.

Numeric data typed at the keyboard should be separated by whitespace, but it does not matter how many whitespace characters are used. The `>>` operator will continue to discard whitespace until it receives values for each of the identifiers in the statement. The values entered from the keyboard must be compatible with the data type of the identifiers in the `cin` statement. Potential input errors will be discussed in Chapter 5.

The following example illustrates the use of `cin`:

```
#include <iostream>        //Required for cin
using namespace std;
int main()
{
    double rate, hours;
    int id;
    char code;
```

```
// Prompt user for input
cout << "Enter the floating point rate of pay "
     << "and hours worked: ";
cin >> rate >> hours;
cout << "Enter the employee's integer id: ";
cin >> id;
cout << "Enter the tax code (h,r,1): "
cin >> code;
cout << rate << endl << hours << endl
     << id << endl << code << endl;
return0;
}
```

If the input stream from the keyboard contained the three lines of input

```
10.5 40
556
r
```

the objects in the input statement would be assigned values as shown in the following memory snapshot:

```
double rate        10.5      double hours       40

int id             556       char code          'r'
```

The cout statement would print the following output to the screen:

```
10.5
40
556
r
```

The >> operator discards whitespace and interprets the input value according to the data type of the identifier that follows. For some applications requiring character data, it may not be desirable to discard whitespace. The function get() is a member function of the istream class and can be called by cin to get a single character from the input stream. The statements

```
char ch;
cin.get(ch);
```

will read the next character from the keyboard and assign the character to the variable ch. The get() function does not discard whitespace, but rather treats whitespace as valid character data, as illustrated in the following example:

```
char ch1, ch2, ch3;
cout << "Enter three characters: ";
cin.get(ch1);
cin.get(ch2);
cin.get(ch3);
cout << ch1 << ch2 << ch3;
```

If the input stream from the keyboard contained the two lines

```
a
1
```

the objects ch1, ch2, and ch3 would be assigned values as shown in the following memory snapshot:

char ch1 $\boxed{\text{'a'}}$ char ch2 $\boxed{\text{'\textbackslash n'}}$ char ch3 $\boxed{\text{'1'}}$

The output would be

```
a
1
```

The get() function treats whitespace as valid character data; thus, the newline character was input from the keyboard, stored in the object ch2 and printed to the screen in the cout statement.

2.6   Building C++ Solutions with IDEs: NetBeans

IDE

We have discussed the general structure of a C++ program and written several simple programs to illustrate the use of data types, arithmetic operators, and input and output operators. In this section, we will illustrate how to develop a C++ solution using an **Integrated Development Environment (IDE)**. An IDE is a software package designed to facilitate the development of software solutions. IDEs include an editor, a compiler, a debugger, and many additional tools to aide in the design and development of large software solutions. As with most software packages, there is a learning curve, and it takes time and experience to become a productive user of an IDE. In this section, we will develop a C++ solution for program chapter1_1 using **NetBeans**. Developing C++ solutions with **NetBeans** is presented again in Chapter 3, and the **MS Visual C++ Express** IDE is presented in Chapter 4.

NetBeans

The NetBeans IDE is an open source project that provides a development environment for multiple languages including Java, C and C++. When the NetBeans application is launched, a welcome screen appears as shown below:

We will work through a simple example to illustrate the use of the editor and compiler in NetBeans. Notice that NetBeans provides a **Quick Start Tutorial**. We recommend that you view this tutorial to learn how to become a more productive user of the IDE.

To create a new C++ solution, we must first create a new NetBeans project. Select **New Project**... from the **File** menu at the top of the NetBeans window. A New Project screen will appear, similar to the one shown below.

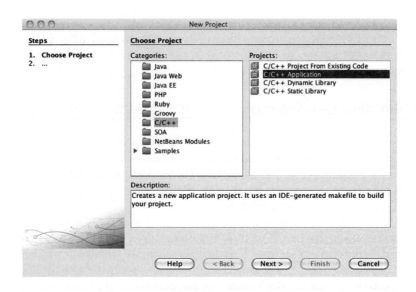

For this C++ project, we will select **C/C++** from the **Categories:** menu, then select **C/C++ Application** from the **Projects:** menu and click the **Next >** button at the bottom of the window. The following **Project Name and Location** window will appear.

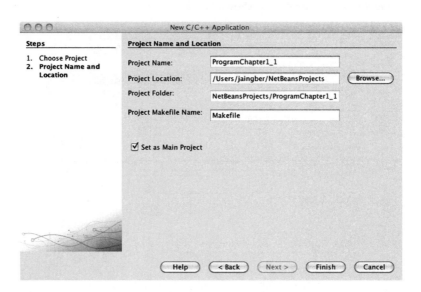

Select the directory of your choice from the **Browse**... button, and name the project `ProgramChapter1_1`. Click on the **Finish** button to complete the creation of your NetBeans project.

Recall that every C++ solution requires exactly one function named *main*. To create main we must add a new file to our project. To add a new file select **New File**... from the **File** menu. The following **Choose File Type** window will appear.

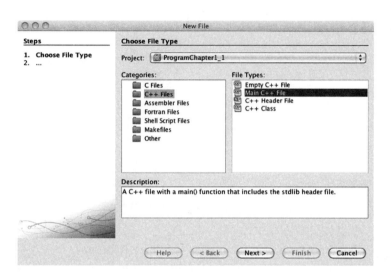

Select **C++ Files** from the Categories: menu and **Main C++ File** from the File Types: menu, then click the **Next >** button on the bottom of the screen. A **Name and Location** window will appear, as shown below.

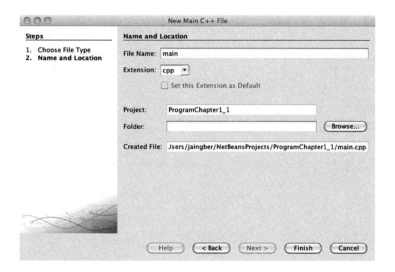

Name the file main and click the **Finish** button at the bottom of the screen. A new file with the following content will be created within an editor window.

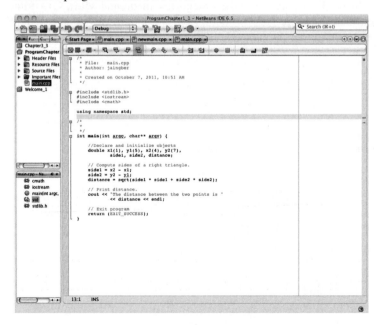

Notice that the header for main() has the parameters int argc, char** argv. These optional parameters will be discussed later in the text. We will modify the main program by adding statements from program chapter1_1 found on page 28 of this text. The modified program is shown below.

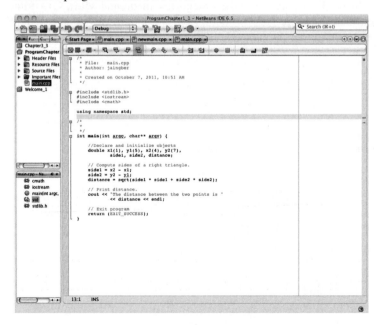

To compile the program, select **Build Main Project** from the **Run** menu at the top of the NetBeans window. An output window will appear as shown below.

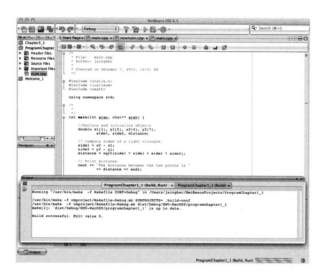

We see from the contents of the window that the build was successful, thus we can attempt to execute the program and view the results. To execute the program, choose **Run Main Project** from the **Run** menu. Our program executes and the output is displayed in a separate window, as shown below.

Next we will add the programmer defined Point class to the project. Select **New File**... from the **File** menu. Select **C++ Files** from the **Categories:** menu and **C++ Class** from the **File Types**: menu then select the **Next >** button, as illustrated below.

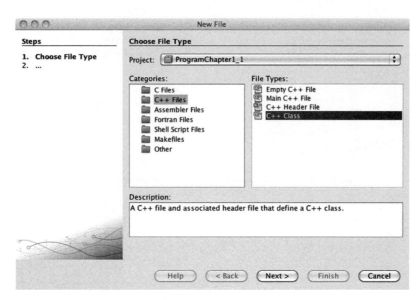

Notice that the IDE created both the point.cpp file and the point.h file. Both files include basic constructors and destructors to facilitate the development of the new class. The file `point.h` also includes the compiler directives #ifndef, #define, #endif. These compiler directives prevent the file `point.h` from being included multiple times, and will be discussed again in Chapter 10. We will use the editor to modify the files by adding the statements to define the `Point` class declaration, found on page 48 of this text and the `Point` class implementation found on page 49 of this text.

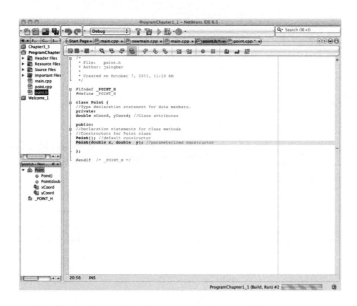

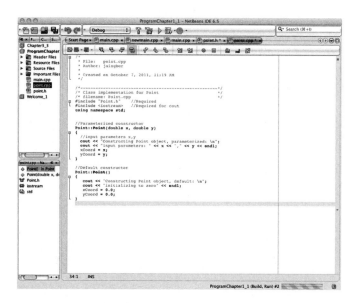

When we build and run this project, we should get the same output as before, because we have not yet modified main.cpp. To test our programmer-defined `Point` class, we will add the following statements from page 50 of this text to main.cpp, as shown below.

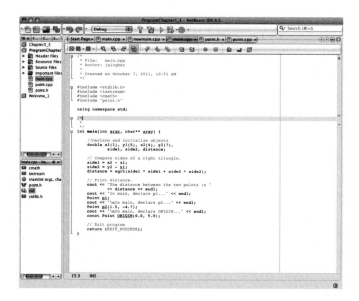

Next, we will again build and run our project, resulting in the following output.

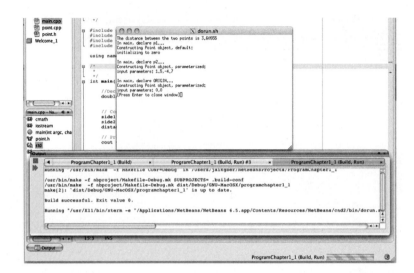

We see in the output window that three `Point` objects have been declared and initialized.

Modify!

These problems relate to the project `ProgramChapter1_1` developed in this section to illustrate the use of NetBeans.

1. Comment out (`//#using namespace std;`), the using directive from `main.cpp`, and build the project. Leaving the using directive as a comment, correct all reported errors and build and run the program.

2. Comment out the `#include "Point.h"` directive and build the project. What errors are reported? How can these errors be corrected?

3. Remove a semicolon from a single statement in `main.cpp` and build the project. What errors are reported?

2.7 Basic Functions Included in the C++ Standard Library

Arithmetic expressions that solve engineering problems often require computations other than addition, subtraction, multiplication, and division. For example, many expressions require the use of logarithms, exponentials, and trigonometric functions. In this section, we discuss predefined mathematical functions and character functions that are available in the Standard C++ library. For example, the following statement computes the sine of an angle `theta` and stores the result in the object `b`:

```
b = sin(theta);
```

The `sin()` function assumes that the argument `theta` is in radians. If `theta` contains a value in degrees, we can convert the degrees to radians with a separate statement. (Recall that 180 degrees $= \pi$ radians.)

```
const double PI = acos(-1.0);
...
theta_rad = theta*PI/180.0;
b = sin(theta_rad);
```

The conversion can also be specified within the function reference

```
b = sin(theta*PI/180.0);
```

function arguments

A function reference, such as `sin(theta)`, represents a single value. The parentheses following the function name contain the inputs to the function, which are called **function arguments.** A function may contain no arguments, one argument, or many arguments, depending on its definition. If a function contains more than one argument, it is very important to list the arguments in the correct order. Some functions also require that the arguments be in specific units. For example, the trigonometric functions assume that arguments are in radians. Most of the mathematical functions assume that the arguments are `double` values; if a different type argument is used, it is promoted to a `double` before the function is executed.

A function reference can also be part of the argument of another function reference. For example, the following statement computes the logarithm of the absolute value of x:

```
b = log(abs(x));
```

composition of functions

When one function is used to compute the argument of another function, be sure to enclose the argument of each function in its own set of parentheses. This nesting of functions is also called **composition of functions**.

We now discuss several categories of functions that are commonly used in engineering computations. Other functions will be presented throughout the remaining chapters as we discuss relevant subjects. Appendix A also contains more information on the functions included in the Standard C++ library.

Elementary Math Functions

The elementary math functions include functions to perform a number of common computations such as computing the absolute value of a number and the square root of a number. In addition, they also include a group of functions used to perform rounding. These functions assume that the type of all arguments is `double`, and the functions all return a `double`; if an argument is not a `double`, a conversion will occur using the rules described in Section 2.2. The following preprocessor directive should be used in programs referencing the mathematical functions available in the Standard C++ library:

```
#include <cmath>
```

We now list these functions with a brief description:

fabs(x)	This function computes the absolute value of x.
sqrt(x)	This function computes the square root of x, where $x >= 0$.
pow(x,y)	This function is used for exponentiation, and computes the value of x to the y power, or x^y. Errors occur if $x = 0$ and $y <= 0$, or if $x < 0$ and y is not an integer.
ceil(x)	This function rounds x to the nearest integer toward infinity. For example, ceil(2.01) is equal to 3.
floor(x)	This function rounds x to the nearest integer toward negative infinity. For example, floor(2.01) is equal to 2.

exp(x)   This function computes the value of e^x,
                 where e is the base for natural logarithms, or approximately 2.718282.

log(x)   This function returns ln x, the natural logarithm of x to the base e.
                 Errors occur if $x <= 0$.

log10(x)   This function returns $\log_{10} x$, the common logarithm of x to the base 10.
                 Errors occur if $x <= 0$.

Remember that the logarithm of a negative value or zero does not exist, and thus an execution error occurs if you use a logarithm function with a negative value for its argument.

Practice!

Evaluate the following expressions:

1. `floor(-2.6)`   2. `ceil(-2.6)`
3. `pow(2.0,-3)`   4. `sqrt(floor(10.7))`
5. `abs(-10*2.5)`   6. `floor(ceil(10.8))`
7. `log10(100) + log10(0.001)`   8. `abs(pow(-2,5.0))`

Trigonometric Functions

trigonometric functions

The **trigonometric functions,** also included in file *cmath,* assume that all arguments are of type `double` and that each function returns a value of `double`. In addition, as previously stated, the trigonometric functions also assume that angles are represented in radians. To convert radians to degrees, or degrees to radians, use the following conversions:

```
const double PI = acos(-1.0);
...
angle_deg = angle_rad*(180/PI);
angle_rad = angle_deg*(PI/180);
```

sin(x)   This function computes the sine of x, where x is in radians.

cos(x)   This function computes the cosine of x, where x is in radians.

tan(x)   This function computes the tangent of x, where x is in radians.

asin(x)   This function computes the arcsine, or inverse sine, of x,
                 where x must be in the range $[-1, 1]$.
                 The function returns an angle in radians in the range $[-\pi/2, \pi/2]$.

acos(x)   This function computes the arccosine, or inverse cosine, of x,
                 where x must be in the range $[-1, 1]$.
                 The function returns an angle in radians in the range $[0, \pi]$.

atan(x)   This function computes the arctangent, or inverse tangent, of x.
                 The function returns an angle in radians in the range $[-\pi/2, \pi/2]$.

atan2(y,x)   This function computes the arctangent or inverse tangent of the value y/x.
                 The function returns an angle in radians in the range $[-\pi, \pi]$.

Note that the *atan* function always returns an angle in Quadrant I or IV, whereas the *atan*2 function returns an angle that can be in any quadrant, depending on the signs of x and y. Thus, in many applications, the *atan*2 function is preferred over the *atan* function.

The other trigonometric and inverse trigonometric functions can be computed using the following equations [10]:

$$\sec x = \frac{1}{\cos x} \qquad a\sec x = a\cos\left(\frac{1}{x}\right)$$

$$\csc x = \frac{1}{\sin x} \qquad a\csc x = a\sin\left(\frac{1}{x}\right)$$

$$\cot x = \frac{1}{\tan x} \qquad a\cot x = a\cos\left(\frac{x}{\sqrt{1+x^2}}\right)$$

 Using degrees instead of radians is a common error in programs with trigonometric functions.

Practice!

In problems 1 through 3, give assignment statements for computing the indicated values, assuming that the objects have been declared and given appropriate values. Also assume that the following declarations have been made:

```
const double g = 9.8:
const double PI = acos(-1.0);
```

1. Velocity computation:

$$\text{Velocity} = \sqrt{v_0^2 + 2a(x - x_0)}$$

2. Length contraction:

$$\text{Length} = \sqrt[k]{1 - \left(\frac{v}{c}\right)^2}$$

3. Distance of the center of gravity from a reference plane in a sector of a hollow cylinder:

$$\text{Center} = \frac{38.1972(r^3 - s^3)\sin a}{(r^2 - s^2)a}$$

In problems 4 through 6, give the equations that correspond to the assignment statement.

4. Electrical oscillation frequency:

```
frequency = 1/sqrt(2*pi*c/L);
```

5. Range for a projectile:

```
range = (v0*v0/g)*sin(2*theta);
```

6. Speed of a disk at the bottom of an incline:

```
v = sqrt(2*g*h/(1 + I/(m*pow(r,2))));
```

Hyperbolic Functions*

Hyperbolic
functions

Hyperbolic functions are functions of the natural exponential function e^x; the inverse hyperbolic functions are functions of the natural logarithm function *ln x*. These functions are useful in specialized applications such as the design of some types of digital filters. The Standard C++ library includes several hyperbolic functions that are described next. The hyperbolic functions are included in the Standard C++ library, and a preprocessor directive including the information in **cmath** should be used with these functions.

cmath

`sinh(x)`   This function computes the hyperbolic sine of *x*, which is equal to

$$\frac{e^x + e^{-x}}{2}.$$

`cosh(x)`   This function computes the hyperbolic cosine of *x*, which is equal to

$$\frac{e^x - e^{-x}}{2}.$$

`tanh(x)`   This function computes the hyperbolic tangent of *x*, which is equal to

$$\frac{\sinh x}{\cosh x}.$$

Additional hyperbolic functions and the inverse hyperbolic functions can be computed using these relationships [10]:

$$\coth\ x\ =\ \frac{\cosh x}{\sinh x}.$$

$$\mathrm{sech}\ x\ =\ \frac{1}{\cosh x}.$$

$$\mathrm{csch}\ x\ =\ \frac{1}{\sinh x}.$$

$$\mathrm{asinh}\ x\ =\ \ln\!\left(x\ +\ \sqrt{x^2\ +\ 1}\right).$$

$$\mathrm{acosh}\ x\ =\ \ln\!\left(x\ +\ \sqrt{x^2\ -\ 1}\right)\ (\text{for}\ |x|\ \geq\ 1).$$

$$\mathrm{atanh}\ x\ =\ \frac{1}{2}\ln\!\left(\frac{1\ +\ x}{1\ -\ x}\right)\ (\text{for}\ |x|\ <\ 1).$$

$$\mathrm{atanh}\ x\ =\ \frac{1}{2}\ln\!\left(\frac{x\ +\ 1}{x\ -\ 1}\right)\ (\text{for}\ |x|\ >\ 1).$$

$$\mathrm{asech}\ x\ =\ \ln\!\left(\frac{1\ +\ \sqrt{1\ -\ x^2}}{x}\right)\ (\text{for}\ 0\ <\ x\ \leq\ 1).$$

$$\mathrm{acsch}\ x\ =\ \ln\!\left(\frac{1}{x}\ +\ \frac{\sqrt{1\ +\ x^2}}{|x|}\right)\ (\text{for}\ x\ \neq\ 0).$$

Many of the hyperbolic functions and inverse trigonometric functions have restrictions on the range of acceptable values for arguments. If the arguments are entered from the keyboard, remind the user of the range restrictions. In the next chapter, we introduce C++ statements that allow you to determine whether a value is in the proper range during program execution.

Give assignment statements for calculating the following values, given the value of x (assume that the value of x is in the proper range of values for the calculations).

1. coth x   2. sech 3 x
3. csch 4 x   4. acots 6 x
5. acosh x   6. acsch x

Character Functions

The Standard C++ library contains many predefined functions for use with character data. These functions fall into two categories: one set of functions is used to convert characters between uppercase and lowercase, and the other set is used to perform character comparisons. The following preprocessor directive should be used in programs referencing these character functions:

```
#include <cctype>
```

The following statement converts the lowercase letter stored in the object ch to an uppercase character and stores the result in the character object ch_upper:

```
ch_upper = toupper(ch);
```

If ch is a lowercase letter, the function toupper() returns the corresponding uppercase letter; otherwise, the function returns ch. **Note that no change is made to the argument** ch.

The character comparison functions return a nonzero value if the comparison is true; otherwise they return zero. The following statement calls the function isdigit(). The function isdigit() will return a nonzero result if the value of ch is a digit (0–9) or the value 0 (false) if ch is not a digit:

```
digit = isdigit(ch);
```

A list of these functions along with a brief explanation is given in Appendix A.

2.8 Problem Solving Applied: Velocity Computation

In this section, we perform computations in an application related to vehicle performance. Turboprop engines, which have been in use for decades, combine the power and reliability of jet engines with the efficiency of propellers. They are a significant improvement over earlier piston-powered propeller engines. Their application has been limited to smaller commuter-type aircraft, however, because they are not as fast or powerful as the fanjet engines used on larger airliners. The unducted fan (UDF) engine employs significant advancements in propeller technology, which narrow the performance gap between turboprops and fanjets. New materials, blade shapes, and higher rotation speeds enable UDF-powered aircraft to fly almost as fast as fanjets, and with greater fuel efficiency. The UDF is also significantly quieter than the conventional turboprop.

During a test flight of a UDF-powered aircraft, the test pilot has set the engine power level at 40,000 N (newtons), which causes the 20,000-kg aircraft to attain a cruise speed of 180 m/s (meters/second). The engine throttles are then set to a power level of 60,000 N and the aircraft begins to accelerate. As the speed of the plane increases, the aerodynamic drag increases in proportion to the square of the airspeed. Eventually, the aircraft reaches a new cruise speed where the thrust from the UDF engines is just offset by the drag. The equations used to estimate the velocity and acceleration of the aircraft from the time that the throttle is reset until the plane reaches its new cruise speed (at approximately 120 s) are the following:

$$\text{Velocity} = 0.00001 * \text{time}^3 - 0.00488 * \text{time}^2 + 0.75795 * \text{time} + 181.3566;$$

$$\text{Acceleration} = 3 - 0.000062 * \text{velocity}^2.$$

Plots of these functions are shown in Figure 2.1. Note that the acceleration approaches zero as the velocity approaches its new cruise speed.

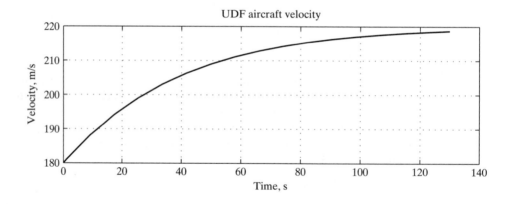

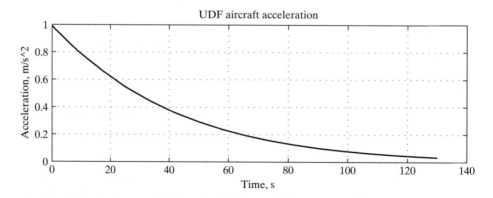

Figure 2.1 UDF aircraft velocity and acceleration.

Write a program that asks the user to enter a time value that represents the time elapsed (in seconds) since the power level was increased. Compute and print the corresponding acceleration and velocity of the aircraft at the new time value.

1. PROBLEM STATEMENT

Compute the new velocity and acceleration of the aircraft after a change in power level.

2. INPUT/OUTPUT DESCRIPTION

The following diagram shows that the input to the program is a time value, and that the output of the program is the pair of new velocity and acceleration values. The built-in data type `double` can be used to represent these values.

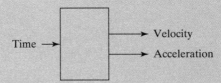

3. HAND EXAMPLE

Suppose that the new time value is 50 seconds. Using the equations given for the velocity and accelerations, we can compute these values:

Velocity = 208.3 m/s;
Acceleration = 0.31 m/s^2.

4. ALGORITHM DEVELOPMENT

The first step in the development of an algorithm is the decomposition of the problem solution into a set of sequentially executed steps:

Decomposition Outline

1. Read new time value.

2. Compute corresponding velocity and acceleration values.

3. Print new velocity and acceleration.

Because this program is a very simple program, we can convert the decomposition directly to C++.

```
/*-----------------------------------------------------------------*/
/*  Program chapter2_6                                             */
/*                                                                 */
/*  This program estimates new velocity and                       */
/*  acceleration values for a specified time.                     */

#include<iostream>   //Required for cin,cout
#include<iomanip>    //Required for setprecision(), setw()
#include<cmath>      //Required for pow()
using namespace std;

int main()
{
   //  Declare objects.
   double time, velocity, acceleration;

   //  Get time value from the keyboard.
   cout << "Enter new time value in seconds: \n";
   cin >> time;

   //  Compute velocity and acceleration.
   velocity = 0.00001*pow(time,3) - 0.00488*pow(time,2)
              + 0.75795*time + 181.3566;
   acceleration = 3 - 0.000062*velocity*velocity;
   //  Print velocity and acceleration.
   cout << fixed << setprecision(3);
   cout << "Velocity = " << setw(10)
        << velocity << " m/s" << endl;
   cout << "Acceleration = " << setw( 14)
        << acceleration << "m/s^2" << endl;

   //  Exit program.
   return 0;
}
/*-----------------------------------------------------------------*/
```

5. TESTING

We first test the program using the data from the hand example. This generates the following interaction:

```
Enter new time value in seconds:
50
Velocity = 208.304 m/s
Acceleration =    0.310 m/s^2
```

Because the values computed match the hand example, we can then test the program with other time values. If the values had not matched the hand example, we would need to determine whether the error is in the hand example or in the program.

These problems relate to the program developed in this section for computing velocity and acceleration values.

1. Enter different values of time until you find one that gives a velocity between 210 m/s and 211 m/s.

2. Enter different values of time until you find one that gives an acceleration between 0.5 m/s and 0.6 m/s.

3. Modify the program so that the input values are entered in minutes instead of seconds. Remember that the equations will still assume that the time values are in seconds.

4. Modify the program so that the output values are printed in feet per second, and feet per second^2. (Recall that 1 meter = 39.37 inches.)

2.9   System Limitations

In Section 2.2, we presented a table that contained the maximum values for the various types of integers and floating-point values for the Microsoft Visual C++ 6.0 compiler. To print a similar table for your system, use the program presented next. Note that the program includes three header files. The `iostream` header file is necessary because the program uses `cout`; the `climits` header file is necessary because it contains information relative to the ranges of integer types; and the `cfloat` header file is necessary because it contains information relative to the ranges of floating-point types. Appendix A contains more information on the constants and limits that are system dependent.

```
/*-------------------------------------------------------------------*/
/*  Program chapter2_7                                               */
/*                                                                   */
/*  This program prints the system limitations.                     */

#include<iostream>
#include<climits>
#include<cfloat>
using namespace std;
int main()
{
   //  Print integer type maxima. /
   cout << "short maximum: " << sizeof(short) << endl;
   cout << "int maximum: " << sizeof(int) << endl;
   cout << "long maximum: " << sizeof(long) << endl << endl;
```

```
// Print float precision, range, maximum.  /
cout << "float precision digits: " << FLTDIG << endl;
cout << "float maximum exponent: "
     << FLT_MAX_10_EXP << endl;
cout << "float maximum: " << sizeof(float) << endl << endl;

// Print double precision, range, maximum.  /
cout << "double precision digits: " << DBL_DIG << endl;
cout << "double maximum exponent: "
     << DBL_MAX_10_EXP << endl;
cout << "double maximum: " << sizeof(double) << endl << endl;

// Print long precision, range, maximum.  /
cout << "long double precision: " << LDBL_DIG << endl;
cout << "long double maximum exponent: "
     << LDBL_MAX_10_EXP << endl;
cout << "long double maximum: " << sizeof(long double) << endl;

// Exit program.
return 0;
}
/*-----------------------------------------------------------------*/
```

SUMMARY

In this chapter, we presented the C++ statements necessary to write simple programs that compute and print new values. We also presented the statement that allows us to enter information through the keyboard when the program is executing. The computations that were presented included the standard arithmetic operations and a large number of functions that can be used to perform the types of computations needed for engineering solutions.

Key Terms

abbreviated assignment	field width
ANSI code	floating-point value
argument	garbage value
assignment statement	hyperbolic function
associativity	identifier
binary codes	initial value
binary operator	keyword
case sensitive	linear interpolation
cast operator	mantissa
character	math function
comment	memory snapshot
composition	modulus
constant	multiple assignment
declaration	object
exponential notation	overflow
expression	parameter

postfix	statement
precedence	symbolic constant
precision	system dependent
prefix	trigonometric function
preprocessor directive	truncate
prompt	unary operator
range	underflow
scientific notation	whitespace
Standard C++ library	

C++ Statement Summary

Preprocessor directives to include information from the files in the Standard C++ library:

General Form:

```
#include<filename>
```

Example:

```
#include <iostream>
#include <cmath>
#include <string>
```

Type Declaration Statement

General Form:

```
datatype identifier [,identifier];
```

Examples: Declarations for integers:

```
short sum=(0);
int year_1, year_2;
long k;
```

Declarations for floating-point values:

```
float height_1, height_2;
double length=(10), side1, side2;
long double distance, velocity;
```

Declarations for characters and strings:

```
char ch;
string name;   //Requires #include<string>
```

Declarations for symbolic constants: General Form:

```
const datatype identifier = expression;
```

Example:

```
const double PI = acos(-1.0);
const int MAX_SIZE = 100;
```

Assignment statement: General Form:

```
identifier = expression;
```

Example:

```
area = 0.5*base*(height_1 + height_2);
```

Keyboard input statement: General Form:

```
cin >> identifier [>> identifier];
```

Example:

```
cin >> hours;
cin >> minutes >> seconds;
```

Character input from keyboard: General Form:

```
cin.get(identifier);
```

Example:

```
cin.get(ch);
```

Screen output statement: General Form:

```
cout << expression [<< expression];
```

Example:

```
cout << "The area is " << area << " square feet. " << endl;
```

Program exit statement: General Form:

```
return integer;
```

Example:

```
return 0;
```

Style

Notes

1. Use comments throughout a program to improve the readability and to document the steps in it.
2. Use blank lines and indenting to identify the structure of a program.

3. Use the units in an object name when possible.
4. Symbolic constants should be used for engineering constants such as π, and they should be uppercase so that they are easily identified.
5. Use consistent spacing around arithmetic and assignment operators.
6. Use parentheses in complicated expressions to improve readability.
7. The evaluation of long expressions should be broken into several statements.
8. Be sure to include units along with numerical values in the output of a program.
9. Use a prompt to the user to describe the information and units for values to be entered from the keyboard.

Debugging Notes

1. Remember that declarations and C++ statements must end with a semicolon.
2. Preprocessor directives do not end with a semicolon.
3. If possible, avoid mixed assignments that could potentially cause information to be lost.
4. Use parentheses in a long expression to be sure that it is evaluated as desired.
5. Use double precision or extended precision to avoid problems with exponent overflow or underflow.
6. Errors can occur if user input values do not match the data type of the variable used in the cin statement.
7. Be sure to use the operator $\gg$ with *cin* (not $\ll$).
8. Be sure to use the operator $\ll$ with *cout* (not $\gg$) .
9. In nested function references, each set of arguments must be in its own set of parentheses.
10. Remember that the logarithm functions cannot be used with negative values for arguments.
11. Be sure to use angles in radians with the trigonometric functions.
12. Remember that many of the inverse trigonometric functions and hyperbolic functions have restrictions on the ranges of allowable input values.
13. Remember that the integer representation for a character digit is not the same as the integer representation of the numerical digit.

Problems

Exam Practice!

Indicate whether the following statements are true (T) or false (F)

1. The execution of a program begins with the `main` function. T F
2. C++ is not case sensitive.   T F
3. Declarations can be placed anywhere in the program.   T F
4. Statement and declarations must end with a semicolon.   T F
5. The result of an integer division is a rounded result.   T F

Indicate if the following declaration statements are correct or not. If the statement is incorrect, modify it so that it is a correct statement.

```
6. int i, j, k,
7. float f1(11), f2(202.00);
```

8. `DOUBLE D1, D2, D3;`
9. `float al(a2);`
10. `int n, m_m;`
11. Which of the following is NOT a C++ keyword?
    (a) `const`
    (b) `goto`
    (c) `static`
    (d) `when`
    (e) `unsigned`
12. In a declaration, the type specifier and the object name are separated by
    (a) a period.
    (b) a space.
    (c) an equal sign.
    (d) a semicolon.
    (e) none of the above.
13. Which of the following declarations would properly define x, y, and z as double objects?
    (a) `double x, y, z;`
    (b) `long double x,y,z`
    (c) `double x=y=z;`
    (d) `double X, Y, Z`
14. In C++, the binary operator % is applied to compute
    (a) integer division.
    (b) floating-point division.
    (c) the remainder of integer division.
    (d) the remainder of floating-point division.
    (e) none of the above.
15. Which of the following assignments produces a value of zero?
    (a) `result = 9%3 - 1;`
    (b) `result = 8%3 - 1;`
    (c) `result = 2 - 5%2;`
    (d) `result = 2 - 6%2;`
    (e) `result = 2 - 8%3;`

Give the corresponding snapshots of memory after each of the following set of statements has been executed.

16. `int x1;`
    ```
    . . .
    x1 = 3 + 4%5 - 5;
    int x(1), z(5);
    . . .
    z = z/++x;
    ```
17. `double a(3.8), z;`
    ```
    int n(2), y;
    . . .
    x = (y=a/n)*2;
    ```

Give the output generated by the sets of statements in Problems 21 through 23.

18. `float value_1(5.78263);`

    `. . .`

    `cout << "value_1 = " << value_1;`
19. `double value_4(66.45832);`

    `. . .`

    `cout << scientific << "value_4 = " << value_4`
20. `int value_5(7750);`

    `. . .`

    `cout << "value_5 = " << fixed << value_5 << endl;`

Programming Problems

Conversions.   This set of problems involves conversions of a value in one unit to another unit. Each program should prompt the user for a value in the specified units and then print the converted value, along with the new units.

21. Write a program to convert miles to kilometers. (Recall that 1 mi = 1.6093440 km.)
22. Write a program to convert meters to miles. (Recall that 1 mi = 1.6093440 km.)
23. Write a program to convert pounds to kilograms. (Recall that 1 kg = 2.205 lb.)
24. Write a program to convert newtons to pounds. (Recall that 1 lb = 4.448 N.)
25. Write a program that converts degrees Fahrenheit (TF) to degrees Rankin (TR). (Recall that TF = TR − 459.67 degrees Rankin.)
26. Write a program that converts degrees Celsius (TC) to degrees Rankin (TR). (Recall that TF = TR − 459.67 degrees Rankin and that TF = (9/5) TC + 32 degrees Fahrenheit.)
27. Write a program that converts degrees Kelvin (TK) to degrees Fahrenheit (TF). (Recall that TR = (9/5) TK and that TF = TR − 459.67 degrees Rankin.)

Areas and Volumes.   These problems involve computing an area or a volume using input from the user. Each program should include a prompt to the user to enter the objects needed.

28. Write a program to compute the area A of a rectangle with sides a and b. (Recall that $A = a * b$.)
29. Write a program to compute the area A of a triangle with base b and height h. (Recall that $A = \frac{1}{2}(b * h)$.)
30. Write a program to compute the area A of a circle with radius r. (Recall that $A = \pi r^2$.)
31. Write a program to compute the area A of a sector of a circle when u is the angle in radians between the radii. (Recall that $A = r^2\theta/2$.)
32. Write a program to compute the area A of a sector of a circle when d is the angle in degrees between the radii. (Recall that $A = r^2\theta/2$, where θ is in radians.)
33. Write a program to compute the area A of an ellipse with semiaxes a and b. (Recall that $A = \pi a * b$.)
34. Write a program to compute the area A of the surface of a sphere of radius r. (Recall that $A = 4\pi r^2$.)
35. Write a program to compute the volume V of a sphere of radius r. (Recall that $V = (4/3)\pi r^3$.)
36. Write a program to compute the volume V of a cylinder of radius r and height h. (Recall that $V = \pi r^2 h$.)

Amino Acid Molecular Weights.   The amino acids in proteins are composed of atoms of oxygen, carbon, nitrogen, sulfur, and hydrogen, as shown in Table 2.8. The molecular weights of the individual elements are as follows:

Element	Atomic Weight
Oxygen	15.9994
Carbon	12.011
Nitrogen	14.00674
Sulfur	32.066
Hydrogen	1.00794

37. Write a program to compute and print the molecular weight of glycine.
38. Write a program to compute and print the molecular weights of glutamic and glutamine.
39. Write a program that asks the user to enter the number of atoms of each of the five elements for an amino acid. Then compute and print the molecular weight for this amino acid.

TABLE 2.8 Amino Acid Molecules

Amino Acid	O	C	N	S	H
Alanine	2	3	1	0	7
Arginine	2	6	4	0	15
Asparagine	3	4	2	0	8
Aspartic	4	4	1	0	6
Cysteine	2	3	1	1	7
Glutamic	4	5	1	0	8
Glutamine	3	5	2	0	10
Glycine	2	2	1	0	5
Histidine	2	6	3	0	10
Isoleucine	2	6	1	0	13
Leucine	2	6	1	0	13
Lysine	2	6	2	0	15
Methionine	2	5	1	1	11
Phenylanlanine	2	9	1	0	11
Proline	2	5	1	0	10
Serine	3	3	1	0	7
Threonine	3	4	1	0	9
Tryptophan	2	11	2	0	11
Tyrosine	3	9	1	0	11
Valine	2	5	1	0	11

40. Write a program that asks the user to enter the number of atoms of each of the five elements for an amino acid. Then compute and print the average weight of the atoms in the amino acid.

  Logarithms to the base b. To compute the logarithm of x to base b, we can use the following relationship

$$\log_b x = \frac{\log_e x}{\log_e b}.$$

41. Write a program that reads a positive number and then computes and prints the logarithm of the value to base 2. For example, the logarithm of 8 to base 2 is 3 because $2^3 = 8$.

42. Write a program that reads a positive number and then computes and prints the logarithm of the value to base 8. For example, the logarithm of 64 to base 8 is 2 because $8^2 = 64$.

3

ENGINEERING CHALLENGE:
Global Change

Seawater is primarily water with about 3.5% dissolved materials (salts, metals, and gases) from volcanic eruptions and the weathering of rocks. The saltiest ocean waters are in the Atlantic around the equator, where evaporation exceeds precipitation. The salinity of seawater is a measure of the amount of dissolved material in the seawater. Chlorine represents about 55% of the constituents, while sodium is about 30.6%. The remaining primary constituents are sulfate (7.7%), magnesium (3.7%), calcium (1.2%), and potassium (1.1). Salinity varies from one location to another in the ocean, but typically falls in the range of 33 to 38 parts per thousand (ppt), or a percentage of 3.3 to 3.8. Salinity is often measured using an instrument that measures the electrical conductivity of the water; the more dissolved materials in the water, the better it conducts electricity. Later in this chapter, we discuss the relationship between salinity and freezing temperatures, and then use linear interpolation to determine the freezing point of seawater with a specified salinity.

CONTROL STRUCTURES: SELECTION

CHAPTER OUTLINE

OBJECTIVES

In this chapter we develop problem solutions containing:

- conditional expressions that evaluate to either true or false
- selection structures that allow us to provide alternative paths in a program

- algorithm development and descriptions of algorithms using flowcharts and pseudocode

3.1 Algorithm Development

In Chapter 2, the C++ programs that we developed were very simple. The steps were sequential, and typically involved reading information from the keyboard, computing new information, and then printing the new information. In solving engineering problems, most of the solutions require more complicated steps, and thus we need to expand the algorithm development part of our problem-solving process.

Top-Down Design

Top-down design presents a "big picture" description of the problem solution in sequential steps. This overall description of the problem is then refined until the steps are detailed enough to translate to language statements. We used decomposition outlines in Chapters 1 and 2 to provide the first definition of a problem solution. This outline is written in sequential steps, and can be shown in a diagram or a step-by-step outline. For very simple problems, such as the one that follows, which was developed in Chapter 2, we can go from the decomposition outline directly to the C++ statements:

Decomposition Outline

1. Read the new time value.

2. Compute the corresponding velocity and acceleration values.

3. Print the new velocity and acceleration.

divide-and-conquer

However, for most problem solutions, we need to refine the decomposition outline into a description with more detail. This process is often referred to as a **divide-and-conquer** strategy, because we keep breaking the problem solution into smaller and smaller portions. To describe this stepwise refinement, we use pseudocode or flowcharts.

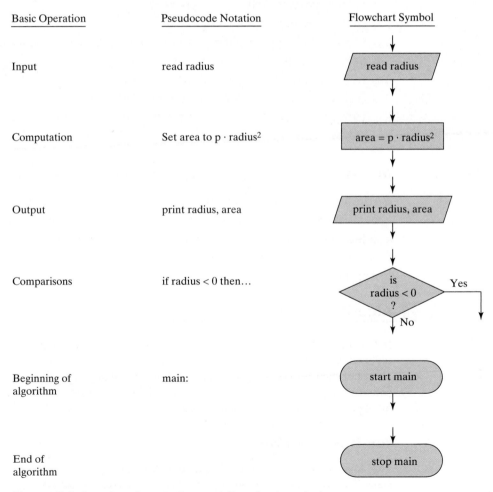

Figure 3.1 Pseudocode notation and flowchart symbols.

pseudocode
flowchart

The refinement of an outline into more detailed steps can be done with **pseudocode** or a **flowchart.** Pseudocode uses English-like statements to describe the steps in an algorithm, and a flowchart uses a diagram to describe the steps in an algorithm. The fundamental steps in most algorithms are shown in Figure 3.1, along with the corresponding notation in pseudocode and flowcharts.

Pseudocode and flowcharts are tools to help us determine the order of steps to solve a problem. Both tools are commonly used, although they are not generally both used with the same problem. In order to give examples of both tools, some problem solutions will use pseudocode and others will use flowcharts; the choice between pseudocode and flowcharts is usually a personal preference. Sometimes we need to go through several levels of pseudocode or flowcharts to develop complex problem solutions; this is the stepwise refinement that we mentioned previously in this section. Decomposition outlines, pseudocode, and flowcharts are working models of the solution, and thus are not unique. Each person working on a solution will have different decomposition outlines and pseudocode or flowchart descriptions, just like the C++ programs developed by different people will be somewhat different, although they solve the same problem.

3.2 Structured Programming

sequence
selection
repetition

A structured program is one written using simple control structures to organize the solution to a problem. A simple structure is usually defined to be a **sequence,** a **selection,** or a **repetition.** A sequence structure contains steps that are performed one after another; a selection structure contains one set of steps that is performed if a condition is true and another set of steps that is performed if the condition is false; a repetition structure contains a set of steps that is repeated as long as a condition is true. We now discuss the sequence and selection structures and use pseudocode and flowcharts to give specific examples. Repetition will be discussed in Chapter 4.

A sequence contains steps that are performed one after another. All the programs developed in Chapter 2 have a sequence structure. For example, the pseudocode and the flowchart for the program that computed the velocity and acceleration of the aircraft with the unducted engine is shown in Figure 3.2.

Pseudocode

```
main: read time
set velocity to 10⁻⁶ * time³ - 0.00488*time² +
                0.75795*time + 181.3566
set acceleration to 3 - 0.000062*velocity²
print velocity and acceleration
```

A selection structure contains a condition that can be evaluated as either true or false. If the condition is true, then one set of statements is executed; if the condition is false, then another set of statements is executed. For example, suppose that we have computed values for the numerator and denominator of a fraction. Before we compute the division, we want to be sure that the denominator is not close to zero. Therefore, the condition that we want to test is "denominator close to zero." If the condition is true, then we want to print a message indicating that we cannot compute the value. If the condition is false, which means that the denominator is not close to zero, then we compute and print the value of the fraction. In defining this condition, we need to define "close to zero." For this example, we will assume

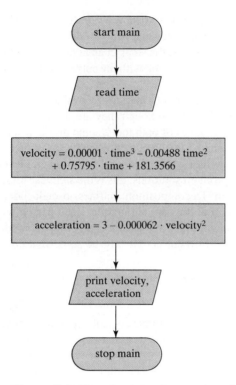

Figure 3.2 Flowchart and pseudocode for unducted fan problem solution from Section 2.8.

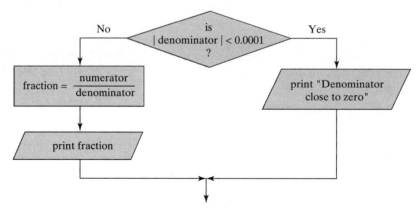

Figure 3.3 Flowchart for selection structure.

that close to zero means that the absolute value is less than 0.0001. A pseudocode description follows, and a flowchart description of this structure is shown in Figure 3.3.

```
if |denominator| < 0.0001
        print "Denominator close to zero"
else
        set fraction to numerator/denominator
        print fraction
```

Note that this structure also contains a sequence structure (compute a fraction and then print the fraction) that is executed when the condition is false.

In the remaining sections of this chapter, we present the C++ statements for performing selections and repetitions and then develop example programs that use these structures.

Evaluation of Alternative Solutions

There are usually many ways to solve the same problem. In most cases, there is not a single best solution, but some solutions are better than others. Selecting a good solution becomes easier with experience, and we will give examples of the elements that contribute to good solutions in this text. For example, a good solution is one that is readable; therefore, a good solution is not necessarily the shortest solution, because short solutions are often not very readable. We will strive to avoid subtle or clever steps that shorten a program, but are difficult to understand.

As you begin to develop a solution to a problem, it is a good idea to try to think of several ways to solve it. Sketch the decomposition outline and pseudocode or flowchart for several solutions. Then choose the solution that you think will be the easiest to translate into C++ statements. Some algorithms fit different languages better than others, so you also want to pick a solution that is a good fit to the C++ language. Occasionally, other aspects of a solution must also be considered, such as execution speed and memory requirements.

3.3   Conditional Expressions

conditions

relational operators
logical operators
evaluation order

Because both selection and repetition structures use **conditions,** we must discuss conditions before presenting the statements that implement selection and repetition structures. A condition is an expression that can be evaluated to be true or false, and it is composed of expressions combined with **relational operators;** a condition can also include **logical operators.** In this section, we present relational operators and logical operators and discuss the **evaluation order** when they are combined in a single condition.

Relational Operators

The relational operators that can be used to compare two expressions in C++ are shown in the following list:

Relational Operator	Interpretation
<	is less than
<=	is less than or equal to
>	is greater than
>=	is greater than or equal to
==	is equal to
!=	is not equal to

 Blanks can be used on either side of a relational operator, but blanks cannot be used to separate a two-character operator such as ==.

Sample conditions are the following:

```
a < b
x+y >= 10.5
fabs(denominator) < 0.0001
```

Given the values of the identifiers in these conditions, we can evaluate each one to be true or false. For example, if a is equal to 5 and b is equal to 8.4, then a<b is a true condition. If x is equal to 2.3 and y is equal to 4.1, then x+y >= 10.5 is a false condition. If denominator is equal to 20.0025, then fabs(denominator) < 0.0001 is a false condition.

 For readability, we use spaces around the relational operator in a logical expression, but not around the arithmetic operators in the conditions.

In C++, a true condition is assigned a value of 1 and a false condition is assigned a value of zero. Therefore, the following statement is valid:

```
d = b > c;
```

If b > c, then d is assigned a value of 1; otherwise, a value of zero is assigned to d. A single value can be used in place of a condition. For example, consider the following statement:

```
if (a)
    ++count;
```

If the value of a is zero, then the condition is assumed to be false; if the value of a is nonzero, then the condition is assumed to be true. Therefore, in the previous statement, the value of count will be incremented if a is nonzero.

Logical Operators

logical operators

Logical operators can also be used within conditions. However, logical operators compare conditions, not expressions. C++ supports three **logical operators: and, or,** and **not.** These logical operators are represented by the following symbols:

Logical Operation	Symbol
and	&&
or	||
not	!

For example, consider the following condition:

```
a<b && b<c
```

 The relational operators have higher precedence than the logical operator; therefore, this condition is read "a is less than b, and b is less than c." *In order to make a condition more readable, we insert spaces around the logical operator, but not around the relational operators.* Given

TABLE 3.1	Logical	Operators			
A	*B*	*A && B*	*A ‖ B*	*!A*	*!B*
False	False	False	False	True	True
False	True	False	True	True	False
True	False	False	True	False	True
True	True	True	True	False	False

values for a, b, and c, we can evaluate this condition as true or false. For example, if a is equal to 1, b is equal to 5, and c is equal to 8, then the condition is true. If a is equal to -2, b is equal to 9, and c is equal to 2, then the condition is false.

If *A* and *B* are conditions, then the logical operators can be used to generate new conditions *A && B*, *A‖B*, *!A*, and *!B*. The condition *A && B* is true only if both *A* and *B* are true. The condition *A‖B* is true if either or both *A* and *B* are true. The ! operator changes the value of the condition which it precedes. Thus, the condition *!A* is true only if *A* is false, and the condition *!B* is true only if *B* is false. These definitions are summarized in Table 3.1.

truth table

Table 3.1 provides a **truth table** for the four conditions

```
A && B, A || B, !A, and !B.
```

Truth tables provide the truth values of a condition given the truth values of the boolean operands. In Table 3.1 there are two boolean operands, *A* and *B*, and there are $2^2 = 4$ unique combinations of values these boolean operands can represent. Each additional boolean operand doubles the number of unique combinations. Consider the condition

```
A && B || B && C.
```

The truth value of this expression depends on the truth values of the three boolean operands *A*, *B* and *C*, thus there are $2^3 = 8$ unique combinations, as illustrated in Table 3.2.

The following program illustrates the use of logical and relational operators to generate the truth table provided in Table 3.2.

TABLE 3.2			
A	*B*	*C*	*A && B ‖ B && C*
0	0	0	0
0	0	1	0
0	1	0	0
0	1	1	1
1	0	0	0
1	0	1	0
1	1	0	1
1	1	1	1

```cpp
/*-------------------------------------------------------------------*/
/*  Program chapter3_1 generates a truth table                       */
/*  for the condition:                                               */
/*   A && B || B && C                                                */

#include<iostream>
using namespace std;

int main()
{
  //Declare and initialize objects
   bool A(false), B(false), C(false);

  //Print table header
  cout << " TABLE 3.2\n A\tB\tC\t\tA && B || B && C"
       << endl;
  cout << "_____"
       << endl;
  cout << A << '\t' << B << '\t' << C << "\t\t\t"
       << (A && B || B && C) << endl;

  //Toggle C
  C = !C;
  cout << A << '\t' << B << '\t' << C << "\t\t\t"
       << (A && B || B && C) << endl;

  //Toggle B and C
  B = !B;
  C = !C;
  cout << A << '\t' << B << '\t' << C << "\t\t\t"
       << (A && B || B && C) << endl;

  //Toggle C
  C = !C;
  cout << A << '\t' << B << '\t' << C << "\t\t\t"
       << (A && B || B && C) << endl;

  //Toggle A, B and C
  A = !A;
  B = !B;
  C = !C;
  cout << A << '\t' << B << '\t' << C << "\t\t\t"
       << (A && B || B && C) << endl;

  //Repeat the pattern for B and C..

  //Toggle C
  C = !C;
  cout << A << '\t' << B << '\t' << C << "\t\t\t"
       << (A && B || B && C) << endl;
```

```
//Toggle B and C
B = !B;
C = !C;
cout << A << '\t' << B << '\t' << C << "\t\t\t"
     << (A && B || B && C) << endl;

//Toggle C
C = !C;
cout << A << '\t' << B << '\t' << C << "\t\t\t"
     << (A && B || B && C) << endl;
return 0;
}
```

short circuiting

When expressions with logical operators are executed, C++ will only evaluate as much of the expression as necessary to evaluate it. This is known as **short circuiting**. For example, if *A* is false, then the expression

```
A && B
```

is also false, and there is no need to evaluate *B*. Similarly, if *A* is true, then the expression

```
A || B
```

is true, and there is no need to evaluate *B*. To verify the correctness of Table 3.2, you must be aware that the && operator takes precedence over the || operator. The precedence of operators is discussed in the following section.

Modify!

1. Modify program `chapter3_1` to generate a truth table for the condition A&&B&&C.

2. Modify program `chapter3_1` to generate a truth table for the condition A||B||C.

3. Modify program `chapter3_1` to generate a truth table for the condition A&&!B.

Precedence and Associativity

A condition can contain several logical operators, as in the following:

```
!(b==c || b==5.5)
```

The hierarchy, from highest to lowest, is !, &&, ||, but parentheses can be used to change the hierarchy. In the previous example, the expressions b==c and b==5.5 are evaluated first. Suppose b is equal to 3 and c is equal to 5. Then neither expression is true, so the expression b==c || b==5.5 is false. We then apply the ! operator to the false condition, which gives a true condition.

A condition can contain both arithmetic operators and relational operators, as well as logical operators. Table 3.3 contains the precedence and the associativity order for the elements in a condition.

TABLE 3.3 Operator Precedence for Arithmetic, Relational, and Logical Operators

Precedence	Operation	Associativity
1	( )	innermost first
2	++ -- + - ! (type)	right to left (unary)
3	* / %	left to right
4	+ -	left to right
5	< <= > >=	left to right
6	== !=	left to right
7	&&	left to right
8	||	left to right
9	= += -= *= /= %=	right to left

Practice!

Determine whether the following conditions in problems 1 through 8 are true or false. Assume that the following objects have been declared and initialized as shown:

$$a = 5.5 \quad b = 1.5 \quad k = 3$$

1. $a < 10.0 + k$
2. $a + b >= 6.5$
3. $k != a - b$
4. $b - k > a$
5. $!(a == 3 * b)$
6. $-k <= k + 6$
7. $a < 10 \;\&\&\; a > 5$
8. $fabs(k) > 3 \;\|\|\; k < b - a$

3.4 Selection Statements: `if` Statement

The `if` statement allows us to test conditions and then perform statements based on whether the conditions are true or false. C++ contains two forms of `if` statements—the simple `if` statement and the **if else** statement. C++ also contains a `switch` statement that allows us to test multiple conditions and then execute groups of statements based on whether the conditions are true or false.

Simple `if` Statements

The simplest form of an `if` statement has the following general form:

```
if (condition)
    statement 1;
```

If the condition is true, we execute statement 1; if the condition is false, we skip statement 1.

The statement within the if statement is indented so that it is easier to visualize the structure of the program from the statements.

statement block

If we wish to execute several statements (or a sequence structure) when the condition is true, we use a **statement block** which is composed of a set of statements enclosed in braces. The location of the braces is a matter of style; two common styles are shown:

```
Style 1                    Style 2
if (condition)                if (condition) {
{                                 statement 1;
    statement 1;                  statement 2;
    statement 2;                  . . .
    . . .                         statement n;
    statement n;              }
}
```

In the text solutions, we use the first style convention; thus, both braces are on lines by themselves. *Although this makes the program a little longer, it also makes it easier to notice if a brace has been mistakenly omitted.* Figure 3.4 contains flowcharts of the control flow with simple if statements containing either one statement to execute, or a statement block to execute, if the condition is true.

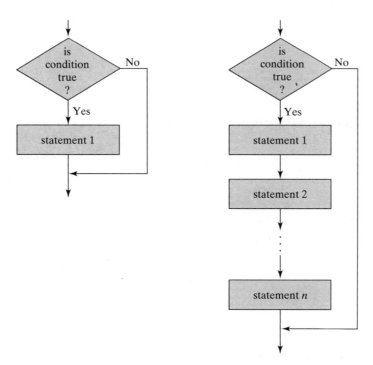

Figure 3.4 Flowcharts for selection statements.

if **Statement:** The if statement allows us to test conditions and then perform statements based on whether the conditions are true or false.

Syntax:

```
if (condition)          if (condition)
   statement;           {
[else                        statement block
   statement;]          }
                        [else
                        {
                             statement block
                        }]
```

Example:

```
if (!error && x > 0)                    if(x > y)
{                                       {
   sum += x;                                ++c1;
   ++count;                                 --x;
}                                       }
                                        else if(x < y)
                                        {
                                            ++c2;
                                            --y;
                                        {
                                        else
                                        {
                                            ++c0;
                                        }
```

A specific example of an if statement follows:

```
#include<iostream>    //Required for cout
using namespace std;
int main()
{
   int a, count(0), sum(0);
   cin >> a;
   if (a < 50)
   {
      ++count;
      sum += a;
   }
   cout << (double) sum/count;
   return 0;
}
```

If a is less than 50, then count is incremented by 1 and a is added to sum; otherwise, these two statements are skipped.

nesting of if
statements

The statements inside an `if` statement block can be any C++ statement, including another `if` statement. This **nesting of if statements** is illustrated in the following example:

```
if(count < 50)
{
    ++count;
    sum = sum + a;
    if(count < 40)
    {
        ++a;
    }
}
```

If `count` is less than 50, we increment `count` by 1 and add `a` to `sum`. In addition, if `count` is less than 40, then we also increment `a`. If `count` is not less than 50, then we skip all of these statements. *For readability, indent the statements in each if statement block.*

`if/else` **Statement**

An `if/else` statement allows us to execute one statement block if a condition is true and a different statement block if the condition is false. The simplest form of an `if/else` statement is the following:

```
if (condition)
    statement 1;
else
    statement 2;
```

empty statement

Statements 1 and 2 can be replaced by statement blocks. Statement 1 or statement 2 can also be an **empty statement,** which is just a semicolon. If statement 2 is an empty statement, then the `if/else` statement should probably be posed as a simple `if` statement. There are situations in which it is convenient to use an empty statement for statement 1; however, these statements can also be rewritten as simple `if` statements with the conditions reversed. For example, the following two statements are equivalent:

```
if (a < b)             if (a >= b)
    ;                      ++count;
else
    ++count;
```

Consider this if/else statement:

```
if (d <= 30)
    velocity = 0.425 + 0.00175*d*d;
else
    velocity = 0.625 + 0.12*d - 0.0025*d*d;
```

In this example, velocity is computed with the first assignment statement if the distance d is less than or equal to 30; otherwise, velocity is computed with the second assignment statement. A flowchart for this `if/else` statement is shown in Figure 3.5.

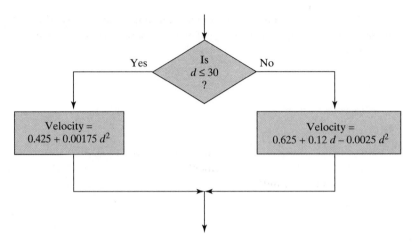

Figure 3.5 Flowchart for if/else statement.

Another example of the if/else statement is

```
if (fabs(denominator) < 0.0001)
   cout << "Denominator close to zero" << endl;
else
{
   x = numerator/denominator;
   cout << "x = " << x << endl;
}
```

In this example, we examine the absolute value of the object denominator. If this value is close to zero, we print a message indicating that we cannot perform the division. If the value of denominator is not close to zero, we compute and print the value of x. The flowchart for this statement was shown in Figure 3.3.

Consider the following set of nested if/else statements:

```
if (x > y)
   if (y < z)
      ++k;
   else
      ++m;
else
   ++j;
```

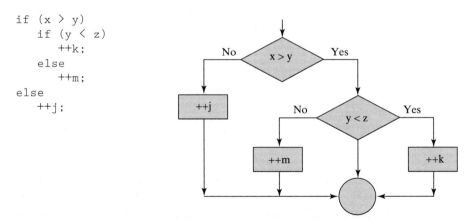

The value of k is incremented when x>y and y<z. The value of m is incremented when x>y and y>=z. The value of j is incremented when x<=y. With careful indenting, this statement is straightforward to follow. Suppose that we now eliminate the `else` portion of the inner `if` statement. If we keep the same indention, the statements become the following:

```
if (x > y)
    if (y < z)
        ++k;
else
    ++j;
```

It might appear that `j` is incremented when $x <= y$, but that is not correct. The C++ compiler will associate an `else` statement with the closest `if` statement within a block. Therefore, no matter what indenting is used, the previous statement is executed as if it were the following:

```
if (x > y)
    if (y < z)
        k++;
    else
        j++;
```

Thus, `j` is incremented when `x>y` and `y>=z`. If we intended for `j` to be incremented when `x<=y`, then we would need to use braces to define the inner statement as a block:

```
if (x > y)
{
    if (y < z)
        ++k;
}
else
    ++j;
```

conditional operator

To avoid confusion and possible errors when using **if/else** statements, you should routinely use braces to clearly define the statement blocks.

C++ allows a **conditional operator** to be used in place of a simple `if/else` statement. This conditional operator is a ternary operator because it has three arguments: a condition, a statement to perform if the condition is true, and a statement to perform if the condition is false. The operation is indicated with a question mark following the condition and with a colon between the two statements. To illustrate, the following two statements are equivalent:

```
if (a<b)                          a<b ? ++count : c = a + b;
    ++count;
else
    c = a + b;
```

The conditional operator (specified as ?:) is evaluated before assignment operators, and if there is more than one conditional operator in an expression, they are associated from right to left.

In this section, we have presented a number of ways to compare values in selection statements. A caution is necessary when comparing floating-point values. As we saw in Chapter 2, floating-point values can sometimes be slightly different than we expect them to be because of the conversions between binary and decimal values. For example, earlier in this section, we did not compare `denominator` with zero, but instead used a condition to see if the absolute value of `denominator` was less than a small value. Similarly, if we wanted to know whether y was close to the value 10.5, we should use a condition such as `fabs(y - 10.5) <= 0.0001` instead of `y == 10.5`. In general, do not use the equality operator with floating-point values.

A second caution is necessary when using the equality operator (==) with integers. A common error is to use the assignment operator (=) instead of the logical operator (==). Consider the following C++ program:

```
#include<iostream>
using namespace std;

int main()
{
    int x(4), y(5);
    if (x = y)
    {
        cout << x << " is equal to " << y << endl;
    }
    return 0;
}
```

The above program compiles and executes without any error messages from the compiler or the operating system, and the output from the program is:

```
5 is equal to 5
```

This bug is the result of using the assignment operator instead of the equality operator to form the condition in the `if` statement. An assignment of y to x is made and since y is not zero (ie y is not `false`), the assignment statement evaluates to true and the `cout` statement inside the `if` statement block is executed. If y were initialized to 0 instead of 5, the statement block would not be executed. Virtually every programmer makes this programming error more than once, so if your program output is not what you expect it to be, check all conditions that are intended to use the equality operator.

Practice!

In problems 1 through 7, draw a flowchart to perform the steps indicated. Then give the corresponding C++ statements. Assume that the objects have been declared and have reasonable values.

1. If time is greater than 15.0, increment time by 1.0.

2. When the square root of *poly* is less than 0.5, print the value of *poly*.

3. If the difference between *volt_1* and *volt_2* is larger than 10.0, print the values of *volt_1* and *volt_2*.

4. If the value of *den* is less than 0.05, set *result* to zero; otherwise, set *result* equal to *num* divided by *den*.

5. If the natural logarithm of *x* is greater than or equal to 3, set *time* equal to zero and decrement *count*.

6. If *dist* is less than 50.0 and *time* is greater than 10.0, increment *time* by 2; otherwise, increment *time* by 2.5.

7. If *dist* is greater than or equal to 100.0, increment *time* by 2.0. If *dist* is between
50 and 100, increment *time* by 1. Otherwise, increment *time* by 0.5.

3.5 Numerical Technique: Linear Interpolation

The collection of data from an experiment or from observing a physical phenomenon is an important step in developing a problem solution. These data points can generally be considered
to be coordinates of points of a function $f(x)$. We would often like to use these data points to
determine estimates of the function $f(x)$ for values of x that were not part of the original set
of data. For example, suppose that we have data points $(a, f(a))$ and $(c, f(c))$. If we want
to estimate the value of $f(b)$, where $a < b < c$, we could assume that a straight line joined
$f(a)$ and $f(c)$ and then use linear interpolation to obtain the value of $f(b)$. If we assume
that the points $f(a)$ and $f(c)$ are joined by a cubic (third-degree) polynomial, we could use
a cubic-spline interpolation method to obtain the value of $f(b)$. Most interpolation problems
can be solved using one of these two methods. Figure 3.6 contains a set of six data points

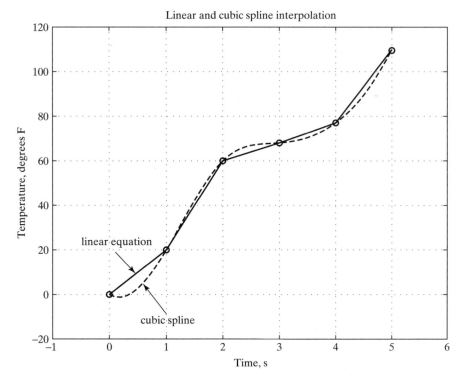

Figure 3.6 Linear and cubic spline interpolation.

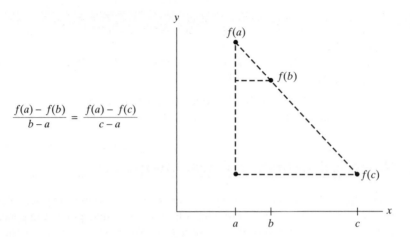

$$\frac{f(a) - f(b)}{b - a} = \frac{f(a) - f(c)}{c - a}$$

Figure 3.7 Similar triangles.

that have been connected with straight-line segments and that have been connected with cubic degree polynomial segments. It should be clear that the values determined for the function between sample points depend on the type of interpolation that we select. In this section, we discuss linear interpolation.

A graph with two arbitrary data points $f(a)$ and $f(c)$ is shown in Figure 3.7. If we assume that the function between the two points can be estimated by a straight line, we can then compute the function value at any point $f(b)$ using an equation derived from similar triangles:

$$f(b) = f(a) + \frac{b - a}{c - a} \left[f(c) - f(a) \right].$$

Recall that we are also assuming that $a < b < c$.

To illustrate using this interpolation equation, assume that we have a set of temperature measurements taken from the cylinder head in a new engine that is being tested for possible use in a race car. These data are plotted with straight lines connecting the points in Figure 3.8, and they are also listed here:

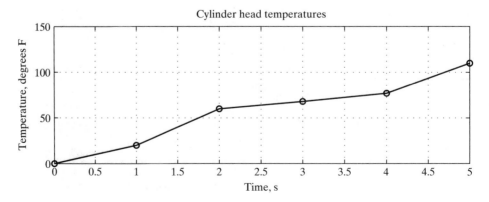

Figure 3.8 Cylinder head temperatures.

Time, s	Temperature, degrees F
0.0	0.0
1.0	20.0
2.0	60.0
3.0	68.0
4.0	77.0
5.0	110.0

Assume that we want to interpolate a temperature to correspond to the value 2.6 seconds. We then have the following situation:

a	2.0	f(a)	60.0
b	2.6	f(b)	?
c	3.0	f(c)	68.0

Using the interpolation formula, we have

$$f(b) = f(a) + \frac{b-a}{c-a}\left[f(c) - f(a)\right]$$

$$= 60.0 + \frac{2.6 - 2.0}{3.0 - 2.0}[68.0 - 60.0]$$

$$= 64.8.$$

In this example, we used linear interpolation to find the temperature that corresponds to a specified time. We could also interchange the roles of temperature and time so that we plot temperature on the x-axis and time on the y-axis. In this case, we can use the same process to compute the time that a specified temperature occurred, assuming that we have a pair of data points with temperatures below and above the specified temperature.

Practice!

Assume that we have the following set of data points, which is also plotted in Figure 3.9:

Time (s)	Temperature (degrees F)
0.0	72.5
0.5	78.1
1.0	86.4
1.5	92.3
2.0	110.6
2.5	111.5
3.0	109.3
3.5	110.2
4.0	110.5
4.5	109.9
5.0	110.2

1. Use your calculator to compute temperatures at the following times, using linear interpolation:

    0.3, 1.25, 2.36, 4.48

2. Use your calculator to compute time values that correspond to the following temperatures, using linear interpolation:

    81, 96, 100, 106

3. Suppose Problem 2 asked you to compute the time value that corresponds to the temperature 110 degrees Fahrenheit. What complicates this problem? How many time values correspond to the temperature 110 degrees Fahrenheit? Find each of the corresponding time values, using linear interpolation. (You may want to refer to Figure 3.10, which contains a plot of these data with the temperature data on the x-axis and the time values on the y-axis.)

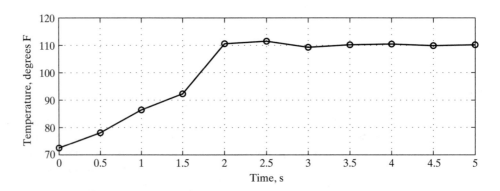

Figure 3.9 Temperature values.

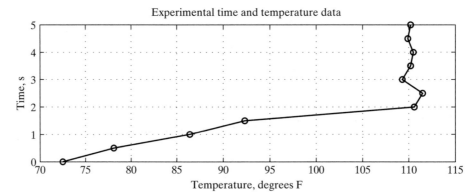

Figure 3.10 Time values.

3.6 Problem Solving Applied: Freezing Temperature of Seawater

In this section, we use linear interpolation to solve a problem related to the salinity of seawater. Recall from the chapter opening discussion that the salinity of seawater is a measure of the amount of dissolved material in the seawater. Salinity varies from one location to another in the ocean, but typically falls in the range of 33 to 38 parts per thousand (ppt), or a percentage of 3.3 to 3.8.

Salinity is often measured using an instrument that measures the electrical conductivity of the water; the more dissolved materials in the water, the better it conducts electricity. Measurements of salinity are especially important in colder regions because the temperature at which seawater freezes is dependent upon its salinity. The higher the salinity, the lower the temperature at which seawater freezes. The following table contains a set of salinity measurements and corresponding freezing temperatures; the values are also plotted in Figure 3.11

Salinity (ppt)	Freezing Temperature (degrees F)
0 (fresh water)	32
10	31.1
20	30.1
24.7	29.6
30	29.1
35	28.6

Assume that we would like to use linear interpolation to determine the freezing temperature of water for which we have measured the salinity. Write a program that allows the user to enter the data for two points and a salinity measure between those points. The program should verify that the value entered for the salinity lies between the values entered for the salinity of the two data points. If the input data is valid, the program should compute the corresponding freezing temperature. If the data is invalid, the program should print an error message and the invalid data.

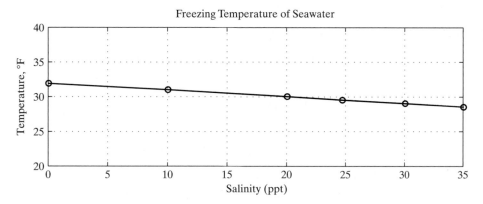

Figure 3.11 Freezing temperature of seawater.

1. PROBLEM STATEMENT

Use linear interpolation to compute a new freezing temperature for water with a specified salinity.

2. INPUT/OUTPUT DESCRIPTION

The following diagram shows that the input to the program includes two consecutive points $(a, f(a))$ and $(c, f(c))$ and the new salinity measurement b. The output is the new freezing temperature.

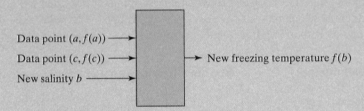

Data point $(a, f(a))$ ⟶

Data point $(c, f(c))$ ⟶   ⟶ New freezing temperature $f(b)$

New salinity b ⟶

3. HAND EXAMPLE

Suppose that we want to determine the freezing temperature for water with a salinity measurement of 33 ppt. From the data, we see that this point falls between 30 and 35 ppt:

```
a     30        29.1        f(a)
b     33        ?           f(b)
c     35        28.6        f(c)
```

Using the linear equation formula, we can compute $f(b)$:

```
f(b) = f(a) + (b-a)/(c-a) . (f(c)-f(a))

     = 29.1 + 3/5 . (28.6 -29.1)

     = 28.8
```

As expected, this value falls between $f(a)$ and $f(c)$.

4. ALGORITHM DEVELOPMENT

The first step in the development of an algorithm is the decomposition of the problem solution into a set of sequentially executed steps:

Decomposition Outline

1. Read the coordinates of the adjacent points and the new salinity value.

2. Validate input.

3. Compute the new freezing temperature.

4. Print the new freezing temperature.

The second step in the decomposition outline requires a selection structure. If the value entered for the salinity does not lie between the salinity values of the two data points, an error message will be printed, along with the erroneous data, and the program will terminate. The following refinement, described in a flowchart, outlines these steps.

The steps in the flowchart are now detailed enough to convert into C++. We will use an `if` statement to implement the selection structure.

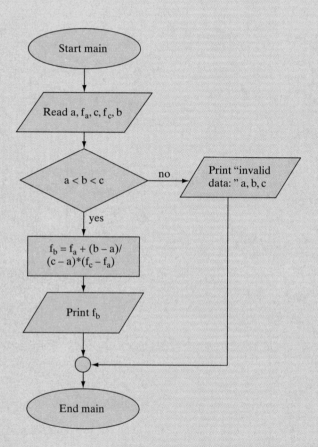

```
/*-------------------------------------------------------------------*/
/*   Program chapter3_2                                              */
/*                                                                   */
/*   This program uses linear interpolation to                      */
/*   compute the freezing temperature of seawater.                  */

#include<iostream> //Required for cin, cout, endl.
#include<iomanip>  //Required for fixed, setprecision()
using namespace std;
```

```
int main()
{
  // Declare objects.
  double a, f_a, b, f_b, c, f_c;

  // Prompt and get user input from the keyboard.
  cout << "Use ppt for salinity values." << endl
       << "Use degrees F for temperatures." << endl
       << "Enter first salinity and freezing temperature: \n";
  cin >> a >> f_a;
  cout << "Enter second salinity and freezing temperature: \n";
  cin >> c >> f_c;
  cout << "Enter new salinity: \n";
  cin >> b;
  if( !(a < b && b < c) )
  {
      cout  << "Invalid data: " << a  << ","
            << b << "," << c << endl;
  }
  else
  {
    // Use linear interpolaltion to compute
    // new freezing  temperature.
    f_b = f_a + (b-a)/(c-a)*(f_c - f_a);
    // Print new freezing temperature to the screen.
    cout << " New freezing temperature in degrees F: "
         << fixed  << setprecision(1) << f_b  << endl;
  }// end else

  // Exit program.
  return 0;
}
```

5. TESTING

We first test the program using the data from the hand example. This generates the following interaction:

```
Use ppt for salinity values.
Use degrees F for temperatures.
Enter first salinity and freezing temperature:
30 29.1
Enter second salinity and freezing temperature:
35 28.6
Enter new salinity:
33
New freezing temperature in degrees F: 28.8
```

The value computed matches the hand example, so we can then test the program with other time values. If the new coefficient value had not matched the result from the hand example, we would then need to determine if the error is in the hand example or in the C++ program.

Modify!

These problems relate to the program developed in this section for computing new freezing points with linear interpolation.

1. Use the program to determine the freezing temperatures to go with the following salinity measurements in ppt:

   3   8.5   19   23.5   26.8   30.5

2. Modify the program so that it converts and prints the new temperature in degrees Centigrade. (Recall that $T_F = 9/5\ T_C + 32$, where T_F represents a temperature in degrees Fahrenheit and T_C represents a temperature in degrees Centigrade.)

3. Suppose that the data used with the program contained values with the degrees in Centigrade. Would the program need to be changed? Explain.

4. Modify the program so that it interpolates for a salinity, instead of a new freezing temperature. (You may want to refer to Figure 3.12, which contains a plot of this data with the freezing temperature on the x axis and the salinity on the y axis.)

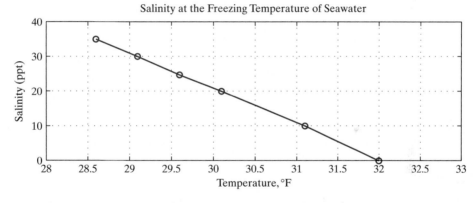

Figure 3.12 Salinity at the freezing temperature of seawater.

3.7   Selection Statements: `switch` Statement

The `switch` statement is used for multiple-selection decision making. In particular, it is often used to replace nested `if/else` statements. Before giving the general discussion of the `switch` statement, we present a simple example that uses nested `if/else` statements and then an equivalent solution that uses the `switch` statement.

Suppose that we have a temperature reading from a sensor inside a large piece of machinery. We want to print a message on the control screen to inform the operator of the temperature status. If the status code is 10, the temperature is too hot, and the equipment should be turned off; if the status code is 11, the operator should check the temperature every

5 minutes; if the status code is 13, the operator should turn on the circulating fan; for all other status codes, the equipment is operating in a normal mode. The correct message could be printed with the following set of nested if/else statements:

```
if (code == 10)
{
   cout << "Too hot - turn equipment off." << endl;
}
else
{
   if (code == 11)
   {
      cout << "Caution - recheck in 5 minutes." << endl;
   }
   else
   {
      if (code == 13)
      {
         cout << "Turn on circulating fan." << endl;
      }
      else
      {
         cout << "Normal mode of operation." << endl;
      }
   }
}
```

An equivalent statement is the following switch statement:

```
switch (code)
{
   case 10:
      cout << "Too hot - turn equipment off." << endl;
      break;
   case 11:
      cout << "Caution - recheck in 5 minutes." << endl;
      break;
   case 13:
      cout << "Turn on circulating fan." << endl;
      break;
   default:
      cout << "Normal temperature range." << endl;
      break;
}
cout << code << endl;
```

The break statement causes execution of the program to continue with the statement following the switch statement (cout << code << endl; in this example), thus skipping the rest of the statements in the braces.

Nested if/else statements do not always easily translate to a switch statement. However, when the conversion works, the switch statement is usually easier to read. It is also easier to determine the statement grouping needed for the switch statement.

controlling
expression

case structure

The `switch` statement selects the statements to perform based on a **controlling expression,** which must be an expression of type integer or character. In the general form given below, the `case` labels (`label_1, label_2, ...`) determine which statements are executed, and thus in some languages this structure is called a **case structure.** The statements executed are the ones that correspond to the `case` for which the label is equal to the controlling expression. The `case` labels must be unique constants; an error occurs if two or more of the `case` labels have the same value. The `default` clause is used to give a statement to execute if none of the other statements is executed; the `default` clause is optional.

```
switch (controlling expression)
{
    case label_1:
        statements;
    case label_2:
        statements;
    ...
    default:
        statements;
}
```

The statements in the `switch` structure usually contain the `break` statement. When the `break` statement is executed, the execution of the program breaks out of the `switch` structure and continues executing with the statement following the `switch` structure. Without the break statement, all statements will be executed that follow the ones selected with the case label.

Although the `default` clause in the `switch` statement is optional, we recommend that it be included so that the steps are clearly specified for the situation in which none of the `case` labels is equal to the controlling expression. We also use the `break` statement in the `default` clause to emphasize that the program continues with the statement following the `switch` statement.

It is valid to use several `case` labels with the same statement, as in

```
switch (op_code)
{
    case 'N':
    case 'R':
        cout << "Normal operating range." << endl;
        break;
    case 'M':
        cout << "Maintenance needed." << endl;
        break;
    default:
        cout << "Error in code value." << endl;
        break;
}
```

When more than one `case` label is used for the same statement, the evaluation is performed as if the logical **or** operator joined the cases. For this example, the first statement is executed if `op_code` is equal to 'N' **or** if `op_code` is equal to 'R'.

Practice!

Convert the following nested `if`/`else` statements to a `switch` statement:

```
if (rank==1 || rank==2)
{
    cout << "Lower division" << endl;
}
else
{
    if (rank==3 || rank==4)
    {
        cout << "Upper division" << endl;
    }
    else
    {
        if (rank==5)
        {
            cout << "Graduate student" << endl;
        }
        else
        {
            cout << "Invalid rank" << endl;
        }
    }
}
```

3.8 Building C++ Solutions with IDEs: NetBeans

In this section, we will develop a C++ solution using the NetBeans IDE. Our C++ program will perform currency conversion. The pseudocode for our currency conversion program is given below:

```
Pseudocode
main: read amount in dollars, currency code
      case currency code E
          convert dollars to euros
      case currency code P
          convert dollars to Mexican pesos
      case currency code S
          convert dollars to British pounds sterling
      print equivalent currency
```

The steps in the pseudocode are detailed enough to convert into C++, using the NetBeans IDE.

NetBeans

NetBeans is an IDE developed by Oracle Corporation and available for free download. The IDE is written in Java and can run on any platform—including Windows, Mac OS, Linux, and Solaris—as long as a Java Virtual Machine (JVM) has been installed. When the NetBeans application is launched, a welcome screen appears as shown below:

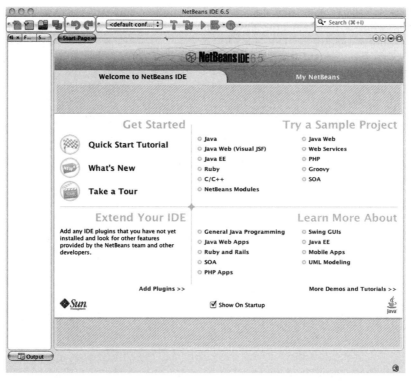

To create a new C++ solution, we must first create a new project. From the welcome screen, select the **C/C++** link. A New Project window will appear similar to the one shown below.

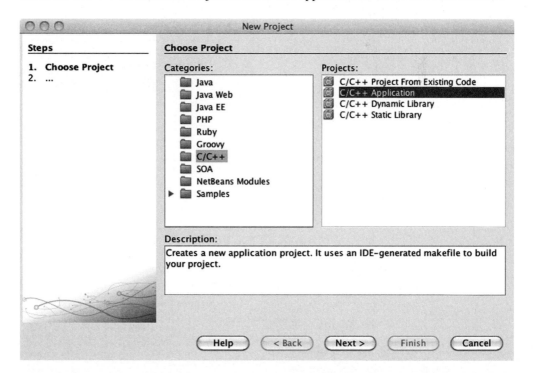

Select **C/C++** from the **Categories** window and **C/C++ Application** from the **Projects** window, then select the **Next >** button. A new window will appear to allow you to name your project and select a directory. The project name window is shown below.

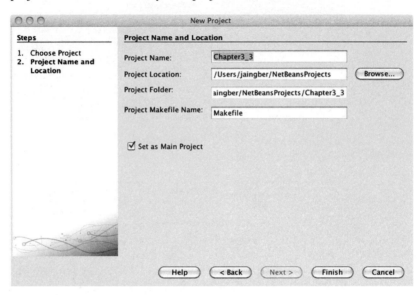

Select the directory of your choice and name the file `chapter3_3`, then click on the **Finish** button to complete the creation of your NetBeans project. The next window that will appear is the **Project** window. The **Project** window provides access to the project files and tools provided by NetBeans.

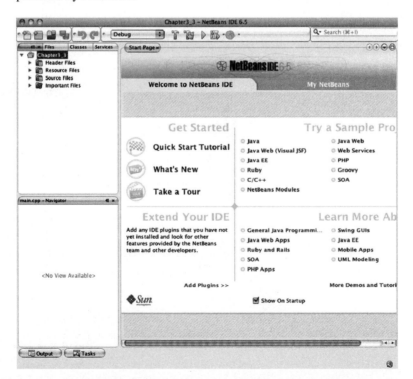

To create a C++ program, select **Chapter3_3** from the left window, then select **New File** from the **NetBeans File** menu at the top of the window. The following window to add a new file will appear.

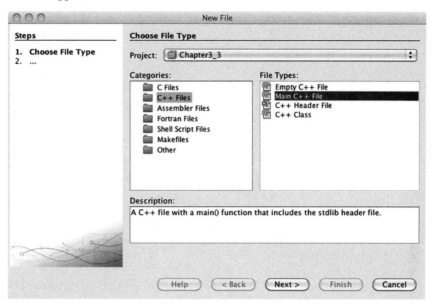

Select **C++Files** from the **Categories** window and **Main C++ File** from the **File Types** window. A new window will appear to allow you to name the file and choose a directory. The new file name window is shown next.

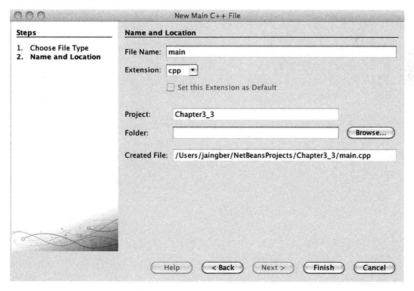

Name the file main and select **Finish**. The Editor window will appear, as shown below. We see that some basic statements have been added to the file main.cpp.

We will now write the C++ implementation of the pseudocode for the currency converter in the file main.cpp. The code and completed file window are shown below:

```cpp
/*
 * File:    main.cpp
 * Author: jaingber
 *
 * Created on May 21, 2011, 10:08 AM
 */

#include <stdlib.h>
#include <iostream>
using namespace std;

/*--------------------------------------------------------------------*/
/*  Program chapter3_3
 *
 *  This program performs currency conversion from dollars to
 *  E => euros
 *  P => pesos
 *  S => pounds sterling
 */
int main(int argc, char** argv)
{
  double dollars, equivalentCurr;
  char currencyCode;
  const double ECONVERTION(0.7041), PCONVERTION(11.6325),
      SCONVERTION(0.6144);
```

```cpp
//Prompt user for input
cout << "enter dollar amount"  << endl;
cin >> dollars;
cout << "enter currency code:\n"
     << "E => Euros\nP => Mexican Pesos\nS => British Pounds
        Sterling\n" ;
cin >> currencyCode;
switch(toupper(currencyCode))
{
    case 'E':
        cout << "converting dollars to euros..\n" ;
        equivalentCurr = dollars*ECONVERTION
        break;
    case 'P':
        cout << "converting dollars to pesos..\n" ;
        equivalentCurr = dollars*PCONVERTION;
        break;
    case 'S':
        cout << "converting dollars to pounds sterling..\n" ;
        equivalentCurr = dollars*SCONVERTION;
        break;
    default:
        cout << currencyCode << "not supported at this time\n" ;
        equivalentCurr = dollars;
}
cout << "Equivalent amount: "<< equivalentCurr << endl;

return (EXIT_SUCCESS);
}
```

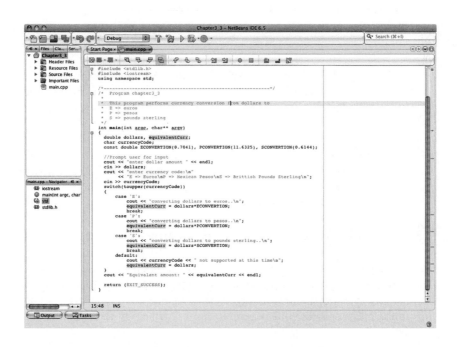

This project can be compiled by selecting the **Build Main Project** from the **NetBeans Run** menu. The build window is shown below, and we can see that the build was successful.

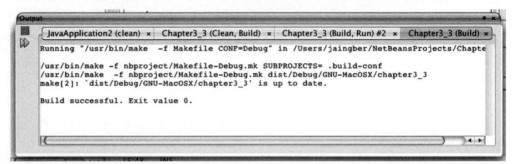

To execute the program, select **Run Main Project** from the **NetBeans Run** menu. An output window will appear, as shown below. Enter the required dollar amount and currency code, and verify the output.

Modify!

1. Look up the current exchange rates for Euros, Mexican Pesos and British Pounds Sterling and modify the constants in program `chapter3_3` to reflect the current values.

2. Modify program `chapter3_3` to also perform conversion from U.S. dollars to Hong Kong dollars.

3. Modify program `chaper3_3` by replacing the `switch` statement with an `if` statement.

3.9 Defining Operators for Programmer-Defined Data Types

We have looked at arithmetic and relational operators and have used these operators with built-in data types to build conditional expressions. However, these operators are not defined for programmer-defined data types such as `Point`. Recall from Chapter 2 that the assignment operator is the only operator that is defined by the compiler for programmer-defined types. Additional operators can be defined for programmer-defined types provided there is a reasonable definition for the operator. Defining operators for programmer-defined types is referred to as **operator overloading**. Operator overloading provides a new definition for an existing operator and allows a programmer-defined type to use operators in the same way that built-in types do. Operators can only be overloaded for programmer-defined types. You cannot overload operators for built-in types.

operator
overloading

In this section, we will add two binary operators to the `Point` class, developed in Chapter 2. The arithmetic operator (–) will be add to the `Point` class and defined to return the distance between two points in a plane. The relational operator (==) will also be added to the `Point` class and defined to return true if and only if all corresponding data members of two operands are equal. To illustrate the syntax of overloading operators, we begin by adding the method declarations to the `Point` class declaration.

```
/*-----------------------------------------------------------*/
/* Point class chapter3_7                                    */
/* Filename: Point.h                                         */
class Point
{
  //Type declaration statements
  //Data members.
  private:
  double xCoord, yCoord; //Class attributes

  public:
  //Declaration statements for class methods
  //Constructors for Point class
  Point(); //default constructor
  Point(double x, double y); //parameterized constructor

  //Overloaded operators
  double operator-(const Point& rhs) const;
  bool operator ==(const Point& rhs) const;
};
/*-----------------------------------------------------------*/
```

Notice that we use the `const` modifier twice in each of the operator declarations. The use of the `const` modifier prevents an overloaded operator from modifying the data members of its operands. The `const` modifier inside the parentheses protects the data members of the right-hand side operand, and the `const` modifier at the end of the declaration protects the data members of the left-hand side operand. Any attempt to modify the data members of either object from within these methods will result in a compilation error.

To complete the definition of our overloaded operators, we must add these two methods to our class implementation. The updated class implementation is provided below.

```
/*-----------------------------------------------------------*/
/* Class implementation for Point                            */
/* filename: Point.cpp                                       */
#include "Point.h"        //Required for Point
#include <iostream>       //Required for cout
#include <cmath>          //Required for sqrt() and pow()
using namespace std;
```

```
/*------------------------------------------------------------*/
/* Parameterized constructor                                  */
Point::Point(double x, double y)
{
  //input parameters x,y
  cout << "Constructing Point object, parameterized: \n";
  cout << "input parameters: " << x << "," << y << endl;
  xCoord = x;
  yCoord = y;
}

/*------------------------------------------------------------*/
/* Default constructor                                        */
Point::Point()
{
    cout << "Constructing Point object, default: \n";
    cout << "initializing to zero"  << endl;
    xCoord = 0.0;
    yCoord = 0.0;
}
/*------------------------------------------------------------*/
/* This method returns the distance between two               */
/* points in a plane.                                         */
double Point::operator -(const Point& rhs) const
{
  double diffX, diffY, distance;
  diffX = rhs.xCoord - xCoord; //(x2-x1)
  diffY = rhs.yCoord - yCoord; //(y2-y1)
  distance = sqrt( pow(diffX,2) + pow(diffY,2) );
  return distance;
}
/*------------------------------------------------------------*/
/* This method returns:                                       */
/*    true if two points are equal                            */
/*    false if two points are not equal.                      */
/* equal means that all corresponding data                    */
/* members are equal.                                         */
bool Point::operator ==(const Point& rhs) const
{
  if(rhs.xCoord == xCoord &&
     rhs.yCoord == yCoord )
  {
    return true;
  }
  else
  {
    return false;
  }
}
```

We have completed the definition of two binary operators for the Point class. These new operators are tested in program `chapter3_3`, provided below. We will use memory snapshots to illustrate the use of the overloaded operators as we trace the execution of the main program.

```
/*------------------------------------------------------------*/
/* Program chapter3_3                                         */
/*                                                            */
/* This program illustrates the use of the                   */
/* programmer-defined data type Point                        */

#include <iostream>   //Required for cout
#include "Point.h"    //Required for Point
using namespace std;

int main()
{
  //Declare and initialize objects.
  Point p1;
  Point p2(1.5, -4.7);

  //Test operators
  if( p1 == p2)
  {
    cout << "p1 is equal to p2"  << endl;
  }
  else
  {
    cout << "Distance between p1 and p2 is"  << p1 - p2
         << endl;
  }

  return 0;
}
/*------------------------------------------------------------*/
```

memory snapshot:
  Point p1;
  Point p2(1.5, -4.7);

Point p1 -> | 0.0 | double xCoord

              | 0.0 | double yCoord

Point p2 -> | 1.5 | double xCoord

              | -4.7 | double yCoord

memory snapshot:
if(p1 == p2)

Point& rhs-> | |

In the expression

```
p1 == p2
```

p1 is the **calling object**. The calling object is the object that calls the method. For overloaded binary operators, the left operand is always the calling object. When the `operator ==(const Point& rhs)` method is called, we see from the memory snapshot that `rhs` is defined and references the same object that `p2` references. The data type of `rhs` is the type `Point&`. The operator (`&`) is called the reference operator, and `rhs` is said to reference an object of type `Point`. The reference operator and calling objects will be discussed in detail in Chapter 6. For now, it is important to note that and `rhs` and `p2` reference the same object.

Class methods have access to the data members of the calling object, by name. Thus, when the statement

```
if(rhs.xCoord == xCoord &&
    rhs.yCoord == yCoord )
  {
    return true;
  }
  else
  {
    return false;
  }
}
```

is evaluated, `xCoord` and `yCoord` refer to the data members of the calling object, `p1`, and the conditional expression inside the parentheses reduces to (`1.5 == 0.0 && -4.7 == 0.0`). This expression is false, so the `return` statement inside the else block is executed and a value of `false` is returned to the `if` statement in `main()`. Since `false` is returned to the `if` statement in `main()`, the `cout` statement inside the `else` block is executed.

memory snapshot:

```
cout << "Distance between p1 and p2 is " << p1 - p2
        << endl;
```

The value of distance is returned to the `cout` statement and printed to standard output. The output from a test run of program `chapter3_3` is show below.

```
Constructing Point object, default:
initializing to zero
Constructing Point object, parameterized:
```

```
input parameters: 1.5,-4.7
Constructing Point object, parameterized:
input parameters: 0,0
Distance between p1 and p2 is 4.93356
```

We will continue to develop the `Point` class as we learn new features of the C++ programming language.

Practice!

1. Create the flowchart for the method `bool Point::operator ==(const Point& rhs) const`

2. Write the pseudocode for the method `double Point::operator -(const Point& rhs) const`

Modify!

1. Add the following declaration to program `chapter3_3`:
   `const Point ORIGIN(0.0, 0.0);`
   then modify the program to test for equality between `p1` and `ORIGIN`.

2. Add the following assignment statement to program `chapter3_3`:
   `p2 = ORIGIN;`
   and the declaration for `ORIGIN` from problem 1, then modify the program to test for equality between `p2` and `ORIGIN`.

3. Add the following assignment statement to program `chapter3_3`:
   `ORIGIN = p2;`
   What message do you receive when you compile your program?

SUMMARY

In this chapter, we covered the use of conditions and `if` statements and `switch` statements to select the proper statements to be executed. These selection structures are used in most programs.

Key Terms

case structure
condition
controlling expression
data file
decomposition outline
divide and conquer
flowchart
logical operator
pseudocode

relational operator
selection
sequence
statement block
stepwise refinement
test data
top-down design
validation and verification

C++ Statement Summary

`if` statement:

```
if (temp > 100)
    cout << "Temperature exceeds limit" << endl;
```

`if/else` statement:

```
if (d <= 30)
    velocity = 4.25 + 0.00175*d*d;
else
    velocity = 0.65 + 0.12*d - 0.0025*d*d;
```

conditional statement:

```
temp>100 ? cout << "Caution \n" : cout << "Normal \n";
```

`switch` statement:

```
switch (op_code)
{
    case 'n':
    case 'r':
        cout << "Normal Operating range \n";
        break;
    case 'm':
        cout << "Maintenance needed \n";
        break;
    default:
        cout << "Error in code value \n";
        break;
}
```

`break` statement:

```
break;
```

Notes

1. Use spaces around the relational operator in a logical expression in a simple condition; use spaces around the logical operator and not around the relational operators in a complicated condition.
2. Indent the statements within a statement block or inside a selection structure. If compound statements are nested, indent each nested set of statements from the previous statement.
3. Use braces even when they are not required to clearly identify the structure of a complicated statement.
4. Use the `default` case within the `switch` statement to emphasize the action to take when none of the case labels matches the controlling expression.

Debugging Notes

1. When you discover and correct an error in a program, start the testing step over again. In particular, rerun the program with all the test data sets again.
2. Be sure to use the relational operator == instead of = in a condition for equality.

3. Put the braces surrounding a block of statements on lines by themselves; this will help you avoid omitting them.
4. Do not use the equality operator with floating-point values; instead, test for values "close to" a desired value.
5. Recompile your program frequently when correcting syntax errors; correcting one error may remove many error messages.
6. Use *cout* statements to give memory snapshots of the values of key objects when debugging loops. Remember to use the *endl* manipulator instead of '\n' to ensure that the values are printed immediately after the statement is executed.

Problems

Exam Practice!

True/False Problems
Indicate whether the following statements are true (T) or false (F).

1. If a condition's value is zero, then the condition is evaluated as false. T F
2. If the condition's value is neither zero nor 1, then it is an invalid condition. T F
3. The expression $a == 2$ is used to determine whether the value of a is equal to 2, and the expression $a = 2$ assigns the value of 2 to the object a. T F
4. The logical operators && and || have the same level precedence. T F
5. The keyword `else` is always associated with the closest `if` statement unless braces are used to define blocks of statements. T F

Syntax Problems
Identify any syntax errors in the following statements. Assume that the objects have all been defined as integers.

```
6. switch (sqrt (x))
   {
       case 1:
         cout << "Too low. \n";
         break;
       case 2:
         cout << "Correct range. \n";
         break;
       case 3:
         cout << "Too high.\n";
         break
   }
```

Multiple-Choice Problems
Circle the letter for the best answer to complete each statement or for the correct answer to each question.

7. Consider the following statement:
```
int i=100, j=0;
```
Which of the following statements are true?
(a) `i<3`
(b) `!(j<1)`
(c) `(i>0) || (j>50)`
(d) `(j<i) && (i <= 10)`

8. If *a*1 is true and *a*2 is false, then which of the following expressions are true?

  (a) `a1 && a2`

  (b) `a1 || a2`

  (c) `!(a1 || a2)`

  (d) `!a1 && a2`

9. Which of the following are unary operators?

  (a) `!`

  (b) `||`

  (c) `&&`

10. The expression

  `(!((3-4%3) < 5 && (6/4 > 3)))` is

  (a) true.

  (b) false.

  (c) invalid.

  (d) none of the above.

Problems 11 through 13 refer to the following statements:

```
int sum(0), count(4);
if(sum <= count)
    sum += count;
cout << "sum = " << sum << endl;
```

11. What would you see on the screen if these statements are executed?

  (a) sum = 0

  (b) sum = 4

  (c) sum = 8

  (d) no output

12. What is the value of count after execution of these statements?

  (a) 0

  (b) 4

  (c) 5

  (d) an unpredictable integer

13. How many times is the statement `sum += count;` executed?

  (a) 0

  (b) 1

  (c) 2

  (d) 4

Memory Snapshot Problems

Give the corresponding snapshots of memory after the following set of statements is executed:

14.
```
int a = 750;
if(a > 0)
    if(a >= 1000)
        a = 0;
    else
        a *= 2;
else
    a *= 10;
```

15.
```
char ch = '*';
switch(ch)
```

```
{
  case '+':
     cout << "addition\n";
     break;
  case '-':
     cout << "subtraction\n";
     break;
  case '*':
     cout << "multiplication\n";
     break;
  case '/':
     cout << "division\n";
     break;
  default:
     cout << "other\n";
}
```

Boolean Expressions

16. Write a program that receives the values of three boolean variables, a, b, and c, from standard input and determines if the value of the condition

```
! (a&&b&&c) && !(a||b||c)
```

is true or false. Format your output as follows:

The condition:

```
! (xx&&xx&&xx) && !(a||b||c)
```

```
is false (if the condition is false) OR
is true (if the condition is true).
```

17. Write a program that receives the values of three boolean variables, a, b, and c, from standard input and determines if the value of the condition

```
!(a || b) && c
```

is true or false. Check for errors in the input data. Format your output as follows:

The condition:

```
!(xx||xx)&&xx
```

```
is false (if the condition is false) OR
is true (if the condition is true).
```

These problems relate to program `chapter3_1`, developed in this section to generate a truth table.

18. Modify this program to determine if the condition is a tautology. **(Hint: A tautology is always true. If even one of the combinations is false then the condition is not a tautology.)**
19. Modify this program to determine if the condition is a contradiction.
20. Modify this program to determine if the condition is a contingency.

4

ENGINEERING CHALLENGE:
Data Collection

Weather balloons are used to collect data from the upper atmosphere. The balloons are filled with helium and rise to an equilibrium point where the difference between the densities of the helium inside the balloon and the air outside the balloon is just enough to support the weight of the balloon. During the day, the sun warms the balloon, causing it to rise to a new equilibrium point; in the evening, the balloon cools, and it descends to a lower altitude. The balloon can be used to measure the temperature, pressure, humidity, chemical concentrations, or other properties of the air around the balloon. A weather balloon may stay aloft for only a few hours or as long as several years collecting environmental data. The balloon falls back to earth as the helium leaks out or is released.

CONTROL STRUCTURES: REPETITION

CHAPTER OUTLINE

OBJECTIVES **In this chapter we develop problem solutions containing:**

- repetition structures that allow us to repeat a set of steps as long as a condition is true
- algorithm development and descriptions of loops using flowcharts and pseudocode

- three common forms of input loops

4.1 Algorithm Development

In Chapter 3 we developed algorithms that used selection structures to provide alternative paths during program execution. In this chapter we develop algorithms and write C++ programs that use repetition structures. The repetition structure allows us to repeat (or loop through) a set of steps as long as a condition is true. For example, we might want to compute a set of velocity values that correspond to time values of 0, 1, 2, . . . , 10 seconds. We do not want to develop a sequential structure that has a statement to compute the velocity for a time of 0, another statement to compute the velocity for a time of 1, then another statement to compute the velocity for a time of 2, and so on. Although this structure would require only eleven statements in this case, it could require hundreds of statements if we wanted to compute the velocity values over a long period. If we use the repetition structure, we can develop a solution in which we initialize the time to 0. Then, as long as the time value is less than or equal to 10, we compute and print a velocity value and increment the time value by 1. When the time value is greater than 10, we exit the structure.

Pseudocode and Flowchart Description

Algorithms using repetition structures can be described with pseudocode or flowcharts. Figure 4.1 contains the flowchart for a repetition structure that will compute and print a velocity value as long as the time value is less than or equal to 10. The time value is incremented by 1 at the end of each repetition. The pseudocode for this structure is given below:

```
set time to 0
while time <= 10
    compute velocity
    print velocity
    increment time by 1
```

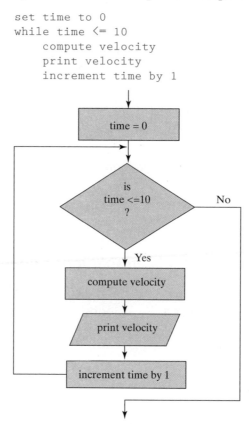

Figure 4.1 Flowchart for repetition structure.

Loops are used to implement repetition structures. C++ contains three different loop structures: the while loop, the do/while loop, and the for loop. C++ also supports the use of two additional statements with loops to modify their performance: the break statement (which we used with the switch statement) and the continue statement. In the remaining sections of this chapter, we present these loop structures and develop example programs that illustrate the use of each of these repetition structures.

4.2 Repetition Structures

The most general looping structure in C++ is the while loop.

`while` **Loop**

The general form of a `while` loop follows:

```
while (condition)
    statement;
```

`while` **Statement:** The `while` statement allows a program to repeatedly execute a block of statements while the specified condition is true.

Syntax:

```
while(condition)                  while(condition)
    statement;                    {
                                      statement block
                                  }
```

Example:

```
while(!isspace(ch))               while(x > y)
{                                 {
   cin.get(ch);                      ++c1;
}                                     --x;
                                  }
```

The condition is evaluated before the statements within the loop are executed. If the condition is false, the statement block is skipped, and execution continues with the statement following the `while` loop. If the condition is true, then the statement block is executed, and the condition is evaluated again. This repetition continues until the condition is false as indicated in the flowchart in Figure 4.2.

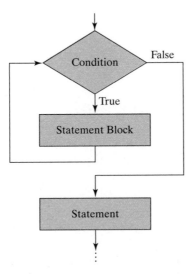

Figure 4.2 Flowchart for while statement.

Program `chapter4_1` uses a while loop to implement the flowchart in Figure 4.1. The program, and the output generated by the program, is provided below.

```
/*******************************************************/
/*  Program chapter4_1                                */
/*  This program computes ands prints a velocity      */
/*  for time values in the range of: 0 <= time <= 10 */

#include<iostream> //required for cout
using namespace std;

int main()
{
  // Declare and initialize objects
  const double V0(0.0);   //initial velocity m/s
  const double A(2.537);  //constant acceleration m/s*s
  double time, velocity;

  //print heading
  cout << " Time, s\t\tVelocity, m/s\n" ;

  time = 0;
  while(time <= 10.0)
  {
    velocity = A*time + V0;
    cout << time << "\t\t"  << velocity << endl;
    ++time;
  }
  return 0;
}
```

Program output:

```
Time, s    Velocity, m/s
0          0
1          2.537
2          5.074
3          7.611
4          10.148
5          12.685
6          15.222
7          17.759
8          20.296
9          22.833
10         25.37
```

The statements that form a loop must modify objects that are used in the condition; otherwise, the value of the condition will never change, and we will either never execute the

infinite loop

statements in the loop or we will never be able to exit the loop. An **infinite loop** is generated if the condition in a `while` loop is always true.

Most systems have a defined limit on the amount of time that can be used by a program, and will generate an execution error when this limit is exceeded. Other systems require that the user enter a special sequence of characters, such as the control key followed by the character c (abbreviated as <cntrl> c) to stop or abort the execution of a program. Nearly everyone eventually writes a program that inadvertently contains an infinite loop, so be sure you know the special characters to abort the execution of a program for your system.

Here, we would like to present two debugging suggestions that are useful when trying to find errors in programs that contain loops. When compiling longer programs, it is not uncommon to have a large number of compiler errors. Rather than trying to correct all errors after compiling, we suggest that you recompile your program after correcting one or two obvious syntax errors. One error will often generate several error messages. Some of these error messages may describe errors that are not in your program, but were printed because the original error confused the compiler.

The second debugging suggestion relates to errors inside a loop. When you want to determine whether the steps in a loop are working the way that you want, include `cout` statements in the loop to provide a memory snapshot of key objects each time the loop is executed. Then, if there is an error, you have much of the information that you need to determine what is causing the error. Remember to use the `endl` manipulator in your `cout` statements to be sure that the output buffer is printed to the screen after each debugging statement.

The following pseudocode and program use a `while` loop to generate a conversion table for converting degrees to radians. The degree values start at 0 degrees, increment by 10 degrees, and go through 360 degrees.

Refinement in Pseudocode

```
main:    set degrees to zero
         while degrees <= 360
                 convert degrees to radians
                 print degrees, radians
                 add 10 to degrees
```

C++ Program

```
/*-------------------------------------------------------------*/
/*   Program chapter4_2                                        */
/*                                                             */
/*   This program prints a degree-to-radian table             */
/*   using a while loop structure.                            */

#include<iostream>   //Required for cout
#include<iomanip>    //Required for setw()
using namespace std;

const double PI = 3.141593;
```

```cpp
int main()
{
   //  Declare and initialize objects.
   int degrees(0);
   double radians;

   //  Set formats.
   cout.setf(ios::fixed);
   cout.precision(6);

   //  Print radians and degrees in a loop.
   cout << "Degrees to Radians \n";
   while (degrees <= 360)
   {
      radians = degrees*PI/180;
      cout << setw(6) << degrees << setw(10) << radians << endl;
      degrees += 10;
   }

   //  Exit program.
   return 0;
}
/*-------------------------------------------------------------------*/
```

The first few lines of output from the program follow:

```
Degrees to Radians
     0   0.000000
    10   0.174533
    20   0.349066
     .    ...
```

To further illustrate the while loop, we provide a program trace and memory snapshot for the first three iterations of the loop. Notice that the value of degrees is printed inside the while loop before the value is incremented by 10.

Program Trace

```
main()
Step 1: int degrees(0);
Step 2: double radians;
Step 3: while(degrees <= 360)
        {
          radians = degrees*PI/180;
          cout << setw(6) << degrees << setw(10)
              << radians << endl;
          degrees += 10;
        }
```

Memory Snapshot

	main()

Step 1:   integer degrees $\boxed{0}$

Step 2:   double radians $\boxed{?}$

Step 3:

    End first iteration

           integer degrees $\boxed{10}$

           double radians $\boxed{0.0}$

    End second iteration

           integer degrees $\boxed{20}$

           double radians $\boxed{0.174533}$

    End third iteration

           integer degrees $\boxed{30}$

    . . .   double radians $\boxed{0.349066}$

We see that degrees is initialized to zero in the type declaration statement, thus the condition degrees <= 360 is true the first time it is tested and the statement block that defines the while loop is executed. Inside the statement block the first line of the conversion table is printed, and degrees is incremented by 10. When the end of the statement block is encountered, control branches back to the condition and it is tested a second time. Again the condition is true and the statement block is executed, this time with a value of 10 for degrees. This repetition continues until the value of degrees reaches 370. Since 370 is greater than 360, the condition is false and the while loop terminates. Termination of the while loop results in control branching down to the first statement following the statement block, the return 0; statement in this case. Note that the directed arrows in the flowchart in Figure 4.2; illustrate the branching associated with the while loop.

do/while **Loop**

The do/while loop is similar to the while loop, except that the condition is tested at the end of the loop instead of at the beginning of the loop, as illustrated in Figure 4.3. Testing the condition at the end of the loop ensures that the do/while loop is always executed at least once; a while loop will not be executed at all if the condition is initially false. The general form of the do/while loop is as follows:

```
do
{
   statements;
} while (condition);
```

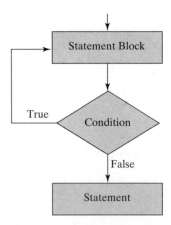

Figure 4.3 Flowchart for `do/while`.

`do/while` **Statement:** The `do/while` statement allows a program to execute a block of statements repeatedly while the specified condition is true. The statement or statement block in a `do/while` statement will always be executed at least once.

Syntax:

```
do                          do
    statement;                  {
  while (condition);                statement block
                              } while(condition);
```

Example:

```
do                          do
    cin.get(ch);                {
  while (ch != '\n')                v = a*t + v0;
                                    cout << t << " " << v << endl;
                                    t += 0.5;
                              } while(t<10);
```

The following pseudocode and program print the degree-to-radian conversion table using a `do/while` loop instead of a while loop:

Refinement in Pseudocode

```
main: set degrees to zero
        do
            convert degrees to radians
            print degrees, radians
            add 10 to degrees
        while degrees <= 360
```

```
/*------------------------------------------------------------------*/
/*  Program chapter4_3                                              */
/*                                                                  */
/*  This program prints a degree-to-radian table                   */
/*  using a do-while loop structure.                               */

#include<iostream>  //Required for cout
#include<iomanip>   //Required for setw()

const double PI = 3.141593;

int main()
{
   //  Declare and initialize objects.
   int degrees(0);
   double radians;

   //  Set formats.
   cout.setf(ios::fixed);
   cout.precision(6);

   //  Print degrees and radians in a loop.
   cout << "Degrees to Radians \n";
   do
   {
      radians = degrees*PI/180;
      cout << setw(6) << degrees << setw(10) << radians << endl;
      degrees += 10;
   } while (degrees <= 360);

   //  Exit program.
   return 0;
}
/*------------------------------------------------------------------*/
```

Practice!

For problems 1 through 4, show what is printed to standard output. If the cout statement is not executed, please explain why.

```
1. int count(1);          2. int count(1);
   while(count < 5)          while(count < 5)
   {                         {
     ++count;                  -count;
   }                         }
   cout << count << endl;    cout << count << endl;
```

```
3. int count(10);          4. int count(0);
   while(count >= 0)          do
   {                          {
      count -= 2;                count = count +3;
   }                          } while (count >=10)
   cout << count << endl;     cout << count << endl;
```

1. Modify program chapter4_1 by replacing the while loop with a do/while loop. Verify that the output is the same.

2. Modify program chapter4_1 by adding the necessary C++ statements to prompt the user to enter the values for initial velocity and constant acceleration. Use these values to compute and print velocity.

3. Modify program chapter4_1 by adding the necessary C++ statements to prompt the user to enter the initial and final values for time. Use these values to compute and print velocity.

for **Loop**

Many programs require loops that are based on the value of a counter that increments (or decrements) by the same amount each time through the loop. When the counter reaches a specified value, we then want to exit the loop. This type of loop can be implemented as a while loop, but it can also be easily implemented with the for loop. The general form of the for loop is as follows:

```
for (expression_1; expression_2; expression_3)
{
    statements;
}
```

loop-control variable

The first expression is used to initialize the **loop-control variable,** expression_2 specifies the condition that must be true to continue the loop repetition, and expression_3 specifies the modification to the loop-control object that follows the execution of the statement block.

Note that expression_1 is executed one time only. The condition, expression_2 is tested 1 to $(n + 1)$ times and expression_3 is executed 0 to n times, where n is the number of times the statement block is executed. The syntax box is provided below, and a flowchart is provided in Figure 4.4.

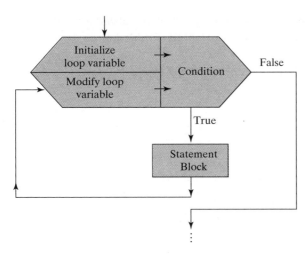

Figure 4.4 Flowchart for simple for statement.

`for` **Statement:** The `for` statement allows a program to execute a block of statements repeatedly based on the value of a counter that is modified by the same amount each time through the loop.

Syntax:

```
for (initialization; condition;)   for (initialization; condition;)
     modification)                      modification)
          statement;                    {
                                            statement block
                                        }
```

Example:

```
for (int count=1; count<=10;       for(int i=counter; i>0; --i)
++count)                           {
    sum = sum + count;                 cin >> degrees;
                                       radians = degrees * PI/180
                                       cout << degress_<< " "
                                            <<_radians << endl;
                                   }
```

If, for example, we want to execute a loop 10 times, with the value of the variable k going from 1 to 10 in increments of 1, we could use the following `for` loop structure:

```
for (int k=1; k<=10; ++k)
{
    statements;
}
```

In this example, the variable k is declared and initialized in the the first expression and can be referenced inside the statement block of the for loop.

If we want to execute a loop with the value of the object n going from 20 to 0 in increments of -2, we could use this loop structure:

```
for (n=20; n>=0; n-=2)
{
    statements;
}
```

In this form, the variable n is assigned an initial value in the first expression, but must be declared before the for statement. The for loop could also have been written in the form

```
for (n=20; n>=0; n=n-2)
{
    statements;
}
```

Both forms are valid, but the abbreviated form for expression_3 is commonly used because it is shorter.

The following expression computes the number of times that a for loop will be executed:

$$\text{floor}\left(\frac{\text{final value} - \text{initial value}}{\text{increment}}\right) + 1.$$

If this value is negative, the loop is not executed. Thus, if a for statement has the structure

```
for (int k=5; k<=83; k+=4)
{
    statements;
}
```

then it would be executed the following number of times:

$$\text{floor}\left(\frac{83 - 5}{4}\right) + 1 = \text{floor}\left(\frac{78}{4}\right) + 1 = 20.$$

The value of k would be 5, 9, 13, and so on, until the final value of 81. The loop would not be executed with the value of 85 because the loop condition is not true when k is equal to 85.

nested for
statements

Consider the following set of **nested for statements**:

```
for(int k=1; k<=3; ++k)
{
    for(int j=0; j<2; ++j)
    {
        ++count;
    }
}
```

The outer for loop will be executed three times. The inner for loop will be executed twice each time the outer for loop is executed. Thus, the variable count will be incremented six times.

The following pseudocode and program print the degree-to-radian conversion table shown earlier with a `while` loop, now modified to use a `for` loop. Note that the pseudocode for the `while` loop solution to this problem and the pseudocode for the `for` loop solution to this problem are identical.

```
Refinement in Pseudocode
main:     set degrees to zero
          while degrees <= 360
                  convert degrees to radians
                  print degrees, radians
                  add 10 to degrees
```

```cpp
/*-------------------------------------------------------------*/
/*   Program chapter4_4                                        */
/*                                                             */
/*   This program prints a degree-to-radian table             */
/*   using a for loop structure.                              */

#include<iostream>  // Required for setw()
#include<iomanip>   // Required for cout
using namespace std;

const double PI = 3.141593;

int main()
{
   // Declare the objects.
   double radians;

   // Set formats.
   cout.setf(ios::fixed);
   cout.precision(6);

   // Print degrees and radians in a loop.
   cout << "Degrees to Radians \n";
   for (int degrees=0; degrees<=360; degrees+=10)
   {
     radians = degrees*PI/180;
     cout << setw(6) << degrees << setw(10) << radians << endl;
   }
   // Exit program.
   return 0;
}
/*-------------------------------------------------------------*/
```

The initialization and modification expressions in a `for` loop can contain more than one statement, as shown in this `for` statement that initializes and updates two objects in the loop:

```
for (int k=1, j=5; k<=10; k++, j++)
{
    sum_1 += k;
    sum_2 += j;
}
```

comma operator

When more than one statement is used, they are separated by commas, and are executed from left to right. This **comma operator** is executed last in operator precedence.

Practice!

For problems 1 through 5, determine the number of times that the for loop is executed.

1. ```
   for (int k=3; k<=20; k++)
   {
   statements;
   }
   ```

2. ```
   for (int k=3; k<=20; ++k)
   {
   statements;
   }
   ```

3. ```
   for (int count=-2; count<=14; count++)
   {
   statements;
   }
   ```

4. ```
   for (int k=2; k>=10; k)
   {
   statements;
   }
   ```

5. ```
   for (int time=10; time>=5; time++)
   {
       statements;
   }
   ```

6. What is the value of count after the nested for loops are executed?

   ```
   int count(0);
   for(int k=-1; k<4; k++)
   {
           for(int j=3; j>0; j--)
           {
                   count++;
           }
   }
   ```
   ```

4.3 Problem Solving Applied: GPS

The Global Positioning System (GPS) originated as a constellation of 24 satellites that broadcasts position, velocity, and time information worldwide. A GPS receiver, using data received from a minimum of four satellites, can determine very precise measurements of the receiver's location.

To determine a GPS receiver's location, the time information received from a satellite broadcast is used to determine the transit time of the broadcast. The **transit time**, or the time it takes for the data to travel between the satellite and the receiver, is used to calculate the distance between the satellite and the receiver. This distance is referred to as the **pseudorange**. Assuming that data travels at the speed of light, the pseudorange, p, is defined as:

$$P = (t_r - t_b)C$$

where:
t_r is the time the data was received,
t_b is the time the data was broadcast,
c is the speed of light, and
$(t_r - t_b)$ is the transit time.

The position and pseudorange of a satellite define a sphere centered at the satellite, with a radius equal to the pseudorange, as illustrated in Figure 4.5.

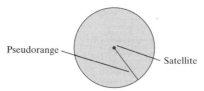

Figure 4.5 Cross-sectional view of sphere centered at satellite.

The GPS receiver is located somewhere on the surface of this sphere. Using position and time data from four satellites, the location of the receiver can be determined by the intersection of the surfaces of the four spheres.[1]

Assume the transit time for four satellite broadcasts is known relative to a GPS receiver. Write a program that prompts the user to enter the satellite ID code and transit time for each of the four satellites. The program should then compute and print the pseudorange for each satellite and the ID code of the satellite that is closest to the GPS receiver.

1. PROBLEM STATEMENT

Given the satellite ID and the transit time of broadcasts from four satellites, compute and print the pseudorange for each satellite. Also print the satellite ID code of the satellite that is closest to the GPS receiver.

---

[1]The article "Trileration" at *http://en.wikipedia.org/wiki/Trilateration* provides a derivation of the mathematics for determining the interscetion of sphere surfaces.

2. INPUT/OUTPUT DESCRIPTION

The following diagram shows that the input to the program includes four consecutive pairs of data (satellite ID code, transit time). The output is the pseudorange for each satellite, followed by the ID of the satellite that is closest to the receiver.

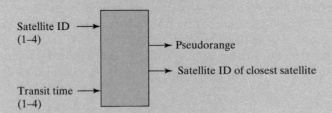

3. HAND EXAMPLE

Assume that the ID of the first satellite is 23 and the corresponding transit time is .001 seconds; then the pseudorange of the first satellite is calculated as transit_time*c = 299792 m.

4. ALGORITHM DEVELOPMENT

We first develop the decomposition outline because it breaks the solution into a series of sequential steps:

Decomposition Outline
For each satellite:

1. Prompt user to enter satellite ID and transit time.

2. Input ID and transit time.

3. Calculate pseudorange.

4. Determine if satellite is closest to the receiver.

5. Print ID and pseudorange.

6. Print ID of satellite that is closest to the receiver.

Steps 1 to 5 will be repeated for each of the four satellites. This suggests a counting loop, or `for` loop. As we refine this algorithm, we will pay particular attention to step 4. To determine which satellite is closest to the receiver, we must keep track of the smallest pseudorange that has been calculated. Each time we calculate a new pseudorange, we will compare that value to the smallest value. If the new value is smaller, we will update the smallest value and keep track of the corresponding satellite number. We will use an `if` statement, nested within our `for` loop, to implement the selection structure required in step 4. The refinement of the algorithm is described in the following flowchart.

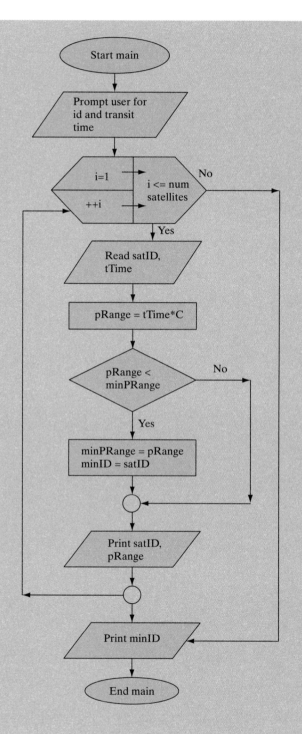

The steps described in the flowchart are now detailed enough to convert into C++:

```
/*******************************************************************/
/* Program chapter4_5                                              */
/*                                                                 */
/* This program computes and prints the pseudorange for           */
/* 4 satellites.  It also prints the number of the satellite      */
/* that is closest to the receiver.                               */

#include<iostream>  //Required for cout
#include<cfloat>    //required for DBL_MAX
using namespace std;

int main()
{
  //Declare and initialize objects
  const double C(299792458.0);  //meters per second
  const int NUMBER_OF_SATELLITES(4);
  int satID, minID;
  double tTime, pRange, minPRange(DBL_MAX);

  //Prompt user for input
  cout << "Enter id and transit time for "
       << NUMBER_OF_SATELLITES << " satellites:\n"
       << "Use whitespace to separate the values(ie: 25 0.00257)\n"
       << endl;

  for(int i=1; i<=NUMBER_OF_SATELLITES; ++i)
  {
    cin >> satID >> tTime;
    pRange = tTime*C;

    //Check for closest satellite
    if(pRange < minPRange)
    {
      minPRange = pRange;
      minID = satID;
    }
    cout << "Satellite " << satID << " has a pseudorange of "
         << pRange << " m\n" << endl;
  }
  //Output ID of closest satellite
  cout << "\nSatellite " << minID
       << " is closest to GPS receiver." << endl;
  return 0;
}
/*******************************************************************/
```

5. TESTING

Using the data from the hand example as the input, along with three additional pairs of satellite data, we get the following program output:

```
Enter id and transit time for 4 satellites:
Use whitespace to separate the values(ie: 25 0.00257)

23 0.001
Satellite 23 has a pseudorange of 299792 m

25 0.00257
Satellite 25 has a pseudorange of 770467 m

18 0.00529
Satellite 18 has a pseudorange of 1.5859e+06 m

20 0.00176
Satellite 20 has a pseudorange of 527635 m

Satellite 23 is closest to GPS receiver.
```

The pseudorange calculated for satellite 23 matches our hand example, and is also the closest to the GPS receiver.

Modify!

These problems relate to the program developed in this section.

1. Modify the program to use the transit time instead of the pseudorange to find the satellite that is closest to the receiver.

2. Modify the program to find the satellite that is farthest from the receiver.

3. Modify the program to handle input from five satellites instead of three.

4.4 break and continue Statements

We used the break statement in the previous chapter with the switch statement. The break statement can also be used with any of the loop structures presented in this chapter to immediately exit from the loop in which it is contained. In contrast, the continue statement is used to skip the remaining statements in the current pass or **iteration** of the loop and then continue with the next iteration of the loop. Thus, in a while loop or a do/while loop the condition is evaluated after the continue statement is executed to determine if the statements in the loop are to be executed again. In a for loop, the loop-control object is modified, and the repetition–continuation condition is evaluated to determine whether the statements in the loop are to be executed again. Both the break and continue statements are useful in exiting either the current iteration or the entire loop, respectively, when error conditions are encountered.

To illustrate the difference between the break and the continue statements, consider the following loop that reads values from the keyboard:

```
sum = 0;
for (int k=1; k<=20; ++k)
{
    cin >> x;
    if (x > 10.0)
        break;
    sum += x;
}
cout << "Sum = " << sum << endl;
```

This loop reads up to 20 values from the keyboard. If all 20 values are less than or equal to 10.0, then the statements compute the sum of the values and print the sum. But, if a value is read that is greater than 10.0, then the break statement causes control to break out of the loop, and execute the cout statement. Thus, the sum printed is only the sum of the values up to the value greater than 10.0.

Now, consider this variation of the previous loop:

```
sum = 0;
for (int k=1; k<=20; ++k)
{
    cin >> x;
    if (x > 10.0)
        continue;
    sum += x;
}
cout << "Sum = " << sum << endl;
```

In this loop, the sum of all 20 values is printed if all values are less than or equal to 10.0. However, if a value is greater than 10.0, then the continue statement causes control to skip the rest of the statements in that iteration of the loop, and to continue with the next iteration of the loop, Hence, the sum printed is the sum of all values in the 20 values that are less than or equal to 10.

4.5 Structuring Input Loops

Loops are often required for reading data from the keyboard or from a data file. Data files will be discussed in Chapter 5. In this section we introduce three common forms of input. We illustrate how each of these loops is implemented when reading data from standard input.

Counter-Controlled Loops

A **counter-controlled** loop can be used for reading input data if the number of data values is known before the data are entered. The number of data values to be input is read from the

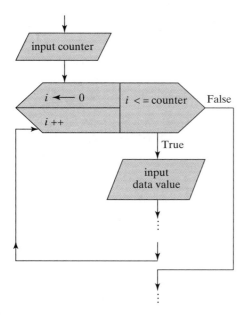

Figure 4.6 Counter-controlled loop.

keyboard and stored in a counter. The counter is then used to control the number of iterations of the input loop. A flowchart of this looping structure is given in Figure 4.6.

This loop is easily implemented using a `while` loop or a `for` loop. We use a `for` loop in the following example to calculate the average of a set of exam scores entered from the keyboard:

```
/*-------------------------------------------------------------*/
/*  Program chapter4_6                                         */
/*  This programs finds the average of a set of exam scores.  */

#include<iostream>//Required for cin, cout
using namespace std;

int main()
{
// Declare and initialize objects.
   double exam_score, sum(0), average;
   int counter;

// Prompt user for input.
   cout << "Enter the number of exam scores to be read ";
   cin >> counter;
   cout << "Enter " << counter << " exam scores separated "
        << " by whitespace ";

// Input exam scores using counter-controlled loop.
   for(int i=1; i<=counter; ++i)
```

```
   {
      cin >> exam_score;
      sum = sum + exam_score;
   }

// Calculate average exam score.
   average = sum/counter;
   cout << counter << " students took the exam.\n";
   cout << "The exam average is " << average << endl;

// Exit program
   return 0;
}
/*--------------------------------------------------------------*/
```

Sentinel-Controlled Loop

A **sentinel-controlled loop** can be used to input data if a special data value exists that can be used to indicate the end of data. This value must be a value that cannot occur naturally in the input data. A flowchart of this looping structure is given in Figure 4.7.

We will use a while loop to implement this structure. To calculate the average of a set of exam scores, we can use this loop structure, with a negative value as the sentinel value, as illustrated in the next example.

```
/*--------------------------------------------------------------*/
/*  Program chapter4_7                                          */
/*  This programs finds the average of a set of exam scores.    */
```

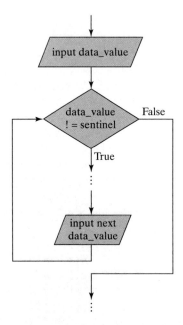

Figure 4.7 Sentinel-controlled loop.

```
#include<iostream>//Required for cin, cout
using namespace std;

int main()
{
// Declare and initialize objects.
   double exam_score, sum(0), average;
   int count(0);

// Prompt user for input.
   cout << "Enter exam scores separated by whitespace.\n";
   cout << "Enter a negative value to indicate the end of data. ";

// Input exam scores using sentinel-controlled loop.
   cin >> exam_score;
   while(exam_score >= 0)
   {
      sum = sum + exam_score;
      ++count;
      cin >> exam_score;
   }

// Calculate average exam score.
   average = sum/count;
   cout << count << " students took the exam.\n";
   cout << "The exam average is " << average << endl;

// Exit program
   return 0;
}
/*-------------------------------------------------------------------*/
```

End-Of-Data Loop

The **end-of-data loop** is the most flexible loop for reading input data. The loop is structured to continue executing the statements inside the loop while new data are available. No prior knowledge of the number of data values is required, and no sentinel value is required. Execution of the loop terminates when the end of data is encountered. Recall that `cin` is an object of type `istream`. The `eof()` function can be called by `cin` to determine whether the end of data has been encountered. The `eof()` function is a member of the `istream` class, and it returns a value of `true` if the end of data has been encountered by the calling object. A flowchart of this looping structure is given in Figure 4.8. The end-of-data loop is easily implemented using a `while` loop, as illustrated in the following example, which calculates the average of a set of exam scores, entered from the keyboard:

```
/*-------------------------------------------------------------------*/
/*   Program chapter4_7                                              */
/*   This programs finds the average of a set of exam scores.       */

#include<iostream>//Required for cin, cout
using namespace std;
```

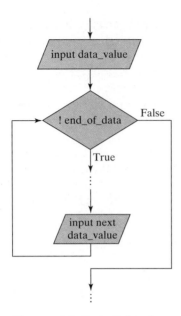

Figure 4.8 End-of-data loop.

```
int main()
{
// Declare and initialize objects.
double exam_score, sum(0), average;
int count(0);

// Prompt user for input.
cout << "Enter exam scores separated by whitespace. ";

// Input exam scores using end-of-data loop.
cin >> exam_score;
while(!cin.eof())
{
   sum = sum + exam_score;
   ++count;
   cin >> exam_score;
}

// Calculate average exam score.
average = sum/count;
cout << count << " students took the exam.\n";
cout << "The exam average is " << average << endl;

// Exit program
return 0;
}
/*-------------------------------------------------------------------*/
```

In program `chapter4_7`, the first input statement attempts to read an exam score from the keyboard. If a data value is read, the `eof()` function returns a value of false, and the statement block is executed. Notice the use of the ! operator in the expression controlling the `while` statement. The last statement in the `while` loop is another input statement that attempts to read the next exam score from the keyboard. This is a correct structure for an end-of-data loop. The `while` loop will continue to execute while the end of data has not been reached. The `eof()` function will not return a value of true until after the end of data is encountered. For this reason it is common to be off by one when reading and counting data if the correct structure of the end-of-data loop is not used. When using the end-of-data loop with standard input you need to know what key sequence your system recognizes as the end of data indicator. Many Unix and Linux systems recognize the <cntrl> d key sequence as an end-of-data indicator.

4.6 Problem Solving Applied: Weather Balloons

Weather balloons are used to gather temperature and pressure data at various altitudes in the atmosphere. The balloon rises because the density of the helium in the balloon is less than the density of the surrounding air outside the balloon. As the balloon rises, the surrounding air becomes less dense, and thus the balloon's ascent slows until it reaches a point of equilibrium. During the day, sunlight warms the helium trapped inside the balloon, which causes the helium to expand and become less dense and the balloon to rise higher. During the night, however, the helium in the balloon cools and becomes more dense, causing the balloon to descend to a lower altitude. The next day, the sun heats the helium again and the balloon rises. Over time, this process generates a set of altitude measurements that can be approximated with a polynomial equation.

Assume that the polynomial $alt(t) = -0.12t^4 + 12t^3 - 380t^2 + 4100t + 220$, where the units of t are hours, represents the altitude or height in meters during the first 48 hours following the launch of a weather balloon. The corresponding polynomial model for the velocity in meters per hour of the weather balloon is $v(t) = -0.48t^3 + 36t^2 - 760t + 4100$.

Print a table of the altitude and the velocity for this weather balloon using units of meters and meters per second. Let the user enter the start time, increment in time between lines of the table, and ending time, where all the time values must be less than 48 hours. In addition to printing the table, also print the peak altitude and its corresponding time.

1. PROBLEM STATEMENT

Using the polynomials that represent the altitude and velocity for a weather balloon, print a table using units of meters and meters per second. Also find the maximum altitude (or height) and its corresponding time.

2. INPUT/OUTPUT DESCRIPTION

The following I/O diagram shows the user input that represents the starting time, time increment, and ending time for the table. The output is the table of altitude and velocity values and the maximum altitude and its corresponding time. We can use the built-in data type `double` for our input and output objects.

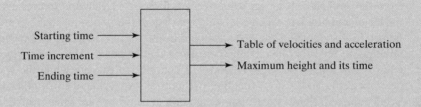

3. HAND EXAMPLE

Assume that the starting time is 0 hours, the time increment is 1 hour, and the ending time is 5 hours. To obtain the correct units, we need to divide the velocity value in meters per hour by 3600 in order to get meters per second. Using our calculator, we can then compute the following values:

Time	Altitude (m)	Velocity (m/s)
0	220.00	1.14
1	3,951.88	0.94
2	6,994.08	0.76
3	9,414.28	0.59
4	11,277.28	0.45
5	12,645.00	0.32

We can also determine the maximum altitude for this table, which is 12,645.00 meters; it occurred at 5 hours.

4. ALGORITHM DEVELOPMENT

We first develop the decomposition outline because it breaks the solution into a series of sequential steps.

Decomposition Outline

1. Get user input to specify times for the table.

2. Generate and print conversion table and find maximum height and corresponding time.

3. Print maximum height and corresponding time.

The second step in the decomposition outline represents a loop in which we generate the table and, at the same time, keep track of the maximum height. As we refine this outline, and particularly step 2 into more detail, we need to think carefully about finding the maximum height. Look back at the hand example. Once the table has been printed, it is easy to look at it and select the maximum height. However, when the computer is computing and printing the table, it does not have all the data at one time; it only has the information for the current line in the table. Therefore, to keep track of the maximum, we need to specify a separate object to store the maximum value. Each time that we compute a new height, we will compare that value to the maximum value. If the new value is larger, we replace the maximum with this new value. We will also need to keep track of the corresponding time. The following refinement in pseudocode outlines these new steps:

```
Refinement in Pseudocode
main: read initial, increment, final values from keyboard
        set max_height to zero
        set max_time to zero
        print table heading
        set time to initial
        while time <= final
                compute height and velocity
                print height and velocity
                if height > max_height
                        set max_height to height
                        set max_time to time
                add increment to time
        print max_time and max_height
```

The steps in the pseudocode are now detailed enough to convert into C++. Note that we convert the velocity from meters per hour to meters per second in the *cout* statement.

```cpp
/*-----------------------------------------------------------*/
/*  Program chapter4_8                                       */
/*                                                           */
/*  This program prints a table of height and               */
/*  velocity values for a weather balloon.                  */

#include <iostream>//Required for cin, cout
#include <iomanip>//Required for setw()
#include <cmath>//Required for pow()
using namespace std;

int main()
{
// Declare and initialize objects.
   double initial, increment, final, time, height,
         velocity, max_time(0), max_height(0);
   int loops;

// Get user input.
   cout << "Enter initial value for table (in hours) \n";
   cin >> initial;
   cout << "Enter increment between lines (in hours) \n";
   cin >> increment;
   cout << "Enter final value for table (in hours) \n";
   cin >> final;
```

```
            //  Print report heading.
            cout << "\n\nWeather Balloon Information \n";
            cout << "Time    Height    Velocity \n";
            cout << "(hrs)   (meters)  (meters/s) \n";

            // Set formats.
            cout.setf(ios::fixed);
            cout.precision(2);

            //  Compute and print report information.
            //  Determine number of iterations required.
            //  Use integer index to avoid rounding error.
            loops = (int)( (final - initial)/increment );

            for (int count=0; count<=loops; ++count)
            {
               time = initial + count*increment;
               height = -0.12*pow(time,4) + 12*pow(time,3)
                        - 380*time*time + 4100*time + 220;
               velocity = -0.48*pow(time,3) + 36*time*time
                          - 760*time + 4100;
               cout << setw(6) << time << setw(10) << height
                    << setw(10) << velocity/3600 << endl;
               if (height > max_height)
               {
                  max_height = height;
                  max_time = time;
               }
            }
            //  Print maximum height and corresponding time.
            cout << "\nMaximum balloon height was " << setw(8)
                 << max_height << " meters \n";

            cout << "and it occurred at " << setw(6) << max_time
                 << " hours \n";

            /*  Exit program.  */
            return 0;
         }
/*-------------------------------------------------------------*/
```

5. TESTING

If we use the data from the hand example, we have the following interaction with the program:

```
Enter initial value for table (in hours)
0
Enter increment between lines (in hours)
1
Enter final value for table (in hours)
5
```

```
Weather Balloon Information

Time        Height        Velocity
(hrs)       (meters)      (meters/s)
0             220.00      1.14
1            3951.88      0.94
2            6994.08      0.76
3            9414.28      0.59
4           11277.28      0.45
5           12645.00      0.32 Maximum balloon height was
                               12645.00 meters, and it occurred at
                               5.00 hours.
```

Figure 4.9 contains a plot of the altitude and velocity of the balloon for a period of 48 hours. From the plots, we can see the periods during which the balloon rises or falls.

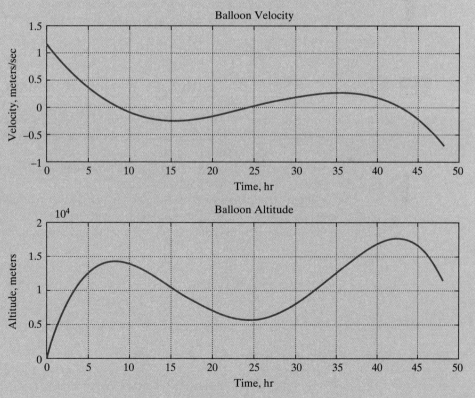

Figure 4.9 Weather balloon altitude and velocity.

Modify!

These problems relate to the program developed in this section that prints a table of weather balloon information.

1. Use this program to generate a table showing the weather balloon information for every 10 minutes for 2 hours, starting at 4 hours after the balloon was launched.

2. Modify the program to include a check to be sure that the final time is greater than the initial. If it is not, ask the user to reenter the complete set of report information.

3. The equations given in this section were developed to be accurate only for time from 0 to 48 hours, so modify the program to print a message to the user that specifies an upper bound of 48 hours. Also, check the user input to be sure that it stays within the proper bounds. If there are any errors, ask the user to reenter the complete set of report information.

4. If there are two times with the same maximum height, this program will print the first time that the maximum height occurred. Modify the program so that it will print the last time that the maximum height occurred.

4.7 Building C++ Solutions with IDEs: Microsoft Visual C++

In this section we develop a C++ solution using Microsoft Visual C++ to illustrate the use of nested control structures. Our program implements the divide-and-conquer algorithm to guess a number between 1 and 20. The divide-and-conquer algorithm divides the range of possible guesses by two at each iteration by adjusting either the high or low value that defines the range. The guess is always the midpoint of the range.

Our program terminates when the number is guessed or the high value in the range becomes less than the low value. The second case will happen if the user does not answer each question correctly. The pseudocode for our number-guessing algorithm is given below:

```
Pseudocode
main: print greeting to user
     while(!done && high > = low)
         guess = (high + low)/2
         print guess
         if guess equals number
            print number of trys required to guess number
            done = true
         else if guess is larger than number
            increment number of tries
            high = guess - 1
         else if guess is smaller than number
             increment number of tries
             low = guess + 1
      end while
```

The steps in the pseudocode are detailed enough to convert into C++. We use the `ceil()` function and the natural log function, `log()`, to predict how many tries it should take to guess the number, using our divide-and-conquer algorithm.

```cpp
/*****************************************************************/
/* Program chapter4_9                                          */
/* This program guesses a number between 1 and 20 inclusive.   */

#include<iostream>  //Required for cout, cin
#include<cmath>     //Required for ceil, log
using namespace std;

int main()
{
  // Declare and initialize objects
  int high(20), low(1), guess, count(1), ceiling;
  bool done(false);
  char answer;
  const char YES('Y'), NO('N');

  // Print greeting to user
  ceiling = ( ceil(log( (double)high ) ) + 1 );
  cout << "Think of a number between "  << low << "and"  << high
       << "and I will guess it in\n"  << ceiling
       << "or fewer trys. Just answer y(es) or n(o) to my questions.\n"
       << "Are you thinking of a number? "  << endl;
  cin >> answer;
  switch(toupper(answer))
  {
  case YES:
    // While number has not been guessed
    while(!done && high >= low)
    {
      guess = (high + low)/2;
      cout << " Are you thinking of "  << guess << '?' << endl;
      cin >> answer;
      switch(toupper(answer))
      {
      case YES:
        cout << " I guessed it in "  << count << "  trys."  << endl;
        if(count > ceiling) cout << " Good pick.."  << endl;
        done = true;
        break;
      case NO:
        //Must guess again.
        ++count;
        cout << " Is "  << guess << "  larger?"  << endl;
        cin >> answer;
```

```
                     if(toupper(answer) == YES) high = guess - 1;
                     else low = guess + 1;
                     break;  //case NO
               default:
                  cout << " Don't support "  << answer << endl;
                  done = true;
               } //end switch
            } //end while
         break;
      case NO:
         cout << " OK..Goodbye. "  << endl;
         break;
      default:
         cout << " Dont support "  << answer << endl;
      }
      return 0;
}//end main
```

Microsoft Visual C++

Visual C++ is an IDE developed by Microsoft for the design and development of C and C++
program solutions. When the Visual C++ application is launched, a Start page appears, similar
to what is shown below:

To create a new project, select **New Project** ... from the **File** menu at the top of the
window, or select **Create: Project** ... from the **Recent Projects** window. A new project
screen will appear, similar to the one shown below.

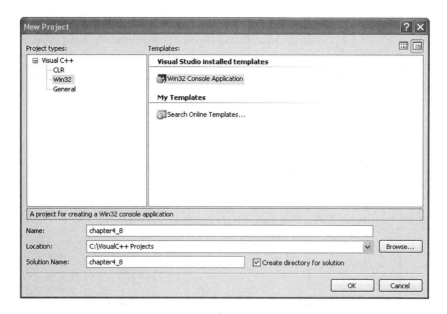

For this example we will select **Win32 Console Application**. We name the file `chapter4_8` and click the **OK** ... button at the bottom of the window. A new **Win32 Application** Wizard window will appear, as shown below.

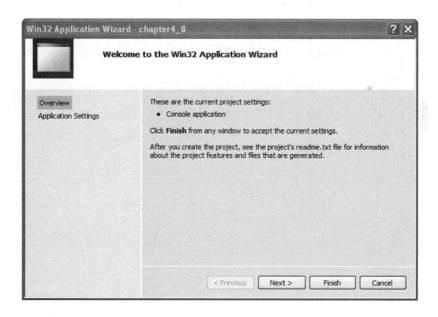

If the **Finish** button is selected at this time, a new project will be created with a pre-compiled header. For simplicity, in this example we want to create an empty project with no added header files, so we click the **Next** > button at the bottom of the window. The following **Finish** screen will appear.

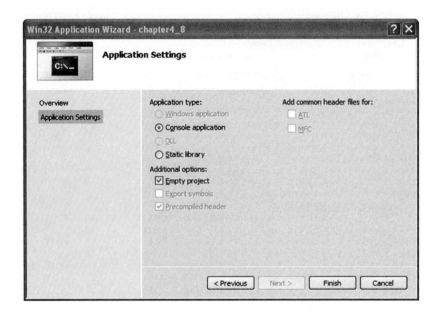

From this screen we select **Console application** and **Empty project**, then click the **Finish** button. A new empty project named `chapter4_8` is created, as shown below in the left window of the `chapter4_8` Visual C++ project screen.

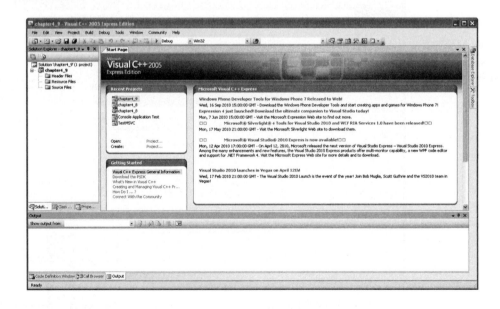

To add a new file to a project, select **Add New Item** from the **Project** menu at the top of the window. The following **Add New Item** window will appear.

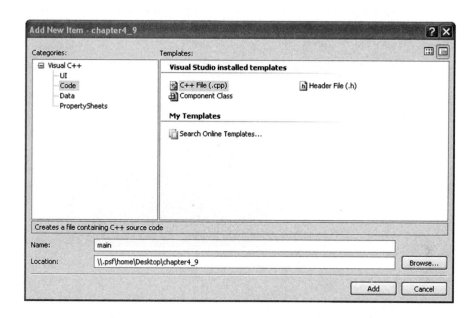

Select **Code** from the left window and **C++ file (.cpp)** from the right window. Name the file main and click the **Add** button. The **Editor** window will open. Enter the code for program chapter4_9, as shown below.

Select **Build Solution** from the **Build** menu. If the build is successful, choose **Start without Debugging** from the **Debug** menu to execute the program. A **Console** window will appear, and all standard I/O can be viewed from this window. Results from a run of our program are provided in the screen image below. The number 7 was guessed in only three tries. Are there any numbers that require more than three tries to guess?

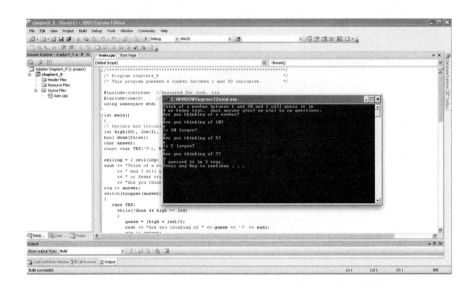

Visual C++ and Visual Studio are powerful IDEs with many tools that facilitate the development of large software projects. If you will be working in a Windows environment, we recommend that you view the help materials and tutorials that are provided as part of the Microsoft Visual environment.

Modify!

These problems relate to the program `chapter4_9` developed in this section.

1. Modify the program by replacing all `switch` statements with if statements.

2. Modify the program by replacing the `while` loop with a `do/while` loop.

3. Modify the program by having it guess a number between 1 and 100.

SUMMARY

In this chapter, we have presented techniques for repeating sets of statements that used loops. These loops can be implemented as `while` loops `do/while` loops or as `for` loops. These repetition structures are used in most programs.

Key Terms

counter-controlled loop	loop
divide and conquer	loop-control variable
end-of-data loop	pseudocode
flowchart	repetition
for loop	sentinel-controlled loop
iteration	while loop

C++ Statement Summary

`while` loop:

```
while (degrees <= 360)
{
    radians = degrees*PI/180;
    cout << degrees << '\t' << radians << endl;
    degrees += 10;
}
```

`do/while` loop:

```
do
{
    radians = degrees*PI/180;
    cout << degrees << '\t' << radians << endl;
    degrees += 10;
} while (degrees <= 360);
```

`for` loop:

```
for (int degrees=0; degrees<=360; degrees+=10)
{
    radians = degrees*PI/180;
    cout << degrees << '\t' << radians << endl;
}
```

`break` statement:

```
break;
```

`continue` statement;

```
continue;
```

Notes

Style

1. Indent the statements within a statement block or inside a loop. If loops or compound statements are nested, indent each nested set of statements from the previous statement.
2. Use braces to identify the body of every loop; put each brace on a line by itself so that the body of the loop is easily identified.

Debugging Notes

1. Use `cout` statements to give memory snapshots of the values of key objects when debugging loops. Remember to use the `endl` manipulator instead of '\n' to ensure that the values are printed immediately after the statement is executed.
2. It is easier than you think to generate an infinite loop; be sure you know the special characters needed to abort the execution of a program on your system if it goes into an infinite loop.

Problems

Exam Practice!

True/False Problems

Indicate whether the following statements are true (T) or false (F).

1. A `break` statement is used to immediately exit from a loop. T F
2. The `continue` statement forces the next iteration of a loop. T F
3. A `break` statement is required in a sentinel-controlled loop. T F
4. The end-of-data loop is easily implemented using a `while` loop. T F
5. A counter-controlled loop is often used to count the number of lines of data received from standard input. T F
6. To debug a loop, we can use `cout` statements in the loop to provide memory snapshots of objects. T F

Syntax Problems

Identify any syntax errors in the following statements. Assume that the objects have all been defined as integers.

```
7. for (b=1, b=<25, b++)
8.   while (k =1)
9. int count(0);
   do
   {
     cout << count << endl;
     ++count;
   }; while(count < 10)
```

Multiple-Choice Problems

Circle the letter for the best answer to complete each statement or for the correct answer to each question.

10. Consider the following statement:
```
int i=100, j=0;
```
Which of the following statements are true?
(a) i<3
(b) !(j<1)
(c) (i>0) || (j>50)
(d) (j<i) && (i <= 10)

11. If $a1$ is true and $a2$ is false, then which of the following expressions are true?
    (a) `a1 && a2`
    (b) `a1 || a2`
    (c) `!(a1 || a2)`
    (d) `!a1 && a2`
12. Which of the following are unary operators?
    (a) `!`
    (b) `||`
    (c) `&&`
13. The expression

    `(!((3-4%3) < 5 && (6/4 > 3)))` is

    (a) true.
    (b) false.
    (c) invalid.
    (d) none of the above.

Problems 14 through 16 refer to the following statements:

```
int sum(0), count;
for (count=0; count<=4; count++)
    sum += count;
cout << "sum = " << sum << endl;
```

14. What would you see on the screen if these statements were executed?
    (a) sum = 1
    (b) sum = 6
    (c) sum = 10
    (d) four lines of output
    (e) error message
15. What is the value of `count` after execution of the `for` loop?
    (a) 0
    (b) 4
    (c) 5
    (d) an unpredictable integer
16. How many times is the `for` loop executed?
    (a) 0
    (b) 4
    (c) 5
    (d) 6

Programming Problems

Unit Conversions.   Problems 19 through 23 generate tables of unit conversions. Include a table heading and column headings for the tables. Choose the number of decimal places based on the values to be printed.

17. Generate a table of conversions from radians to degrees. Start the radian column at 0.0, and increment by $\pi/10$ until the radian amount is 2π.

18. Generate a table of conversions from degrees, to radians. The first line should contain the value for 0 degrees, and the last line should contain the value for 360 degrees. Allow the user to enter the increment to use between lines in the table.

19. Generate a table of conversions from inches to centimeters. Start the inches column at 0.0 and increment by 0.5 in. The last line should contain the value 20.0 in. (Recall that 1 in. = 2.54 cm.)

20. Generate a table of conversions from mph to ft/s. Start the mph column at 0 and increment by 5 mph. The last line should contain the value 65 mph. (Recall that 1 mi = 5,280 ft.)

21. Generate a table of conversions from ft/s to mph. Start the ft/s column at 0 and increment by 5 ft/s. The last line should contain the value 100 ft/s. (Recall that 1 mi = 5,280 ft.)

Currency Conversions.   Problems 24 through 27 generate tables of currency conversions. Use title and column headings. Assume the following conversion rates or check the Web for current rates:

```
1 dollar ($) = 9.02 Mexican pesos
1 yen (Y) = $ 0.01 U.S. dollars
1 dollar ($) = 11.30 South African rand
```

22. Generate a table of conversions from pesos to dollars. Start the pesos column at 5 pesos and increment by 5 pesos. Print 25 lines in the table.

23. Generate a table of conversions from yen to pesos. Start the yen column at 1 Y and increment by 2 Y. Print 30 lines in the table.

24. Generate a table of conversions from yen to South African rand. Start the yen column at 100 Y and print 25 lines, with the final line containing the value 10,000 Y.

25. Generate a table of conversions from dollars to pesos, South African rand, and yen. Start the column with $1 and increment by $1. Print 50 lines in the table.

Temperature Conversions.   Problems 28 through 30 generate temperature-conversion tables. Use the following equations that give relationships between temperatures in degrees Fahrenheit (TF), degrees Celsius (TC), degrees Kelvin (TK), and degrees Rankin (TR):

```
TF = TR - 459.67 degrees R
TF = (9/5)TC + 32 degrees F
TR = (9/5)TK
```

26. Write a program to generate a table of conversions from Fahrenheit to Celsius for values from 0 degrees F to 100 degrees F. Print a line in the table for each 5-degree change. Use a while loop in your solution.

27. Write a program to generate a table of conversions from Fahrenheit to Kelvin for values from 0 degrees F to 200 degrees F. Allow the user to enter the increment in degrees Fahrenheit between lines. Use a do/while loop in your solution.

28. Write a program to generate a table of conversions from Celcius to Rankin. Allow the user to enter the starting temperature and increment between lines. Print 25 lines in the table. Use a for loop in your solution.

Timber Regrowth.   A problem in timber management is to determine how much of an area to leave uncut so that the harvested area is reforested in a certain period. It is assumed that reforestation takes place at a known rate per year, depending on climate and soil conditions. A reforestation equation expresses this growth as a function of the amount of timber standing and the reforestation rate. For example, if 100 acres are left standing after harvesting and the reforestation rate is 0.05, then $100 + 0.05 * 100$, or 105 acres, are forested at the end of the first year. At the end of the second year, the number of acres forested is $105 + 0.05 * 105$, or 110.25 acres.

29. Assume that there are 14,000 acres total with 2,500 acres uncut and that the reforestation rate is 0.02. Print a table showing the number of acres forested at the end of each year, for a total of 20 years.
30. Modify the program developed in problem 31 so that the user can enter the number of years to be used for the table.
31. Modify the program developed in problem 31 so that the user can enter a number of acres and the program will determine how many years are required for the number of acres to be completely reforested.

Loops   These problems relate to program chapter3_1 developed in chapter 3 to generate a truth table.

32. Rewrite program `chapter 3_1`, developed in Chapter 3, and use nested `for` loops.
33. Modify program `chapter 4_5`, developed in this chapter, by replacing the `for` loop with a `do/while` loop.
34. Modify program `chapter 4_5`, developed in this chapter, by replacing the `for` loop with a `while` loop.

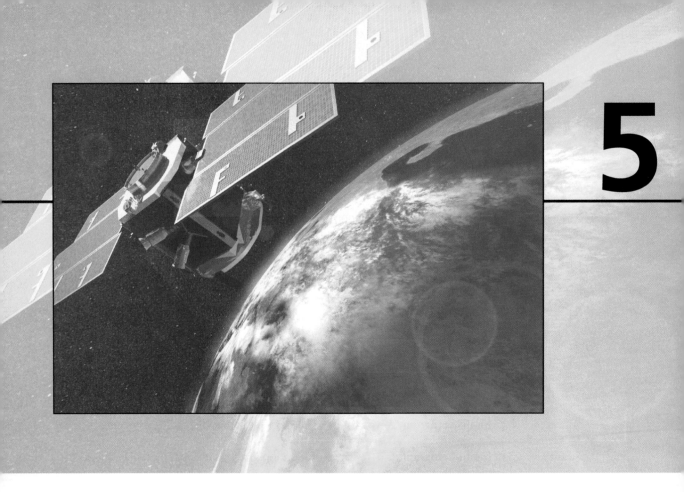

5

ENGINEERING CHALLENGE:
Weather Prediction

Weather satellites provide information to scientists and meteorologists. Large volumes of data are collected and analyzed, and historic data is used to test models for predicting weather. Data can be analyzed to identify factors, such as clouds and greenhouse gases, associated with global climate change. Understanding, for example, how clouds affect solar energy distribution in the atmosphere can help scientists better understand weather patterns and aid in the development of tools for weather prediction and simulation of changes in the global climate.

WORKING WITH DATA FILES

CHAPTER OUTLINE

OBJECTIVES *In this chapter, we develop problem solutions that:*

- open and close data files for input and output
- read data from files using common looping structures

- check the state of an input stream
- recover from input stream errors
- apply the numerical technique of linear modeling

5.1 Defining File Streams

Engineering problem solutions often involve large amounts of data. These data can be generated by the program as output, or they can be input data that are used by the program. It is not generally feasible either to print large amounts of data to the screen or to read large amounts of data from the keyboard. In these cases, we usually use data files to store the data. These data files are similar to the program files that we create to store our C++ program. In fact, a C++ program file is an input data file to the C++ compiler and the object program is an output file from the C++ compiler. In this section, we discuss the C++ statements for interacting with data files and give examples that generate and read information from data files.

Stream Class Hierarchy

In Chapter 2, we introduced the standard stream objects cin and cout. Recall that these class objects are defined by the compiler to correspond with the system's standard input device and

standard error

file stream classes

standard output device, respectively. Another standard stream class object that we will use in this chapter, and the following chapters, is `cerr`. The stream object `cerr` is defined by the compiler to stream output to the system's **standard error** output device. `cerr` is an unbuffered stream meaning that the output will be streamed directly to standard error. Buffered streams, such as `cout`, stream data to a buffer, and the data is displayed when the buffer is flushed. A program must include the header file `iostream` to use these standard streams.

When working with data files, new streams must be defined that support the general properties of reading (`>>`) and writing (`<<`) and also support the ability to be attached to a specific file. The C++ Standard Library provides **file stream classes** to support file input and file output. The `ifstream` class is used to define input file streams that can stream data from a file, and the `ofstream` class is used to define output file streams that can stream output to a file. A portion of the C++ stream class hierarchy is illustrated in Figure 5.1.

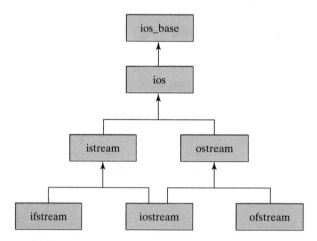

Figure 5.1 C++ stream class hierarchy.

Figure 5.1 uses directed arrows to indicate that `ios` inherits from `ios_base`. Both `istream` and `ostream` inherit from `ios`, and `ifstream` and `ofstream` are derived from `istream` and `ostream` respectively. We also see that `iostream` inherits from both `istream` and `ostream`. This is an example of **multiple inheritance**.

multiple inheritance

We will discuss the `ifstream` class and the `ofstream` class in the following sections, but first we will illustrate the use of these classes in program `chapter5_1`. To use the `ifstream` and `ofstream` classes, a program must include the header file `fstream`. Program `chapter5_1` also uses the C++ standard library function `exit()`. The function `exit()` requires a single integer argument. Like the return value of `main()`, `exit()` returns its integer argument to the system. Thus, a call to `exit(1)` in the following program will terminate the program and return a value of 1 as the return value of `main()`.

```
/*------------------------------------------------------------*/
/* Program 5_1                                               */
/* This program reads data pairs from the                    */
/* the file sensor.dat and writes valid data pairs           */
```

```
/* to the file checkedSensor.dat. Valid data pairs          */
/* may not be negative. Invalid data is written to          */
/* to standard error(cerr)                                  */

#include<iostream> //Required for cerr
#include<fstream> //Required for ifstream, ofstream
using namespace std;

int main()
{
  //Define file streams for input and output.
  ifstream fin("sensor.dat");
  ofstream fout("checkedSensor.dat");

  //Check for possible errors.
  if(fin. fail())
  {
    cerr << "could not open input file sensor.dat\n";
    exit(1);
  }
  if(fout. fail())
  {
    cerr << "could not open output file checkedSensor.dat\n";
    exit(1);
  }

  //All files are open.
  double t, motion;
  int count(0);
  fin >> t >> motion;
  while(!fin.eof())
  {
    ++count;

    //Write valid data to output file.
    if(t >= 0 && motion >= 0)
    {
      fout << t << " " << motion << endl;
    }
    //Write invalid data to standard error output.
    else
    {
      cerr << "Bad data encountered on line"
           << count << endl
           << t << " " << motion << endl;
    }

    //Input next data pair.
    fin >> t >> motion;
  }//end while
```

```
//close all files.
fin.close();
fout.close();

return 0;
}
```

If the data file `sensor.dat` contained the following data,

```
0  45
1  48
2  56
3  -1
4  10
-5  8
-6  -4
6  12
```

the output displayed to standard error, in this case the screen, would be as follows:

```
Bad data encountered on line 4
3  -1
Bad data encountered on line 6
-5  8
Bad data encountered on line 7
-6  -4
```

The data file `checkedSensor.dat` would then contain the following data:

```
0  45
1  48
2  56
4  10
6  12
```

`ifstream` **Class**

The `ifstream` class is derived from the `istream` class, thus it inherits all of the functionality of the `istream` class including the input operator and the member functions `eof()`, and `fail()`. Additional member functions required to open and close data files are also provided in the `istream` class.

Each data file used for input in a program must have an ifstream object associated with it. A type declaration statement is used to define an object of type `ifstream`, as in

```
ifstream sensor1;
```

After an `ifstream` object is defined, it must then be associated with a specific file. The `ifstream` class includes a member function named `open()`. This function is called by the `ifstream` object and a file name is passed as an argument to this function. The file name needs to be a string constant or a C-style string object. Thus, the following statement specifies that the `ifstream` object `sensor1` is going to be used with a file named `sensor1.dat` from which we will read information:

```
sensor1.open("sensor1.dat");
```

It is also possible to initialize an `ifstream` object at the time it is defined:

```
ifstream sensor1("sensor1.dat");
```

Here the `open()` function is called automatically when the `ifstream` object `sensor1` is created.

When a data file is being used for input, the file must exist and contain data values to be used by the program. If the file cannot be opened, an error flag is set. No error message will be generated, and your program will continue to execute, but all attempts to read from the data file will be ignored. Thus, when opening a file for input, it is always good practice to check the state of the file stream object to insure that the file open was successful. One method of checking the state of the file stream object is to have the object call the member function `fail()`. The `fail()` function returns a value of true if the data file failed to open, as shown in the following example:

```
ifstream sensor1;
sensor1.open("sensor1.dat");
if( sensor1.fail() ) //open failed
{
    cerr << "File sensor1.dat could not be opened";
    exit(1); //end execution of the program
}
```

The state of a file stream object can also be checked directly:

```
ifstream sensor1("sensor1.dat);
if( !sensor1 ) //open failed
{
    cerr << "File sensor1.dat could not be opened";
    exit(1); //end execution of the program
}
```

For clarity, we will usually use the first method for opening a data file and checking the state of the file stream. Stream states are discussed in more detail in section 5.5.

Once an input file stream has been defined and successfully attached to a data file, it can be used in the same way that `cin` is used. If each line in the `sensor1.dat` file contains a time and sensor reading, we can read one line of this information and store the values in the objects `t` and `motion` with this statement:

```
sensor1 >> t >> motion;
```

Note that we used the input operator with `sensor1` to input numeric values from the `sensor1.dat` file. If the data file held character data, the `get()` function could also be used with `sensor1`.

When reading information from a data file, print a few lines of the information to be sure that the data are being read correctly.

`ofstream` **Class**

The `ofstream` class is derived from the `ostream` class, thus it inherits all of the functionality of the `ostream` class. Additional member functions required to open and close data files are also provided in the `ostream` class.

A type declaration statement is used to define an object of type `ofstream`, as in

```
ofstream balloon;
```

After an `ofstream` object is defined, it must be associated with a specific file. The `of-stream` class includes a member function named `open()`. This function is called by the `ofstream` object and a file name is passed as an argument to this function. Thus, the following statement specifies that the `ofstream` object `balloon` will write data to a file named `balloon.dat`:

```
balloon.open("balloon.dat");
```

It is also possible to initialize an `ofstream` object at the time it is defined, as in

```
ofstream balloon("balloon.dat");
```

When an `ofstream` object calls the `open()` function, a new file with the specified name is created if a file by that name does not already exist. If the file already exists, it is opened and the old contents of the file are overwritten by the new data. It is possible to open an existing file for output and append new data to the end of the existing data by adding a second argument to the open function, as in

```
balloon.open("balloon.data", ios::app);
```

Because the `open()` function defined in the `ofstream` class creates a new file if an existing file does not already exist, it is rare to have an error occur when opening a file for output. For this reason we will not check the state of an `ofstream` object after opening a file in the remainder of our example programs.

Once an `ofstream` object has been defined and associated with a data file, the `ofstream` object can be used in the same way that `cout` is used. As an example, consider the program developed in Chapter 3 that computed and printed a table of time, altitude, and velocity data. If we wanted to modify this program so that it generated a data file containing this set of data, we could use the `ofstream` object `balloon` that has been associated with an output file named `balloon.dat` using these statements:

```
balloon << time << ' ' << height << ' '
        << velocity/3600 << endl;
```

A blank space is used to separate the values, and the `endl` manipulator causes a skip to a new line after each group of three values is written to the file.

The `close()` function is used to close a file after we are finished with it; the function is called by a file stream object. To close the two files used in these example statements, we use the following statements:

```
sensor1.close();
balloon.close();
```

If a file has not been closed when the `return 0` statement is executed, it will be closed automatically. A call to `exit()` will also close all files.

A `string` object is often used to specify the name of a data file because we frequently use the same program with different data files. It is often desirable to prompt the user to enter the name of a data file at run time and store the name of the file as a `string` object.

This string can then be used by the `open()` function as illustrated in the following code segment:

```
...
string filename;
cout << "enter the name of the output file";
cin >> filename;
balloon.open(filename.c_str());
...
```

We declared filename to be a `string` object, since these are easy to work with. However, the `open()` function requires a C-style string as an argument, so `filename` must call the function `c_str()`. The function `c_str()` is a member function of the `string` class, and it returns a C-style string that is equivalent to the calling object. We will use this combination of statements in all the sample programs that use files in this and the chapters that follow.

5.2 Reading Data Files

To read information from a data file, we must first know some details about the file. Obviously, we must know the file name so that we can open the file. We must also know the order and data type of the values stored in the file so that we can declare corresponding identifiers correctly. Finally, we need to know if there is any special information in the file to help us determine how much information is in the file. If we attempt to execute an input statement after we have read all the data in the file, the value of the input object will remain unchanged. This may cause unexpected results in our program. To avoid this situation, we need to know when we have read all the data.

Data files generally have one of three common structures. Some files have been generated such that the first line in the file contains the number of lines (also called records) with information that follow. For example, suppose that a file containing sensor data has 150 sets of time and sensor information. The data file could be constructed such that the first line contains only the value 150, and that line would then be followed by 150 lines containing the sensor data. To read the data from this file, we use a counter-controlled loop, as discussed in Chapter 4.

trailer signal
    Another form of file structure uses a **trailer signal** or sentinel signal. These signals are special data values that are used to indicate or signal the last record of a file. For example, the sensor data file constructed with a sentinel signal would contain the 150 lines of information followed by a line with special values, such as -999.0 for the time and sensor value. These sentinel signals must be values that could not appear as regular data in order to avoid confusion. To read data from this type of file, we use a while loop, as discussed in Chapter 4.

    The third data file structure does not contain an initial line with the number of valid data records that follow, and it does not contain a trailer or sentinel signal. For this type of data file, we use the value returned by the file stream object to help us determine when we have

end-of-file loop
reached the end of the file. To read data from this type of file, we use and **end-of-file loop,** as discussed in Chapter 4.

    We now present programs for reading sensor information and printing a summary report that contains the number of sensor readings, the average value, the maximum value, and the minimum value. Each of the three common file formats discussed will be used in the following programs.

Specified Number of Records

Assume that the first record in the sensor data file contains an integer that specifies the number of records of sensor information that follow. Each of the following lines contains a time and sensor reading:

```
    sensor1.dat
10
0.0   132.5
0.1   147.2
0.2   148.3
0.3   157.3
0.4   163.2
0.5   158.2
0.6   169.3
0.7   148.2
0.8   137.6
0.9   135.9
```

The process of first reading the number of data points and then using that to specify the number of times to read data and accumulate information is easily described using a variable-controlled loop. In the program shown next, the first actual data value is used to initialize the max and min values. If we set the min value initially to zero and all the sensor values were greater than zero, the program would print the erroneous value of zero for the minimum sensor reading. The program for this solution is as follows:

```
/*----------------------------------------------------------*/
/* Program chapter5_2                                       */
/*                                                          */
/* This program generates a summary report from            */
/* a data file that has the number of data points          */
/* in the first record.                                     */

#include <iostream> //Required for cerr, cin, cout.
#include <fstream> //Required for ifstream, ofstream.
#include <string> //Required for string.
using namespace std;

int main()
{
  // Declare and initialize objects.
  int num_data_pts, k;
  double time, motion, sum=0, max, min;
  string filename;
  ifstream sensor1;
  ofstream report;

  // Prompt user for name of input file.
  cout << "Enter the name of the input file";
  cin >> filename;

  // Open file and read the number of data points.
```

```cpp
sensor1. open(filename.c_str());
if( sensor1.fail() )
{
    cerr << "Error opening input file" << filename << endl;
    exit (1);
}
// Open report file.
report.open ("sensor1Report.txt");

sensor1 >> num_data_pts;

// Read first data pair and initial max and min.
sensor1 >> time >> motion;
max=min=motion;
sum += motion;

// Read remaining data and compute summary information.
for (k=1; k<num_data_pts; k++)
{
  sensor1 >> time >> motion;
  sum += motion;
  if (motion > max)
  {
     max = motion;
  }
  if (motion < min)
  {
     min = motion;
  }
}

// Set format flags.
report.setf(ios::fixed);
report.setf(ios::showpoint);
report.precision(2);
// Print summary information.
report << "Number of sensor readings: "
       << num_data_pts << endl;
report << "Average reading:           "
       << sum/num_data_pts << endl;
report << "Maximum reading:           "
       << max << endl;
report << "Minimum reading:           "
       << min << endl;

// Close files and exit program.
sensor1.close();
report.close();
return 0;
} //end main
/*-------------------------------------------------------------*/
```

The report printed by this program using the `sensor1.dat` file is as follows:

```
Number of sensor readings: 10
Average reading:            149.77
Maximum reading:            169.30
Minimum reading:            132.50
```

Trailer or Sentinel Signals

Assume that the data file `sensor2.dat` contains the same information as the `sensor1.dat` file, but instead of giving the number of valid data records at the beginning of the file, a final record contains a trailer signal. The time value on the last line in the file will contain a negative value so that we know that it is not a valid line of information. The contents of the data file are as follows:

```
sensor2.dat
0.0   132.5
0.1   147.2
0.2   148.3
0.3   157.3
0.4   163.2
0.5   158.2
0.6   169.3
0.7   148.2
0.8   137.6
0.9   135.9
-99   -99
```

The process of reading and accumulating information until we read the trailer signal is easily described using a do/while loop structure, as shown in the following pseudocode and program:

```
Pseudocode
main:     set sum to zero
          set number of points to 0
          read time, motion
          set max to motion
          set min to motion
          do
                    add motion to sum
                    if motion > max
                            set max to motion
                    if motion < min
                            set min to motion
                    increment number of points by 1
                    read time, motion
          while time >= 0
          set average to sum/number of data points
          print average, max, min

/*-----------------------------------------------------------*/
/*  Program chapter5_3                                      */
/*                                                         */
/*  This program generates a summary report from          */
```

```
/*  a data file that has a trailer record with        */
/*  negative values.                                   */

#include <iostream>  //Required for cin, cout, cerr
#include <fstream>   //Required for ifstream, ofstream
#include <string>    //Required for string.
using namespace std;

int main()
{
   // Declare and initialize objects.
   int num_data_pts(0), k;
   double time, motion, sum(0), max, min;
   string filename;
   ifstream sensor2;
   ofstream report;

   // Prompt user for name of input file.
   cout << "Enter the name of the input file";
   cin >> filename;

   // Open file and read the first data point.
   sensor2.open(filename.c_str());
   if(sensor2.fail())
   {
       cerr << "Error opening input file\n";
       exit(1);
   }

   // Open report file.
   report.open("sensor2Report.txt");
   sensor2 >> time >> motion;

   // Initialize objects using first data point.
      max = min = motion;

   // Update summary data until trailer record read.
      do
       {
          sum += motion;
          if (motion > max)
          {
             max = motion;
          }
          if (motion < min)
          {
             min = motion;
          }
          num_data_pts++;
          sensor2 >> time >> motion;
       } while (time >= 0);
```

```
//   Set format flags.
     report.setf(ios::fixed);
     report.setf(ios::showpoint);
     report.precision(2);

//   Print summary information.
     report << "Number of sensor readings:   "
            << num_data_pts << endl
            << "Average reading:             "
            << sum/num_data_pts << endl
            << "Maximum reading:             "
            << max << endl
            << "Minimum reading:             "
            << min << endl;

//   Close files and exit program.
     sensor2.close();
     report.close();
   return 0;
}   //end main
/*---------------------------------------------------------*/
```

The report printed by this program using the `sensor2.dat` file is exactly the same as the report printed using the `sensor1.dat` file.

End-of-File

A special system dependent end-of-file indicator is automatically inserted at the end of every data file. The `eof()` function, can be used to detect when this indicator has been reached in a data file. The function returns a value of true if the end-of-file indicator has been read in the data file associated with the file stream object. Consider the following statements:

```
sum = count = 0;
data1 >> x;
while ( !data1.eof() )
{
    ++count;
    sum += x;
    data1 >> x;
}
avg = sum/count;
```

The first input statement attempts to read a value for x from the data file associated with the input file stream object `data1`. If a data value is read, the `eof()` function returns a value of 0, and the statements within the loop are executed. The last statement inside the while loop is an input statement that attempts to read the next value of x from the data file. The `while` loop will continue to execute while the end of the data file has not been reached. When there is no more data in the file and the end-of-file indicator is read, the next call to the `eof()` function will return a value of 1, and control will pass to the statement following the `while` loop. This is the correct structure for an end-of-file loop. The `eof()` function will not return a value of true until after the end of file indicator has been read. For this reason, it is important to test for the end of file immediately after an input statement.

You can also detect an end-of-file indicator automatically, as illustrated in the following statements:

```
while ( data1 >> x )
{
   ++count;
   sum += x;
}
```

This `while` loop uses the value returned by the input request to control execution. The input request will return a value of `true` if a data value is read from the `data1` file stream and a value of `false` if a data value cannot be read from the file stream. In our examples, we will use the `eof()` function for clarity.

We now assume that the data file `sensor3.dat` contains the same information as the `sensor2.dat` file, except that it does not include the trailer signal. In the following program, we read and accumulate information until we reach the end of the data file:

```
/*-------------------------------------------------------*/
/*   Program chapter5_4                                  */
/*                                                       */
/*   This program generates a summary report from        */
/*   a data file that does not have a header record      */
/*   or a trailer record.                                */

#include <iostream> //Required for cin, cout, cerr
#include <fstream> //Required for ifstream, ofstream.
#include <string> //Required for string.
using namespace std;

int main()
{
   // Declare and initialize objects.
   int num_data_pts(0), k;
   double time, motion, sum(0), max, min;
   string filename;
   ifstream sensor3;
   ofstream report;

   // Prompt user for name of input file.
   cout << "Enter the name of the input file";
   cin >> filename;

   // Open file and read the first data point.
   sensor3.open(filename.c_str());
```

```cpp
        if(sensor3.fail())
        {
           cerr << "Error opening input file\n";
           exit(1);
        }

   //  open report file.
        report.open("sensor3Report.txt");

   //  While not at the end of the file,
   //  read and accumulate information
        sensor3 >> time >> motion;  // initial input
        while ( !sensor3.eof() )
        {
           num_data_pts++;
           if (num_data_pts == 1)
           {
              max = min = motion;
           }
           sum += motion;
           if (motion > max)
           {
              max = motion;
           }
           if (motion < min)
           {
              min = motion;
           }
           sensor3 >> time >> motion;  // input next
        }

   //  Set format flags.
        report.setf(ios::fixed);
        report.setf(ios::showpoint);
        report.precision(2);
   //  Print summary information.
        report << "Number of sensor readings: "
               << num_data_pts << endl
               << "Average reading:            "
               << sum/num_data_pts << endl
               << "Maximum reading:            "
               << max << endl
               << "Minimum reading:            "
               << min << endl;

   //  Close file and exit program.
        sensor3.close();
        report.close();
     return 0;
} //end main
/*-------------------------------------------------------*/
```

The report printed using the `sensor3.dat` file is exactly the same as the report printed using `sensor1.dat` or `sensor2.dat`.

The programs in this section work properly if the data files exist and contain the information expected. If this program is going to be used routinely with sensor data, statements should be included to be sure that the file structure is the one expected. Also, a division-by-zero would occur if the number of points were zero. A division-by-zero could be avoided by comparing the number of points to zero before printing the report.

All three file structures are commonly used in engineering and scientific applications. Therefore, it is important to know which type of structure is used when you work with a data file. If you make the wrong assumption, you may get incorrect answers instead of an error message. Sometimes the only way to be sure of the file structure is to print the first few lines and the last few lines of the file.

Modify!

In program `chapter5_3` developed in this chapter, the loop contained a condition that tested for the first time that the loop was executed. When the condition was true, the `max` and `min` values were initialized to the first motion value. If the data files used with these programs were very long, the time required to execute this selection statement could begin to be substantial. One way to avoid this test is to read the first set of data and initialize the objects before entering the loop. This change may also require other changes in the program.

1. Modify program `chapter5_3` so that it works correctly after the condition is removed that tests for the first time that the loop is executed.

2. Run program `chapter5_4` with an empty data file. If the output is in error, modify the program to correct the error.

5.3   Generating a Data File

Generating a data file is similar to printing a report; instead of writing the line to the terminal screen, we write it to a data file. Before we generate the data file, though, we must decide what file structure we want to use. In the previous discussion, we presented the three most common file structures—files with an initial record giving the number of valid records that follow, files with a trailer or sentinel record to indicate the end of the valid data, and files with only valid data records and no special beginning or ending records.

There are advantages and disadvantages to each of the three file structures discussed. A file with a trailer signal is simple to use, but choosing a value for the trailer signal must be done carefully so that it does not contain values that could occur in the valid data. If the first record in the data file will contain the number of lines of actual data, we must know how many lines of data will be in the file before we begin to generate the file. It may not always be easy to determine the number of lines before executing the program that generates the file. The simplest file to generate is the one that contains only the valid information, with no special information at the beginning or end of the file. If the information in the file is going to be used with a plotting package, it is usually best to use this third file structure which includes only valid information.

We now present a program that is a modification of the program presented in Chapter 4 that printed a table of time, height, and velocity values for a weather balloon. In addition to generating a table of information that is displayed on the screen, we also write the time, height, and velocity information to a data file. Compare this program to program `chapter4_8`:

```
/*-----------------------------------------------------------*/
/*  Program chapter5_5                                        */
/*                                                            */
/*  This program generates a file of height and              */
/*  velocity values for a weather balloon. The               */
/*  information is also printed in a report.                 */

#include <iostream> //Required for cin, cout.
#include <fstream> //Required for ofstream.
#include <iomanip> //Required for setw().
#include <cmath> //Required for pow().
#include <string> //Required for string.
using namespace std;

int main()
{
   // Declare and initialize objects.
   double initial, increment, final, time, height,
          velocity, max_time(0), max_height(0);
   int loops, itime;
   string filename;
   ofstream balloon;

   // Prompt user for name of output file.
   cout << "Enter the name of the output file";
   cin >> filename;

   // Open output file
   balloon.open(filename.c_str());

   // Get user input.
   cout << "Enter initial value for table (in hours) \n";
   cin >> initial;
   cout << "Enter increment between lines (in hours) \n";
   cin >> increment;
   cout << "Enter final value for table (in hours) \n";
   cin >> final;

   // Set format flags for standard output.
   cout.setf(ios::fixed);
   cout.precision(2);

   // Set format flags for file output.
   balloon.setf(ios::fixed);
   balloon.precision(2);
```

```
// Print report heading.
cout << "\n\nWeather Balloon Information \n";
cout << "Time     Height     Velocity \n";
cout << "(hrs)    (meters)   (meters/s) \n";

// Determine number of iterations required.
// Use integer index to avoid rounding error.
loops = (int)((final - initial)/increment);
for (itime=0; itime<=loops; itime++)
{
    time = initial + itime*increment;

    height = -0.12*pow(time,4) + 12*pow(time,3)
            - 380*time*time + 4100*time + 220;
    velocity = -0.48*pow(time,3) + 36*time*time
            - 760*time + 4100;

// Print report information to the screen.
    cout << setw(6) << time << setw(10) << height
        << setw(10) << velocity/3600 << endl;

// Write report information to a file.
    balloon << setw(6) << time << setw(10) << height
            << setw(10) << velocity/3600 << endl;

    if (height > max_height)
    {
        max_height = height;
        max_time = itime;
    }
}

// Report maximum height and corresponding time.
cout << "\nMaximum balloon height was "
    << setw(8) << max_height
    << " meters\nand it occurred at "
    << setw(6) << max_time << endl;

// Close file and exit program.
balloon.close();
return 0;
}
/*---------------------------------------------------------*/
```

The first few lines of a data file generated by this program, using an initial time of 0 hours, an increment of 0.5 hours, and a final time of 48 hours, are as follows:

```
0.00    220.00    1.14
0.50    2176.49   1.04
1.00    3951.88   0.94
...
```

This file is in a form to be easily plotted using a package such as Matlab, as discussed in Appendix C; a plot of this specific file was shown in Figure 4.7 in Chapter 4.

Modify!

1. Modify program `chapter5_5` so that it generates a file in which the last line of the data file contains negative values for the time, height, and velocity.

2. Modify program `chapter5_5` so that it generates a file in which the first line contains a number that specifies the number of valid lines of data that follow in the data file.

5.4 Problem Solving Applied: Data Filters—Modifying an HTML File

data filters

Programs called **data filters** are often used to read the information in a data file, modify the contents of the file, and write the modified data to a new file. Suppose we have found an html document on the Web with important information that we would like save as plain text with all of the hypertext markup language (html) commands removed. An html command, also called a tag, has the following general form:

```
<html command>
```

We can write a C++ program that reads an html file and filters out all of the tags. The text from the file, minus the tags, is output to a new file.

1. PROBLEM STATEMENT

Write a program to remove the tags from an html file and save the text to a new file.

2. INPUT/OUTPUT DESCRIPTION

The following diagram shows that the input to the program is an html file. The output of the program is the text from the html file with the tags removed.

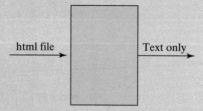

html file →   → Text only

3. HAND EXAMPLE

For the hand example, we will use a very small html file that just has a few lines. Here is the sample html file:

```
<HTML>
<HEAD>
<META HTTP-EQUIV="Content-Type" CONTENT="text/html;
 charset=ISO-8859-1">
<TITLE>HomePage</TITLE>

<META NAME="GENERATOR" CONTENT="Internet Assistant for
 Microsoft Word 2.04z">
</HEAD>
<BODY BGCOLOR = "#118187" >
<HR>
<b><font size=4>
<p>
J. Ingber
<br>
Accurate Solutions in Applied Physics, LLC
<br>
Albuquerque, New Mexico
</b></font>
</BODY>
</HTML>
```

The text without tags should be

```
HomePage
J. Ingber
Accurate Solutions in Applied Physics, LLC
Albuquerque, New Mexico
```

4. ALGORITHM DEVELOPMENT

We first develop the decomposition outline because it breaks the solution into a series of sequential steps.

Decomposition Outline

1. Read a character from the file.

2. Determine if character is part of an html tag.

3. Print all characters that are not part of an html tag.

The first step in the decomposition outline involves a loop in which we read each character from the file. The condition to exit the loop will be a test for the end of the file. Our program will have two distinct states. In one state, we will be reading the text of the file (not a tag), so we will output each character as we read it. In the other state, we will be reading a tag, so the character will not be printed. We will use an object of type `bool` to keep track of which state we are in. If we are in the text state, the character '<' will mark the beginning of a tag. If we are in the tag state, the character '>' will mark the end of a tag. The refinement in pseudocode is as follows:

```
Refinement in Pseudocode
main:   set text_state to true
        read character
        while not end-of-file
        if text_state is true
           if character = '<'
               set text_state to false
           else
               print character to file
        else
           if character = '>'
               set text_state to true
        read next character
```

The steps in the pseudocode are now detailed enough to convert into C++:

```cpp
/*-------------------------------------------------------------------*/
/* Program chapter5_6                                                */
/* This program reads an html file, and writes the text             */
/* without the tags to a new file.                                  */

#include<iostream> //Required for cin, cout, cerr.
#include<fstream> //Required for ifstream, ofstream.
#include<string> //Required for string.
using namespace std;

int main()
{
  // Declare objects.
  char character;
  bool text_state(TRUE);
  string infile, outfile;
  ifstream html;
  ofstream htmltext;

  // Prompt user for name of input file.
  cout << "enter the name of the input file";
  cin >> infile;

  // Prompt user for name of output file.
  cout << "enter the name of the output file";
  cin >> outfile;

  // Open files.
  html.open(infile.c_str());
  if(html.fail())
  {
     cerr << "Error opening input file\n";
     exit(1);
  }
  htmltext.open(outfile.c_str());
```

```
// Read first character from html file.
html.get(character);

while(!html.eof())
{
// Check state.
    if(text_state)
    {
        if(character == '<')            // Beginning of a tag.
            text_state=FALSE;           // Change States.
        else
            htmltext << character;      // Still text, write to
                                            the file.

    }
    else
    {

// Command state, no output required.
        if(character == '>')            // End of tag.
            text_state = TRUE;          // Change States.
    }

// Read next character from html file.
    html.get(character);
}
    html.close();
    htmltext.close();
    return 0;
}
```

5. TESTING

Using the html file from the hand example, we get the following output:

```
HomePage
J. Ingber
Accurate Solutions in Applied Physics, LLC
Albuquerque, New Mexico
```

This matches the output from the hand example.

Modify!

1. Modify program chapter5_6 by replacing the if statements with switch statements

2. The pseudocode for program chapter5_6 is provided. Write the corresponding flowchart.

5.5 Error Checking

error state

In the previous sections, we used the `fail()` function to test the state of an input stream to determine if an error had occurred while trying to open a file. Errors can also occur while attempting to read data from a file or from standard input. An input stream will be set to an **error state** if the input data is not what the input statement is expecting.

Consider the following statements that attempt to read two values from standard input:

```
int iVar1(0), iVar2(0);
cin >> iVar1 >> iVar2;
cout << iVar1 << " " << iVar2 << endl;
```

whitespace

Since the variables `iVar1` and `iVar2` are declared to be of type `int`, the data entered from the keyboard must be two integer numbers, separated by **whitespace**. In C++, whitespace is defined as blank, tab, newline, formfeed, and carriage return. If any other type of data is encountered, such as a decimal point, a comma, or any non numeric character other than whitespace, `cin` will be set to an error state.

Suppose the following data were entered at the keyboard:

```
10,20
```

When the enter key is pressed at the end of the line, the data is stored in the standard input buffer. The contents of the standard input buffer and its associated pointer, after pressing the enter key, is illustrated in Figure 5.2:

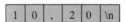

Figure 5.2 Standard input buffer.

Note that the newline character, generated by pressing the enter key, is stored as a single character in the input buffer. A trace of statements attempting to read from the input buffer is shown below.

Statement Trace:	
Statement	**Memory Snapshot**
`int iVar1(0), iVar2(0);`	integer iVar1 ⬚0⬚ integer iVar2 ⬚0⬚
`cin >> iVar1 >> iVar2;`	integer iVar1 ⬚10⬚ integer iVar2 ⬚0⬚
`cout << iVar1 << " "` `     << iVar2 << endl;`	
Standard Output	
`10 0`	

We can see that the characters 1 and 0 are extracted from the input buffer, converted to the integer value 10, and assigned to `iVar1`. Since a comma cannot be interpreted as integer data, the comma is left in the input buffer. No error occurs after the first extraction since the integer value 10 was successfully extracted and assigned to `iVar1`. When the $>>$ operator attempts to extract a value for the integer variable `iVar2`, the comma is encountered. Since a comma is not a numeric character, and it is not whitespace, the comma is left in the input buffer. No value is extracted, and thus, no value is assigned to `iVar2`.

Since the extraction for `iVar2` was unsuccessful, the value of `iVar2` is unchanged and `cin` is now in an error state. The `cout` statement is executed next and the output 10 0 is display on the screen. The standard input buffer has been modified as illustrated in Figure 5.3.

| , | 2 | 0 | n |

Figure 5.3 Standard input buffer.

When an input stream is in an error state, the program continues to execute but input operations applied to the stream will result in a null operation, which means that the input buffer will not be modified.

In order to access the input buffer and extract the value 20, we must first set `cin` back to an error free state. Once `cin` is in a good state, the comma can be extracted from the input stream and then the value 20 can be extracted and assigned to `iVar2`. The function `clear()` can be used to set `cin` to an error free state. We illustrate the use of the `clear()` function, and other functions defined in the stream class hierarchy and designed to handle stream errors, in the following section.

The Stream State

state
state flags

Every stream has an associated **state**. The state of a stream is represented as a set of variables defined in the class `ios_base`. These variables are often referred to as **state flags**. Recall that all classes in the stream class hierarchy inherit from `ios_base`. Thus, every stream has an associated set of state flags. State flags indicate a Boolean state which can be represented by a value of 0 or 1. These flags can be set and tested to handle potential errors.

The state of a stream is affected by events that occur when operations are applied to the stream, as illustrated in Table 5.1. Note that the names of the state flags include the word bit. Recall that a bit is a binary digit and can represent a value of 0 or 1. Thus, the names indicate the Boolean nature of the flags.

We see from Table 5.1 that the `goodbit` is initialized to true when a stream is first created and remains true as long as the `eofbit`, the `failbit`, and the `badbit` remain false. The `eofbit` is set to true when an end of file is encountered. The `failbit` of a stream is set to true when an attempt to open a file fails, an end-of-file is encountered, or unexpected data corrupts the input stream. The state of these bits determines the state of the associated stream.

TABLE 5.1   Stream State Flags

Event	badbit	failbit	eofbit	goodbit
Initialization of a stream.	0	0	0	1
Failure to open a file.	0	1	0	0
Unexpected data encountered.	0	1	0	0
End of file encountered.	0	1	1	0

TABLE 5.2   Stream Class Functions

Function	Description
bool bad()	Returns true if badbit is set.
bool eof()	Returns true if eofbit is set.
bool fail()	Returns true if failbit is set.
bool good()	Returns true if goodbit is set.
void clear(iostate flag=goodbit)	Sets the state flags.
iostate rdstate()	Returns value of state flags.

The `badbit` will be set to true if the stream becomes corrupted and data is assumed to be lost. Input routines in some user-defined class types and class templates set the bad bit to true when input data does not match the required format.

The state of a stream can be tested and directly modified using functions defined within the stream class hierarchy. These functions are designed to facilitate error handling, and should be used in all programs that rely on correct input for correct results. Table 5.2 provides a partial list of functions defined within the stream class hierarchy.

Program `chapter5_7` illustrates the use of these functions to handle input errors.

```
/*-------------------------------------------------------*/
/* Program chapter5_7                                    */
/* This program illustrates the use of stream            */
/* flags and stream functions for detecting              */
/* and handling input errors.                            */

#include<iostream> //Required for cin, cout, cerr.
#include<fstream> //Required for ifstream, ofstream.
#include<string> //Required of string
#include<iomanip> //Required for setw()
using namespace std;

int main()
{
  //Declare variables.
  ifstream fin;
  ofstream fout;
  int iVar1, count (0);
  string filename;
  char junk;

  //Request name of input file.
  cout << "Enter the name of input file";
  cin >> filename;

  //Open file and check for failure.
  fin.open(filename.c_str());
  while(fin.fail())
  {
    ++count;
```

```
//Open failed. Attempt to recover.
//rdstate() returns the iostate of a stream
//Print the state of the fin stream
cout << "could not open" << filename
     <<". The state of the fin stream is"
     << fin.rdstate() << endl;
cerr << setw(10) << "badbit:" << setw(10)
     << fin.bad() << endl;
cerr << setw(10) << "failbit:" << setw(10)
     << fin.fail() << endl;
cerr << setw(10) << "eofbit:" << setw(10)
     << fin.eof() << endl;
cerr << setw(10) << "goodbit:" << setw(10)
     << fin.good() << endl;
cerr << "*********************" << endl;

fin.clear(); //reset fin to good state

//Print the state of fin after clearing.
cout << "fin state reset to"
     << fin.rdstate() << endl;
cout << setw(10) << "badbit:" << setw(10)
     << fin.bad() << endl;
cout << setw(10) << "failbit:" << setw(10)
     << fin.fail() << endl;
cout << stew(10) << "eofbit:" << setw(10)
     << fin.eof() << endl;
cout << setw(10) << "goodbit:" << setw(10)
     << fin.good() << endl;
cout << "*********************" << endl;
if(count >= 5)
{
  cerr << "Failed to open an input file.";
  exit(1);
}
cout << "enter the name of a file";
cin >> filename;
fin.open(filename.c_str());
}
//File has been successfully opened.
//Get state of fin.
cout << "File" << filename
     << "is open. State of fin is"
     << fin.rdstate() << endl;

//Open file for output.
fout.open("output.dat");

//Print table of values to output file.
//Print heading.
fout << "Count iVar2" << endl;
fout << "--------------------" << endl;
```

```
//Read and print data from file
count = 0;//Reset count to zero.
fin >> iVar1;
while(!fin.eof())
{
  //Test state of fin.
  if(!fin) //if fin is bad
  {
    cerr << "Bad data encountered.\n";
    cerr << "The state of fin is:"
         << fin.rdstate()<<endl;
    cerr << setw(10) << "badbit:"
         << setw(10) << fin.bad() << endl;
    cerr << setw(10) << "failbit:"
         << setw(10) << fin.fail() << endl;
    cerr << setw(10) << "eofbit:"
         << setw(10) << fin.eof() << endl;
    cerr << setw(10) << "goodbit:"
         << setw(10) << fin.good() << endl;
    cerr << "*******************" << endl;
    //Reset fin to good state
    fin.clear();
    //Remove bad character from input stream.
    fin.get(junk);
    cerr << "The bad character is:" << junk << endl;
    continue; //Force next iteration of while loop.
  }
  ++count;
  fout << setw(5) << count
       << setw(10) << iVar1 << endl;
  fin >> iVar1;
}
//Print current state of fin to standard output.
cout << "Outside of while, state of fin is:"
     << fin.rdstate() << endl;
cout << setw(10) << "badbit:" <<
     setw(10) << fin.bad() << endl;
cout << setw(10) << "failbit:"
     << setw(10) << fin.fail() << endl;
cout << setw(10) << "eofbit:"
     << setw(10) << fin.eof() << endl;
cout << setw(10) << "goodbit:"
     << setw(10) << fin.good() << endl;
cout << "*******************" << endl;
fin.close();
fout.close();
return 0;
}
```

A sample run of this program is shown below. First we enter the name of a file that does not exist. When prompted for a new file name we enter the filename `test.dat`. The file `test.dat` contains the following data:

```
20 30
5 9
1,5
8 9
-7 4
```

Sample run:

```
enter the name of input file badfilename
could not open badfilename. The state of the fin stream is 4
    badbit:         0
   failbit:         1
    eofbit:         0
   goodbit:         0
* * * * * * * * * * * * * * * * * * * * * *
fin state reset to 0
    badbit:         0
   failbit:         0
    eofbit:         0
   goodbit:         1
* * * * * * * * * * * * * * * * * * * * * *
enter the name of a file test.dat
File test.dat is open. State of fin is 0
Bad data encountered.
The state of fin is: 4
    badbit:         0
   failbit:         1
    eofbit:         0
   goodbit:         0
* * * * * * * * * * * * * * * * * * * * * *
The bad character is:,
Outside of while, state of fin is: 6
    badbit:         0
   failbit:         1
    eofbit:         1
   goodbit:         0
* * * * * * * * * * * * * * * * * * * * * *
```

After running the program, the output file `output.dat` contains the following data:

```
Count       iVar2
- - - - - - - - - - - - - - - -
    1          20
    2          30
    3           5
    4           9
    5           1
    6           1
    7           5
    8           8
    9           9
   10          -7
   11           4
```

Modify!

1. Program `chapter5_7` allows the user 5 additional attempts to input the name of a valid input file after the first attempt fails. Modify the program to allow the user only 1 additional attempt, and use a boolean control variable instead of the integer variable `count`.

2. Modify program `chapter5_7` by deactivating the block of code that tests the state of `fin` directly. Compile and run the modified program. What is displayed to standard output? What is written to the output file? Explain the results. Note: A block of code can be deactivated by placing comments lines around the block to instruct the compiler to treat the code as if it were a block of comment lines.

Practice!

Assume the following line of data is entered at the keyboard:

```
1,2.3
```

Give the corresponding snapshots of memory, and the value of the stream state flags, after each of the following sets of statements are executed:

1. ```
   int i(0), j(0);
   cin >> i >> j;
   ```

2. ```
   double x(0), y(0);
   cin >> x >> y;
   ```

3. ```
   char ch1, ch2;
   cin >> ch1 >> ch2;
   ```

4. ```
   char ch;
   double x, y;
   cin >> x >> ch >> y;
   ```

5.6 Numerical Technique: Linear Modeling*

linear regression

Linear modeling is the name given to the process that determines the linear equation that is the best fit to a set of data points in terms of minimizing the sum of the squared distances between the line and the data points. (This process is also called **linear regression**.) To understand the process, we first consider the set of temperature values presented in Section 2.5 that were collected from the cylinder head of a new engine.

Time, s	Temperature, degrees F
0	0
1	20
2	60
3	68
4	77
5	110

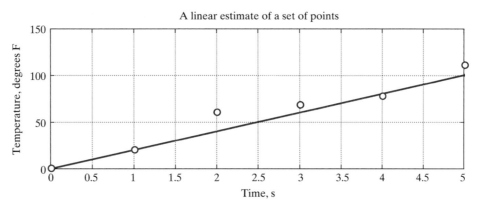

Figure 5.4 A linear estimate to model a set of points.

If we plot these data points, we find that they appear to be close to a straight line. In fact, we could determine a good estimate of a straight line through these points by drawing it on a graph and then computing the slope and y-intercept. Figure 5.4 contains a plot of the points (with time on the x-axis and temperature on the y-axis), along with the straight line with the equation

$$y = 20x.$$

To measure the quality of the fit of this linear estimate to the data, we first determine the vertical distance from each point to the linear estimate; these distances are shown in Figure 5.5. The first two points fall exactly on the line, so d_1 and d_2 are zero. The value of d_3 is equal to $60 - 40$, or 20; the rest of the distances can be computed in a similar way. If we compute the sum of the distances, some of the positive and negative values would cancel each other and give a sum that is smaller than it should be. To avoid this problem, we could add absolute values or squared values; linear regression uses squared values. Therefore, the measure of the quality of the fit of this linear estimate is the sum of the squared distances between the points and the linear estimates. This sum can be easily computed and is 573.

If we drew another line through the points, we could compute the sum of squares that corresponds to this new line. Of the two lines, the best fit is provided by the line with the

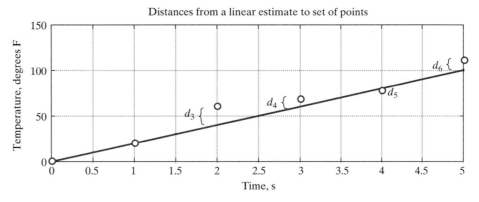

Figure 5.5 Distances between points and linear estimates.

least-squares smaller sum of squared distances, or the **least-squares** distance. To find the line with the smallest sum of squared distances, we begin with a general linear equation:

$$y = mx + b$$

We then write an equation that computes the sum of the squared distances between the given data points and this general equation. Using techniques from calculus, we can then compute the derivatives of the equation with respect to m and b, and set the derivatives equal to zero. The values of m and b that are determined in this way represent the straight line with the minimum sum of squared distances. Before giving these equations for m and b, we define

summation notation **summation notation**.

The set of data points given at the beginning of this section can be represented by the points $(x_1, y_1), (x_2, y_2), \ldots, (x_6, y_6)$. The symbol $\sum$ represents a summation, and thus the sum of the x-coordinates can be expressed in the following notation:

$$\sum_{k=1}^{6} x_k$$

This summation is read as "the sum of x_k as k goes from 1 to 6." The value of this summation for the example data points is $(0+1+2+3+4+5)$, or 15. Other sums that could be computed using the example data points are as follows:

$$\sum_{k=1}^{6} y_k = 0 + 20 + 60 + 68 + 77 + 110 = 335,$$

$$\sum_{k=1}^{6} y_k^2 = 0^2 + 20^2 + 60^2 + 68^2 + 77^2 + 110^2 = 26,653,$$

$$\sum_{k=1}^{6} x_k y_k = 0 \times 0 + 1 \times 20 + 2 \times 60 + 3 \times 68 + 4 \times 77 + 5 \times 110 = 1,202.$$

We now return to the problem of finding the best linear fit to a set of points. Using the procedure described before that is based on results from calculus, we find that the slope and y-intercept for the best linear fit to a set of n data points, in a least-squares sense, are the following:

$$m = \frac{\sum_{k=1}^{n} x_k \cdot \sum_{k=1}^{n} y_k - n \cdot \sum_{k=1}^{n} x_k y_k}{\left(\sum_{k=1}^{n} x_k\right)^2 - n \cdot \sum_{k=1}^{n} x_k^2}, \tag{5.1}$$

$$b = \frac{\sum_{k=1}^{n} x_k \cdot \sum_{k=1}^{n} x_k y_k - \sum_{k=1}^{n} x_k^2 \cdot \sum_{k=1}^{n} y_k}{\left(\sum_{k=1}^{n} x_k\right)^2 - n \cdot \sum_{k=1}^{n} x_k^2}. \tag{5.2}$$

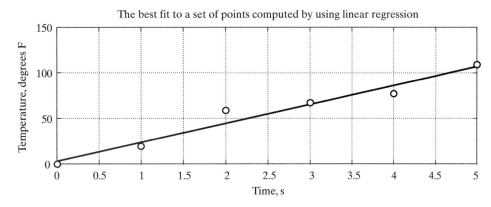

Figure 5.6 Least-squares linear regression model.

For the sample set of data, the optimum value for m is 20.83, and the optimum value for b is 3.76. The set of data points and this best-fit linear equation are shown in Figure 5.6. The sum of squares for this best fit is 356.82, compared with 573 for the straight line in Figure 5.5.

One of the advantages of performing a linear regression for a set of data points that is nearly linear in nature is that we can then estimate or predict points for which we had no data. For example, in the cylinder-head temperature example, suppose that we want to estimate the temperature for the cylinder head at 3.3 seconds. By using the equation computed with linear regression, we find that the estimated temperature is

$$y = mx + b$$

$$= (20.83)(3.3) + 3.76$$

$$= 72.5.$$

With an equation model, we can compute estimates that we could not compute with linear interpolation. For example, using the linear model, we can compute an estimate of the temperature for 8 seconds, but we could not compute an estimate at 8 seconds using linear interpolation, because we do not have a point with a time greater than 8 seconds. (This would be extrapolation, not interpolation.)

It is also important to remember that linear models do not provide a good fit to all sets of data. Therefore, it is important to first determine whether a linear model is a good model for the data before using it to predict new data points. Techniques for measuring the quality of a linear model for a set of data is presented in Chapter 6.

In the next section, we develop a problem solution that determines the best fit for a set of sensor data collected from a satellite, and then we use that model to estimate or predict other sensor values.

5.7 Problem Solving Applied: Ozone Measurements*

Satellite sensors can be used to measure many different pieces of information that help us understand more about the atmosphere, which is composed of a number of layers around the earth [12]. Starting at the earth's surface, we know that the layers are the troposphere,

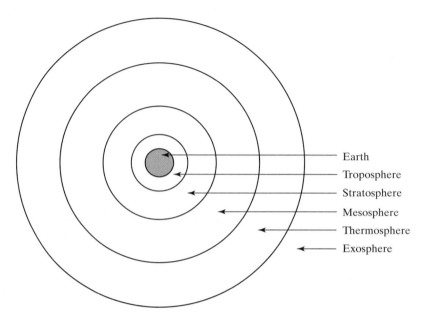

Figure 5.7 Atmospheric layers around the earth.

stratosphere, mesosphere, thermosphere, and exosphere, as shown in Figure 5.7. Each layer of the atmosphere can be characterized by its temperature profile. The troposphere is the inner layer of the atmosphere, varying in height from around 5 km at the poles to 18 km at the equator. Most cloud formations occur in the troposphere, and there is a steady fall of temperature with increasing altitude. The stratosphere is characterized by relatively uniform temperatures over considerable differences in altitude. It extends from the troposphere to about 50 km (about 31 miles) above the earth. Pollutants that drift into the stratosphere may remain there for many years before they drift back to the troposphere, where they can be diluted and removed by the weather. The mesosphere extends from 50 to approximately 85 km (about 53 miles) above the earth's surface. In this layer, the air mixes fairly readily. Above the mesosphere is the thermosphere, which extends from 85 to about 140 km (about 87 miles) above the earth. In this region, the heating is due to the absorption of solar energy by atomic oxygen. The ionosphere is a relatively dense band of charged particles within the thermosphere. Some types of communications use the reflection of radio waves off the ionosphere. Finally, the exosphere is the highest region of the atmosphere. In the exosphere, the air density is so low that an air molecule moving upward is more likely to escape the atmosphere than it is to hit another molecule.

A satellite experiment was launched on the NIMBUS 7 spacecraft in 1978 to collect data on the composition and structure of the middle atmosphere [13]. The instrumentation and sensors collected data from October 25, 1978, to May 28, 1979, returning more than 7,000 sets of data to the earth each day. These data were used to determine temperature, ozone, water vapor, nitric acid, and nitrogen dioxide distributions in the stratosphere and mesosphere.

Consider a problem in which we have collected a set of data measuring the ozone mixing ratio in parts per million volume (ppmv). Over small regions, these data are nearly linear, and thus we can use a linear model to estimate the ozone at altitudes other than ones for which we have specific data. Write a program that reads a data file named *zone1.dat* containing the altitude in km and the corresponding ozone mixing ratios in ppmv for a region over which we want to determine a linear model. The data file contains only valid data and thus does not have a special header line or trailer line. Use the least-squares technique presented in the previous section to determine and print the model. Also, print the beginning and ending altitudes to indicate the region over which the model is accurate.

1. PROBLEM STATEMENT

Use the least-squares technique to determine a linear model for estimating the ozone mixing ratio at a specified altitude.

2. INPUT/OUTPUT DESCRIPTION

The following I/O diagram shows that the data file *zone1.dat* is the input and that the output is the range of altitudes and the linear model:

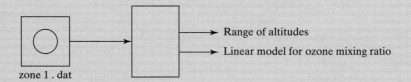

3. HAND EXAMPLE

Assume that the data consist of the following four data points:

Altitude (km)	Ozone Mixing Ratio (ppmv)
20	3
24	4
26	5
28	6

We now need to evaluate equations (5.1) and (5.2), which are repeated here for convenience:

$$m = \frac{\sum_{k=1}^{n} x_k \cdot \sum_{k=1}^{n} y_k - n \cdot \sum_{k=1}^{n} x_k y_k}{\left(\sum_{k=1}^{n} x_k\right)^2 - n \cdot \sum_{k=1}^{n} x_k^2}, \tag{5.1}$$

$$b = \frac{\sum_{k=1}^{n} x_k \cdot \sum_{k=1}^{n} x_k y_k - \sum_{k=1}^{n} x_k^2 \cdot \sum_{k=1}^{n} y_k}{\left(\sum_{k=1}^{n} x_k\right)^2 - n \cdot \sum_{k=1}^{n} x_k^2}. \tag{5.2}$$

To evaluate these equations using the hand-example data, we need to compute the following group of sums:

$$\sum_{k=1}^{4} x_k = 20 + 24 + 26 + 28 = 98,$$

$$\sum_{k=1}^{4} y_k = 3 + 4 + 5 + 6 = 18,$$

$$\sum_{k=1}^{4} x_k y_k = 20 \cdot 3 + 24 \cdot 4 + 26 \cdot 5 + 28 \cdot 6 = 454,$$

$$\sum_{k=1}^{4} x_k^2 = (20)^2 + (24)^2 + (26)^2 + (28)^2 = 2436.$$

Using these sums, we can now compute the values of m and b:

$$m = 0.37;$$
$$b = -4.6.$$

4. ALGORITHM DEVELOPMENT

We first develop the decomposition outline because it divides the solution into a series of sequential steps.

Decomposition Outline

1. Read data file values and compute corresponding sums and ranges.

2. Compute slope and y-intercept.

3. Print range of altitudes and linear model.

The first step in the decomposition outline involves a loop in which we read the data from the file and at the same time add the corresponding values to the sums needed for computing the linear model. We will also need to determine the number of data points as we read the file. The condition to exit the loop will be a test for the end-of-file, because there is no header or trailer information. Since the end-of-file flag must be tested immediately after the input statement, we will use a `while` loop instead of `do-while` loop. A `for` loop would not be an appropriate choice because we do not know how many data points are contained in the file. Because we want to keep track of the altitude ranges, we also need to save the first and last altitude values. Steps 2 and 3 of the decomposition outline are sequential steps involving computations and printing. Therefore, the refinement in pseudocode is as follows:

```
Refinement in Pseudocode
main:   set count to zero
        set sumx, sumy, sumxy, sumx2 to zero
        while not at end-of-file
                read x, y
                increment count by 1
                if count = 1
                        set first to x
                add x to sumx
                add y to sumy
                add x2 to sumx2
                add xy to sumxy
        set last to x
        compute slope and y intercept
        print first, last, slope, y intercept
```

The steps in the pseudocode are now detailed enough to convert into C++:

```
/*----------------------------------------------------------------*/
/*  Program chapter5_8                                            */
/*                                                                */
/*  This program computes a linear model for a set               */
/*  of altitude and ozone mixing ratio values.                   */
#include <iostream> //Required for cin, cout
#include <fstream>  //Required for ifstream
#include <string>   //Required for string
using namespace std;

int main()
{
   // Declare and initialize objects.
   int count(0);
   double x, y, first, last, sumx(0), sumy(0), sumx2(0),
          sumxy(0), denominator, m, b;
   string filename;
   ifstream zone1;
   cout << "Enter name of input file:";
   cin >> filename;

   // Open input file.
   zone1.open(filename.c_str());
   if(zone1.fail())
   {
      cerr << "Error opening input file\n";
      exit(1);
   }
```

```
//  While not at the end of the file,
//  read and accumulate information.
zone1 >> x >> y;
while ( !zone1.eof() )
{
  ++count;
  if (count == 1)
    first = x;
  sumx += x;
  sumy += y;
  sumx2 += x*x;
  sumxy += x*y;
  zone1 >> x >> y;
}
last = x;

//  Compute slope and y-intercept.
denominator = sumx*sumx - count*sumx2;
m = (sumx*sumy - count*sumxy)/denominator;
b = (sumx*sumxy - sumx2*sumy)/denominator;

//  Set format flags
cout.setf(ios::fixed);
cout.precision(2);

//  Print summary information.
cout << "Range of altitudes in km: \n";
cout << first << " to " << last << endl << endl;
cout << "Linear model: \n";
cout << "ozone-mix-ratio = " << m << "  altitude + "
        << b << endl;

//  Close file and exit program.
zone1.close();
return 0;
}
/*-----------------------------------------------------------*/
```

5. TESTING

Using the data from the hand example as the contents of the data file *zone1.dat*, we get the following program output:

```
Range of altitudes in km:
20.00 to 28.00

Linear model:
ozone-mix-ratio = 0.37 altitude + -4.60
```

This matches the values computed from the hand example. The range also indicates that the measurements used in this problem were taken in the stratosphere.

Modify!

These problems relate to the program developed in this section. You may need to use the following relationship in some of the problems:

$$1\,km = 0.621\,mi$$

1. Add statements to the program so that it allows you to enter an altitude in km, and then uses the model to estimate a corresponding ozone mix ratio.

2. Modify your program in problem 1 so that it checks that the altitude that you enter is within the range that is appropriate for this model.

3. Modify the program in problem 2 so that it allows you to enter the altitude in miles. (The program should convert miles to kilometers.)

4. Modify the original program so that it also prints a linear model so that it can be used with altitudes that are in miles instead of kilometers. Assume that the data file still contains altitudes in kilometers.

SUMMARY

In this chapter, we covered the statements necessary to read information from a data file so that we could use the information in a program. We also presented the statements to generate a data file from a program. Data files are commonly used in solving engineering problems; therefore, this concept was presented early in the text so that we could use it in many of the later problem solutions. We introduced a technique for handling errors that may occur when inputting data. Finally, we covered the concept of generating a linear model for a set of data points and included the equations for determining the best fit in terms of least squares.

Key Terms

data file	output file stream
data filters	sentinel signal
end-of-file indicator	standard input buffer
error condition	stream class inheritances
input file stream	stream flags
least squares	stream state
linear modeling	summation notation
linear regression	trailer signal

C++ Statement Summary

Declaration for file stream objects:

```
ifstream sensor1;
ofstream balloon;
```

File open function:

```
//filename is a string object
sensor1.open(filename.c_str());
balloon.open(filename.c_str());
```

File fail function:

```
if (sensor1.fail())
```

File input:

```
sensor1 >> t >> motion;
```

File output:

```
balloon << setw(8) << time << setw(8) << height << setw(8) << velocity;
```

Output to standard error:

```
cerr << "Error encountered on input";
```

File close function:

```
sensor1.close();
stream clear function
sensor1.clear()
standard error output stream
```

Notes

1. Prompt the user to enter filenames so that they can be determined at run time.

Debugging Notes

1. When debugging a program that reads data from a data file, print the values as soon as they are read to check for errors in reading the information.
2. When debugging a program that reads a data file, be sure that your program checks for successful opening of the file.
3. To avoid infinite loops when inputting data, check the error status of the istream object before each iteration of the loop.
4. To avoid problems with operating systems that are case sensitive, use filenames with lowercase letters.

Problems

Exam Practice!

True/False Problems
Indicate whether the following statements are true (T) or false (F).

1. cin, cout and cerr are C++ keywords. T F
2. When a program attempts to open a data file for input, and the file is not found, the program will terminate. T F
3. The statement block of a while loop will be executed at least once. T F

4. The statement block of a `for` loop will be executed at least once. T F
5. If a comma is encountered when attempting to read an integer value from standard input, the program will terminate. T F

Multiple-Choice Problems

6. When an end of file is encountered, which of the following stream state flags are set to true?
   (a) `badbit`
   (b) `failbit`
   (c) `eofbit`
   (d) `goodbit`
7. When an input stream is in an error state, the program will
   (a) terminate.
   (b) continue normal execution.
   (c) continue to execute but input operations applied to the stream will result in a null operation.
   (d) send a warning message to `cerr` and continue normal execution.

Memory Snapshot Problems

Assume the following line of data is entered at the keyboard:

1 5.2 a,b

Give the corresponding memory snapshot, and the value of the stream state flags, after each of the following sets of statements is executed:

8.  ```
    int i(0), j(0);
    double x, y;
    char ch1, ch2;
    cin >> x >> y >> ch1 >> ch2;
    ```
9.  ```
    int i(0), j(0);
    double x, y;
    char ch1, ch2;
    cin >> x >> i >> j >> ch1 >> ch2;
    ```
10. ```
    int i(0), j(0);
    double x, y;
    char ch1, ch2;
    cin >> i >> j >> ch1 >> ch2;
    ```
11. ```
    int i(0), j(0);
    double x, y;
    char ch1, ch2;
    cin >> i >> j >> x >> ch1 >> ch2;
    ```

Data Filters. Programs called data filters are often used to read the information in a data file and then analyze the contents. In many cases, this data filter program is designed to remove any data errors that would cause problems with other programs that read the information from the data file. The next set of programs is designed to perform error checking and data analysis on information in a data file. Generate data files to test all features of the programs.

12. Write a program that reads a data file that should contain only integer values and thus should contain only digits, plus or minus signs, and whitespace. The program

should print any invalid characters located in the file, and at the end it should print a count of the invalid characters located.

13. Write a program that analyzes a data file that has been determined to contain only integer values and whitespace. The program should print the number of lines in the file and the number of integer values (not integer digits).

14. Write a program that reads a file that contains only integers, but some of the integers have embedded commas, as in 145,020. The program should copy the information to a new file, removing any commas from the information. Do not change the number of values per line in the file.

15. Write a program that reads a file containing integer and floating-point values separated by commas, which may or may not be followed by additional whitespace. Generate a new file that contains the integers and floating-point values separated only by spaces; remove all whitespace characters between the values, and insert a single space between the values. Do not change the number of values per line in the file.

16. Write a program that reads a file containing data values computed by an accounting software package. While the file contains only numerical information, the values may contain embedded commas and dollar signs, as in $3,200, and negative values are enclosed in parentheses, as in (200.56). Write a program to generate a new file that contains the values with the commas and dollar signs removed, and with a leading minus sign instead of the parentheses. Do not change the number of values per line in the file.

17. A very useful program is one that compares two files, character by character, to determine whether they are exactly the same. Write a program to compare two files. The program should print a message indicating that the files are exactly the same or that there are differences. If the files are different, the program should print the line numbers for lines that are not the same.

18. Developing secret codes has interested people for centuries. A simple coding scheme can be developed by replacing each character in a text file by another character that is a fixed number of positions away in the collating sequence. For example, if each character is replaced by the character that is two characters to its right in the alphabet, then the letter a is replaced by the letter c, the letter b is replaced by the letter d and so on. Write a program that reads the text in a file and then generates a new file that contains the coded text using this scheme. Change only the alphanumeric characters.

19. Write a program to decode the scheme presented in problem 7. Test the program by using files generated by problem 7.

Sounding Rocket Trajectory. Sounding rockets are used to probe different levels of the atmosphere to collect information such as that used to monitor the levels of ozone in the atmosphere. In addition to carrying the scientific package for collecting data in the upper atmosphere, the rocket carries a telemetry system in its nose to transmit data to a receiver at the launch site. Besides the scientific data, performance measurements on the rocket itself are transmitted to be monitored by range safety personnel and to be later analyzed by engineers. These performance data include altitude, velocity, and acceleration data. Assume that this information is stored in a file and that each line contains contains four values: time, altitude, velocity, and acceleration. Assume that the units are s, m, m/s, and m/s^2, respectively.

20. Assume that the file `rocket1.dat` contains an initial line that specifies the number of actual data lines that follows. Write a program that reads these data and determines

 the time at which the rocket begins falling back to earth. (*Hint:* Determine the time at which the altitude begins to decrease.)

21. The number of stages in the rocket can be determined by the number of times that the velocity increases to some peak and then begins decreasing. Write a program that reads these data and determines the number of stages on the rocket. Use the data file `rocket2.dat`. It contains a trailer line with the value −99 for all four values.

22. Modify the program in problem 10 so that it prints the times that correspond to the firing of each stage. Assume that the firing corresponds to the point at which the velocity begins to increase.

23. After each stage of the rocket is fired, the acceleration will initially increase and then decrease to −9.8 m/s^2, which is the downward acceleration due to gravity. Find the periods of the rocket flight during which the acceleration is due only to gravity. Allow the acceleration to range within 65% of theoretical value for these periods. Use the data file `rocket3.dat`, which does not contain a header line or a trailer line.

Suture Packaging. Sutures are strands or fibers used to sew living tissue together after an injury or an operation. Packages of sutures must be sealed carefully before they are shipped to hospitals so that contaminants cannot enter the packages. The object that seals the package is referred to as a *sealing die*. Generally, sealing dies are heated with an electric heater. For the sealing process to be a success, the sealing die is maintained at an established temperature and must contact the package with a predetermined pressure for an established time period. The period in which the sealing die contacts the package is called the dwell time. Assume that the acceptable range of parameters for an acceptable seal are the following:

```
Temperature:        150-170 degrees C
Pressure:           60-70 psi
Dwell time:         2-2.5 s
```

24. A data file named `suture.dat` contains information on batches of sutures that have been rejected during a one-week period. Each line in the data file contains the batch number, temperature, pressure, and dwell time for a rejected batch. The quality control engineer would like to analyze this information and needs a report that computes the percent of the batches rejected due to temperature, the percent rejected due to pressure, and the percent rejected due to dwell time. It is possible that a specific batch may have been rejected for more than one reason, and it should be counted in all applicable totals. Write a program to compute and print these three percentages.

25. Modify the program developed in problem 13 so that it also prints the number of batches in each rejection category and the total number of batches rejected. (Remember that a rejected batch should appear only once in the total, but could appear in more that one rejection category.)

26. Write a program to read the data file `suture.dat` and make sure that the information relates only to batches that should have been rejected. If any batch should not be in the data file, print an appropriate message with the batch information.

Timber Regrowth. A problem in timber management is to determine how much of an area to leave uncut so that the harvested area is reforested in a certain period. It is assumed that reforestation takes place at a known rate per year, depending on climate and soil conditions. A reforestation equation expresses this growth as a function of the amount of timber standing and the reforestation rate. For example, if 100 acres are left standing after harvesting and the reforestation rate is 0.05, then 100 + 0.05 * 100, or 105 acres, are forested at the end of the first year. At the end of the second year, the number of acres forested is 105 + 0.05 * 105, or 110.25 acres.

27. Assume that there are 14,000 acres total with 2,500 acres uncut and that the reforestation rate is 0.02. Print a table showing the number of acres forested at the end of each year for a total of 20 years.
28. Modify the program developed in problem 16 so that the user can enter the number of years to be used for the table.
29. Modify the program developed in problem 16 so that the user can enter a number of acres and the program will determine how many years are required for the number of acres to be completely reforested.

Weather Patterns. In Chapter 1, we discussed the types of information that are collected by the National Weather Bureau. Figure 1.5 contained a sample of the reports that are available with weather information. A group of data files included in the instructors CD that accompanies this text contains weather information for Stapleton International Airport for the period January–December 1991. Each file contains data from 1 month; each line in the file contains 32 pieces of information, in the order shown in Figure 1.5. The data have been edited so that they are totally numeric. If a field of information contained T, for a trace amount, the corresponding value in the data file contains 0.001. There are nine possible weather types, and because several weather types can occur during a single day, nine fields are used to store this information. For example, if weather type 1 occurred, the first of the nine fields will contain a 1; otherwise, it will contain a 0. If weather type 2 occurred, the second of the nine fields will contain a 1; otherwise, it will contain a 0. The peak wind-gust direction has been converted to an integer using the following:

```
N   1
NE  2
E   3
SE  4
S   5
SW  6
W   7
NW  8
```

The values on each line in the data file are separated by blanks, and the data files are named jan91.dat, feb91.dat, and so on.

30. Write a program to determine the number of days that had temperatures in the following categories for January 1991:
    a. Below 0
    b. 0–32
    c. 33–50
    d. 51–60

e. 61–70

f. Over 70

Note that the range of temperatures in one day may fall in several of the categories.

31. Modify the program developed in problem 19 so that it prints percentages instead of the number of days.

32. Modify the program developed in problem 19 so that it uses the period May–August 1991.

33. Write a program that computes the average temperature for days with fog in November 1991.

34. Write a program that determines the date in December 1991 with the largest difference between the maximum temperature and the minimum temperature. Print the date, both temperatures, and the difference.

Critical-Path Analysis. A critical-path analysis is a technique used to determine the schedule for a project. This information is important in the planning stages before a project is begun, and it is also useful to evaluate the progress of a project that is partially completed. One method for this analysis starts by dividing a project into sequential events and then dividing each event into various tasks. Although one event must be completed before the next one is started, various tasks within an event can occur simultaneously. The time it takes to complete an event, therefore, depends on the number of days required to finish its longest task. Similarly, the total time it takes to finish a project is the sum of time it takes to finish each event. Assume that the critical path information for a major construction project has been stored in a data file. Each line of the data file contains an event number, a task number, and the number of days required to complete the task. The data have been stored such that all the task data for event 1 are followed by all the task data for event 2, and so on. Thus, a typical set of data might be as follows:

```
Event        Task        Number of Days
1            15          3
1            27          6
1            36          4
2            15          5
3            18          4
3            26          1
4            15          2
4            26          7
4            27          7
5            16          4
```

35. Write a program to read the critical-path information and print a project completion timetable that lists each event number, the maximum number of days for a task within the event, and the total number of days for the project completion.

36. Write a program to read the critical-path information and print a report that lists the event number and task number for all tasks requiring more than five days.

37. Write a program to read the critical path information and print a report that lists the number of each event and a count of the number of tasks within the event.

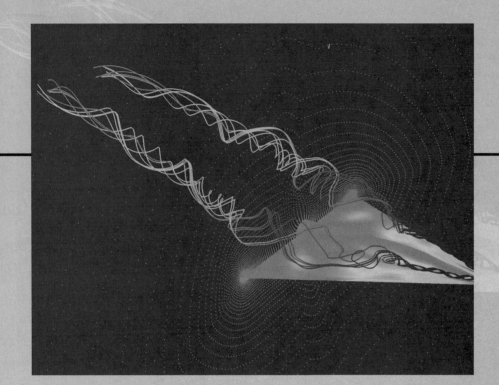

6

ENGINEERING CHALLENGE:
Simulation

Simulation has become recognized as the third paradigm of science, the first two being experimentation and theory. In some cases, simulation is the only approach available for obtaining knowledge that affects good decision making in engineering design. Experimentation may not be possible due to the size of the experiment, the cost of the experiment, or the dangers associated with conducting an experiment. In simulations, mathematical models of physical phenomena are translated into computer software, and simulations are conducted using different data sets and input parameters. The knowledge gained from running simulations can reduce risk, and improve the speed and quality of the design process.

MODULAR PROGRAMMING WITH FUNCTIONS

CHAPTER OUTLINE

OBJECTIVES *In this chapter, we develop problem solutions containing:*

- functions from the standard C++ library
- programmer-defined functions
- functions that generate random numbers

- simulation techniques
- techniques for finding real roots to polynomials
- numerical integration techniques

6.1 Modularity

In the previous chapters, we developed problem solutions that contained a single function named `main()`. When a problem solution is executed, the operating system begins execution with the block of statements defined in `main()`. Thus, every C++ problem solution must contain one, and only one, function named `main()`. If a problem solution does not contain a `main()` function, or if more than one function named `main()` is included, a linking error will occur and the executable file will not be built.

modules

A problem solution can contain additional functions that can be called within `main()`. These functions, or **modules**, are independent blocks of statements, defined outside of `main()`, that typically perform an operation or compute a value. For example, the function `sqrt()`, defined in `cmath`, calculates the square root of a value and can be called by `main()` or any function that requires this computation, provided the header file `<cmath>` has been included.

To maintain simplicity and readability in longer and more complex problem solutions, we develop solutions that use multiple functions rather than writing one long `main()` function. By separating a solution into a group of modules, we make each module simpler and easier to understand, thus adhering to the basic guidelines of structured programming presented in Chapters 3 and 4.

The process of developing a problem solution is often one of "divide and conquer," as was discussed in Chapter 3 when we first presented the decomposition outline. The decomposition outline is a set of sequentially executed steps that solves the problem, so it provides a good starting point for selecting potential functions. In fact, it is not uncommon for each step in the decomposition outline to correspond to one or more function references in the `main()` function.

Breaking a problem solution into a set of modules has many advantages. Because a module has a specific purpose, it can be written and tested separately from the rest of the problem solution. An individual module is smaller than the complete solution, so testing it is easier. Also, once a module has been carefully tested, it can be used in new problem solutions without being retested. For example, suppose that a module is developed to find the average of a group of values. Once this module is written and tested, it can be used in other programs that need to compute an average. This reusability is a very important issue in the development of large software systems because it can save development time. In fact, libraries of commonly used modules (such as the Standard C++ library) are often available on computer systems.

modularity

The use of modules (called **modularity**) often reduces the overall length of a program because many problem solutions include steps that are repeated several places in the program. By placing these repeated steps in a function, the steps can be written once and referenced with a single statement each time that they are needed.

Several programmers can work on the same project if it is separated into modules because the individual modules can be developed and tested independently of each other. This allows the development schedule to be accelerated because some of the work can be done in parallel.

abstraction

The use of modules that have been written to accomplish specific tasks supports the concept of **abstraction.** The modules contain the details of the tasks, and the programmer can reference the modules without worrying about these details. The I/O diagrams that we use in developing a problem solution are an example of abstraction: We specify the input information and the output information without giving the details of how the output information is determined. In a similar way, we can think of modules as "black boxes" that have a specified input and that compute specified information; we can use these modules to help develop a solution. Thus, we are able to operate at a higher level of abstraction to solve problems. For example, the Standard C++ library contains functions that compute the logarithms of values. We can reference these functions without being concerned about the specific details, such as whether the functions are using infinite-series approximations or lookup tables to compute the specified logarithms. By using abstraction, we can reduce the development time of software at the same time that we increase its quality.

To summarize, some of the advantages of modularity are listed below:

- A module can be written and tested separately, thus module development can be done in parallel for large projects.

- A module is a small part of the solution, and thus testing it separately is easier.

- A module is written once and tested, then it can be used many times within a problem solution.

- Once a module is tested carefully, it does not need to be retested before it can be used in new problem solutions.

- The use of modules usually reduces the length of a program, making it more readable.

- The use of modules promotes the concept of abstraction that allows the programmer to "hide" the details in modules; this allows us to use modules in a functional sense without being concerned about the specific details.

Additional benefits of modules will be pointed out as we progress through this chapter.

Structure charts
module charts

Structure charts, or **module charts,** show the module structure of a program. The `main` function references additional functions, which may also reference other functions themselves. Figure 6.1 contains structure charts for some of the programs developed in the Problem Solving Applied sections in this chapter and in the next two chapters. Note that a structure chart does not indicate the sequence of steps that are contained in the decomposition outline. The structure chart shows the separation of the program tasks into modules and indicates which modules reference other modules. Therefore, both the decomposition outline and the structure chart provide different but useful views of a problem solution. Also, note that the structure chart does not contain the modules referenced from the Standard C++ library, because they are used so frequently and because they are an integral part of the C++ environment.

As we begin to develop solutions to more complicated problems, the programs become longer. Therefore, we include here three suggestions for debugging longer programs. First, it is sometimes helpful to run a program using a different compiler because different compilers have different error messages; in fact, some compilers have extensive error messages, whereas others give very little information about some errors. Another useful step in debugging a long program is to add comment indicators (`/*` and `*/`) around some sections of the code so that you can focus on other parts of the program. Of course, you must be careful that you do not comment out statements that affect objects needed for the parts of the program that you want to test. Finally, test complicated functions by themselves. This is usually done with a special program called a **driver,** whose purpose is to provide a simple interface between you and the function that you are testing. Typically, this program will have a `main()` function that asks you to enter the parameters that you want passed to the function, and it then prints the value returned by the function. The usefulness of a driver program will become more apparent as we cover the next few sections.

driver

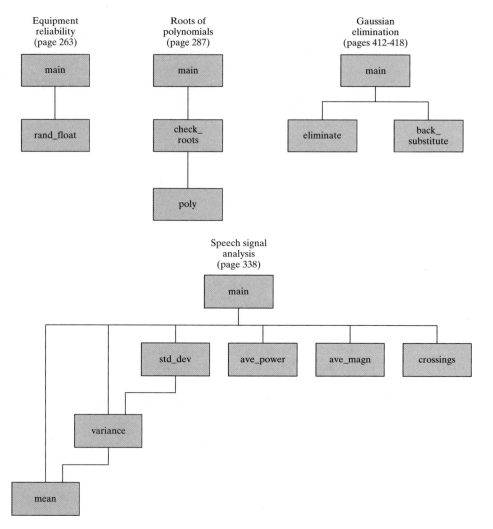

Figure 6.1 Example structure chart.

6.2 Programmer-Defined Functions

The execution of a program always begins with the `main` function. Additional functions are called, or invoked, when the program encounters function names. These additional functions must be defined in the file containing the main function or in another available file or library of files. (If the function is included in a system library file, such as the `sqrt` function, it is often called a **library function;** other functions are usually called **programmer-written,** or **programmer-defined, functions.**) After executing the statements in a function, the program execution continues with the statement that called the function.

library function
programmer-
defined functions

Consider the the simple task of converting from degrees Celsius to degrees Fahrenheit. We can write a programmer defined function to perform this calculation, and call the function from any program solution that requires this conversion. Our conversion function will have one input parameter, a temperature in degrees Celsius, and will return the equivalent temperature in degrees Fahrenheit. To illustrate, we will write a program solution that reads temperatures in degrees Celsius from an input file and writes the degrees Fahrenheit to an output file. The program solution will contain two programmer-defined functions, the function `main()` to perform the input and output, and the function `CelsiusToFahr()` to perform the conversion. The structure chart and flowchart for our conversion program are provided in Figure 6.2 followed by our solution and a Program Trace.

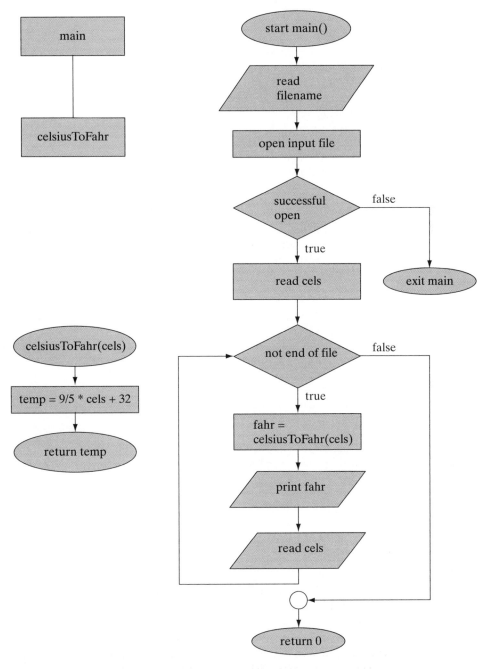

Figure 6.2 Structure chart and flowchart for temperature conversion program.

```cpp
#include<iostream> //Required for cin, cerr
#include<fstream> //Required for ifstream, ofstream
#include<string> //Required for string, c_str()
using namespace std;

//Function prototype.
double celsiusToFahr(double celsius); //Programmer defined function.

/*-------------------------------------------------------------*/
/* Program chapter6_1                                          */
/* This program reads temperatures in degrees Celsius          */
/* from an input file, calls a conversion function             */
/* and writes converted temperatures to an output file.        */
int main()
{
  //Declare variables.
  ifstream fin;
  ofstream fout;
  string filename;
  double cels, fahr;;

  //Open files.
  cout << "Enter name of input file\n ";
  cin >> filename;
  fin.open(filename.c_str());
  if(fin.fail())
  {
    cerr << "Could not open the file " << filename << endl;
    exit(1);
  }
  fout.open( (filename + "ToFahr").c_str() );
  fin >> cels;

  //while not end of file
  while(!fin.eof())
  {
    //Convert temperature and write to file.
    fahr = celsiusToFahr(cels); //Function call.
    fout << fahr << endl;
    fin >> cels;
  }
  fin.close();
  fout.close();
  return 0;
}
/*-------------------------------------------------------------*/
/* This function performs a conversion from                    */
/* degrees Celsius to degrees Fahrenheit.                      */
/* Precondition: celsius holds a temperature in degrees Celsius */
/* Postcondition: returns degrees Fahrenheit                   */
```

```
double celsiusToFahr(double celsius) //Function header.
{
  //Declare local variables.
  double temp;

  //Convert from degrees celsius to degrees Fahrenheit.
  temp = (9.5/5.0)*celsius + 32.0;

  return temp;
}
```

Notice that the function celsiusToFahr() includes no input statements and no output statements, only the statements required to perform the temperature conversion and to return the new value. The input and output is performed in main(). We will now provide a partial program trace for program chapter6_1, beginning with the fin >> cels; statement.

Program Trace

main( )

Step 1: fin >> cels;
Step 2: while(!end of file)
     Step 2A: fahr = celsiusToRahr(cels);
 	
     Step 2E: fout << fahr;
     Step 2F: fin   << cels;
Step 3: fin.close(.);
Step 4: fout.close();
Step 5: return 0;

celsiusToFahr (double cels)
Step 2B: double temp; Step 2C: temp = 9.5/5 * cels + 32; Step 2D: return temp;

Function Definition

function header

parameter list

As we look more closely at the functions we have defined thus far in the text, we see that a function definition consists of a **function header** followed by a statement block. A function header defines the type of value that is returned by the function: int for main() and double for celsiusToFahr() in the example given in the previous section. If a function does not return a value, the return type is void. The function name and a **parameter list** follow the return type. Note, that the parameter list may be empty as in our definition of main(). The general form of a function definition is

```
return_type function_name(parameter list)
{
    declarations;
    statements;
}
```

function body

The parameter list represents the information passed to the function; if there are no input parameters the parameter list can be omitted. However, the function name must always be followed by a set of parentheses, as we do when defining int main(). Additional objects used by a function are defined in the statement block that defines the **function body**.

A function name should be selected to help document the purpose of the function. Comments should also be included within the function to further describe the purpose of the function and to document the steps. *We also use a comment line with dashes to separate a programmer-defined function from the main function and from other programmer-defined functions.*

All functions that return a value must include a `return` statement. The general form of the `return` statement is

```
return expression;
```

The expression specifies the value to be returned to the statement that referenced the function. The expression type used in the `return` statement should match the return_type indicated in the function definition to avoid potential errors. The cast operator (discussed in Chapter 2) can be used to explicitly specify the type of the expression if necessary. A `void` function does not return a value, and thus has this general function header:

```
void function_name(parameter declarations)
```

The `return` statement in a `void` function is optional, and it does not contain an expression. The general form is

```
return;
```

Function Definition: A function definition consists of a function header followed by a statement block.

Syntax:

```
return-type function name([parameter list]) //function header
{
   //Statement block
}
```

Examples:

```
int main()
{
  cout << "hello world" << endl;
  return 0;
}

void drawBlock(ostream& out, int size)
{
  int width, height;
  for(height=0; height<size; ++height)
  {
    for(width=0; width<size; ++width)
    {
      out << "*";
    }
    out << endl;
  }
}
```

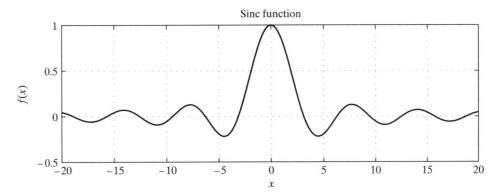

Figure 6.3 Sinc function in [−20, 20].

Functions can be defined before or after the main function. Remember that a right brace specifies the end of the statement block that defines the body of a function. However, one function must be completely defined before another function definition begins; function definitions cannot be nested within each other. *In our programs, we include the main function first, and then additional functions are included in the order in which they are referenced in the program.*

We will now present second example of a program that uses a programmer-defined function. The *sinc(x)* function, plotted in Figure 6.3, is commonly used in many engineering applications. The most common definition for *sinc(x)* is the following:

$$f(x) = sinc(x)$$

$$= \frac{sin(x)}{x}.$$

The values of this function can be easily computed, except for *sinc(0)*, which gives an indeterminant form of 0/0. In this case, l'Hopital's theorem from calculus can be used to prove that *sinc(0) = 1*.

Assume that we want to develop a program that allows the user to enter interval limits, a and b. The program should then compute and print 21 values of *sinc(x)* for values of *x* evenly spaced between a and b, inclusively. Thus, the first value of *x* should be a. An increment should then be added to obtain the next value of *x*, and so on, until the 21st value, which should be b. Therefore, the increment in *x* is

$$x\_increment = \frac{interval\_width}{20} = \frac{b - a}{20}.$$

Select values for a and b, and convince yourself that, with this increment, and with a as the first value, the 21st value will be b.

Because *sinc(x)* is not part of the mathematical functions provided by the Standard C++ library, we implement this problem solution two ways. In one solution, we include the statements to perform the computations of *sinc(x)* in the main function; in the other solution, we write a programmer-defined function to compute *sinc(x),* and then reference the programmer-defined function each time that the computations are needed. Both solutions are now presented so that you can compare them:

Solution 1

```
/*------------------------------------------------------*/
/*   Program chapter6_2                                 */
/*                                                      */
/*   This program prints 21 values of the sinc          */
/*   function in the interval [a,b] using               */
/*   computations within the main function.             */

#include<iostream> //Required for cin, cout.
#include<cmath> //Required for sin().
using namespace std;

int main()
{
   // Declare objects.
   double a, b, x_incr, new_x, sinc_x;


   // Get interval endpoints from the user.
   cout << "Enter end points a and b (a<b): \n";
   cin >> a >> b;
   x_incr = (b - a)/20;


   // Set Formats
   cout.setf(ios::fixed);
   cout.precision(6);


   // Compute and print table of sinc(x) values.
   cout << "x and sinc(x) \n";
   for (int k=0; k<=20; ++k)
   {
      new_x = a + k*x_incr;
      if (fabs(new_x) < 0.0001)
      {
         sinc_x = 1.0;
      }
```

```
        else
        {
            sinc_x = sin(new_x)/new_x;
        }
        cout << new_x << " " << sinc_x << endl;
    }


    //  Exit program.
    return 0;
}
/*-------------------------------------------------------*/
```

Solution 2

```
/*-------------------------------------------------------*/
/*  Program chapter6_3                                   */
/*                                                       */
/*  This program prints 21 values of the sinc            */
/*  function in the interval [a,b] using a               */
/*  programmer-defined function.                         */
/*                                                       */

#include<iostream> //Required for cin, cout
#include<cmath> //Required for sin().
using namespace std;

//Function Prototype
//Programmer defined function.
double sinc(double x);

int main()
{
    //  Declare objects
    double a, b, x_incr, new_x;

    //  Get interval endpoints from the user.
    cout << "Enter endpoints a and b (a<b): \n";
    cin >> a >> b;
    x_incr = (b- a)/20;

    //  Set Formats
    cout.setf(ios::fixed);
    cout.precision(6);
```

```
        //  Compute and print table of sinc(x) values.
        cout << "x and sinc(x) \n";
        for (int k=0; k<=20; k++)
        {
           new_x = a + k*x_incr;
           cout << new_x << " " << sinc(new_x) << endl;
        }


        //  Exit program.
        return 0;
   }
/*------------------------------------------------------*/
/*  This function evaluates the sinc function.        */

double sinc(double x)
{
   if (fabs(x) < 0.0001)
   {
      return 1.0;
   }
   else
   {
      return sin(x)/x;
   }
 }
/*------------------------------------------------------*/
```

The following output represents a sample interaction that could occur with either program:

```
Enter endpoints a and b  (a<b):
-5 5
x and sinc(x)
-5.000000 -0.191785
-4.500000 -0.217229
-4.000000 -0.189201
-3.500000 -0.100224
-3.000000 -0.047040
-2.500000 0.239389
-2.000000 0.454649
-1.500000 0.664997
-1.000000 0.841471
-0.500000 0.958851
0.000000 1.000000
0.500000 0.958851
1.000000 0.841471
1.500000 0.664997
```

```
2.000000  0.454649
2.500000  0.239389
3.000000  0.047040
3.500000  -0.100224
4.000000  -0.189201
4.500000  -0.217229
5.000000  -0.191785
```

Figure 6.4 contains plots of the 21 values computed for four different intervals [a, b]. The program computes only 21 values, so the resolution in the plots is affected by the size of the interval: A smaller interval has better resolution than a larger interval. Note that the main function of solution 2 is easier to read because it is shorter than the main function in the first solution.

The main function in solution 2, and the main function in program chapter6_1 each contained a function prototype statement that was placed above the main function. In the following section we discuss function prototypes and look more closely at the interaction between a statement that references a function and the function definition itself.

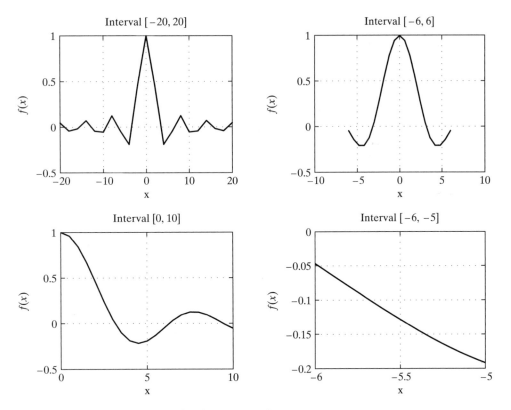

Figure 6.4 Program output for four intervals.

Function Prototype

The solution presented in program `chapter6_3` contained the following statement above the `main` function definition:

```
double sinc(double x);
```

function prototype

This statement is called a **function prototype**. The prototype declares that `sinc()` expects an argument of type `double` and returns a value of type `double`. The compiler can now check all future references to `sinc()` to insure that the reference is compatible with the function prototype. Note that the compiler does not need the identifier `x` to check future references to `sinc()`. In fact, the following function prototype statement is also valid for program `chapter 6_3`.

```
double sinc(double);
```

Both of these function prototypes provide the same information to the compiler. *We recommend using identifiers in function prototypes because the identifiers help document the order and definition of the parameters.*

Function Prototype Statements: A function prototype provides information to the compiler to allow the compiler to detect potential errors when a function is referenced.

Syntax:

        return-type function name([parameter list]);

Examples:

  Prototype:
```
double sinc(double x);
```
  Valid references:
```
double y(-5);
cout << sinc(y);
cout << sinc(1.5);
cout << sinc(10);
y = sinc(0.0);
```
  Invalid reference: ERROR MESSAGE:
```
sinc("1.5");
sinc('0');
```
                                     Invalid string argument, expected double

                                     Invalid char argument, expected double

  Prototype:
```
void clearScreen(ostream&);
```
  Valid reference:
```
clearScreen(cout);
```
  Invalid reference: ERROR MESSAGE
```
cout<<clearScreen(cout);
```
                                     std::operator<<error, clearScreen() is a void function

Function prototypes should be included at the top of a program file, outside of any statement block, in order to make the function prototypes available to all functions defined within the file. In other words, including function prototypes at the top of the program file, outside all statement blocks, gives the function prototypes **file scope** or **global scope.** Scope will be discussed in more detail in the following section. Header files, such as `cmath`, contain function prototypes for the functions included in the library files; otherwise, we would need to include individual prototypes for functions such as `log()` and `sqrt()` in our programs.

file scope
global scope

If a program references a large number of programmer-defined functions, it becomes cumbersome to include all the function prototype statements. In these cases, a **custom header file** can be defined that contains the function prototypes and any related symbolic constants. A header file should have a file name that ends with a suffix of .h. The file is then referenced with an include statement, using double quotes around the file name. In this chapter, we develop a set of functions for computing common statistics from a set of values. If a header file containing the corresponding function prototypes is named `stat_lib.h`, then the prototypes are all included in a program with this statement:

custom header file

```
#include "stat_lib.h"
```

Custom header files are often used to accompany routines that are shared by programmers. Note that custom header files are programmer defined so the name of the file is enclosed within double quotes, rather than < > characters. If the custom header file is not in the same directory as the executable file, the complete path to the file must preceed the filename.

6.3 Parameter Passing

A function header defines the parameters required to reference a function; these are called **formal parameters.** Any statement that references a function must provide values that correspond to the parameters; these are called **actual parameters** or **function arguments.** For example, consider the `sinc` function developed earlier in this section. The function header is

formal parameters
function arguments

```
double sinc (double x).
```

Suppose a `main` function references this function with the following statement:

```
cout << newX << " " << sinc(newX) << endl;
```

The formal parameter is `x` and the function argument is `newX`. When the `sinc` function is referenced in the `cout` statement, the value of the function argument is assigned to the formal parameter `x` and the statement block following the function header is executed. The value returned by `sinc()` is streamed to the standard output buffer and printed to the screen along with the value of `newX`.

It is important to note that the value of a formal parameter is not assigned back to the function argument. We illustrate these steps with a memory snapshot that shows the transfer of the value from the function argument to the formal parameter, assuming that the value of `newX` is 5.0 at the time the `sinc` function is called:

```
main()                          sinc(double x)
function argument               formal parameter

double newX 5.0                 double x 5.0
```

local

After the value in the function argument is copied to the formal parameter, the steps in the `sinc()` function are executed. When debugging a function, it is a good idea to use `cout` statements to provide a memory snapshot of the function arguments before the function is referenced, and of the formal parameters at the beginning of the function. Formal parameters are defined only within the statement block that defines the body of the function and cannot be referenced outside of the block. Thus, formal parameters are refered to as **local** parameters.

Pass by Value

pass by value

pass by reference

The C++ programming language uses a **pass by value** for parameter passing, as illustrated by the `sinc()` function. When a function reference is made, the value of the argument is passed to the function and assigned as the value of the corresponding formal parameter. In general, a C++ function cannot change the value of the function argument. Exceptions occur when the function arguments are arrays (discussed in Chapter 8) or the formal parameters are declared to be **pass by reference,** which will be discussed in the next section.

Since the formal parameter, x, in the `sinc` function is a pass by value parameter, valid arguments to the *sinc* function can be expressions, and other function calls, as shown in the following statement:

```
cout << sinc(x+2.5) << endl;   //argument is expression x+2.5

double y;
cin >> y;
cout << sinc(y) << endl;

z = x*x + sinc(2.0*x); //argument is expression 2.0*x

w = sinc(fabs(y));   //argument is value returned by fabs (y).
```

coercion of
arguments

If a function has formal parameters, the formal parameters and the function arguments must match in number, type, and order. A mismatch between the number of formal parameters and function arguments can be detected by the compiler by referring to the function prototype. If the type of a function argument is not the same as the corresponding formal parameter, then the value of the function arguments may be converted to the appropriate type; this conversion is also called **coercion of arguments** and may cause errors. The coercion occurs according to the discussion given in Chapter 2, which discussed moving values stored as one type to an object with a different type. Converting values to a higher type (such as from `float` to `double`) generally works correctly; converting values to a lower type (such as from `double` to `int`) often introduces errors. To illustrate the coercion of arguments, consider the following function that returns the maximum of two values:

```
/*-----------------------------------------------------------*/
/*   This function returns the maximum of two       */
/*   integer values.                                */

int theMax(int a, int b)
{
   if (a > b)
   {
      return a;
   }
```

```
   else
   {
      return b;
   }
}
/*-----------------------------------------------------*/
```

Assume that a reference to this function is theMax(xSum, ySum) and that xSum and ySum are integers containing the values 3 and 8, respectively. Then the following memory snapshot shows the transfer of values from the function arguments to the formal parameters when the reference theMax(xSum, ySum) is made:

function arguments	formal parameters	
int xSum 3	int a 3	a receives the value of xSum
int ySum 8	int b 8	b receives the value of ySum

The statements in the function will then return the value 8 as the value of the reference theMax(xSum, ySum).

Now suppose that a reference to the function theMax() is made using double objects t1 and t2. If t1 and t2 contain the values 2.8 and 4.6, respectively, then the following transfer of parameters occurs when the reference theMax(t1, t2) is executed:

function arguments	formal parameters	
double t1 2.8	int a 2	a receives the value 2
double t2 4.6	int b 4	b receives the value 4

The statements in the function will then return the value 4 to the statement containing the reference theMax(t1, t2). Obviously, the wrong value has been returned by the function. However, the problem is not in the function; the problem is that the function was referenced with the wrong types of function arguments.

Additional errors can be introduced if the function arguments are out of order. These errors may not be detected by the compiler and can be difficult to detect upon examination of the code; therefore, be especially careful that the order of the formal parameters and the function arguments match.

Practice!

Consider the following function:

```
/*-----------------------------------------------------*/
/*  This function counts positive parameters.     */

int positive(double a, double b, double c)
{
   int count;
```

```
count = 0;
if (a >= 0)
{
    ++count;
}
if (b >= 0)
{
    ++count;
}
if (c >= 0)
{
    ++count;
}
return count;
}
/*- - - - - - - - - - - - - - - - - - - - - - - - - - - - - - - - - - - - - - - - - - - - - */
```

Assume that the function is referenced with the following statements:

```
x = 25;
total = positive(x, sqrt(x), x-30);
```

1. Show the memory snapshot of the formal parameters and the function arguments.

2. What is the new value of `total`?

Pass by Reference

When a formal parameter is a pass by value parameter, the value of the corresponding function argument cannot be modified within the function body. When the purpose of a function is to modify one or more of the function arguments, the corresponding formal parameters

address

must receive the **address** of the arguments to be modified, instead of the value. This type of parameter passing is referred to as pass by reference.

To illustrate when we need to use pass by reference parameters, we develop a function that exchanges, or swaps, the contents of two integer variables. Three assignment statements and a temporary integer variable are required to exchange two values. A statement block performing the swap and a memory snapshot are provided below.

	integer a	integer b	integer hold
`{`			
`int hold, a(5), b(10);`	5	10	?
`hold = a;`	5	10	5
`a = b;`	10	10	5
`b = hold;`	10	5	5
`}`			

In problem solutions that require frequent swapping of values, such as sorting programs, it is convenient to write a function to perform this task. Consider the following function, that attempts to perform a swap of two integer arguments using pass-by-value parameters.

```
/********************************************************************/
/* Incorrect function that attempts to swap two integer value      */
/* using pass-by-value parameters.                                  */

void swapIntegers(int a, int b)
{
   //Define temporary variable;
   int hold=a;

   //Swap the values in a and b
   a = b;
   b = hold;

   //exit void function
   return;
}
```

We will test this function with the following driver program:

```
/********************************************************************/
/* Driver program to test swapIntegers(int a, int b)               */

#include<iostream>//Required for cin, cout.
using namespace std;

//Function prototype
void swapIntegers(int, int);

int main()
{
   //Declare variables.
   int a, b;

   //Get values for a and b.
   cout << "enter two integer values: ";
   cin >> a >> b;

   //Print values of a and b before the swap
   cout << "Before swap:\n a is " << a << " b is " << b << endl;

   //Call swap function and print values
   swapIntegers(a, b);
   cout << "After call to swapIntegers\n a is " << a << " b is "
        << b << endl;

   //Exit main
   return 0;
}
```

A sample run of our driver program produces the following results:

```
enter two integer values: 5 10                    Pass by value
  Before swap:                              main()          swapIntegers
  a is 5 b is 10                          a  5            a  5
After call to swapIntegers                b  10           b  10
  a is 5 b is 10
```

We see that the function arguments were not modified. Since the function swapIntegers uses pass-by-value parameters, the values of the function arguments, not the addresses, are passed to the formal parameters. The values of the formal parameters are correctly swapped, but no change is made to the function arguments.

After considering this incorrect solution, we see that we need two pass by reference parameters in order to correctly modify the two corresponding function arguments. To specify a pass by reference, an ampersand (&) is appended to the data type of each formal parameter in the function header and the function prototype. This is the only modification that we need to make. The ampersand instructs the compiler to pass the address of the function argument to the corresponding formal parameter, instead of the value. The correct solution, and a program trace, are provided below.

```
/***************************************************************/
/* Correct function to swap two integer value                 */
/* using pass-by-reference parameters.                        */

void swapIntegers(int& a, int& b)
{
  //Define temporary variable;
  int hold=a;

  //Swap the values in a and b
  a = b;
  b = hold;

  //exit void function
  return;
}
```

We will test this function with the following driver program:

```
#include<iostream> //Required for cin, cout.
using namespace std;

//Function prototype
void swapIntegers(int&, int&);
int main()
{
  //Declare variables.
  int a, b;
```

```
//Get values for a and b.
cout << "enter two integer values: ";
cin >> a >> b;

//Print values of a and b before the swap
cout << "Before swap:\n a is " << a << " b is " << b << endl;

//Call swap function and print values
swapIntegers(a,b);
cout << "After call to swapIntegers\n a is " << a
     << " b is " << b << endl;

//Exit main
return 0;
}
```

A sample run of our driver program produces the following results:

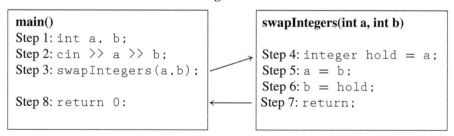

```
enter two integer values: 5 10
Before swap:
 a is 5 b is 10
After call to swapIntegers
 a is 10 b is 5
```

To further illustrate pass by reference, we provide a trace of the execution of our program, omitting the `cout` statements. Note that directed arrows are used to indicate that the formal parameters reference, or point to the function arguments when pass by reference is used.

Program Trace

main()	**swapIntegers(int a, int b)**
Step 1: `int a, b;` Step 2: `cin >> a >> b;` Step 3: `swapIntegers(a,b);` Step 8: `return 0:`	Step 4: `integer hold = a;` Step 5: `a = b;` Step 6: `b = hold;` Step 7: `return;`

Memory Snapshot

	main()	**swapIntegers(int a, int b)**
Step 1:	integer a `?` integer b `?`	
Step 2:	integer a `5` integer b `10`	

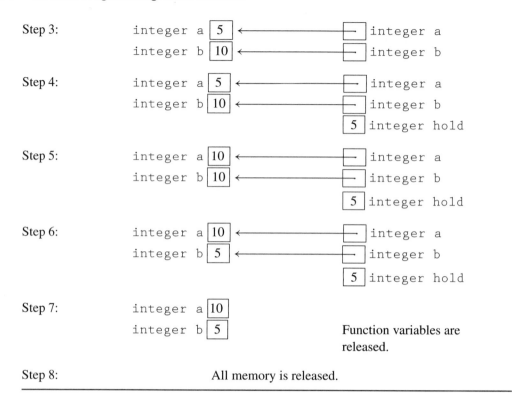

Step 3: integer a [5] ← [—] integer a
         integer b [10] ← [—] integer b

Step 4: integer a [5] ← [—] integer a
         integer b [10] ← [—] integer b
                                [5] integer hold

Step 5: integer a [10] ← [—] integer a
         integer b [10] ← [—] integer b
                                [5] integer hold

Step 6: integer a [10] ← [—] integer a
         integer b [5] ← [—] integer b
                                [5] integer hold

Step 7: integer a [10]
         integer b [5]   Function variables are
                                          released.

Step 8:   All memory is released.

Recall that function arguments and formal parameters must agree in order, type and number, but the names do not have to be the same. In the above example we chose to use the same identifiers for the function arguments and the formal parameters. This is allowable because the identifiers are defined within different statement blocks. However, it is important to realize that a and b defined in the `main` function occupy different memory locations than a and b defined in the function header. Function arguments that correspond to pass by reference parameters must be variables, since their values can be modified. Constants and expressions cannot be passed as arguments to pass-by-reference parameters.

Modify!

1. Modify the driver program developed in the previous section by adding the following function call:

```
swapIntegers(10, 5);
```

What results do you see when you attempt to compile and execute the program? Explain.

Modify!

2. Modify the driver program developed in the previous section by adding the following function call:

```
swapIntegers(a, a * b);
```

What results do you see when you attempt to compile and execute this program? Explain.

Practice!

In problems 1–4, consider the references to the swapIntegers function. For invalid reference, explain why the reference is invalid. For valid references, give a memory snapshot before and after the reference.

1. ```
   int x=1, y=3;
   . . .
   swapIntegers(x,y);
   ```

2. ```
   . . .
   swapIntegers(10,5);
   ```

3. ```
   int x=1, y=3;
   . . .
   swapIntegers(x, y+5);
   ```

4. ```
   double x=1.5, y=3.2;
   . . .
   swapIntegers(x,y);
   ```

5. What is output by the following program?

```
#include<iostream>
using namespace std;

void fun_ch6(int first, int& second);

int main()
{
    int n1(0), n2(0);
    fun_ch6(n1,n2);
    cout << n1 << endl << n2 << endl;
    return 0;
}
void fun_ch6(int first, int& second)
{
        first++;
        second += 2;
        return;
}
```

Storage Class and Scope

scope

In the sample programs presented thus far, we have declared objects within a `main` function and within programmer-defined functions, and we have placed our function prototypes before the main function. It is also possible to define an object before the `main` function. This affects the **scope** of the object, where scope refers to the portion of the program in which it is valid to reference the object. Scope is also sometimes defined in terms of the portion of the program in which the object is visible or accessible. It is important to be able to determine the scope of a function or object. Because the scope of an object is directly related to its **storage class,** we also discuss the four storage classes: automatic, external, `static`, and `register`.

storage class

local
global

First, we define the difference between **local** and **global** or **file** scope. Local objects are defined within a function and thus include the formal parameters and any other objects declared in the function. A local object can be accessed only in the function that defines it. A local object has a value when its function is being executed, but its value is not retained when the function is completed. Global objects are defined outside the main function or other programmer-defined functions. The definition of a global object is outside of all functions, so it can be accessed by any function within the program file. The **automatic storage class** is used to represent local objects; this is the default storage class, but it can also be specified with the keyword `auto` before the type designation. The **external storage class** is used to represent global objects.

automatic storage
class
external storage
class

Consider a program that contains the following statements:

```cpp
#include <iostream>
using namespace std;

int count(0);
...
int main()
{
   int x, y, z;
   ...
}
int calc(int a, int b)
{
   int x;
   count += x;
   ...
}
void check(int sum)
{
   count += sum;
   ...
}
```

The object `count` is global and thus can be referenced by the functions `calc()` and `check()`. The objects x, y, and z are local objects that can be referenced only in the `main` function; similarly, the objects a, b, and x are local objects that can be referenced only in the function `calc()`, and sum is a local object that can be referenced only in the function `check()`. Note that there are two local objects named x—these are two different objects with different scopes.

The memory assigned to a global object is retained for the duration of the program. Although a global object can be referenced from a function, using global objects is generally discouraged. *In general, parameters are preferred for transferring information to a function because the parameter is evident in the function prototype, whereas the global object is not visible in the function prototype. The use of nonconstant global objects should be avoided.*

Style

Function names also have external storage class, and thus can be referenced from other functions. Function prototypes, and #include directives included outside of any function are also global, and thus are available to all other functions in the program; this explains why we do not need to include the header file cmath in every function that references a mathematical function.

static storage class

The **static storage class** is used to specify that the memory for a local object should be retained during the entire program execution. Therefore, if a local object in a function is given a static storage class assignment by using the keyword static before its type specification, the object will not lose its value when the program exits the function in which it is defined. A static object could be used to count the number of times that a function was invoked, because the value of the count would be preserved from one function call to another. The following program illustrates the use of the static storage class:

```
#include<iostream>
using namespace std;

void ch6_static();

int main()
{
    ch6_static();
    ch6_static();
    ch6_static();
}

void ch6_static()
{
    int x(0);
    static int count(0);
    x++;
    count++;
    cout << x << ',' << count;
    return;
}
```

The first time the function ch6_static() is called the objects x and count are defined and initialized. Since count is static and retains its value, the initialization is ignored on all subsequent calls to the function. The output from this program is as follows:

```
1,1
1,2
1,3
```

The keyword register is used before the type designation of an object to specify that it should be placed in a register or high speed memory location. Accessing registers is faster than accessing memory, so this class of storage is used for frequently accessed values.

Because the availability of high speed memory is limited, it may not be possible to honor the request and the object will be placed in a regular memory location.

6.4 Problem Solving Applied: Calculating a Center of Gravity

When piloting an aircraft, it is necessary to know the weight and center of gravity of the aircraft before takeoff. If the aircraft is overloaded, it may be difficult or impossible to achieve lift. If the center of gravity is outside of the designated limits, the aircraft may be difficult to control. In this section, we perform computations to determine the total weight and center of gravity of an aircraft.

1. PROBLEM STATEMENT

Determine the total weight and center of gravity of an aircraft, based on the number of crew members (a maximum of two is allowed) and the weight of the cargo (a maximum of 5,000 pounds is allowed). To compute the center of gravity, the program will take each weight and multiply it by its distance from the nose of the airplane. These products, called moments, are added together, and the sum is divided by the total weight to give us the center of gravity. The empty weight of the aircraft is known to be 9,021 pounds, and its empty center of gravity is 305 inches from the nose of the aircraft. Thus, the empty moment is 2,751,405 inch–pounds. The aircraft can hold a maximum of 540 gallons of fuel. For simplicity, we will assume that the tank is full at the time of takeoff and, with a fuel weight of 6.7 pounds per gallon, the fuel moment is known to be 1169167.3 inch–pounds.

2. INPUT/OUTPUT DESCRIPTION

The I/O diagram illustrates that the inputs to this program are the number of crew members (one to two) and the weight of the cargo. The output is a report of the total weight of the aircraft and the center of gravity. Built in data types `int` and `double` will be used for all data objects.

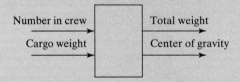

3. HAND EXAMPLE

Suppose two crew members board the aircraft with a total cargo weight of 100 pounds. Assuming an average weight of 160 pounds per person, we calculate the crew moment as follows:

Number of crew members * average weight per person *
distance from crew to nose of aircraft.

The cargo moment is calculated as follows:

cargo weight * distance from cargo bay to nose of aircraft.

The aircraft manual gives the distance in inches from nose of aircraft to the crew seats as 120 inches and the distance from the nose of the aircraft to the cargo bay as 345 inches. Thus, the crew moment is

$$2 * 160 * 120 = 38400 \text{ inch–pounds.}$$

The cargo moment is

$$100 * 345 = 34500 \text{ inch–pounds.}$$

The total weight of the aircraft is

crew weight + cargo weight + fuel weight + weight of the empty aircraft, or

$$320 + 100 + 3618 + 9021 = 13059 \text{ pounds.}$$

The center of gravity is the sum of the moments divided by the total weight:

$$= (38400 + 34500 + 2751405 + 1169167.3) \text{ inch–pounds/13059 pounds}$$
$$= 1438172.3 \text{ inch–pounds/13059 pounds} = 305.802 \text{ inches.}$$

4. ALGORITHM DEVELOPMENT

We first develop the decomposition outline because it divides the solution into a series of sequential steps:

Decomposition Outline

1. Read the number of crew members and the cargo weight.

2. Calculate total weight.

3. Calculate the center of gravity.

Step 1 involves prompting the user to enter the necessary information. Since the number of crew and the amount of cargo have limits, error checking on the data is required. This step is a good candidate for a function. Step 3 requires the value of each moment. We will write value returning functions to calculate the required moments. We will use global constants for the values assumed in the problem statement. The refinement in pseudocode is as follows:

```
Refinement in Pseudocode
main:  Get_Data(crew, cargo)
       calculate total_weight
       calculate center_of_gravity
       print center_of_gravity, total_weight
```

The steps in the pseudocode are detailed enough to convert to C++:

```
/*---------------------------------------------------------------------*/
/* Program chapter6_4                                                  */
/* This program calculates the total weight and                       */
/* center of gravity of an aircraft.                                  */
#include<iostream>   //Required for cin, cout
using namespace std;

//Program Assumptions

const double PERSON_WT(160.0);          //Average weight/person
const double FUEL_MOMENT(1169167.3);    //Fuel moment for full tank
const double EMPTY_WT(9021.0);          //Standard empty weight
const double EMPTY_MOMENT(2751405.0);   //Standard empty moment
const double FUEL_WT(3618.0);           //Full fuel weight
const double CARGO_DIST(345.0);
const double CREW_DIST(120.0);

//function prototypes

double CargoMoment(double);
double CrewMoment(int);
void GetData(int&, double&);

int main()
{

   //Declare objects.
   int crew; //number of crew on board (1 or 2)
   double cargo;   //weight of baggage, pounds
   double total_weight, center_of_gravity;

   //Set format flags.
   cout.setf(ios::fixed);
   cout.setf(ios::showpoint);
   cout.precision(1);

   GetData(crew, cargo);

   total_weight = EMPTY_WT + crew*PERSON_WT + cargo
                  + FUEL_WT;

   center_of_gravity = (CargoMoment(cargo) + CrewMoment(crew)
                     + FUEL_MOMENT + EMPTY_MOMENT)/total_weight;

   cout << endl << "The total weight is " << total_weight
                << " pounds. \n"
        << "The center of gravity is " << center_of_gravity
        << " inches from the nose of the plane.\n";
   return(0);
}//end main
```

```
/*---------------------------------------------------------------*/
double CargoMoment(double weight)
{
    return(CARGO_DIST*weight);
}//end CargoMoment
/*---------------------------------------------------------------*/
double CrewMoment(int crew)
{
    return(CREW_DIST*crew*PERSON_WT);
}//end CrewMoment
/*---------------------------------------------------------------*/
void GetData(int& crew, double& cargo)
{
  cout << "enter number of crew members (Maximum of 2) ";
  cin >> crew;
  while(crew <= 0 || crew > 2)
  {
    cout << endl << crew
         << " is an invalid entry\n"
         << " re-enter number of crew, 0 < crew <= 2  ";
    cin >> crew;
  }//end while
  cout << crew << " crew members, thank you.\n\n";
  cout << "enter weight of cargo (Maximum of 5000 lbs) ";
  cin >> cargo;
  while(cargo < 0 || cargo > 5000)
  {
    cout << endl << cargo
         << " is an invalid entry"
         << " re-enter cargo weight, 0 < cargo <= 5000\n  ";
    cin >> cargo;
  }//end while
  cout << cargo << " pounds of cargo loaded.  Thank you.\n\n";
  return;
}//end getdata
/*---------------------------------------------------------------*/
```

5. TESTING

If we use the data from the hand example, we have the following interaction with the program (the total weight and center of gravity match the one that we computed by hand):

```
enter number of crew members (Maximum of 2) 2
2 crew members, thank you.
enter weight of cargo (Maximum of 5000 lbs) 100
100.0 pounds of cargo loaded.  Thank you.

The total weight is 13059.0 pounds.
The center of gravity is 332.3 inches from the nose of the plane.
```

Modify!

1. Modify the `GetData()` function to perform error checking and correcting for bad data, such as floating point data for the number of crew or character data. Test your function.

2. Modify the program by adding a second cargo bay that is 522 inches from the nose of the aircraft and has a maximum cargo weight of 1000 pounds.

6.5 Random Numbers

random numbers

A sequence of **random numbers** is not defined by an equation; instead, it has certain characteristics that define it. These characteristics include the minimum and maximum values, the average, and whether the possible values are equally likely to occur or whether some values are more likely to occur than others. Sequences of random numbers can be generated from experiments, such as tossing a coin, rolling a die, or selecting numbered balls. Sequences of random numbers can also be generated using the computer.

Many engineering problems require the use of random numbers in the development of a solution. In some cases, the numbers are used to develop a simulation of a complicated problem. The simulation can be run over and over to analyze the results, and each run represents a repetition of the experiment. We also use random numbers to approximate noise sequences. For example, the static that we hear on a radio is a noise sequence. If we are testing a program that uses an input data file that represents a radio signal, we may want to generate noise and add it to a speech signal or a music signal in order to provide a more realistic signal.

Engineering applications often require random numbers distributed between specified values. For example, we may want to generate random integers between 1 and 500, or we may want to generate random floating-point values between 5 and −5. We now present discussions on generating random numbers between two specified values. The random numbers generated are equally likely to occur; that is, if the random number is supposed to be an integer between 1 and 5, each of the integers in the set 1, 2, 3, 4, 5 is equally likely to occur. Another way of saying this is that each integer has a probability of 0.20 of occurring for each run. Any values in a specified set are also called uniform random numbers or uniformly distributed random numbers.

Integer Sequences

The Standard C++ library contains a function `rand` that generates a random integer between 0 and RAND_MAX, where RAND_MAX is a system-dependent integer defined in `cstdlib`. (A common value for RAND_MAX is 32,767.) The rand function has no input arguments and is referenced by the expression `rand()`. Thus, to generate and print a sequence of two random numbers, we could use this statement:

```
cout << "random numbers: " << rand() << " " << rand() << endl;
```

The same two values are printed each time that a program containing this statement is executed because the `rand` function generates integers in a specified sequence. (Because this sequence eventually begins to repeat, it is sometimes called a pseudorandom sequence instead of a random sequence.) However, if we generate additional random numbers in the same program, they will be different. Thus, this pair of statements generates four random numbers:

```
cout << "random numbers: " << rand() << " " << rand() << endl;
cout << "random numbers: " << rand() << " " << rand() << endl;
```

Each time that the `rand()` function is referenced in a program, it generates a new value; however, each time that the program is run, it generates the same sequence of values.

random number
seed

To cause a program to generate a new sequence of random values each time that it is executed, we need to give a new **random number seed** to the random-number generator. The function `srand()` (from `cstdlib`) specifies the seed for the random-number generator; for each seed value, a new sequence of random numbers is generated by `rand()`. The argument of the `srand()` function is an unsigned integer that is used in computations that initialize the sequence; the seed value is not the first value in the sequence. If an `srand()` function is not used before the `rand()` function is referenced, the computer assumes that the seed value is 1. Therefore, if you specify a seed value of 1, you will get the same sequence of values from the `rand()` function that you will get without specifying a seed value.

In the next program, the user is asked to enter a seed value, and then the program generates 10 random numbers. Each time that the user executes the program and enters the same seed, the same set of 10 random integers is generated; each time that a different seed is entered, a different set of 10 random integers is generated. The function prototype statements for `rand()` and `srand()` are included in `cstdlib`.

```
/*------------------------------------------------------*/
/*   Program chapter6_5                                 */
/*                                                      */
/*   This program generates and prints ten             */
/*   random integers between 1 and RAND_MAX.           */

#include <iostream> //Required for cin, cout
#include <cstdlib> //Required for srand(), rand(),
using namespace std;

int main()
{
   //  Declare objects.
   unsigned int seed;

   //  Get seed value from the user.
   cout << "Enter a positive integer seed value: \n";
   cin >> seed;
   srand(seed);   //Seed random number generator.

   //  Generate and print ten random numbers.
   cout << "Random Numbers: \n";
   for (int k=1; k<=10; ++k)
```

```
    {
        cout << rand() << ' ';  //Print a random number.
    }
    cout << endl;
    //  Exit program.
    return 0;
}
/*-------------------------------------------------------------*/
```

A sample output follows, using g++ on a Linux system:

```
Enter a positive integer seed value:
123
Random Numbers:
128959393 1692901013 436085873 748533630 776550279 289139331
807385195 556889022 95168426 1888844001
```

Experiment with the program on your computer system; use the same seed to generate the same numbers, and use different seeds to generate different numbers.

Because the prototype statements for `rand()` and `srand()` are included in `cstdlib`, we do not need to include them separately in a program. However, it is instructive to analyze these prototype statements. Because the `rand()` function returns an integer and has no input, its prototype statement is

```
int rand();
```

Because the `srand()` function returns no value and has an unsigned integer as an argument, its prototype statement is

```
void srand(unsigned int);
```

Generating random integers over a specified range is simple to do with the `rand()` function. For example, suppose that we want to generate random integers between 0 and 7. The following statement first generates a random number that will be between 0 and RAND_MAX and then uses the modulus operator to compute the modulus of the random number and the integer 8:

```
x = rand()%8;
```

The result of the modulus operation is the remainder after `rand()` is divided by 8, so the value of x can assume integer values between 0 and 7.

Suppose that we want to generate a random integer between −25 and 25. The total number of possible integers is 51, and a single random number in this range can be computed with the statement

```
y = rand()%51 - 25;
```

This statement first generates a value between 0 and 50, and then subtracts 25 from the value, yielding a new value between −25 and 25.

We can now write a function that generates an integer between two specified integers, a and b. The function first computes n, which is the number of all integers between a and b, inclusive; this value is equal to b − a + 1. The function then uses the modulus operation with the rand() function to generate a new integer between 0 and $n - 1$. Finally, the lower limit, a, is added to the new integer to give a value between a and b. All three steps can be combined in one expression on the return statement in the function:

```
/*-----------------------------------------------------*/
/*   This function generates a random integer          */
/*   between specified limits a and b (a<b).           */

int rand_int(int a, int b)
{
    return rand()%(b-a+1) + a;
}
/*-----------------------------------------------------*/
```

To illustrate the use of this function, the next program generates and prints 10 random integers between user-specified limits. The user also enters the seed to initiate the sequence:

```
/*-----------------------------------------------------*/
/*   Program chapter6_6                                */
/*                                                     */
/*   This program generates and prints ten random      */
/*   integers between user-specified limits.           */

#include <cstdlib>  //Required for srand(), rand().
#include <iostream> //Required for cin, cout.
using namespace std;

//  Function prototype.
int rand_int(int a, int b);

int main()
{
    //  Declare objects.
    unsigned int seed;
    int a, b;

    //  Get seed value and interval limits.
    cout << "Enter a positive integer seed value: \n";
    cin >> seed;

    //Seed the random number generator.
    srand(seed);
    cout << "Enter integer limits a and b (a<b): \n";
    cin >> a >> b;

    //  Generate and print ten random numbers.
    cout << "Random Numbers: \n";
    for (int k=1; k<=10; ++k)
    {
        cout << rand_int(a,b) << ' ';
    }
    cout << endl;
```

```
    //  Exit program.
    return 0;
}


/*-----------------------------------------------------*/
/*  This function generates a random integer           */
/*  between specified limits a and b (a<b).             */

int rand_int(int a, int b)
{
    return rand()%(b-a+1) + a;
}
/*-----------------------------------------------------*/
```

A sample set of values generated from this program's as follows:

```
Enter a positive integer seed value:
13
Enter integer limits a and b (a<b):
-5 5
Random Numbers:
3  1  4  -4  0  4  0  0  -3  0
```

Remember that the values generated are system dependent; you should not expect to get this same set of random numbers from a different compiler.

Modify!

Use the program developed in this section to generate several sets of random integers in each of the following ranges using different seed values.

1. 0 through 500

2. -10 through 200

3. -50 through -10

4. -5 through 5

Floating-Point Sequences

In many engineering problems, we need to generate random floating-point values in a specified interval $[a, b]$. The computation to convert an integer between 0 and RAND_MAX to a floating-point value between a and b has three steps. The value from the rand() function is first divided by RAND_MAX to generate a floating-point value between 0 and 1. The value between 0 and 1 is then multiplied by $(b - a)$, which is the width of the interval $[a, b]$, to give a value between 0 and $(b - a)$. The value between 0 and $b - a$ is then added to a to adjust it so that it will be between a and b. These three steps are combined in the expression on the return statement in the following function.

```
/*------------------------------------------------------------*/
/*   This function generates a random                         */
/*   double value between a and b.                            */

double rand_float(double a, double b)
{
  return ((double)rand()/RAND_MAX)*(b-a) + a;
}
/*------------------------------------------------------------*/
```

Note that a cast operator was needed to convert the integer `rand()` to a `double` value so that the result of the division would be a `double` value.

The program presented earlier in this section can easily be modified to generate and print floating-point values. A sample set of values from such a modification is the following:

```
Enter a positive integer seed value:
82
Enter limits a and b (a<b):
-5 5
Random Numbers:
3.64335 -1.51118 2.9090 2.21546 -4.37439 -4.23527
0.709869 -3.41159 -4.86308 -0.958863
```

Modify!

Modify the program for generating integers to one that generates 10 random floating-point values within a user-specified range. Then, generate several sets of numbers from each of the following ranges, using different seed values:

1. 0.0 through 1.0

2. 0.1 through 1.0

3. −5.0 through −4.5

4. −5.1 through 5.1

6.6 Problem Solving Applied: Instrumentation Reliability

An analysis of the reliability of a piece of equipment is especially important if it is going to be used in situations that would be dangerous if it should fail or in environments that are not easily accessible.

Equations for analyzing the reliability of instrumentation can be developed from the study of statistics and probability, where the reliability is the proportion of the time that the component works properly. Thus, if a component has a reliability of 0.8, then it should work properly 80% of the time. The reliability of combinations of components can also be determined if the individual component reliabilities are known. Consider the diagrams in Figure 6.5. For information to flow from point a to point b in the series design, all three components must work properly. In the parallel design, only one of the three components must work properly for information to flow from point a to point b. If we know the reliability

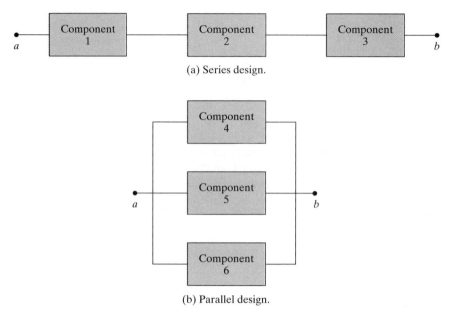

(a) Series design.

(b) Parallel design.

Figure 6.5 Series and parallel configurations.

of an individual component, then the reliability of a specific combination of components can be determined in two ways; an analytical reliability can be computed using theorems and results from probability and statistics, and a computer simulation can be developed to give an estimate of the reliability.

Consider the series configuration of Figure 6.5(a). If r is the reliability of a component and if all three components have the same reliability, then it can be shown that the reliability of the series configuration is r^3. Thus, if the reliability of each component is 0.8 (which means that a component works properly 80% of the time), then the analytical reliability of the series configuration is 0.8^3, or 0.512. That is, this series configuration should work properly 51.2% of the time.

Consider the parallel configuration of Figure 6.5(b). At least one of the components must not fail for this configuration to work properly. The equation that describes a parallel configuration is:

$$R = 1 - \prod_{i=0}^{n}(1 - r_i)$$

where:

R is the reliability of the configuration

n is the number of components

r_i is the reliability of the ith component.

If all three components have the same reliability, then the reliability equation for the parallel configuration in Figure 6.5(b) reduces to $3r - 3r^2 + r^3$. Thus, if the reliability of each component is 0.8, then the analytical reliability of the parallel configuration is $3(0.8) - 3(0.8)^2 + (0.8)^3$, or 0.992. The parallel configuration should work properly 99.2% of the time.

Your intuition probably also tells you that the parallel configuration is more reliable, because only one of the components must be working for the overall configuration to perform properly, whereas all three components must work properly for the series configuration to perform properly.

We can also estimate the reliability of these two designs using random numbers from a computer simulation. First, we need to simulate the performance of a single component. If the reliability of a component is 0.8, then it works properly 80% of the time. To simulate this performance, we could generate a random value between 0 and 1. If the value is between 0 and 0.8, we can assume that the component worked properly; otherwise, we assume that it failed. (We could also have used the values 0 to 0.2 to signify a failure and 0.2 to 1.0 to signify that a component worked properly.) To simulate the series design with three components, we would generate three floating-point random numbers between 0 and 1. If all three numbers are less than or equal to 0.8, then the design works for this one trial; if any one of the numbers is greater than 0.8, then the design does not work for this one trial. If we run hundreds or thousands of trials, we can compute the proportion of the time that the overall design works. This simulation estimate is an approximation to the analytically computed reliability.

To estimate the reliability of the parallel design with a component reliability of 0.8, we again generate three random floating-point numbers between 0 and 1. If any one of the three numbers is less than or equal to 0.8, then the design works for this one trial; if all of the numbers are greater than 0.8, then the design does not work for one trial. To estimate the reliability determined by the simulation, we divide the number of trials for which the design works by the total number of trials performed.

As indicated by the previous discussion, we can use computer simulations to provide a validation for the analytical results because the simulated reliability should approach the analytically computed reliability as the number of trials increases. There are also cases in which it is very difficult to analytically compute the reliability of a piece of instrumentation. In these cases, a computer simulation can be used to provide a good estimate of the reliability.

Develop a program to compare the analytical reliabilities of the series and parallel configurations in Figure 6.5 with simulation results. Allow the user to enter the individual component reliability and the number of trials to use in the simulation.

1. PROBLEM STATEMENT

Compare the analytical and simulation reliabilities for a series configuration with three components and for a parallel configuration with three components. Assume that all components have the same reliability.

2. INPUT/OUTPUT DESCRIPTION

The I/O diagram shows that the input values are the component reliability, the number of trials, and a random-number seed for initiating the sequence. The output consists of the analytical reliability and the simulation reliability for the series and the parallel configurations.

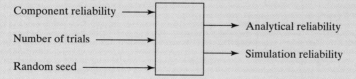

3. HAND EXAMPLE

For the hand example, we use a component reliability of 0.8 and three trials. Since each trial requires three random numbers, assume that the first nine random numbers generated are the following. (These were generated from the *rand_float* function using a seed of 6,666 for values between 0 and 1.)

The first set of three random values is

```
0.939775    0.0422243    0.929037
```

The second set of three random values is

```
0.817733    0.211689    0.9909
```

The third set of three random values is

```
0.0377037    0.103508    0.407272
```

From each group of three random numbers, we can determine whether a series configuration would work properly and whether a parallel configuration would work properly. For the first and second groups of three random numbers, two of the values are greater than 0.8, so only the parallel configuration would work properly. Both configurations work properly with the third set of random numbers. Thus, the analytical results (computed earlier in this section) and the simulation results for three trials are the following:

```
Analytical Reliability:
Series: 0.512 Parallel:  0.992
Simulation for 3 Trials
Series: 0.333333 Parallel:  1
```

As we increase the number of trials, the simulation results should approach the analytical results. If we change the random-number seed, the simulation results may also change, even with only three trials.

4. ALGORITHM DEVELOPMENT

We first develop the decomposition outline because it divides the solution into a series of sequential steps.

Decomposition Outline

1. Read component reliability, number of trials, and random-number seed.

2. Compute analytical reliabilities.

3. Compute simulation reliabilities.

4. Print comparison of reliabilities.

Step 1 involves prompting the user to enter the necessary information and then reading it. Step 2 uses the equations given earlier to compute the analytical reliabilities. Because the computations are straightforward, we compute them in the main function.

Step 3 involves a loop to generate the random numbers and to determine whether the configurations would perform properly for each trial. The *rand_float()* function is used to compute the random numbers in the loop. In step 4, we print the results of the computations. The structure chart for this solution was shown in Figure 6.1. The refinement in pseudocode is the following:

Refinement in Pseudocode

```
main:   read component reliability, number of trials,
            and random number seed
        compute analytical reliabilities
        set series_success to zero
        set parallel_success to zero
        set k to 1
        while k <= number of trials
            generate three random numbers between 0 and 1
            if each number <= component reliability,
                increment series_success by 1
            if any number <= component reliability,
                increment parallel_success by 1
            increment k by 1
        print analytical reliabilities
        print simulation reliabilities
```

The steps in the pseudocode are now detailed enough to convert to C++. We also include the *rand_float()* function in the program:

```
/*-------------------------------------------------------*/
/*  Program chapter6_7                                   */
/*                                                       */
/* This program estimates the reliability               */
/* of a series and a parallel configuration             */
/* using a computer simulation.                          */

#include <iostream> //Required for cin, cout.
#include <cstdlib> //Required for srand(), rand().
#include <cmath>   //Required for pow().
using namespace std;

//  Function prototypes
double rand_float(double a, double b);

int main()
{
   //  Declare objects.
   unsigned int seed;
   int n;
   double component_reliability, a_series, a_parallel,
          series_success(0), parallel_success(0),
          num1, num2, num3;
   //  Get information for the simulation.
```

```
       cout << "Enter individual component reliability: \n";
       cin >> component_reliability;
       cout << "Enter number of trials: \n";
       cin >> n;
       cout << "Enter unsigned integer seed: \n";
       cin >> seed;
       srand(seed);
       cout << endl;

       //  Compute analytical reliabilities.
       a_series = pow(component_reliability,3);
       a_parallel = 3*component_reliability
                    - 3*pow(component_reliability,2)
                    + pow(component_reliability,3);

       //  Determine simulation reliability estimates.
       for (int k=1; k<=n; k++)
       {
         num1 = rand_float(0,1);
         num2 = rand_float(0,1);
         num3 = rand_float(0,1);
         if (((num1<=component_reliability) &&
              (num2<=component_reliability)) &&
              (num3<=component_reliability))
         {
               series_success++;
         }

         if (((num1<=component_reliability) ||
              (num2<=component_reliability)) ||
              (num3<=component_reliability))
         {
               parallel_success++;
         }
       }

       //  Print results.
       cout << "Analytical Reliability \n";
       cout << "Series: " << a_series << "   "
            << "Parallel: " << a_parallel << endl;
       cout << "Simulation Reliability " << n << " trials \n";
       cout << "Series: " << (double)series_success/n << " Parallel: "
            << (double)parallel_success/n << endl;

       //  Exit program.
       return 0;
}
/*-----------------------------------------------------------*/
/*  This function generates a random                         */
```

```
/*   double value between a and b.                           */
double rand_float(double a, double b)
{
   return ((double)rand()/RAND_MAX)*(b-a) + a;
}
/*---------------------------------------------------------*/
```

5. TESTING

If we use the data from the hand example, we have the following interaction, and the output matches the data that we computed by hand:

```
Enter individual component reliability:
0.8
Enter number of trials:
3
Enter unsigned integer seed:
6666

Analytical Reliability
Series: 0.512  Parallel: 0.992
Simulation Reliability, 3 trials
Series: 0.333333  Parallel: 1
```

Here are results from two more simulations that demonstrate that the simulation results approach the analytical results as the number of trials increases:

```
Enter individual component reliability:
0.8
Enter number of trials:
100
Enter unsigned integer seed:
123

Analytical Reliability
Series: 0.512  Parallel: 0.992
Simulation Reliability, 100 trials
Series: 0.54  Parallel: 0.97
Enter individual component reliability:
0.8
Enter number of trials:
1000
Enter unsigned integer seed:
3535

Analytical Reliability
Series: 0.512  Parallel: 0.992
Simulation Reliability, 1000 trials
Series: 0.514  Parallel: 0.995
```

Modify!

These problems relate to the program developed in this section, which compares the analytical and simulated reliabilities.

1. Use this program to compute information comparing the simulation results for 10, 100, 1,000, and 10,000 trials, assuming that the component reliability is 0.85.

2. Use this program to compute information comparing the simulation results for 1,000 trials, using five different random-number seeds. Assume that the component reliability is 0.75.

3. What component reliability is necessary to give a series reliability of 0.7? (*Hint:* Use the analytical reliability equation.) Validate your answer using this program.

4. What component reliability is necessary to give a parallel reliability of 0.9? Using the analytical reliability equation is not as easy in this case. If your calculator does not find roots of polynomial equations, just experiment with the program until you are close to the desired reliability.

5. Perform the required algebra to show that the equation $R = 1 - \prod_{c=0}^{3} (1 - r_c)$ reduces to $3r - 3r^2 + r^3$ when r_c is the same for each component.

6.7 Defining Class Methods

In Chapters 2 and 3, we developed a partial programmer-defined data type named `Point`, resulting in the following `class` declaration.

```
/*------------------------------------------------------------*/
/* Point class Chapter3_7                                     */
/* Filename: Point.h                                          */
class Point
{
   //Type declaration statements
   //Data members.
   private:
   double xCoord, yCoord; //Class attributes

   public:
   //Declaration statements for class methods
   //Constructors for Point class
   Point(); //default constructor
   Point(double x, double y); //parameterized constructor

   //Overloaded operators
   double operator -(const Point& p2) const;
   bool operator ==(const Point& p2) const;
};
/*------------------------------------------------------------*/
```

The constructors and overloaded operators declared in the `Point` class declaration are methods or member functions of the `Point` class. Recall from Chapter 2 that methods define the operations that can be performed on a `class` object. The current definition of our `Point` class has a very limited set of operations. An application can declare and initialize `Point` objects using either of the two constructor methods, but an application does not have access to the attributes of `Point` objects. Thus, once a `Point` object is initialized, its value cannot be modified, and the value of the private attributes cannot be accessed by the application. In this section, we will define a set of accessor methods and a set of mutator methods to provide a better public interface for our user-defined data type, `Point`.

Public Interface

encapsulation

The public interface of a well-designed data type provides a complete, yet minimal, set of `public` methods and hides the implementation of the data type through **encapsulation**. Encapsulation requires that direct access to the `class` attributes be restricted to the member functions defined within the `class` and `friend` functions. The keyword `friend` will be discussed in Chapter 10. Encapsulation and a good public interface allow for efficient maintenance and expansion of a data type. We have used the keyword `private` in the `Point` class declaration to restrict access to the attributes. Thus, with the current `public` interface, an application cannot access or modify the value of a `Point` object. Consider the test program shown below:

```
#include <iostream>
#include " Point.h"
using namespace std;
int main()
{
  Point p1;
  cout << p1.xCoord << endl;
  return 0;
}
```

This program attempts to print the value of the private data member, `xCoord`, of the `Point` object p1. The syntax `p1.xCoord` is correct, but the compiler will generate an error message in this case because `xCoord` is a private attribute. The error message generated when this program was compiled using the **g++** compiler on a **MacBook Pro** is shown below.

Ingbers-MacBook-Pro:Programs jaingber$ g++ main.cpp Point.cpp
Point.h: In function 'int main()':
Point.h:9: error: 'double Point::xCoord' is private
main.cpp:7: error: within this context

A good `public` interface requires a complete set of `public` methods to support the `private` attributes of the class. Since our `Point` class has two `private` attributes, we will add four additional methods to our `public` interface: two accessor methods and two mutator methods. The expanded `class` declaration is given below.

```
/*------------------------------------------------------------*/
/* Point class Chapter6_7                                     */
/* Filename: Point.h                                          */
class Point
{
  //Type declaration statements
  //Data members.
  private:
  double xCoord, yCoord; //Class attributes

  public:
  //Declaration statements for class methods
  //Constructors for Point class
  Point(); //default constructor
  Point(double x, double y); //parameterized constructor

  //Overloaded operators
  double operator -(const Point& rhs) const;
  bool operator = =(const Point& rhs) const;

  //Accessor Methods
  double getX() const {return xCoord;}
  double getY() const {return yCoord;}


  //Mutator Methods
  void setX(double newX);
  void setY(double newY);

};
/*------------------------------------------------------------*/
```

Accessor Methods

Accessor methods are value-returning member functions with an empty parameter list. The sole purpose of an accessor method is to *return* the value of an attribute. Because accessor methods are small, simple methods, they can be defined within the `class` declaration. The current convention is to name these methods get *Attribute*(). Notice that we use the `const` modifier in the definition of our accessor methods. Accessor methods are intended to provide read-only access to an attribute, and the use of the `const` modifier enforces this. Any attempt to modify a `private` attribute within a `const` method will result in a compilation error, as illustrated in our test program. To illustrate the use of accessor methods, we will modify our test program to use the accessor method `getX()`, to print the value of the x coordinate of a point.

```
#include <iostream>
#include " Point.h"
using namespace std;
```

```
int main()
{
   Point p1(2.3, -7.1);
   cout << p1.getX() << endl;
   return 0;
}
```

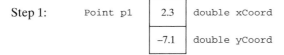

```
main()

Step1: Point p1 (2.3, -7.1)



Step6: cout << p1.getX () << endl;

Step8: return 0;
```

```
Point::Point (double x, double y)
Step2: cout << "Constructing Point object,
                  parameterized: \n";
Step3: cout << "input parameters: " << x
                  << "," << y << endl;
Step4:  XCoord = X;
Step5:  yCoord = y;
```

```
Point::getX ()

Step7: return xCoord;
```

Memory snapshot: main()

Step 1:   Point p1

2.3	double xCoord
–7.1	double yCoord

Figure 6.6 Program trace and memory snapshot.

Since the accessor method `getX()` is `public`, the test program now compiles without error and prints the value 2.3 to standard output when executed as shown below. A program trace and memory snapshot is provided for illustration in Figure 6.6

```
Ingbers-MacBook-Pro:Programs jaingber$ g++ main.cpp Point.cpp
Ingbers-MacBook-Pro:Programs jaingber$ ./a.out
Constructing Point object, parameterized:
input parameters: 2.3,-7.1
2.3
```

Note that the g++ compiler writes the executable code to a file named `a.out`. The command `./a.out` asks the operating system to executes the file `a.out`, found in the current working directory (`./`).

Mutator Methods

Mutator methods are defined as `void` member functions with one or more input parameter. The sole purpose of a mutator method is to *mutate*, or change, the value of the calling object. Input parameters allow an application to specify a new value to be assigned to an attribute. The current convention is to name these methods `set` *Attribute*(). Notice that we do not use the `const` modifier in the prototypes of the mutator methods as we did with the accessor methods. We have defined the mutator methods in the `class` implementation. The expanded `class` implementation is given below.

```cpp
/*-----------------------------------------------------------*/
/* Point Class Chapter6_7                                    */
/* filename: Point.cpp                                       */
#include " Point.h"        //Required for Point
#include <iostream>    //Required for cout
#include <cmath>        //Required for sqrt() and pow()
using namespace std;

//Parameterized constructor
Point::Point(double x, double y)
{
  //input parameters x,y
  cout << " Constructing Point object, parameterized: \n" ;
  cout << " input parameters: "  << x << " ,"  << y << endl;
  xCoord = x;
  yCoord = y;
}

//Default constructor
Point::Point()
{
   cout << " Constructing Point object, default: \n" ;
   cout << " initializing to zero"  << endl;
   xCoord = 0.0;
   yCoord = 0.0;
}
//Distance Formula
double Point::operator -(const Point& rhs) const
{
  double t1, t2, d;
  t1 = rhs.xCoord - xCoord; //(x2-x1)
  t2 = rhs.yCoord - yCoord; //(y2-y1)
  d = sqrt( pow(t1,2) + pow(t2,2) );
  return d;
}
bool Point::operator ==(const Point& rhs) const
{
  if(rhs.xCoord == xCoord &&
     rhs.yCoord == yCoord )
  {
    return true;
  }
  else
  {
    return false;
  }

}
```

```
void Point::setX(double xVal)
{
    xCoord = xVal;
}
void Point::setY(double yVal)
{
    yCoord = yVal;
}
```

A `class` method has access to all of the data members of the calling object. We see in the implementation of the mutator method `setX()` that the value of the input parameter `xVal` is assigned to the private attribute `xCoord`. Similarly, in the mutator method `setY()`, the value of the input parameter `yVal` is assigned to `private` attribute `yCoord`.

Method Definition: A method is a function that is a member of a `class`. The definition of a method consists of a header followed by a statement block. The header must include the name of the `class`, followed by the scope resolution operator and the name of the method.

Syntax:

> *return-type class-name::method-name([parameter list])[modifier]*
> *{*
> *   //Statement block*
> *}*

Examples:

```
double Point::getX() const
{
    return xCoord;
}

void Point::setX(double newX)
{
    xCoord = newX;
}
```

Our definition of a point in plane does not restrict the set of values that can reasonably be assigned to the x and y coordinates. Any value in the set of real numbers is reasonable, so no validation of the input parameter is required in the mutator methods. It is often the case when defining a new data type that a natural restriction may exist on the value that can be assigned to one or more of the data members. If we defined a new data type to represent a circle and we defined the circle as a point in a plane and a radius, it would not be reasonable to assign a negative value to the radius. To avoid creating a meaningless object, a test can be performed within each mutator method before assigning a new value. If the input data is not within the range of allowable values, the error can be handled within the method. Thus, a mutator method allows an application to modify the value, or state of an object, yet maintains control over the state of the object. This is extremely beneficial in reducing the propagation of error that can occur when bad data is inadvertently processed. Validating data within a mutator method is illustrated in Chapter 10.

We will now write a small driver program to test the mutator methods in our `Point` class. The output generated by the driver is given below. A program trace and memory snapshot are provided in Figure 6.7.

```
/*------------------------------------------------------------*/
/* Driver program to test Point class                        */
/* filename main.cpp                                         */
#include " Point.h"
#include <iostream>
using namespace std;
```

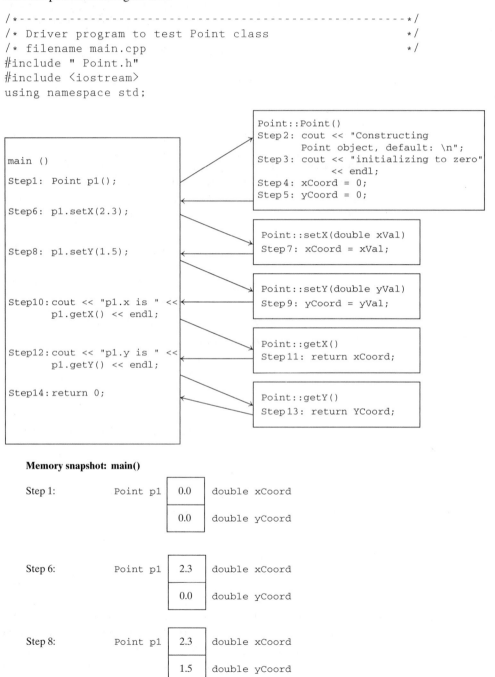

Memory snapshot: main()

Step 1:   Point p1 | 0.0 | double xCoord
                         | 0.0 | double yCoord

Step 6:   Point p1 | 2.3 | double xCoord
                         | 0.0 | double yCoord

Step 8:   Point p1 | 2.3 | double xCoord
                         | 1.5 | double yCoord

Figure 6.7 Program trace and memory snapshot of driver program.

```
int main()
{
  Point p1;
  p1.setX(2.3);
  p1.setY(1.5);
  cout <<   " p1.x is " << p1.getX() << endl;
  cout <<   " p1.y is " << p1.getY() << endl;
  return 0;
}
```

```
Ingbers-MacBook-Pro:Programs jaingber$ g++ main.cpp Point.cpp
Ingbers-MacBook-Pro:Programs jaingber$ ./a.out
Constructing Point object, default:
initializing to zero
p1.x is 2.3
p1.y is 1.5
```

Practice!

The following questions refer to the Point class developed in this section.
Consider the program given below:

```
#include "Point.h"
#include <iostream>
using namespace std;
int main()
{
  Point p1, p2; //line 1
  p1.xCoord = 3; //line 2
  cout <<p1.getY(); //line 3
  cout << p1 - p2 << endl; //line 4
  return 0;
}
```

1. Will this program compile?

2. Is line 1 a valid statement? Explain.

3. Is line 2 a valid statement? Explain.

4. Is line 3 a valid statement? Explain.

5. Is line 4 a valid statement? Explain.

6. Add a mutator method to the Point class that will allow an application to modify both the x and y coordinates. The prototype is: void setXY(double xVal, double yVal);

6.8 Problem Solving Applied: Design of Composite Materials

The design of advanced composite materials is an important problem in many areas of science and engineering. As an example of their application, encapsulating materials are now being engineered to insulate critical components in electronic assemblies from thermal and mechanical shock. It may be important for an encapsulating material to be tough against penetration on the outside while providing damping from vibration on the inside near the electronic assembly. In this simulation, we are modeling a molten plastic material containing suspended alumina particles in a space between two cylinders. Initially, the alumina particles are uniformly distributed. When the inner cylinder is rotated, the alumina particles migrate away from the inner cylinder towards the outer cylinder. More toughness exists with a higher concentration of alumina particles, and better vibrational dampening occurs with fewer particles. For this exercise, we are interested in determining the percentage of particles that lie outside the critical radius, as illustrated in Figure 6.8. We will use a data file named `composite-MaterialsSim1.dat`, created during a simulation, as our input file.

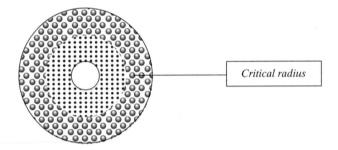

Figure 6.8 Particles suspended between two cylinders.

1. PROBLEM STATEMENT

A data file named `compositMaterialsSim1.dat` holds the x,y location of particles recorded during a simulation. Write a C++ program to determine the percentage of the particles that lie outside a user-specified critical radius.

2. INPUT/OUTPUT DESCRIPTION

The inputs to this program are a data file named *compositMaterialsSim1.dat* and the critical radius. The first line in the data file holds the radius of the outer cylinder, followed by the radius of the inner cylinder. Each remaining line holds the x and y location of a particle. The critical radius may vary and is entered by the user from the keyboard.

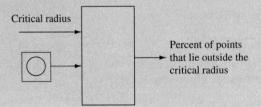

3. HAND EXAMPLE

We will work a hand example using only four particles, as illustrated in the following diagram:

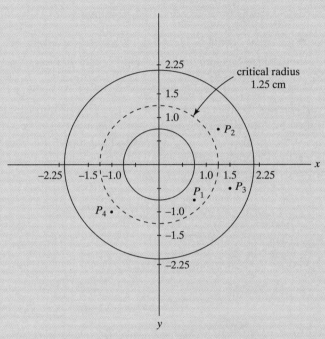

Our data file for this hand example is

2.0	0.75
0.75	−0.75
1.25	0.75
1.5	−0.5
−1.0	−1.0

and we are using a critical radius of 1.25.

We see in Figure 6.8 that the center of the two cylinders is at the origin. Using the distance formula to calculate the distance from the origin to each point in the data file, we get the following results:

Distance from p1 to the origin: 1.06066
Distance from p2 to the origin: 1.45774
Distance from p3 to the origin: 1.58114
Distance from p4 to the origin: 1.41421

There are a total of four points, and three of them lie outside of the critical radius. Thus, 3/4*100 or 75% of the points lie outside of the critical radius.

4. ALGORITHM DEVELOPMENT

Decomposition Outline

1. Initialize counters for calculating percentage.

2. Input critical radius from user and data from input file.

3. Calculate distance from origin for each point.

4. Compare distance and increment the appropriate counters.

5. Print percentage of points that lie outside the critical radius.

Step 2 involves reading the data. The critical radius is read once, as is the first line of input file. To read the remaining point data from the input file, we will use an end-of-file loop, because the number of points is not specified in the file. Steps 3 and 4 will be performed inside the loop. We will write a value-returning function to perform step 3. Step 5 is performed outside the loop, after all of the data has been read from the input file.

```
Refinement in Pseudocode
      main:  Initialize counters for percentage
             Read critical radius
             Read radius of outer cylinder and inner cylinder
             Read x and y
             while not end-of-file
                 increment point counter
                 calculate distance from origin
                 if distance is greater than origin
                         increment outside counter
             Print percentage of points outside critical radius
```

The steps in the pseudocode are now detailed enough to convert to C++. We will provide two solutions to this application. The first solution uses our programmer-defined `Point` class. The second solution uses only built-in C++ data types.

Solution 1:

```cpp
/*-------------------------------------------------------------------*/
/*  Program chapter6_8                                               */
/*                                                                   */
/*  This program calculates the percentage points that lie          */
/*  outside of a critical radius.                                    */

#include <iostream>  //Required for cin, cout
#include <fstream>   //Required for file input
#include "Point.h"   //Programmer-defined data type
using namespace std;

int main()
{
  //Declare objects
  const Point ORIGIN(0,0);
```

```
Point p;
int pointCount(0), outside(0);
double x,y,criticalRad;
double dist, radiusOuter, radiusInner;

//open input file
ifstream fin("compositeMaterialsSim1.dat");
if(fin.fail())
{
  cout << "Could not open data file compositeMaterialsSim1.dat"
       << endl;
  exit(1);
}

//Input critical radius from user
cout << "Enter critical radius ";
cin  >> criticalRad;

//Input radius of outer and inner cylinders
fin  >> radiusOuter >> radiusInner;

//While not end of file, input point data
fin >> x >> y;
while(!fin.eof())
{
  ++pointCount;  //increment point count
  p.setX(x);
  p.setY(y);
  dist = p - ORIGIN;
  if(dist > criticalRad)
  {
     ++outside;  //increment outside counter
  }
  fin >> x >> y;
}

//Print results
//Pre-Multiply by 100.0 to force floating point arithmetic
cout << (100.0*outside/pointCount)
     << "% lie outside the critical radius" << endl;
return 0;
}
```

Solution 2:

```
/*-------------------------------------------------------------*/
/*  Program chapter6_9                                         */
/*                                                             */
/*  This program calculates the percentage points that lie    */
/*  outside of a critical radius.                              */
```

```cpp
#include <iostream>  //Required for cin, cout
#include <fstream>   //Required for file input
using namespace std;

//Function Prototypes
double distance(double x1, double y1, double x2, double y2);

int main()
{
  //Declare objects
  int pointCount(0), outside(0);
  double x,y,criticalRad;
  const double xORIGIN(0), yORIGIN(0);
  double dist, radiusOuter, radiusInner;

  //open input file
  ifstream fin("compositeMaterialsSim1.dat");
  if(fin.fail())
  {
    cout << "Could not open data file compositeMaterialsSim1.dat"
        << endl;
    exit(1);
  }

  //Input critical radius from user
  cout << "Enter critical radius ";
  cin >> criticalRad;

  //Input radius of outer and inner cylinders
  fin >> radiusOuter >> radiusInner;

  //While not end of file, input point data
  fin >> x >> y;
  while(!fin.eof())
  {
    ++pointCount;  //increment point count
    dist = distance(x,y,xORIGIN, yORIGIN);
    if(dist > criticalRad)
    {
      ++outside;  //increment outside counter
    }
    fin >> x >> y;
  }
  //Print results
  //Pre-Multiply by 100.0 to force floating point arithmetic
  cout << (100.0*outside/pointCount)
      << "% lie outside the critical radius" << endl;
  return 0;
}
#include <cmath>  //Required for sqrt and pow
double distance(double x1, double y1, double x2, double y2)
```

```
{
    double d1, d2, d;
    d1 = x2-x1;
    d2 = y2-y1;
    d = sqrt( pow(d1,2) + pow(d2,2) );
    return d;
}
```

5. TESTING

Using an input file from the hand example, we get the following output from solution 1:

```
Ingbers-MacBook-Pro:Programs jaingber$ g++ chapter6_8.cpp
    Point.cpp
Ingbers-MacBook-Pro:Programs jaingber$ ./a.out
Constructing Point object, parameterized:
input parameters: 0,0
Constructing Point object, default:
initializing to zero
Enter critical radius 1.25
75% lie outside the critical radius
```

Using the same input file, we get the following output from solution 2:

```
Ingbers-MacBook-Pro:Programs jaingber$ g++ chapter6_9.cpp
Ingbers-MacBook-Pro:Programs jaingber$ ./a.out
Enter critical radius 1.25
75% lie outside the critical radius
```

Modify!

1. Write a value returning function with the following prototype:

   ```
   bool validate(double rad1, double rad2, double critic-
   alRadius);
   ```

   the function should return `true` if `rad1 < critical radius < rad2` and `false` otherwise. Use this function in program `chapter6_8` to verify that the critical radius entered by the user lies in between the inner and outer radius read from the data file. Allow the user three tries to input a correct value for the critical radius. Your program should terminate with a message after three invalid entries for the critical radius.

2. Add a new method to the `Point` class. The prototype for the new method is:

   ```
   void Point::input(istream& in);
   ```

   The statement: `p.input(fin);` will input two floating point values from the input file stream `fin` and assign them to the x and y coordinates of the calling object. Use this method in program `chapter6_8` to replace the two `fin >> x >> y` statements. Note: When you use `p.input(fin)`, you do not need to call either set methods.

6.9 Numerical Technique: Roots of Polynomials*

A polynomial is a function of a single object that can be expressed in the general form

$$f(x) = a_0 x^N + a_1 x^{N-1} + a_2 x^{N-2} + \cdots + a_{N-2}x^2 + a_{N-1}x + a_N, \tag{6.1}$$

where the object is x and the coefficients are represented by $a_0, a_1, \ldots, a_N$. The degree of a polynomial is equal to the largest nonzero exponent. Therefore, the general form for a cubic (third-degree) polynomial is

$$g(x) = a_0 x^3 + a_1 x^2 + a_2 x + a_3,$$

and a specific example of a cubic polynomial is

$$h(x) = x^3 - 2x^2 + 0.5x - 6.5.$$

Note that, for each term in the equation, the sum of the coefficient subscript and the object exponent is equal to the polynomial degree using the notation in Equation (6.1).

Polynomial Roots

The solutions to many engineering problems involve finding the roots of an equation of the form

$$y = f(x),$$

where the roots are the values of x for which y is equal to zero. Examples of applications in which we need to find roots of equations include designing the control system for a robot arm, designing springs and shock absorbers for an automobile, analyzing the response of a motor, and analyzing the stability of a digital filter.

If a function $f(x)$ is a polynomial of degree N, then $f(x)$ has exactly N roots. These N roots may contain real roots or complex roots, as will be shown in the examples that follow. If we assume that the coefficients $(a_0, a_1, \ldots, a_N)$ of the polynomial are real values, then complex roots will always occur in complex conjugate pairs. (Recall that a complex number can be expressed as $\alpha + i\beta$, where $i = \sqrt{-1}$. The complex conjugate of $\alpha + i\beta$ is $\alpha - i\beta$.)

If a polynomial is factored into linear terms, it is easy to identify the roots of the polynomial by setting each term to zero. For example, consider the following equation:

$$\begin{aligned} f(x) &= x^2 + x - 6 \\ &= (x-2)(x+3). \end{aligned}$$

If $f(x)$ is equal to zero, we have

$$(x-2)(x+3) = 0.$$

The roots of the equation, or the values of x for which $f(x)$ is equal to zero, are then $x = 2$ and $x = -3$. These roots also correspond to the values of x where the polynomial crosses the x-axis, as shown in Figure 6.9.

If a quadratic equation (polynomial of degree two) cannot easily be factored, we can use the quadratic formula to determine the two roots of the equation. Recall that for a general quadratic equation

$$y = ax^2 + bx + c,$$

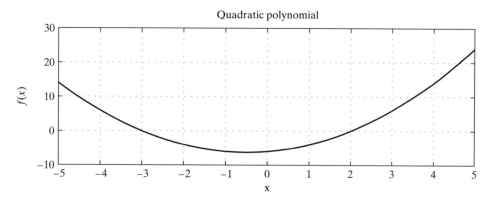

Figure 6.9 Polynomial with two real roots.

the roots can be computed as

$$x_1 = \frac{-b + \sqrt{b^2 - 4ac}}{2a}$$

and

$$x_2 = \frac{-b - \sqrt{b^2 - 4ac}}{2a}.$$

Thus, for the quadratic equation

$$f(x) = x^2 + 3x + 3,$$

the roots are

$$x_1 = \frac{-3 + \sqrt{-3}}{2} = -1.5 + 0.87\sqrt{-1}$$

and

$$x_2 = \frac{-3 - \sqrt{-3}}{2} = -1.5 - 0.87\sqrt{-1}.$$

Because a cubic polynomial is of degree three, it has exactly three roots. If we assume that the coefficients are real, then there are only these four possibilities:

- three real roots at different values (distinct roots)
- three real roots at the same value (multiple roots)
- one distinct real root and two multiple real roots
- one real root and a complex conjugate pair of roots

Examples of functions that illustrate each of these cases are as follows:

$$f_1(x) = (x - 3)(x + 1)(x - 1)$$
$$= x^3 - 3x^2 - x + 3;$$
$$f_2(x) = (x - 2)^3$$
$$= x^3 - 6x^2 + 12x - 8;$$

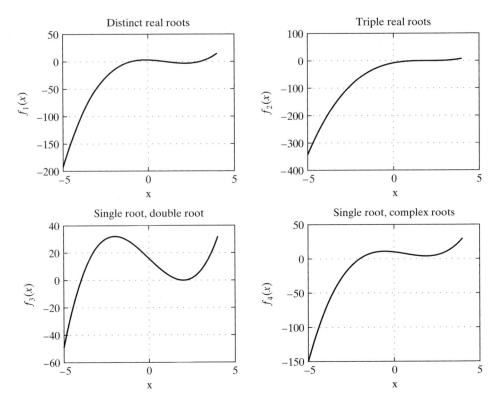

Figure 6.10 Cubic polynomials.

$$f_3(x) = (x + 4)(x - 2)^2$$
$$= x^3 - 12x + 16;$$

$$f_4(x) = (x + 2)[x - (2 + i)][x - (2 - i)]$$
$$= x^3 - 2x^2 - 3x + 10.$$

Figure 6.10 contains plots of these functions. Note again that the real roots correspond to the points where the function crosses the x-axis.

It is relatively easy to determine the roots of polynomials of degree one or two, but it can be difficult to determine the roots of polynomials of degree three or higher. A number of numerical techniques exist for determining the roots of polynomials. Techniques such as the incremental search, the bisection method, and the false-position technique identify the real roots by searching for intervals in which the function changes sign because this indicates that the function has crossed the x-axis. Additional techniques, such as the Newton–Raphson method, can be used to find complex roots.

Incremental-Search Technique

incremental-search

The **incremental-search** technique is often used to determine the real roots of a function in an interval $[a, b]$. This technique searches for a subinterval $[a_k, b_k]$ such that the function value is negative on one end and positive on the other. We are then assured that there is at least one root in this subinterval.

There are many variations of the incremental-search technique. The one that we discuss begins with the selection of a step size that is used to subdivide the original interval into a group of smaller subintervals, as shown in Figure 6.11. For each subinterval, we evaluate the function at both endpoints. If the product of the function values is negative, then there is a root in this subinterval. (A negative product implies that one function value is positive, whereas the other function value is negative; hence, the function must cross the x-axis in the interval.) At this point, we can estimate the root to be the midpoint of this small segment, as shown in Figure 6.12(a). It is also possible that one of the subinterval endpoints might be a root, or be very close to a root, as shown in Figure 6.12(b). Remember that it is not likely that a floating-point value will be exactly equal to zero, so the test to determine whether an endpoint is a root should compare the function value with a very small number, but not with zero.

It is also important to recognize that there are cases in which this incremental-search technique fails. For example, suppose that there are two roots in one of the subintervals. In this case, because the function values at the endpoints will have the same sign, their product will be positive, and the algorithm will skip to the next subinterval. As another example, consider the case with three roots in one of the subintervals. In this case, because the function values at the endpoints have different signs, the estimate of the root is the midpoint of the subinterval. We then continue with the next subinterval and thus miss the other two roots in

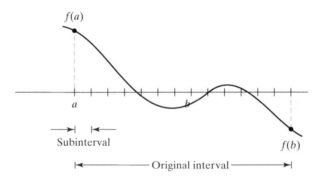

Figure 6.11 Incremental search.

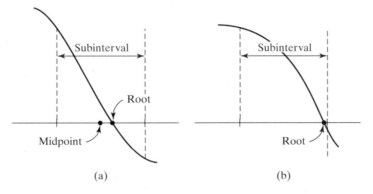

Figure 6.12 Subinterval analysis.

the previous subinterval. These examples are used to illustrate the fact that the incremental-search technique has some flaws, although, in general, it works reasonably well. If a technique is needed that has better performance characteristics, other root-finding methods [16] should be investigated.

6.10 Problem Solving Applied: System Stability*

system

stable system

The term **system** is often used to represent instrumentation or equipment for which specfied inputs generate specified outputs or actions. Examples of systems include the cooling equipment connected to the supports of a pipeline, a robot arm used in a manufacturing facility, and a fast "bullet" train. A simple definition of a **stable system** is the following: A system is stable if a reasonable input causes a reasonable output. For example, consider the control system of a robot arm. A reasonable input to the system would specify that the arm should move in a direction that is valid for the robot arm. If a reasonable input causes the arm to become erratic or to attempt to move in invalid directions, then the system is not stable. The analysis of the stability of the design of a system involves determining dynamic properties of the system. A discussion of the types of analyses involved, or of the functions involved, is beyond the scope of this text, but one component of the analysis requires the determination of the roots of polynomials. Usually, both the real and complex roots are needed, but the techniques for finding complex roots involve using the derivative of the polynomial, and thus they become more involved mathematically. Therefore, we reduce the scope of this problem to finding only the real roots of a polynomial given a specified interval in which to search. We also assume that the polynomial is a cubic polynomial, but the solution developed can easily be extended to handle higher degree polynomials.

Develop a program to determine the real roots of a cubic polynomial. Allow the user to enter the coefficients of the polynomial, the interval to be searched, and the step size of the subintervals used in the search.

1. PROBLEM STATEMENT

Determine the real roots of a cubic polynomial.

2. INPUT/OUTPUT DESCRIPTION

The I/O diagram shows that the input values are the polynomial coefficients, the interval endpoints, and the step size of the subintervals. The output values are the roots identified in the specified interval.

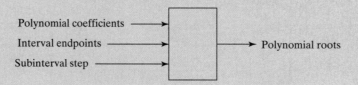

Polynomial coefficients ⟶
Interval endpoints ⟶   ⟶ Polynomial roots
Subinterval step ⟶

3. HAND EXAMPLE

For the hand example, we use the equation

$$y = 2x - 4.$$

This function can be described as a cubic polynomial with $a_0 = 0$, $a_1 = 0$, $a_2 = 2$, and $a_3 = -4$. If we set the polynomial to zero, we easily observe that the root is 2. To examine the incremental-search technique, we first use a step size such that the root falls on one of the endpoints of a subinterval, and then we use a step size such that the root does not fall on one of the endpoints of a subinterval. If the root falls on an endpoint, we can easily identify it because the polynomial value will be very close to zero. If the root falls within a subinterval, the product of the function values at the endpoints will be negative, and we then estimate the root to be the midpoint of the interval.

First, consider the interval [1, 3] with a step size of 0.5. The subintervals and the corresponding information derived from them are as follows:

Subinterval 1:   [1.0, 1.5]
$f(1.0) * f(1.5) = (-2) * (-1) = 2$
No root in this interval.

Subinterval 2:   [1.5, 2.0]
When we evaluate the endpoints, we detect the root
at $x = 2.0$.

Subinterval 3:   [2.0, 2.5]
When we evaluate the endpoints, we again detect the
root at $x = 2.0$. Note that we will need to be careful
that we do not identify this root twice in the program.

Subinterval 4:   [2.5, 3.0]
$f(2.5) * f(3.0) = (1) * (2) = 2$
No root in this interval.

We now consider the interval [1,3] with a step size of 0.3. The subintervals and the corresponding information derived from them are as follows:

Subinterval 1:   [1.0, 1.3]
$f(1.0) * f(1.3) = (-2) * (-1.4) = 2.8$
No root in this interval.

Subinterval 2:   [1.3, 1.6]
$f(1.3) * f(1.6) = (-1.4) * (-0.8) = 1.12$
No root in this interval.

Subinterval 3:   [1.6, 1.9]
$f(1.6) * f(1.9) = (-0.8) * (-0.2) = 1.6$
No root in this interval.

Subinterval 4:   [1.9, 2.2]
$f(1.9) * f(2.2) = (-0.2) * (0.4) = -0.08$
The root in this interval is estimated to occur
at the midpoint.

Subinterval 5:   [2.2, 2.5]

$f(2.2) * f(2.5) = (0.4) * (1.0) = 0.4$

No root in this interval.

Subinterval 6:   [2.5, 2.8]

$f(2.5) * f(2.8) = (1.0) * (1.6) = 1.6$

No root in this interval.

Subinterval 7:   [2.8, 3.1]

Note that the right endpoint exceeds the overall
endpoint. In the program, we will modify
such an interval so that it ends on the original
right endpoint.

$f(2.8) * f(3.0) = (1.6) * (2.0) = 3.2$

No root in this interval.

4. ALGORITHM DEVELOPMENT

We first develop the decomposition outline because it breaks the solution into a series of sequential steps.

Decomposition Outline

1. Read polynomial coefficients, interval of interest, and step size.

2. Locate roots using subintervals.

Step 1 involves prompting the user to enter the necessary information and then reading it. Step 2 requires a loop to compute the subinterval endpoints and then to determine whether a root occurs on an endpoint or in the subinterval. When a root is located, a corresponding message is printed. There are a number of operations involved in step 2, so we should consider using functions to keep the main function from getting long. Because we need to evaluate the cubic polynomial several places in the program, it is a good candidate for a function. Within each subinterval, we need to search for a root; this search is also a good candidate for a function. The structure chart for this solution was shown in Figure 6.1. The refinement in pseudocode is the following:

```
Refinement in Pseudocode
main:   read coefficients, interval endpoints a and b,
              and step size
        compute the number of subintervals, n
        set k to 0
        while k<= n-1
              compute left subinterval endpoint
              compute right subinterval endpoint
              check_roots (left, right, coefficients)
              increment k by 1
        check_roots (b,b,coefficients)

check_roots (left, right, coefficients):
        set f_left to poly(left,coefficients)
        set f_right to poly(right,coefficients)
        if f_left is near zero
              print root at left endpoint
```

```
            else
                if f_left * f_right < 0
                      print root at midpoint of subinterval
            return
poly(x,a0,a1,a2,a3):
        return a0x^3 + a1x^2 + a2x + a3
```

Note in the pseudocode for the *check_root()* function that we check to see whether the left subinterval endpoint is a root, but we do not check the right subinterval endpoint. This is necessary to avoid identifying the same root twice: when it is a right endpoint for one interval and also when it is a left endpoint for the next subinterval. Because we only check the left endpoints, we need to check the final point in the interval because it never becomes a left endpoint.

The steps in the pseudocode are detailed enough to convert to C++:

```cpp
/*------------------------------------------------------------*/
/*  Program chapter6_10                                       */
/*                                                            */
/*  This program estimates the real roots of a               */
/*  polynomial function using incremental search.            */

#include<iostream>  //Required for cin, cout
#include<cmath>  //Required for cell()
using namespace std;

// Function Prototypes
void check_roots(double left, double right, double a0,
                 double a1, double a2, double a3);
double poly(double x, double a0, double a1,
            double a2, double a3);

int main()
{
   // Declare objects and function prototypes.
   int n;
   double a0, a1, a2, a3, a, b, step, left, right;

   // Get user input.
   cout << "Enter coefficients a0, a1, a2, a3: \n";
   cin >> a0 >> a1 >> a2 >> a3;
   cout << "Enter interval limits a, b (a<b): \n";
   cin >> a >> b;
   cout << "Enter step size: \n";
   cin >> step;

   //Check subintervals for roots.
   n = ceil((b - a)/step);
   for (int k=0; k<=n-1; k++)
   {
      left = a + k*step;
      if (k == n-1)
      {
          right = b;
      }
```

```
            else
            {
                right = left + step;
            }
            check_roots(left,right,a0,a1,a2,a3);
        }
        check_roots(b,b,a0,a1,a2,a3);

        //  Exit program.
        return 0;
}
/*------------------------------------------------------*/
/*  This function checks a subinterval for a root.    */

void check_roots(double left, double right, double a0,
                 double a1, double a2, double a3)
{
    //  Declare objects and function prototypes.
    double f_left, f_right;

    //  Evaluate subinterval endpoints and
    //  test for roots.
    f_left = poly(left,a0,a1,a2,a3);
    f_right = poly(right,a0,a1,a2,a3);
    if (fabs(f_left) < 0.1e-04)
    {
        cout << "Root detected at " << left << endl;
    }
    else
    {
        if (fabs(f_right) < 0.1e-04)
            ;
        else
        {
            if (f_left*f_right < 0)
            {
                cout << "Root detected at " << (left+right)/2 << endl;
            }
        }
    }
    // Exit function.
    return;
}
/*------------------------------------------------------*/
/*  This function evaluates a cubic polynomial.       */

double poly(double x, double a0, double a1, double a2,
            double a3)
{
    return a0*x*x*x + a1*x*x + a2*x + a3;
}
/*------------------------------------------------------*/
```

5. TESTING

If we use the data from the hand example, we have the following interaction with the program (the roots match the ones that we computed by hand):

```
Enter coefficients a0, a1, a2, a3:
0 0 2 -4
Enter interval limits a, b (a<b):
1 3
Enter step size:
0.5
Root detected at 2.000
Enter coefficients a0, a1, a2, a3:
0 0 2 -4
Enter interval limits a, b (a<b):
1 3
Enter step size:
0.3
Root detected at 2.050
```

Use the polynomials given on page 281 to test this program. Use intervals and step sizes so that the roots do not always fall on subinterval endpoints.

Modify!

1. The size of the interval affects the estimate of the root if the root is not on an endpoint of a subinterval. Using the polynomial from the hand example, experiment with several step sizes, including 1.1, 0.75, 0.5, 0.3, and 0.14, for the interval [0.5, 3].

2. Using the first cubic polynomial given on page 281, test the program using intervals in which the roots fall on the endpoints of the interval [a, b] entered as input.

3. Using the first cubic polynomial given on page 281, find a step size that causes the program to miss some of the roots for an initial interval of [−10, 10]. Explain why the roots were missed by the program. Is this an error in the program?

4. Modify the program so that it checks to see whether the right endpoint of a subinterval is a root, instead of checking the left endpoint of a subinterval. Be sure to include a check for the first point of the interval [a, b].

5. Modify the program so that it can accept and locate the real roots of a fourth-degree polynomial.

6. Use this program to help answer problem 4 of the previous Modify! problems on page 266.

Newton–Raphson Method*

Newton–Raphson
method

The **Newton–Raphson method** is a popular root-finding technique that relies on information about the equation. It is also known as the tangent method because of the root-estimation technique it uses. The Newton–Raphson method uses both the function $f(x)$ and its derivative $f'(x)$ to compute the slope of a tangent line, which is then used as a straight-line approximation of the curve at each iteration point. The intersection of the tangent line and the x-axis becomes the next estimate for the root and the next point at which the tangent line is computed. The process is repeated until the root is found. Since the Newton–Raphson method makes a better estimate for the root at each step, it typically requires significantly fewer iterations to converge than the incremental-search technique.

Using the graph shown in Figure 6.13, we find that the Newton–Raphson method can be described with the following series of steps. An initial guess, x_1, is made for the root of the function $f(x)$. The slope of the curve at x_1 is then computed using $f'(x_1)$, and a tangent line with that slope is drawn through $f(x_1)$. The point x_2 where the tangent line intersects the x-axis becomes the new estimate for the root. The process then repeats using $f'(x_2)$ as the slope of the tangent line drawn through $f(x_2)$, which intersects the x-axis at x_3 and so on until it converges on the root at x_r.

The algorithm for finding the next estimate for the root, x_{k+1}, given the current estimate for the root, x_k, is obtained by noting that the slope of the tangent line at $f(x_k)$ can be computed by dividing the change in y by the change in x:

$$f'(x_k) = \frac{f(x_k) - 0}{x_k - x_{k+1}}.$$

Solving this equation for x_{k+1} provides the algorithm we need for the next estimate of the root:

$$x_{k+1} = x_k - \frac{f(x_k)}{f'(x_k)}.$$

As stated earlier, an advantage of the Newton–Raphson method is that it generally requires fewer iterations and, therefore, is computationally more efficient than the incremental-search method. In addition, it can be used to find complex roots when complex objects are used and when the initial guess is a complex value. The method can also be generalized to multiple dimensions for use in solving systems of nonlinear equations.

The method also has some limitations. The most important limitation relates to the initial guess; if the initial guess for the root is not good enough, the algorithm may miss the

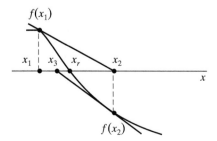

Figure 6.13 Newton–Raphson method.

root entirely, finding instead one of the other roots or not finding a root at all. Other problems can arise, depending on the equation itself. Places where $f'(x)$ is zero or close to zero at peaks or inflection points in the curve can cause both the function and its derivative to be zero and result in the method failing at the origin. But these problems can usually be avoided if the initial guess for a root is close enough. It may also not be easy or even possible to compute the derivative of the function. Methods that do not require the derivative, such as the secant method, can be used in these situations.

To illustrate the Newton–Raphson method, we will write a program to determine the real roots of a polynomial $p(x)$ where $p(x)$ has the following form:

$$y = p(x)$$
$$= a_0x^3 + a_1x^2 + a_2x + a_3.$$

We will assume that a root has been located if the absolute value of $p(x)$ is less than 0.001. For a test case, assume that the polynomial equation is

$$y = p(x)$$
$$= x^2 + 4x + 3.$$

We can use factoring to determine that the roots of this equation are $x = -1$ and $x = -3$. The Newton–Raphson method also requires the derivative of the polynomial, which in this case is

$$p'(x) = 2x + 4.$$

We begin with an initial guess and compute the value of the function and its derivative. The tolerance measure is the absolute value of the function. When the tolerance is less than 0.001, the process is terminated; otherwise, the next estimate for the root is determined using the equation for x_{k+1} given previously.

We now present a program to implement the Newton–Raphson method. Since the program is short and straightforward, no modules are needed:

```
/*-----------------------------------------------------------*/
/*   Program chapter6_11                                      */
/*                                                           */
/*   This program finds the real roots of a cubic polynomial  */
/*   using the Newton-Raphson method.                         */

#include<iostream> //Required for cin, cout
#include<cmath>    //Required for pow()
using namespace std;

int main()
{
//   Declare objects.
        int iterations(0);
        double a0, a1, a2, a3, x, p, dp, tol;

//   Get user input.
        cout << "Enter coefficients a0, a1, a2, a3\n";
        cin >> a0 >> a1 >> a2 >> a3;
        cout << "Enter initial guess for root\n";
        cin >> x;
```

```
        // Evaluate p at initial guess.
        p = a0*pow(x,3) + a1*x*x + a2*x + a3;

    //  Determine tolerance.
        tol = fabs(p);
        while(tol > 0.001 && iterations < 100)
        {
                //  Calculate the derivative.
                dp = 3*a0*x*x + 2*a1*x + a2;

                //  Calculate next estimated root.
                x = x - p/dp;
                //  Evaluate p at estimated root.
                p = a0*x*x*x + a1*x*x + a2*x + a3;
                tol = fabs(p);
                iterations++;
        }
        if(tol < 0.001)
        {
                cout << "Root is " << x << endl
                        << iterations << " iterations\n";
        }
        else
                cout << "Did not converge after 100 iterations\n";
        return 0;
}
```

The following are some sample runs of the program:

```
Enter coefficients a0, a1, a2, a3
0 1 4 3
Enter initial guess for root
0
Root is -0.999695
 3 iterations
-------------------------------------------------------------------
Enter coefficients a0, a1, a2, a3
0 1 4 3
Enter initial guess for root
5
Root is -0.999799
5 iterations
-------------------------------------------------------------------
Enter coefficients a0, a1, a2, a3
0 1 4 3
Enter initial guess for root
-4
Root is -3.000305
 3 iterations
```

Modify!

1. Run the Newton–Raphson program using the same coefficients and an initial guess of −1.

2. Run the Newton–Raphson program using the same coefficients and an initial guess of −2. Explain what happens.

3. Modify the Newton–Raphson program to allow the user to input the tolerance used to stop the iterations.

4. Modify the Newton–Raphson program to find the roots of a fifth-degree polynomial.

6.11 Numerical Technique: Integration*

The operation of integration gives engineers and scientists important information about functions or data sets. For example, distance, velocity and acceleration all relate to each other through integration. Velocity is the integral of acceleration and distance is the integral of velocity. The topic of integration is covered in detail in calculus courses, but the underlying principles can be explained simply in terms of area. The integral of a function over an interval represents the area under the graph of the function. Integration can be numerically approximated using any one of several different techniques. In this chapter, we will present a technique for performing numerical integration using the **trapezoidal rule.**

trapezoidal rule

Integration Using the Trapezoidal Rule

To use the analytical techniques of calculus to obtain the integral of a function over an interval, we must have an equation for the function. In many engineering and scientific applications, we have data points or measurements from the function, but we do not have an explicit equation. Therefore, we need a method that requires only points of the function to numerically compute the integral. In other applications, we may have an equation that defines the function, but it is difficult or impossible to determine the integral analytically. In this case, we would also like to have a method that allows us to compute points or values of the function and then numerically evaluate the integral. The technique that we present in this section is a simple way to numerically estimate the area under a curve, given points on the curve. The technique uses the areas of trapezoids and thus is called integration using the trapezoidal rule.

The integral of the function $f(x)$, evaluated from a to b, is expressed as

$$\int_a^b f(x)\, dx$$

and represents the area under the function $f(x)$ from $x = a$ to $x = b$, as shown in Figure 6.14. If we are given the function that represents the curve, we can evaluate the function at points spaced along the interval of interest, as shown in Figure 6.15. Note that since $y = f(x)$, we can represent $f(x_1)$ as y_1, $f(x_2)$ as y_2, and so on.

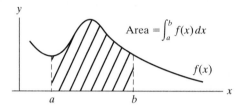

Figure 6.14 Area under a curve.

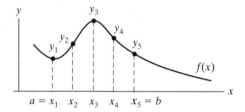

Figure 6.15 Spaced intervals.

If we join the points on the curve with straight-line segments, we form a group of trapezoids whose combined areas approximate the area under the curve. The closer the points are together on the curve, the more trapezoids there are in the interval, and thus the more accurate will be our approximation to the integral. In Figure 6.16, we use five points on the curve to generate four trapezoids, and the sum of the areas of the four trapezoids is then an approximation to the integral of the function between a and b.

The area of a trapezoid is one-half times the base times the sum of the two heights (or sides):

$$Area = 1/2 * base * (height_1 + height_2).$$

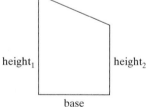

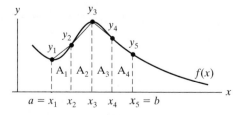

Figure 6.16 Four trapezoids.

Thus, the area of the first trapezoid, A_1, is computed using the pair of points (x_1, y_1) and (x_2, y_2):

$$A_1 = 1/2 * (x_2 - x_1) * (y_1 + y_2).$$

Since the points on the curve are equally spaced along the x-axis in this example, the base of each of the trapezoids is the same value. We can then compute the individual areas of the trapezoids as

$$A1 = 1/2 * base * (y_1 + y_2),$$

$$A2 = 1/2 * base * (y_2 + y_3),$$

$$A3 = 1/2 * base * (y_3 + y_4),$$

$$A4 = 1/2 * base * (y_4 + y_5).$$

Thus, the total area between a and b can be approximated by the sum of the areas of the four trapezoids:

$$\int_a^b f(x)\,dx \approx \frac{base}{2}((y_1 + y_2) + (y_2 + y_3) + (y_3 + y_4) + (y_4 + y_5))$$

$$\approx \frac{base}{2}(y_1 + 2y_2 + 2y_3 + 2y_4 + y_5).$$

In general, if the area under a curve is divided into N trapezoids with equal bases, the area can be approximated by the following equation:

$$\int_a^b f(x)\,dx \approx \frac{base}{2}\left(y_1 + 2\sum_{k=2}^{N} y_k + y_{N+1}\right).$$

This equation is referred to as the trapezoidal rule.

When computing an integral with this numerical technique, we need to remember that the data points on the curve could come from different sources. If we have the equation for the curve, a C++ program can compute the data points that we use as the height of the trapezoids; in this case, we can choose the data points to be as close together or as far apart as we wish. Another possibility is that the points are experimentally collected data; in this case, we have a set of x-coordinates that represent the trapezoid base values and the y-coordinates that represent the heights of the trapezoids. We can still use the trapezoid areas to estimate the integral, but we cannot choose data points that are closer together or farther apart, because we do not have a function to evaluate; we only have the available data to use. If the bases of the trapezoids determined by the data points are not of equal value, we have to add the areas of the trapezoids individually instead of using the equation that assumes that the bases are equal.

We will now present a C++ program that determines an estimate of the integral (between two specified points) of the following equation:

$$y = f(x)$$

$$= 4e^{-x}.$$

```
/*-----------------------------------------------------------------*/
/*   Program chapter6_12                                           */
/*                                                                 */
/*   This program estimates the area under a given curve           */
/*   using trapezoids with equal bases.                            */

#include<iostream> //Required for cin, cout
#include<cmath> //Required for exp()
using namespace std;

//  Function prototypes.
double integrate(double a, double b, int n);
double f(double x);

int main()
{
   //  Declare objects
   int num_trapezoids;
   double a, b, area;

   //  Get input from user.
   cout << "Enter the interval endpoints, a and b\n";
   cin >> a >> b;
   cout << "Enter the number of trapezoids\n";
   cin >> num_trapezoids;

   //  Estimate area under the curve of 4e^-x
   area = integrate(a, b, num_trapezoids);

   //  Print result.
   cout << "Using " << num_trapezoids
        << " trapezoids, the estimated area is "
        << area << endl;

   return 0;
}
/*-----------------------------------------------------------------*/

/*-----------------------------------------------------------------*/
double integrate(double a, double b, int n)
{
   //  Declare objects.
      double sum(0), x, base, area;

      base = (b-a)/n;
      for(int k=2; k<=n; k++)
      {
            x = a + base*(k-1);
            sum = sum + f(x);
      }
      area = 0.5*base*(f(a) + 2*sum + f(b));
      return area;
}
```

```
double f(double x)
{
        return(4*exp(-x));
}
/*--------------------------------------------------------------------*/
```

The following are some sample runs of the preceding program:

```
Enter the interval endpoints, a and b
0 1
Enter the number of trapezoids
5
Using 5 trapezoids, the estimated area is 2.536905
-----------------------------------------------------------
Enter the interval endpoints, a and b
0 1
Enter the number of trapezoids
50
Using 50 trapezoids, the estimated area is 2.528567
-----------------------------------------------------------
Enter the interval endpoints, a and b
0 1
Enter the number of trapezoids
100
Using 100 trapezoids, the estimated area is 2.528503
```

If we use calculus to integrate the specified function over the interval [0, 1], the theoretical answer to seven digits of accuracy is 2.528482.

SUMMARY

Most programs in C++ benefit from using both library and programmer-defined functions. Functions allow us to reuse software and to employ abstraction in our solution, and, hence, reduce development time and increase the quality of the software. Numerous examples were developed to illustrate using value returning programmer-defined functions to solve problems, including examples of recursive functions. Specific applications were presented to illustrate generating random numbers (integers or floating-point values) and to implement the incremental search technique and Newton–Raphson method for identifying real roots of polynomials as well as numerical integration using the trapezoidal rule.

Key Terms

abstraction	computer simulation
accessor methods	custom header file
address operator	encapsulation
automatic storage class	external storage class
center of gravity	function argument
coercion of arguments	formal parameter
composite materials	function

function argument	pass by value
function body	public interface
function header	programmer-defined function
function prototype	random number
global scope	random number seed
incremental search	register class
library function	reliability
local scope	re-usability
modularity	root
module	scope
module chart	simulation
moment	stable system
mutator methods	static storage class
Newton–Raphson method	storage class
numerical integration	structure chart
parameter declarations	system
pass by reference	trapezoidal rule

C++ Statement Summary

Function definition:

```
return_type function_name(parameter types)
{
   declarations;
   statements;
}
```

Method definition:

```
return_type class_name::function_name(parameter types)
{
  declarations;
  statements;
}
```

Return statements:

void function:

```
return;
```

Value returning function:

```
return (a + b)/2;
```

Function prototype:

```
double sinc(double x);
double sinc(double);
void check_roots(double left, double right, double a0,
                double a1, double a2, double a3);
```

Notes

1. A program with several modules is easier to read and understand than one long `main` function.
2. Select the name of the function to indicate the purpose of the function.
3. Use a special line, such as a line of dashes, to separate programmer-defined functions from the `main` function and other programmer-defined functions.
4. Use a consistent order for functions, such as the `main` function first, followed by additional functions in the order in which they are referenced.
5. Use parameter identifiers in prototype statements to help document the order and definition of the parameters.
6. List the function prototypes on separate lines so that they are easy to identify.
7. Use the parameter list instead of global objects to transmit information to a function.

Debugging Notes

1. If you are having difficulty understanding the error messages from a compiler, try running the program on another compiler to obtain different error messages.
2. When debugging a long program, add comment indicators (/ * and * /) around some sections of the code so that you can focus on other parts of the program.
3. Test a complicated function by itself using a driver program.
4. Make sure that the value returned from a function matches the function return type. If necessary, use the cast operator to convert a value to the proper type.
5. Functions can be defined before or after the `main` function, but not within it.
6. Always use function prototype statements to avoid errors in parameter passing.
7. Use `cout` statements to generate memory snapshots of the function argument before a function is referenced, and of the formal arguments at the beginning of the function.
8. Carefully match the type, order, and number of function argument with the formal parameters of a function.
9. System-dependent limitations can occasionally cause problems with recursive solutions to a problem.

Problems

Exam Practice!

True/False Problems

Indicate whether the following statements are true (T) or false (F).

1. The body of a function is contained in braces. T F
2. The parameter list (or argument list) contains all objects used by the function. T F
3. In a call by value, a function cannot change the value of an function argument. T F
4. A static object is declared inside a function, but it retains its value from one reference call to another. T F
5. All data members, or attributes, of a class must be of the same data type. T F
6. Member functions, or methods, have access to the private data members of the calling object. T F
7. A mutator method can change the state of the calling object. T F

Multiple Choice Problems
Circle the letter for the best answer to complete each statement or for the correct answer to each question.

8. Which of the following is a valid function definition statement?
   (a) function cube (double x)
   (b) double cube (double x)
   (c) double cube (x)
   (d) cube (double x)

9. In a function call, the function arguments are separated by
   (a) commas.
   (b) semicolons.
   (c) colons.
   (d) spaces.

10. The definition of the statements in which an identifier is known (or can be used) is its
    (a) global.
    (b) local.
    (c) static.
    (d) scope.

Program Analysis
Use the following function for problems 11–14:

```
/*-------------------------------------------------- */
/* This function returns 0 or 1.                   */
/*                                                 */
int fives (int n)
{
//  Declare objects.
    int result;
//   Compute result to return.
    if ((n%5) == 0)
    {
        return 1;
    }
    else
    {
        return 0;
    }
 }
/*-------------------------------------------------- */
```

11. What is the value of fives(15) ;
12. What is the value of fives(26) ;
13. What is the value fives(ceil(sqrt(62.5))) ;
    (*Hint:* You don't need a calculator to determine this value.)
14. Does the function work properly for all integers? If not, what are its limitations?

Memory Snapshot Problem
Use the following class definition to answer questions 15–17.

```
//Class Declaration
class UnitVector
{
private:
//data members
  double x, y; //vector anchor point
  double orientation; //vector orientation
public:
//constructor functions
  UnitVector(); //default constructor
  UnitVector(double x_val, // constructor with 3 parameters
             double y_val,
             double or);
};
//Class implementation
UnitVector::UnitVector()
{
    x = y = 1;
    orientation = 3.1415;
}

UnitVector::UnitVector(double x_val, double y_val, double o)
{
    x = x_val;
    y = y_val;
    orientation = o;
}
```

Provide a memory snapshot for each of the following set of statements.

15. UnitVector v1, v2;
16. UnitVector v1(0,0,0), v2;
17. UnitVector v1(2.1, 3.0, 1.6), v2; v2 = v1;

Programming Problems
18. Write a void function that uses two nested for loops and the modulus (%) operator to detect and print to standard output the first *n* prime integers. Recall that a prime number is a number that is evenly divisible only by 1 and itself. *Hint:* the function prototype is: `primeGen(int n);`
19. Write a void function that uses two nested for loops and the modulus (%) operator to detect and print to a specified output file, the first *n* prime integers. Recall that a prime number is a number that is evenly divisible only by 1 and itself. *Hint:* the function prototype is: `primeGen(int n, ostream& file);` and a precondition is that *file* is defined.
20. Write a value returning function that prints the number of valid integer values contained in a data file. If the file contains any data that cannot be read as an integer, the function should return the number of integers that were successfully read prior

to encountering the bad data, and print a message to standard error indicating that not all of the data in the file could be read. *Hint:* use the function header: `int countInts (ifstream& file);` and a precondition that *file* is defined.

21. Write a void function that prints the values of the state flags *badbit, failbit, eofbit* and *goodbit* of a file stream. The file stream in an input parameter.

Simple Simulations.   In the problems that follow, develop simple simulations using the functions *randint* and *randfloat* developed in this chapter.

22. Write a program to simulate tossing a "fair" coin. Allow the user to enter the number of tosses. Print the number of tosses that yielded heads and the number of tosses that yielded tails. What should be the percentage distribution of heads and tails?

23. Write a program to simulate tossing a coin that has been weighted such that it lands with heads up 60 percent of the time. Have the user enter the number of tosses. Print the number of tosses that yielded heads and the number of tosses that yielded tails.

24. Define a programmer-defined data type named Coin. A Coin has only one attribute and that is its face value. Represent the face value as a char. 'H'=> heads, 'T'=>tails. Use the Coin class to write solutions for problems 22 and 23.

25. Write a program to simulate rolling a six-sided "fair" die with one dot on one side, two dots on another side, three dots on another side, and so on. Allow the user to enter the number of rolls. Print the number of rolls that gave one dot, the number of rolls that gave two dots, and so on. What should be the percentage distribution of the number of dots from the rolls?

26. Write a program to simulate an experiment rolling two six-sided "fair" dice. Allow the user to enter the number of rolls of the dice to simulate. What percentage of the time does the sum of the dots on the dice equal eight in the simulation?

27. Write a program to simulate a lottery drawing that uses balls numbered from 1 to 10. Assume that three balls are drawn at random. Allow the user to enter the number of lottery drawings to simulate. What percentage of the time does the result contain three even numbers in the simulation? What percentage of the time does the number 7 occur in the three numbers in the simulation? What percentage of the time do the numbers 1, 2, and 3 occur in the simulation?

Component Reliability.   The following problems specify computer simulations to evaluate the reliability of several component configurations. Use the function *randfloat* developed in this chapter.

28. Write a program that simulates the design shown in Figure 6.17 using a component reliability of 0.8 for component 1, 0.85 for component 2, and 0.95 for component 3. Print the estimate of the reliability using 5,000 simulations. (The analytical reliability of this system is 0.794.)

29. Write a program that simulates the design shown in Figure 6.18, using a component reliability of 0.8 for components 1 and 2, and 0.95 for components 3 and 4. Print the estimate of the reliability, using 5,000 simulations. (The analytical reliability of this system is 0.9649.)

30. Write a program that simulates the design shown in Figure 6.19, using a component reliability of 0.95 for all components. Print the estimate of the reliability using 5000 simulations. (The analytical reliability of this system is 0.99976.)

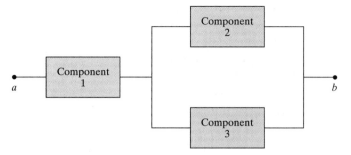

Figure 6.17 Configuration 1.

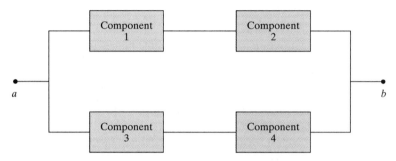

Figure 6.18 Configuration 2.

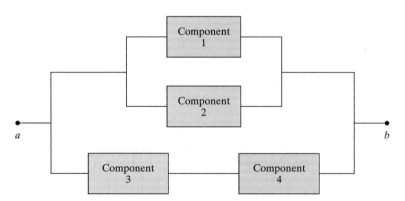

Figure 6.19 Configuration 3.

Flight Simulator Wind Speed.   This set of problems relates to a computer simulation of wind speed for a flight simulator. Assume that the wind speed for a particular region can be modeled by using an average value and a range of gust values that is added to the average. For example, the wind speed might be 10 miles an hour, with added noise (which represents gusts) that ranges from 22 miles per hour to 2 miles per hour, as shown in Figure 6.20. Use the function *randfloat* developed in this chapter.

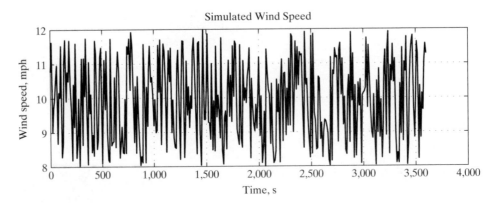

Figure 6.20 Simulated wind speed.

31. Write a program to generate a data file named **wind.dat** that contains 1 hour of simulated wind speeds. Each line of the data file should contain the time in seconds and the corresponding wind speed. The time should start with 0 seconds. The increment in time should be 10 seconds and the final line of the data file should correspond to 3,600 seconds. The user should be prompted to enter the average wind speed and the range of values of the gusts.

32. In problem 31, assume that we want the flight simulator wind data to include a 0.5% possibility of encountering a small storm at each time step. Therefore, modify the solution to problem 31 so that the average wind speed is increased by 10 mph for a period of 5 minutes when a storm is encountered. A plot of an example data file with three storms is shown in Figure 6.21.

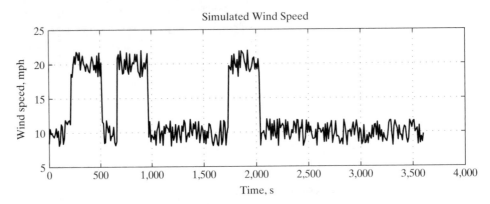

Figure 6.21 Simulated wind speeds with three storms.

33. In problem 32, assume that there is a 1% possibility of encountering a microburst at each time step in a small storm. Therefore, modify the solution to problem 32 so that the wind speed is increased by 50 mph over the storm values for a period of 1 minute if a microburst is encountered. A plot of a sample data file with a microburst within a storm is shown in Figure 6.22.

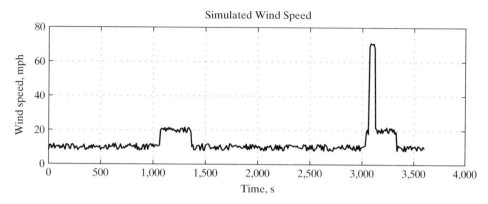

Figure 6.22 Simulated wind speeds with a microburst.

34. Modify the program in problem 32 so that the user enters the possibility of encountering a storm.

35. Modify the program in problem 32 so that the user enters the length in minutes for the duration of a storm.

36. Modify the program in problem 35 so that the length of a storm is a random number that varies between 3 and 5 minutes.

Roots of Functions.   The following problems relate to finding real roots for functions:

37. Write a program to determine the real roots of a quadratic equation, assuming that the user enters the coefficients of the quadratic equation. If the roots are complex, print an appropriate message.

38. Modify the program in problem 37 so that the program also computes the real and imaginary parts of the roots if they are complex.

39. Write a C++ function to evaluate this mathematical function:

$$f(x) = 0.1x^2 - x \ln x.$$

Assume that the corresponding function prototype is

```
double f(double x);
```

Then modify the program developed in Section 6.10 so that it searches for roots of this new function instead of searching for roots of polynomials. Test the program by searching for a root in [1, 2] for this new function.

40. Modify the program developed in Section 6.10 to find the roots of this function in a user-specified interval:

$$f(x) = sinc(x).$$

Use the sinc function developed in this chapter.

41. In the program developed in Section 6.10, we searched for subintervals for which the function values at the endpoints had different signs; we then estimated the root location to be the midpoint of the subinterval. A more accurate estimate of the root location is usually the intersection of a straight line through the function values with the x-axis, as shown in Figure 6.23.

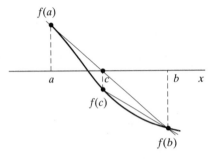

Figure 6.23 Straight line intersection in (a, b).

Using similar triangles, it can be shown that the intersection point c can be computed using the following equation:

$$c = \frac{a * f(b) - b * f(a)}{f(b) - f(a)}.$$

Modify program `chapter6_10` to estimate the root of a subinterval using this approximation.

42. Write functions that could be used by the Newton–Raphson method program to evaluate the polynomial and its derivative. These functions would be useful if the evaluations of the polynomial and its derivative were complicated. Show the changes that would be necessary in the program.

Numerical Integration. The following set of problems relates to performing numerical integration using the trapezoidal rule.

43. Modify program `chapter6_11` to estimate the integral of the function

$$f(x) = 3x - 2x^2.$$

44. Modify program `chapter6_11` so that it stores the x- and y-coordinates of the endpoints of the trapezoids in a data file so that they can be plotted later.

45. Write a program that estimates the integral of a function where the function is represented by a collection of experimental data points stored in a file rather than by an equation. The file contains a set of x-coordinates that represent the trapezoid base values and the y-coordinates that represent the heights of the trapezoids. Note that the number of data points determines the number of trapezoids. You must recalculate the base of the trapezoid for each new pair of data points because you cannot assume that all of the x-coordinates are equally spaced across the interval.

Value Returning Functions

46. Suppose that we have n distinct objects. There are many different orders that we can select to line up the objects in a row. In fact, there are $n!$ orderings, or permutations, that can be obtained with n objects. If we have n objects and select k of the objects, then there are $n!/(n-k)!$ possible orderings of k objects. That is, the number of different permutations of n different objects taken k at a time is $n!/(n-k)!$. Write a function named **permute** that receives values for n and k, and then returns the number of permutations of the n objects taken k at a time. (If we consider the set of digits 1, 2, 3, the different permutations of two digits are 1, 2, 2, 1, 1, 3, 3, 1, 2, 3 and 3, 2.) Assume that the corresponding prototype is

```
int permute(int n; int k);
```

47. Whereas permutations (problem 46) are concerned with order; combinations are not. Thus, given n distinct objects, there is only one combination of n objects taken k at a time, but there are $n!$ permutations of n distinct objects taken n at a time. The number of combinations of n objects, taken k at a time, is equal to $n!/((k!)(n-k)!)$. Write a function named combine that receives values for n and k and then returns the number of combinations of the n objects taken k at a time. (If we consider the set of digits 1, 2, 3, the different combinations of two digits are 1, 2, 1, 3 and 2, 3.) Assume that the corresponding prototype is

```
int combine(int n, int k);
```

48. The cosine of an angle can be computed from the following infinite series:

$$\cos x = 1 - \frac{x^2}{2!} + \frac{x^4}{4!} - \frac{x^6}{6!} + \cdots.$$

Write a program that reads an angle x (in radians) from the keyboard. Then, in a function, compute the cosine of the angle using the first five terms of this series. Print the value computed along with the value of the cosine computed using the C++ library function.

49. Modify the program in problem 48 so that the approximation uses terms from the series as long as the absolute value of a term is greater than 0.0001. Also, print the number of terms used in the series approximation.

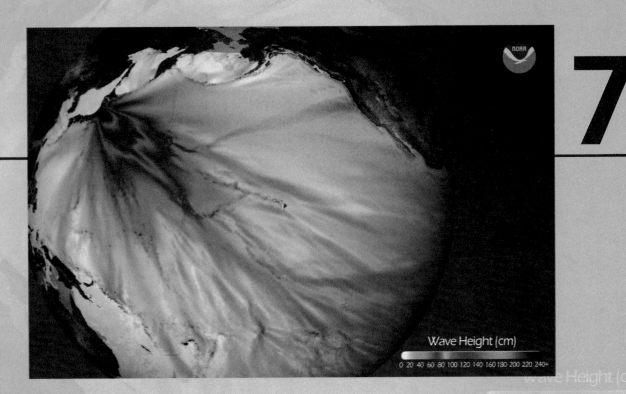

Wave Height (cm)

0 20 40 60 80 100 120 140 160 180 200 220 240+

ENGINEERING CHALLENGE:
Tsunami Warning Systems

Tsunami waves rolled thousands of miles across the Pacific Ocean after an 8.9-magnitude quake hit Japan, the largest ever recorded in the nation's history. Low-lying areas were evacuated as the Pacific Tsunami Warning Center (PTWC) issued warnings. This National Oceanic and Atmospheric Administration (NOAA) image released on March 11, 2011, shows the expected wave heights of the tsunami as it travels across the Pacific basin. The largest wave heights are expected near the earthquake epicenter. The wave will decrease in height as it travels across the deep Pacific, but the wave will grow taller as it nears coastal areas. In general, as the energy of the wave decreases with distance, the near-shore heights will also decrease. The PTWC uses seismic data and real-time oceanographic data to calculate possible threats. Tide gauges and DART (Deep-ocean Assessment and Reporting of Tsunamis) buoys are monitored to determine the formation of a tsunami. When this is established, forecasts of the tsunami are generated and warnings are issued. In this chapter, we use buoy data to calculate the significant wave height over a 20-minute period.

ONE-DIMENSIONAL ARRAYS

CHAPTER OUTLINE

OBJECTIVES

In this chapter, we develop problem solutions containing:

- one-dimensional arrays and vectors
- programmer-defined modules for statistical analysis of data
- functions that sort data and search data
- functions that calculate the probability of an event

- character strings and string objects
- functions defined in the header files `cstring` and `string`
- custom header files

7.1 Arrays

When solving engineering problems, it is important to be able to visualize the data related to the problem. Sometimes the data consist of just a single number, such as the radius of a circle. Other times the data may be a coordinate in a plane that can be represented as a pair of numbers, with one number representing the *x*-coordinate and the other number representing the *y*-coordinate. There are also times when we want to work with a set of similar data values, but we do not want to give each value a separate name. For example, suppose that we have

309

a set of 100 temperature measurements that we want to use to perform several computations. Obviously, we do not want to use 100 different names for the temperature measurements, so we need a method for working with a group of values using a single identifier. One solution to this problem uses a data structure called an **array.**

one-dimensional array

A **one-dimensional array** can be visualized as a list of values arranged in either a row or a column, as follows:

```
double s[]  | 0.5 | 0.0 | –0.1 | 0.2 | 0.15 | 0.2 |
             s[0]  s[1]  s[2]  s[3]  s[4]   s[5]
```

```
char v[]  | 'a' | v[0]
          | 'e' | v[1]
          | 'i' | v[2]
          | 'o' | v[3]
          | 'u' | v[4]
```

elements

offsets

We assign a type and an identifier to an array and then distinguish between **elements,** or values, in the array using **offsets,** also referred to as indicies or subscripts. Thus, by using the example arrays, the first value in the s array is referenced by s[0], the second value in the s array is reference by s[1], and the last value in the array v is referenced by v[4]. In C++, the array identifier holds the *address of the first element,* so the offset always starts at 0 and is incremented by 1.

Definition and Initialization

An array is defined using declaration statements. An integer expression in brackets follows the identifier and specifies the number of elements in the array. Note that all elements in an array must be of the same data type. The declaration statements for the two example arrays are as follows:

```
double s[6];
char v[5];
```

An array can be initialized with declaration statements or assigned values with program statements. To initialize an array with a declaration statement, we use an **initialization list.** An initialization list is a block of values, specified in a sequence and separated by commas. The following statements define and initialize the sample arrays s and v:

initialization list

```
int s[6]={0.5, 0.0, -0.1, 0.2, 0.15, 0.2};
char v[5] = {'a', 'e', 'i', 'o', 'u'};
```

If the initializing sequence is shorter than the array, then the rest of the values are initialized to zero. Hence, the following statement defines an integer array of 100 values; each value is also initialized to zero:

```
int t[100]={0};
```

If an array is specified without a size, but with an initialization list, the size is defined to be equal to the number of values in the sequence:

```
double s[]={0.5, 0.0, -0.1, 0.2, 0.15, 0.2};
int t[]={0, 1, 2, 3};
```

A memory snapshot of s and t is given below:

```
double s  | 0.5 | 0.0 | -0.1 | 0.2 | 0.15 | 0.2 | ← data values
           [0]   [1]   [2]    [3]   [4]    [5]  ← offsets

int t        | 0 | 1 | 2 | 3 | ← data values
             [0][1][2][3] ← offsets
```

The size of an array must be specified in the declaration statement, using either a constant within brackets or by an initialization list.

Array Declaration Statements: The declaration of a 1-dimensional array allocates a consecutive block of memory addresses, and the name of the array holds the first address in the block. The array name and an offset are used to access individual values, thus the data type of each value must be the same.

Syntax:
   data type identifier[size] [= initialization list];

Example:
   `int data[5];` //allocates consecutive memory for 5 integer values
      Memory diagram: data | ? | ? | ? | ? | ? |
      Offsets: 0 1 2 3 4

   `char vowels[5] = {'a', 'e', 'i', 'o', 'u'};` //allocates and initializes
      Memory diagram: vowels |'a'|'e'|'i'|'o'|'u'|
      Offsets: 0 1 2 3 4

   `double t[100] = {0.0};` //allocates and initialized all values to 0.0
      Memory diagram: t | 0 | 0 | 0 | ... | 0 |
      Offsets: 0 1 2 ... 99

Valid References:
`cout << vowels[0];`
`cout <<t[2];`

Invalid References:
`cout << vowel[5];` //invalid offset.
`cout << t[-1];` //invalid offset

Arrays can also be assigned values after they have been declared. For example, suppose that we want to fill a `double` array g with the values 0.0, 0.5, 1.0, 1.5, ..., 10.0. Because there are 21 different values, listing the values in an initialization list would be tedious, but assigning the values to the array within a `for` loop is very easy, as illustrated in program `chapter7_1`.

Pseudocode

```
main: set i to 0
      while i<21
          assign i*0.5 to t[i]
          increment i by 1
      print heading
      set i to 0
      while i<21
          print t[i]
          increment i by 1
```

```cpp
/*-----------------------------------------------------------*/
/* Program chapter7_1                                        */
/* This program assigns a set of values to a                 */
/* one-dimensional array then prints a list of the array     */
/* offsets and values to standard output.                    */
/*-----------------------------------------------------------*/

#include<iostream> //Required for cout.
#include<iomanip> //Required for setw().
using namespace std;

int main()
{
   //Declare varialbles.
   double t[21]; //The array.
   int i; //The loop index.

   //Assign 21 value to array t.
   for(i=0; i<21; ++i)
   {
      t[i] = i*0.5; //i provides offset and value.
   }

   //Print list of array offsets and values.
   //Print heading.
   cout << "21 values assigned to t"<< endl
        << "Offset Value" << endl;
   //Print list inside for loop.
   for(i=0; i<21; ++i)
   {
      cout << setw(6) << i << setw(10) << t[i] << endl;
   }
   return 0;
}
```

The output from program chapter7_1 is given below.

```
21 values assigned to t
  Offset      Value
     0          0
     1          0.5
     2          1
```

3	1.5
4	2
5	2.5
6	3
7	3.5
8	4
9	4.5
10	5
11	5.5
12	6
13	6.5
14	7
15	7.5
16	8
17	8.5
18	9
19	9.5
20	10

It is important to recognize that the final offset value is 20, not 21. This is because the offset of the first element is 0, not 1, thus the offset of the last element is 20, not 21. It is a common mistake to specify an offset that is one greater than the largest valid offset. This error can be very difficult to find because it is not reported by the compiler and it accesses a memory location outside of the declared memory space of the array. Accessing memory locations outside the bounds of an array can produce execution errors such as "segmentation fault" or "bus error". More often this error is not detected during the program execution, but will cause unpredictable program results, since your program has potentially modified a memory location allocated for a different use.

Arrays are often used to store information that is read from data files. For example, suppose that we have a data file named sensor3.dat that contains ten time and motion measurements collected from a seismometer. Program chapter7_2 illustrates how these values can be read from the data file and assigned to the arrays named time and motion.

```
/*-------------------------------------------------------------------*/
/* Program chapter7_2                                                */
/*                                                                   */
/* This program reads time and motion values from an input file      */
/* and assigns the values to the arrays time and motion.             */
/* Input values are printed to standard output for verification.     */

#include<iostream> //required for cout
#include<fstream>  //required for ifstream

using namespace std;

int main()
{
   // Declare objects.
   double time[10], motion[10];
   ifstream sensor3(" sensor3.dat" );
```

```
// Check for successful open and read data into arrays.
if(!sensor3.fail())
{
    for (int k=0; k<10; ++k)
    {
        sensor3 >> time[k] >> motion[k];
        cout << time[k] << '\t' << motion[k] << endl;
    }
}
else
{
    cout << " Could not open file sensor3.dat..goodbye." << endl;
}
return 0;
}
```

If the data file `sensor3.dat` held the set of data

```
0.0       1
0.1       1
0.2       2.5
0.3       1.7
0.4       2
0.5       2.5
0.6       3.5
0.7       1.5
0.8       1.5
0.9       1
```

then the arrays time and motion would contain the following values:

double time		double motion	
	0.0		1.0
	0.1		1.0
	0.2		2.5
	0.3		1.7
	0.4		2.0
	0.5		2.5
	0.6		3.5
	0.7		1.5
	0.8		1.5
	0.9		1.0

The output from program `chapter7_2` is given below:

```
0         1
0.1       1
0.2       2.5
0.3       1.7
0.4       2
0.5       2.5
```

```
0.6        3.5
0.7        1.5
0.8        1.5
0.9        1
```

Show the contents of the arrays defined in each of the following sets of statements.

1. `int x[10]={-5, 4, 3};`

2. `char letters[] = {'a', 'b', 'c'};`

3. `double z[4];`
   ```
   ...
   z[1] = -5.5;
   z[2] = z[3] = fabs(z[1]);
   ```

4. `double time[9];`
   ```
   ...
   for (int k=0; k<=8; k++)
   {
       time[k] = (k-4)*0.1;
   }
   ```

5. Show the output generated by the following program:

   ```
   #include<iostream>
   using namespace std;
   int main()
   {
     int arr[5], i, k;
     for(i=0; i<5; ++i)
     {
         for(k=1; k<3; ++k)
         {
           arr[i] += k*i;
         }
         cout << "arr[" << i << "] is " << arr[i] << endl;
     }
     return 0;
   }
   ```

Computation and Output

Computations with array elements are specified just like computations with simple objects, but an offset must be used to specify an individual array element. To illustrate, the next program uses a `for` loop to read a specified number of floating-point values from a data file and assign the values to the array y. The declared size of y is 100, thus the program will allow at most 100 values to be assigned to y to avoid exceeding the bounds of the array. The program determines the average value of the data and stores it in yAve. Then, the number of values in the array that are greater than the average are counted and printed.

```
/*------------------------------------------------------------*/
/* Program chapter7_3                                         */
/*                                                            */
/* This program reads at most 100 values from a data          */
/* file and determines the number of values greater          */
/* than the average.                                          */

#include<iostream> //Required for cin, cout, cerr.
#include<fstream> //Required for ifstream.
#include<string> //Required for string.
using namespace std;

int main()
{
  // Define maximum array size constant
  const int N = 100;

  // Declare and initialize objects.
  string filename;
  int count=0, numberOfValues;
  double y[N], yAve, sum=0;
  ifstream lab;

  // Prompt user for name of input file
  cout << "Enter name of the input file";
  cin >> filename;

  // Open data file and read data into an array.
  // Compute a sum of the values.
  lab.open(filename.c_str());
  if (lab. fail())
  {
    cerr << "Error opening input file\n";
    exit(1);
  }
  /* File has been opened.                                    */
  /* Read number of data values.                              */
  lab >>numberOfValues;
  // Don't exceed the bound of the array.
  if(numberOfValues > N)
  {
    cerr << "Number of data values," << numberOfValues
         << "exceeds maximum array size of" << N << endl
         << N << "values will be read." << endl;
    numberOfValues = N;
  }
  int k;
  for (k=0; k<numberOfValues; ++k)
  {
        lab >> y[k];
        sum += y[k];
  }
```

```
// Compute average and count values that
// are greater than the average.
yAve = sum/numberOfValues;
for (int k=0; k<numberOfValues; ++k)
{
     if (y[k] > y_ave)
        count++;
}

// Print count.
cout << count << "values greater than the average \n";

// Close file and exit program.
lab.close();
return 0;
}
/*-------------------------------------------------------------*/
```

If the purpose of this program had been to determine the average of the values in the data file, an array would not have been necessary. The loop to read values could read each value into the same object, adding its value to a sum before the next value is read. However, because we needed to compare each value to the average in order to count the number of values greater than the average, we chose to use an array to store the values so we could access them a second time.

Array values are printed using an offset to specify the individual value desired. For example, the following statement prints the first and last values of the array y used in the previous example:

```
cout << "first and last array values: \n";
cout << y[0] << " " << y[numberOfValues-1] << endl;
```

The following loop prints all 100 values of y, one per line:

```
cout << "y values: \n";
for (int k=0; k<N; ++k)
{
   cout << y[k] << endl;
}
```

Note that the values in an array must be printed one value at a time since C++ does not, in general, support aggregate output operations on arrays. When printing a large array such as this one, we probably would like to print several numbers on the same line. The following statements use the modulus operator to skip to a new line before each group of five values is printed:

```
cout << "y values: \n";
for (int k=0; k<numberOfValues; ++k)
{
    if (k%5 == 0)
       cout << y[k] << endl;
    else
       cout << y[k] << " ";
}
cout << endl;
```

Statements similar to the ones illustrated here can also be used to write array values to a data file. For example, the following statement will print the value of y[k] on a line in a data file using the file stream `sensor`:

```
sensor << y[k] << endl;
```

Since the `endl` manipulator is included, the next value written to the file will be on a new line.

Modify!

1. Rewrite program `chapter7_3` without using an array. Hint: calculate the average, then close and reopen the input file and count the number of values greater than the average. Did you need to clear the `eofbit` before reading the file for a second time?

2. Consider the following program:

```
#include<iostream>
using namespace std;

int main()
{
    char greeting[] = "HelloWorld";
    int numbers[] = {1,2,3,4,5};
    cout << greeting << endl;
    cout << numbers << endl;
    return 0;
}
```

Compile and run this program. Explain the output.

maximum size of an array

The **maximum size of an array**, that is, the number of elements that can be assigned to an array, is determined in the type declaration statement and can be referenced later in the program to avoid exceeding the bounds of the array. If the maximum size is changed, then there may be several places in the program that need to be modified. *Changing the maximum size of an array is simplified if a symbolic constant is used to specify the declared size of the array.* Then, to change the maximum size, only the value of the symbolic constant needs to be changed. This style suggestion is especially important in programs that contain many modules or in programming environments in which several programmers are working on the same software project. Many of the following programs illustrate the use of a symbolic constant to define the maximum size of an array.

Table 7.1 gives an updated precedence order that includes offset brackets. Brackets and parentheses are associated before the other operators. If parentheses and brackets are in the same statement, they are associated from left to right; if they are nested, the innermost set is evaluated first.

TABLE 7.1 Operator Precedence

Precedence	Operation	Associativity
1	() []	innermost first
2	++ -- + - ! (type)	right to left (unary)
3	* / %	left to right
4	+ -	left to right
5	< <= > >=	left to right
6	== !=	left to right
7	&&	left to right
8	||	left to right
9	? :	right to left
10	= += -= *= /= %=	right to left
11	,	left to right

Practice!

Assume that the array *s* has been defined with the following statement:

```
int s[]={3, 8, 15, 21, 30, 41};
```

Determine, by hand, the output for each of the following sets of statements:

```
1. for (int k=0; k<=5; k+=2)
   {
       cout << s[k] << ' ' <<  s[k+1] << endl;
   }

2. for (int k=0; k<=5; k++)
   {
       if (s[k]%2 == 0)
           cout << s[k] << ' ';
   }
   cout << endl;
```

Function Arguments

When the information in an array is passed to a function, two parameters are usually used; one parameter specifies the specific array and the other parameter specifies the number of elements used in the array. By specifying the number of elements of the array that are to be used, the function becomes more flexible. For example, if the function specifies an integer array, then the function can be used with any integer array; the parameter that specifies the number of elements assures that we use the correct size. Also, the number of elements used in an array may vary from one time to another. For example, the array may use elements read from a data file; the number of elements then depends on the specific data file used when the program is run. In all these examples, though, the array must be declared to be a maximum size, and then the actual number of elements used can be less than or equal to that maximum size.

Consider program `chapter7_4` provided below, which reads an array from a data file and then references a function to determine the maximum value in the array. The object `npts` is used to count the actual number of values that are read from the data file and stored in the array; the value of `npts` can be less than or equal to the defined size of the array, which is 100. We must be careful not to assign more than 100 values to the array, and we must also keep an accurate count of the actual number of values that are assigned to the array. The function has two formal parameters, the name of the array and the actual number of points in the array, as indicated in the function prototype statement. A flowchart for program `chapter7_4` is provided in Figure 7.1.

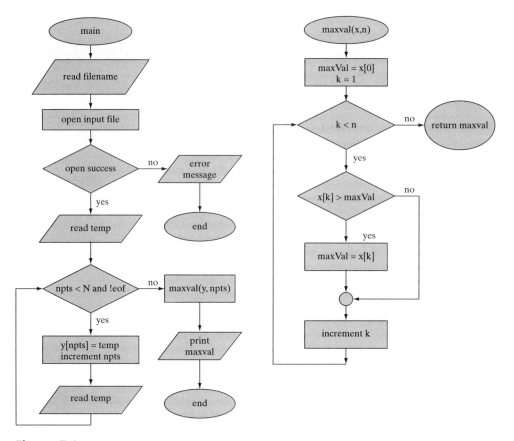

Figure 7.1

```
/*-------------------------------------------------------*/
/* Program chapter7_4                                    */
/*                                                       */
/* This program reads values from a data file and        */
/* calls a function to determine the maximum value       */
/* with a function.                                      */

#include<iostream> //Required for cin, cerr.
#include<fstream> //Required for ifstream.
#include<string> //Required for string.
using namespace std;

// Define function prototypes.
double maxval (const double x[], int n);

int main()
{
  // Declare objects.
  const int N = 100;
  int npts=0;
  double y[N], temp;
  string filename;
  ifstream lab;

  // Prompt user for file name and open data file.
  cout << "Enter the name of the data file:";
  cin >> filename;
  lab.open(filename.c_str());
  if(lab.fail())
  {
    cerr << "Error opening input file\n";
    exit(1);
  }
  // Read a data value from the file.
  lab >> temp;

  // While there is room in the array and
  // and end of file was not encountered,
  // assign the value to the array and
  // input the next value.

  while (npts < N && !lab.eof() )
  {
      y[npts] = temp; // Assign data value to array.
      ++npts;         // Increment npts.
      lab >> temp;    // Input next value
  }

  // Find and print the maximum value.
  cout << "Maximum value: " << maxval(y,npts) << endl;
```

```
  // Close file and exit program.
  lab.close();

  return 0;
}
/*------------------------------------------------------------*/
/* This function returns the maximum                          */
/* value in the array x with n elements.                      */

double maxval (const double x[], int n)
{
  // Declare local objects.
  double maxVal;

  // Determine maximum value in the array.
  maxVal = x[0];
  for (int k=1; k<n; ++k)
  {
    if (x[k] > maxVal)
    maxVal = x[k];
  }

  // Return maximum value. /
  return maxVal;
}
/*------------------------------------------------------*/
```

A program trace and memory snapshot for program `chapter7_4` are provided in Figure 7.2. A separate program trace and memory snapshot for the function `maxval()` are provided in Figure 7.3.

There is a very significant difference in using arrays as parameters, and using simple objects as parameters. When a simple object is used as a parameter, the default is always a pass by value. When an array is used as a parameter, it is always a pass by reference. Recall that a pass by reference means that the memory address of the argument, rather than the value, is passed to the formal parameter. When an array is used as a parameter, the address of the first element is passed to the function. The function uses this address, along with an integer offset, to reference values in the original array, as illustrated in Figure 7.2 and Figure 7.3. Any changes made to the array in the function are made directly to the array argument. Because a function accesses the array argument directly, we must be very careful not to inadvertently change values in an array within a function. Of course, there may be occasions when we wish to change the values in the array, as we will see in later examples in this chapter.

Since we want to insure that the `maxval` function will not change the values in the array argument, we use the `const` modifier in the function prototype and the function header. This will prevent the function from assigning new values to the array. Any attempt to assign a value to an element in the array x will result in a compilation error.

Memory Snapshot

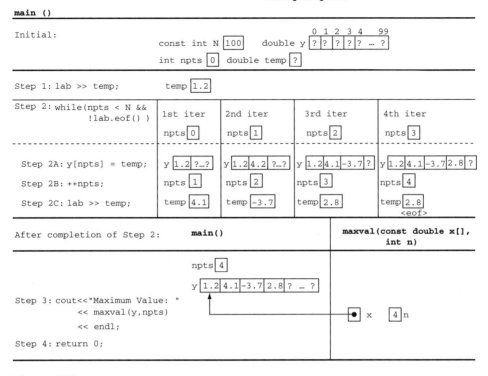

Figure 7.2

Memory Snapshot

maxval(const double x[ ], int n)

Initial:	**main( )**	**maxval(const double x[ ],** **int n)**
	npts 4 　　0　1　2　3　4　99 y 1.2 4.1 -3.7 2.8 ? ... ?	4 n ? maxVal ● x
Step 1: maxVal = x[0]; Step 2: for(int k=1;		1.2 maxVal 1 int k

	1st iter k 1 true	2nd iter k 2 true	3rd iter k 3 true	4th iter k 4 false
Step 3: k<n;				
Step 3A: if(x [k]>maxVal)	true	false	false	
Step 3A1: maxVal = x[k];	4.1 maxVal			
Step 3B: ++k;	k 2	k 3	k 4	
Step 4: return maxVal;				

Figure 7.3

Assume that the following objects are defined:

```
int k=6;
double data[]={1.5, 3.2, -6.1, 9.8, 8.7, 5.2};
```

Give the values of the expressions that follow, which reference the `maxval` function presented in this section.

1. maxval(data,6);
2. maxval(data,5);
3. maxval(data,k-3);
4. maxval(data,k%5);

7.2 Problem Solving Applied: Hurricane Categories

Hurricanes are tropical storms with very strong winds and heavy rains. (They are called typhoons in the western North Pacific Ocean, and cyclones in the Indian Ocean.) These tropical storms, or cyclones, are low-pressure cells that typically form in the summer and early fall. The large rotating air masses are easily seen on satellite images, and the storms are carefully tracked because of the potential for damage in populated areas. If the winds in a storm are between 38 and 74 miles per hour, it called a tropical storm; if the wind exceeds 74 miles per hour, the storm is a tropical cyclone, or hurricane. The Saffir-Simpson scale defines categories of hurricane intensity based on the wind speed. In this section, we define the Saffir-Simpson scale in more detail, and we then develop a program that reads a data file containing current storms and their peak wind speeds. Then, based on the wind speeds, we print a report with information on the storms that are strong enough to be classified as hurricanes.

The Saffir-Simpson scale of hurricane intensities is used to classify hurricanes according to the amount of damage that the storm is likely to generate if it hits a populated area. The main characteristics of the five categories are described below:

Category 1	wind speeds of 74–95 mph storm surge of 4–5 feet minimal damage to property
Category 2	wind speeds of 96–110 mph storm surge of 6–8 feet moderate damage to property
Category 3	wind speeds of 111–130 mph storm surge of 9–12 feet extensive damage to property
Category 4	wind speeds of 131–155 mph storm surge of 13–18 feet extreme damage to property
Category 5	wind speeds over 155 mph storm surge greater than 18 feet catastrophic damage to property

Table 7.2 contains a list of the twelve strongest hurricanes to hit the U.S. during the period 1950 to 2002. (You will find it interesting to obtain more details on these hurricanes using the Internet.)

TABLE 7.2	Strongest Hurricanes in the U.S. during 1950–2002	
Hurricane	**Year**	**Category**
Hazel	1954	4
Audrey	1957	4
Donna	1960	4
Carla	1961	4
Camille	1969	5
Celia	1970	3
Frederic	1979	3
Allen	1980	3
Gloria	1985	3
Hugo	1989	4
Andrew	1992	5
Opal	1995	3

Each year there are over 100 storms with the potential to become hurricanes. Write a program that will read a data file containing information on the current storms that consists of an identification number and the highest wind speed (in miles per hour, or mph) measured so far in the storm. The program should print a list of all storms that have wind speeds high enough to make them a hurricane. In addition to the identification number (an integer), also print the peak wind speed and the corresponding hurricane intensity category. Also, print an asterisk after the identification number of the hurricane with the largest wind speed.

1. PROBLEM STATEMENT

Determine the storms that are hurricanes using a data file of current storm information.

2. INPUT/OUTPUT DESCRIPTION

The I/O diagram shows the data file as the input and the hurricane information as output.

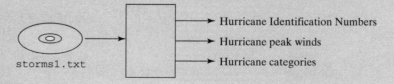

storms1.txt → [ ] → Hurricane Identification Numbers
→ Hurricane peak winds
→ Hurricane categories

3. HAND EXAMPLE

Assume that the data file contained the following five sets of data:

Identification	Peak Wind
142	38
153	135
162	59
177	76
181	63

The corresponding output would then be the following report:

Storms that Qualify as Hurricanes

Identification	Peak Wind (mph)	Category
153*	135	4
177	76	1

Recall that the asterisk identifies the storm with the largest wind speed.

4. ALGORITHM DEVELOPMENT

We first develop the decomposition outline because it divides the solution into a series of sequential steps. To print the information for storms that are hurricanes, we do not need an array. We could do that as we read through the file, since the hurricane status is dependent only on the wind speed. However, since we also need to use an asterisk to indicate the storm with the peak wind, we will need to store all the information in arrays. After we have determined the maximum, we can then go back through the data printing the hurricane information with the asterisk for the maximum wind speed.

Decomposition Outline

1. Read the storm data into arrays, and determine the maximum wind speed.

2. Compute the intensity categories and print information for storms that are hurricanes, with an asterisk at the maximum.

We will put the steps that determine the intensity category into a function.

Refinement in Pseudocode

```
main: if file cannot be opened
            print error mesage
      else
            read data into arrays, and determine max speed, npts
            set k to 0
            while k ≤ npts-1
                    if mph[k] > 74
                            if mph[k] = max speed
                                    print id[k], *, mph[k], cateory(mph[k])
```

```
                        else
                                print id[k], mph[k], category(mph[k])
                        add 1 to k

category(mph):
        category =1;
        if mph ≥ 96
                category =2
        if mph ≥ 111
                category =3
        if mph ≥ 131
                category =4
        if mph ≥ 155
                category =5
```

The steps in the pseudocode are now detailed enough to convert into C++.

```cpp
/*-------------------------------------------------------------*/
/* Program chapter7_5                                          */
/*                                                             */
/* This program reads storm values from a data file           */

#include<iostream> //Required for cin, cout, cerr.
#include<fstream> //Required for fin.
using namespace std;


//Function Prototypes.
double category(double speed);

int main()
{
  //Declare and initialize variables.
  const int MAX_SIZE = 500;
  int k(0), npts, id[MAX_SIZE];
  double mph [MAX_SIZE], max(0);
  ifstream fin("storm1.txt");
  if(fin.fail())
  {
    cerr << "Could not open file storm1.txt" << endl;
    exit(1);
  }
  //Read data and determine maximum mph.
  fin >> id[k] >> mph[k];
  while(!fin.fail())
  {
    if(mph[k] > max)
    {
      max = mph[k];
    }
```

```
         ++k;
         fin >> id[k] >> mph[k];
      }//end while
      npts = k;

      //Print hurricane report.
      if(max >= 74)
      {
         cout << "Storms that Qualify as Hurricanes \n"
              << "Identification\t Peak Wind(mph)\t Category\n";
      }
      else
      {
         cout << "No hurricanes in the file \n";
      }
      for(k=0; k<npts; ++k)
      {
         if(mph[k] >= 74)
         {
            if(mph[k] == max)
            {
               cout << "\t" << id[k] << "*\t\t" << mph[k] << "\t
                    << category(mph[k]) << endl;
            }
            else
            {
               cout << "\t" << id[k] << "\t\t" <<mph[k] << "\t
                    << category(mph[k]) << endl;
            }
         }//end if k
      }//end for
      fin.close();
      return 0;
}
/*------------------------------------------------------------*/
/* This function determines the hurricane intensity           */
/* category.                                                  */

double category(double speed)
{
   //Declare variables.
   int intensity(1);

   //Determine category.
   if(speed >= 155)
   {
       intensity=5;
   }
```

```
        else if(speed >= 131)
        {
            intensity = 4;
        }
        else if(speed >= 111)
        {
            intensity = 3;
        }
        else if(speed >= 96)
        {
            intensity = 2;
        }
        return intensity;
    }
/*-------------------------------------------------------------------*/
```

5. TESTING

We start testing with a file containing the hand example, which gives the following interaction:

Storms that Qualify as Hurricanes

Identification	Peak Wind (mph)	Category
153*	135	4
177	76	1

Modify!

These problems relate to the program developed in this section for printing a hurricane intensity report.

1. Modify the program so that it only prints the information for the hurricane with the largest wind speed.

2. Modify the program so that it also prints the number of storms from the data file.

3. Modify the program so that it also prints the number of hurricanes from the data file.

4. Modify the program so that it prints the number of hurricanes in each category at the end of the report.

5. Modify the program so that it generates a new data file containing information on each hurricane, along with its intensity.

7.3   Statistical Measurements

statistical
measurements

Analyzing data collected from engineering experiments is an important part of evaluating the experiments. This analysis ranges from simple computations on the data, such as calculating the average value, to more complicated analysis. Many of the computations or measurements using data are **statistical measurements** because they have statistical properties that change from one set of data to another. For example, the sine of 60 degrees is an exact value that is the same value every time we compute it, but the number of miles to the gallon that we get with our car is a statistical measurement because it varies somewhat, depending on parameters such as the temperature, the speed that we travel, the type of road, and whether we are in the mountains or the desert.

Simple Analysis

mean
median

When evaluating a set of experimental data, we often compute the maximum value, minimum value, **mean** or average value, and the **median**. In this section, we develop functions that can be used to compute these values using an array as input. These functions (stored in a file *stat_lib.cpp*) will be useful in many of the programs that we develop later in the text and in solutions to problems at the end of the chapters. It is important to note that the functions assume that there is at least one value in the array. The functions also assume that the array contains `double` values.

Maximum, Minimum.   A function for determining the maximum value in an array was presented in the previous section; a similar function for determining the minimum value is presented here:

```
/*-----------------------------------------------------*/
/*   This function returns the minimum                 */
/*   value in an array x with n elements.              */

double minval(const double x[], int n)
{
// Declare objects.
   double min_x;
// Determine minimum value in the array.
   min_x = x[0];
   for (int k=1; k<=n-1; ++k)
   {
      if (x[k] < min_x)
         min_x = x[k];
   }

// Return minimum value.
   return min_x;
}
/*-----------------------------------------------------*/
```

Average.   The Greek symbol μ is used to represent the average, or mean, value, as shown in the following equation, which uses summation notation:

$$\mu = \frac{\sum_{k=0}^{n-1} x_k}{n},$$

where

$$\sum_{k=0}^{n-1} x_k = x_0 + x_1 + x_2 + \cdots + x_{n-1}.$$

This function computes the mean value of a `double` array of n values:

```
/*-----------------------------------------------------------*/
/*   This function returns the average or                    */
/*   mean value of an array with n elements.                 */

double mean(const double x[], int n)
{
    //  Declare and initialize objects.
    double sum(0);

    //  Determine mean value.
    for (int k=0; k<n; ++k)
    {
        sum += x[k];
    }

    //  Return mean value.
    return sum/n;
}
/*-----------------------------------------------------------*/
```

Note that the object `sum` was initialized to zero in the declaration statement. It could also have been initialized to zero with an assignment statement. In either case, the value of `sum` is initialized to zero when the function is referenced.

median

Median.   The **median** is the value in the middle of a group of values, assuming that the values are sorted. If there is an odd number of values, the median is the value in the middle; if there is an even number of values, the median is the average of the values in the two middle positions. For example, the median of the values 1, 6, 18, 39, 86 is the middle value, or 18; the median of the values 1, 6, 18, 39, 86, 91 is the average of the two middle values, or $(18 + 39)/2$, or 28.5. Assume that a group of sorted values is stored in an array, and that n contains the number of values in the array. If n is odd, then the offset of the middle value can be represented by `floor(n/2)`, as in `floor(5/2)`, which is 2. If n is even, then the offsets of the two middle values can be represented by `floor(n/2)-1` and `floor(n/2)`, as in `floor(6/2)-1` and `floor(6/2)`, which are 2 and 3. The next function determines the median of a set of values stored in an array. We assume that the values are sorted (into either ascending or descending order). If the array is not sorted, a function developed later in this chapter can be referenced from the median function to sort the values.

```
/*-------------------------------------------------------------*/
/*  This function returns the median                        */
/*  value in an array x with n elements                     */
/*  The values in x are assumed to be ordered.              */

double median(const double x[], int n)
{
   //  Declare objects.
   double median_x;
   int k;

   //  Determine median value.
   k = floor(n/2);
   if (n%2 != 0)
      median_x = x[k];
   else
      median_x = (x[k-1] + x[k])/2;

   //  Return median value.
   return median_x;
}
/*-------------------------------------------------------------*/
```

Go through this function by hand, using the two sets of data values given in this discussion.

Variance and Standard Deviation

One of the most important statistical measurements for a set of data is the variance. Before we give the mathematical definition for variance, it is useful to develop an intuitive understanding. Consider the values of arrays data1 and data2 that are plotted in Figure 7.4. If we attempted to draw a horizontal line through the middle of the values in each plot, this line would be at approximately 3.0.

Thus, both arrays have approximately the same average, or mean, value of 3.0. However, the data in the two arrays clearly have some distinguishing characteristics. The values in data2 vary more from the mean, or deviate more from the mean value. The **variance** of a set of values is defined to be the average squared deviation from the mean; the **standard deviation** is defined to be the square root of the variance. Thus, the variance and the standard deviation of the values in data2 are greater than the variance and standard deviation for the values in data1. Intuitively, the larger the variance (or the standard deviation), the further the values fluctuate around the mean value.

variance
standard deviation

Mathematically, the variance is represented by σ^2, where σ is the Greek symbol sigma. The variance for a set of data values (which we assume are stored in an array x) can be computed using the following equation:

$$\sigma^2 = \frac{\sum_{k=0}^{n-1}(x_k - \mu)^2}{n - 1}. \tag{7.1}$$

This equation is a bit intimidating at first, but if you look at it closely, it becomes much simpler. The term $x_k - \mu$ is the difference between x_k and the mean, or the deviation of x_k

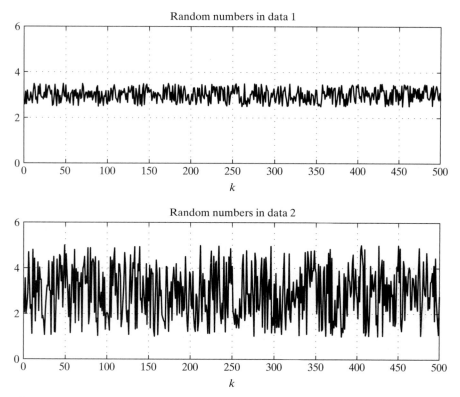

Figure 7.4 Random sequence.

from the mean. This value is squared so that we always have a positive value. We then add the squared deviations for all data points. This sum is then divided by $n - 1$, which approximates an average. The definition of variance has two forms: The denominator of a **sample variance** is $n - 1$, and the denominator of a **population variance** is n. Most engineering applications use the sample variance, as shown in equation (7.1). Thus, equation (7.1) computes the average squared deviation of the data from the mean. The standard deviation is defined to be the square root of the variance:

sample variance
population variance

$$\sigma = \sqrt{\sigma^2}. \tag{7.2}$$

Both the variance and the standard deviation are commonly used in analyzing engineering data, so we give functions for computing both values. Note that the function for computing the standard deviation references the variance function and that the variance function references the mean function; thus, these functions must include the proper function prototype statements. Also, note that there must be at least two values in the array, or the variance function will attempt to perform a division by zero.

```
/*-----------------------------------------------------------*/
/*   This function returns the variance                      */
/*   of an array with n elements.                            */
```

```
//  Function prototype.
double mean(const double x[], int n);

double variance(const double x[], int n) // Function header.
{
    //  Declare objects.
    double sum(0), mu;

    //  Determine variance.
    mu = mean(x,n);
    for (int k=0; k<n; ++k)
    {
        sum += (x[k] - mu)*(x[k] - mu);
    }

    //  Return variance.
    return sum/(n-1);
}
/*-------------------------------------------------------------*/
/*  This function returns the standard deviation              */
/*  of an array with n elements.                              */

//  Declare function prototypes.
double variance(const double x[], int n);

double std_dev(const double x[], int n) // Function header.
{

    //  Return standard deviation.
    return sqrt(variance(x,n));
}
/*-------------------------------------------------------------*/
```

Practice!

Assume that the array *x* is defined and initialized with the following statement:

```
double x[]={2.5, 5.5, 6.0, 6.25, 9.0};
```

Compute by hand the values returned by the following function references:

1. maxval(x,5)

2. median(x,5)

3. variance(x,5)

4. std_dev(x,5)

5. minval(x,4)

6. median(x,4)

Custom Header Files

The functions developed in the previous sections are frequently used in solving engineering problems. To facilitate their use, we generate a custom header file that contains the prototypes for these function. Then, instead of writing all the function prototypes in a main function, a preprocessor directive can be used that includes the custom header file.

The custom header file named `stat_lib.h` contains the following function prototypes:

```
double maxval(const double x[], int n);
double minval(const double x[], int n);
double mean(const double x[], int n);
double median(const double x[], int n);
double variance(const double x[], int n);
double std_dev(const double x[], int n);
```

The statement that includes these in a `main` function is

```
#include "stat_lib.h"
```

The use of this custom header is illustrated in the program in the next section.

In addition to accessing the custom header file with the include statement, a program must also have access to the file `stat_lib.cpp` containing the statistical functions. The specific details of providing this access are platform dependent and may involve adding a file name to the operating system command that performs the compilation and linking/loading operations.

7.4 Problem Solving Applied: Speech Signal Analysis

A speech signal is an acoustical signal that can be converted into an electrical signal with a microphone. The electrical signal can then be converted into a series of numbers that represents the amplitudes of the electrical signal values. These numbers can be stored in data files so that the speech signal can be analyzed using computer programs. Suppose that we are interested in analyzing speech signals for the words "zero," "one," "two," ..., "nine." The goal of this analysis would be to develop ways of identifying the correct digit from a data file containing the utterance of an unknown digit.

Figure 7.5 contains a plot of an utterance of the digit "zero." The analysis of a complicated signal like this one often starts with computing some of the statistical measurements

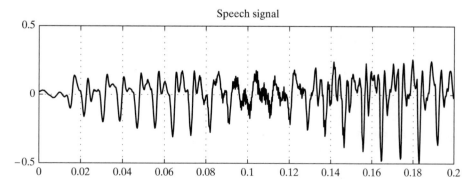

Figure 7.5 Utterance of the word *zero*.

discussed in the previous section. Other measurements used with speech signals include the average magnitude, or average absolute value, which is computed as shown, where n is the number of data values:

$$\text{Average magnitude} = \frac{\sum_{k=0}^{n-1} |x_k|}{n}.$$

(7.3)

Another metric used in speech analysis is the average power of the signal, which is the average squared value:

$$\text{Average power} = \frac{\sum_{k=0}^{n-1} x_k^2}{n}.$$

(7.4)

The number of zero crossings in a speech signal is also a useful statistical measurement. This value is the number of times that the speech signal transitions from a negative to a positive value or from a positive value to a negative value: Transition from a nonzero value to a zero value is not a zero crossing.

Write a program to read a speech signal from a data file named *zero.dat*. This file contains values that represent an utterance of the word "zero." Each line of the file contains a single value representing a measurement from the microphone taken in time increments of 0.0002 second, so 5,000 measurements represent 1 second of data. The data file contains only valid data, with no header or trailer line; a maximum of 2,500 values is contained in the file. Compute and print the following statistical measurements from the file: mean, standard deviation, variance, average power, average magnitude, and number of zero crossings.

1. PROBLEM STATEMENT

Compute the following statistical measurements for a speech utterance: mean, standard deviation, variance, average power, average magnitude, and number of zero crossings.

2. INPUT/OUTPUT DESCRIPTION

The I/O diagram shows the data file as the input and the statistical measurements as output.

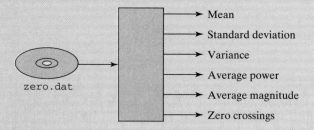

3. HAND EXAMPLE

For a hand example, assume that the file contains the following values:

```
2.5   8.2   -1.1   -0.2   1.5
```

Using a calculator, we can compute the following values:

$$\text{Mean} = \mu = \frac{(2.5 + 8.2 - 1.1 - 0.2 + 1.5)}{5}$$

$$= 2.18;$$

$$\text{Variance} = [(2.5 - \mu)^2 + (8.2 - \mu)^2 + (-1.1 - \mu)^2$$
$$+ (-0.2 - \mu)^2 + (1.5 - \mu)^2]/4$$

$$= 13.307;$$

$$\text{Standard deviation} = \sqrt{13.307}$$

$$= 3.648;$$

$$\text{Average power} = \frac{[(2.5)^2 + (8.2)^2 + (-1.1)^2 + (-0.2)^2 + (1.5)^2]}{5}$$

$$= 15.398;$$

$$\text{Average magnitude} = \frac{(|2.5| + |8.2| + |-1.1| + |-0.2| + |1.5|)}{5}$$

$$= 2.7;$$

$$\text{Number of zero crossings} = 2.$$

4. ALGORITHM DEVELOPMENT

We first develop the decomposition outline, because it divides the solution into a series of sequential steps.

Decomposition Outline

1. Read the speech signal into an array.

2. Compute and print statistical measurements.

Step 1 involves reading the data file and determining the number of data points. Step 2 involves computing and printing the statistical k measurements, using the functions already developed when possible. The refinement in pseudocode for the `main` function and for the additional statistical functions needed is shown next; the structure chart was shown in Figure 5.1 to illustrate an example of a main function that references several programmer-defined functions.

Refinement in Pseudocode

```
main:   read speech signal from data file and
        determine the number of points, n
        compute and print mean
        compute and print standard deviation
```

```
                    compute and print variance
                    compute and print average power
                    compute and print average magnitude
                    compute and print zero crossings
Additional Functions
ave_power(x, n):
        set sum to zero
        set k to zero
        while k <=n - 1
         add x[k]^2 to sum
         increment k by 1
        return sum/n
ave_magn(x, n):
        set sum to zero
        set k to zero
        while k <= n - 1
         add | x[k] | to sum
         increment k by 1
        return sum/n
crossings(x, n):
        set count to zero
        set k to zero
        while k <= n-2
         if x[k]*x[k + 1] < 0
            increment count by 1
         increment k by 1
        return count
```

Note that the number of potential zero crossings for a set of n data points is $n - 1$ crossings, because each crossing is determined by a pair of values. Thus, the last pair of values tested will be at offsets $n - 2$ and $n - 1$. The steps in the pseudocode are detailed enough to convert to C++:

```
/*-----------------------------------------------------------------*/
/*  Program chapter7_6                                             */
/*                                                                 */
/*  This program computes a set of statistical                    */
/*  measurements from a speech signal.                            */

#include<iostream> //Required for cin, cout.
#include<fstream>  //Required for ifstream.
#include<string>   //Required for string
#include<cmath>    //Required for abs()
#include "stat_lib.h" //Required for mean(), variance(), std-dev()
using namespace std;

//  Declare function prototypes and define constants.
double ave_power(double x[], int n);
double ave_magn(double x[], int n);
```

```
int crossings(double x[], int n);

int main()
{
   //  Declare objects.
   const int MAXIMUM = 2500;
   int npts(0);
   double speech[MAXIMUM];
   string filename;
   ifstream file_1;

 //  Prompt user for file name and
 //  open file.
 cout << "Enter filename ";
 cin >> filename;
 file_1.open(filename.c_str());
 if( file_1.fail() )
 {
      cout << "error opening file " << filename
           << endl;
      return 0;
 {
 // Read information from a data file.  *
    while (npts <= MAXIMUM-1 && file_1 >> speech[npts])
    {
      npts++;
    } //end while

 //  Compute and print statistics.
    cout << "Digit Statistics \n";
    cout << "\tmean: " << mean(speech,npts) << endl;
    cout << "\tstandard deviation: "
         << std_dev(speech,npts) << endl;
    cout << "\tvariance: " << variance(speech,npts)
         << endl;
    cout << "\taverage power: " << ave_power(speech,npts)
         << endl;
    cout << "\taverage magnitude: "
         << ave_magn(speech,npts) << endl;
    cout << "\tzero crossings: " << crossings(speech,npts)
         << endl;

   //  Close file and exit program.
   file_1.close();
   return 0;
}
/*-------------------------------------------------------------------*/
/*  This function returns the average power                        */
```

```cpp
/*  of an array x with n elements.                                 */

double ave_power(double x[], int n)
{
   //  Declare and initialize objects.
   double sum(0);

   //  Determine average power.
   for (int k=0; k<=n-1; ++k)
   {
      sum += x[k]*x[k];
   }

   //  Return average power.
   return sum/n;
}
/*-----------------------------------------------------------------*/
/*  This function returns the average magnitude                    */
/*  of an array x with n values.                                   */

double ave_magn(double x[], int n)
{
   //  Declare and initialize objects.
   double sum(0);

   //  Determine average magnitude.
   for (int k=0; k<=n-1; ++k)
   {
      sum += abs(x[k]);
   }

   //  Return average magnitude.
   return sum/n;
}
/*-----------------------------------------------------------------*/
/*  This function returns a count of the number                    */
/*  of zero crossings in an array x with n values.                 */

int crossings(double x[], int n)
{
   //  Declare and initialize objects.
   int count(0);

   //  Determine number of zero crossings.
   for (int k=0; k<=n-2; ++k)
   {
      if (x[k]*x[k+1] < 0)
         count++;
   }
```

```
                    //  Return number of zero crossings.
                    return count;
                }
                /*------------------------------------------------------------*/
```

5. TESTING

This program requires access to the *stat_lib.h* header file and to the *stat_lib.cpp* file developed in the previous section. The following values were computed for the utterance "zero" using the file zero.dat:

```
Digit Statistics
        mean: 0.002931
        standard deviation: 0.121763
        variance: 0.014826
        average power: 0.014820
        average magnitude: 0.089753
        zero crossings: 106
```

Modify!

1. Run this program using the files *two_a.dat*, *two_b.dat*, and *two_c.dat*, available on your instructor's resource CD. These utterances are all of the word "two," but they are spoken by different people.

2. Compare the program output from Problem 1 for the three files. The output illustrates some of the difficulty in designing speech-recognition systems that are speaker independent.

7.5 Sorting and Searching Algorithms

Sorting

Sorting a group of data values is another operation that is routinely used when analyzing data. Entire texts are available that present many different sorting algorithms. One of the reasons that there are so many sorting algorithms is that there is not one "best" sorting algorithm. Some algorithms are faster if the data are already close to the correct order, but these algorithms may be very inefficient if the order is random or is close to the opposite order. Therefore, to choose the best sorting algorithm for a particular application, you usually need to know something about the order of the original data. Rather than try to present a complete discussion of sorting algorithms, we present two algorithms in this text. We encourage you to reference additional texts for a more complete discussion of sorting algorithms. In this section, we present a selection sort that is simple to understand and simple to code in a function.

Selection Sort

selection sort

The **selection sort** algorithm begins by finding the position of the minimum value and exchanging the minimum with the value in the first position in the array. Then, the algorithm finds the minimum value beginning with the second element, and exchanges this minimum with the second element. This process continues until reaching the next-to-last element, which is compared to the last element; the values are exchanged if they are out of order. At this point, the entire array of values is now in ascending order. This process is illustrated in the following sequences that reorder an array:

Original order:

| 5 | 3 | 12 | 8 | 1 | 9 |

Exchange the minimum with the value in the first position:

| 1 | 3 | 12 | 8 | 5 | 9 |

Exchange the next minimum with the value in the second position:

| 1 | 3 | 12 | 8 | 5 | 9 |

Exchange the next minimum with the value in the third position:

| 1 | 3 | 5 | 8 | 12 | 9 |

Exchange the next minimum with the value in the fourth position:

| 1 | 3 | 5 | 8 | 12 | 9 |

Exchange the next minimum with the value in the fifth position:

| 1 | 3 | 5 | 8 | 9 | 12 |

Array values are now in ascending order:

| 1 | 3 | 5 | 8 | 9 | 12 |

The steps in the following function are short, but it is still a good idea to go through this function using the data in this example. Follow the changes in the subscripts k, m, and j within the loops. Also, note that it takes three steps (not two) to exchange values in two objects. Because the function does not return a value, its return type is void.

```
/*-------------------------------------------------------------*/
/*   This function sorts an array with n elements              */
/*   into ascending order.                                     */

void sort(double x[], int n)
{
   // Declare objects.
   int m;
   double hold;
```

```
//  Implement selection sort algorithm.
for (int k=0; k<=n-2; ++k)
{
   // Find position of smallest value in array
   // beginning at k
   m = k;
   for (int j=k+1; j<=n-1; ++j)
   {
      if (x[j] < x[m])
         m = j;
   }
   // Exchange smallest value with value at k
   hold = x[m];
   x[m] = x[k];
   x[k] = hold;
}

//  Void return.
return;
}
/*- - - - - - - - - - - - - - - - - - - - - - - - - - - - - - - - - - - - - - - - - -*/
```

To change this function into one that sorts an array into descending values, the inner loop should search for a maximum instead of a minimum.

The function prototype statement that should be used to refer to this sort function is

```
void sort(double x[], int n);
```

It is also important to note that this function modifies the original array. To keep the original order, an array should be copied into another array before this function is executed; then the data are available in the original order and in the sorted order.

Modify!

1. Write a `main` function that initializes an array, references this `sort` function, and then prints the array values in the new order.

2. Modify the `sort` function so that it sorts values in descending order instead of ascending order. Test the function with the program written in problem 2.

Search Algorithms

Another very common operation performed with arrays is searching the array for a specific value. We may want to know whether a particular value is in the array, how many times it occurs in the array, or where it first occurs in the array. All these forms of searches determine a single value, and thus are good candidates for functions. Next, we will develop several functions for searching an array; then, when you need to perform a search in a program, you can probably use one of these functions with little or no modification to the function.

Searching algorithms fall into two groups: those for searching an unordered list and those for searching an ordered list.

Unordered Lists

sequential search

We first consider searching an unordered list; thus, we assume that the elements are not necessarily sorted into an ascending numerical order, or any other order that may aid us in searching the array. The algorithm to search an unordered array is just a simple **sequential search**: check the first element, check the second element, and so on. There are several ways that we could implement this function. We could develop the function as an integer function that returns the position of the desired value in the array or the value -1 if the desired value is not in the array. We could develop the function as an integer function that returns the number of times the element occurs in the array. We could also develop the function as a `boolean` function that returns a value of true (1) if the element is in the array or false (0) if the element is not in the array. All of these ideas represent valid functions, and we could think of programs that would use each of these forms. Here we present a function that returns the position of the desired value in an unordered array or -1 if the value is not found.

```
int search(const int A[], int n, int value)
/* This function returns the position of value in array A.  */
/*  Returns -1 if value is not found in A.                  */
/*  Function assumes array A is unordered.                  */
{
   int index(0);
   while (index < n && A[index]!=value)
   {
        ++index;
   }
   if(index < n && A[index] == value)
        return(index);
   else
        return(-1);
}
```

Ordered Lists

We now consider searching an ordered or sorted list of values. Consider the following list of ordered values, and assume that we are searching for the value 25:

-7
2
14
38
52
77
105

As soon as we reach the value 38, we know that 25 is not in the list, because we know that the list is ordered in ascending numerical order. Therefore, we do not have to search the entire list, as we would have to do for an unordered list; we only need to search past the point where the value we are looking for should have been. If the list is in ascending order, we search until the current value in the list is larger than the value we are searching for; if the list is in descending order we search until the current value is smaller than the value we are looking for. We now present a function that performs a **sequential search on an ordered list**. The function returns the position of the desired value in an ordered array or −1 if the value is not found:

sequential search on an ordered list

```
/*--------------------------------------------------------------*/
/*  This function returns the position of value in array A.  */
/*  Returns -1 if value is not found in A.                   */
/*  Function assumes:                                        */
/*     the array A has n elements in ascending order.        */

int search(const int A[], int n, int value)
{
    int index(0);
    while (index < n && A[index] < value)
    {
            ++index;
    }
    if(index < n && A[index] == value)
            return(index);
    else
            return(-1);
}
/*--------------------------------------------------------------*/
```

binary search

Another popular and more efficient algorithm for searching an ordered list is the **binary search**. The binary search algorithm is sometimes referred to as the divide-and-conquer algorithm because it begins at the middle of the list and determines if the value being searched for is in the top half or the bottom half of the list. If the value belongs in the top half of the list, the algorithm checks the middle of the top half and repeats, dividing the search space in half at each iteration until the value is found or it is determined that the value is not in the list. The following is a function that implements a binary search:

```
/*--------------------------------------------------------------*/
/*  This function returns the position of value in array list. */
/*  Returns a value of -1 if value is not found in list.       */
/*  Function assumes:                                          */
/*     the array list has n elements in ascending order.       */

int bSearch(const int list[], int n, int value)
{
    int top(0), bottom(n-1), mid;
```

```
while(top<=bottom)
{
   // Determine mid point of list.
   mid = (top + bottom)/2;

   // Value is found.
   if(list[mid] == value)
       return mid;

   // Look for value in top half of list.
   else if(list[mid] > value)
       bottom=mid-1;

   // Look for value in bottom half of list.
   else
       top=mid+1;
}
// Value was not found in the list.
return -1;
}
```

Modify!

1. Modify the sequential search on an ordered list to return a count of the number of times a specified value occurred in an ordered list.

2. Modify the binary-search function so that it correctly searches a list that is ordered in descending order instead of ascending order. Write a `main` program to test your function.

7.6 Problem Solving Applied: Tsunami Warning Systems

A tsunami is a series of water waves that occurs following a large displacement of water. Underwater explosions, such as volcanoes and earthquakes, have the potential to displace large volumes of water, resulting in tsunamis that flood low-lying areas. The Pacific Tsunami Warning Center (PTWC) uses seismic data and real-time oceanographic data to calculate possible threats and issue warnings when a tsunami is detected. Oceanographic data collected from tide gauges and buoys are monitored to determine the formation of a tsunami. The National Oceanic and Atmospheric Administration (NOAA) National Data Buoy Center (NDBC) develops and maintains a network of data-collecting buoys and coastal stations. Real-time data files are generated that contain the last 45 days of recorded data. Raw data from these files is sampled and analyzed to generate oceanographic data, including wind direction, wind speed, significant wave height, average wave period, and dominant wave period. To support this network and other data-collection projects, the NDBC employs a variety of professionals, including engineers, meteorologists, oceanographers, and computer scientists.

In this application, we use recorded data to calculate the significant wave height (WVHT) over a 20-minute sampling period. The significant wave height is measured in meters and is defined as the average of the highest one-third of all wave heights recorded during a 20-minute sampling period. Write a program that will read a data file containing wave-height measurements over a 20-minute sampling period, and then calculate the WVHT. The program should print the WVHT and the beginning time and ending time of the 20-minute sampling period. The data file consists of a header line followed by 20 lines of data. The header line has the following format:

```
#YY MM DD HH MM WH(m)
```

Each subsequent line in the data file contains time and wave-height measurements, in the following format:

```
year(int) month(int) day(int) hour(int) minute(int)
    wave height(double)
```

1. PROBLEM STATEMENT

Calculate the significant wave height (WVHT) over a 20-minute sampling period.

2. INPUT/OUTPUT DESCRIPTION

The I/O diagram shows the data file as the input and the WVHT and time information as output.

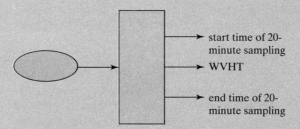

start time of 20-minute sampling

WVHT

end time of 20-minute sampling

3. HAND EXAMPLE

Assume that the data file JulySample.dat contained the following data:

#YY	MM	DD	HH	MM	WH(m)
2011	07	11	03	28	1.23
2011	07	11	03	29	1.27
2011	07	11	03	30	1.29
2011	07	11	03	31	1.51
2011	07	11	03	32	1.72
2011	07	11	03	33	1.85
2011	07	11	03	34	2.01
2011	07	11	03	35	2.12
2011	07	11	03	36	1.92
2011	07	11	03	37	1.71
2011	07	11	03	38	1.32

2011	07	11	03	39	1.26
2011	07	11	03	40	1.21
2011	07	11	03	41	1.02
2011	07	11	03	42	1.12
2011	07	11	03	43	1.24
2011	07	11	03	44	1.27
2011	07	11	03	45	1.29
2011	07	11	03	46	1.33
2011	07	11	03	47	1.73

By observation we see that the top 6 values are:

2.12 2.01 1.92 1.85 1.73 1.72

The corresponding output would be the following:
Starting time:

2011 7 11 3 28

ending time:

2011 7 11 3 47
WVHT is 1.89167

4. ALGORITHM DEVELOPMENT

We first develop the decomposition outline because it divides the solution into a series of sequential steps. To find the significant wave height we must take the average of the highest one-third of the recorded wave heights. Our input file contains 20 wave measurements, so we will calculate the average of the top 20/3, or 6, wave heights. Because the data file is ordered by time, not wave height, our approach will be to read the data and store the wave heights in an array. We will store the wave-height data in descending order, as we read them. This sorting technique is referred to as an **insertion sort**. After all the data has been read, we will take the average of the first six values in the ordered array.

insertion sort

Decomposition Outline

1. Read the header and first line of data.

2. Print starting time.

3. Read wave-height data into array and sort in descending order.

4. Calculate the WVHT.

5. Print ending time and WVHT.

We will put the steps that calculate the WVHT into a function.

Refinement in Pseudocode

```
main: if file cannot be opened
            print error message
            exit
      read header and first line of data
      print starting time
```

```
      //insertion sort
      set i to 1
      while(i < 20)
        read next line of data
        set pos to 0
        while pos < i  and  wave height < array[pos]
          increment pos by 1
        if pos equal to i assign wave height to end of array
          array[i] = wave height
        else insert wave height to maintain order
          set k to i
          while k > pos move values down to make room
              array[k] = array[k-1]
              decrement k by one
          array[pos] = wave height
          increment i by 1
      //end insertion sort
      calculate WVHT
      print ending time and WVHT

WVHT(array,count)
    set i and sum to 0
    while i < count
      add array[i] to sum
      increment i by 1
    return sum/count
```

The steps in the pseudocode are now detailed enough to convert into C++.

```
/*-------------------------------------------------------------*/
/* Program chapter7_7                                          */
/* This program inputs wave height data from an               */
/* input file then calculates the significant wave            */
/* height(WVHT).                                              */

#include<iostream>  //Required for cin, cout, cerr.
#include<fstream>   //Required for ifstream.
#include<string>    //Required for getline().
#include<iomanip>   //Required for setw()
using namespace std;

//Function Prototypes
double average(double[], int);

int main()
{
  //Declare and initialize objects
  const int SAMPLE_SIZE = 20;
  double waveHeights[SAMPLE_SIZE], WVHT, newVal;
  int year, month, day, hour, minute;
  string filename, header;
  ifstream fin;
```

```
            //Get filename and open file
            cout << " Enter name of input file: ";
            cin >> filename;
            fin.open(filename.c_str());
            if(fin.fail())
            {
               cerr << " Could not open the file " << filename
                    << "  Goodbye." << endl;
               exit(1);
            }
            //Read header from input file
            getline(fin,header);

            //Read first line of input data
            int i = 0;
            fin >> year >> month >> day >> hour
                >> minute >> waveHeights[i];

            //Echo header
            cout << header << endl;
        //Print starting date and time.
            cout << " Starting time: " << endl << year
                 << setw(3) << month << setw(3) << day
                 << setw(3) << hour << setw(3) << minute << endl;

            //Read remaining lines of input
            //Order waveHeight in descending order
            int pos;
            for(i=1; i<SAMPLE_SIZE; ++i)
            {
               fin >> year >> month >> day >> hour
                   >> minute >> newVal;
               //find ordered position
               pos = 0;  //start at top
               while(pos < i && newVal < waveHeights[pos])
               {
                  ++pos;
               }
               if(pos == i)
               {
                  //newVal belongs at end of array
                  waveHeights[i] = newVal;
               }
               else
               {
                  //Insert newVal at midpoint in array
                  //Move values down to make room
                  for(int k=i; k>pos; --k)
```

```
                  {
                     waveHeights[k] = waveHeights[k-1];
                  }
               //Assign new value to array
               waveHeights[pos] = newVal;
            }
         }//end for

         //Calculate the WVHT
         //WVHT is defined as the average of the
         //the highest one-third of all wave heights.
         //Average top 1/3 of array elements.
         int top3rd = SAMPLE_SIZE/3;
         WVHT = average(waveHeights, top3rd);

         //Print ending date and time.
         cout << " ending time: "  << endl << year
              << setw(3) << month << setw(3) << day
              << setw(3) << hour << setw(3) << minute << endl;
         cout << " WVHT is "  << WVHT << endl;

         fin.close();
         return 0;
      }
/*------------------------------------------------------------*/
/* This function returns the average of the first size   */
/* elements in array                                     */

double average(double array[], int size)
{
   double sum = 0.0;
   for(int i=0; i<size; ++i)
   {
      sum += array[i];
   }
   sum = sum/size;
  return sum;
}
/*------------------------------------------------------------*/
```

5. TESTING

We start testing with the file used in the hand example, which gives the following output:

```
Enter name of input file: JulySample.dat
#YY  MM DD HH MM WH(m)
Starting time:
2011  7 11  3 28
ending time:
2011  7 11  3 47
WVHT is 1.89167
```

Modify!

These problems relate to the program developed in this section for calculating the WVHT.

1. Modify the program so that it reads all of the wave-height data and stores it in an array, unordered, then calls the function

   ```
   void sort(double x[], int n);
   ```

   developed in this chapter to sort the data before calculating the WVHT.

2. Modify the program to accommodate a sample size of 200 instead of 20.

3. Modify the program to calculate the WVHT without ordering the array of values. Hint: Read and store the first "top3rd" values in a new array, then compare each additional value to the smallest value in the new array.

7.7 Character Strings

character string

C-style string

A character array is an array in which the individual elements are stored as characters. A **character string** can be represented using a character array in which the last array element is a null character, '\0', which has an ASCII integer equivalent of zero. This representation of a string is referred to as a **C-style string**, because it originated with the C programming language and is still supported by C++.

Character strings can also be represented using the string class type introduced in Chapter 2. The string class will be discussed in section 6.9.

C Style String Definition and I/O

Character string constants are enclosed in double quotes, as in "sensor1.dat", "r", and "15762". A character string object can be defined and initialized using string constants or using character constants, as shown in the following statements:

```
// Define string objects using string constants.
char filename1[15] = "sensor1.txt";
char filename2[] = "zero.txt";

// Define string object using character constants.
char filename3[] = {'s','p','e','a','c','h',
                    '.','t','x','t','\0'};
```

Each of the preceding statements defines a C-style string object as illustrated with the following memory snapshot:

char filename1[] | s | e | n | s | o | r | 1 | . | t | x | t | \0 | \0 | \0 | \0 |

char filename2[] | z | e | r | o | . | t | x | t | \0 |

char filename3[] | s | p | e | a | c | h | . | t | x | t | \0 |

Note that the null character occupies one element of the array.

The following statements use the input operator to read two strings from the keyboard and the output operator to print the strings to the screen:

```
// Declare objects.
char unit_length[10], unit_time[10];
...
// Read data into string.
cin >> unit_length >> unit_time;
cout << unit_length << ' ' << unit_time << endl;
...
```

Suppose the following data were entered at the keyboard:

```
inch second
```

The input operator will input a character string and assign the null character to the end of the string, as illustrated with the following memory snapshot:

char unit_length[] | i | n | c | h | \0 | ? | ? | ? | ? | ? |

char unit_time[] | s | e | c | o | n | d | \0 | ? | ? | ? |

However, the input operator does not do any checking on the maximum size of the array. If the input data has more characters than the maximum size of the character array, the input operator will assign values beyond the bounds of the array, and an error will occur.

Recall that the input operator ignores all whitespace. If whitespace is desired as part of a string, the function getline() can be used to read strings, as illustrated in the next example that reads comment lines from the header of an ASCII image file and prints the comment lines on the screen. Our example uses the peek() function to look at the next character on the input stream. The function peek() is a member function of the istream class and can be called by any istream object. The function peek() returns the value of the next character on the input stream but does not remove the character from the input stream:

```
...
// Declare objects
ifstream image("Io.ppm");
char comment_line[100];
...
// Read and print a comment line from a data file.
// Comment lines begin with a #.
```

```
while(image.peek() == '#')
{
        image.getline(comment_line, 100);
        cout << comment_line << endl;
}
...
```

The function `getline()` is a member function of the `istream` class and can be called by any input stream object. The first argument is the name of a character array. The second argument is the maximum length of the array. The `getline()` function will read and store characters until the newline character is encountered or until `maximum_length1` characters have been read. The function will assign the null character as the last character in the string. If the newline character is encountered, the `getline()` function will read and discard the character. A third argument can be used with the `getline()` to specify a character other than the newline to signal the end of the input.

Practice!

Assume that the following text is entered from the keyboard:

```
The mice, Sniff and Scurry,
had only simple brains.
```

Show the output generated by the following program segments (assume that each segment uses the entire input stream):

1. ```
   char cstring1[10], cstring2[] = "Cheese";
   cin >> cstring1;
   cout << cstring1 << ' ' << cstring2 << endl;
   ```
2. ```
   char cstring1[10], cstring2[] = "Cheese";
   cin.getline(cstring1,10);
   cout << cstring1 << cstring2 << endl;
   ```
3. ```
   char cstring1[50], cstring2[50];
   cin.getline(cstring1,50);
   cin.getline(cstring2,50);
   cout << cstring1 << cstring2 << endl;
   ```

String Functions

The Standard C++ library contains numerous functions for working with C-style strings, such as the ones listed below. The header file `cstring` must be included for these functions to be used in a program:

```
strlen(s)    // Returns the length of the string s.
strcpy(s,t)  // Copies string t to string s.
strcat(s,t)  // Concatenates string t to the end of string s.
strcmp(s,t)  // Compares ASCII values of string s to string t
             // in an character-by-character comparison.
             // Returns a negative value if s<t.
             // Returns zero if s is equal to t.
             // Returns a positive value if s>t.
```
```

A complete list of the functions included in the cstring library file can be found in Appendix A. To illustrate the use of these functions, we now present a simple example:

```
/*------------------------------------------------------------*/
/*   Program chapter7_8                                       */
/*   This program illustrates the use of several              */
/*   C style string functions.                                */

#include<iostream> //Required for cout
#include<cstring>  //Required for strlen(), strcmp(), strcpy()
                   //                  strcat().
int main()
{
   // Declare and initialize objects.
   char strg1[]="Engineering Problem Solving: ";
   char strg2[]="Object Based Approach", strg3[75] = "";

   // Print the length of each string.
   cout << "String lengths: " << strlen(strg1) << ' '
        << strlen(strg2) << ' ' << strlen(strg3) << endl;

   // Swap strings if strg1 is larger than strg2
   if(strcmp(strg1,strg2) > 0)

   {
     strcpy(strg3,strg2);
     strcpy(strg2,strg1);
     strcpy(strg1,strg3);
   }

   // Combine two strings into one.
   strcpy(strg3,strg1);
   strcat(strg3,strg2);
   cout << "strg3: " << strg3 << endl;
   cout << "strg3 length: " << strlen(strg3) << endl;
   return 0;
}
/*------------------------------------------------------------*/
```

The output from this program is the following:

```
String lengths: 29 21 0
strg3: Engineering Problem Solving: Object Based Approach
strg3 length: 50
```

7.8 The string Class

The string class provides and object-based alternative to the C-style string. The following are a few of the commonly used member functions included in the string class:

```
size()                  // Returns the length of the calling string.
empty()                 // Returns true if the calling string
                        // contains no characters.
                        // Returns false otherwise.
substr(int start,       // Returns the substring of length len,
       int len)         // Beginning at start of the calling string.
c_str()                 // Returns the equivalent C-style string.
```

Numerous operators have been overloaded in the string class to support the use of string objects. The assignment operator, as well as the relational operators <, >, <=, >=, ==, and the operators + and +=, can be used with string objects. The binary operator + concatenates two strings, and the binary operator += appends one string to the end of the other. To illustrate the use of some of these operators and functions, we will rewrite program7_8, adding a few additional statements and using the string class instead of C-style strings (recall that we must include the header file string in order to use the string class):

```
/*-------------------------------------------------------------*/
/*  Program chapter7_9                                         */
/*  This program illustrates the use of several                */
/*  operators and functions supported by the string class.     */

#include<iostream> //Required for cout
#include<string>   //Required for string, size()

int main()
{
   // Declare and initialize string objects.
   string strg1 = "Engineering Problem Solving: ";
   string strg2 = "Object Based Approach", strg3;

   // Print the length of each string.
   cout << "String lengths: " << strg1.size() << ' '
        << strg2.size() << ' ' << strg3.size() << endl;

   // Swap strings if strg1 is larger than strg2
   if(strg1 > strg2)
   {
      strg3 = strg2;
      strg2 = strg1;
      strg1 = strg3;
   }

   // Append a string.
   strg2 += " Using C++";

   // Concatenate two strings.
   strg3 = strg1 + strg2;
```

```
      cout << "strg3: " << strg3 << endl;
      cout << "strg3 length: " << strg3.size() << endl;
      return 0;
}
/*-----------------------------------------------------*/
```

The output from this program is the following:

```
String lengths: 29 21 0
strg3: Engineering Problem Solving: Object Based Approach Using C++
strg3 length: 60
```

Modify!

1. Modify the sort() function so that it sorts an array of strings in alphabetical order. Use the string class. Write a program to test the function.

2. Modify the bSearch() function so that it searches an ordered list of strings. Use the string class. Write a program to test the function.

7.9 The vector class

The vector class is a pre-defined type included in the C++ Standard Template Library (STL), and provides a generic implementation for the concept of an array. Using the vector class to implement an array has several advantages. When using arrays, we must be careful not to exceed the bounds of the array, and we must also keep track of the actual size of the array. The vector class includes a method that returns the size of a vector, a method that returns the **capacity** of a vector and a method that can increase or decrease the capacity of a vector object dynamically, meaning the capacity can be changed while a program is executing.

capacity

The capacity of a vector is the amount of memory that has been allocated, while the size of a vector is a count of the number of elements that are being used. Due to the dynamic nature of vectors, these numbers are not always the same. Table 7.3 lists a few of the commonly used methods defined in the vector class. These methods are called by an object of type vector, thus the method description refers to the the effect of the method on the calling object.

You will notice that two of these methods return iterators. Iterators and pointers and will be discussed in Chapter 9.

We can define an instance of the vector class in a type declaration statement as illustrated below:

```
vector<char> v1;         //Define vector of type char, capacity 0.
vector<int> v2(10);      //Define v2 with capacity for 10 integers.
vector<string> v3(n);    //Define v3 with capacity for n strings.
vector<double> v4(n,1.0); //Define v4 with capacity for n doubles.
                         //Initialize each element to 1.0.
```

TABLE 7.3 Methods Defined in Vector Class

Method Name	Method Description
back()	Return the value of the last element.
begin()	Return iterator to first element.
capacity()	Return the capacity.
empty()	Return true if size is zero. Return false otherwise.
end()	Return iterator to one past last element.
erase()	Delete element.
insert()	Insert element.
pop_back()	Delete last element.
push_back()	Add element to the end.
resize()	Change the capacity.
size()	Return the size.

Notice the syntax used to specify the type of data that each vector will store. The use of

```
vector<data type>
```

is required because vector is defined as a class template. Templates defined in the STL support generic programming by implementing the concept of a type without specifying the specific type of data that will be stored. For example, the concept of a vector, or an array, is a container that stores a sequential block of data. Data can be added to, or deleted from, the end of a vector very efficiently, and a vector, like an array, supports random access of data, using offsets. Since these concepts are independent of the data, a template for a vector is defined and the compiler generates a concrete instance of the template when a vector is declared with a specific type.

The following example illustrates the use of the vector class and the difference between the size and the capacity of a vector. Notice that we must include the header file vector. Because vector is part of the Standard C++ Library, the linking occurs automatically.

```
/*-------------------------------------------------------------*/
/* Program chapter7_10                                         */

#include<iostream>  //Required for cout
#include<vector>    //Required for vector
using namespace std;

int main()
{
 //Declare and initialize objects.
   vector<int> v(5);

//Print the capacity and the size.
  cout << "Capacity: " << v.capacity() << " Size: " << v.size()
       << endl;
```

```
// Assign values to v.
   for(int i=0; i<v.capacity(); i++)
   {
      v[i] = i;   //Random access
   }

//Print the capacity and the size.
   cout << "Capacity: " << v.capacity() << " Size: " << v.size()
        << endl;

//Add additional data to the end of v
   v.push_back(10);
   v.push_back(20);

//Print the capacity and the size.
   cout << "Capacity: " << v.capacity() << " Size: " << v.size()
        << endl;

   return 0;
}
/*------------------------------------------------------------*/
```

The output from a sample run of this program is:

```
Capacity: 5 Size: 5
Capacity: 5 Size: 5
Capacity: 10 Size: 7
```

For complete and up-to-date information on the STL, visit the website:

```
http://www.sgi.com/tech/stl/table_of_contents.html
```

Modify!

- Modify Program `chapter7_10` by adding statements to print every element in the vector `v`, one value per line, just before the return statement.

- Modify Program `chapter7_10` by replacing the statements

  ```
  //Add additional data to the end of v
    v.push_back(10);
    v.push_back(20);
  ```

  with statements that assign the same values to the end of `v`, using offsets instead of the push_back() method. Does your program run correctly? Explain.

Parameter Passing

When a `vector` is required as a formal parameter in a function definition, the default is pass by value. If we desire to modify the values of a `vector` argument, we must specify a pass by reference, as illustrated in the following program.

```
/*-------------------------------------------------------------*/
/* Program chapter7_11                                         */
/* This program inputs a collection of points and             */
/* finds the Point that is closest to the origin              */
#include<iostream> //Required for cin, cout, cerr.
#include<fstream>  //Required for ifstream.
#include<string>   //Required for string.
#include<vector>   //Required for vector.
#include "Point.h" //Required for Point.
using namespace std;

// Function prototypes.
void readPointFile(istream& in,
                   vector<Point>& v); //Pass by reference
Point closeToOrigin(vector<Point> v);  //Pass by value.

int main()
{
 //Declare objects.
   Point p;
   string filename;
   ifstream file1;

  //Prompt user for file name and
  //open file.
  cout << "Enter filename ";
  cin >> filename;
  file1.open(filename.c_str());
  if( file1.fail() )
  {
       cerr << "error opening file " << filename << endl;
       exit(1);
  }

  //Build Point vector
  vector<Point> v;
  readPointFile(file1, v);

  //Find point closest to orign
  p = closeToOrigin(v);
```

```
      cout << "(" << p.getX() << "," << p.getY() << ")"
           << " is closest to the origin." << endl;
      return 0;
   }
/*------------------------------------------------------------*/
/*------------------------------------------------------------*/
void readPointFile(istream& in,
                   vector<Point>& v)
{
   int npts;
   // Read number of data points.
      in >> npts;
      v.resize(npts);
      Point p;

   // Read Points and store in vector.
   // Points are formatted as x,y
      double x,y;
      char comma;
      for (int i=0; i<npts; ++i)
      {
          in >> x >> comma >> y;
          p.setX(x);
          p.setY(y);
          v[i] = p;;
      }
}
/*------------------------------------------------------------*/
/*------------------------------------------------------------*/
/* This function returns the point                          */
/* closest to the origin                                    */

Point closeToOrigin(vector<Point> v)
{
   Point p1, origin(0.0,0.0);
   int closest(0);  //offset of closest.
   for(int i=1; i<v.size(); ++i)
   {
     if(v[i]-origin < v[closest]-origin)
     {
       closest = i;
     }
   }
   return v[closest];
}
/*------------------------------------------------------------*/
```

A sample run of this program generated the following output:

```
Enter filename pointdata.txt
(1.00,-0.50) is closest to the origin.
```

Classes defined in the C++ STL are supported by a collection of top-level functions defined in the header file `algorithm`. These functions perform sorts, searches, and other common tasks. Using functions defined in `algorithm` can save time in the development of a problem solution and improve the efficiency of a solution. In the next section, we will develop a problem solution that uses the `random_shuffle()` function defined in `algorithm`.

Modify!

1. Modify the `Point class` by adding a `print(ostream&) const` method. When referenced with a `p.print(cout);` statement, the output should look like the output generated by program 7_11; i.e., (X, Y).

7.10 Problem Solving Applied: Calculating Probabilities

The theory of probability has many applications in engineering, including instrumentation reliability as discussed in Chapter 6, structural analysis, and risk management. Risk management is a process that includes identification, analysis, communication, and treatment of risks. In engineering, risk is defined as:

$$Risk = (probability\ of\ an\ event) * (losses\ per\ event).$$

In this section, we will calculate the probability of an event, using formulas developed from the study of set theory, and write a simulation to test our results.

Experimentation and simulation are major paradigms in science and engineering. Simulation uses mathematical models that can be translated into software to better understand experimental results. Many physical experiments do not yield exactly the same results when performed repeatedly. These types of experiments are referred to as **nondeterministic**, or **probabilistic**, **experiments**. For example, if the experiment is to draw a single card from a shuffled deck of 52 playing cards and you conduct the the experiment twice, the results will probably be different. However, it is possible that the results on two consecutive draws from a random deck will be the same.

nondeterministic
probabilistic

In the unlikely event of drawing the same card on two separate draws, no major losses would occur, other than perhaps a financial loss if you happened to place a wager against the occurrence of the event. Engineers design structures and new technologies to improve our quality of life. When unlikely events do occur, the losses can be catastrophic. Thus, the ability to correctly determine the probability of an event is critical in the analysis of risk.

probability of
event E

In probability theory, a number $p(E)$, referred to as the **probability of event E**, is assigned to an event. The number $p(E)$ is the likelihood that event E will occur. Suppose we draw two cards from a shuffled deck of 52 cards and we are interested in the probability that both cards are Kings. In this case, the event, E, is the event of drawing 2 Kings from a deck of 52 cards. To estimate the probability of the event, we can conduct the probabilistic experiment of drawing 2 cards from a deck n times and count the number of times, n_E, that the event E occurred. The fraction n_E/n is a measure of the likelihood that E will occur. Our intuition tells us that if we conducted this experiment twice ($n = 2$), n_E would most likely be zero. However, if we conducted the experiment ten thousand times ($n = 10,000$), n_E would most likely be greater than zero. Thus, $p(E)$ represents a number, n_E/n, as n becomes very large.

To estimate the probability of drawing 2 Kings from a deck of 52 cards, we can conduct the experiment n times by hand and count the number of times the event occurs, or we can write a simulation to conduct the experiment n times and report the results. In either case, we are counting outcomes of a probabilistic experiment, and the results will vary. Probability theory uses formulas based on set theory to count outcomes and calculate probablities.

Suppose we have a set, S, that contains n elements and we choose r such that $1 <= r <= n$. It can be shown that the number of combinations of the elements of S, taken r at a time, is:

$$\frac{n!}{r!(n-r)!}$$

n choose *r*

Note that the number of combinations of S, taken r at at time, depends only on r and n, not on S. This number is the **combination of *n* objects taken *r* at a time**, or ***n* choose *r***, and is written as:

$$_nC_r = \frac{n!}{r!(n-r)!}$$

sample space

event space

We can think about outcomes of experiments, and the occurrences of events, as forming sets. A set consisting of all outcomes of an experiment is called the **sample space** of the experiment, and a set consisting of all outcomes that represent an occurrence of an event is called the **event space**. Note that the event space is a subset of the sample space. Recall that a set is a well-defined collection of unique elements, and the order in which the elements are listed is not important. If we assume that all outcomes of an experiment are equally likely, which is commonly true but difficult to prove, then:

$$p(E) = \frac{size\ of\ the\ event\ space}{size\ of\ the\ sample\ space}.$$

We will now calculate the probability of drawing 2 Kings from a deck of 52 cards. The experiment is drawing 2 cards from a deck of 52 cards; thus, the size of the sample space is the number:

$$_{52}C_2 = \frac{52!}{2!(52-2)!} = \frac{52(51)(50!)}{2!(50!)} = \frac{52(51)}{2} = 1326$$

The event is drawing 2 Kings from a deck of cards that contains exactly 4 Kings; thus, the size of the event space is the number:

$$_4C_2 = \frac{4!}{2!(4-2)!} = \frac{4(3)(2!)}{2!(2!)} = \frac{4(3)}{2} = 6$$

The probability of drawing 2 Kings from a deck of 52 cards is $\frac{6}{1326} = 0.00452489$. Because the size of our event space is 6, we list the elements in the set for illustration.

event space =
{{King of Spades, King of Hearts}, {King of Spades, King of Diamonds}

{King of Spades, King of Clubs}, {King of Hearts, King of Diamonds}

{King of Hearts, King of Clubs}, {King of Diamonds, King of Clubs}}

As indicated by the previous discussion, we can use computer simulations to provide a validation for our analytical results. The simulated probability should approach the analytically computed probability as the number of experiments increases.

Develop a program to compare the analytical probability of an event with simulation results. For this program, the event is drawing 2 cards from a deck of 52 cards, where each card is red and the face value of each card is less than 10. Allow the user to enter the number of experiments to use in the simulation.

1. PROBLEM STATEMENT

Compare the analytical and simulation probabilities for drawing 2 cards from a shuffled deck of 52 cards, where each drawn card is red and has a face value less than 10.

2. INPUT/OUTPUT DESCRIPTION

The I/O diagram shows that the input value is the number of experiments to be conducted in the simulation. The output is the analytical probability and the simulation results.

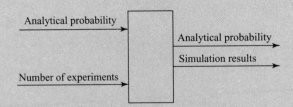

3. HAND EXAMPLE

For the hand example, we will compute the analytical result by determining the size of the event space and then dividing this number by the size of the sample space. In a deck of

52 cards, there are 8 Hearts with a face value less than 10 and 8 Diamonds with a face value less than 10, for a total of 16 red cards with a face value less than 10. Thus, the size of the event space is:

$$_{16}C_2 = \frac{16!}{2!(16-2)!} = \frac{16(15)(14!)}{2!(14!)} = 120$$

The sample space, calculated earlier in this section, is 1,326; thus, the probability of drawing 2 red cards, each with a face value less than 10, is $\frac{120}{1326} = 0.09049774$.

To perform the experiment by hand, we need to:

- Shuffle a deck of cards.

- Draw 2 cards from the deck.

- Look at the results.

- If both cards are red and both cards have a face value less than 10, then we record the event and put back in the deck the 2 cards we drew.

We repeat this experiment n times, then divide the recorded number of events by n. If you have a deck of cards, perform this experiment 10 times. What were your results? Even conducting this experiment times is tedious, and we must be careful to keep accurate counts. Thus, a computer simulation is desirable.

To support our simulation, we will develop a `Card` class and a `CardDeck` class. Our `Card class` requires two attributes: one for the suit and one for the face value, or rank. We need to "look at the results" when we draw a `Card`, so we will include two accessor methods. We will also include a method to display a card in the format:

`Ace of Spades` if the rank is 14 and the suit is 'S', or

`10 of Diamonds` if the rank is 10 and the suit is 'D',

and so on.

We do not include mutators in our `class`, because the concept of a card is that it is not mutable, meaning its value cannot be changed once it has been created.

Our `CardDeck class` requires two attributes: a `vector` to store the 52 cards in a deck and a second `vector` to hold the cards that we draw from the deck. The functionality of `CardDeck` requires a method to shuffle the `CardDeck` and one to draw a `Card` from the `CardDeck`. The shuffle method will be responsible for replacing cards that were drawn from the deck and will use the method `random_shuffle()` defined in `<algorithm>` to perform the shuffle.

Class diagrams for `Card` and `CardDeck` are shown in Figure 7.6. Notice the solid diamond connector joining the two class diagrams. This connector indicates class

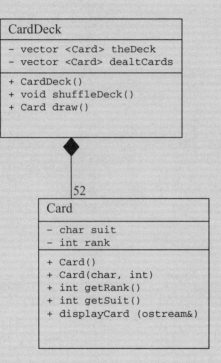

Figure 7.6 UML class diagrams.

composition. We say that a `CardDeck` "has-a" Card. The notation of 52 specifies that a `CardDeck` has exactly 52 `Card` objects. Class composition and UML class diagrams will be discussed in more detail in Chapter 10. The `class` definitions are given below.

Class Definitions:
Card.h
```
/*------------------------------------------------------------*/
/*We use the following compiler directives to avoid          */
/*including the Card.h file muliple times.                   */

/*It is a good idea to always use these directives           */
/*in custom header files.                                    */
#ifndef CARD_H
#define CARD_H

/* Card Class declaration                                    */
/* filename: Card.h                                          */

#include<iostream> //Required for ostream
using namespace std;
```

```
class Card {
   public:
   //Constructors
     Card(); //Default
     Card(char aSuit,
          int aRank);//parameterized
   //Accessors
     int getRank() const;
     char getSuit() const;
   //Formatted Display Method
   //Example: if char is 'S' and rank is 11
   //output will be:

   //Jack of Spades
     void displayCard(ostream& outStream) const;
   private:
     char suit;
     int rank;
};
#endif  //end compiler directive ifndef
/*-----------------------------------------------------------*/
```

Card.cpp

```
/*-----------------------------------------------------------*/
/* Card class implementation                                 */
/* filename: Card.cpp                                        */

#include "Card.h" //Required for Card
#include<cctype> //Required for toupper()
#include<string> //Required for string
#include<iostream> //require for ostream
using namespace std;

//Constructors.
Card::Card():rank(2), suit('S')
{
}
Card::Card(char ch, int i): rank(i)
{
 suit=toupper(ch);
}


//Accessor Methods
int Card::getRank() const
{
  return rank;
}

char Card::getSuit() const
{
  return suit;
}
```

```
//Formatted display method
void Card::displayCard(ostream& out) const
{
   string suitString;
   //Establish suit string
   //Constructors and mutators guarantee uppercase suit
   switch(suit){
    case 'S':
      suitString = "Spades";
      break;
    case 'H':
      suitString = "Hearts";
      break;
    case 'D':
      suitString = "Diamonds";
      break;
    case 'C':
      suitString = "Clubs";
      break;
    default:
      suitString = "Invalid Suit";
   }//end switch suit

   if(rank >= 2 && rank < 11)
   { //output the rank and suit string
     out << rank << " of " << suitString;
   } //end if
   else
   { //Establish rank string(Ace, King, Queen, or Jack)
     switch(rank){
       case 11:
         out << "JACK of " << suitString;
         break;
       case 12:
         out << "QUEEN of " << suitString;
         break;
       case 13:
         out << "KING of " << suitString;
         break;
       case 14:
         out << "ACE of " << suitString;
         break;
      }//end switch rank
   }//end else
   return;
 }//end Display
/*-------------------------------------------------------------*/
```

CardDeck.h

```cpp
/*----------------------------------------------------------------*/
#ifndef CARDDECK_H
#define CARDDECK_H              \
/* CardDeck class declaration                                     */
/* filename: CardDeck.h                                           */
#include "Card.h" //Required for Card
#include <vector> //Required for vector                           */
using namespace std;

class CardDeck {
public:
  CardDeck();
  void shuffleDeck();
  Card draw();
private:
  vector<Card>  theDeck;
  vector<Card>  deltCards;
};
#endif
/*----------------------------------------------------------------*/
```

CardDeck.cpp

```cpp
/*----------------------------------------------------------------*/
/* CardDeck implementation                                        */
/* filename: CardDeck.cpp                                         */

#include "CardDeck.h"
#include<ctime> //Required for time()
#include<algorithm> //Required for random_shuffle()
using namespace std;

CardDeck::CardDeck()
{
  /* 13 cards in each suit.                                       */
  /* 52 new cards.                                                */
  for(int i= 2; i<15; ++i)
  {
    theDeck.push_back(Card('S',i));
    theDeck.push_back(Card('H',i));
    theDeck.push_back(Card('D',i));
    theDeck.push_back(Card('C',i));
  }
  srand(time(NULL)); //Must seed RNG 1 time!
}
```

```
Card CardDeck::draw()
{
/* Draw and return one card.                                    */
  if(theDeck.empty())
  {
    exit(1);
  }
  Card aCard = theDeck.back(); //Draw card.
  theDeck.pop_back();//Remove card.

  //Retain card for shuffle.
  deltCards.push_back(aCard);
  return(aCard);
}

void CardDeck::shuffleDeck()
{
  /* Replace drawn cards                                        */
  for(int i=0; i<deltCards.size(); ++i)
  {
    theDeck.push_back(deltCards[i]);
  }
  //Clear the vector.
  deltCards.resize(0);

  //Use the top level function from algorithm.
  random_shuffle(theDeck.begin(), theDeck.end());
}
/*************************************************************/
```

4. ALGORITHM DEVELOPMENT

We first develop the decomposition outline.

Decomposition Outline

   1. Read number of experiments.

   2. Read analytical probability.

   3. Run simulation.

   4. Print comparison of probabilities.

Step 1 involves prompting the user to enter the number of experiments. Step 2 involves prompting the user to enter the analytical result. Step 3 requires a loop to conduct the experiment *n* times. In step 4, we print the comparison of results. A flowchart of our algorithm is given below.

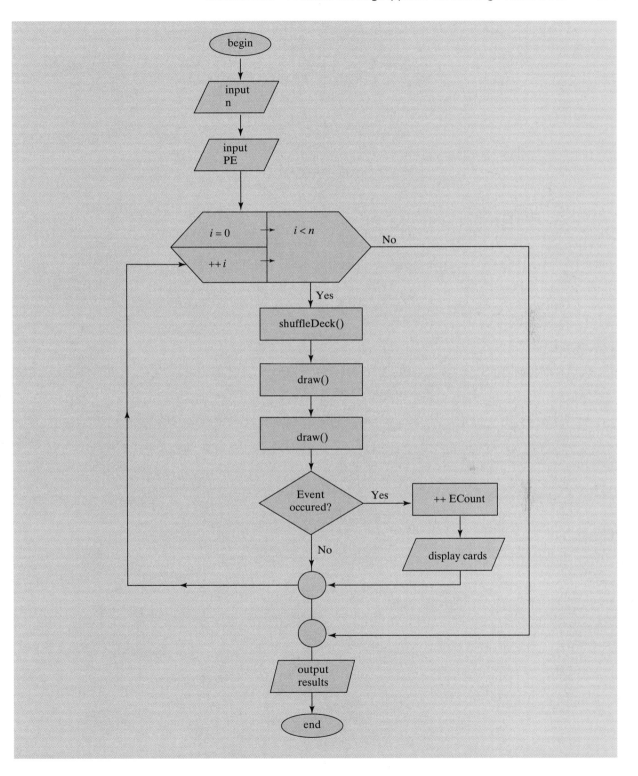

Our flowchart provides enough detail to develop our problem solution.

```cpp
/*-------------------------------------------------------------*/
/* Program chapter7_12                                        */
/* This program runs a simulation to calculate               */
/* the probability of drawing 2 red cards, each              */
/* with a face value less than 10, from a                    */
/* shuffled deck of 52 cards.  The results are               */
/* then compared to analytical results.                      */
#include<iostream> //Required for cout.
#include "Card.h" //Required for Card.
#include "CardDeck.h" //Required for CardDeck.         */
using namespace std;

int main()
{
   //Declare objects.
   CardDeck theDeck;
   Card card1, card2;
   double pE(0), eventCounter(0);
   int n(0);
   bool isRed;

   cout << "Enter the analytical result ";
   cin >> pE;
   cout << "Enter number of experiments to run ";
   cin >> n;

   for(int i=0; i<n; ++i)
   {
      theDeck.shuffleDeck();
      card1 = theDeck.draw();
      card2 = theDeck.draw();

      //Check if the event occured.
      if( (card1.getSuit() == 'H' || card1.getSuit() == 'D')
        &&(card2.getSuit() == 'H' || card2.getSuit() == 'D'))
      {
         isRed = true;
      }
      else
      {
         isRed = false;
      }
      if( isRed && (card1.getRank() < 10 && card2.getRank() < 10) )
      {
         ++eventCounter;
         cout << "Event " << eventCounter << endl;
         card1.displayCard(cout);
         cout << " ";
```

```
         card2.displayCard(cout);
         cout << endl;
      }//end if
   }//end for
   cout << "Analytical results: " << pE << endl
        << "Simulated results: " << eventCounter << '/' << n
        << " = " << eventCounter/n << endl;
   return 0;
}
/*--------------------------------------------------------------*/
```

5. TESTING

We will test our solution twice with a small number of experiments so that we can look at the outcomes to ensure that we are counting the events correctly.

Simulation 1

```
Enter the analytical result 0.0904977
Enter number of experiments to run 97
Event 1
4 of Diamonds 8 of Diamonds
Event 2
5 of Diamonds 2 of Hearts
Event 3
3 of Hearts 2 of Hearts
Event 4
4 of Diamonds 7 of Hearts
Event 5
7 of Hearts 8 of Hearts
Event 6
5 of Hearts 2 of Diamonds
Event 7
8 of Diamonds 4 of Hearts
Event 8
9 of Hearts 8 of Diamonds
Event 9
4 of Diamonds 9 of Hearts
Analytical results: 0.0904977
Simulated results: 9/97 = 0.0927835
```

Simulation 2

```
Enter the analytical result 0.0904977
Enter number of experiments to run 97
Event 1
6 of Hearts 4 of Hearts
Event 2
8 of Hearts 5 of Hearts
Event 3
8 of Diamonds 2 of Hearts
Event 4
6 of Hearts 5 of Diamonds
```

```
Event 5
3 of Diamonds 8 of Hearts
Event 6
4 of Diamonds 3 of Hearts
Event 7
3 of Hearts 4 of Hearts
Analytical results: 0.0904977
Simulated results: 7/97 = 0.0721649
```

To run our simulation for larger values of n, we will comment out the print statements to speed up execution.

Simulation 3

```
Enter the analytical result 0.0904977
Enter number of experiments to run 101371
Analytical results: 0.0904977
Simulated results: 9171/101371 = 0.0904697
```

Simulation 4

```
Enter the analytical result 0.0904977
Enter number of experiments to run 101371
Analytical results: 0.0904977
Simulated results: 9101/101371 = 0.0897791
```

Simulation 5

```
Enter the analytical result 0.0904977
Enter number of experiments to run 1111111
Analytical results: 0.0904977
Simulated results: 100368/1111111 = 0.0903312
```

Modify!

The following exercises require modification of program `chapter7_12`, however, no modification of *Card* or *CardDeck* is required.

1. Modify program `chapter7_12` to calculate the probability of drawing 2 face cards.

2. Modify program `chapter7_12` to calculate the probability of drawing 5 black cards.

3. Modify program `chapter7_12` to calculate the probability of drawing 4 Aces.

SUMMARY

Key Terms

alphanumeric character
array
binary search
event space
C-style string
character string
magnitude
mean
median
null character
offset
one-dimensional array

sample space
selection sort algorithm
sequential search
sorting
standard deviation
statistical measurements
string class
subscripts
variance
vector class
whitespace
zero crossing

C++ Statement Summary

Include C-style string header file

```
#include<cstring>
```

Include string class header file

```
#include<string>
```

Include vector class header file

```
#include<vector>
```

Array and vector declaration:

```
int a[5], b[]={2, 3, -1};
char vowels[]={'a', 'e', 'i', 'o', 'u'};
string words[100];
vector<double> time;
```

Notes

1. The identifier i is commonly used as a subscript for a one-dimensional array.
2. Use symbolic constants to declare the size of an array so that it is easy to modify.

Debugging Notes

1. Use arrays only when it is necessary to keep all the data available in memory.
2. If unexpected characters are printed at the end of a C-style string, the null character may be missing from the string.
3. Be careful not to exceed the maximum offset value when referencing an element in an array.
4. An array must be declared to be as large as, or larger than, the maximum number of values to be stored in it.
5. Because an array reference in a function is always a pass by reference, be careful that you do not inadvertently change values in an array in the function.

Problems

Exam Practice!

True/False Problems

Indicate whether the following statements are true (T) or false (F).

1. If the initializing sequence is shorter than an array, then the rest of the values are initialized to zero. T F
2. If an array is defined without a size, but with an initialization sequence, then the array size is arbitrary. T F
3. When the value of a subscript or offset is greater than the largest valid offset of an array, it will always cause an execution error. T F
4. All values of an array are printed if we specify the identifier of the array without an offset. T F
5. In ASCII, the string "Smith" is less than the string "Johnson". T F

Multiple Choice

6. An array is
   (a) a group of values having a common object name and all of the same data type.
   (b) a collection of elements of different data types which are stored in adjacent memory locations.
   (c) an object that contains multiple values of the same data type.
   (d) a location in memory that holds multiple values of the same data type.
7. An individual element in an array is addressed by specifying
   (a) the name of the array and the offset of the element.
   (b) the name of the array.
   (c) the offset of the element within the array followed by the name of the array.
   (d) the offset of the element in the array.
8. The offset identifies the _____ of a particular element in the array.
   (a) location
   (b) value
   (c) range
   (d) name

Memory Snapshot Problems

Give the corresponding snapshots of memory after each of the following sets of statements is executed. Use ? to indicate an array element that is not initialized.

9. ```
int t[5];
...
t[0] = 5;
for(int k=0; k<4; k++)
    t[k+1] = t[k] + 3;
```
10. ```
char s[] = "Hello", t[] = {'a', 'e', 'i', 'o', 'u'}, name[10];
strcpy(name,"Sue");
```

Program Output

Problems 11–13 refer to the following statements:

```
string strng1 = "K", strng2 = "265", strng3 = "xyz";
```

11. What is the output of the following statement?

    ```
    cout << strng1.size() << endl;
    ```

12. What is the output of the following statement?

    ```
    strng1 = strng2;
    cout << strng1 << endl;
    ```

13. What is the output of the following statements?

    ```
    strng1 += string2;
    cout << strng1 << endl;
    ```

Programming Exercises

Linear Interpolation.   The following problems refer to the wind-tunnel test data stored in the file *tunnel.dat*. The file contains the set of data which consists of a flight-path angle (in degrees) and its corresponding coefficient of lift on each line in the file. The flight-path angles will be in ascending order.

14. Write a program that reads the wind-tunnel test data and then allows the user to enter a flight-path angle. If the angle is within the bounds of the data set, the program should then use linear interpolation to compute the corresponding coefficient of lift. (You may need to refer to the section on linear interpolation in Section 2.5.)

15. Modify the program in Problem 14 so that it prints a message to the user giving the range of angles that are covered in the data file after reading the values.

16. Write a function that could be used to verify that the flight-path angles are in ascending order. The function should return a zero if the angles are not in order and a 1 if they are in order. Assume that the corresponding function prototype is

    ```
    int ordered(double x[], int num_pts);
    ```

17. Write a function that receives two one-dimensional array that correspond to the flight-path angles and the corresponding coefficients of lift. The function should sort the flight-path angles into ascending order while maintaining the correspondence between the flight-path angles and the corresponding coefficients of lift. Assume that the corresponding function prototype is

    ```
    void reorder(double& x, double& y);
    ```

18. Modify the program developed in Problem 14 such that it uses the function developed in Problem 16 to determine whether the data are in the desired order. If they are not in the desired order, use the function developed in Problem 17 to reorder them.

Noise Signals. In engineering simulations, we often want to generate a floating-point sequence of values with a specified mean and variance. The function developed in this chapter allows us to generate numbers between limits a and b, but it does not allow us to specify the mean and variance. By using results from probability, the following relationships can be derived between the limits of a uniform random sequence and its theoretical mean μ and variance σ^2:

$$\sigma^2 = \frac{(b-a)^2}{12}, \qquad \mu = \frac{(a+b)}{2}.$$

19. Write a program that uses the **rand_float** function developed in Chapter 5 to generate sequences of random floating-point values between 4 and 10. Then compare the computed mean and variance to the theoretical values computed. As you use more and more random numbers, the computed values and the theoretical values should become closer.

20. Write a program that uses the **rand_float** function developed in Chapter 5 to generate two sequences of 500 points. Each sequence should have a theoretical mean of 4, but one sequence should have a variance of 0.5, and the other should have a variance of 2. Check the computed means and compare to the theoretical means. (*Hint:* Use the two previous equations to write two equations with two unknowns. Then solve for the unknowns by hand.)

21. Write a program that uses the **rand_float** function developed in Chapter 5 to generate two sequences of 500 points. Each sequence should have the same variance of 3.0, but one sequence should have a mean of 0.0, and the other should have a mean of −4.0. Compare the theoretical and computed values for mean and variance. (*Hint:* Use the two previous equations to write two equations with two unknowns. Then solve for the unknowns by hand.)

22. Write a function named **rand_mv** that generates a random floating-point value with a specified mean and variance that are input parameters to the function. Assume that the corresponding function prototype is

```
double rand_mv(double mean, double var);
```

Use the rand_float function developed in Chapter 5.

Cryptography. The science of developing secret codes has interested many people for centuries. Some of the simplest codes involve replacing a character, or a group of characters with another character, or group of characters. To easily decode these messages, the decoder needs the "key" that shows the replacement characters. In recent times, computers have been used very successfully to decode many codes that initially were assumed to be unbreakable. The next set of problems considers simple codes and schemes for decoding them. Generate files to test the programs.

23. One step in decoding a simple code without knowing the coding scheme, involves counting the number of occurrences of each character. Then, knowing that the most common letter in English is 'e,' the letter that occurs most commonly in the coded message is replaced by 'e.' Similar replacements are then made based on the number of occurrences of characters in the coded message and the known occurrences of

characters in the English language. This decoding often provides enough of the correct replacements that the incorrect replacements can then be determined. For this problem, write a program that reads a data file and determines the number of occurrences of each of the characters in the file. Then, print the characters and the number of times that they occurred. If a character does not occur, do not print it. (*Hint:* Use an array to store the occurrences of the characters based on their ASCII codes.)

24. Another simple code encodes a message in text such that the true message is represented by the first letter of each word. There are no spaces between the words, but the decoded string of characters can easily be separated into words by a person. Write a program to read a data file and determine the secret message stored by the sequence of first letters of the words. (*Hint:* Store the first letter of each word in a character string.)

25. Assume that the true secret message in Problem 24 is stored in the second letter of each word. Write a program to read a data file and determine the secret message stored in the file.

26. Assume that the true secret message in Problem 24 is represented by the characters that are three characters to the right in the collating sequence from the first letters of the words. Write a program to read a data file and determine the secret message stored in the file using this decoding scheme.

27. Write a program that encodes the text in a data file using a character array named **key** that contains 26 characters. This key is read from the keyboard; the first letter contains the character that is to replace the letter *a* in the data file, the second letter contains the letter that is to replace the letter *b* in the data file, and so on. Assume that all punctuation is to be replaced by spaces. Check to be sure that the key does not map two different characters to the same one during the encoding.

28. Write a program which decodes the file that is the output of Problem 27. Assume that the same integer key is read from the keyboard by this program and is used in the decoding steps. Note that you will not be able to restore the punctuation characters.

A **palindrome** is a word (noon), sentence (Draw a level award), or number (18781) that reads the same backward or forward. (Note that whitespace is ignored when determining whether a word, sentence, or number is a palindrome.)

29. Write a program that reads a line of text from standard input and determines whether the line of text is a palindrome.

30. Write a program that reads text from a data file. The program should read each line in the data file (read lines until an end of file is encountered), print each line, and also print a message that indicates whether the line is a palindrome.

Calculating Probabilities.

31. Add a method to the `CardDeck` class named `randomDraw()`. This method should return one card, drawn from a random location in the deck. Use this method to simulation to the probability of drawing two face cards from a shuffled deck.

32. Add a method to the `CardDeck` class named `isEmpty()`. This method should return true if the deck is empty, false otherwise. Write a driver to test the new method.

33. Write a program that uses the Card and `CardDeck` classes to deal a hand of 13 cards and count the value of the hand based on the number of face cards in the hand. Assume an Ace is worth 4 points, a King is worth 3 points, a Queen is worth 2 points and a Jack is worth 1 point. Thus, if the hand held 2 Aces, 1 King and 3 Jacks, the value of the hand would be 14. The program should display the hand that was dealt and the value of the hand.

34. Write a simulation to estimate the probability of drawing a 13-card hand having no face cards, from a deck of 52 cards.

35. Write a simulation to estimate the probability of drawing a 5-card hand that holds 2 Kings and 1 Ace.

36. Write a simulation to estimate the probability of drawing a 5-card hand that holds 2 pairs.

Programmer defined data types.

37. Define a class to implement the concept of a line. Your class should have two private data members; length, fixedPoint. Include a complete set of accessors, mutators, constructors, and additional methods to:

  - print location and length of a line

  - move (translate) a line

  - resize a line

  Draw a UML class diagram and write a driver to test your class.

38. Define a class to implement the concept of a circle. Your class should have two private data members: radius, centerPoint. Include a complete set of accessors, mutators, constructors, and additional methods to:

  - print location and radius of a circle

  - move (translate) a circle

  - resize a circle

  Draw an UML class diagram and write a driver to test your class.

39. Define a class to represent a date. Your class should have three data members: month, day, and year. Include a complete set of accessors, mutators, constructors, and additional functions to:

  - print a date as month/day/year (10/1/1999)

  - print a date as month day, year (October 1, 1999)

  Draw an UML class diagram and write a driver to test your class.

40. Define a class to represent time, in military format. Your class should have three private data member; hours, minutes, and seconds. Military time is represented with times ranging from 00:00:00 (12 am) to 23:59:59 (11:59:59 pm). Include a complete set of accessors, mutators, constructors, and additional methods to:

  - print a time in twelve hour format

  - calculate the difference between two times (overload the - operator)

Tsunami Warning Systems

Wave steepness is the ratio of wave height(WH) to wave length(WL) and is an indicator of wave stability. When wave steepness exceeds a 1/7 ratio; the wave becomes unstable and begins to break. Assume a data file exits with the following header:

#YY MM DD HH MM WH(m) WL(m)

Each subsequent line in the data file contains time and wave height measurements, in the following format:

year(int) month(int) day(int) hour(int) minute(int) wave height(double) wave length(double)

41. Write a program to calculate the average steepness given an input file in the above format. The program should also determine and print what percentage of the time the steepness exceeded the average. The input file can be of any length.
42. Write a program that will generate a report given an input file in the above format. The program should calculate and report the steepness for each entry in the data file and issue a warning message when the steepness exceeds a 1/7 ratio. The program should then print a summary of the wave height, length and steepness of the highest 50% of the waves measured. The input file can be of any length.

ENGINEERING CHALLENGE:
Terrain Navigation

The Mars Exploration Rovers are designed to move across the surface of Mars and examine the soil and rocks in fine detail. The auto-navigation system takes pictures of the nearby terrain using one of the rover's stereo camera pairs. After stereo images are taken, 3-D terrain maps are generated automatically by the rover software. Traversability and safety is then determined from the height and density of rocks or steps, excessive tilts and roughness of the terrain. Dozens of possible paths are considered before the rover chooses the shortest, safest path toward the programmed geographical goal. Moving from place to place, the rovers perform on-site geological investigations. The robotic arm is capable of movement in much the same way as a human arm with an elbow and wrist, and can place instruments directly up against rock and soil targets of interest. In this chapter, we analyze elevation data from a terrain map to determine the number and location of peaks within the terrain.

TWO-DIMENSIONAL ARRAYS

CHAPTER OUTLINE

OBJECTIVES *In this chapter, we develop problem solutions containing:*

- matrix computations
- input from data files
- functions to compute sums and averages

- techniques for solving a system of simultaneous equations
- vectors to implement the concept of two-dimensional arrays

8.1 Two-Dimensional Arrays

A set of data values that is visualized as a row or column is easily represented by a one-dimensional array. However, there are many examples in which the best way to visualize a set of data is with a grid or a table of data.

Suppose we wanted to display a table of temperature values recorded at eight-hour intervals over a period of four days. The values could be displayed as shown in the following array which has four rows corresponding to the number of days and three columns corresponding to the number of temperatures recorded during a 24-hour period:

	col 0	col 1	col 2
row 0 →	50	70	60
row 1 →	48	78	62
row 2 →	51	69	60
row 3 →	52	78	63

row offset
column offset

In C++, a grid or table of data is represented with a two-dimensional array. Each element in a two-dimensional array is referenced using an identifier followed by two offsets: a **row offset** and a **column offset**. The offset values for both rows and columns begin with 0, and each offset has its own set of brackets. Thus, assuming that the previous array has an identifier, `temp`, we see that the value in position `temp[2][1]` is 69. Common errors in array references include using parentheses instead of brackets, as in temp(2)(3), or using only one set of brackets or parentheses, as in temp[2,3] or temp(2,3).

All values in a two dimensional array must have the same data type. An array cannot have a column of integers followed by a column of floating numbers, and so on.

Declaration and Initialization

To declare a two-dimensional array, we specify the number of rows and the number of columns in the declaration statement, with the row number first. Both the row number and the column number are in brackets, as shown in the following declaration statement:

```
int temp[4][3];
```

The declaration statement for `temp` results in the allocation of a consecutive block of memory large enough to hold 12 integer values.

initialization list

A two-dimensional array can be initialized with a declaration statement and an **initialization list**, as in:

```
int temp[4][3] = {50, 70, 60, 48, 75, 62, 51, 69, 60, 52, 78, 63};
```

Notice that we listed the values in the initialization list row by row because this is the order in which a C++ compiler assigns values to memory.

The next declaration statement illustrates the use of blocks within an initialization list to explicitly define the values to be assigned to each row of a two dimensional array. The values assigned to `temp` in this example will be the same as above.

```
int temp[4][3] = {{50, 70, 60}, {48, 75, 62},
                  {51, 69, 60}, {52, 78, 63}};
```

If the initialization list provided in a type declaration statement is shorter than the array, then the rest of the values in the array are initialized to zero. As an example, the following declaration statement:

```
int t2[7][4] = {{50, 70, 60}, {48, 75, 62},
                {51, 69, 60}, {52, 78, 63}};
```

would result in values being assigned to the upper left-hand corner of `t2`, as shown below.

50	70	60	0
48	75	62	0
51	69	60	0
52	78	63	0
0	0	0	0
0	0	0	0
0	0	0	0

Thus, the use of blocks allows us to initialize a specified subset of a two-dimensional array.

A two-dimensional array can be declared with an empty row size, but an initialization list is required. The number of data values, or the number of blocks in the list, determines the row size. Thus, the following two type declaration statements will also correctly define the array `temp`:

```
int temp[][3] = {{50, 70, 60}, {48, 75, 62}, {51, 69, 60},
                 {52, 78, 63}};
int temp[][3] = {50, 70, 60, 48, 75, 62, 51, 69, 60, 52, 78, 63};
```

The row size is the only dimension that can be empty when declaring a two-dimensional array. Leaving the column size empty will result in a compilation error.

Two-Dimensional Arrays: The declaration of a two-dimensional array requires a row size and a column size. A consecutive block of (row size) * (column size) memory addresses is allocated, and the name of the array holds the first address in the block. The array name followed by a row offset and column offset are required to access a value in the array.

Syntax:
  data type identifier[row size][column size] [= initialization list];

Example:
```
int data[2][5];      //allocates consecutive memory for 10 integer values.
```

  Memory snaptshot for `data`:

  int data:
?	?	?	?	?
?	?	?	?	?

```
double t[2][2] = {{3.0, 5.0}, {2.1, 7.2}};  //allocates and initializes
```
  Memory snapshot for `t`:

  double t:
3.0	5.0
2.1	7.2

Valid References:
```
cout << data[0][0];
```

Invalid References:
```
cout << t[2][2];     //invalid offset.
```

Show the memory snapshot for the arrays defined in each of the following statements.

1. `int a[3][2] = {{1},{2},{3}};`

2. `int b[3][3] = {1,2,3,4,5,6};`

3. `int c[][4] = {{1,2,3,4}, {0,3,0,6}, {8,3,-6,-1}};`

4. `int d[][4] = {1,2,3,0,3,0,6,3,-6,-1};`

Arrays can also be assigned values with program statements. *For two-dimensional arrays, two nested* `for` *loops are usually required to initialize an array; i and j are commonly used as offsets.* The following statements define and initialize an array such that each row contains the row number:

```
//  Declare objects.
int t[5][4];
...
//  Assign values to array.
for (int i=0; i<5; ++i)
{
    for (int j=0; j<4; ++j)
    {
        t[i][j] = i;
    }
}
```

A memory snapshot for the array `t` is provided below:

Offset	0	1	2	3	4	5	6	7	8	9	10	11	12	13	14	15	16	17	18	19
int t	0	0	0	0	1	1	1	1	2	2	2	2	3	3	3	3	4	4	4	4

Displayed in row-column form:

0	0	0	0
1	1	1	1
2	2	2	2
3	3	3	3
4	4	4	4

int t

Two-dimensional arrays can also be assigned values read from a data file. In the following program, we read temperature values from a data file named `engine.dat`. The first line of the data file contains two integers. The first integer specifies the number of engines (row size), and the second integer specifies the number of trials (column size). The remaining lines in the data file contain (row size) ∗ (column size) temperature values that will be read and stored in the array. Symbolic constants `NROWS` and `NCOLS` are used to represent the number of rows and columns. *Changing the size of an array is easier to do when the numbers of rows and columns are specified as symbolic constants; otherwise, the change requires modifications to several statements.*

```
/*-------------------------------------------------------------*/
/* Program chapter8_1                                          */
/* This program reads and stores temperature values           */
/* for multiple trials from the input file engine.dat.        */

#include<iostream> //Required for cerr, cout
#include<fstream>  //Required for ifstream
using namespace std;
```

```
int main()
{
// Declare objects.
   int numEngines, numTrials;
   ifstream data1;

   //Open input file.
   data1.open("engine.dat");
   if(data1.fail())
   {
      cerr << "could not open engine.dat";
      exit(1);
   }
   //Input row and column size
   data1 >> numEngines >> numTrials;

   //Declare constants for array declaration
   const int NROWS(numEngines);
   const int NCOLS(numTrials);
   double temps[NROWS][NCOLS];

   //Read temperature data and store in array.
   for (int i=0; i<NROWS; ++i)
   {
      for (int j=0; j<NCOLS; ++j)
      {
         data1 >> temps[i][j];
      }
   }
   data1.close();

   //Echo input
   cout << numEngines << ',' << numTrials << endl;
   for (int i=0; i<NROWS; ++i)
   {
      for (int j=0; j<NCOLS; ++j)
      {
         cout << temps[i][j] << '\t';
      }
      cout << endl;  //end of ith row
   }
   return 0;
}
/*------------------------------------------------------------*/
```

A program trace and memory snapshot for the first iteration of program `chapter8_1` is provided below:

```
      engine.dat
3 3
335.6 339.4 421.7
299.6 332.4 340.5
320.1 329.8 339.3
```

main()	Memory Snapshot

Step 1: data1 >> rows >> cols;   int rows [3]   int cols [3]

Step 2: const int NROWS(rows);   int NROWS [3]

Step 3: const int NCOLS(cols);   int NCOLS [3]

Step 4: double temps[NROWS][NCOLS];   double temps

?	?	?
?	?	?
?	?	?

Step 5: for(int i=0;   int i [0]

    Step 5A: i<NROWS; true(i=0) . . .

Step 6: for(int j=0;   int j [0]

    Step 6A: j<NCOLS)   true(j=0)   true(j=1)   true(j=2)

    Step 6B: data1>>temps[i][j];

    Step 6C: ++j;

temps

335.6	?	?
?	?	?
?	?	?

335.6	339.4	?
?	?	?
?	?	?

335.6	339.4	421.7
?	?	?
?	?	?

    Step 5B: ++i)   i [1]

Step 7: data1.close();

. . .

The output generated by program chapter8_1 is given below:

```
3,3
335.6 339.4 421.7
299.6 332.4 340.5
320.1 329.8 339.3
```

Practice!

Show the memory snapshot for the arrays defined in each of the following sets of statements. Use a question mark to indicate an element that has not been initialized.

    1. int d[3][1]={{1},{4},{6}};

    2. int g[6][2]={{5,2},{-2,3}};

```
3. double h[4][4]={{0,0}};

4. int p[3][3]={{0,0,0}};
   ...
   for (int k=0; k<3; ++k)
   {
      p[k][k] = 1;
   }

5. int g[5][5];
   ...
   for (int i=0; i<5; ++i)
   {
      for (int j=0; j<4; ++j)
      {
         g[i][j] = i + j;
      }
   }

6. int g[5][5];
   ...
   for (int i=0; i<=4; ++i)
   {
      for (int j=0; j<=4; ++j)
      {
         g[i][j] = pow(-1.0,j);
      }
   }
```

Computations and Output

Computations and output with two-dimensional arrays must always specify two offsets when referencing an array element. To illustrate, consider the next program, which reads a data file containing power output for an electrical plant for a 10-week period. Each line of the data file contains seven values representing the daily power output for a week. The data are stored in a two-dimensional array, and then a report is printed giving the average power for the first day of the week during the period, the average power for the second day of the week during the period, and so on:

```
/*-----------------------------------------------------------*/
/*  Program chapter8_2                                       */
/*                                                           */
/*  This program computes power averages                     */
/*  over a 10-week period.                                   */
```

```cpp
#include<iostream>      //Required for cin, cout, cerr
#include<fstream>       //Required for ifstream
#include<string>        //Required for string
using namespace std;

int main()
{

   //  Declare objects.
   const int NROWS = 10;
   const int NCOLS = 7;
   double power[NROWS][NCOLS], col_sum;
   string filename;
   ifstream data1;

   //  Open file and read data into array.
   cout << "Enter name of input file.\n";
   cin >> filename;
   data1.open(filename.c_str());
   if(data1.fail())
   {
     cerr << "Error opening data file\n";
     exit(1);
   }
   // Set format flags.
   cout.setf(ios::fixed);
   cout.setf(ios::showpoint);
   cout.precision(1);
   for (int i=0; i<NROWS; ++i)
   {
      for (int j=0; j<NCOLS; ++j)
      {
        data1 >> power[i][j];
      }
   }

   //  Compute and print daily averages.
   for (int j=0; j<NCOLS; ++j)
   {
     col_sum = 0;
     for (int i=0; i<NROWS; ++i)
     {
        col_sum += power[i][j];
     }
     cout << "Day" << j+1 <<": Average =" << col_sum/NROWS << endl;
   }

   //  Close file and exit program.
   data1.close();
   return 0;
}
/*-------------------------------------------------------------------------*/
```

Note that the daily averages are computed by adding each column and then dividing the column sum by the number of rows (which is also the number of weeks). The column number is then used to compute the day number. A sample output from this program is as follows:

```
Day 1: Average = 238.4
Day 2: Average = 199.5
Day 3: Average = 274.8
Day 4: Average = 239.1
Day 5: Average = 277.0
Day 6: Average = 305.8
Day 7: Average = 276.1
```

Writing information from a two-dimensional array to a data file is similar to writing the information from a one-dimensional array. In both cases, a newline indicator must be used to specify when the values are to begin a new line. The following statements will write a set of distance measurements to a data file named dist.txt, with five values per line:

```
// Declare objects.
double dist[20][5];
ofstream data1;
...
// Write information from the array to a file.
data1.open("dist.txt");
for (int i=0; i<20; ++i)
{
    for (int j=0; j<5; ++j)
    {
        data1 << dist[i][j] << ' ';
    }
    data1 << endl;
}
```

The space printed after the value of dist[i][j] in the output statement is necessary in order that the values be separated by a space.

Practice!

Assume the following declaration for the array g :

```
int g[3][3]={{0,0,0},{1,1,1},{2,2,2}};
```

Give the value of sum after each of the following sets of statements are executed.

Practice!

```
1. sum = 0;
   for (int i=0; i<3; ++i)
   {
     for (int j=0; j<3; ++j)
     {
       sum += g[i][j];
     }
   }

2. sum = 1;
   for (int i=1; i<3; i++)
   {
     for (int j=0; j<i; j++)
     {
       sum *= g[i][j];
     }
   }

3. sum = 0;
   for (int j=0; j<3; ++j)
   {
     sum -= g[2][j];
   }

4. sum = 0;
   for (int i=0; i<3; ++i)
   {
       sum += g[i][1];
   }
```

Function Arguments

When arrays are used as function parameters, the default is pass by reference, instead of pass by value. As discussed in Chapter 7, this means that array parameters in a function refer to the original array and not to a copy of the array. Thus, we must be careful that we do not change values in the original array when we do not intend to make changes.

When using a one-dimensional array as a function argument, the function needs only the address of the first element in the array, which is specified by the array name. When using a two-dimensional array as a function argument, the function also needs information about declared **the declared column size** of the array. In general, the function header and function prototype column need to give the declared column size of a two-dimensional array. To illustrate, suppose that size we need to write a program that computes the sum of the elements in an array containing four rows and four columns. Computing this sum requires two nested loops, so the program will

declared
column
size

be more readable if we put the steps to compute the sum in a function. The program can then reference the function with a single statement, as in the following:

```
*- - - - - - - - - - - - - - - - - - - - - - - - - - - - - - - - - - - - - - - - - - - - - - - - - - - - - - -*
#include <iostream>     //Required for cout
using namespace std;
const int NROWS=4, NCOLS=4;

//  Function prototypes.
int sum(int x[][NCOLS]);
...
int main()
{
   //  Declare objects.
   int a[NROWS][NCOLS];
   ...
   //  Reference function to compute array sum.
   cout << "Array sum = " << sum(a) << endl;
```

If we need to recompute the array sum in several places in the program, the function becomes even more effective. If there are several different arrays, we can use the same function to compute their sums:

```
#include <iostream>     //Required for cout
using namespace std;
const int NROWS=4, NCOLS=4;

//  Function prototypes.
int sum(int x[][NCOLS]);
...
int main()
{
   //  Declare objects.
   int a[NROWS][NCOLS], b[NROWS][NCOLS];
   ...
   //  Reference function to compute array sums.
   cout << "Sum of a = " << sum(a) << endl;
   cout << "Sum of b = " << sum(b) << endl;
```

We now present the function referenced in these statements:

```
/*- - - - - - - - - - - - - - - - - - - - - - - - - - - - - - - - - - - - - - - -*/
/*  This function returns the sum of the values in    */
/*  an array with NROWS rows and NCOLS columns.        */
//  PreCondition: Array X has NROWS and NCOLS.
//  PostCondition: Sum of integer Values is returned.

int sum(int x[][NCOLS])
{
   //  Declare and initialize local objects.
   int total(0);
```

```
//   Compute a sum of the array values.
for (int i=0; i<NROWS; ++i)
{
    for (int j=0; j<NCOLS; ++j)
    {
        total += x[i][j];
    }
}

//   Return sum of array values.
return total;
}
/*-------------------------------------------------------------*/
```

In the next example, we develop a function that computes a partial sum of the elements
in an array. The elements to be summed are assumed to be in a **subarray** in the upper left
corner of the array. The arguments of the function include the original array, and the numbers
of rows and columns in the subarray. The function prototype is

subarray

```
//   Function prototype
int partial_sum(int x[][NCOLS], int m, int n);
```

Thus, if we want to sum the elements shown in the *shaded area* in the array a, we would use
the reference

```
partial_sum(a,2,3);
```

2	3	−1	9
0	−3	5	7
2	6	3	2
−2	10	4	6

This reference should then compute the sum of the elements in the subarray beginning
in the upper left corner and consisting of two rows and three columns; the function should
return a value of 6. This function is as follows:

```
/*-----------------------------------------------------------*/
/*  This function returns the sum of the values       */
/*  in a subarray of an array with a declared         */
/*  NCOLS column size of NCOLS.                       */
int partialSum(int x[][NCOLS],int m, int n)
{
    //   Declare and initialize local objects.
    int total(0);
    //   Compute a sum of subarray values.
    for (int i=0; i<m; ++i)
    {
```

```
   for (int j=0; j<n; ++j)
   {
      total += x[i][j];
   }
}

// Return sum of subarray values.
return total;
}
/*-----------------------------------------------------------*/
```

This function can be used with two-dimensional arrays of various sizes provided the symbolic constant **NCOLS** is within the scope of the function.

Practice!

Assume that the following statement is from a `main` function:

```
int a[4][4] = {{2, 3, -1, 9}, {0, -3, 5, 7},
               {2, 6, 3, 2}, {-2, 10, 4, 6}};
```

Determine by hand the values of the following references to the partialSum function developed in this section.

1. `partialSum(a,1,4);`

2. `partialSum(a,1,1);`

3. `partialSum(a,4,2);`

4. `partialSum(a,2,4);`

As a final example, we will modify program `chapter8_1` by adding two new functions. Suppose we wanted to determine the average engine temperature for each trial in the data file `engine.dat`, then report which engines in each trial performed below the average temperature. Since each trial is stored as a column in an array, we will write a function to return the average of a specified column of a two-dimensional array of type double. We will also write a function to read data from an input file and store the values in a two-dimensional array of type double. The modified program and function definitions are provided below.

```
/*-----------------------------------------------------------*/
/* Program chapter8_3                                        */
/* This program reads and stores temperature values         */
/* for multiple trials from the input file engine.dat,      */
/* then determines which engines performed below the        */
/* average trial temperature.                               */

#include<iostream> //Required for cerr, cout
#include<fstream>  //Required for ifstream
using namespace std;
```

```cpp
//Declare constants and Function Prototypes
const int MAXCOLSIZE(50);
const int MAXROWSIZE(50);
double columnAvg(const double a[][MAXCOLSIZE],
                 int colNum, int rows);
void input2D(istream& in, double a[][MAXCOLSIZE],
             int rows, int cols);
int main()
{
   //Declare objects.
   int numEngines, numTrials;
   ifstream data1;
   double temps[MAXROWSIZE][MAXCOLSIZE];
   double avgTemp;

   //Open input file.
   data1.open("engine.dat");
   if(data1.fail())
   {
      cerr << "could not open engine.dat";
      exit(1);
   }
   //Input row and column size
   data1 >> numEngines >> numTrials;

   //Read temperature data and store in array.
   input2D(data1, temps, numEngines, numTrials);

   data1.close();
   //Generate Report
   for(int i=0; i<numTrials; ++i)
   {
     //Calculate average engine temperature for each trial.
     avgTemp = columnAvg(temps, i, numEngines);

     //Generate Report
     cout << "\nTrial "<<(i+1)<<"\tAverage Engine Temperature "
          << avgTemp << endl;
      cout << "============================================\n";
      for(int j=0; j<numEngines; ++j)
      {
        if(temps[j][i] < avgTemp)
        {
          cout << "Engine " << (j+1)
               << " performed below the average temp." << endl;
        }
      }
   }
   return 0;
}//end main
/*-------------------------------------------------------------*/
```

```
/*-------------------------------------------------------------*/
/* This function reads data from an input stream and           */
/* assigns the data to the 2D array, arr.                      */
/* Pre-conditions:                                             */
/*   The istream in has been defined.                          */
/*   The integer cols is <= MAXCOLSIZE                         */
/*   The integer rows is <= MAXROWSIZE                         */
/* Post-conditions:                                            */
/*   rows*cols values are assigned to the array, arr           */

void input2D(istream& in, double arr[][MAXCOLSIZE],
             int rows, int cols)
{

   for (int i=0; i<rows; ++i)
   {
      for (int j=0; j<cols; ++j)
      {
         in >> arr[i][j];
      }
   }
}
/*-------------------------------------------------------------*/


/*-------------------------------------------------------------*/
/* This function returns the average of a column in the array */
/* arr. The integer colNum specifies the column number.       */
/* Pre-conditions:                                            */
/*   The array arr has rowSize rows of valid data             */
/*   The integer colNum is < MAXCOLSIZE                       */
double columnAvg(const double arr[][MAXCOLSIZE], int colNum,
                 int rowSize)
{
  //Declare and initialize local variables
  double avg = 0.0;

  //Sum all values in column colNum
  for(int i=0; i<rowSize; ++i)
  {
     avg += arr[i][colNum];
  }

  //Return the average
  return(avg/rowSize);
}
/*-------------------------------------------------------------*/
```

pre-conditions
post-conditions

Notice that we have included **pre-conditions** and **post-conditions** in our initial comment block in the function `input2D()`. Pre-conditions describe conditions that are assumed to be true at the time a function is called. If the pre-conditions are not true, there is no guarantee that the function will execute correctly. Post-conditions describe the changes that are made to the formal parameters during execution of the function. The function `columAvg()` has no post-conditions, because the formal parameters are not modified by the function. *When writing functions intended for use in multiple applications, it is always a good practice to include pre- and post-conditions.*

The output generated by program `chapter8_3` is given below:

```
Trial 1 Average Engine Temperature 319.35
=========================================
Engine 2 performed below the average temp.

Trial 2 Average Engine Temperature 340.75
=========================================
Engine 1 performed below the average temp.
Engine 2 performed below the average temp.
Engine 3 performed below the average temp.

Trial 3 Average Engine Temperature 375.85
=========================================
Engine 2 performed below the average temp.
Engine 3 performed below the average temp.
```

Modify!

1. Modify program `chapter8_2` to use the functions `input2D()` and `columnAvg()`. Do not modify the function definitions.

2. Modify program `chapter8_3` to report the engines that performed above the average temperature in each trial.

3. Modify program `chapter8_3` to report the temperatures of the engines that performed below the average in each trial.

8.2 Problem Solving Applied: Terrain Navigation

Terrain navigation is a key component in the design of robotic spacecraft. Robotic spacecraft refers to spacecraft with no humans on board. These spacecraft can travel on land, such as the Mars Exploration Rovers, or above land as in the Mars Reconnaissance Orbiter. A robotic spacecraft contains numerous onboard computers that store terrain information for the area in which it is to be operated. By knowing at any time where it is (perhaps with the aid of a global positioning system [GPS] receiver), the vehicle can then select the best path to get to a designated spot. If the destination changes, the vehicle can refer to its internal maps to recompute the new path.

The computer software that guides these vehicles must be tested over a variety of land formations and topologies. Elevation information for large grids of land is available in computer databases. One way of measuring the "difficulty" of a land grid with respect to terrain navigation is to determine the number of peaks in the grid, where a peak is a point that has lower elevations all around it. For this problem, we will assume that the values in the four positions shown in the following diagram are the ones adjacent to grid position [m][n] for purposes of determining if the value in grid position [m][n] is a peak:

	grid [m−1][n]	
grid [m][n−1]	grid [m][n]	grid [m][n+1]
	grid [m+1][n]	

Write a program that reads elevation data from a data file named *grid1.dat* and then prints the number of peaks and their locations. Assume that the first line of the data file contains the number of rows and the number of columns for the grid of information. These values are then followed by the elevation values, in row order. The maximum size grid is 25 rows by 25 columns.

1. PROBLEM STATEMENT

Determine and print the number of peaks and their locations in an elevation grid.

2. INPUT/OUTPUT DESCRIPTION

The I/O diagram shows that the input is a file containing the elevation data, and that the output is a listing of the locations of the peaks.

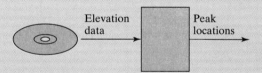

3. HAND EXAMPLE

Assume that the following data represent elevation for a grid that has six points along the side and seven points along the top. The peaks have been underlined in the data:

```
5039 5127 5238 5259 5248 5310 5299
5150 5392 5410 5401 5320 5820 5321
5290 5560 5490 5421 5530 5831 5210
5110 5429 5430 5411 5459 5630 5319
4920 5129 4921 5821 4722 4921 5129
5023 5129 4822 4872 4794 4862 4245
```

To specify the location of the peaks, we need to assign an addressing scheme to the data. Because we are going to be implementing this solution in C++, we choose its two-dimensional array-offset notation. Thus, we assume that the top-left corner is position [0][0], that the row numbers increase by 1 as we move down the page, and that the column numbers increase by 1 as we move to the right. These peaks then occur at positions [2][1], [2][5], and [4][3].

To determine the peaks, we compare a potential peak with its four neighboring points. If all four neighboring points are less than the potential peak, then the potential peak is a real peak. Note that the points on the edges of the array or grid cannot be potential peaks because we do not have elevation information on all four sides of the points.

4. ALGORITHM DEVELOPMENT

We first develop the decomposition outline because it divides the solution into a series of sequential steps:

Decomposition Outline

1. Read the terrain data into an array.

2. Determine and print the location of the peaks.

Step 1 involves reading the data file and storing the information in a two-dimensional array. Step 2 is a loop that evaluates all potential peaks and prints their locations if they are determined to be real peaks. We will write a boolean function to determine whether a location is a peak.

Refinement in Pseudocode

```
main:   read nrows and ncols from the data file
        read the terrain data into an array
        set i to 1
        while i < nrows - 1;
          set j to 1
          while j < ncols - 1;
            if (ispeak(grid,i,j))
              print peak location
            increment j by 1
          increment i by 1
peak:
        if ((grid[i-1][j]<grid[i][j]) &&
            (grid[i+1][j]<grid[i][j]) &&
            (grid[i][j-1]<grid[i][j]) &&
            (grid[i][j+1]<grid[i][j]))
            return true;
        else
            return false;
```

The steps in the pseudocode are now detailed enough to convert to C++:

```
/*-------------------------------------------------------------*/
/*  Program chapter8_4                                         */
/*                                                             */
/*  This program determines the locations of                  */
/*  peaks in an elevation grid of data.                       */

#include <iostream>   //Required for cin, cout
#include <fstream>    //Required for ifstream
```

```cpp
#include <string>      //Required for string
using namespace std;

// Function prototypes.
bool isPeak(const double grid[][N], int r, int c);

int main()
{
   //  Declare objects.
   int const N = 25;
   int nrows, ncols;
   double elevation[N][N];
   string filename;
   ifstream file1;

   // Prompt user for file name and open file for input.
   cout << "Enter the name of the input file.\n";
   cin >> filename;
   file1.open(filename.c_str());
   if(file1.fail())
   {
     cerr << "Error opening input file\n";
     exit(1);
   }
   file1 >> nrows >> ncols;
   if(nrows > N || ncols > N)
   {
     cerr << "Grid is too large, adjust program.";
     exit(1);
   }
   //  Read information from data file into array.
   for (int i=0; i<nrows-1; ++i)
   {
     for (int j=0; j<ncols; ++j)
     {
        file1 >> elevation[i][j];
     }
   }
   //  Determine and print peak locations.
    cout << "Top left point defined as row 0, column 0 \n";
    for (int i=1; i<nrow-1; ++i)
    {
      for (int j=1; j<ncols-1; ++j)
      {
         if(isPeak(elevation, i, j))
         {
               cout << "Peak at row: " << i
                    << " column: " << j << endl;
         }
      }
    }
```

```
                   // close file
                   file1.close();
                   // Exit program.
                   return 0;
               }
               bool isPeak(const double grid[][N], int i, int j)
               {
                 if ((grid[i-1][j]<grid[i][j]) &&
                     (grid[i+1][j]<grid[i][j]) &&
                     (grid[i][j-1]<grid[i][j]) &&
                     (grid[i][j+1]<grid[i][j]))
                     return true;
                 else
                     return false;
               }
               /*--------------------------------------------------------*/
```

5. TESTING

The following output was printed using a data file that corresponds to the hand example (recall that this file must contain a special first line that specifies the number of rows and columns in the elevation data):

```
Top Left point defined as row 0, column 0
Peak at row: 2 column: 1
Peak at row: 2 column: 5
Peak at row: 4 column: 3
```

Modify!

Modify the peak-finding program as follows:

1. Print a count of the number of peaks in the grid.

2. Print the location of valleys instead of peaks. Assume that a valley is a point with an elevation lower than the four surrounding elevations. Write a boolean function named `isvalley` to be called by your program.

3. Find and print the location and elevation of the highest point and the lowest point in the elevation data. Write a function named `extremes` to be called by your program.

4. Assuming that the distance between points in a vertical and horizontal direction is 100 feet, give the location of the peaks in feet from the lower left corner of the grid.

5. Modify the function `isPeak()` to use all eight neighboring points in determining a peak instead of only four neighboring points.

6. Add pre-conditions to the function `isPeak()`.

8.3   Two-Dimensional Arrays and the `vector` Class

The `vector` class can be used to implement the concept of a two-dimensional array. Using the `vector` class has advantages over built-in arrays. It allows variables to be used in a type declaration statement to define the desired row and column size of a `vector`, thus eliminating the need for symbolic constants. The `vector class` also includes a set of useful methods for determining and modifying the size and capacity of a `vector`, dynamically. To define a two-dimensional `vector`, we define a `vector` of vectors of a specified type, as illustrated in the type declaration statements provided below:

```
vector< vector<double> >  arr(3,4);          //3 rows, 4 columns

vector< vector<int> > table(nRows, nCols); //nRows, nCols

vector< vector<char> > tags;                //capacity is 0
```

Notice the space between the last two > > characters in each of the type declaration statements. This space is required for successful compilation.

Two-Dimensional `vector` Declaration: The `vector` class can be used to implement the concept of a two-dimensional array. To use the `vector class`, a program must include the compiler directive `#include <vector>`.

Syntax:
```
vector<vector<type specifier> > identifier[(size,size)];
```

space is required

Example:
```
vector<vector<double> > temp(rows,cols);
vector<vector<int> > table(10,4);
vector<vector<char> > tags;
vector<vector<Point> > image(height,width);
```

To illustrate the use of the `vector` class to implement a two-dimensional array, we will write a program that is similar to program `chapter8_3`; then we will compare these two programs. The following program calls the function `input2DVec()` to read data from the file `engine.dat` and assign it to a `vector`, then calls the function `columnAvgVec()` to compute the average of each column in the `vector`.

```
/*------------------------------------------------------------*/
/* Program chapter8_5                                         */
/* This program illustrates the use of the vector             */
/* class to implement a two-dimensional array.                */

#include<iostream>  //Required for cout
#include<fstream>   //Required for ifstream
#include<vector>    //Required for vector
using namespace std;
```

```
//Function Prototypes
void input2DVec(istream& in,vector<vector<double> >&arr);
double columnAvgVec(vector<vector<double> >arr,int cNum);

int main()
{
   //Open input file
   ifstream fin("engine.dat");
   if(fin.fail())
   {
     cerr << "Could not open file engine.dat" << endl;
     exit(1);
   }
   //File open successful, declare objects
   int rows, cols;
   double colAvg;
   fin >> rows >> cols;


   //Define vector of vectors of type double
   vector< vector<double> > temps(rows,cols);

   //Call function to input data
   input2DVec(fin,temps);

   //Print the average value for each column
   for(int j=0; j<cols; ++j)
   {
     cout << "The average value of column " << j << " is "
          << columnAvgVec(temps,j) << endl;
   }
   return 0;
}
/*-----------------------------------------------------------*/


/*-----------------------------------------------------------*/
/* This function reads data from an input stream and         */
/* assigns the data to the 2D vector, arr.                   */
/* Pre-conditions:                                           */
/*    The istream has been defined.                          */
/*    istream source has sufficient data.                    */
/* Post-condtions:                                           */
/*    The vector arr is filled                               */
void input2DVec(istream&in,vector<vector<double> >&arr)
{

   //Declare and initialize local objects
   double val;
   int rows = arr.size();    //row size
   int cols = arr[0].size(); //all rows have same col size
```

```
      //Fill the array
      for (int i=0; i<rows; ++i)
      {
         for (int j=0; j<cols; ++j)
         {
            in >> arr[i][j];
         }
      }
   }
/*-------------------------------------------------------------*/


/*-------------------------------------------------------------*/
/* This function returns the average of column colNum          */
double columnAvgVec(vector<vector<double> >arr, int colNum)
{
   //Declare and initialize local objects.
   double avg = 0.0;
   int r = arr.size();
   //Sum all values in column colNum
   for(int i=0; i<r; ++i)
   {
      avg += arr[i][colNum];
   }

   //Return the average
   return (avg/r);
}
/*-------------------------------------------------------------*/
```

Recall that the data file `engine.dat` contains the following data:

```
4 3
335.6 339.4 421.7
299.6 332.4 340.5
320.1 329.8 339.3
322.1 361.4 401.9
```

The output generated by program `chapter8_4` is provided below:

```
The average value of column 0 is 319.35
The average value of column 1 is 340.75
The average value of column 2 is 375.85
```

First, we will compare the type declaration statements for the array `temps`.

```
double temps[MAXROWSIZE][MAXCOLSIZE];
vector< vector<double> > temps(rows,cols);
```

We see that program `chapter8_3` uses symbolic constants to define the array `temps`. The program `chapter8_5` does not require symbolic constants. The row size and column size are read from the data file and used directly to define the two-dimensional `vector  temps`.

Function Arguments

When passing a `vector` as an argument to a function, the default is pass-by value. If a function is intended to modify the contents of a `vector` argument, then a pass-by reference is required. The function `input2DVec()` reads data values from an input stream and assigns the values the to the `vector arr`. When this function is called in program `chapter8_5`, the `vector temps` is passed as an argument to the function. We want the values assigned to the formal parameter, `arr`, to also be assigned to the argument `temps`; thus a pass-by reference is required. We will now compare the function prototypes of the two input functions.

```
void input2D(istream& in, double a[][MAXCOLSIZE], int, int);
void input2DVec(istream& in,vector<vector<double> >&arr);
```

Notice that an "&" is used with the formal parameter `arr`, but not with the formal parameter `a`. Recall that arrays are always pass-by references in C++. Notice also that the function `input2D()` requires two additional formal parameters. Since the `vector` class includes a method to return the size of a `vector`, we do not need to pass additional information to the function `input2DVec()`. The function will get this information from the `vector` argument by calling the method `vector::size()`, as illustrated in the function definition.

Finally, we will compare the function prototypes of the two functions that compute column averages.

```
double columnAvg(const double a[][MAXCOLSIZE], int colNum,
                 int rows);
double columnAvgVec(vector<vector<double> >arr,int cNum);
```

Notice that the `const` modifier is used with the formal parameter `a` to prevent modification of the argument, but not with the formal parameter `arr`, because pass-by value is the default for `vector` objects.

Recall that a pass-by value creates a copy of the argument. In program `chapter8_5`, the size of the `vector` is small, so creating a copy of the argument does not require very much additional space or time. However, if we were working with a large `vector`, it would be more efficient to pass the address of the `vector` and use the `const` modifier to prevent modification, as illustrated below:

```
double columnAvgV2(const vector<vector<double> > &arr,
                   int cNum);
```

If the above prototype is used, no change is required to the function call in program `chapter8_5`. However, the function header must be modified to agree with the function prototype.

Practice!

Write a memory snapshot for each of the following code segments:

1. ```
   int r(3), c(5);
   vector<vector<char> > tags(r,c);
   ```

2. ```
   vector<vector<int> > series(4,4);
   ```

Practice!

3. Write a function to find, and return, the largest value in a specified column of a two-dimensional `vector`. Include pre- and post-conditions. Use the following function prototype:

```
double maxColumnVal(vector<vector<double> > v,
                    int colNum);
```

4. Write a function to find, and return, the smallest value in a specified row of a two-dimensional `vector`. Include pre- and post-conditions. Use the following function prototype:

```
double minColumnVal(const vector<vector<double> >
                    &v, int rowNum);
```

8.4 Matrices

matrix

A **matrix** is a set of numbers arranged in a rectangular grid with rows and columns, as shown in the following matrix with four rows and three columns, whose size is also specified as 4×3:

$$A = \begin{bmatrix} -1 & 0 & 0 \\ 1 & 1 & 0 \\ 1 & -2 & 3 \\ 0 & 2 & 1 \end{bmatrix}.$$

Note that the values within a matrix are written within large brackets.

In mathematical notation, matrices are usually given names with uppercase boldface letters. To refer to individual elements in the matrix, the row and column number are used, with both the row and column numbers starting with the value 1. In formal mathematical notation, the uppercase name refers to the entire matrix, and the lowercase name with subscripts refer to a specific element. Thus, by using the matrix **A**, the value of $a_{3,2}$ is -2. If a matrix has the

square matrix

same number of rows and columns, it is a **square matrix**.

A two-dimensional array can be used to store a matrix, but we must be careful translating equations in matrix notation into C++ statements because of the difference in subscripting. Matrix notation assumes that the row and column numbers begin with the value 1, whereas C++ statements assume that the row and column offsets of a two-dimensional array begin with the value 0.

Matrix operations are frequently used in engineering problem solutions, so we now present common operations with matrices. C++ statements for performing some of the operations are included; the problems at the end of the chapter relate to developing C++ statements for the remaining operations.

Determinant

determinant

The **determinant** of a matrix is a value computed from the entries in the matrix. Determinants have various applications in engineering, including computing inverses and solving systems of simultaneous equations. For a 2×2 matrix A, the determinant is defined as

$$|A| = a_{1,1}a_{2,2} - a_{2,1}a_{1,2}.$$

Therefore, the determinant of A is equal to 8 for the following matrix:

$$A = \begin{bmatrix} 1 & 3 \\ -1 & 5 \end{bmatrix}.$$

For a 3×3 matrix A, the determinant is defined to be the following:

$$|A| = a_{1,1}a_{2,2}a_{3,3} + a_{1,2}a_{2,3}a_{3,1} + a_{1,3}a_{2,1}a_{3,2} - a_{3,1}a_{2,2}a_{1,3}$$
$$- a_{3,2}a_{2,3}a_{1,1} - a_{3,3}a_{2,1}a_{1,2}.$$

If A is the matrix

$$A = \begin{bmatrix} 1 & 3 & 0 \\ -1 & 5 & 2 \\ 1 & 2 & 1 \end{bmatrix},$$

then $|A|$ is equal to $5 + 6 + 0 - 0 - 4 - (-3)$, or 10.
The array, a, that stores the matrix is:

	col 0	col 1	col 2
row 0	1	3	0
row 1	−1	5	2
row 2	1	2	1

and the equation to calculate the determinate of a is:

```
determinate =
   a[0][0]*a[1][1]*a[2][2]+a[0][1]*a[1][2]*a[2][0]+a[0][2]
 * a[1][0]*a[2][1] - a[2][0]*a[1][1]*a[0][2] - a[2][1]*a[1][2]
 * a[0][0] - a[2][2]*a[1][0]*a[0][1]
 = 5+ 6+ 0- 0- 4-(-3)
 = 10
```

It is important to note that subscripts used with matrices begin with 1, while offsets used with arrays begin with 0.

A more involved process is necessary for computing determinants of matrices with more than three rows and columns. This process is discussed in the problems at the end of this chapter.

Transpose

transpose

The **transpose** of a matrix is a new matrix in which the rows of the original matrix are the columns of the new matrix. We use a superscript T after a matrix name to refer to the transpose. For example, consider the following matrix and its transpose:

$$B = \begin{bmatrix} 2 & 5 & 1 \\ 7 & 3 & 8 \\ 4 & 5 & 21 \\ 16 & 13 & 0 \end{bmatrix}, \quad B^T = \begin{bmatrix} 2 & 7 & 4 & 16 \\ 5 & 3 & 5 & 13 \\ 1 & 8 & 21 & 0 \end{bmatrix}.$$

If we consider a couple of the elements, we see that the value in position (3, 1), has now moved to position (1, 3) and that the value in position (4, 2) has now moved to position (2, 4). In fact, we have interchanged the row and column offset so that we are moving the value in position (i, j) to position (j, i). Also, note that the size of the transpose is different from the size of the original matrix unless the original is a square matrix (i.e., a matrix with the same number of rows as columns).

We now develop a function that generates the transpose of a matrix. The formal arguments of the function must include two-dimensional arrays that represent the original matrix and the matrix that is to contain the transpose of the original matrix. To allow some flexibility with this function, we assume that symbolic constants have been defined that specify the number of rows and the number of columns in the original matrix; these symbolic constants are *NROWS* and *NCOLS*. Note that the function does not return a value; hence, the return type is void. Note also that the symbolic constants *NROWS* and *NCOLS* must be defined in a program that uses this function:

```
/*-------------------------------------------------------------*/
/*   This function generates a matrix transpose.          */
/*   NROWS and NCOLS are symbolic constants               */
/*   that must be defined in the calling program.         */

void transpose(int b[][NCOLS], int bt[][NROWS])
{
    //  Declare objects.

    //  Transfer values to the transpose matrix.
    for (int i=0; i<=NROWS-1; ++i)
    {
        for (int j=0; j<=NCOLS-1; ++j)
        {
            bt[j][i] = b[i][j];
        }
    }

    //  Void return.
    return;
}
/*-------------------------------------------------------------*/
```

Matrix Addition and Subtraction

The addition (or subtraction) of two matrices is performed by adding (or subtracting) the elements in corresponding positions in the matrices. Therefore, matrices that are added (or subtracted) must be of the same size; the result of the operation is another matrix of the same size. Consider the following matrices:

$$A = \begin{bmatrix} 2 & 5 & 1 \\ 0 & 3 & -1 \end{bmatrix}, \quad B = \begin{bmatrix} 1 & 0 & 2 \\ -1 & 4 & -2 \end{bmatrix}.$$

Several matrix sums and differences follow:

$$A + B = \begin{bmatrix} 3 & 5 & 3 \\ -1 & 7 & -3 \end{bmatrix}, \quad A - B = \begin{bmatrix} 1 & 5 & -1 \\ 1 & -1 & 1 \end{bmatrix},$$

$$B - A = \begin{bmatrix} -1 & -5 & 1 \\ -1 & 1 & -1 \end{bmatrix}.$$

Matrix Multiplication

Matrix multiplication

Matrix multiplication is not computed by multiplying corresponding elements of the two matrices. The value in position $c_{i,j}$ of the product C of two matrices A and B is the product of row i of the first matrix and column j of the second matrix:

$$c_{i,j} = \sum_{k=1}^{n} a_{i,k} b_{k,j}.$$

The product of row i and column j requires that the row i and the column j have the same number of elements. Therefore, the first matrix (A) must have the same number of elements in each row as there are in the columns of the second matrix (B). Thus, if A and B both have five rows and five columns, their product has five rows and five columns. Furthermore, for these matrices, we can compute both AB and BA, but, in general, they will not be equal.

If A has two rows and three columns and B has three rows and three columns, the product AB will have two rows and three columns. To illustrate, consider the following matrices:

$$A = \begin{bmatrix} 2 & 5 & 1 \\ 0 & 3 & -1 \end{bmatrix}, \quad B = \begin{bmatrix} 1 & 0 & 2 \\ -1 & 4 & -2 \\ 5 & 2 & 1 \end{bmatrix}.$$

The first element in the product $C = AB$ is

$$c_{1,1} = \sum_{k=1}^{3} a_{1,k} b_{k,1}$$

$$= a_{1,1} b_{1,1} + a_{1,2} b_{2,1} + a_{1,3} b_{3,1}$$

$$= 2(1) + 5(-1) + 1(5)$$

$$= 2.$$

Similarly, we can compute the rest of the elements in the product of A and B:

$$AB = C = \begin{bmatrix} 2 & 22 & -5 \\ -8 & 10 & -7 \end{bmatrix}.$$

In this example, we cannot compute BA, because B does not have the same number of elements in each row as A has in each column.

An easy way to decide whether a matrix product exists is to write the sizes of the two matrices side by side. If the two inside numbers are the same, the product exists; the size of the product is determined by the two outside numbers. To illustrate, in the previous example, the size of A is 2×3 and the size of B is 3×3. Therefore, if we want to compute AB, we write the sizes side by side:

$2 \times 3 \quad 3 \times 3$

The two inner numbers are both the value 3, so AB exists, and its size is determined by the two outer numbers, 2×3. If we want to compute BA we again write the sizes side by side:

$3 \times 3 \quad 2 \times 3$

The two inner numbers are not the same, so BA does not exist.

We now present a function to compute the product $C = AB$. In this function, the arrays are each of size $N \times N$, where N is a symbolic constant:

```
/*-------------------------------------------------------------*/
/*   This function performs a matrix multiplication    */
/*   of two NxN matrices using sums of products.       */
/*   N is a symbolic constant that must be defined     */
/*   within the scope of the function.                 */

void matrixMult(int a[][N], int b[][N], int c[][N])
{

    //  Compute sums of products.
    for (int i=0; i<N; i++)
    {
        for (int j=0; j<N; ++j)
        {
            c[i][j] = 0;
            for (int k=0; k<N; ++k)
            {
                c[i][j] += a[i][k]*b[k][j];
            }
        }
    }
    //  Void return.
    return;
}
/*-------------------------------------------------------------*/
```

Practice!

Use the matrices A, B, and C presented next to evaluate by hand the expressions in these problems. If the expression can be evaluated, then write programs to test your answers using the functions developed in this section. The functions are available in a file *matrix.cpp* on the instructor's resource CD.

Practice!

$$A = \begin{bmatrix} 2 & 1 \\ 0 & -1 \\ 3 & 0 \end{bmatrix}, \quad B = \begin{bmatrix} -2 & 2 \\ -1 & 5 \end{bmatrix},$$

$$C = \begin{bmatrix} 3 & 2 \\ -1 & -2 \\ 0 & 2 \end{bmatrix}$$

1. $|B|$

2. $C^T + A^T$

3. $A + B$

4. AB

5. BA

6. $B(C^T)$

7. $(CB)C^T$

The problems at the end of the chapter use the matrix operations discussed in this section and also define additional matrix operations.

8.5 Numerical Technique: Solution to Simultaneous Equations

The need to solve a system of simultaneous equations occurs frequently in engineering problems. A number of methods exist for solving a system of equations, and each method has its advantages and disadvantages. In this section, we present the **Gauss elimination** method of solving a set of **simultaneous linear equations**; the equations are called linear equations because the equations contain only linear (degree-1) terms such as x, y, and z. However, before we present the details of this technique, we first present a graphical interpretation of the solution to a set of equations.

Gauss elimination
simultaneous linear
equations

Graphical Interpretation

A linear equation with two variables, such as $2x - y = 3$, defines a straight line and is often written in the form $y = mx + b$, where m represents the slope of the line and b represents the y-intercept. Thus, $2x - y = 3$ can also be written as $y = 2x - 3$. If we have two linear equations, they can represent two different lines that intersect in a single point, they can represent two parallel lines that never intersect, or they can represent the same line; these possibilities are shown in Figure 8.1.

Equations that represent two intersecting lines can be easily identified because they will have different slopes, as in $y = 2x - 3$ and $y = -x + 3$. Equations that represent two parallel

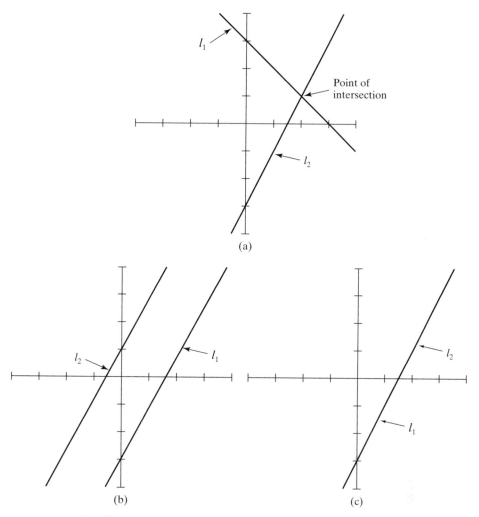

Figure 8.1 Two lines.

lines will have the same slope, but different y-intercepts, as in $y = 2x - 3$ and $y = 2x + 1$. Equations that represent the same line have the same slope and y-intercept, as in $y = 2x - 3$ and $3y = 6x - 9$.

If a linear equation contains three variables, x, y, and z, then it represents a plane in three-dimensional space. If we have two equations with three variables, they can represent two planes that intersect in a straight line, they can represent two parallel planes, or they can represent the same plane; these possibilities are shown in Figure 8.2. If we have three equations with three variables, the three planes can intersect in a single point, they can intersect in a plane, they can have no common intersection point, or they can represent the same plane. Examples of the possibilities that exist if the three equations define three different planes are shown in Figure 8.3. These ideas can be extended to more than three variables, although it is harder to visualize the corresponding situations.

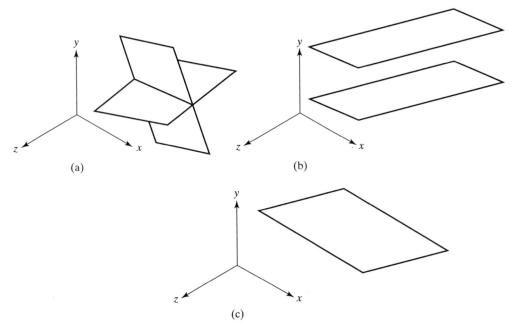

(a)

(b)

(c)

Figure 8.2 Two planes.

hyperplane

We call the set of points defined by an equation with more than three variables a **hyperplane.** In general, we consider a set of m linear equations that contain n unknowns, where each equation defines a hyperplane that is not identical to another hyperplane in the set of equations. If $m < n$ then the system is underspecified, and a unique solution does not exist. If $m = n$, then a unique solution will exist if none of the equations represents parallel hyperplanes. If $m > n$, then the system is overspecified, and a unique solution does not exist. A set of

system of equations

nonsingular

equations is also called a **system of equations**. A system with a unique solution is called a **nonsingular** system of equations, and a system with no unique solution is called a singular set of equations.

As a specific example, consider the following system of equations:

$$3x + 2y - z = 10,$$

$$-x + 3y + 2z = 5,$$

$$x - y - z = -1.$$

The solution to this set of equations is the point $(-2, 5, -6)$. Substitute these values in each of the questions to confirm that this point is a solution to the set of equations.

The material in the previous section on matrices is not required for the development of the solution presented in this section. However, if you did cover that material, it is interesting to observe that a system of linear equations can be expressed in terms of a matrix multiplication. To illustrate, let the information in the previous equations be expressed using the following matrices:

$$A = \begin{bmatrix} 3 & 2 & -1 \\ -1 & 3 & 2 \\ 1 & -1 & -1 \end{bmatrix}, \quad X = \begin{bmatrix} x \\ y \\ z \end{bmatrix}, \quad B = \begin{bmatrix} 10 \\ 5 \\ -1 \end{bmatrix}.$$

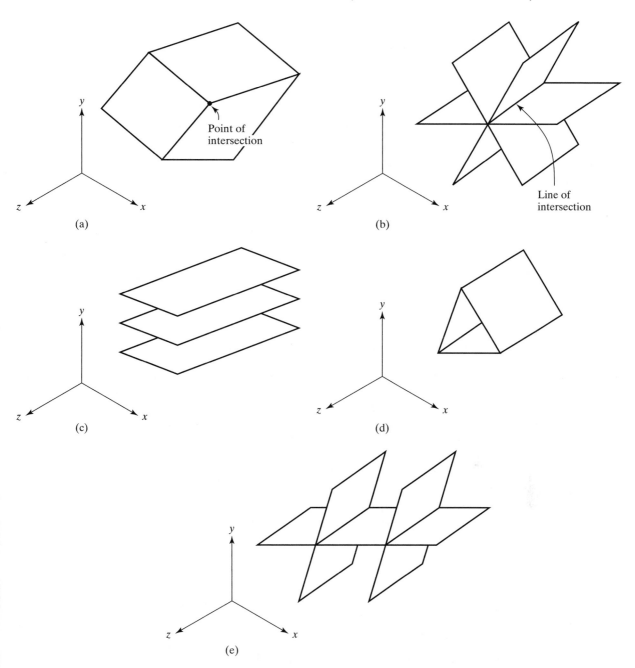

Figure 8.3 Three distinct planes.

Then, using matrix multiplication, we find that the system of equations can be written in the form

$$AX = B.$$

Go through the multiplication to convince yourself that this matrix equation yields the original set of equations.

In many engineering problems, we are interested in determining whether a common solution exists to a system of equations. If the common solution exists, then we want to determine it. In the next part of this section, we present the Gauss elimination technique for solving a set of simultaneous linear equations.

Gauss Elimination

Before presenting a general description of the Gauss elimination technique, we illustrate the technique with a specific example, using the set of equations presented earlier:

$$3x + 2y - z = 10 \quad \text{(first equation)},$$

$$-x + 3y + 2z = 5 \quad \text{(second equation)},$$

$$x - y - z = -1 \quad \text{(third equation)}.$$

elimination
The first step is an **elimination** step in which the first variable is eliminated from each equation that follows the first equation. This elimination is achieved by adding a scaled form of the first equation to each of the other equations. The term involving the first variable, x, in the second equation is $-x$. Therefore, if we multiply the first equation by $1/3$ and add it to equation 2, we obtain a new equation in which the x variable has been eliminated:

$$-x + 3y + 2z = 5 \quad \text{(second equation)}$$

$$x + \frac{2}{3}y - \frac{1}{3}z = \frac{10}{3} \quad \left(\text{first equation times } \frac{1}{3}\right),$$

$$\overline{0x + \frac{11}{3}y + \frac{5}{3}z = \frac{25}{3}} \quad \text{(sum)}.$$

The modified set of equations is then

$$3x + 2y - z = 10,$$

$$0x + \frac{11}{3}y + \frac{5}{3}z = \frac{25}{3},$$

$$x - y - z = -1.$$

We now eliminate the first variable from the third equation, using a similar process:

$$x - y - z = -1 \quad \text{(third equation)},$$

$$-x - \frac{2}{3}y + \frac{1}{3}z = -\frac{10}{3} \quad \left(\text{first equation times } -\frac{1}{3}\right),$$

$$\overline{0x - \frac{5}{3}y - \frac{2}{3}z = -\frac{13}{3}} \quad \text{(sum)}.$$

The modified set of equations is then

$$3x + 2y - z = 10,$$

$$0x + \frac{11}{3}y + \frac{5}{3}z = \frac{25}{3},$$

$$0x - \frac{5}{3}y - \frac{2}{3}z = -\frac{13}{3}.$$

We have now eliminated the first variable in all equations except for the first.

The next step is to eliminate the second variable in all equations except for the first and second, by adding the equations to a scaled form of the second equation:

$$0x - \frac{5}{3}y - \frac{2}{3}z = -\frac{13}{3} \quad \text{(third equation)},$$

$$0x + \frac{5}{3}y + \frac{25}{33}z = \frac{125}{33} \quad \left(\text{second equation times } \frac{5}{11}\right),$$

$$\overline{0x + 0y + \frac{3}{33}z = -\frac{18}{33} \quad \text{(sum)}.}$$

The modified set of equations is then

$$3x + 2y - z = 10,$$

$$0x + \frac{11}{3}y + \frac{5}{3}z = \frac{25}{3},$$

$$0x + 0y + \frac{3}{33}z = -\frac{18}{33}.$$

Because there are no equations following the third equation, this part of the algorithm is completed.

back substitution We now perform a **back substitution** to determine the solution of the equations. The last equation has only one variable, so we can multiply the equation by a scale factor chosen to make the variable's coefficient equal to 1. Thus, we multiply the last equation by $\frac{33}{3}$, or 11, giving

$$0x + 0y + z = -6.$$

This value of z is substituted in the next-to-last equation, giving

$$0x + \frac{11}{3}y + \frac{5}{3}(-6) = \frac{25}{3}.$$

Reducing the equation so that all constant terms are on the right side, we have

$$0x + \frac{11}{3}y = \frac{55}{3}.$$

This equation has only one variable, so we now multiply it by a scale factor chosen to make the new coefficient equal to 1:

$$0x + y = 5.$$

We back up to the next equation, which is the last equation in this example:

$$3x + 2y - z = 10.$$

Substituting the values already determined, we have

$$3x + 2(5) - (-6) = 10,$$

or

$$3x = -6$$

Thus, the value of x is -2.

The Gauss elimination technique thus has two parts: elimination and back substitution. First, the equations are modified such that the kth variable is eliminated in all equations following the kth equation. Then, starting with the last equation, we compute the value of the last variable. Next, using this value and the next-to-last equation, we compute the value of the next-to-last variable. This back substitution continues until we have determined the values of

ill conditioned

all the variables. The system is **ill conditioned** or does not have a unique solution if all the coefficients for a variable are zero or are very close to zero.

pivoting

A process called **pivoting** can be applied to improve the accuracy of Gauss elimination. Row pivoting involves reordering the rows before perfoming Gauss elimination, and column pivoting involves reordering the columns before performing the process. Complete pivoting involves reordering both rows and columns. These processes are discussed in the problems at the end of the chapter.

Practice!

Use the Gauss elimination numerical technique to find the solution of the following sets of simultaneous linear equations:

1. $-2x + y = -3$
    $x + y = 3$

2. $3x + 5y + 2z = 8$
    $2x + 3y - z = 1$
    $x - 2y - 3z = -1$

8.6 Problem Solving Applied: Electrical Circuit Analysis

The analysis of an electrical circuit frequently involves finding the solution of a set of simultaneous equations. These equations are often derived using either current equations that describe the currents entering and leaving a node or voltage equations that describe the voltages around mesh loops in the circuit. For example, consider the circuit shown in Figure 8.4. The equations that describe the voltages around the three loops are the following:

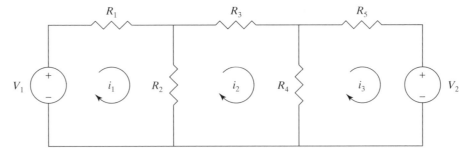

Figure 8.4 Circuit with two voltage sources.

$$-V_1 + R_1 i_1 + R_2(i_1 - i_2) = 0,$$
$$R_2(i_2 - i_1) + R_3 i_2 + R_4(i_2 - i_3) = 0,$$
$$R_4(i_3 - i_2) + R_5 i_3 + V_2 = 0.$$

If we assume that the values of the resistors (R_1, R_2, R_3, R_4, and R_5) and the voltage sources (V_1 and V_2) are known, then the unknowns in the system of equations are the mesh currents (i_1, i_2, and i_3). We can then rearrange the system of equations to the following form:

$$(R_1 + R_2)i_1 - R_2 i_2 + 0i_3 = V_1,$$
$$-R_2 i_1 + (R_2 + R_3 + R_4)i_2 - R_4 i_3 = 0,$$
$$0i_1 - R_4 i_2 + (R_4 + R_5)i_3 = -V_2.$$

Write a program that allows the user to enter the values of the five resistors and the values of the two voltage sources and store these values in a two-dimensional array. The program should then compute the three mesh currents.

1. PROBLEM STATEMENT

Compute the three mesh currents in the circuit shown in Figure 8.4.

2. INPUT/OUTPUT DESCRIPTION

The I/O diagram shows that the resistor values and the voltage values are the input values. The three mesh currents are the output values.

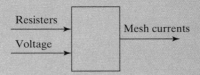

3. HAND EXAMPLE

By using the resistor values and the voltage values, a system of three equations can be defined, using this rearranged set of equations from the definition of the problem:

$$(R_1 + R_2)i_1 - R_2i_2 + 0i_3 = V_1,$$

$$-R_2i_1 + (R_2 + R_3 + R_4)i_2 - R_4i_3 = 0,$$

$$0i_1 - R_4i_2 + (R_4 + R_5)i_3 = -V_2.$$

For example, suppose that each of the resistor values is 1 ohm and that both of the voltage sources are 5 volts. Then the corresponding set of equations is the following:

$$2i_1 - i_2 + 0i_3 = 5,$$

$$-i_1 + 3i_2 - i_3 = 0,$$

$$0i_1 - i_2 + 2i_3 = -5.$$

Once the system of equations is determined, the solution follows the steps illustrated in the hand example in the previous section. For this set of equations, the solution is $i_1 = 2.5$, $i_2 = 0$, and $i_3 = -2.5$.

4. ALGORITHM DEVELOPMENT

We first develop the decomposition outline, because it breaks the solution into a series of sequential steps:

Decomposition Outline

1. Read the resistor values and the voltage values.

2. Specify the coefficients for the system of equations.

3. Perform Gauss elimination to determine currents.

4. Print currents.

In step 1 we read the information necessary to specify the circuit values, and in step 2 we use this information to specify the coefficients for the system of equations. Then, in step 3, we develop the details of the elimination and back-substitution steps. To keep the main function short and readable, functions are used for both the elimination and the back substitution. The structure chart for this solution was used in Figure [?].

The coefficients of the simultaneous equations are stored in a two-dimensional array; the solution is stored in a one-dimensional array. The variable index indicates which variable is being eliminated in the elimination function; this variable ranges from 0 to $n - 1$ to match the subscripting in C++.

The algorithm for Gauss elimination is a difficult algorithm to describe in pseudocode because of the detailed subscripting that must be specified. Go through this pseudocode with the hand example to be sure that you are comfortable with the subscript handling.

```
Refinement in Pseudocode
main:      read resistor values and voltage values
           specify array coefficients, a[i][j]
           set index to zero
           while index <= n - 2
                   eliminate(a,n,index)
                   increment index by 1
           back-substitute(a,n,soln)
           print current values
eliminate(a,n,index):
           set row to index +1
           while row <= n-1
```

$$\text{set scale-factor to } \frac{-a[row][index]}{a[index][index]}$$

```
                   set a[row][index] to zero


                   set col to index +1
                   while col <= n
                           add a[index][col] · scale-factor
                                   to a[row][col]
                           increment col by 1
                   increment row by 1
back-substitute(a,n,soln):
```

$$\text{set soln[n-1] to } \frac{a[n-1][n]}{a[n-1][n-1]}$$

```
           set row to n-2
           while row >= 0
                   set col to n-1
                   while col >= row +1
                           subtract soln[col] · a[row][col]
                                   from a[row][n]
                           subtract 1 from col
```

$$\text{set soln[row] to } \frac{a[row][n]}{a[row][row]}$$

```
                   subtract 1 from row
```

Once we are comfortable with the pseudocode, it is relatively straightforward to convert it to C++:

```
/*-----------------------------------------------------------*/
/*  Program chapter8_6                                       */
/*                                                           */
/*  This program uses Gauss elimination to                   */
/*  determine the mesh currents for a circuit.               */

#include <iostream>   //Required for cin, cout
using namespace std;

// Define global constant for number of unknowns.
const int N = 3;
```

```
// Declare function prototypes.
void eliminate(double a[][N+1], int n, int index);
void back_substitute(double a[][N+1],
                     int n, double soln[N]);
int main()
{
  // Declare objects.
  double r1, r2, r3, r4, r5, v1, v2,
         a[N][N+1], soln[N];

  // Get user input.
  cout << "Enter resistor values in ohms: \n"
       << "(R1, R2, R3, R4, R5) \n";
  cin >> r1 >> r2 >> r3 >> r4 >> r5;
  cout << "Enter voltage values in volts: \n"
       << "(V1, V2) \n";
  cin >> v1 >> v2;

  // Specify equation coefficients.
  a[0][0] = r1 + r2;
  a[0][1] = a[1][0] = -r2;
  a[0][2] = a[2][0] = a[1][3] = 0;
  a[1][1] = r2 + r3 + r4;
  a[1][2] = a[2][1] = -r4;
  a[2][2] = r4 + r5;
  a[0][3] = v1;
  a[2][3] = -v2;

  // Perform elimination step.
  for (int index=0; index<N-1; index++)
  {
    eliminate(a,N,index);
  }

  // Perform back substitution step.
  back_substitute(a,N,soln);

  // Print solution.
  cout << "\nSolution: \n";
  for (int i=0; i<N; ++i)
  {
    cout << "Mesh Current " << i+1 << ": "<< soln[i] << endl;
  }

  // Exit program.
  return 0;
}
/*------------------------------------------------------------*/
/*  This function performs the elimination step.          */
```

```cpp
void eliminate(double a[][N+1], int n, int index)
{
   //  Declare objects.
   double scale_factor;

   //  Eliminate object from equations.
   for (int row=index+1; row<n; ++row)
   {
      scale_factor = -a[row][index]/a[index][index];
      a[row][index] = 0;
      for (int col=index+1; col<=n; ++col)
      {
         a[row][col] += a[index][col]*scale_factor;
      }
   }

   //  Void return.
   return;
}
/*-------------------------------------------------------------*/
/*  This function performs the back substitution.            */

void back_substitute(double a[][N+1], int n,
                     double soln[])
{
   //  Perform back substitution in each equation.
   soln[n-1] = a[n-1][n]/a[n-1][n-1];
   for (int row=n-2; row>=0; --row)
   {
      for (int col=n-1; col>=row+1; --col)
      {
         a[row][n] -= soln[col]*a[row][col];
      }
      soln[row] = a[row][n]/a[row][row];
   }

   //  Void return.
   return;
}
/*-------------------------------------------------------------*/
```

To handle larger systems of equations, the symbolic constant N must be changed; the steps in the Gauss elimination do not need any modifications. The program interaction using the data from the hand example is as follows:

```
Enter resistor values in ohms:
(R1, R2, R3, R4, R5)
1 1 1 1 1
Enter voltage values in volts:
(V1, V2)
5 5
```

```
Solution:
Mesh Current 1: 2.5
Mesh Current 2: 0
Mesh Current 3: -2.5
```

The program assumes that the system of equations has a solution, which means that none of the equations represents the same equation or parallel equations. Modifications to the program to check for these conditions could be added with additional statements or functions.

Modify!

Use the program developed in this section to answer the following questions:

1. Determine the mesh currents if all five resistors are 5 ohms and both voltage sources are 10 volts.

2. Verify your answer in problem 1 by using matrix multiplication as discussed in this section. (This problem assumes that you covered the previous section on matrices and vectors.)

3. Determine the mesh currents if the resistors have the values of 2, 8, 6, 6, and 4 ohms and the voltage sources have the values of 40 and 20 volts.

4. Verify your answer from problem 3 by substituting back in the original set of three equations.

8.7 Higher Dimensional Arrays

C++ allows arrays to be defined with more than two dimensions. For example, the following statement defines a **three-dimensional array**:

```
int b[3][4][2];
```

The three offsets, which are necessary to specify a specific element, correspond to the x-, y-, and z-coordinates if you position the array at the origin of a three-dimensional space, as shown in Figure 8.5. Thus, the position that is shaded corresponds to b[2][0][1].

Most engineering problems that need arrays can be solved using one-dimensional or two-dimensional arrays. However, there are occasionally problems that are good candidates for using higher dimensional arrays. These problems typically involve data that are specified by several parameters; in addition, the parameters either are integers that are sequential or parameters that can easily be converted into sequential parameters. For example, suppose that a set of data representing temperature measurements is taken from the floor of a large chemical reaction chamber. Furthermore, this set of temperatures is taken at specified intervals of time during a chemical reaction. In this case, we might choose to use a three-dimensional array, using the first offset to indicate a specific time, and the other two offset to indicate the location

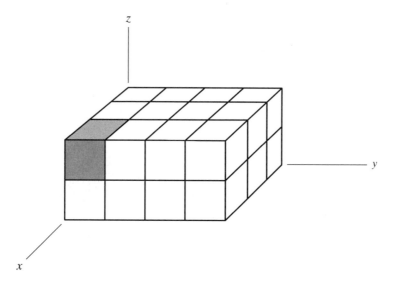

Figure 8.5 Three-dimensional array.

within the floor. The offsets would need to begin with zero to match the requirements of C++ offsets. The offsets [3][2][5] would then specify the value taken at the fourth time value and at position [2][5] in the grid of temperatures.

Arrays with more than three offsets are seldom used because it is difficult to visualize them. However, a simple way to visualize arrays with more than three offsets can be developed. First, consider a three-dimensional array to be a building. The building has floors and a rectangular grid of rooms on each floor. Assume that each room can contain a single value. The three-dimensional array representing the building uses three offsets to specify a room; the first offset is the floor number, and the other two offsets specify the row and column number of the room on the specified floor.

A **four-dimensional array** is a row of buildings, as shown in Figure 8.6. The first offset specifies the building, and the remaining three offsets specify the room in the building.

A **five-dimensional array** is a block of buildings, as shown in Figure 8.7. The first two offsets specify the building in the block, and the remaining three offsets specify the room in the building.

This analogy could continue with a row of blocks, a city of blocks, a group of cities, a state of cities, and so on. Although we have shown you how to visualize higher dimensional arrays, we also want to caution you about using higher order arrays. Higher order arrays have

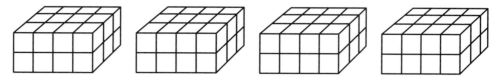

Figure 8.6 Four-dimensional array.

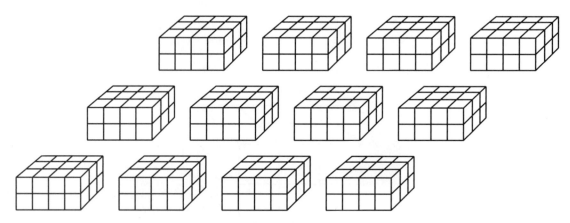

Figure 8.7 Five-dimensional array.

a lot of overhead related to the offsetting; not only are there extra offsets required, but extra loops are necessary each time you want to work with groups of values in the array. In general, higher order arrays also complicate the debugging and maintenance of the program. Therefore, higher order arrays should be used only when they simplify the overall visualization of the problem and the steps to solve it.

SUMMARY

An array is a data structure often used to store engineering data that are analyzed in a program. If the data are best represented by a table or grid of information, a two-dimensional array is used. Many examples were developed in this chapter to illustrate definitions, initializations, computations and input and output with two-dimensional arrays, and two-dimensional arrays as function parameters. The Gauss elimination technique for solving a system of simultaneous linear equations was also presented, and a C++ program developed to implement this technique. The `vector` class was used in an example to model a two-dimensional array.

Key Terms

column offset
declared column size
determinant
Gauss elimination
hyperplane
ill conditioned
inner product
matrix
matrix multiplication
nonsingular
pivoting

post-conditions
pre-conditions
row offset
simultaneous linear equations
square matrix
subarray
system of equations
transpose
two-dimensional array
two-dimensional vector

C++ Statement Summary

Two-dimensional array declaration:

```
double x[10][5];
```

Notes

1. Use symbolic constants to declare the size of an array so that it is easy to modify.
2. In documentation, describe a two-dimensional array as a grid with rows and columns.
3. The objects i and j are commonly used as offsets for a two-dimensional array.
4. Include pre- and post-conditions in function definition.

Debugging Notes

1. The declared column size of an array must be specified in the formal parameter list and in the function prototype.
2. Be careful not to exceed the maximum offset value when referencing an element in a multidimensional array.
3. Be sure to enclose each offset in its own set of brackets when referencing elements of a multidimensional array.
4. When translating matrix notation to C++, remember that the first row and column in a matrix is referenced with the number 1, not 0.
5. Multidimensional matrices complicate the logic of a program and should be used only when they are necessary.
6. When declaring a two-dimensional vector, remember that the space between the last two >> characters in the type declaration statement is required.

Problems

Exam Practice!

Give the corresponding snapshots of memory after each of the following sets of statements is executed. Use ? to indicate an array element that is not initialized.

```
1.  int x[4][5];
    ...
    for(int r=0; r<=3; ++r)
      for(int c=0; c<=4; ++c)
        x[r][c] = r + c;
2.  int x[4][5];
    for(int c=0; c<=4; ++c)
      for(int r=0; r<=3; ++r)
        x[r][c] = r;
```

Program Output

Problems 3 and 4 refer to the following statements:

```
int sum, k, i, j;
int x[4][4] = {{1,2,3,4}, {5,6,7,8}, {9,8,7,3}, {2,1,7,1}};
```

3. Give the value in sum after the following statements are executed.

```
sum = x[0][0];
for(int k=1; k<=3; ++k)
  sum += x[k][k];
```

4. Give the value in sum after the following statements are executed.

```
sum = 0;
for(int i=1; i<=3; ++i)
  for(int j=0; j<=3; ++j)
    if(x[i][j] > x[i-1][j])
      sum++;
```

5. Give the value in size after the following statements are executed.

```
vector<vector<double> > power(5,10);
int size = power.size();
```

6. Give the value of size after the following statements are executed.

```
vector<vector<int> > power(5,10);
int size = power[0].size();
```

Multiple-Choice Problems

7. What value will be assigned to A[1][2] after the following type declaration statement is executed? `int A[3][3] = {1,2,3,4,5,6,7,8,9};`
   (a) 2
   (b) 3
   (c) 4
   (d) 5
   (e) 6

8. What value will be assigned to the array B[2][2] after the following type declaration statement is executed? `int B[3][3] = {{1,2},[3,4],[5,6]};`
   (a) 0
   (b) 2
   (c) 4
   (d) 6
   (e) Value of B[2][2] is undefined.

9. Which of the following is the correct prototype for a function that returns the largest
   value in the nth row of a two-dimensional array of type `int`?
   (a) `void fun(int[][], int n, int largest);`
   (b) `int fun(const int a[n][COLSIZE]);`

(c) `int fun(const int a[][COLSIZE], int n);`
(d) `int fun(const int [n] [COLSIZE], int n);`
(e) `void fun(const int[][], COLSIZE, int n);`

10. Which of the following is the correct prototype for a function that subtracts the integer value n from every element of a two-dimensional array of type `int`?
(a) `void fun(int[][], int n);`
(b) `int fun(const int a[][COLMAX], int n);`
(c) `void fun(const int a[][n], int COLSIZE);`
(d) `void fun(int a[][COLSIZE], int n);`
(e) `int fun(const int[][], int n);`

Programming Exercises

Power Plant Data.   The data file *power1.dat* contains a power plant output in megawatts over a period of 10 weeks. Each row of data contains 7 floating-point numbers that represent 1 week's data. In developing the following programs, use symbolic constants NROWS and NCOLS to represent the number of rows and columns in the array used to store the data.

11. Write a program to compute and print the average power output over this period. Also print the number of days with greater-than-average power output.

12. Write a program to print the day of the week and the number of the week on which the minimum power output occurred. If there are several days with the minimum power output, print the information for each of these days.

13. Write a function to compute the average of a specified column of a two dimensional array that has NROWS rows and NCOLS columns. The parameters should be the floating-point array and the desired column. Assume that the corresponding function prototype is

```
double col_ave(double x[]NCOLS],int col);
```

14. Write a function to compute and return the average value in a two-dimensional `vector` of type `double`. Assume that the corresponding function prototype is

```
double avgVec(const vector<vector<double> > &x);
```

15. Write a program to print a report that lists the average power output for the first day of the week, then for the second day of the week, and so on. Print the information in the following format:

```
Day x: Average Power Output in Megawatts:   xxxx.xx
```

16. Write a function to compute the average of a specified row of a two-dimensional array that has NROWS rows and NCOLS columns. The parameters should be the floating-point array and the desired row. Assume that the corresponding function prototype is

```
double row_ave(double x[]NCOLS],int row);
```

17. Write a program to print a report that lists the average power output for the first week, the second week, and so on. Print the information in the following format:

```
Week x: Average Power Output in Megawatts:   xxxx.xx
```

18. Write a program to compute and print the mean and variance of the power plant output data.

Temperature Distribution. The temperature distribution in a thin metal plate with constant (or isothermal) temperatures on each side can be modeled using a two-dimensional grid, as shown in Figure 8.8. Typically, the number of points in the grid are specified, as are the constant temperatures on the four sides. The temperatures of the interior points are usually initialized to zero, but they change according to the temperatures around them. Assume that the temperature of an interior point can be computed as the average of the four adjacent temperatures; the points shaded in Figure 8.8 represent the adjacent temperatures for the point labeled x in the grid. Each time that the temperature of an interior point changes, the temperatures of the points adjacent to it change. These changes continue until a thermal equilibrium is achieved and all temperatures become constant.

19. Write a program to model this temperature distribution for a grid with six rows and eight columns. Allow the user to enter the temperatures for the four sides. Use one grid to store the temperatures. Thus, when a point is updated, its new value is used to update the next point. Continue updating the points, moving across the rows until the temperature differences for all updates are less than a user-entered tolerance value. Use the `vector` class to implement the grid.

20. Modify the program generated in problem 19 so that the updates are performed down the columns. Compare the equilibrium values for the two programs using different tolerance values. The equilibrium values should be very close for small tolerance values.

21. Modify the program in problem 19 so that two grids are used and so that the program can perform the updates as if they all happen at the same time. Thus, all temperatures are updated using one set of grid values. The two grids are needed so that all the old temperatures are available to compute each new temperature.

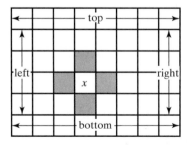

Figure 8.8 Temperature grid in a metal plate.

22. Modify the program in problem 19 to use an array instead of the `vector` class to implement the grid.

Gauss Elimination.   The accuracy of the Gauss elimination technique can be improved using a process called pivoting. To perform row pivoting, we first reorder the equations so that the equation with the largest absolute value for the first coefficient is the first equation. We then eliminate the first object from the equations that follow the first equation. Then, starting with the second equation, we reorder the equations such that the second equation has the largest coefficient (in absolute value) for the second object. We then eliminate the second object from all equations after the second equation. The process continues similarly for the rest of the objects. Assume that a symbolic constant N contains the number of equations.

23. Use the program developed in Section 8.4 as a guide to develop a function that receives a `double` array a of size N by $N+1$. A second parameter is a `double` array soln of size $N + 1$. The function should solve the system of equations represented by array a, and return the solution in array *soln*. Assume that the corresponding function prototype is

    ```
    void gauss(double a[][N+1], double soln[N+1]);
    ```

24. Write a function that receives a two-dimensional array and a pivot value that specifies the coefficient of interest j. The function should then reorder all equations starting with the jth equation such that the jth equation will have the largest coefficient (in absolute value) in the jth position. Assume that the function can reference the size of the array as N by $N+1$, and that the corresponding function prototype is

    ```
    void pivot_r(double a[][N+1], int j);
    ```

25. Modify the function developed for problem 23 so that the row pivoting is performed before each variable is eliminated. Use the function developed in problem 24.

26. Column pivoting is performed in a similar fashion to row pivoting by exchanging columns such that the largest coefficient (in absolute value) will be in the position of interest. When columns are exchanged, it is important to keep track of the changes in the order of the objects. Write a function to perform column pivoting. Include parameters to specify changes in the order of the objects. Assume that the corresponding function prototype is

    ```
    void pivot_c(double a[][N+1], int j, int reorder k[N]);
    ```

27. Modify the function developed for problem 23 so that column pivoting is performed before each object is eliminated. Use the function developed in problem 26.

28. Modify the function developed for problem 23 so that both row pivoting and column pivoting are performed before each object is eliminated. Use the functions developed in problems 24 and 26.

Determinants. The following problems define cofactors and minors of a square matrix; use them to evaluate a determinant.

29. The **minor** of an element $a(i, j)$ of a matrix A is the determinant of the matrix obtained by removing the row and column to which the given element $a(i, j)$ belongs. Thus, if the original matrix has four rows and four columns, the minor is the determinant of a matrix with three rows and columns. Write a function to compute the minor of a square matrix with four rows and four columns. The input arguments should be the matrix A and the values of i and j. Assume that the corresponding function prototype is

```
double minor(double a[][4], int i, int j);
```

30. A **cofactor** $A(i, j)$ of a matrix A is the product of the minor of $a(i, j)$ and the factor $(-1)i + j$. Write a function to compute a cofactor of a square matrix with four rows and four columns. The arguments should be the matrix A and the values of i and j. You may want to reference the function in problem 29. Assume that the corresponding function prototype is

```
double cofactor(double a[][4], int i, int j);
```

The determinant of a square matrix A can be computed in the following way:
(a) Select any column.
(b) Multiply each element in the column by its cofactor.
(c) Add the products obtained in step (b).

31. Write a function **det_c** to compute the determinant of a square matrix with four rows and four columns using this technique. You may want to reference the function developed in problem 30. Assume that the corresponding function prototype is

```
double det_c(double a[][4]);
```

32. The determinant of a square matrix A can be computed in the following way:
(a) Select any row.
(b) Multiply each element in the row by its cofactor.
(c) Add the products obtained in step (b).

33. Write a function det_r to compute the determinant of a square matrix with four rows and four columns using this technique. You may want to reference the function developed in problem 32. Assume that the corresponding function prototype is:

```
double det_r(double a[][4]);
```

34. Write a function to find the transpose of a two-dimensional vector. Assume that the corresponding function prototype is:

```
void transpose(const vector<vector<int> > &b, vector
                                  <vector<int> > &bT);
```

35. Write a function to perform matrix multiplication. Assume that the corresponding function prototype is:

```
void matrixMult(const vector<vector<int> > &a,
                const vector<vector<int> > &b,
                vector<vector<int> > &c);
```

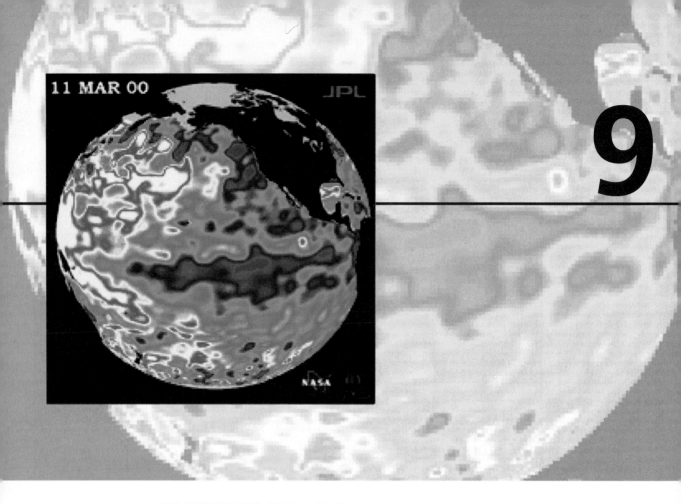

ENGINEERING CHALLENGE:
Weather Patterns

Normal sea-surface temperatures along the equator are warm along the western side of the Pacific Ocean and cold along the eastern side of the Pacific Ocean. In a reoccurring phenomenon, a warm current causes the ocean temperatures on the eastern side of the Pacific (along the western shores of California, Mexico, and South America) to increase as much as 18° F. This phenomenon often occurs near Christmas and thus is often called El Niño. (In Spanish, El Niño means a male child.) A reverse phenomenon also occurs in which the temperatures on the western side of the Pacific Ocean become colder, and this is called La Niña. (In Spanish, La Niña means a female child.) These conditions relate to the Southern Oscillation between warm currents and east-west atmospheric pressure changes. The ENSO (El Niño-Southern Oscillation) index is a metric that is computed from a number of variables, including atmospheric pressure, wind, and ocean temperature. When the ENSO index is positive, the ocean temperatures represent the El Niño condition; when the ENSO index is negative, the ocean temperatures represent the La Niña condition. The larger the index, the larger the variation in temperatures from normal. In this chapter, we develop a program that reads a set of ENSO indices, and determines the periods of El Niño.

AN INTRODUCTION TO POINTERS

CHAPTER OUTLINE

OBJECTIVES

In this chapter, we develop problem solutions containing:

- addresses and pointers
- pointers to arrays
- dynamic memory allocation
- pointers with character strings
- `new` and `delete`

- linked data structures
- classes from the C++ Standard Template Library (STL)
- iterators

9.1 Addresses and Pointers

When a C++ program is executed, memory locations are assigned to the objects used in the program. Each of these memory locations has a positive integer address that uniquely defines the location. When an object is assigned a value, this value is stored in the corresponding memory location. The value of an object can be used by statements in the program, and it can be changed by statements in the program. The specific addresses used for the objects are determined each time that the program is executed, and may vary from one execution to another.

It is sometimes helpful to compare memory allocation with the allocation of a group of post office boxes. If the post office has 100 boxes numbered from 1 to 100, then the box number corresponds to the memory address. Each box is assigned to an individual, using the individual's name; this name corresponds to the identifier assigned to a memory location. The contents of the box corresponds to the value in the memory location; this value can be examined, and it can be changed:

post office box number	individual name	contents
78	John Ruiz	utility bill

memory address	identifier	contents
oxbffff8d8	x	105

This analogy is not completely valid, because two individuals might have the same name, but two identifiers cannot be exactly the same. Also, a mail box might be empty, or it might contain a number of items, whereas a memory location always contains a single value.

Address Operator

address operator

In C++, the address of an object can be referenced using the **address operator &.** This operator was introduced in Chapter 6 in conjunction with pass by reference. Recall that when the address operator is appended to the data type of a formal parameter in a function prototype and function header, the formal parameter receives the address of the corresponding argument when the function is called. To illustrate the use of the address operator to obtain the memory address of a object, consider the following program:

```
/*-------------------------------------------------------------*/
/*  Program chapter9_1                                         */
/*                                                             */
/*  This program demonstrates the relationship                 */
/*  between objects and addresses.                             */

#include <iostream> //Required for cout
using namespace std;
int main()
{
//  Declare and initialize objects.
    int a(1), b(2);

//  Print the contents and addresses of a and b.
    cout << "a= " << a << ";  address of a = " << &a << endl;
    cout << "b= " << b << ";  address of b = " << &b << endl;
    return 0;
}
/*-------------------------------------------------------------*/
```

A sample output from this program is the following:

```
a = 1;  address of a = 0xbffff8d8
b = 2;  address of b = 0xbffff8d4
```

The following memory snapshot shows the contents of the two memory locations at the time the cout statements are executed. This memory snapshot also shows the memory address of each of the variables.

int a [0xbffff8d8] $\boxed{1}$

int b [0xbffff8d4] $\boxed{2}$

We do not usually indicate the memory addresses in these diagrams because the addresses used are system dependent and change with every run of the program.

In the next example, which is a modification to the previous program, there are no initial values given to objects a and b:

```
/*------------------------------------------------------------------*/
/*   Program chapter9_2                                             */
/*                                                                  */
/*   This program demonstrates the relationship                    */
/*   between objects and addresses.                                */

#include <iostream>//Required for cout
using namespace std;
int main()
{
// Declare and initialize objects.
    int a, b;

//  Print the contents and addresses of a and b.
    cout << "a= " << a << ";  address of a = " << &a << endl;
    cout << "b= " << b << ";  address of b = " << &b << endl;
    return 0;
}
/*------------------------------------------------------------------*/
```

A sample output from this program is the following:

```
a = -1073743608;  address of a = 0xbffff8e8
b = 1073784016;  address of b = 0xbffff8e4
```

A memory snapshot at the time the `cout` statements are executed shows a question mark for the contents of the memory locations because the variables have not been initialized. However, memory has been allocated for the variables, thus the memory addresses for each of the variables has been established.

int a [0xbffff8e8] $\boxed{?}$

int b [0xbffff8e4] $\boxed{?}$

While we see that there are values in the variables, even though we have not assigned any in the program, we should not assume anything about these values. This example illustrates the importance of being sure that a program initializes an object before using its value in other statements in a program.

Modify!

1. Run program `chapter9_1` two times on the computer that you are using for class assignments. Did your computer use the same addresses or different addresses? Compare the results with your classmates.

2. Run program `chapter9_2` presented in this section. What values were in the locations assigned to `a` and `b`? Do the values change from one execution of the program to another?

Pointer Assignment

pointer

base type

dereference
indirection

The C++ language allows us to store the address of a memory location in a special type of object called a **pointer.** When a pointer is defined, the type of object to which it will point must also be defined. The type of object to which a pointer will point is referred to as the pointer's **base type.** The base type of a pointer determines how the object being pointed to will be interpreted. Thus, a pointer defined to point to an integer object cannot also be used to point to a floating-point object. The following statement declares two integer objects and a pointer to an integer object. Note that an asterisk is used to indicate that the object is a pointer; this asterisk is also called a **dereference** or **indirection** operator:

```
int a, b, *ptr;
```

This statement specifies that memory addresses should be assigned to three objects—two integer objects and a pointer to an integer object. The statement does not specify the initial values for a, b, and `ptr`. Thus, the memory snapshot after this declaration indicates that the initial contents of all objects are not specified; the diagram uses an arrow, and a question mark, to indicate that `prt` is a pointer, and that what `ptr` points to has not been specified:

```
int   a      ?
int   b      ?
int*  ptr    ?⟶
```

To specify that `ptr` should point to the object a, we could use an assignment statement that stores the address of a in `ptr`:

```
int a, b, *ptr;
ptr = &a;
```

We could have initialized `ptr` in the declaration statement:

```
int a, b, *ptr=&a;
```

In either case, the memory snapshot after the declaration is the following:

```
int*  ptr
          ↓
int   a   ?        int b ?
```

Note that it is not necessary to show the contents of `ptr`, as long as the object to which it points is specified.

Consider this set of statements:

```
//  Declare and initialize objects.
int a(5), b(9), *ptr(&a);
...
//  Assign the value pointed to by ptr to b.
b = *ptr;
```

This last statement is read as "b is assigned the value at the address contained in `ptr`," or "b is assigned the value pointed to by `ptr`." The memory snapshot before the assignment statement is executed is the following:

```
int* ptr
int  a    5        int b 9
```

The memory snapshot after the assignment statement is executed is the following:

```
int* ptr
int  a    5        int b 5
```

Thus, b is assigned the value pointed to by `ptr`. Now consider this set of statements:

```
//  Declare and initialize objects.
int a=5, b=9, *ptr=&a;
...
//  Assign the value of b to the object
//  pointed to by ptr.
*ptr = b;
```

The assignment statement in this set of statements is read "what is pointed to by `ptr` is assigned the value of b." The memory snapshot before the assignment statement is executed is the following:

```
int* ptr
int  a    5        int b 9
```

The memory snapshot after the assignment statement is executed is the following:

```
int* ptr
int  a    9        int b 9
```

Thus, the value pointed to by `ptr` is assigned the value in b.

Declaration of Pointer Types: Pointer types are declared using type declaration statements and the pointer operator (*). Pointer types can be initialized using the address operator (&).

Syntax: Declaration of a pointer

type * identifier[=&identifier];

Example: Declare two pointers to int

int *iPtr, *jPtr;
Example: Declare and initialize a pointer to int

int a=5;
int *aPtr = &a;

We now extend program `chapter9_1` to demonstrate the relationship between objects, addresses, and pointers. Consider the following program:

```
/*-------------------------------------------------------------------*/
/*  Program chapter9_3                                               */
/*                                                                   */
/*  This program demonstrates the relationship                      */
/*  between objects, addresses, and pointers.                       */

#include <iostream> //Required for cout
using namespace std;
int main()
{
//  Declare and initialize objects.
int a(1), b(2), *ptr(&a);

//  Print address and contents of all objects.
    cout << "a = " << a << "; address of a = " << &a << endl;
    cout << "b = " << b << "; address of b = " << &b << endl;
    cout << "ptr = " << ptr << "; address of ptr = " << &ptr << endl;
    cout << "ptr points to the value " << *ptr << endl;
    return 0;
}
/*-------------------------------------------------------------------*/
```

A sample output from this program is the following:

```
a = 1; address of a = 0xbffff8d8
b = 2; address of b = 0xbffff8d4
ptr = 0xbffff8d8; address of ptr = 0xbffff8d0
ptr points to the value 1
```

Note that the values of the pointer to a and the address of a are the same.

Practice!

Give memory snapshots after each of these sets of statements are executed.

```
1. int a(1), b(2), *ptr;
   ptr = &b;

2. int a(1), b(2), *ptr=&b;
   a = *ptr;

3. int a(1), b(2), c(5), *ptr=&c;
   b = *ptr;
   *ptr = a;

4. int a(1), b(2), c(5), *ptr;
   ptr = &c;
   c = b;
   a = *ptr;
```

Pointer Arithmetic

The operations that can be performed with pointers (or addresses) are limited to the following:

- A pointer can be assigned to another pointer of the same type

- An integer value can be added to or subtracted from a pointer

- A pointer can be assigned or compared to the integer zero, or, equivalently, to the symbolic constant NULL, which is defined in <iostream>

In addition, pointers to elements of the same array can be subtracted or compared as a means to accessing elements in the array.

A pointer can point to only one location at a time, but several pointers can point to the same location, as illustrated in this next example. Both ptr_1 and ptr_2 point to the same object after the following statements are executed:

```
// Declare and initialize objects.
int x(-5), y(8), *ptr_1, *ptr_2;
...
// Assign both pointers to x.
ptr_1 = &x;
ptr_2 = ptr_1;
```

The memory snapshot after these statements are executed is

We now present several invalid statements using these objects to illustrate some common errors that can be made when working with pointers:

```
&y = ptr_1;        // invalid statement: attempts
                   // to change the address of y

ptr_1 = y;         // invalid statement: attempts
                   // to change ptr_1 to a
                   // nonaddress value

*ptr_1 = ptr_2;    // invalid statement: attempts
                   // to assign an address to an
                   // integer object

ptr_1 = *ptr_2;    // invalid statement: attempts
                   // to assign a
                   // nonaddress value to ptr_1
```

It is recommended, as an instructive exercise, to attempt to draw memory snapshots of these invalid statements; in each statement we are attempting to store an object value in a pointer, or we are attempting to store a pointer in an object. *To help avoid these errors, use identifier names for pointers that clearly indicate that the identifiers are associated with pointers.*

When simple objects are defined, we should not make any assumptions about the relationships of the memory locations assigned to the objects. For example, if a declaration statement defines two integers, a and b, we should not assume that the values are adjacent in memory; we also should not make assumptions about which value occurs first in memory. The memory assignments of simple objects are system dependent. However, the memory assignment for an array is guaranteed to be a sequential group of memory locations. Thus, if array x contains five integers, then the memory location for x[1] will immediately follow the memory location for x[0], the memory location for x[2] will follow the memory location for x[1], and so on. Therefore, if ptr_x is a pointer to an integer, we can initialize it to point to the integer x[0] with the statement

```
ptr_x = &x[0];
```

The statement

```
ptr_x = x;
```

is equivalent, since the identifier x holds the address of the first element in x. To move the pointer to x[1], we can increment ptr_x by 1, which causes it to point to the value that follows x[0], or we can assign ptr_x the address of x[1]. Thus, any of the following statements would cause ptr_x, which currently points to x[0], to be changed to point to x[1]:

```
++ptr_x;           // increment ptr_x to point to the
                   // next value in memory

ptr_x++;           // increment ptr_x to point to the
                   // next value in memory
```

```
ptr_x = ptr_x + 1;  // increment ptr_x to point to
                    // the next value in memory

ptr_x += 1;         // increment ptr_x to point to
                    // the next value in memory

ptr_x = &x[1];      // ptr_x is assigned the
                    // address of x[1]
```

Similarly, the statement

```
ptr_x += k;
```

refers to the address of the value that is k values past the one pointed to by ptr_x before this statement was executed. These are all examples of adding integers to pointers. Similarly, integers can also be subtracted from pointers. Section 9.2 expands this discussion for one-dimensional arrays.

When an integer value is added to or subtracted from a pointer, it is assumed that the integer refers to the number of values from the one referenced by the pointer before the addition or subtraction is performed. For example, the statement

```
ptr++;
```

indicates that ptr should be modified such that it points to the next value in memory, which is the value that follows the one pointed to by ptr before ptr is incremented. Because different types of values require different amounts of memory, the actual integer value added to ptr depends on the base type of the pointer. A value of type double requires more memory than an integer, and thus the address increment for a pointer to double will be more than an address increment for a pointer to int. For example, if the size of an int on your system is four bytes, and the size of a double is eight bytes, the memory addresses for consecutive integers might be 0xbffff8e4 and 0xbffff8e8, and memory addresses for consecutive values of type double might be 0xbffff8f4 and 0xbffff8fc. In this case, an address increment for a pointer to int will add 4 to the address and an address increment for a pointer to double will add 8. Fortunately, the compiler will determine the correct address increment for us when we add an integer to a pointer or when we subtract an integer from a pointer.

A pointer operation can be included in a statement with other operations, so it is important to be sure that the precedence of the operations is specified correctly. An address operator is a unary operation, and thus it is performed before binary operations; unary operations are also performed from right to left if there are more than one in a statement. These precedence rules are summarized in Table 9.1. Remember that parentheses can always be used to change the precedence of operations.

Errors with pointers can cause problems that are difficult to debug. Even worse, pointer errors can often cause a program to give incorrect results while appearing to work properly. Many pointer errors are caused by pointers that were not initialized before being used. *Therefore, it is a good habit to initialize all pointers at the beginning of the program. If a pointer is not initially assigned to a memory location, assign it a NULL value.* A pointer that is assigned a NULL value does not point to any memory location. You can determine whether the pointer named ptr_1 has been assigned to a memory location at some point in the program in an if statement that contains a condition such as (NULL == ptr_1).

TABLE 9.1 Operator Precedence

Precedence	Operation	Associativity
1	( ) [ ]	innermost first
2	++ -- + - ! (type) & *	right to left (unary)
3	* / %	left to right
4	+ -	left to right
5	< <= > >=	left to right
6	== !=	left to right
7	&&	left to right
8	||	left to right
9	?:	right to left
10	= += -= *= /= %=	right to left
11	,	left to right

Practice!

For each of the problems that follow, give a memory snapshot that includes all objects after the problem statements are executed. Include as much information as possible. Use question marks to indicate memory locations that have not been initialized.

1. ```
   double x(15.6), y(10.2), *ptr_1(&y), *ptr_2(&x);
   *ptr_1 = *ptr_2 + x;
   ```

2. ```
   int w(10), x(2), *ptr_2(&x);
   *ptr_2 -= w;
   ```

3. ```
   int x[5]={2,4,6,8,3};
   int *ptr_1=NULL, *ptr_2=NULL, *ptr_3=NULL;
   ptr_3 = &x[0];
   ptr_1 = ptr_2 = ptr_3 + 2;
   ```

4. ```
   int w[4], *first_ptr(NULL), *last_ptr(NULL);
   first_ptr = w;
   last_ptr =first_ptr + 3;
   ```

9.2 Pointers to Array Elements

Arrays and array handling were covered in detail in Chapters 7 and 8 using offsets to specify individual array elements. Pointers can also be used to specify individual array elements. Array references using pointers and addresses are almost always faster than references using offsets; thus, pointer references for arrays are generally preferred if speed is a concern. As discussed in this section, pointer references to array values are based on the knowledge that memory assignment of array values is always sequential.

One-Dimensional Arrays

Consider the following declaration that defines and initializes a one-dimensional array with floating-point values:

```
double x[6]={1.5, 2.2, 4.3, 7.5, 9.1, 10.5};
```

The memory snapshot after this statement is executed is the following:

```
double x[0]   1.5
double x[1]   2.2
double x[2]   4.3
double x[3]   7.5
double x[4]   9.1
double x[5]  10.5
```

In referencing the array x using standard array notation, reference x[0] refers to the first element in the array, reference x[1] refers to the second element in the array, and reference x[k] refers to the (k+1)th element in the array. Similar references to an array can be generated with pointers. Assume that a pointer ptr has been defined to be a pointer to double and is then initialized with the statement

```
ptr = &x[0];
```

The address of the first element in the array is then stored in the pointer ptr. Thus, reference *ptr refers to x[0], reference *(ptr+1) refers to x[1], and reference *(ptr+k) refers to x[k]. The value of k in reference *(ptr+k) is the offset from the first element in the array.

The following statements compute the sum of the values in the array x using array notation and a for loop:

```
//  Declare and initialize objects.
double x[6], sum(0);
. . .
//  Sum the values in the array x.
for (int k=0; k<5; ++k)
{
    sum += x[k];
}
```

An equivalent set of statements that uses pointers instead of array notation is the following:

```
//  Declare and initialize objects.
double x[6], sum(0), *ptr=&x[0];
. . .
//  Sum the values in the array x.
for (int k=0; k<5; ++k)
{
    sum += *(ptr+k);
}
```

Note that reference *(ptr+k) requires parentheses to perform the operations in the correct order; *k* is added to the address in ptr, and then the indirection operator is used to refer to the value pointed to by ptr+k. Reference *ptr+k would be computed as (*ptr)+k because a unary operator has precedence over a binary operator.

In the discussion on arrays in Chapter 7, we saw that the name of an array is the address of the first element. Thus, an array name can also be used as a pointer to reference elements in the array. For example, the following two statements are equivalent:

```
ptr = &x[0];
ptr = x;
```

Similarly, reference *(ptr+k) is also equivalent to *(x+k). Thus, the statements to sum array x can be simplified to the following:

```
// Declare and initialize objects.
double x[6], sum(0);
...
// Sum the values in the array x.
for (int k=0; k<=5; ++k)
{
    sum += *(x+k);
}
```

This example illustrates the use of an array name as an address. The array name can be used in most statements in place of a pointer, but it cannot be used on the left side of an assignment statement, because its value cannot be changed.

Practice!

Assume that an array g is defined with the following statement:

```
int g[] = {2, 4, 5, 8, 10, 32, 78};
int *ptr1(g), *ptr2(&g[3]);
```

Give a memory snapshot, including the array values. Also indicate the offset values from the initial value in the array. Using this information, give the value of the following references.

1. *g
2. *(g+1)
3. *g+1
4. *(g+5)
5. *ptr1
6. *ptr2
7. *(ptr1 + 1)
8. *(ptr2 + 2)

Character Strings

Recall from Chapter 7 that a character array is an array in which the individual elements are stored as characters. A C-style character string is a character array in which the last array element is a null character. Character strings are used in many engineering applications, including cryptography and pattern recognition. It is often convenient to manipulate character strings via pointers to the strings. Many of the character functions in the header file `cstring`, introduced in Chapter 6, require pointers to strings as arguments, and many return pointers to strings. In this section, we will look at the syntax required to reference C-style character strings using pointers.

One of the functions included in the header file `cstring` is the function named `strstr()`. The function `strstr(ps,pt)` takes a pointer to string s and a pointer to string t as arguments and returns a pointer to the start of the string t within the string s. If t does not occur in s, a `NULL` pointer is returned. We will use this function in our next example.

Assume that we want to count the occurrences of one string in another string. For example, suppose we want to count the number of times that the string *"bb"* occurs in the string *"abbcfgwdbibbw"*. The `strstr()` function will return a pointer to the start of the first occurrence of *"bb"* in *"abbcfgwdbibbw"*, or a `NULL` pointer if *"bb"* is not found. In this example, the `strstr()` function will return a pointer to the beginning of the first occurrence of *"bb"*, as follows:

```
"abbcfgwdbibbw"
  ^
```

To find the next occurrence of the string *"bb"*, we need to search the portion of the string that follows the first position of the occurrence of *"bb"*. The *strstr()* function will then return a pointer to the beginning of the first occurrence of *"bb"* in the new portion of the string as follows:

```
"bcfgwdbibbw"
          ^
```

We repeat the process until the `strstr()` function returns a `NULL` value. The complete program to implement this process follows:

```
/*-------------------------------------------------------------------*/
/* Program chapter9_4                                                */
/*                                                                   */
/*   This program counts and prints the number of                   */
/*   times one string appears within another string.                */
/*
#include <iostream> //Required for cout
#include <cstring> //Required for strstr
using namespace std;

int main()
{
// Declare and initialize objects.
int count(0);
char strg1[] ="abbcfgwdbibbw" , strg2[] = "bb";
char *ptr1(strg1), *ptr2(strg2);
```

```
//  Count  number of occurrences of strg2 in strg1.
//  While function strstr does not return NULL
//  increment count and move ptr1 to next section
//  of strg1.
while ((ptr1=strstr(ptr1,ptr2)) != NULL)
{
  count++;
  ptr1++;
}

//  Print the number of occurrences.
cout << "Count: " << count << endl;

return 0;
}
/*-----------------------------------------------------------------------*/
```

The output from this program is:

```
count: 2
```

Pointers as Function Arguments

When a pointer is passed as an argument to a function, the pointer can be passed by value or passed by reference. If a pointer is passed by value, the pointer can be used to modify the object it points to, but the value of the pointer argument cannot be modified by the function. If a pointer is passed by reference, the pointer can be used to modify the object it points to, and the value of the pointer argument can also be modified.

Consider the following program that calls a function to convert a string to uppercase:

```
/*-----------------------------------------------------------------------*/
/* Program chapter9_5                                                   */
/*                                                                      */
/* This program converts a string to all upper case.                   */
/*                                                                      */
#include <iostream> //Required for cout
#include <cctype> //Required for toupper()
using namespace std;

//Function prototypes
void stringupper(char*);

int main()
{
// Declare and initialize objects.
char strg1[] ="abbcfgwdbibbw";
char *ptr_strg1(strg1);

// Ouput string before and after call to function.
cout << ptr_strg1 << endl;
```

```
stringupper(ptr_strg1);
cout << ptr_strg1 << endl;

return 0;
}
/*-----------------------------------------------------------------*/
/*-----------------------------------------------------------------*/
/*                                                                 */
/*  This function converts each character in                       */
/*  the string pointed to by ptr_strg to upper case.               */
/*                                                                 */
void stringupper(char* ptr_strg)
{
  // While not end of string (while character is not null).
  while(*ptr_strg)
  {
    // Convert character to upper case
    *ptr_strg = toupper(*ptr_strg);

    // Mover pointer to next character
    ptr_strg++;
  }
}
/*-----------------------------------------------------------------*/
```

In this example, the pointer `ptr_str1` is passed to the function `stringupper()`, and the string pointed to by `ptr_str` is converted to uppercase. The formal parameter `ptr_strg` is incremented in the function to traverse the string, but no change is made to the argument in `main` because a pass by value is used. The output from this program is

```
abbcfgwdbibbw
ABBCFGWDBIBBW
```

The next program modifies the function in program 9_5 to use pass by reference instead of pass by value:

```
/*-----------------------------------------------------------------*/
/* Program chapter9_6                                              */
/*                                                                 */
/*  This program converts a string to all upper case.              */
/*                                                                 */
#include <iostream> //Required for cout
#include <cctype> //Required for toupper
using namespace std;

//Function prototypes
void stringupper(char*&);

int main()
{
// Declare and initialize objects.
char strg1[] ="abbcfgwdbibbw";
char *ptr_strg1 = strg1;
```

```
               // Ouput string before and after call to function.
               cout << ptr_strg1 << endl;
               stringupper(ptr_strg1);
               cout << ptr_strg1 << endl;
               return 0;
               }
               /*------------------------------------------------------------------*/
               /*------------------------------------------------------------------*/
               /*                                                                */
               /*   This function converts each character in the string          */
               /*    pointed to by ptr_strg to upper case.                       */
               /*                                                                */
               void stringupper(char* &ptr_strg)
               {
                 // While not end of string.
                 while(*ptr_strg)
                 {
                     // Convert character to upper case
                     *ptr_strg = toupper(*ptr_strg);

                     // Mover pointer to next character
                     ptr_strg++;
                 }
               }
               /*------------------------------------------------------------------*/
```

Notice the order of operators in the function prototype and the function header. When passing a pointer by reference the address operator must follow the dereference operator.

In this version of the program, the string is converted to uppercase just as it was in program `chapter9_6`. However, in this version, incrementing the formal parameter in the function changes the argument in `main` because a pass by reference is used. After the call to the function `stringupper()`, the pointer `ptr_strg1` points to the null character at the end of the string. Thus, the uppercase string will not be printed. A sample output from this program is

`abbcfgwdbibbw`

In both examples, the function `stringupper()` was able to modify the string being pointed to by the formal parameter.

Sometimes it is desirable to pass a pointer as an argument to a function and also ensure that the function will not inadvertently modify the object being pointed to. We can use the `const` modifier in the function prototype, and the function header, to protect the object being pointer to, as illustrated in the next example. The definition for the function `stringupper()` is not included in this example:

```
               /*------------------------------------------------------------------*/
               /* Program chapter9_7                                             */
               /*                                                                */
               /*   This program counts the number of times a specified          */
               /*    letter appears in an upper case string.                     */
               /*                                                                */
```

```cpp
#include <iostream> //Required for cout
#include <cctype> //Required for toupper()
using namespace std;

//Function prototypes.
void stringupper(char*);
int countchar(const char*, char);

int main()
{
// Declare and initialize objects.
char strg1[] ="abbcfgwdbibbw";
char *ptr_strg1 =strg1, ch='B';

// Convert string to upper case.
stringupper(ptr_strg1);

cout << "The letter " << ch << " appears "
     << countchar(ptr_strg1, ch) << " times in the string "
     << ptr_strg1 << endl;

return 0;
}
/*--------------------------------------------------------------------*/
/*--------------------------------------------------------------------*/
/*                                                                    */
/*  This function counts the number of times the character ch         */
/*  appears in the string pointed to by ptr_strg.                     */
/*                                                                    */
int countchar(const char* ptr_strg, char ch)
{
   // Declare and initialize local objects.
   int cnt(0);

   // While not end of string.
   while(*ptr_strg)
   {
   // Look for ch and increment cnt.
     if( *ptr_strg == ch)
        cnt++;

   // Mover pointer to next character
     ptr_strg++;
   }
   return cnt;
}
/*--------------------------------------------------------------------*/
```

This program generates the following output:

```
The letter B appears 5 times in the string ABBCFGWDBIBBW
```

The function `countchar()` cannot modify the object pointed to by `ptr_strg`. For example, if we were to make the nagging error of using the assignment operator instead of the equality operator in the `if` statement, as in

```
if ( *ptr_strg = ch);
```

the compiler would flag it as an error.

The **const** modifier can also be used in a type declaration statement when defining pointers, as in the following statement:

```
const char *cptr = "abbcfgwdbibbw";
```

pointer to a
constant

In the preceding statement, `cptr` is defined to be a **pointer to a constant.** It is important to note that the pointer `cptr` is not constant, but what's pointed to by `cptr` is treated as a constant. Thus, the value of `cptr` can be reassigned, but we cannot use `cptr` to modify an object. The following code segment illustrates this use of the `const` modifier:

```
// Declare and initialize objects.
int x(5), y(10), *ptr1(&x);
const int *cptr(&y);

// Print values.
cout << *ptr1 <<',' << *cptr << endl;
cout << x << ',' << y << endl;

// Increment x.
(*ptr1)++;

// Print values.
cout << *ptr1 <<',' << *cptr << endl;
cout << x << ',' << y << endl;

// Reassign both pointers.
ptr1 = &y;
cptr = &x;

// Increment y.
(*ptr1)++;

// Print values.
cout << *ptr1 <<',' << *cptr << endl;
cout << x << ',' << y << endl;
```

The output generated by this code segment is shown below:

```
5,10
5,10
6,10
6,10
11,6
6,11
```

constant pointer

A **constant pointer** can be declared in a type declaration statement, as in the statement

```
char *const cptr = "A standard message.";
```

Using this syntax, the value of `cptr` cannot be reassigned, but the object pointed to by `cptr` can be modified.

Practice!

Assume that objects have been defined with the following statements:

```
int i(5), j(10);
int *iptr(&i);
const int *cptr(&j);
int *const jptr(&j);
```

Determine whether the following statements are valid or invalid.

1. `cptr = jptr;`

2. `jptr = cptr;`

3. `*cptr = *jptr;`

4. `*cptr = *iptr;`

5. `*jptr = *cptr;`

6. `iptr = cptr;`

9.3 Problem Solving Applied: El Niño-Southern Oscillation Data

In the chapter opening discussion, we discussed sea surface temperatures. In particular, normal sea-surface temperatures along the equator are warm along the western side of the Pacific Ocean and cold along the eastern side of the Pacific Ocean. In a reoccurring phenomenon, a warm current causes the ocean temperatures on the eastern side of the Pacific (along the western shores of California, Mexico, and South America) to increase as much as 18° F. This phenomenon often occurs near Christmas and thus is often called El Niño. (In Spanish, El Niño means a male child.) A reverse phenomenon also occurs in which the temperatures on the western side of the Pacific Ocean become colder, and this is called La Niña. (In Spanish, La Niña means a female child.) These conditions relate to the Southern Oscillation between warm currents and east-west atmospheric pressure changes. The ENSO (El Niño-Southern Oscillation) index is a metric that is computed from a number of variables, including atmospheric pressure, wind, and ocean temperature. When the ENSO index is positive, the ocean temperatures represent the El Niño condition; when the ENSO index is negative, the ocean temperatures represent the La Niña condition. The larger the index, the larger the variation in temperatures from normal. Write a program that reads a data file that contains the year, quarter, and ENSO index for a period of time. The program should determine and print the year and quarter with the strongest El Niño conditions.

1. PROBLEM STATEMENT

Determine the year and quarter with the strongest El Niño conditions.

2. INPUT/OUTPUT DESCRIPTION

The I/O diagram shows the data file as the input and the year and quarter as output.

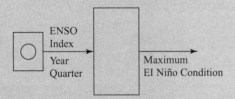

3. HAND EXAMPLE

Assume that the data file contained the following data:

Year	Quarter	ENSO Index
1990	1	0.6
1991	1	0.2
1992	1	1.1
1993	1	0.5
1994	1	0.1
1995	1	1.2
1996	1	−0.3
1997	1	−0.1
1998	1	2.2
1999	1	−0.7
2000	1	−1.1

The corresponding output would then be the following report:

```
Maximum El Nino Conditions in Data file
Year: 1998, Quarter: 1
```

4. ALGORITHM DEVELOPMENT

We first develop the decomposition outline because it divides the solution into a set of sequential steps.

Decomposition Outline

1. Read the ENOS data into arrays and determine the maximum positive index.

2. Print the year and quarter that go with the maximum intensity.

The refinement in pseudocode follows.

Refinement in Pseudocode

```
main: if file cannot be opened
          print error message

     else
             read data and determine maximum intensity
             print the year and quarter that go with maximum intensity
```

The steps in the pseudocode are now detailed enough to convert to C++.

```
/*--------------------------------------------------------------------*/
/* Program chapter 9_2                                                */
/*                                                                    */
/* This program reads a data file of ENSO index values and           */
/* determines the maximum El Nino condition in the file.             */

#include<iostream> //Required for cout
#include<fstream> //Required for ifstream

const int MAX_SIZE = 1000;

using namespace std;

int main()
{
  //Declare variables
  int k=0, year[MAX_SIZE],qtr[MAX_SIZE], maxK=0;
  double index[MAX_SIZE];
  ifstream fin("ENSO1.txt");
  if(fin.fail())
  {
    cerr <<"Could not open file ENSO1.txt" <<endl;
    exit(1);
  }
  fin >> *year, *qtr, *index;
  while(fin)
  {
    if(*(index+k) > *(index+maxK))
    {
      maxK = k;
    }
    k++;

    fin >> *(year+k) >> *(qtr+k) >> *(index+k);
}//end while

  /* Print data for maximum El Nino condition.                       */
  cout << "Maximum El Nino conditions in Data File \n";
```

```
        cout << "Year:" << *(year+maxK) <<" Quarter:"
             << *(qtr+maxK) << endl;
        return 0;
   }


   /*- - - - - - - - - - - - - - - - - - - - - - - - - - - - - - - - - - - - - - - - - - - - - - - - - -*/
```

5. TESTING

The output from the program using the data from the hand example follows:

```
Maximum El Nino conditions in Data File
Year: 1998 Quarter: 1
```

Modify!

1. Modify the program to find and print the maximum La Niña Conditions.

2. Modify the program to find the conditions closest to zero. These would be the closest to normal conditions.

3. Modify the program so that it prints all years and quarters with El Niño conditions.

4. Modify the program so that it counts the number of years with El Niño conditions and the number with La Niña conditions. Print both values.

5. Modify the program so that it computes and prints the average intensity for the years with El Niño conditions.

9.4 Dynamic Memory Allocation

Dynamic memory allocation allows a program to allocate memory for objects during execution of the program rather than determining memory requirements at the time the program is compiled. This is important when a program uses an array thats size cannot be determined until the program is executing; without dynamic memory allocation, the program would have to specify the maximum size anticipated for the array. For systems with limited memory, it is possible that there would not be enough memory to run a program if all arrays had to be specified to the maximum size anticipated. Dynamic memory is allocated from a region of available memory referred to as the program's **heap.** Dynamic memory is allocated on the heap using the `new` operator and returned to the heap using the `delete` operator.

heap

The `new` Operator

Dynamic memory allocation is specified using the keyword `new`, followed by a type specifier to indicate the data type of the object to be allocated. The `new` operator returns the address of the new object in memory. To allocate memory for a single object of type int we could use either of the following sets of statements:

```
//   Example 1
//   Dynamically allocate memory for one integer object.
//   No initial value is given to the object.
int *ptr;
ptr = new int;
```

```
//   Example 2
//   Dynamically allocate memory for one integer object.
//   Give an initial value of -1 to the object.
int *ptr;
ptr = new int(-1);
```

In both of the preceding examples, the new operator returns a value that is assigned to a pointer. If memory is available on the heap, the pointer will contain the address of the allocated memory. In the first example, no initial value is assigned to the newly allocated memory, as illustrated in Figure 9.1. In the second example, a value of −1 is specified as an initial value and is assigned to the newly allocated memory, as illustrated in Figure 9.2.

Since the heap is finite there is always a possibility that a request for new memory cannot be honored. If there is insufficient memory on the heap for a memory request, in general, the new operator will **throw an exception** called bad_alloc. This exception will terminate execution of the program. There is a mechanism supported by C++ that allows a program to detect an exception and recover from the potential error. This mechanism is referred to as **exception handling.** Exception handling is not covered in this text.

throw an
exception

exception handling

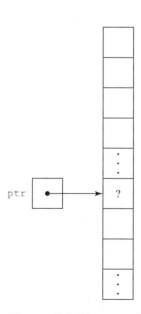

Figure 9.1 Diagram of heap. Example 1.

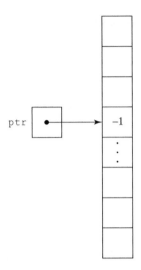

Figure 9.2 Diagram of heap. Example 2.

Dynamically Allocated Arrays

Dynamic memory allocation is very useful in solving engineering problems that require large arrays. Assume that we want to dynamically allocate a block of memory to store a `double` array containing `npts` elements. (In this example, we assign a small value to `npts` for illustration, but more commonly it would be a large value, computed by other statements in the program or read from the keyboard or a data file.) The following set of statements specify the desired allocation:

```
//  Declare objects.
int npts = 10;
double *dptr;
...
//  Dynamically allocate memory.
dptr = new double[npts];
```

As illustrated in Figure 9.3, a contiguous block of memory is allocated on the heap to hold 10 objects of type `double`. The pointer `dptr` is assigned the memory address of the first element in the array. References to the array can be made using pointer notation, such as `*(dptr+2)`. References to the array can also be made using standard array notation, such as `dptr[2]`.

When using `new` to dynamically allocate objects, the data type specified for the object can be any built in data type or any programmer-defined class type.

The `delete` Operator

de-allocated

When a program is finished using memory that has been dynamically allocated using `new`, the memory can be returned to the heap, or **de-allocated,** using the operator `delete`. The following program illustrates the use of the operators `new` and `delete`:

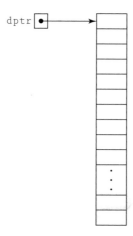

Figure 9.3 Block of memory allocated on the heap.

```
/*--------------------------------------------------------------------*/
/*   Program chapter9_9                                               */
/*   This program illustrates the use of operators new and delete.   */

#include<iostream>  //Required for cout
using namespace std;

int main()
{
// Declare objects.
int *ptr, npts(10);
double *darr_ptr;

// Dynamically allocate one integer object.
ptr = new int(-1);

// Dynamically allocate array of type double.
darr_ptr = new double[npts];

// Assign what is pointed to by ptr to all elements of dynamic array.
for(int i=0; i<npts; ++i)
{
    darr_ptr[i] = *ptr;
}

// Print all values in dynamic array.
for(int i=0; i<=npts-1; ++i)
{
    cout << darr_ptr[i] << ' ';
}
cout << endl;
```

```
//   Return memory to free-store.
delete ptr;
delete [] darr_ptr;
return 0;
}
/*-----------------------------------------------------------------------*/
```

The output from this program is as follows:

```
-1 -1 -1 -1 -1 -1 -1 -1 -1 -1
```

When deallocating an array, the empty square brackets are required with the `delete` operator. If we omit the brackets, our program may not continue to execute correctly.

9.5 | Problem Solving Applied: Seismic Event Detection

Special sensors called seismometers are used to collect earth motion information. These seismometers can be used in a passive environment, in which they record the earth's motion, which includes earthquakes and tidal motion. By analyzing ground motion from an earthquake using data from several seismometers, it is possible to determine the epicenter of the earthquake and the intensity of the earthquake. The earthquake intensity is usually measured using the Richter scale, which is a scale from 1 to 10 named after U.S. seismologist C. F. Richter.

Write a program that reads a set of seismometer data from a data file named *seismic.dat*. The first line of the file contains two values: the number of seismometer data readings that follow in the file and the time interval in seconds that occurred between consecutive measurements. Array memory is dynamically allocated based on the number of seismometer data readings in the seismic data file. The time interval is a floating-point value, and we assume that all the measurements were taken with the same time interval between them. After reading and storing the data measurements, the program should identify possible earthquakes, which are also called seismic events, using a power ratio. At a specific point in time, this ratio is the quotient of a short-time power measurement divided by a longtime power measurement. If the ratio is greater than a given threshold, an event may have occurred at that point in time. Given a specific point in the data measurements, the short-time power is the average power, or average squared value, of the measurements using the specified point plus a small number of points that occurred just previous to the specified point. The longtime power is the average power of the measurements using the specified point plus a larger number of points that occurred just previous to the specified point. (The set of points used in a calculation is sometimes referred to as a data window.) The threshold is generally greater than 1 to avoid detecting events in constant data because the short-time power is equal to the longtime power if the data values are all the same value. Assume that the numbers of measurements for the short-time power and for the longtime power are read from the keyboard. Set the threshold value to 1.5.

1. PROBLEM STATEMENT

Determine the locations of possible seismic events using a set of seismometer measurements from a data file.

2. INPUT/OUTPUT DESCRIPTION

The inputs to this program are a data file named *seismic.dat* and the number of measurements to use for short-time power and longtime power. The output is a report giving the times of potential seismic events.

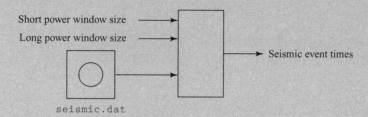

3. HAND EXAMPLE

Suppose that a data file contains the following data, which includes number of points to follow (11) and time interval between points (0.01), followed by the 11 values that correspond to a sequence of values $x_0, x_1, \ldots x_1 0$:

```
11 0.01
1    2    1    1    1    5    4    2    1    1    1
```

If the short-time power measurement is made using two samples and the longtime power measurement is made using five measurements, then we can compute power ratios, beginning with the rightmost point, in a window:

```
1 2 1 1 1 5 4 2 1 1 1
       └─┘
short window
└─────────┘
long window

Point x4:    Short-time power = (1 + 1)/2 = 1

Long-time power= (1 + 1 + 1 + 4 + 1 )/5 = 1.6
Ratio = 1/1.6 = 0.63

1 2 1 1 1 5 4 2 1 1 1
     └─┘
short window
  └─────────┘
long window
```

Point x5:   Short-time power = (25 + 1)/2 = 13

Long-time power = (25 + 1 + 1 + 1 + 4)/5 = 6.4

Ratio = 13/6.4 = 2.03

1 2 1 1 1 5 4 2 1 1 1

short window

long window

Point x6:   Short-time power = (16 + 25)/2 = 20.5

Long-time power = (16 + 25 + 1 + 1 + 1)/5 = 8.8

Ratio = 20.5/8.8 = 2.33

1 2 1 1 1 5 4 2 1 1 1

short window

long window

Point x7:   Short-time power = (4 + 16)/2 = 10

Long-time power = (4 + 16 + 25 + 1 + 1)/5 = 9.4

Ratio = 10/9.4 = 1.06

1 2 1 1 1 5 4 2 1 1 1
short window

long window

Point x8:   Short-time power = (1 + 4)/2 = 2.5

Long-time power = (1 + 4 + 16 + 25 + 1)/5 = 9.4

Ratio = 2.5/9.4 = 0.27

1 2 1 1 1 5 4 2 1 1 1

short window

long window

```
Point x9:     Short-time power = (1 + 1)/2 = 1

Long-time power = (1 + 1 + 4 + 16 + 25 )/5 = 9.4

Ratio = 1/9.4 = 0.11

1 2 1 1 1 5 4 2 1 1 1
                  └─┘
short window

long window  └─────────┘

Point x10:    Short-time power = (1 + 1)/2 = 1

Long-time power = (1 + 1 + 1 + 4 + 16 )/5 = 4.6

Ratio = 1/4.6 = 0.22
```

By using the previous ratios computed, possible seismic events occurred at points x5 and x6. Because the time interval between points is 0.01 second, the times that correspond to the seismic events are 0.05 and 0.06 second. (We assume that the first point in the file occurred at 0.0 second.)

4. ALGORITHM DEVELOPMENT

We first develop the decomposition outline because it divides the solution into a series of sequential steps.

Decomposition Outline

1. Read data header and allocate memory.

2. Read seismic data from the data file and read numbers of measurement for power from the keyboard.

3. Compute power ratios and print possible seismic event times.

Step 3 involves computing power ratios and comparing them to the threshold to determine whether a possible event occurred. Because we need to compute two power measurements for each possible event location, we implement the power measurement as a function. The refinement in pseudocode for the main function and the power function can now be developed:

Refinement in Pseudocode

```
main:  set threshold to 1.5
       read npts and time-interval
       allocate memory for sensor array
```

```
                    read the values into sensor array
                    read short-window, long-window from keyboard
                    set k to long-window - 1
                    while k<= npts-1
                        set short-power to power(sensor,short-window,k)
                        set long-power to power(sensor,long-window,k)
                        set ratio to short-power/long-power
                        if ratio > threshold
                            print k*time-interval
                        increment k by 1
power(x,length,n):
        set xsquare to zero
        set k to 0
        while k<=n-1
            add x[length-k]*x[length-k] to xsquare
        return xsquare/length
```

We are now ready to convert the pseudocode to C++:

```
/*-------------------------------------------------------------*/
/*  Program chapter9_10                                        */
/*                                                             */
/*  This program reads a seismic data file and then           */
/*  determines the times of possible seismic events.          */
/*  Dynamic memory allocation is used.                        */

#include <fstream>//Required for ifstream
#include <string>//Required for string
#include <cmath>//Required for pow()
using namespace std;

//  Set threshold.
const double THRESHOLD = 1.5;

//  Function prototypes.
double power_w(double arr[], int length, int n);
int main()
{
   //  Declare objects.
   int k, npts, short_window, long_window;
   double time_incr, *sensor, short_power, long_power,
          ratio;
   string filename;
   ifstream fin;

   //  Prompt user for file name and open file for input.
   cout << "Enter name of input file\n";
   cin >> filename;
   fin.open(filename.c_str());
```

```cpp
      if(fin.fail())
      {
         cerr << "error opening input file" << endl;
      }
      else
      {
   //  Read data header and allocate memory.
         fin >> npts >> time_incr;
         sensor = new double[npts];

   //  Program continues if no exception is thrown.
         cout << "Memory allocated." << endl;

   //  Read data into an array.
         for (k=0; k<npts; ++k)
            fin >> sensor[k];
   //  Read window sizes from the keyboard.
         cout << "Enter number of points for short-window: \n";
         cin >> short_window;
         cout << "Enter number of points for long-window: \n";
         cin >> long_window;

   //  Compute power ratios and search for events.
         for (k=long_window-1; k<npts; ++k)
         {
            short_power = power_w(sensor, k, short_window);
            long_power = power_w(sensor, k, long_window);
            ratio = short_power/long_power;
            if (ratio > THRESHOLD)
               cout << "Possible event at " << time_incr*k
                                           << " seconds \n";
         }
   //  Return memory to free-store, close file, and exit program.
         delete [] sensor;
         fin.close();
      }
   return 0;
}
/*------------------------------------------------------------*/
/*------------------------------------------------------------*/
/*  This function computes the average power in a    */
/*  specified window of a double array.              */
double power_w(double arr[], int length,  int n)
{
   //  Declare and initialize objects.
   double xsquare(0);

   //  Compute sum of values squared in the array x.
   for (int k=0; k<n; ++k)
```

```
      {
          xsquare += pow(arr[length-k],2);
      }

      /*  Return the average squared value.  */
      return xsquare/n;
}
/*-------------------------------------------------------------*/
```

5. TESTING

The output from the program using the data file from the hand example is as follows:

```
Memory allocated.
Enter number of points for short-window:
2
Enter number of points for long-window:
5
Possible event at 0.05 seconds
Possible event at 0.06 seconds
```

Modify!

Modify the event-detection program to include the following new capabilities:

1. Allow the user to enter the threshold value. Check the value to be sure that it is a positive value greater than 1.

2. Print the number of events detected by the program. (Assume that events with contiguous times are all part of the same event. Thus, for the hand example, one event was detected.)

3. Use the `vector` class instead of an array, eliminating the need for `new` and `delete`.

9.6 Common Errors Using `new` and `delete`

Dynamically allocated memory should always be returned to the heap once it is no longer needed so that the memory becomes available for use with another dynamic allocation. This requires being careful to keep track of all pointers to the memory space. After the `delete` operator is used with a pointer to return memory to the heap, the pointer will point to an invalid memory space or, depending on the compiler, it may retain the memory address of the deleted memory. In either case, the pointer should not be referenced again until it has been assigned a new, valid address.

It is easy to make errors when working with pointers and dynamic memory allocation and difficult to find these errors. The following are some of the more common errors:

memory leak

- Referencing a pointer to dynamically allocated memory after the delete operator has been used to return the memory to the heap.

- Failing to return memory to the heap when it is no longer being used. This is often referred to as a **memory leak.**

- Using the delete operator with a pointer that does not reference memory that has been dynamically allocated using the new operator.

- Omitting the square brackets when using delete to free a dynamically allocated array.

To avoid many of the errors associated with dynamic memory allocation of arrays, we recommend using the vector class.

Practice!

Assume that the pointers iptr, jptr, and arr_ptr have been defined with the following statements:

```
int *iptr, *jptr, *arr_ptr;
iptr = new int(10);
arr_ptr = new int[5];
```

Draw a memory allocation diagram, and show the output line (or lines) generated by each of the following set of statements. We recommend that you program each example and run it to determine the output generated on your system.

```
1. jptr = iptr;
   cout << *iptr << ' ' << *jptr << endl;
   cout <<  iptr << ' ' <<  jptr << endl;
   delete iptr;
   cout << iptr  << ' ' <<  jptr << endl;

2. cout << arr_ptr << endl;
   for(int i=0; i<4; ++i)
      arr_ptr[i] = i;
   for(int i=0; i<4; ++i)
      cout << *(arr_ptr)++ << ' ';
   cout << endl << arr_ptr << endl;
   for(int i=0; i<4; ++i)
      cout << arr_ptr[i] << ' ';
```

```
3. for(int i=0; i<4; ++i)
      arr_ptr[i] = i;
   jptr = &arr_ptr[2];
   cout << arr_ptr << ' ' << jptr << endl;
   cout << *arr_ptr << ' ' << *jptr << endl;
   delete [] arr_ptr;
   cout << arr_ptr << ' ' << jptr << ' ' << *jptr << endl;
```

9.7 Linked Data Structures

When we work with data structures such as arrays and vectors, we are working with a contiguous block of memory. It is easy to access individual elements of an array or a `vector` because each access is a fixed offset from the starting address. However, it is not easy to insert or remove an element unless the element is the last element. To insert or remove an element at any location other than the last requires copying all elements below the inserted or removed element into a new memory location. This is very inefficient, especially when working with very large amounts of data.

Linked data structures, such as **linked lists, stacks** and **queues,** are designed for efficient inserts and removals. Memory is allocated and deleted as needed during execution of the program, and pointers are used to link the elements, since the elements do not form a contiguous block of memory. Using pointers to link the elements allows for efficient inserting and removing of elements; links need to be reassigned, but no coping of elements is required. However, accessing elements in a linked structure is less efficient than array access because we must **traverse** the structure for each access. To traverse a linked data structure, we must begin at the first element in the structure and follow the links to successive elements until we reach the element to be accessed.

traverse

Linked Lists

linked list

A **linked list** is a data structure organized as a group of elements that are linked by pointers. An individual element consists of data and a pointer to the next element. We generally assume that there is some order to the data stored in the elements, such as an ascending order, and that we may want to insert new elements or remove elements from this ordered list.

Figure 9.4 illustrates a linked list with four elements, containing the ordered information 10, 14, 21, 35. A separate pointer, which we have labeled *head,* points to the first element in the linked list.

To access data in a linked list, we use the *head* pointer to reference the information in the first element (the element containing the value 10 in this example). Then, since the first element contains a pointer to the next element (the element containing the value 14), we can use this information to move to the second element. Similarly, we use the pointer in the second element to move to the third element. The last element in a linked list will contain a pointer value of NULL to indicate that we have reached the last element in the list. We use the symbol Ω to indicate a value of NULL in our diagrams.

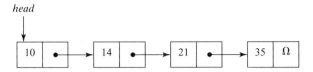

Figure 9.4 Linked list.

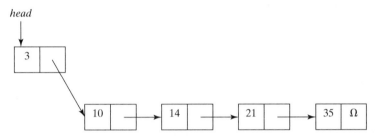

Figure 9.5 Insert before the first element (requires updating the head pointer).

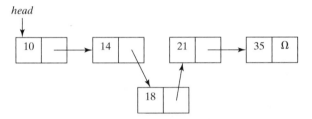

Figure 9.6 Insert between two elements.

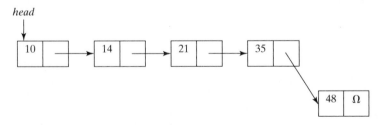

Figure 9.7 Insert after last element.

To insert a value into a linked list, we must traverse the list to find the location for the insert. We begin at the *head* of the list and move from one element to another using the pointer in the current element, until we find the desired location for the insert. The insertion location can be one of four places: before the first element, between two elements, after the last element, or in an empty list. Figures 9.5 through 9.8 outline each of these cases assuming that we started with the linked list given in Figure 9.4 for each of the first three cases.

To delete a value from a linked list, we must traverse the list to find the element to be deleted. We begin at the head of the list and move from one element to another using the pointer in the current element. If the element to be deleted is found, it can be the first element,

Figure 9.8 Insert in an empty list (requires updating the head pointer).

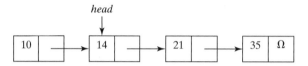

Figure 9.9 Delete first element (requires updating the head pointer).

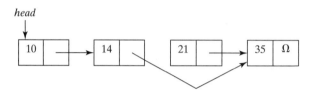

Figure 9.10 Delete an element between two elements.

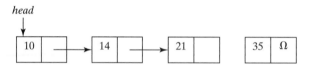

Figure 9.11 Delete the last element.

an element between two other elements, or the last element. Figures 9.9 through 9.11 outline each of these three cases. For each case we start with the linked list given in Figure 9.4.

Stacks

A stack is known as a last-in-first-out (LIFO) data structure. You can insert (push) and remove (pop) elements only from the top of the stack. Thus, the element removed from a stack is always the last element that was added. Stacks are essential in the design of compilers and in unraveling the flow of function calls within a program. For example, each time a function is called, a return address is added to the stack. Each return statement references the last address added to the stack. Figure 9.12 illustrates the behavior of a stack.

Queue

A queue is known as a first-in-first-out (FIFO) data structure. You can add (push) elements only to the back of a queue and remove (pop) elements only from the front of the queue. Thus, the element removed from a queue is always the first element that was added to the queue. Queues are useful data structures in computer engineering and computer science application. For example, operating systems use queues to process job requests. Job requests, such as a request for a printer, wait in a queue to be processed. The job request at the front of the queue is the first to be processed. Figure 9.13 illustrates the behavior of a queue.

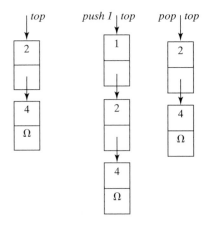

Figure 9.12 Behavior of a stack.

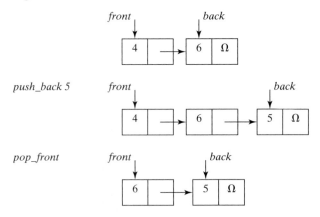

Figure 9.13 Behavior of a queue.

Practice!

1. Write the implementation of a `stack` class, as given in the following class declaration:

```
class stack
{
int* a;
int sizeOfStack;
public:
stack();
void push(int);          //add value to top of stack
int pop();               //remove top element
int top();               //return value of top element
                         //element is not removed

int isempty();

};
```

> 2. Modify your `stack class` to be a stack of type `double`.
>
> 3. Modify your `stack class` to be a stack of type `point`.

9.8 The C++ Standard Template Library

Writing programmer-defined functions to insert and remove elements from a linked data structure requires careful memory management and reassignment of pointers, as illustrated in the development of a programmer-defined type to implement the concept of a binary tree, provided in Chapter 10. However, as an alternative to implementing your own library of data structures, you may choose to use the container classes defined in the C++ STL. A container class is a class, such as the `vector class`, that is designed to hold objects. The SGI website (http://www.sgi.com/tech/stl/) is a good source for complete and current documentation. Our first example will illustrate the use of the `list class`.

The `list` class

The compiler directive `#include<list>` must be included to use the `list class`. When defining a new list, the data type of the objects in the `list` must be specified. The following type declaration statement defines an empty list of integers, named `alist`:

```
list<int> alist;
```

To systematically insert and remove elements from a `list`, we must be able to traverse the list. The `list class` provides a special type of pointer, called an `iterator`, to support accessing successive elements in a list. An `iterator` is basically a pointer to an element in a list. We can define an `iterator` named `iter` to access elements in our `list` of integers with the following statement:

```
list<int>::iterator iter;
```

The `list class` includes numerous member functions to support a `list` structure, including functions to insert and remove elements from a list. Table 9.2 lists several of the commonly used member functions of the `list class`.

TABLE 9.2   Member Functions of the `list class`

begin( )	returns an iterator that points to first element in the list.
end( )	returns an iterator that points to *one past the last element in the list.*
empty( )	returns true if the list is empty, false otherwise.
insert(iterator, value)	insert value at location specified by the iterator.
remove(value)	remove all instances of value from the list.
sort( )	arranges elements in ascending order.

The following program illustrates the use of several of these functions:

```
/*------------------------------------------------------------------*/
/* Program chapter9_10                                              */
/*                                                                  */
/* This programs creates a list of data entered from
   standard input.                                                 */
/* The list is sorted and printed to standard output.             */

#include<iostream>//Required for cout, cin
#include<list>//Required for list, begin(), end(), insert(), sort()
using namespace std;

int main()
{

  // Declare objects.
  list<int> alist;
  list<int>::iterator iter;
  int ivalue;

  // Set iter to beginning of alist.
  iter = alist.begin();

  cout << "enter integer values, 's' to stop\n";

  // While valid data, read value and insert into list.
  while(cin >> ivalue)
  {
    alist.insert(iter, ivalue);
    ++iter;
  }

  // Sort the list in ascending order.
  alist.sort();

  // Print the list to standard output.
  cout << "Sorted list: \n";
  for(iter=alist.begin(); iter!=alist.end(); ++iter)
  {
    cout << *iter << endl;
  }
  return 0;
}
```

If the data

```
35 18 21 14 10 2 s
```

were entered from the keyboard, the program would generate the following output:

```
Enter integer values, 's' to stop
Sorted List:
2
10
14
18
21
35
```

The statement

```
++iter;
```

does not do standard pointer arithmetic, but rather reassigns `iter` to point to the next element in the `list`.

The `stack class`

The C++ STL includes the `stack class`, which provides an object-based implementation of a stack. The compiler directive #include<stack> must be included to use the `stack class`.

When a `stack` is defined, the data type of the objects in the `stack` must be specified. The following type declaration statement defines an empty `stack` of integers named `astack`:

```
stack<int> astack;
```

TABLE 9.3 Member Functions of the `stack class`

empty( )	returns true if the stack is empty and false otherwise.
pop( )	removes top element from the stack. Does not return a value.
push(value)	adds *value* to top of stack.
size( )	returns the number of elements in the stack.
top( )	returns the value of the first element in the stack. The element is not removed from the stack.

Table 9.3 lists member functions of the `stack class`. The following program illustrates the use of several of these functions:

```
/*-------------------------------------------------------------------*/
/* Program chapter9_11                                               */
/*                                                                   */
/* This programs creates a stack of data entered from               */
/*    standard input.                                                */
/* The stack is printed to standard output.                         */
```

```
#include<iostream>//Required for cout, cin
#include<stack>//Required for stack, push(), top(), empty()
using namespace std;
int main()
{

   // Declare objects.
   stack<int> astack;
   int ivalue;

   cout << "enter integer values, 's' to stop\n";

   // While valid data, read value and add to stack.
   while(cin >> ivalue)
   {
      astack.push(ivalue);
   }

   // Print values to standard output.
   cout << "Elements from the stack: \n";
   while(!astack.empty())
   {
   // Access the top element.
      cout << astack.top() << endl;

   // Remove top element from the stack.
      astack.pop();
   }
   return 0;
}
```

If the data

```
35 18 21 14 s
```

were entered from the keyboard, the program would generate the following output:

```
Enter integer values, 's' to stop
Elements from the stack:
14
21
18
35
```

Notice that the order of the elements has been reversed.

The queue class

The C++ STL includes the queue class, which provides an object-based implementation of a queue. The compiler directive #include<queue> must be included to use the queue class. When a queue is defined, the data type of the elements in the queue must be specified. The following statement defines an empty queue of integers, named aqueue:

```
queue<int> aqueue;
```

TABLE 9.4 Member Functions of the queue class

empty( )	returns true if the queue is empty and false otherwise.
pop( )	removes front element from the queue. Does not return a value.
push(value)	adds value to front of queue.
size( )	returns the number of elements in the queue.
top( )	returns the value of the element at the front of the queue. The element is not removed from the queue.

Table 9.4 lists some of the member functions of the queue class. The following program illustrates the use of several of these functions:

```
/*-------------------------------------------------------------------*/
/* Program chapter9_12                                               */
/*                                                                   */
/* This programs creates a queue of data entered from
   standard input.                                                   */
/* The queue is printed to standard output.                          */
#include<iostream>//Required for cout, cin
#include<queue>//Required for queue, push(), empty(), top()
using namespace std;
int main()
{

  // Declare objects.
  queue<int> aqueue;
  int ivalue;

  cout << "enter integer values, 's' to stop\n";

  // While valid data, read value and add to back of queue.
  while(cin >> ivalue)
  {
     aqueue.push(ivalue);
  }

  // Print values to standard output.
  cout << "Elements in the queue: \n";
```

```
while(!aqueue.empty())
{
// Access element at the front of the queue.
   cout << aqueue.top() << endl;

// Remove element from the front of the queue.
   aqueue.pop();
}
return 0;
}
```

If the data

```
35 18 21 14 s
```

were entered from the keyboard, the program would generate the following output:

```
Enter integer values, 's' to stop
Elements in the queue:
35
18
21
14
```

9.9   Problem Solving Applied: Concordance of a Text File

A concordance of a text file is an alphabetical list of the unique words in the text file. Here is a concordance of the preceding sentence:

```
a
an
alphabetical
concordance
file
in
is
list
of
text
the
unique
words
```

Write a program that prompts the user for the name of an input text file, and output file. Build a concordance of the file and print the concordance to an output file.

1. PROBLEM STATEMENT

Build a concordance of a text file. Write the concordance, along with a count of the unique words in the text file, to an output file.

2. INPUT/OUTPUT DESCRIPTION

The following diagram shows that the input to the program is a text file, and that the output is a concordance of the text file along with the count of unique words. We will use the `list` class to define a list, where each element in the list is of type `string`.

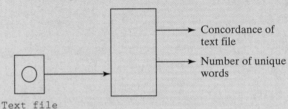

Text file

Concordance of text file

Number of unique words

3. HAND EXAMPLE

Suppose our text file contained only the following text:

```
A concordance of a text file is an alphabetical list of
the unique words in the text file.
```

Our program would generate the following output file:

```
There are 13 distinct words in the text file:
a
an
alphabetical
concordance
file
in
is
list
of
text
the
unique
words
```

4. ALGORITHM DEVELOPMENT

We first develop the decomposition outline to break the solution into a series of sequential steps:

Decomposition Outline

1. Open input and output files.

2. Read a word from the input file.

3. Insert word if the word is not already in the list.

4. Alphabetize list of unique words.

5. Write the size and contents of the list to output file.

Step 2 in the decomposition outline involves a loop that reads the text file one character at a time until a nonalpha character is reached. A nonalpha character will signal the end of a word. Other than their use as delimiters between words, all nonalpha characters will be ignored. All alpha characters will be converted to lowercase. We will use a function to perform this task. Step 3 requires that we insert a word if it is not already in the list. We will use a function that utilizes member functions of the *list* class. Step 4 involves sorting the list in ascending order. We will use the generic *sort()* function. Since the list may be long, step 5 will print the list three words per line. We will use a function to perform this task. The refinement in pseudocode is the following:

Refinement in Pseudocode

```
main:  open input file
          get_word(istream,string)
          while(string size in not 0)
            insert_word(list,string)
            get_word(string)
          sort(list)
          print size of list
          display_list(ostream,list)
get_word(istream,string):
        clear string
        read a character
        while(not end of file and character is not alpha)
            read next character
        while(not end of file and character is an alpha)
            append lower case character to string
            input next character
insert_word(list, string)
        if(string is not in list)
            insert string
display_list(ostream,list)
        set counter to 0
        while(not end of list)
          print list element
          increment counter
          if(counter mod 3 is zero)
            print newline
```

The steps in the pseudocode are now detailed enough to convert into C++ code:

```
/*-------------------------------------------------------------------*/
/* Program chapter9_13                                               */
/* This program builds a concordance of a text file.                */
/*                                                                  */
#include <fstream>//Required for ifstream, ofstream
```

```
#include <string>//Required for string
#include <cctype>//Required for isalpha(), tolower()
#include <iomanip>//Required for setw()
#include <list>//Required for list, sort(), begin(), end()
#include <algorithm>//Required for find()
using namespace std;

// Function prototypes.
void get_word(istream& in_stream, string& w);
void insert_word(string word, list<string> &wordlist);
void display_list(ostream& out_stream, list <string> wordlist);

int main()
{
// Declare objects.
ifstream in_stream;
ofstream out_stream;

string infile, outfile;//filenames
string word;           // string to hold current word

// Prompt for filenames and open files
cout << "Enter the input file name ";
cin >> infile;
cout << "Enter the output file name ";
cin >> outfile;

in_stream.open(infile.c_str());
if(in_stream.fail())
  cout << "fail to open file " << infile << endl;
else
{
  out_stream.open(outfile.c_str());
  list <string> wordlist;
  list <string>::iterator iter;
  get_word(in_stream,word);  // get a word

  // While non-empty word was returned
  while(word.size())
  {
    insert_word(word, wordlist);
    get_word(in_stream,word);  // get a word
  }
  wordlist.sort();
  out_stream << "There were " << wordlist.size()
           << " distinct words. \n";
  out_stream << "\nHere is the ordered list of words\n";
  display_list(out_stream,wordlist);

}//end else
return 0;
}
/*------------------------------------------------------------------*/
```

```cpp
/*------------------------------------------------------------------*/
/* This function will insert word into wordlist                     */
/* if word is not found in wordlist.                                */
/*                                                                  */
void insert_word(string word, list<string> &wordlist)
{
  list<string>::iterator iter;

  iter = find(wordlist.begin(), wordlist.end(), word);

  if( iter == wordlist.end() )
  {
  // Word is not in list.  Insert word.
    wordlist.insert(iter, word);
  }
}
/*------------------------------------------------------------------*/
/*------------------------------------------------------------------*/
/* This function returns the next word from the input stream.       */
/* All non-alpha characters are treated as delimiters.              */
/* The function will ignore all leading non-alpha characters,       */
/* then read and store the following alpha characters               */
/* until it reaches the next non alpha character.                   */
void get_word(istream& in_stream, string& w)
{
  char ch;
  w = ""; //clear word

  in_stream.get(ch);
  while( !isalpha(ch)&& !in_stream.eof() )// skip non-alpha
  {
    in_stream.get(ch);
  }

  while( isalpha(ch) && !in_stream.eof() ) // read and store alpha
  {
    ch = tolower(ch);
    w += ch;
    in_stream.get(ch);
  }
}
/*------------------------------------------------------------------*/

/*------------------------------------------------------------------*/
/* This function outputs the list of words to an output stream.     */
/* Three words per column are printer.                              */
void display_list(ostream& out_stream, list<string> wordlist)
{
  int columns(3), counter(0);
  list<string>::iterator iter;
  out_stream << setiosflags(ios::left);
```

```
      // Position iter at beginning of list.
      iter = wordlist.begin();
      while(iter != wordlist.end())
      {
         out_stream << setw(20) << (*iter).c_str();
         iter++;
         counter++;
         if(counter%columns == 0)
         {
            out_stream << endl;
         }
      }
   }
```

5. TESTING

If we use the text from the hand example, we get the following information written to a data file:

```
There are 13 distinct words in the text file:
a                an              alphabetical
concordance      file            in
is               list            of
text             the             unique
words
```

SUMMARY

In this chapter, we looked at the relationships between the value stored in an object, the identifier assigned to an object, and the address of the memory location used to store the value of an object. A new pointer data type was defined that can be used to hold the address of another object. Examples were presented to demonstrate the use of pointers to reference array elements and character strings. The process of dynamic memory allocation was defined. The operators new and delete were examined, and the *vector* class was revisited as an alternative to dynamic memory allocation. Data structures, including linked list, stacks and queues, were discussed, with examples that utilize the *list*, *stack*, and *queue* classes.

Key Terms

address	indirection
address operator	linked data structures
container	list
deallocation	pointer
dereference	queue
dynamic data structures	stack
dynamic memory allocation	

C++ Statement Summary

Pointer declaration:

General Form:

```
data type *identifier [,*identifier];
```

Example:

```
int *ptr_1;
double a, *ptr_2=&a;
```

Dynamic memory allocation:

General Form:

```
pointer_object = new datatype;
```

Example:

```
ptr = new double;
```

Deallocation of dynamic memory:

General Form:

```
delete pointer_object;
```

Dynamic array memory allocation:

```
arr_ptr = new double[100];
```

Deallocation of dynamic array:

General Form:

```
delete pointer_object[];
```

Notes

1. Choose identifiers for pointers that clearly indicate that the identifiers are associated with pointer objects.
2. If a pointer is not initially assigned to a memory location, give it a value of NULL to indicate that it has not yet been assigned.

Debugging Notes

1. Be sure that a program initializes an object before using its value in other statements.
2. Be sure that a pointer object is initialized before it is used to reference a value.
3. The actual parameter that corresponds to a pointer argument in a function must be an address or a pointer.

Problems

Exam Practice!

True/False Problems
Indicate whether the following statements are true (T) or false (F).

1. Both the address operator and the indirection operator are unary operators. T F
2. A pointer provides an indirect means of accessing the value of a particular data item. T F
3. An object must always be declared and initialized before a pointer can point to it. T F
4. The memory locations given to dynamic memory space are determined when the program is compiled. T F

Multiple Choice Problems
Circle the letter for the best answer to complete each statement or for the correct answer to each question.

5. A location in memory
   (a) is reserved whenever an object is declared.
   (b) is reserved when an object is used in a program.
   (c) can hold several different values at the same time.
   (d) cannot be reused once it is assigned a value.
6. A pointer object
   (a) contains the data stored at a location in memory.
   (b) contains the address of a memory location.
   (c) can be used in input statements, but not output statements.
   (d) can be changed to different values in both input and output statements.
7. How would you assign to the object `name` the value of an object referenced by the pointer `a`?
   (a) `a = &name;`
   (b) `name = &a;`
   (c) `a = *name;`
   (d) `name = *a;`
8. Assume that *a* and *b* are pointers to integers and that *a* points to the object *name*. What is the effect of the statement

   ```
   b = a;
   ```

   (a) The value of *name* is copied into *b*.
   (b) The memory address stored in *a* is copied into *b*.
   (c) The memory address stored in *b* is copied into *a*.
   (d) The pointer *a* is now pointing to a different object.

Memory Snapshot Problem

9. Give the corresponding snapshot of memory after the following set of statements is executed:

```
double name, x(20.5);
double *a = &x;
name = *a;
```

Assume the address of name is 10 and the address of x is 14. (That is, name is stored in memory location 10, and x is stored in memory location 14.) problems 10–13 refer to the following statements:

```
int i1, i2;
int *p1, *p2;
i1 = 5;
p1 =  &i1;
i2 = *p1/2 + 10;
p2 = p1;
```

10. What is the value of i1?
11. What is the value of i2?
12. What is the value of *p1?
13. What is the value of *p2?

Vector Functions.   These problems develop functions for manipulating values within a vector.

14. Write a function that creates a vector of size n, with each element assigned the value v. Assume that the function prototype statement is

```
void assign_n(vector <double> &x, int n, double v);
```

15. Write a function that creates a vector of n random numbers between a and b. Assume that the function prototype statement is

```
void assign_random(vector <int> &x, int n, int a, int b);
```

16. Write a function that computes the sum of a vector. Assume that the function prototype statement is

```
int v_sum(vector<int> x);
```

17. Write a function that replaces values in a vector with their absolute values. Assume that the function prototype statement is

```
void v_abs(vector<int>&x);
```

Character Functions: Pattern Recognition.   Many areas of engineering use problem solutions in which we search for a specific pattern of information in a signal. Problems 17–24 develop a set of functions for this purpose.

18. Write a function that receives a pointer to a character string and a character. The function should return the number of times that the character occurred in the string. Assume that the function has the prototype statement

```
int charcnt(char *ptr, char c);
```

19. Write a function that receives a pointer to a character string and returns the number of repeated characters that occur in the string. For example, the string "Mississippi" has three repeated characters. Do not count repeated blanks in the string. If a character occurs more than two times, it should still only count as one repeated character; thus, "hisssss" would have only one repeated character. Assume that the function has the prototype statement

```
int repeat(char *ptr);
```

20. Rewrite the function from problem 19 so that each pair of characters is counted as a repeat. Thus, the string "hisssss" would have four repeated characters. Assume that the function has the prototype statement

```
int repeat2(char *ptr);
```

21. Write a function that receives pointers to two character strings and returns a count of the number of times that the second character string occurs in the first character string. Do not allow overlap of the occurrences. Thus, the string "110101" contains only one occurrence of "101." Assume that the function has the prototype statement

```
int overlap(char *ptr1, char *ptr2);
```

22. Rewrite the function from problem 21 so that overlap of the occurrences of the second string in the first string is allowed. Thus, the string "110101" contains two occurrences of "101." Assume that the function has the prototype statement

```
int overlap(char *ptr1, char *ptr2);
```

23. Rewrite the function in problem 19 using the **string** class instead of C-style strings. Assume that the function has the prototype statement

```
int repeat(string);
```

24. Rewrite the function in problem 20 using the **string** class instead of C-style strings. Assume that the function has the prototype statement

```
int repeat2(string);
```

25. Rewrite the function in problem 21 using the **string** class instead of C-style strings. Assume that the function has the prototype statement

```
int pattern(string, string);
```

26. Modify program `chapter 9_13` to insert all words into the list, then call the member function *unique()* to remove duplicate words.
27. Modify program `chapter 9_13` to keep a count of how many times each unique word appears in the text file.
28. Write a function that assigns the value v to the first *n* elements of the array *x*. Use the prototype:

```
void assignV(double *x, int n, double v);
```

29. Write a function that assigns a random value to the first *n* elements of the array *x*. Use the prototype:

```
void assignRandom(double *x, int n);
```

10

ENGINEERING CHALLENGE:
Artificial Intelligence

Artificial Intelligence (AI) is an intriguing area of science that focuses on creating intelligent machines that have the ability to "think." Research in the areas of robotics, cognitive science, language, computing, and sensory perception have advanced the creation of intelligent machines. Today, software exists that can conduct a dialog with human client, beat a world-class chess player, and aid in the diagnosis of disease. Virtual pets are available that "learn" about their environment and respond to their owners. The intelligent software that exists today is only a hint of what is to come.

ADVANCED TOPICS

CHAPTER OUTLINE

OBJECTIVES   *In this chapter, we develop problem solutions containing:*

- function templates
- overloaded operators
- image processing examples
- recursive member functions

- class templates
- class hierarchies
- an implementation of the iterated prisoner's dilemma game

10.1   Generic Programming

templates

Generic programming is a form of programming that supports the implementation of an algorithm, or a type, using a set of parameters rather than a specific type. The C++ programming language supports generic programming through the use of **templates**. A `template` is a formal definition of a generic algorithm, or generic type, and can be implemented, or instantiated, by the compiler when referenced with a specific type. The ability to define a concept once, and have the concept implemented automatically for many different types, saves time in the development and testing of problem solutions.

In previous chapters we developed problem solutions that used pre-defined templates from the C++ Standard Library, including `vector <type>` and `random_shuffle()`. In this chapter we will illustrate the use of programmer defined templates by writing a set of function templates to perform statistical measures on various sets of data, and a `class template` to implement the concept of a binary tree.

489

The ability to define algorithms and types using templates is a powerful feature of the C++ programming language, but there are some limitations. Templates are not well supported by all compilers, linkers and debuggers. Thus, using templates can result in code that is harder to compile and debug, and code that is less portable.

To minimize the time spent debugging a `template`, it is a good idea to first develop a working version of a function, or `class`, for a specific type. Once a working version has been throughly tested and debugged, a `template` can be defined and the `template` can be tested against the working version to compare results and performance. *For portability, and to eliminate some of the potential linker errors, we will use* `#include` *statements in our problem solutions to include the source files that define our templates, thus eliminating the need to link to the object files.*

Function Templates

A function `template` uses a parameter in the function definition rather than a data type. When a function `template` is referenced with an argument of a specific type, the compiler generates an instance of the `template`, replacing the parameter with the specific type of the function argument. Thus, a function template is written once, and multiple versions of the template are instantiated, as needed, by the compiler.

In Chapter 7, we wrote a set of functions to perform statistical measures on a set of data. Each function assumed that the data was in an array of type `double`. In this section, we will develop a set of function templates to perform statistical measures, then test these templates against the functions developed in Chapter 7. We will begin with the function `minval()`. The definition of `minval()`, taken from Chapter 7, is repeated below:

```
/*-----------------------------------------------------------*/
/* This function returns the minimum                        */
/* value in an array x with n elements.                     */
double minval(const double x[], int n)
{
// Declare objects.
double min_x;
// Determine minimum value in the array.
min_x = x[0];
for (int k=1; k<n; ++k)
{
   if (x[k] < minX)
      min_x = x[k];
}
// Return minimum value.
return min_x;
}
/*-----------------------------------------------------------*/
```

The function `minval()` returns the smallest value found in an array of type `double`. The algorithm for finding the smallest value in an array is independent of the data type of the array, thus `minval()` is a good candidate for a function `template`.

The definition of a function `template` begins with an expression of the form:

```
template<typename identifier>.
```

The identifier in this expression provides a name for a parameterized type, and this identifier is used in the function definition in place of a specific type. The definition of a function `template` named `minVal()` is provided below:

```
/*------------------------------------------------------*/
/* Function returns the minimum value in an             */
/* array of type Dtype and size n.                      */

template <typename Dtype>
Dtype minVal(const Dtype x[], int n)
{

// Declare objects.
   Dtype minX;
// Determine minimum value in the array.
   minX = x[0];
   for (int k=1; k<n; ++k)
   {
      if (x[k] < minX)
         minX = x[k];
   }
// Return minimum value.
   return minX;
}
/*------------------------------------------------------*/
```

Note that the only difference between the statement block that defines `minval()` and the statement block that defines the function `template minVal()` is that the data type `double` in `minval()` has been replaced with the parameter `Dtype`. The prototype for this function template is:

```
template <typename Dtype>
Dtype minVal(const Dtype x[], int n);
```

Function Templates: A function template is a parameterized function definition.

Syntax:
 	
    template<typename identifier1 [,typename identifier2,....] >
    return-type function name(parameter list)
    {
      //Statement block
    }

Example:
 	
`    template<typename Dtype>`
`    void swapTwo(Dtype& a, Dtype& b)`
`    {`
`      Dtype temp = a;`
`      a = b;`
`      b = temp;`
`    }`
 	
Prototype:
`    template<typename Dtype>`
`    void swapTwo(Dtype& a, Dtype& b);`

The keyword `template`, followed by a parameter list enclosed within `<>` symbols, must precede a function template definition and a function template prototype. Within the parameter list the keyword `typename` precedes each identifier in the list, indicating that the identifier represents a data type. The template parameter list must include at least one parameter. If multiple parameters are used, they are separated with commas, as in:

```
template <typename T1, typename T2, typename T3>
```

The following program calls the function template `minVal()` four times to find the smallest value in arrays of type `int`, `char`, `double`, and `string`.

```
/*-------------------------------------------------------------------*/
/* Program chapter10_1                                               */
/* This program demonstrates the use of the function                */
/* template minVal.                                                 */

   #include<iostream> //Required for cout.
   #include<string> //Required for string.
   using namespace std;

   //Function Prototype
   template <typename Dtype>
   Dtype minVal(const Dtype x[], int n);

   int main()
   {
    //Declare objects.
    const int SIZE = 10;
    char ch[SIZE] = {'h','e','l','l','o','w','o','r','l','d'};
    int iDat[SIZE] = {5,2,7,8,2,5,9,8,1,9};
    double dDat[SIZE] = {-2.1,4.3,0.0,9.3,0.4,-4.2};
    string sDat[SIZE] = {"this","short","the","list","of","strings"};

    //Print smallest value in each array.
    cout << "smallest char in ch is "
         << minVal(ch,SIZE) << endl;        // Char
    cout << "smallest integer in iDat is "
         << minVal(iDat,SIZE) << endl;      // int
    cout << "smallest double in dDat is "
         << minVal(dDat,6) << endl;         // double
    cout << "smallest string in sDat is: "
         << minVal(sDat,6) << endl;         // string

      return 0;
    }
/*-------------------------------------------------------------------*/
```

The output from a sample run is given below:

```
smallest char in ch is: d
smallest integer in iDat is: 1
smallest double in dDat is: -4.2
smallest string in sDat is: list
```

The function `template minVal()` uses two operators, < and =, to find the smallest value in the array, x. Thus, `minVal()` can be called with any data type that has these operators defined. The operator = is, by default, defined for all types, but the same is not true for the operator <. If we tried to call `minVal()` with an array of type `Card`, for example, the result would be a long list of compiler errors because we did not overload this operator in our `Card class` definition.

We can add a boolean method to our `Card class` to overload the < operator, if we can define what it means for one card to be less than another card. When overloading the operator < for a new type, it should always hold that if $c1 < c2$ and $c2 < c3$ then $c1 < c3$ for all objects of the type. This is true for all relational operator. Overloading operators is discussed in the following section.

Modify!

Questions 1–4 refer to the functions defined in Chapter 7.

1. Write a function template for the function:

   ```
   double mean(const double x[], int n);
   ```

   Test your template with at least 2 data types.

2. Write a function template for the function:

   ```
   double median(const double x[], int n);
   ```

   Test your template with at least 2 data types.

3. Write a function template for the function:

   ```
   double variance(const double x[], int n);
   ```

   Test your template with at least 2 data types.

4. Write a function template for the function:

   ```
   double std_dev(const double x[], int n);
   ```

   Test your template with at least 2 data types.

10.2 Data Abstraction

In real-world applications it is very common to work with concepts that are not available as built-in or predefined data types. Problem solutions to real-world applications often require multiple programmers working separately on different aspects of a solution. In these situations, an objected oriented approach to the design and implementation of a solution is desirable. Defining a new type to represent a concept ensures that all programmers are working with the same physical definition of the concept and adhering to the same rules of operation, thus reducing the potential for errors and increasing productivity. Programmer-defined types can also be used as building blocks to define more-complex concepts.

data abstraction

encapsulation

The C++ programming language supports object-oriented programming through the use of programmer defined types, or **data abstraction**. C++ supports the use of classes to define new types that can be used as easily as built-in types and receive nearly as much compiler support as built-in types. A well-designed type provides a good public interface and hides the implementation of the type through **encapsulation**. Encapsulation requires that direct access to the data members of a type be restricted to the `class` methods. Recall that the programmer-defined `Point class` uses the keyword `private` to restrict access to the data members. Encapsulation and a good public interface allow for efficient maintenance and expansion of a type without requiring changes to the applications that depend on the use of the type.

Operator overloading is supported in C++ to allow programmer-defined types to be used as easily as predefined types. We first introduced overloading operators in Chapter 3, where we defined the operator `Point::operator-()` to calculate the distance between two points in a plane. In this section, we look at overloading operators in more detail and introduce the use of the keyword `friend` for overloading the input and output operators $<<$ and $>>$.

Overloading Operators

Operator overloading allows programmer-defined types to redefine the behavior of an existing operator, with some restrictions. All of the predefined operators in C++, with the exception of four, can be overloaded. It is not possible to define new operators, such as $**$, for exponentiation. The four predefined operators that cannot be overloaded are listed in Table 10.1.

Operators in C++ have a syntax that defines their usage. Unary operators such as $++x$ require a single operand, and binary operators such as $x + y$ require two operands. When overloading operators in C++, you must adhere to the syntax that defines the operator. Thus, when overloading a binary operator you must provide two operands, and when overloading a unary operator you must provide one operand. To illustrate operator overloading, we will develop a new type to implement the concept of a pixel.

TABLE 10.1	Operators That Cannot Be Overloaded
Operator	**Description**
::	Scope Resolution Operator
.	Dot Operator
.*	Pointer to Member Operator
?:	Conditional Operator

The Pixel class

picture elements
pixel
red, green, and blue
triple

A digital image can be represented as a collection of **picture elements**. A picture element is a small rectangular region, also referred to as a **pixel**. In the case of a color image, each pixel represents a **red, green, and blue triple**. Typically, each value in the triple ranges from 0 to 255, where 0 indicates that none of that primary color is present in the pixel and 255 indicates a maximum amount of that primary color. Thus, a pixel displaying the color white will have a value of (255,255,255), and a black pixel will have a value of (0,0,0).

brighten
darken

Digital images can be modified by manipulating the pixels that represent an image. For example, we can uniformly **brighten** an image by multiplying each pixel by a small positive value greater than 1, bringing each pixel closer to white. We can uniformly **darken** an image by multiplying each pixel by a positive value less than 1, bringing each pixel closer to black.

When we multiply a pixel by a value, we want to multiply each of the three color values of the pixel—the red value, the green value, and the blue value—by the same amount, and we would like to do this in a single multiplication using the multiplication ∗ operator. Thus, we will overload the multiplication operator when we define our pixel class.

smoothing

neighborhood

Another modification we can perform on a digital image is called **smoothing**. To smooth an image, we replace each pixel with an average of the surrounding pixels. The number of surrounding pixels we choose to include is referred to as the **neighborhood**. The size of the neighborhood determines the degree of smoothing: the larger the neighborhood, the more dramatic the smoothing. For example, we can uniformly smooth an image by replacing each pixel, except the pixels on the boundaries of the image, with an average of four surrounding pixels: the pixel above, the pixel below, the pixel to the right, and the pixel to the left. To calculate an average, we need to sum the pixel values and divide by the number of pixels. When we sum two pixels, we want to add the red values, the green values, and the blue values of the two pixels. When we divide a pixel by a value, we want to divide the red value, the green value, and the blue value by the same value. Thus, we will overload the addition operator and the division operator.

We have identified the attributes of a pixel as a red, green, and blue triple, and we have defined three arithmetic operations (addition, multiplication, and division) required to modify the value of a pixel. The declaration of a Pixel class is provided below. We will now implement a Pixel class, using the class declaration provided below.

```
/*------------------------------------------------------------------*/
/* Pixel class declaration.                                         */
/* File name: Pixel.h                                               */
/* This class implements the concept of a pixel                     */
#include <iostream> //Required for istream, ostream
using namespace std;
class Pixel
{
  public:
  //Constructors
  Pixel();                            //Default
  Pixel(unsigned );                   //Gray scale
  Pixel(unsigned,unsigned,unsigned);  //Full color range
```

```
//Overloaded operators.
//Addition.
Pixel operator+(const Pixel& p) const;

//Multiplication of a Pixel by a floating point value.
Pixel operator*(double v) const;

//Division of a Pixel by an integer value.
Pixel operator/(unsigned v) const;

//Input operator.
friend istream& operator >>(istream& in, Pixel& p);

//Output operator.
friend ostream& operator <<(ostream& out, const Pixel& p);

private:
unsigned int red, green, blue;
};
/*--------------------------------------------------------------------*/
```

The `class` declaration includes prototypes for a set of constructors; the arithmetic operators $+$, $-$, and $*$; and the operators $\ll$ and $\gg$. The keyword `friend` is used in the prototypes for the input and output operators. A `friend` function is not a member function; however, the keyword `friend` provides the function with access to the `private` and `protected` data members of the friendly class. This violates the guidelines for encapsulation but allows for programmer-defined types to be used in the same way as built-in types. Overloading of operators and `friend` functions are discussed in the sections that follow.

Arithmetic Operators

Our `Pixel class` declaration includes the following prototypes:

```
Pixel operator+(Pixel p) const;
Pixel operator*(double v) const;
Pixel operator/(unsigned v) const;
```

Each prototype specifies a return type of `Pixel`, indicating that each method will return a value of type `Pixel` and that each method has one formal parameter. In each method, the formal parameter is a pass-by-value parameter, which prevents modification of the argument. The keyword `const` prevents modification of the calling object.

The + Operator   The method `Pixel operator+(Pixel p) const` has one formal parameter of type `Pixel`. Because this method is a member of the `Pixel class`, it will be called by a `Pixel` object. The calling object will provide the first operand for the + operator, and the argument will provide the second operand. The implementation of the overloaded addition operator is provided below.

```
/*--------------------------------------------------------------------*/
/* Addition (+) operator.                                             */
/* File name: Pixel.cpp                                               */
#include "Pixel.h"

Pixel Pixel:: operator+(Pixel p) const
{
    Pixel temp;
```

```
    temp.red = red + p.red;
    temp.green = green + p.green;
    temp.blue = blue + p.blue;
    return temp;
}
/*-------------------------------------------------------------------*/
```

We can call the + operator as illustrated here:

```
Pixel p1, p2(100,200,100), p3(10,20,30);
p1 = p2 + p3;   //function call
cout << p1;
...
```

In the statement

```
p1 = p2 + p3;
```

p2 is the calling object and p3 is the argument. When the + operator is called, the formal parameter p receives the value of the argument, p3. The method references the `private` data members (`red`, `green`, and `blue`) of the calling object and the `private` data members (`p.red`, `p.green`, and `p.blue`) of the formal parameter. The function also references the `private` data members of the local object `temp` (`temp.red`, `temp.green`, and `temp.blue`). The three assignment statements in the function definition

```
temp.red = red + p.red;
temp.green = green + p.green;
temp.blue = blue + p.blue;
```

assign to the local object `temp` the result of adding the function argument to the calling object. The value of `temp` is returned and assigned to the `Pixel` `p1`. The output generated when `p1` is printed to the screen is

```
110 220 130
```

A program trace of these statements is provided in Figure 10.1.

The ∗ Operator   The function `Pixel operator*(double v) const` has one formal parameter of type `double`. The calling object will provide the first operand for the ∗ operator, and the function argument will provide the second operand. The following is the function definition:

```
/*-------------------------------------------------------------------*/
/* Multiplication (*) operator.                                      */
/* File name: Pixel.cpp                                              */
Pixel Pixel:: operator*(double v) const
{
    Pixel temp;
    temp.red = red*v;
    temp.green = green*v;
    temp.blue = blue*v;
    return temp;
}
/*-------------------------------------------------------------------*/
```

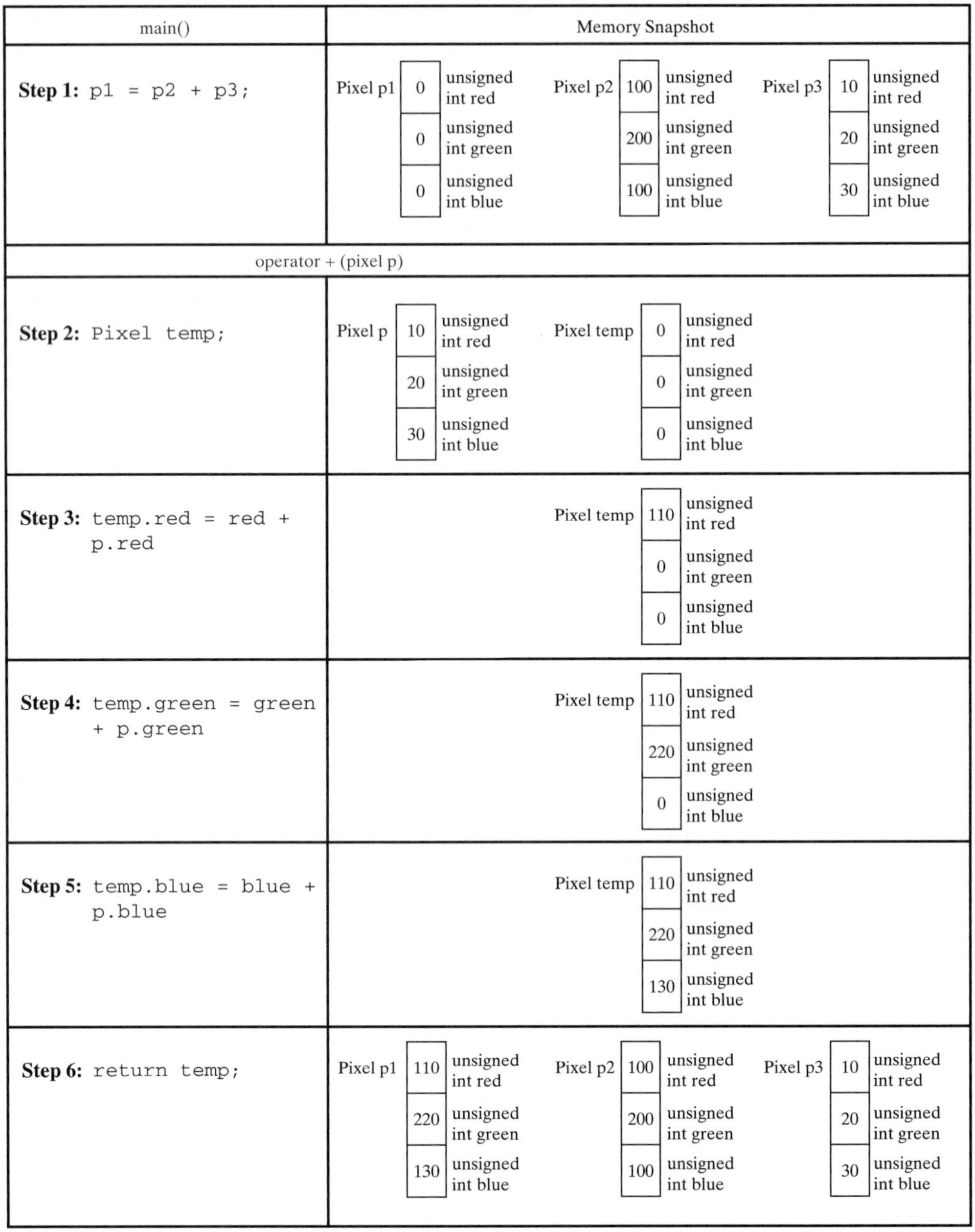

main()	Memory Snapshot
Step 1: p1 = p2 + p3;	Pixel p1: 0 unsigned int red, 0 unsigned int green, 0 unsigned int blue; Pixel p2: 100 unsigned int red, 200 unsigned int green, 100 unsigned int blue; Pixel p3: 10 unsigned int red, 20 unsigned int green, 30 unsigned int blue

operator + (pixel p)	
Step 2: Pixel temp;	Pixel p: 10 red, 20 green, 30 blue; Pixel temp: 0 red, 0 green, 0 blue
Step 3: temp.red = red + p.red	Pixel temp: 110 red, 0 green, 0 blue
Step 4: temp.green = green + p.green	Pixel temp: 110 red, 220 green, 0 blue
Step 5: temp.blue = blue + p.blue	Pixel temp: 110 red, 220 green, 130 blue
Step 6: return temp;	Pixel p1: 110 red, 220 green, 130 blue; Pixel p2: 100 red, 200 green, 100 blue; Pixel p3: 10 red, 20 green, 30 blue

Figure 10.1 Program trace.

We can call the operator* function as follows:

```
Pixel p1, p2(100,200,100);
double factor(1.2);
p1 = p2*factor;
cout << p1;
...
```

In this example, p2 is the calling object and `factor` is the function argument. When the function `operator*` is called, the formal parameter v receives the value of `factor`. The local object `temp` is assigned the result of multiplying each data member of the calling object by the floating-point value v. The value of `temp` is returned and assigned to the `Pixel p1`. The output generated when `p1` is printed to the screen is

```
120 240 120
```

A program trace is provided in Figure 10.2 to illustrate the passing of information.

Note that this function does not define multiplication of two pixels, but rather defines multiplication of a `pixel` by a `double`. If we want to define multiplication of two pixels,

main()	Memory Snapshot
Step 1: `Pixel p1, p2` `(100, 200, 100);`	Pixel p1 [0] unsigned int red; [0] unsigned int green; [0] unsigned int blue — Pixel p2 [100] unsigned int red; [200] unsigned int green; [100] unsigned int blue
Step 2: `double factor (1.2)`	double factor [1.2]
Step 3: `p1 = p2*factor;`	
operator *(double v)	
Step 4: `Pixel temp;`	Pixel temp [0] unsigned int red; [0] unsigned int green; [0] unsigned int blue — double v [1.2]
Step 5: `temp.red = red*v;` **Step 6:** `temp.green = green*v;` **Step 7:** `temp.blue = blue*v;`	Pixel temp [120] unsigned int red; [240] unsigned int green; [120] unsigned int blue
Step 8: `return temp;`	
	Pixel p1 [120] unsigned int red; [240] unsigned int green; [120] unsigned int blue — Pixel p2 [100] unsigned int red; [200] unsigned int green; [100] unsigned int blue

Figure 10.2 Program trace.

we can include a function with the following prototype in our `Pixel class` definition:

```
Pixel operator*(Pixel p) const;
```

The / Operator   The function `Pixel operator/(int v) const` has one formal parameter of type `int`. The calling object will provide the first operand for the / operator, and the function argument will provide the second operand. The function definition is the following:

```
/*--------------------------------------------------------------------*/
/* Division (/) operator.                                             */
/* File name: Pixel.cpp                                               */

Pixel Pixel:: operator/(int v) const
{
    Pixel temp;
    temp.red = red/v;
    temp.green = green/v;
    temp.blue = blue/v;
    return temp;
}
/*--------------------------------------------------------------------*/
```

We can call this function as illustrated below:

```
Pixel p1, p2(100,200,100);
p1 = p2/2;
cout << p1;
...
```

In this example, `p2` is the calling object, and the integer 2 is the function argument. When the function is called, the formal parameter `v` receives the value of the argument. The local object `temp` is assigned the result of dividing the calling object by an integer value. The value of `temp` is returned and assigned to the `Pixel p1`. The output generated when `p1` is printed to the screen is

```
50 100 50
```

Note that this function does not define division of two Pixels, but rather defines division of a `Pixel` by an `int`. If we want to define division of two pixels, we can include a function with the following prototype in our pixel class definition:

```
Pixel operator/(Pixel p) const;
```

The overloaded operator functions defined above are member functions of the `pixel class`. Thus, each function must be called by a `pixel` object. This creates a limitation in the use of these operators; the first operand must be a pixel object. Consider the following code segment that uses the + operator:

```
Pixel p1, p2(100,200,100), p3(10,20,30);
p1 = p2 + p3; // Valid.
p1 = p2 + 100; // Valid.
p1 = 100 + p2; // Invalid!
```

The first assignment statement

```
p1 = p2 + p3; // Valid.
```

is valid, since both operands of the + operator are `Pixel` objects. The second assignment statement

```
p1 = p2 + 100; // Valid.
```

is also valid, since the first operand, the calling object, is a `Pixel` object. The second operand is an integer, not a `Pixel`. However, since our `pixel class` includes a constructor with one integer argument, this constructor is used to promote the integer 100 to a `Pixel` object with the value (100,100,100) and the function call is successful. The third statement

```
p1 = 100 + p2; // Invalid!
```

is not valid, since the first operand, the calling object, is an integer object, rather than a `Pixel` object. This statement will generate an error at compile time. This limitation can be removed by defining operators as `friend` functions instead of member functions.

Practice!

Assume the following prototypes have been added to the Pixel class declaration. Write function definitions for each of the following methods.

1. `pixel operator/(pixel p1); //divide a pixel by a pixel`
2. `bool operator==(pixel p1); //return true if p1 is`
   `                          //equivalent to calling object`

---

friend **Functions**

A `friend` function is not a member function; however, a `friend` function does have access to the `private` data members of the `class` in which it is included. To declare a function as a `friend` function, the function prototype in the `class` declaration must begin with the keyword `friend`. Since a `friend` function is not a member function, the function is not affected by the `public` or `private` keywords. In our `Pixel class`, we include the `friend` functions in the `public` section, along with the other operator functions.

   If we wanted to define the + operator as a `friend` function rather than as a member function, the prototype would be:

```
friend Pixel operator+(Pixel p1, Pixel p2);
```

Notice that this function prototype requires two formal parameters. Because `friend` functions are not member functions, there is no calling object. Instead, we must include both operands as formal parameters in the function prototype and the function header. The following code segment illustrates the use of this function:

```
Pixel p1, p2(100,200,100), p3(10,20,30);
p1 = p2 + p3; // Valid.
p1 = p2 + 100; // Valid.
p1 = 100 + p2; // Valid!
```

The third assignment statement

```
p1 = 100 + p2; // Valid!
```

is now a valid statement. The integer 100 provides the first argument of the + function, and p2 provides the second argument. Since the function is expecting `Pixel` objects as arguments, a constructor is used to promote the integer 100 to the `Pixel` object (100,100,100), and the function call is successful. The definition of the function is as follows:

```
/*-----------------------------------------------------------------*/
/* Addition (+) operator as friend function.                       */
/* File name: Pixel.cpp                                            */

Pixel operator+(pixel p1, pixel p2)
{
    Pixel temp;
    temp.red = p1.red + p2.red;
    temp.green = p1.green + p2.green;
    temp.blue = p1.blue + p2.blue;
    return temp;
}
/*-----------------------------------------------------------------*/
```

Notice that the keyword `friend` is not included in the function definition. `friend` status can only be granted in the `class` declaration. Compare this function definition with the member function definition. Since this function is not a member function, there is no calling object, and the references to `red`, `green`, and `blue` in the member function definition have been replaced by references to `p1.red`, `p1.green`, and `p1.blue` in the definition of the `friend` function.

Practice!

Assume that the following function prototypes have been added to the Pixel `class` declaration. Write function definitions for each of the functions.

1. `friend Pixel operator*(Pixel p1, Pixel p2);`

2. `friend Pixel operator/(Pixel p1, Pixel p2);`

3. `friend Pixel operator-(Pixel p1, Pixel p2);`

The ≪ Operator   Our Pixel class declaration includes a function to overload the ≪ operator. The function has the following prototype:

```
friend ostream& operator<<(ostream& out, const Pixel& p);
```

This function is defined as a `friend` function with two formal parameters, and the function returns an `ostream` reference. Returning an `ostream` reference supports chaining. Thus, we can output multiple expressions in a single output statement, as illustrated in the following statement:

```
cout << p1 << ',' << p2 << endl;
```

The ≪ operator cannot be defined as a member function of the `pixel class` because the first argument of the function must be an `ostream` reference. However, the function needs to access the private data members of the `Pixel` argument, so we declare it to be a `friend` function of the `Pixel class`. *For efficiency, we have chosen to make the second formal parameter a `const` pass by reference instead of a pass by value.* This allows a reference to be passed, but prevents modification of the argument pointed to by the reference. The function definition is as follows:

```
/*-------------------------------------------------------------------*/
/* Output << operator.                                               */
/* File name: Pixel.cpp                                              */
ostream& operator<<(ostream& out, const Pixel& p)
{
    out << p.red << ' ';
    out << p.green << ' ';
    out << p.blue;
    return out;
}
/*-------------------------------------------------------------------*/
```

The function must return an `ostream` reference, thus the statement
```
return out;
```
is required.

Our function outputs the `red`, `green`, and `blue` values of the `Pixel p`, separated by whitespace. We can use the function as follows:

```
Pixel p1, p2(100,200,100);
cout << "P1: " << p1 <<"  P2: " << p2 << endl;
. . .
```

The output printed to the screen is

```
P1: 0 0 0  P2: 100 200 100
```

We can also use our ≪ function to send output to a file. Recall that the `ofstream class` is derived from the `ostream class`. Thus, all `ostream` operations can also be applied to `ofstream` objects. The following code segment uses our ≪ function to write to the file `pixel.dat`:

```
. . .
pixel p1, p2(255);
ofstream outfile("pixel.dat");
outfile << "P1: " << p1 <<"  P2: " << p2 << endl;
. . .
```

The output written to the file `pixel.dat` is

```
P1:  0  0  0    P2:  255  255  255
```

Notice that our ≪ function does not output a newline following the value of the `Pixel`. *This allows us to output multiple* `Pixel` *values on the same line and is consistent with the performance of output operators defined for the built-in data types.*

The ≫ Operator   Our `Pixel class` declaration includes a function to overload the ≫ operator. The function has the following prototype:

```
friend istream& operator>>(istream& in, Pixel& p);
```

This function is defined as a `friend` function with two formal parameters, and the function returns an `istream` reference. The ≫ operator cannot be defined as a member function of the `Pixel class` because the first argument must be an `istream` reference. However, the function needs access to the `private` data members of the `pixel` argument, so we have declared the function to be a `friend` function of the `Pixel class`.

Since the function is defined to input a `Pixel` value, the function must modify the object referenced by the formal parameter, `p`. Therefore, this formal parameter must be a pass by reference. The function definition follows:

```
/*------------------------------------------------------------------*/
/* Input (>>) operator.                                             */
/* File name: Pixel.cpp                                             */

istream& operator>>(istream& in, Pixel& p)
{
    in >> p.red >> p.green >> p.blue;
    return in;
}
/*------------------------------------------------------------------*/
```

This function must return an `istream` reference.

Overloading the ≫ operator is similar to overloading the ≪ operator, except that the potential for encountering errors on input is greater. The function attempts to input three integer values to be assigned to the `red`, `green`, and `blue` data members of `p`. This function looks to the input stream for three integer values, separated by whitespace. Any unexpected character in the input stream, such as a comma or a colon, will place the `istream` in a fail state.

If our `Pixel class` required a special format for input, our ≫ function would need to check for the required format. If the required format was not encountered, the function would need to place the `istream` in a fail state. For illustration, assume that the format for entering a Pixel value required the integer values to be separated by a colon, as in

```
100:150:100
```

Our function can be modified to check for this format and place the `istream` in a fail state if the format is not correct:

```
/*-------------------------------------------------------------------*/
/* Input (>>) operator.                                              */
/* Expected Pixel format is 100:150:100                             */
/* File name: Pixel.cpp                                             */

istream& operator>>(istream& in, Pixel& p)
{
// Declare local objects.
   char ch;

// Input integer value for red data member.
   in >> p.red;

// Input colon.  If colon not encountered,
// set error state and return.
   in >> ch;
   if(ch != ':')
   {
      in.setstate(ios::failbit);
      return in;
   }

// Input integer value for green data member.
   in >> p.green;

// Input colon.  If colon not encountered,
// set error state and return.
   in >> ch;
   if(ch != ':')
   {
      in.setstate(ios::failbit);
      return in;
   }

// Input integer value for blue data member.
   in >> p.blue;

   return in;
}
/*-------------------------------------------------------------------*/
```

In this function definition, the function `setstate()` is used to place the `istream` in a fail state. The function `setstate()` is a member function of the `istream` class. In the statement

```
in.setstate(ios::failbit);
```

the `istream` object referenced by `in` calls the `setstate` function, and the `failbit` is set to true.

Another potential error when using the `Pixel` class is assigning a value greater than 255 to one or more of the data members. Handling potential overflow errors is discussed in the following section.

Validating Objects

Recall that we defined a pixel as red, green, and blue triple, where each value in the triple ranges from 0 to 255. The `Pixel` class includes three data members (`red`, `green`, and `blue`) of type `unsigned int`. The data type `unsigned int` prevents the occurrence of a negative value, but it does not prevent a value from exceeding the maximum of 255. Consider the following example that uses the `Pixel` class:

```
/*-----------------------------------------------------------------*/
/* Program chapter10_2                                             */
/* Driver program for testing Pixel class                         */
#include "Pixel.h"  //Required for Pixel
#include <iostream> //Required for cout
using namespace std;
int main()
{
  //Test constructors
  Pixel defaultP;
  Pixel grayP(100);
  Pixel redP(255,0,0);

  //Test output operator
  cout << "Default pixel: " << defaultP << endl;
  cout << "Gray pixel: " << grayP << endl;
  cout << "Red pixel: " << redP << endl;

  //Test arithmetic operators
  //Addition
  defaultP = grayP + redP;
  cout << "After addition, defaultP: " << defaultP << endl;
  return 0;
}
```

A sample run of this program is provided below:

```
Ingbers-MacBook-Pro:Programs jaingber$ g++ main.cpp Pixel.cpp
Ingbers-MacBook-Pro:Programs jaingber$ ./a.out
Default pixel: 0 0 0
Gray pixel: 100 100 100
Red pixel: 255 0 0
After addition, defaultP: 355 100 100
```

We see that the red value of `defaultP` has exceeded the maximum of 255. If any of the data members of a `Pixel` object exceeds the maximum value, unexpected results can occur when using the `Pixel` class to modify an image. To handle this situation, we will follow the model of the `istream` class, discussed in the previous section. The `Pixel` class will maintain an overflow flag and will set the appropriate bit in the overflow flag whenever overflow is detected. Applications using the Pixel class will be responsible for checking the state of the overflow flag. Public methods will be provided to allow access to the overflow flag, and a private validation method will be provided to help maintain its state. The validation method will be called by all mutator methods of the Pixel class. The expanded Pixel class declaration is provided below:

```
/*-----------------------------------------------------*/
/* Pixel class declaration.                            */
/* File name: pixel.h                                  */
/* This class implements the concept of a pixel        */
#ifndef PIXEL_H
#define PIXEL_H
#include <iostream> //Required for istream, ostream
using namespace std;
class Pixel
{
  public:
  static const unsigned int MAXVAL = 255;

  //Constructors
  Pixel(); //Default
  Pixel(unsigned ); //Gray scale
  Pixel(unsigned,unsigned,unsigned); //Full color range

  //Overloaded operators.
  Pixel operator+(const Pixel& p) const;
  Pixel operator*(double v) const;
  Pixel operator/(unsigned v) const;

  //IO Operators.
  friend istream& operator >>(istream& in, Pixel& p);
  friend ostream& operator <<(ostream& out, const Pixel& p);

  bool overflow() const; //check overflow state
  void reset(); //reset overflow state

  private:
  unsigned int red, green, blue;
  unsigned short overflowFlag;

  static const unsigned short RMASK = 4;
  static const unsigned short GMASK = 2;
  static const unsigned short BMASK = 1;
  static const unsigned short CHECK = 7;

  void validate(); //set overflow bits
};
```

Notice that we have added five static constants to the Pixel class. The public constant MAXVAL is set to 255 and is part of the public interface. The four private

bit masks

constants are referenced in various `class` methods and have been assigned the integer values 1, 2, 4, and 7. Recall that the binary value 1, in 8 bits, can be represented as 00000001; binary 2 as 00000010; binary 4 as 0000100; and binary 7 as 00000111. These constants are used as **bit masks** to set and check the state of `overflowFlag`. A bit mask is integer data that is used with bitwise operators to manipulate bits in a single bitwise operation. The implementation of the extended `Pixel class` is provided below:

```cpp
#include "Pixel.h"
/*-----------------------------------------------------------*/
/* Pixel class implementation.                               */
/* File name: Pixel.cpp                                      */
/* Addition (+) operator.                                    */
Pixel Pixel:: operator+(const Pixel& p) const
{
  Pixel temp;
  temp.red = red + p.red;
  temp.green = green + p.green;
  temp.blue = blue + p.blue;
  temp.validate();
  return temp;
}
/*-----------------------------------------------------------*/
/* Multiplication (*) operator.                              */
Pixel Pixel:: operator*(double v) const
{
  Pixel temp;
  temp.red = red*v;
  temp.green = green*v;
  temp.blue = blue*v;
  temp.validate();
  return temp;
}
/*-----------------------------------------------------------*/
/* Division (/) operator.                                    */
Pixel Pixel:: operator/(unsigned int v) const
{
  Pixel temp;
  temp.red = red/v;
  temp.green = green/v;
  temp.blue = blue/v;
  temp.validate();
  return temp;
}

/*-----------------------------------------------------------*/
ostream& operator<<(ostream& out, const Pixel& p)
{
  out << p.red << ' ';
  out << p.green << ' ';
```

```cpp
  out << p.blue;
  return out;
}
/*-------------------------------------------------------------*/

istream& operator>>(istream& in, Pixel& p)
{
  in >> p.red >> p.green >> p.blue;
  p.validate();
  return in;
}
/*-------------------------------------------------------------*/
Pixel::Pixel()
{
  //Black
  red=green=blue=0;
  return;
}
/*-------------------------------------------------------------*/
Pixel::Pixel(unsigned int value)
{
  //Gray scale
  red=green=blue=value;
  validate();
  return;
}
/*-------------------------------------------------------------*/
Pixel::Pixel(unsigned int r,unsigned int g,unsigned int b)
{
  //Full color range
  red=r;
  green=g;
  blue=b;
  validate();
  return;
}
/*-------------------------------------------------------------*/
bool Pixel::overflow() const
{
  return(overflowFlag&CHECK);
}
/*-------------------------------------------------------------*/
void Pixel::reset()
{
  if(red > MAXVAL) red = MAXVAL;
  if(green > MAXVAL) green = MAXVAL;
  if(blue > MAXVAL) blue = MAXVAL;
  overflowFlag = 0;
}
```

```
/*------------------------------------------------------------------*/
void Pixel::validate()
{
  if(red > MAXVAL) overflowFlag = overflowFlag|RMASK;
  if(green > MAXVAL) overflowFlag = overflowFlag|GMASK;
  if(blue > MAXVAL) overflowFlag = overflowFlag|BMASK;
}
```

Notice that the private mutator method `void Pixel::validate()` uses the bit-wise operator | to set the state of `overflowFlag`. The method `validate()` must be called by all mutator methods of the `Pixel class` to guarantee the correct state of `over-flowFlag`. The `public` accessor method `bool Pixel::overflow()` uses the bitwise operator & to return the state of `overflowFlag`. We will look at these two methods in more detail and also discuss bitwise operators.

Bitwise Operators

A bitwise operator performs an operation on each bit of its operand. C++ supports three binary bitwise operators: the bitwise or (|), the bitwise and (&) and the bitwise exclusive or (^), and a unary bitwise not operator(~). The operands for these operators are restricted to be of an integral type, such as `int` or `char`. Table 10.2 provides a truth table for bitwise operators.

TABLE 10.2		**Truth Table for C++ Bitwise Operators**			
A	**B**	**~A**	**A|B**	**A^B**	**A$B**
0001	0001	1110	0001	0000	0001
0010	0010	1101	0010	0000	0010
0011	0100	1100	0111	0111	0000
0100	0111	1011	0111	0011	0100

To illustrate the use of bitwise operators, assume that a `Pixel` object has been defined and has the following value:

Pixel p1	278	unsigned red
	298	unsigned green
	150	unsigned blue
	0	unsigned short overflowFlag

The statement `p1.validate();` results in the following program trace and memory snapshot:

Validate()	Memory Snapshot		
Step 1: `if(red > MAXVAL)` `    overflowFlag = overflowFlag|RMASK;`	Pixel p1	278	unsigned red
		298	unsigned green
		150	unsigned blue
		4	unsigned short overflowFlag
Step 2: `if(green > MAXVAL)` `    overflowFlag = overflowFlag|GMASK;`	Pixel p1	278	unsigned red
		298	unsigned green
		150	unsigned blue
		6	unsigned short overflowFlag
Step 3: `if(blue > MAXVAL)` `    overflowFlag = overflowFlag|BMASK;`			

When the bitwise or is performed in step 1 with the operands `overflowFlag` (`00000000`) and `RMASK` (`00000100`), the result is 4, as illustrated below:

```
00000000    overflowFlag
00000100    RMASK

00000100    result of bitwise or
```

The result of the operation is assigned to `overflowFlag`, thus replacing the previous value. When the bitwise or is performed in step 2 with the operands `overflowFlag` (`00000100`) and `GMASK` (`00000010`), the result is 6, as illustrated below:

```
00000100    overflowFlag
00000010    GMASK

00000110    result of bitwise or
```

The resulting value of `overflowFlag` indicates that there is overflow in the data member `red`, overflow in the data member `green`, and no overflow in the data member `blue`. Thus, the statement `p1.overflow()` will return a Boolean value of true, as illustrated below:

```
00000110    overflowFlag
00000111    CHECK

00000110    result of bitwise and
```

We will now write a small driver program to test the new methods of the `Pixel` class.

```
/*------------------------------------------------------------*/
/* Program chapter10_3                                        */
/* Driver program to test overflow state of Pixel            */

#include "Pixel.h"
#include <iostream>
using namespace std;
int main()
{
  //Declare objects
  Pixel defaultP;
  Pixel grayP(100);
  Pixel redP(255,255,0);

  //Create overflow in red
  defaultP = grayP + redP;
  cout << defaultP << endl;
  if(defaultP.overflow() )
  {
     defaultP.reset();
  }
  cout << defaultP << endl;

  return 0;
}
```

The output from a sample run is provided below:

```
Ingbers-MacBook-Pro:Programs jaingber$ g++ main.cpp Pixel.cpp
Ingbers-MacBook-Pro:Programs jaingber$ ./a.out
355 100 100
255 100 100
```

We see that the expression `defalutp.overflow()` returned a value of true, indicating that overflow was detected and that the statement `defaultP.reset();` was executed, resetting the value of `defaultP` to a valid state.

Modify!

1. Add the following methods to the `Pixel class`:

```
bool checkRed() const;
bool checkGreen() const;
bool checkBlue() const;
```

Each method should check the `overflowFlag` of the calling object and returns `true` if overflow has occurred in the specified data member, `false` otherwise.

Modify!

2. Add the following methods to the `Pixel class`:

```
void resetRed();
void resetGreen();
void resetBlue();
```

Each method should set the specified data member of the calling object to MAX-VAL and reset the appropriate bit of `overflowFlag`.

3. Modify the output function

```
friend ostream& operator<<(ostream& out, const pixel& p)
```

so that the value of a `pixel` is output using colons, instead of whitespace, to separate the red, green and blue values.

4. Modify the input function

```
/*------------------------------------------------------------*/
/* Input >> operator. Expected pixel format is 100:150:100*/

friend istream& operator>>(istream& in, pixel& p)
```

to handle incorrect format by alerting the user and requesting new input. (*Hint:* Refer to error handling discussed in Chapter 5.)

10.3   Problem Solving Applied: Color Image Processing

The following is a picture of Io, one of Jupiter's moons, taken by the Galileo spacecraft:

This image was downloaded from the nasa.gov home page following a search for Io images.

bitmap

The image was converted to an ASCII file format, using the unix utility *xv*. The following is a sampling of the underlying pixel values, called a **bitmap**, taken from the ASCII file:

```
 43   56 100 147 160 204 148 160 208 147 159 207 146 158 210
149 161 213 146 159 212 145 158 211 143 158 213 143 158 213
143 159 211 143 159 211 142 160 210 142 160 210 142 160 208
140 161 208 136 158 208 135 158 208 136 156 207 138 155 207
139 155 207 140 153 206 142 151 206 142 151 206 148 155 210
149 156 211 148 157 212 148 159 213 147 158 212 143 159 211
142 158 210 141 156 211 142 154 212 142 152 213 141 151 212
140 150 211 139 149 210 139 149 210 140 150 211 140 150 211
142 152 213 142 152 213 143 153 214 144 154 215 144 154 215
143 153 214 142 152 213 142 152 211 145 154 211 144 153 208
143 152 207 143 152 207 144 153 208 145 154 209 147 156 211
148 157 212 146 155 210 147 156 211 148 157 212 148 157 212
149 158 213 150 159 214 151 160 215 151 161 214 152 162 215
152 162 213 152 162 213 152 162 213 152 162 213 152 162 213
```

ppm file format

The first pixel in the bitmap is represented by the triple 43 56 100. Each row of the bitmap holds five pixel values. The complete image is stored as an ASCII file, using a **ppm file format**. A *ppm* file contains a header that must be preserved in order to view or convert the image. The header contains a "magic number" (P3 for ppm files), possible comment lines (comment lines begin with a # in column 1), the width and height of the image, and the maximum color value. The header for this image is

```
P3
# CREATOR: XV Version 3.10a  Rev: 12/29/94
259 256
255
```

Once the image has been modified, the ASCII file can be viewed using the xv utility, or converted back to a jpg or gif file for viewing on other platforms. The "smoothed" image of Io is shown in the following:

Write a program that inputs an image from an ASCII ppm file and performs a smoothing operation on the image. The smoothed image is written to a new ppm file.

1. PROBLEM STATEMENT

Modify a color digital image by performing a smoothing process on the image.

2. INPUT/OUTPUT DESCRIPTION

The input to this program is the data in the image file Io.ppm. The output is the modified image. We must first read the header information to determine the size of the image. We can then use the information in the header to allocate memory and input the pixel values.

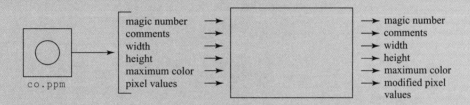

3. HAND EXAMPLE

To perform the smoothing process on the image, we will take an average of the current pixel and the four adjacent pixels; the pixel to the left, the pixel above, the pixel to the right, and the pixel below. We will replace the original pixel value with the smoothed pixel value as we perform the calculations. For our hand example, we will determine the smoothed value for one pixel from the image of Io.

Original image:

```
143  159  211  142  160  210  142  160  210
136  158  208  135  158  208  136  156  207
140  153  206  142  151  206  142  151  206
```

The current pixel has a red value of 135, a green value of 158, and a blue value of 208. The smoothed value for this pixel is calculated as follows:

```
red value -> (135 + 136 + 142 +136 +142)/5 = 138
green value -> (158 +158 + 160 + 156 +151)/5 = 156
blue value -> (208 + 208 + 210 + 207 + 206)/5 = 207
```

Modified image:

```
143  159  211  142  160  210  142  160  210
136  158  208  138  156  207  136  156  207
140  153  206  142  151  206  142  151  206
```

This process is repeated for every interior pixel in the image. Pixels on the boundaries are missing one of the four adjacent pixels just described (corner pixels are missing two) and will not be modified in this application.

4. ALGORITHM DEVELOPMENT

We first develop the decomposition outline because it breaks the solution into a series of sequential steps.

Decomposition Outline

(1) Read the header information.

(2) Write header information to the new file.

(3) Read the pixel values.

(4) Perform smoothing on each interior pixel.

(5) Write smoothed pixel values to the new file.

Steps 1 and 2 involve reading the header information from the data file and preserving this information by writing it to a new file. We will write a function to perform this task. Step 3 requires reading the pixel values into a two dimensional array. The array size depends on the information in the header, so we will use the *vector* class to define a two-dimensional array type pixel. Step 4 involves performing a smoothing modification on the image. We will write a second function to perform this task. To easily store and modify the pixel elements in the image, we will use the *pixel* `class` developed in Section 10.2. The refinement in pseudocode can now be developed:

Refinement in Pseudocode

```
main():
    open data files
    read_header(fin, fout, width, height, max_color)
    read image
    smooth(image,width, height)
    write image
read_header(fin, fout, width, height, max_color):
        read magic_num
        while(next_ch == '#')
            read comment_line
            write comment_line to new file
        read width, height, max_color
        write width, height, max_color
smooth(image, width, height):
    set i to 0
    set j to 0
```

```
      while(i<height)
        while(j<width)
          image[i][j] = (image[i][j] + image[i][j-1] + image[i-1][j]
                         + image[i][j+1] + image[i+1][j])/5
```

We are now ready to convert the pseudocode to C++:

```
/*-------------------------------------------------------------------*/
/* Program chapter10_4                                               */
/*                                                                   */
/* This program reads an ASCII digital image and perform a           */
/* smoothing operation on the on the image. The smoothed image       */
/* is written to a new file.                                         */

#include "Pixel.h"
#include <fstream>//Required for ifstream, ofstream
#include <string>//Required for string
#include <vector>//Required for vector
using namespace std;

//Function prototypes.
void read_header(istream& fin, ostream& fout,
                 int& width, int& height, int& max);
void smooth(vector <vector<Pixel> >& , int w, int h);

int main()
{
   // Declare objects.
   int height, width, max, i, j;
   string filename;
   ifstream fin;
   ofstream fout;

   // Prompt user for file name and open file for input.
   cout << "enter name of input file ";
   cin >> filename;
   fin.open(filename.c_str());
   if(fin.fail())
   {
      cerr << "Error opening input file\n";
   }
   else
   {
   // Open new file for output.
      filename = "smoothed_"+filename;
      fout.open(filename.c_str());

   // Read and write header information.
      read_header(fin,fout, width, height, max);
```

```
                // Declare image array.
                   vector< vector<Pixel> > image(height, width);

                // Read the image.
                   for(i=0; i<height; i++)
                    for(j=0; j<width; j++)
                    {
                        fin >> image[i][j];
                    }
                // Smooth the image.
                    smooth(image, width, height);

                // Write modified image to new file.
                   for(i=0; i<height; i++)
                     for(j=0; j<width; j++)
                     {
                        fout << image[i][j] << ' ';
                        if((j+1)%5 == 0) fout<<endl;
                     }
                 }

                // Exit program.
                return 0;
            }
            void read_header(istream& fin, ostream& fout, int& width,
                             int& height, int& max)
            {
              char header[100];
              char ch;
            // Get magic number.
              fin.getline(header, 100);
            // Write magic number.
              fout << header << endl;
              cout << header << endl;

            // Get all comment lines and write to new file.
              fin >> ch;
              while(ch == '#')
              {
                fin.getline(header, 100);
                fout <<ch << header << endl;
                cout << ch <<header << endl;
                fin >> ch;
              }
              fin.putback(ch);
            // Input width and height of image.
              fin >> width >> height;
              cout << width <<" " <<  height << endl;
              fout << width << " " << height << endl;
            // Input maximum color value.
```

```
    fin >> max;
    cout << max << endl;
    fout << max << endl;
    return;
}
void smooth(vector< vector<Pixel> > &image, int w, int h)
{
    for(int i=1; i<h-1; i++)
      for(int j=1; j<w-1; j++)
        image[i][j] = (image[i][j] + image[i+1][j] + image[i-1][j]
                         + image[i][j+1] + image[i][j-1])/5;
}
```

5. TESTING

The following is the smoothed image of Io alongside the original to illustrate the effect:

Modify!

1. Modify the smooth function in program `chapter10_4` to include eight adjacent pixels in the average, instead of four.

2. Modify the smooth function in program `chapter10_4` to include the pixels on the boundrys, including the corners, in smoothing process. Be careful not to include references to pixels that are outside the bounds of the image.

10.4   Recursion

Recursion is a powerful tool for solving certain classes of problems in which the solution can be defined in terms of a similar but smaller problem, and then the smaller problem can be defined in terms of a similar but still smaller problem. This redefinition of the problem into recursive function

smaller problems continues until the smaller problem has a unique solution that is then used to determine the overall solution.

Programming languages that support recursion allow functions to reference, or call, themselves. A function that references itself is called a **recursive function**. To solve a problem recursively, a function is written in such a way that each time the function calls itself it reduces the problem to a similar but smaller problem. The function continues to call itself until it finally returns, to itself, the unique solution to a small part of the problem. This unique solution is passed back up the calling chain resulting in the determination of the overall solution.

stack

Each time a recursive function calls itself, information regarding that instance of the function is stored on a portion of memory known as the **stack**. Recall from Chapter 9 that a stack is a First In Last Out (FILO) data structure. Each successive call to a recursive function pushes information onto the stack. Each successive `return` pops information off the stack. There are system-dependent limitations to the number of times that a recursive function can call itself, due to the finite size of the stack, but these limitations do not usually cause difficulties if your recursive function is written correctly.

A recursive function requires two blocks:

1. a block that defines a terminating condition, or return point, where a unique solution to a smaller version of the problem is returned,

2. a recursive block that reduces the problem to a similar but smaller version of the problem.

To illustrate recursion we will begin by developing a recursive algorithm for calculating the factorial function.

Factorial Function

Recall that $n!$ (read as n factorial) is defined in the following way:

$$n! = (n)(n-1)(n-2)...(1)$$

where n is a nonnegative integer, and $0! = 1$, by definition. A recursive definition of this problem is given below:

$$f(n) = n! = \begin{cases} 1 & : \quad n = 0 \\ n * f(n-1) & : \quad n > 1 \end{cases}$$

The recursive definition provides the terminating condition, ($f(0) = 1$) for this example, and the reduction statement for the recursive block, ($f(n) = n * f(n-1)$). The reduction statement reduces the problem of solving $f(n)$ to the problem of solving $f(n-1)$ and multiplying the result by n.

To illustrate, we will compute 5! by hand using the following steps:

$$5! = 5 * 4!$$
$$4! = 4 * 3!$$
$$3! = 3 * 2!$$
$$2! = 2 * 1!$$
$$1! = 1 * 0!$$
$$0! = 1$$

Thus, we have defined a factorial in terms of a product that involves smaller factorials. The smaller factorial is continually redefined until we reach 0!. We substitute the unique solution to 0! in the last equation, and then begin going back up the list of equations, substituting values for the factorials:

$$1! = 1 * 1$$
$$2! = 2 * 1! = 2$$
$$3! = 3 * 2! = 6$$
$$4! = 4 * 3! = 24$$
$$5! = 5 * 4! = 120$$

We have now developed a recursive algorithm for computing a factorial.

We present a program with a recursive function to calculate the factorial function. A factorial value becomes large quickly, so we use long integers for the factorial value. Note that the function call in main() looks the same as a call to a non-recursive function.

```
/*-------------------------------------------------------------*/
/*  Program chapter10_5                                        */
/*                                                             */
/*  This program calls a recursive function to                */
/*  compute a factorial.                                       */

#include <iostream> //Required for cout
using namespace std;

// Function prototypes.
long factorialR(int n);

int main()
{
   //  Declare objects
   int n;

   //  Get user input.
   cout << "Enter positive integer: \n";
   cin >> n;

   //  Compute and print factorials.
   cout << "Recursive: " << n << "! = " << factorialR(n) << endl;
```

```
    //  Exit program.
    return 0;
}
/*-------------------------------------------------------------------*/
/*  This function computes a factorial recursively.               */

long factorialR(int n)
{
    /*  Recursive reference until n is equal to 0.               */
    if (n == 0)   //Solution is known
    {
        return 1;   //Return unique solution.
    }
    return n*factorialR(n - 1);   //Reduce the  problem
}
/*-------------------------------------------------------------------*/
```

The terminating condition n == 0 keeps the recursive routine from becoming an infinite loop. The recursive block calls itself with an argument that is continually being decremented by 1, until the argument reaches zero.

For large values of *n*, the value of *n*! can exceed even long integers. In these cases, the computations should be done using double values. An interesting approximation to *n*! is also discussed in the end-of-chapter problems.

A program trace of program chapter10_5 is provided in Figure 10.3.

Fibonacci Sequence

A Fibonacci sequence is a sequence of numbers f0, f1, f2, f3, ... in which the first two values (f0 and f1) are equal to 1, and each succeeding number is the sum of the previous two numbers. Thus, the first few values of the Fibonacci sequence are

1   1   2   3   5   8   13   21   34...

This sequence was first described in the year 1202, and it has applications that range from biology to electrical engineering. For example, Fibonacci sequences are often used in studies of rabbit population growth.

A function to compute the kth value in the Fibonacci sequence is a good candidate for a recursive function because each new value in the sequence is computed from the two previous values, as shown in the following recursive definition:

$$f(n) = \begin{cases} 1 & n = 0, n = 1 \\ f(n-1) + f(n-2) & n > 1 \end{cases}$$

We next provide a definition for a recursive function to compute the kth term in the Fibonacci sequence.

```
/*-------------------------------------------------------------------*/
/*                                                               */
/*  This function computes the kth Fibonacci                     */
/*  number using a recursive algorithm.                          */
```

main()	Memory Snapshot
Step 1: `int n;` **Step 2:** `cin >>n;` **Step 3:** `cout << ... << factorialR(n);`	int n ⟨ ? ⟩ int n ⟨ 4 ⟩
factorialR(n)	
Step 4: `return n*factorialR(3)`	int n ⟨ 4 ⟩ stack ⟨ 4*factorialR(3) ⟩
factorialR(3)	
Step 5: `return 3*factorialR(2)`	int n ⟨ 3 ⟩ stack ⟨ 3*factorialR(2) ⟩
factorialR(2)	
Step 6: `return 2*factorialR(1)`	int n ⟨ 2 ⟩ stack ⟨ 2*factorialR(1) ⟩
factorialR(1)	
Step 7: `return n*factorialR(0)`	int n ⟨ 1 ⟩ stack ⟨ 1*factorialR(0) ⟩
factorialR(0)	
Step 8: `return 1`	factorialR(0) returns 1 factorialR(1) returns 1*1 factorialR(2) returns 2*1 factorialR(3) returns 3*2 factorialR(4) returns 4*6

Figure 10.3 Program trace.

```
int fibonacciR(int k)
{
   //  Declare objects.
   int term = 1;

   //  Compute kth Fibonacci number recursively
   if (k <=1)
   {
      return term;  //Unique solution.
   }
   return  fibonacciR(k-1) + fibonacciR(k-2);  //Reduce.
}
/*------------------------------------------------------*/
```

In the recursive function, the condition $k <= 1$ keeps the function from getting into an infinite loop.

Modify!

1. Use program `chapter10_3` to compute values of 1!, 2!, and so on, until you reach the limits for long integers. What kind of error message occurred when the value of k! exceeded the limits on your system?

2. Modify `chapter10_3` so that it uses **double** values instead of integers to compute factorials. Explain why the number of digits of precision determines the maximum value of k! that can be correctly computed using **double** values. What is the maximum value of k! that can be computed using **double** values on your system?

3. Write a main function to test the Fibonacci functions. What is the maximum Fibonacci value that can be correctly computed with integers on your system?

The `BinaryTree class`

In this section, we will implement a new programmer-defined type to represent the concept of a binary tree. Our implementation will include the use of `class` composition, and the definition of several recursive methods. In Section 10.5, we will use the `BinaryTree class` to develop a `class` template.

root
node
left child
right child
leaf node

A binary tree is a dynamic, linked, data structure that represents a collection of nodes that extend from a single **root**. The root of a binary tree references the first `node`. Each node in a binary tree consists of a data value and at most two links to other nodes. The links to other nodes are referred to as the **left child** and the **right child**. The left child is the root of the left subtree, and the right child is the root of the right subtree. If both the left child and the right child of a node are null, the node is referred to as a **leaf node**. A diagram of a binary tree with five nodes is provided in Figure 10.4.

Figure 10.4 illustrates a binary tree with five nodes. The root of the tree references the first node, which has a value of 7. The first node has a left child that references a node with a value of 14, and a right child that references a node with the value of 21. The node with a value of 14 has a left child that references a leaf node, and a right child that references a leaf node. Note that the left child and the right child of each node is the root of a smaller subtree.

When developing a new type, we need to consider both the physical description of the type, and operations supported by the public interface of the type. The physical description of a binary tree suggests a *root*, where *root* is a pointer, to a *node*. Three basic operations performed on a binary tree are inserting a node, printing a node value, and clearing a tree by removing all nodes. A `class` diagram for a minimal `BinaryTree` is provided in Figure 10.5.

Notice that the `class` diagram in Figure 10.5 uses a data type named `Node` and overloads the methods `print()`, `insert()` and `clear()`. The structure of a binary tree is recursive in nature since each node in a binary tree is the first node of a smaller subtree. Thus the basic operations performed on a binary tree are implemented using recursion. The `private` methods are the recursive methods, and they are called by the non-recursive `public` methods. We will discuss this in more detail after we develop a new type to implement the concept of a node.

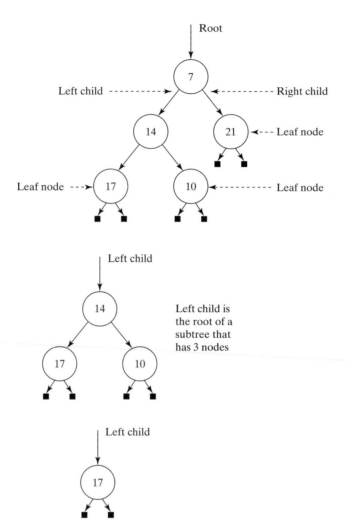

Figure 10.4 Binary tree with 5 nodes.

The `Node class`   Since there is no built in type to represent a node, we will define a new type to implement the concept of a node. A node in a binary tree is a type defined as a data value, a left child, and a right child. These three attributes are mutable so we will provide a `public` interface that includes three accessor methods and three mutator methods. A `class` diagram for a `Node class` is provided in Figure 10.6.

The `class` diagram in Figure 10.6 specifies an integer type for the data value of a `Node`. Note that the operations performed on a binary tree are independent of the type of the data value stored in each node. Thus, `Node` is a good candidate for a `class template`, where the type of the data value is the parameterized type. A `class template` for a generic node type will be developed after implementing and testing the data specific `Node class`.

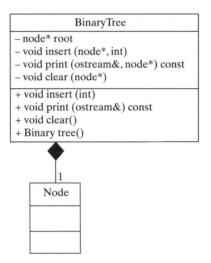

Figure 10.5 UML `BinaryTree` class diagram.

The implementation of the `Node` `class` described in Figure 10.6 is provided below. Notice the use of the preprocessor directives #ifndef, #define and #endif. These directives should be used in all header files to prevent the header file from being included more than once. If, for example, the header file `Node.h` is included in more than one file during compilation, the compiler will generate an error message similar to the one shown below.

```
error: redefinition of 'class Node'
```

This error is generated because the compiler is attempting to define the `Node` `class` for a second time. The preprocessor directive #ifndef is read "if not defined" and is followed by an identifier that is chosen, by convention, to be all uppercase letters and to reflect the name of the header file. The first time the header file is included, the preprocessor directive #ifndef returns `true` because the uppercase identifier has not yet been defined. Because

#ifndef returns true, everything between #ifndef and #endif is processed, including the preprocessor directive #define NODE_H, which defines the identifier NODE_H. The next time the header file is included, the directive #ifndef NODE_H returns false; thus everything between #ifndef and #endif is ignored and a multiple include of the Node class is avoided.

```cpp
/*-----------------------------------------------------------*/
/* class declaration for node:                            */
/* filename node.h                                        */

#ifndef NODE_H
#define NODE_H
class Node
{
    //Private attributes
   private:
        int data;
        Node *left;
        Node *right;

    //Public interface.
    public:
        Node();  //Default constructor
        Node(int); //Parameterized constructor

        //Accessors
        Node* getLeft() const;
        Node* getRight() const;
        int getData() const;

        //Mutators
        void setLeft(Node*);
        void setRight(Node*);
        void setData(int v);

};
#endif
/*-----------------------------------------------------------*/
/*-----------------------------------------------------------*/
/* Class implementation for node                          */
/* filename: node.cpp                                     */

#include "node.h" //Required for Node.
using namespace std;

//Constructors.
Node::Node() : data(0),left(0),right(0)
{
}
```

```
Node::Node(int v):data(v), left(0), right(0)
{
}
//Accessors
Node* Node::getLeft() const
{
  return left;
}
Node* Node::getRight() const
{
  return right;
}
int Node::getData() const
{
  return data;
}

//Mutators
void Node::setLeft(Node* l)
{
  left=l;
}
void Node::setRight(Node* r)
{
  right=r;
}
void Node::setData(int v)
{
  data=v;
}
/*---------------------------------------------------*/
```

To test the Node class, we will write a driver program that calls each of the methods at least once and prints the state of the attributes after each method is called.

```
/*-----------------------------------------------------------------*/
/* Program chapter10_6                                             */
/* This program tests the node class                              */
/* filename: nodeTest.cpp                                         */

#include<iostream> //Required for cout.
#include "node.h" //Required for Node.
using namespace std;

int main(){

  Node n1,n3; //Test default constructor.
  Node n2(4); //Test parameterized constructor.

  //Test accessor methods.
  cout << "Value of n1 after default construction: "
       << endl << n1.getData() << "," << n1.getLeft() << ","
       << n1.getRight() << endl;
```

```
    cout << "Value of n2 after parameterized construction: "
         << endl << n2.getData() << "," << n2.getLeft() << ","
         << n2.getRight() << endl;

    //Test mutator methods.
    n1.setData(13);
    n1.setLeft(&n2);
    n1.setRight(&n3);
    cout << "Value of n1 after modification: " << endl
         << n1.getData() << "," << n1.getLeft() << ","
         << n1.getRight() << endl;
    cout << "Value of n2 after modification: " << endl
         << n2.getData() << "," << n2.getLeft() << ","
         << n2.getRight() << endl;
    cout << "Value of n3 after modification: " << endl
         << n3.getData() << "," << n3.getLeft() << ","
         << n3.getRight() << endl;
    return 0;
}
/*----------------------------------------------------------------*/
```

A sample run of our test program generated the following output:

```
Value of n1 after default construction:
0,0,0
Value of n2 after parameterized construction:
4,0,0
Value of n1 after modification:
13,0xbffffaf0,0xbffffae4
Value of n2 after modification:
4,0,0
Value of n3 after modification:
0,0,0
```

Practice!

Use the `Node class` developed in this section to answer the following questions. Consider the program given below:

```
#include<iostream>
#include "node.h"
using namespace std;

int main()
{
    Node n1, n2(5);
    cout << n1.getRight() << endl; //Line 1
```

```
cout << n2.getLeft() << endl; //Line 2
cout << n2.getData() << endl; //Line 3
n1.setLeft(&n2);
cout << n1.getLeft() << ',' << n1.getRight()
        << ',' << n1.getData() << endl; //Line 4
return 0;
}
```

1. Show the output generated by Line 1.

2. Show the output generated by Line 2.

3. Show the output generated by Line 3.

4. Show the output generated by Line 4.

Recursive Member Functions   To continue the development of our `BinaryTree` `class` as diagramed in Figure 10.5, we must consider how we want to arrange the nodes in our tree and how we will traverse our binary tree. A binary tree may be ordered or unordered. An unordered binary tree assumes that there is no order imposed on the data values of the nodes that define the tree. An ordered binary tree imposes an ordering on the nodes of the tree.

binary search tree

A **binary search tree** is an example of an ordered binary tree. A binary search tree is defined as a binary tree where:

1. each node has a value,

2. the left subtree of a node contains only nodes with values less than the node's value.

3. the right subtree of a node contains only nodes with values greater than or equal to the node's value.

A binary search tree with six nodes is displayed in Figure 10.7.

Binary search trees are popular data structures for storing large amounts of ordered data because of the speed with which a binary search tree can be traversed and modified. Notice in the diagram in Figure 10.7 that there is a unique path from the root of the tree to every other node in the tree. Notice also that each right child of a node and each left child of a node is the root of a smaller subtree. These two features allow for the development of efficient recursive algorithms for **tree traversal**.

tree traversal

Traversing a tree refers to the process of visiting each node in a tree structure, exactly once, in a systematic way. Traversal algorithms are classified by the order in which the nodes are visited. For example, if we want the `print()` method to print the ordered data stored in the binary search tree represented in Figure 10.7, we would perform an **in order** traversal of the tree, printing the value of a node when it is visited. The recursive algorithm for an in order traversal of a tree is given below:

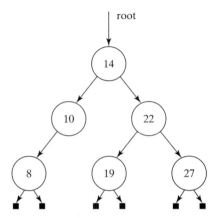

Figure 10.7 Binary search tree with 6 nodes.

```
inOrder traverse:

if(root == null)
   return
inOrder traverse left child
visit node
inOrder traverse right child
```

This algorithm begins at the root of a binary tree and calls itself recursively on the left child of each successive node until a null value is encountered. When a node with a null left child is eventually found, the node is "visited", and the algorithm calls itself recursively on the right child of this node. The condition root == null is the terminating condition, and each recursive call reduces the problem to the traversal of a smaller subtree. Applying an in order traversal of the tree in Figure 10.7, and printing each nodes as it was visited would result in the following output: 8 10 14 19 22 27.

The algorithm for inserting a new node in the correct position to maintain the ordering of a binary search tree begins at the root of the tree. If the tree is empty, the new node is inserted as the first node in the tree. If the tree is not empty, the value of the new node is compared to the value of the first node. If the value of the new node is less than the root node, the algorithm calls itself on the left child, else the algorithm calls itself on the right child. The recursive algorithm is described below:

```
insert( node* root, int value):

  if(root == null)
     root = new node(value)
     return
  else
     if( value < root->value)
       insert(root->left child,value)
     else
       insert(root->right child,value)
```

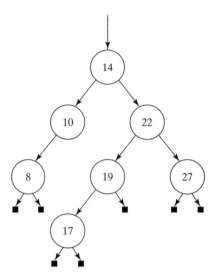

Figure 10.8 Binary search tree after insertion of a new node.

If the value 17 was inserted into the binary search tree in Figure 10.7, the resulting tree would look like the tree in Figure 10.8.

The algorithm for clearing a tree is described next.

```
clear(node* root):

if(root == null)
  return
else
  clear(root->left)
  clear(root->right)
  delete root
```

We can now complete the definition of the BinaryTree class as described in Figure 10.5.

```
/*------------------------------------------------------*/
/* Binary tree declaration                              */
/* filename: binaryTree.h                               */

#include "node.h" //Required for node.
#include <iostream> //Required for ostream.
using namespace std;

class BinaryTree {
public:
  //Default constructor.
  BinaryTree();

  //public, non recursive print and insert
  void print(ostream& out) const;
  void insert(int value);
  void clear();
```

```
private:
  //private recursive overloaded print and insert
  void print(ostream& out, node* rt) const;
  void insert(node* rt, int value);
  void clear(node* rt);

  //private attribute
  Node* root;
};
/*--------------------------------------------------*/
```

Notice in the declaration of the BinaryTree class that the methods `print()`, `insert()`, and `clear()` are overloaded. The `public` versions of these methods are not recursive. The `private` versions of these methods are recursive, and each has a formal parameter of type `Node*`.

The `public` versions of these methods must be called by a `BinaryTree` object, thus the root of the tree is provided by the calling object. The `private` versions of these methods calls themselves recursively, on the right and left subtree of the calling object, to traverse the tree. Thus the value of the formal parameter, `rt`, is different for each subsequent call and must be passed as an argument to support the recursive nature of these methods. The definition of a minimal `BinaryTree class` is given below:

```
/*------------------------------------------------------------------*/
/* Binary tree implementation                                       */
/* filename: binaryTree.cpp                                         */

#include "bTree.h" //Required for BinaryTree.
#include <iostream> //Required for ostream.
using namespace std;

//Constructor
  BinaryTree::BinaryTree():root(0)
  {
  }

//print: Public method
  void BinaryTree::print(ostream& os) const
  {
    if(root == NULL)
    {
     cout << "tree is empty ";
     return;
    }
    else
      print(os, root); //call private print()
  }

//print: private, recursive method
  void BinaryTree::print(ostream& os, node* theRoot) const
  {
   if(theRoot == NULL)
     return;
```

```
        else
        {
          print(os, theRoot->getLeft());
          os << theRoot->getData() << ' ';
          print(os,theRoot->getRight());
        }
      }
//insert: public method
  void BinaryTree::insert(int value)
  {
    if(root == NULL)
      root = new node(value);
    else
      insert(root,value); //call private insert
  }
//insert: private method
void BinaryTree::insert(node* root, int val){
    if(val < root->getData())
    {
      //Traverse the left subtree
      if(root->getLeft() == NULL)
      {
          //insert new node here.
          root->setLeft(new node(val));
      }
      else
      {
          //recursive call to traverse left subtree
          insert(root->getLeft(),val);
      }
    }
    else
    {
      //Traverse the right subtree
      if(root->getRight() == NULL)
      {
        //insert new node here
        root->setRight(new node(val));
      }
      else
      {
        //recursive call to traverse right subtree
        insert(root->getRight(),val);
      }
    }
  }//end insert
//clear: Public method
  void BinaryTree::clear()
  {
    if(root == NULL)
      return;
```

```
        else
        {
          clear(root); //call private clear()
          root = 0; //tree is empty
        }
    }//end clear

//clear: private, recursive method
    void BinaryTree::clear(node* theRoot)
    {
      if(theRoot == NULL)
        return;
      else
      {
        clear(theRoot->getLeft());
        clear(theRoot->getRight());
        delete theRoot;
      }
    }//end clear

/*-------------------------------------------------------------------*/
```

The following program tests the `BinaryTree` class.

```
/*-------------------------------------------------------------------*/
/* filename: testBTree                                             */

#include<iostream> //Required for cout.
#include "BinaryTree.h" //Required for BinaryTree.
using namespace std;

int main(){
  BinaryTree bt;        //Test default constructor
  bt.insert(2);         //Test insert on empty tree.
  bt.insert(10);        //Test insert to right subtree.
  bt.insert(-2);        //Test insert to left subtree.
  bt.print(cout);       //Test print method.
  bt.clear();           //Test clear method.
  bt.print(cout);
  return 0;
}
```

The output from a sample run of our test program is shown below:

```
-2 2 10
tree is empty
```

Now that a working version of a BinaryTree has been written and tested, we will write a class template to represent a generic binary tree, and test it against the working version.

10.5 Class Templates

The declaration of a `class template` must begin with an expression of the form:

```
template < typename identifier >
```

as illustrated in the following declaration of a class template to represent a node on a binary tree:

```
/*-------------------------------------------------------------*/
/* class declaration for node template:                        */
/* filename nodeTemplate.h                                     */

#ifndef TNODE_H
#define TNODE_H
template<typename T>
class Node
{
    //Private attributes
    private:
        T data;
        Node *left;
        Node *right;

    //Public interface.
    public:
        Node();  //Default constructor
        Node(T); //Parameterized constructor

        //Accessors
        Node* getLeft() const;
        Node* getRight() const;
        T getData() const;

        //Mutators
        void setLeft(Node*);
        void setRight(Node*);
        void setData(T v);
};
#endif
/*-------------------------------------------------------------*/
```

Notice that the identifier T replaces int in the class template declaration. The implementation of this `class template` follows.

```
/*-------------------------------------------------------------*/
/* Class implementation for Node template                      */
/* filename: nodeTemplate.cpp                                  */

#include "nodeTemplate.h" //Required for Node.
using namespace std;
```

```
//Constructors.
template<typename T>
Node<T>::Node() : data(0),left(0),right(0)
{
}
template<typename T>
Node<T>::Node(T v):data(v), left(0), right(0)
{
}
//Accessors
template<typename T>
node<T>* Node<T>::getLeft() const
{
  return left;
}
template<typename T>
Node<T>* Node<T>::getRight() const
{
  return right;
}
template<typename T>
T Node<T>::getData() const
{
  return data;
}

//Mutators
template<typename T>
void Node<T>::setLeft(Node<T>* l)
{
  left=l;
}
template<typename T>
void Node<T>::setRight(Node<T>* r)
{
  right=r;
}
template<typename T>
void Node<T>::setData(T v)
{
  data=v;
}
/*-------------------------------------------------------------*/
```

Notice that the class implementation requires that each method be defined as a method `template`.

The `class template` definition for `BinaryTree` follows:

```
/*-------------------------------------------------------------*/
/* Binary tree declaration                                     */
/* filename: binaryTreeTemplate.h                              */
```

```
#include "nodeTemplate.h" //Required for node.
#include "nodeTemplate.cpp" //Required for node implementation.
#include <iostream> //Required for ostream.
using namespace std;

template<typename T>
class BinaryTree {
public:
  //Default constructor.
  BinaryTree();

  //public, non recursive print and insert
  void print(ostream& out) const;
  void insert(T value);
  void clear();

private:
  //private recursive overloaded print and insert
  void print(ostream& out, Node<T>* rt) const;
  void insert(Node<T>* rt, T value);
  void clear(Node<T>* rt);

  //private attribute
  Node<T>* root;
};
/*------------------------------------------------------------------------*/
/*------------------------------------------------------------------------*/
/* Binary tree implementation                                             */
/* filename: binaryTreeTemplate.cpp                                       */

#include "binaryTreeTemplate.h" //Required for BinaryTree.
#include <iostream> //Required for ostream.
using namespace std;

//Constructor
  template<typename T>
  BinaryTree<T>::BinaryTree():root(0)
  {
  }

//clear: Public method
  template<typename T>
  void BinaryTree<T>::clear()
  {
    if(root == NULL)
    {
     return;
    }
    else
    {
```

```
      clear(root); //call private clear()
      root = 0; //tree is empty
    }
  }//end clear

//clear: private, recursive method
  template<typename T>
  void BinaryTree<T>::clear(Node<T>* theRoot)
  {
   if(theRoot == NULL)
     return;
   else
   {
     clear(theRoot->getLeft());
     clear(theRoot->getRight());
     delete theRoot;
   }
  }//end clear

//print: Public method
  template<typename T>
  void BinaryTree<T>::print(ostream& os) const
  {
     if(root == NULL)
     {
      cout << "tree is empty ";
      return;
     }
     else
      print(os, root); //call private print()
  }//end print

//print: private, recursive method
  template<typename T>
  void BinaryTree<T>::print(ostream& os, Node<T>* theRoot) const
  {
   if(theRoot == NULL)
     return;
   else
   {
     print(os, theRoot->getLeft());
     os << theRoot->getData() << ' ';
     print(os,theRoot->getRight());
   }
  }//end print

//insert: public method
  template<typename T>
  void BinaryTree<T>::insert(T value)
  {
    if(root == NULL)
```

```
          root = new node<T>(value);
        else
          insert(root,value); //call private insert
    }//end insert

//insert: private method
  template<typename T>
void BinaryTree<T>::insert(Node<T>* root, T val){
    if(val < root->getData())
    {
      //Traverse the left subtree
      if(root->getLeft() == NULL)
      {
          //insert new node here.
          root->setLeft(new Node<T>(val));
      }
      else
      {
          //recursive call to traverse left subtree
          insert(root->getLeft(),val);
      }
    }
    else
    {
      //Traverse the right subtree
      if(root->getRight() == NULL)
      {
        //insert new node here
        root->setRight(new Node<T>(val));
      }
      else
      {
        //recursive call to traverse right subtree
        insert(root->getRight(),val);
        insert(root->getRight(),val);
      }
    }
  }//end insert
/*------------------------------------------------------------------*/
```

Generic programming through the use of programmer defined `class templates` is a powerful feature of the C++ programming language, but the required syntax can be a bit cumbersome. A `class template` should always be developed from a working version of a specific `class` implementation.

The following program tests our class templates:

```
/*------------------------------------------------------------------*/
/* filename: testBTree                                             */

#include<iostream> //Required for cout.
#include "BinaryTreeTemplate.cpp" //Required for BinaryTree.
using namespace std;
```

```
int main(){
  BinaryTree<int> bt;    //Test default constructor
  bt.insert(2);          //Test insert on empty tree.
  bt.insert(10);         //Test insert to right subtree.
  bt.insert(-2);         //Test insert to left subtree.
  bt.print(cout);        //Test print method.
  bt.clear();            // Test clear method.
  bt.print(cout);
  return 0;
}
```

A sample run of the test program produced the following output:

```
-2 2 10
tree is empty
```

The output matches the output of the test of the specific definition.

Modify!

1. Add a `public` method named `printPreOrder(ostream&)` and a `private` recursive method named `printPreOrder(ostream&, Node*)` that will perform a preOrder print of a tree. The recursive preOrder algorithm is:

   ```
   preOrder traverse:

   if(root == null)
      return
   visit node
   preOrder traverse left child
   preOrder traverse right child
   ```

   A preOrder print of the tree in Figure 10.8 would result in the output : 14 10 8 22 19 17 27.

2. Add a *public* method named printPostOrder(ostream&) and a *private* recursive method named printPostOrder(ostream&, Node*) that will perform a postOrder print of a tree. The recursive postOrder algorithm is:

   ```
   postOrder traverse:

   if(root == null)
      return
   postOrder traverse left child
   postOrder traverse right child
   visit node
   ```

   A postOrder print of the tree in Figure 10.8 would result in the following output: 8 10 17 19 27 22 14.

10.6 Inheritance

polymorphism

In this section, we will introduce features of the C++ programming language that support **polymorphism** through the use of inheritance and `virtual` methods. Polymorphism is the ability to assign many meanings to the same name. This is an important concept in object oriented programming because it allows objects of many different types to be assigned to an object of a single type. Thus, a single type name can have more than one meaning.

base type
derived type

Inheritance provides a mechanism for defining a new `class` type from an existing `class` type. The existing type is referred to as the **base type**, and the new type is referred to as the **derived type**. The derived type is derived from the base type and inherits properties from the base type. An object of a derived type is compatible with an object of its base type, thus an object of a base type can be assigned the value of many different derived types.

In addition to supporting polymorphism, inheritance maximizes the reuse of code through the inheritance of `class` type attributes and methods. To illustrate the implementation of inheritance in C++, we will develop a `Rectangle class` and a `Square class`, as illustrated in Figure 10.9. Notice that UML uses an open arrowhead to indicate inheritance. Inheritance models an is–a relationship only in the direction of the arrowhead. It is important to remember that a square is a rectangle, but a rectangle is not necessarily a square.

The `Rectangle class`

A rectangle can be described by a width, a height, and a point of origin. Thus, the `class` declaration will require three private attributes plus mutator and accessor methods to support these attributes. We also include a print method, a method to move a rectangle to a new location in a plane, and a method to determine the area of a rectangle. The move method is a mutator method because it will modify the point of origin of the calling object. The method to calculate the area of a rectangle should not modify the attributes of the calling object, so we will use the `const` modifier when defining the area method. The `class` declaration for `Rectangle` is given below:

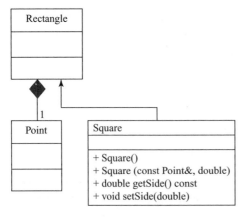

Figure 10.9 UML `class` hierarchy.

```
/*------------------------------------------------------------------*/
/* Class declaration for Rectangle.                                 */
/* filename: rectangle.h                                            */
#include "Point.h" //Required for Point
class Rectangle
{
private:
// Declaration of data members;
double width, height;
Point origin;

public:
// Public interface
// Default constructor
Rectangle();
// Parameterized constructor
Rectangle(double w, double p, double x, double y);
// Accessor methods.
double getWidth() const;
double getHeight() const;
Point getOrigin() const;

//Mutator methods.
void setWidth(double w);
void setHeight(double h);
void setOrigin(Point p);


//Additional operations
void move(double dx, double dy);
double area() const;
void print(ostream&) const;

};
/*------------------------------------------------------------------*/


/*------------------------------------------------------------------*/
/* Class Implementation for Rectangle.                              */
/* filename: Rectangle.cpp                                          */
#include "Rectangle.h" //Required for Rectangle

Rectangle::Rectangle():origin(0,0)
{
   cout << "Constructing Rectangle() ..." << this << endl;
   width=height=1;
}
Rectangle::Rectangle(double w, double h,
                     double x, double y):origin(x,y)
{
   cout << "Constructing Rectangle(parameter list)..."
        << this <<endl;
```

```
    width=w;
    height=h;
}
void Rectangle::print(ostream& out) const
{
   out << "Width: " << getWidth() << " Height: " << getHeight();
   out << "\nOrigin at: (" << this->getOrigin().getX()
       << "," << this->getOrigin().getY() << ")";
}
double Rectangle::getWidth() const
{
   return width;
}
double Rectangle::getHeight() const
{
   return height;
}
Point Rectangle::getOrigin() const
{
   return origin;
}
double Rectangle::area() const
{
   return width*height;
}
void Rectangle::setWidth(double w)
{
   width = w;
}
void Rectangle::setHeight(double h)
{
   height = h;
}
void Rectangle::setOrigin(Point p)
{
   origin = p;
}
void Rectangle::move(double dx, double dy)
{
   origin.setX( origin.getX() + dx);
   origin.setY( origin.getY() + dy);
}
/*-------------------------------------------------------------------*/
```

Notice the syntax used in the definition of the constructors of the Rectangle class. Recall that a constructor is responsible for the initialization of the data members. If a data member is a class object, as when using class composition, it is more efficient to initialize the class attribute in an initialization list rather than assign a value to the attribute in the body of the constructor. An initialization list requires a colon to separate the method header from the initialization list. The initialization of the attribute origin, in both constructors, will result in a call to the parameterized constructor of the Point class. The use of initialization lists in the Rectangle class is not required, but it does improve efficiency. An initialization list is required when a class has non-static const attributes or attributes that are references.

Constructors: A constructor is a method that builds an instance of a class. A constructor has the same name as the class in which it is a member, and no return value.

Syntax:
```
class-name::class-name([parameter list])[:initialization list]
{
    //Statement block
}
```

Examples:
```
Point::Point(double x, double y)
{
    xCoord = x;
    yCoord = y;
}
Rectangle::Rectangle():origin(1.0,1.0)
{
    width = height = 1.0;
}
Valid References:
Point p (1.5, 2.7);
Rectangle r;
```

In the body of the Rectangle constructors, we use the C++ keyword this in the cout statement to print the address of the object that is being constructed. The keyword this identifies a pointer to a class object. The this pointer is always defined within a member function to hold the address of the calling object. The calling object of a constructor is the object that is being constructed. Notice that the this pointer is also used in Rectangle::print() to explicitly call the getOrigin() method.

The Square class

A square is a rectangle with four equal sides. Because a square is a rectangle, the public interface for Rectangle should apply to all Rectangle objects, even those rectangles that happen to be square. If we want to define a new class to implement the concept of a square, then we can use inheritance to inherit the attributes and methods from Rectangle and add new public methods to support the specific concept of a Square. The class declaration for Square is provided below:

```
#ifndef SQUARE_H
#define SQUARE_H
/*--------------------------------------*/
/* Class Declaration for Square         */
/* filename Square.h                    */
```

```
#include "Rectangle.h"
using namespace std;

class Square : public Rectangle
{
  public:
  //Constructors
  Square();
  Square(const Point&, double s);
  double getSide() const;
  void setSide(double);
};
/*-------------------------------*/
#endif
```

Notice the first line of the class declaration:

```
class Square : public Rectangle
```

`: public` specifies that `Square` will inherit all `public` and `protected` members of `Rectangle`. However, a derived `class` does not inherit constructors from its base class, thus new constructors must be defined for each derived class.

The constructors defined for a derived class will always call a constructor of their base `class`. The base `class` default constructor will be called implicitly at the beginning of execution of a derived constructor, or the derived constructor may explicitly call a parameterized constructor of its base `class`. When a derived class constructor makes an explicit call to a parameterized constructor of its base `class` the explicit call must be the first executable statement in the default constructor.

The implementation of `Square` is given below:

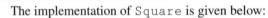

```
/*---------------------------------------------------------------------------*/
/* Class implementation for Square                                           */
/* filename: Square.cpp                                                      */

#include "Square.h"

//Constructors
Square::Square()
{
  //Rectangle constructor called implicitly.
  cout << "Construction Square().. " << this
       << endl;
}

Square::Square(const Point& p, double s):Rectangle(s,s,
                                              p.getX(),
                                              p.getY())
{
  //Parameterized constructor explicitly called in parameter list.
  cout << "Constructing Square( Point, double).. " << this
       << endl;
}
```

```
double Square::getSide() const
{
   return getWidth();
}
void Square::setSide(double s)
{
   setWidth(s);
   setHeight(s);
}
/*----------------------------------------------------------------*/
```

We will look first at the default constructor of `Square`. Since the `Square class` has no additional attributes to initialize, a call to the default constructor of the `Rectangle` class is all that is needed. The call to the default constructor is done implicitly, thus the only statement in the block that defines the default constructor for `Square` is a print statement to trace the construction of objects at run time. The print statement outputs the value of `this`. `this` is a keyword in C++ and it is defined to hold the address of the calling object. Thus, the print statement will print the address of the object being constructed. A similar print statement has been added to the default constructor of the `Rectangle class` for illustration.

The parameterized constructor for `Square` explicitly calls the parameterized constructor of the `Rectangle` class in the initialization list. We have added a print statement to the parameterized constructor in both the `Square  class` and the `Rectangle class` to trace the construction of objects.

The methods `getSide()` and `setSide()` use the `public` interface of the `Rect-angle` class to access the `private` attributes of `Rectangle`. We could have allowed `Square` to inherit the attributes of `Rectangle` by making these attributes `protected` instead of `private`, but that would be a poor design decision. If a derived `class` references the attributes of its base `class` by name, the derived `class` becomes dependent on the implementation of its base `class`. *A derived class should use the public interface of its base* *class to avoid being highly dependent on the implementation of its base class.*

A program to test the `Square class` is given below:

```
/*----------------------------------------------*/
/* Program chapter10_7                          */
/*   filename: testSquare.cpp                   */
/* This program tests the Square class.         */
#include<iostream>
#include "Square.h"
using namespace std;

int main()
{
   //Test constructors.
   Point p1(5,4);
   Square s1, s2(p1, 4);

   /* Test print()                              */
   /* inherited from Rectangle.                 */
   cout << "Square s2 has: " << endl;
```

```
        s2.print(cout);
        cout << endl;

        //Test getSide().
        cout << "Lenth of side of s2 is "
             << s2.getSide() << endl;

        //Test area method from Rectangle
        cout << "Area of s2 is "
             << s2.area() << endl;

         cout << "**********************\n";
        //Test setSide()
        s1.setSide(3.2);

        //Test print()
        cout << "Square s1 has: " << endl
        s1.print(cout);
        cout <<  endl;
        return 0;
}
/*---------------------------------------*/
```

The output from a sample run of program `chapter10_7` is shown below:

```
Constructing Rectangle() ...0xbffffb68
Construction Square().. 0xbffffb68
Constructing Rectangle(parameter list)...0xbffffb88
Constructing Square( Point, double).. 0xbffffb88
Square s2 has:
Width: 4 Height: 4
Origin at: (5,4)
Length of side of s2 is 4
Area of s2 is 16
**********************
Square s1 has:
Width: 3.2 Height: 3.2
Origin at: (0,0)
```

The output from Program `chapter10_7` traces the construction of Square $s1$ and $s2$. $s1$ is defined by the default constructor and has an address of `0xbffffb68`. $s2$ is defined by the parameterized constructor and has an address of `0xbffffb88`. We see from the output that a `Rectangle` is constructed before a `Square` is constructed. This is understandable since a `Square` is derived from a `Rectangle`.

The `Cube class`

A cube is a three-dimensional representation of a square. This relationship suggests that a new type to implement the concept of a cube can be derived from `Square`. A method to

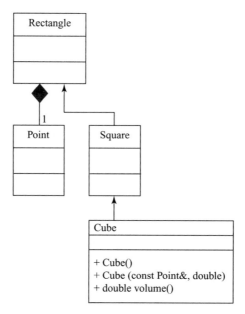

Figure 10.10 UML diagram for cube.

calculate the volume of a cube will be added to the derived class, and we will overload the << to print the value of a cube instead of a rectangle. A class diagram of `Cube` is provided in Figure10.10.

     The definition of `Cube` is given below:

```
#ifndef CUBE_H
#define CUBE_H
/*--------------------------------------------------------*/
/* Class declaration for Cube                             */
/* filename: Cube.h                                       */

#include "Square.h"//Required for Square
#include "Point.h" //Required for Point
#include <iostream> //Required for ostream

class Cube : public Square
{
   public:
   Cube();
   Cube(const Point& p, double);
   double volume();
   void print(ostream&) const;
};
#endif
/*--------------------------------------------------------*/
/* Class implmentation for Cube                           */
/* filename: cube.cpp                                     */
```

```cpp
#include "Cube.h" //Required for Cube
#include <cmath> //Required for pow()

    Cube::Cube():Square()
    {
      cout << "Constructing Cube()..."
           << this << endl;
    }
    Cube::Cube(const Point& p, double s):Square(p,s)
    {
      cout << "Constructing Cube(Point, double)..."
           << this << endl;
    }
    double Cube::volume()
    {
      return pow(getSide(), 3);
    }

    void Cube::print(ostream& out) const
    {
      Rectangle r;
      r = *this;  //A cube is a rectangle.

      //Print the depth
      out << "Depth: " << this.getSide() << " ";

      //Call Rectangle << to finish the job.
      Rectangle::print(out);
    }
/*----------------------------------------------------------*/
```

A program to test the Cube class is provided next.

```cpp
/*----------------------------------------------------------*/
/* Program chapter10_8                                      */
/* filename: testCube.cpp                                   */
/* This program tests the Cube class                        */

#include<iostream>//Required for cout
#include "Point.h"//Required for Point
#include "Cube.h"//Required for Cube
using namespace std;

int main()
{
  Point p1(4,2);

  //Test constructors.
  Cube c1, c2(p1, 3);
```

```
//Test << operator
cout << "c1: ";
c1.print(cout);
cout << endl;
cout << "c2: " ;
c2.print(cout);
cout << endl;

//Test volume.
cout << "Volume of a c2 is " << c2.volume()
     << endl;
return 0;
}
/*-------------------------------------------------------------*/
```

Program `chapter10_8` generated the following output on a sample run:

```
Constructing Rectangle() ...0xbffffb68
Construction Square().. 0xbffffb68
Constructing Cube()...0xbffffb68
Constructing Rectangle(parameter list)...0xbffffb88
Constructing Square( Point, double).. 0xbffffb88
Constructing Cube(Point, double)...0xbffffb88
c1: Depth: 1 Width: 1 Height: 1
Origin at: (0,0)
c2: Depth: 3 Width: 3 Height: 3
Origin at: (4,2)
Volume of a c2 is 27
```

Again we see the order in which constructors are called when building objects of derived types.

10.7 virtual **Methods**

All methods defined in Rectangle, Square, and Cube classes are, by default, non-virtual methods. When a non-virtual method is called, the method executed is the method defined by the `static class` type of the calling object. Consider the following example:

```
...
Point p1(2,1);
Cube c1(p1,4);
Rectangle r1(1, 3, 5,4.5);
r1 = c1;
r1.print(cout);
...
```

In the above example, r1 is assigned the value of c1. This is valid since a Cube is a Rectangle. However, when r1 calls the print method, it calls the print method defined in Rectangle, not Cube, because the `static class` type of r1 is Rectangle. The output from the above code segment would be as follows:

```
Constructing Rectangle(parameter list)...0xbffffb68
Constructing Square( Point, double).. 0xbffffb68
Constructing Cube(Point, double)...0xbffffb68
Constructing Rectangle(parameter list)...0xbffffb88
Width: 4 Height: 4
Origin at: (2,1)
```

dynamic binding If a method is defined to be `virtual`, and pointers or references to objects are used instead of statically defined objects, then C++ supports **dynamic binding**. Dynamic binding refers to the binding of an object to a specific type at run time. Consider the following example that uses pointers to objects:

```
...
//Define an array of pointers to Rectangles
Rectangle* rPtrs[4];

//Define 2 Cubes and 2 Squares.
Point p1(2,1), p2;
Cube c1(p1,4);
Cube c2(p1,5);
Square s1, s2(p2,5);

rPtrs[0] = &c1;
rPtrs[1] = &c2;
rPtrs[2] = &s1;
rPtrs[3] = &s2;

for(int i=0; i<4; ++i)
{
    rPtrs[i]->print(cout);
    cout << endl;
}
...
```

The array `rPtrs` holds pointers to `Rectangles`, but the pointers are referencing Cubes and Squares. Since the `print` method defined in `Rectangle` is non-virtual, the `print` method defined in the `Rectangle class` will be called four times, as illustrated in the output generated from the above code segment:

```
Constructing Rectangle(parameter list)...0xbffffb20
Constructing Square( Point, double).. 0xbffffb20
Constructing Cube(Point, double)...0xbffffb20
Constructing Rectangle(parameter list)...0xbffffb40
Constructing Square( Point, double).. 0xbffffb40
Constructing Cube(Point, double)...0xbffffb40
Constructing Rectangle() ...0xbffffb60
Constructing Square().. 0xbffffb60
Constructing Rectangle(parameter list)...0xbffffb80
Constructing Square( Point, double).. 0xbffffb80
Width: 4 Height: 4
Origin at: (2,1)
Width: 5 Height: 5
```

```
Origin at: (2,1)
Width: 1 Height: 1
Origin at: (0,0)
Width: 5 Height: 5
Origin at: (0,0)
```

When the keyword virtual is applied to the print method prototype, as in:

```
virtual void print(ostream&) const;
```

the above code segment generates the following output:

```
Constructing Rectangle(parameter list)...0xbffffb10
Constructing Square( Point, double).. 0xbffffb10
Constructing Cube(Point, double)...0xbffffb10
Constructing Rectangle(parameter list)...0xbffffb34
Constructing Square( Point, double).. 0xbffffb34
Constructing Cube(Point, double)...0xbffffb34
Constructing Rectangle() ...0xbffffb58
Constructing Square().. 0xbffffb58
Constructing Rectangle(parameter list)...0xbffffb7c
Constructing Square( Point, double).. 0xbffffb7c
Depth: 4 Width: 4 Height: 4
Origin at: (2,1)
Depth: 5 Width: 5 Height: 5
Origin at: (2,1)
Width: 1 Height: 1
Origin at: (0,0)
Width: 5 Height: 5
Origin at: (0,0)
```

Notice that cubes and squares are printed using the version of the method that corresponds to the dynamic type of the pointer in the array rPtrs. No change to Square or Cube is required. In C++ dynamic binding is only supported through the use of virtual methods, and pointers or references.

Practice!

Assume that the print() function defined in the Rectangle class is a virtual function. Given the declaration statements:

```
Point p1(1,2), p2;
Cube *cPtr, c1(p1,4);
Square *sptr, s1(p2,5);
Rectangle *rptr, r1(2,2,7,9);
```

show the output generated by the following code segments: Use the Cube class and the Square class defined in this section.

Practice!

Show the output generated by the following code segments: Use the `Cube class` and the `Square class` defined in this section.

```
1. cptr = &c1;
   c1.print(cout);
   cptr->print(cout);

2. r1 = c1;
   r1.print(cout);

3. sptr = &s1;
   r1 = s1;
   rptr = sptr;
   r1.print(cout);
   cout << endl;
   rptr->print(cout);
```

10.8 Problem Solving Applied: Iterated Prisoner's Dilemma

The iterated prisoner's dilemma (IPD) is a popular game from game theory. The traditional form of the prisoner's dilemma game has two players. Each player must choose between one of two possible *moves:* defect or cooperate. The combination of your *move* and your opponent's *move* determines some form of payoff, usually represented as a score.

The name "prisoner's dilemma" is derived from the following situation: Two prisoners are serving time for a minor offense. However, both are suspected of having committed a far more serious crime. The police approach each prisoner, privately, with the same deal. Each is given the choice between

1. implicating the other prisoner (i.e., defect, relative to the other prisoner) and thereby getting paroled

2. not implicating the other prisoner (i.e., cooperate, relative to the other prisoner) and thereby continuing to serve time for the minor offense.

In this example, each suspect has only one move and one payoff. If both cooperate, each continues to serve their remaining time in prison. If both defect, each gets paroled; however, each is then convicted of the more serious crime and must serve a new, longer jail sentence. If one defects and the other cooperates, the defector goes free, and the cooperator spends a lot of time behind bars. What would you do in this situation? What do you hope your fellow prisoner does? How will you behave towards your fellow prisoner in the future if he or she implicates you in the crime? This situation is the basis for interesting research in many areas, including political science, biology, and economics.

In the implementation of the IPD game, you will have repeated interactions with your opponent, rather than just one, thus the name *iterated* prisoner's dilemma. Your first move in the game, cooperate or defect, will be decided with no knowledge of how your opponent will move. However, on all subsequent moves you can decide whether to cooperate or defect based on your opponent's last move. This is when the strategy becomes interesting.

You will be competing with your opponent, and you will also be competing with other players who will be playing against you and your opponents. The goal of the game is to accumulate the maximum number of points in a given number of moves. The payoff table for the prisoner's dilemma is as follows:

IPD Payoff Table

	cooperate	defect
cooperate	3,3	0,5
defect	5,0	1,1

If you look at the table carefully, you will notice that the highest payoff occurs when your opponent cooperates and you defect. However, if both players cooperate, each player will receive a higher payoff than if both had defected.

If the game consisted of only one move, then you could argue that it is rational to defect on the first move to give yourself the best chance of winning the game, since you will not encounter your opponent again. However, since you will encounter your opponent multiple times, and your opponent will know your behavior, you may have a better chance of accumulating points if you attempt to form a cooperative relationship with your opponent. Developing a cooperative strategy, while protecting oneself from defectors, is what makes this game an interesting behavior model, and a challenging programming assignment. The Web is a good source for information on the IPD. Good strategies incorporate AI algorithms that attempt to learn their opponents strategy and optimize their own. One very simple and effective strategy is called "tit for tat." With this strategy, your next move is always your opponents last move. "Tit for Tat" is one of the strategies we will develop.

To implement the iterated prisoner's dilemma game in C++, we will define a player `class` to be used as the base `class`. The `virtual` member functions of the player `class` will define the play of the game. However, the actual moves of the individual players will be defined by classes derived from the player `class`. The derived classes will override the functions defined in the player `class`. The definition of the base `Player` class is

```
/*-----------------------------------------------------------*/
/* The Player class declaration.                             */
/* File Player.h                                             */

#ifndef PLAYER_H
#define PLAYER_H
#include <iostream>
class Player
{
public:
// Constructor
  Player();
// Accessor Function
  virtual int get_score() const;

// Print player's name.
  virtual void print_name();

// Print name of the player's algorithm.
  virtual void print_algorithm();
```

```cpp
// Player's first move.
  virtual bool play();

// Player's subsequent moves.
  virtual bool play(bool opponents_last_play);

// Cumulative score.
  virtual void accumulate(int);
protected:
int score;
};
#endif
/*----------------------------------------------------------*/
/*----------------------------------------------------------*/
/*                                                          */
/* The Player class implementation.                         */
/* This implements the always cooperate strategy.           */
/* File Player.cpp                                          */

#include "Player.h"

// Constructor
  Player::Player() : score(0)
  {
  }

// Accessor function
  int Player::get_score() const
  {
      return score;
  }

// Print player's name.
  void Player::print_name()
  {
   cout << "Base Class Player";
  }

// Print name of the player's algorithm.
  void Player::print_algorithm()
  {
   cout << "Always Cooperate\n";
  }

// Implement player's first move.
  bool Player::play()
  {
   return true;
  }

// Implements player's subsequent moves.
  bool Player::play(bool opponents_last_play)
  {
   return true;
  }
```

```
// Keep a cumulative score.
   void Player::accumulate(int s)
   {
      score+=s;
   }
```

1. PROBLEM STATEMENT

Write a program to implement the iterated prisoner's dilemma for two players. Using the *player* class as a base class, derive a new class that implements the "Tit for Tat" strategy. Play this strategy against the default strategy of the player class.

2. INPUT/OUTPUT DESCRIPTION

The input to this program is the number of iterations in a game. The output is the total score of each player and the winner of the game.

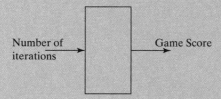

3. HAND EXAMPLE

If both players cooperate at each play and the game runs for 10 iterations, the score for each player will be 30. The program will output the following results:

```
Player1 and Player 2 tied at 30 points each.
```

4. ALGORITHM DEVELOPMENT

We first develop the decomposition outline to break the problem into a sequence of steps:

Decomposition Outline

(1) Define a player object for each player, and setup the game.

(2) Input the number of iterations.

(3) Player 1 makes first move.

(4) Player 2 makes first move.

(5) Determine payoff.

(6) Additional moves and payoffs for the specified number of iteration.

(7) Report the score.

Step 1 requires that each player develop a strategy for playing the game and define a `class`, derived from the base *player* `class`, to implement their strategy. Objects of each player `class` are then defined, and the game reports on the players. We will write a function to set up the game. Steps 2–6 form the heart of the game. We will write a function to perform these steps for the desired number of iterations. We will also write a function to determine the payoff of each move. This function will be used in steps 5 and 6. Step 7 reports the final scores. This will also be done in a function. We will now develop the refinement in pseudo code:

Refinement in Pseudocode

```
main():
    setup(player*, player*)
    play_game(player1* ,player2*)
    report(player1*, player2*)
end main
play_game(player* player1, player* player2):
    input number of iterations.
    p1move = player1->play()
    p2move = player2->play()
    player1->accumulate(payoff(p1move, p2move))
    player2->accumulate(payoff(p2move, p1move))
    for(count =1, count < iterations, count++)
        p1save = p1move
        p1move = player1->play(p2move)
        p2move = player2->play(p1save)
        player1->accumulate(payoff(p1move, p2move))
        player2->accumulate(payoff(p2move, p1move))
end play_game
payoff(p1move, p2move):
    if(p1move)
        if(p2move)
            return 3
        else
            return 0
    else
        if(p2move)
            return 5
        else
            return 1
end payoff
report(player* player1, player* player2):
    if(player1->score > player2->score)
        output player 1 wins
    elseif(player1->score < player2->score)
        output player 2 wins
    else
        output tie
end report
```

Our `main` function calls three functions to implement the game. Each function has formal parameters of type *player**. Since the *player* `class` uses the keyword `virtual` in its class declaration, the dynamic objects referenced by the formal parameters will call the overriding functions defined by the dynamic data type of the object, and the game will function properly for multiple players. We are now ready to convert the pseudocode to C++ code:

```cpp
/*--------------------------------------------*/
/* Program chapter10_9                        */
/* This program implements a version of the Iterated
Prisoner's Dilemma */
#include <iostream>
using namespace std;

#include "player.h"      //base class player
#include "TitforTat.h"   //TitforTat player

//Function prototypes
void setup(player*, player*);
void play_game(player*, player*);
void report(player*, player*);
int payoff(bool move, bool opponent_move);

int main()
{
// Declare objects.
   player p1;
   TitforTat p2;
   player* ptr1 = &p1;
   player* ptr2 = &p2;

// Notify players.
   setup(ptr1, ptr2);
   play_game(ptr1, ptr2);
   cout << endl;
   report(ptr1, ptr2);

   return 0;
}
void setup(player* p1, player* p2)
{
  // Announce players.
  p1->print_name();
  cout << " is playing ";
  p1->print_algorithm();
  cout << endl;
  p2->print_name();
  cout << " is playing ";
  p2->print_algorithm();
  cout << endl;
}
```

```
int payoff(bool move, bool opponent_move)
{
  if (move)
  {
    if (opponent_move)
    {
      return 3; // Both cooperate.
    }
    else
    {
      return 0; // I cooperate, opponent defects.
    }
  }
  else
  {
    if (opponent_move)
    {
      return 5; // I defect, opponent cooperates.
    }
    else
    {
      return 1; // Both defect.
    }
  }
}
/* Play a single game of the iterated
 * prisoner's dilemma between two players.
 */
void play_game(player* p1, player* p2)
{
// Declare objects.
  int max_iterations;
  bool p1_move, p2_move, old_p1_move;
  cout << "Enter the number of iterations for the game: ";
  cin >> max_iterations;

  p1_move = p1->play();  // get the first move.
  p2_move = p2->play();  // get the first move.
  for(int i=1; i<max_iterations; i++)
  {
    old_p1_move = p1_move;
    p1_move = p1->play(p2_move);        // get the next move
    p2_move = p2->play(old_p1_move);  // get the next move

    // Update the scores for this round of play.
    p1->accumulate(payoff(p1_move, p2_move));
    p2->accumulate(payoff(p2_move, p1_move));
  }
}
```

```
void report(player *p1, player *p2)
{
  if (p1->get_score() > p2->get_score())  // Player 1 won.
  {
    p1->print_name();
    cout << " (" << p1->get_score() << ") beat ";
    p2->print_name();
    cout << " (" << p2->get_score() << ").\n";
  }
  else if (p2->get_score() > p1->get_score()) // Player 2 won.
  {
    p2->print_name();
    cout << " (" << p2->get_score() << ") beat ";
    p1->print_name();
    cout << " (" << p1->get_score() << ").\n";
  }
  else // The players tied.
  {
    p1->print_name();
    cout << " and ";
    p2->print_name();
    cout << " tied at " << p1->get_score() << " each.\n";
  }
}
```

The class `TitforTat` is derived from the `player` class. The complete definition of the `TitforTat` class is

```
#ifndef TITFORTAT_H
#define TITFORTAT_H

#include "player.h"
/*-------------------------------------------------------------------*/
/*                                                                   */
/* This implements the Tit for Tat strategy.                         */
/* filename TitforTat.h                                              */
class TitforTat : public Player
{
public:

// Print player's name.
  void print_name();

// Print name of the player's algorithm.
  void print_algorithm();

// Implement player's first move.
  bool play();
```

```
// Implements player's subsequent moves.
  bool play(bool opponents_last_play);

};
#endif

/* This implements the Tit for Tat strategy with initial defect. */
#include <iostream>
using namespace std;

#include "TitforTat.h"

  void TitforTat::print_name()
  {
    cout << "Jeanine ";
  }

// Print name of the player's algorithm.
  void TitforTat::print_algorithm()
  {
      cout << "Tit for Tat";
  }

// Implement player's first move.
  bool TitforTat::play()
  {
    return false;
  }

// Implements player's subsequent moves.
  bool TitforTat::play(bool opponents_last_play)
  {
    return opponents_last_play;
  }
```

5. TESTING

A sample run of the program is as follows, with Jeanine playing the base class player:

```
Base Class Player is playing Always Cooperate.

Jeanine is playing Tit for Tat.

Enter the number of iterations for the game: 10

Jeanine (32) beat Base Class Player (27).
```

The difference in the score is the result of the first move, when player Jeanine defected and Base Class Player cooperated. On the remaining plays, both players cooperated.

Modify!

Define a player class, derived from the base class, to implement an always-defect algorithm.

1. Run program `chapter10_9` playing always defect against always cooperate. What are the results after 25 iterations?

2. Run program `chapter10_9` playing always defect against tit for tat. What are the results after 25 iterations?

3. Remove the keyword `virtual` from the player `class` declaration. Run program `chapter10_9`. What is the output?

SUMMARY

In C++ the `class` mechanism supports object-based programming. Classes are used to define new abstract data types, and overloading of operators allows these new data types to provide definitions for the existing, built in operators. Friend functions and overloading of operators provide for easy, convenient use of these new data types. The use of inheritance and `virtual` functions form the basis for object-oriented design of large programs. The utilization of these advanced topics are illustrated with the development of a `Pixel class` and the development of two new classes derived from the `Rectangle class`. The power of inheritance and `virtual` functions is demonstrated in a program to implement the iterated prisoner's dilemma.

Key Terms

base `class`	overloading operators
binary tree	pixel
derived class	polymorphism
dynamic binding	`protected`
generic programming	public inheritance
image processing	`this` pointer
inheritance	tree traversal
iterated prisoner's dilemma	`virtual` function

C++ Statement Summary

Prototype for member function of overloaded + operator:

return data type operator +(*data type*);

Example:

```
Pixel operator +(Pixel) const;
```

Prototype for `friend` function of overloaded + operator:

`friend` *return data type* operator +(*data type, data type*);

Example:

```
friend Pixel operator +(Pixel, Pixel);
```

Prototype for `friend` function of overloaded ≪ operator:

friend ostream& operator ≪(ostream&, data type);

Example:

```
friend ostream& operator <<(ostream&, Pixel);
```

Prototype for `friend` function of overloaded ≫ operator:

friend istream& operator ≫(istream&, data type&);

Example:

```
friend istream& operator >>(istream&, Pixel&);
```

Class definition for public inheritance

`class` *classname* : `public` *base class name*

Example:

```
class square : public rectangle
{
public:
...
protected:
...
};
```

Specification of virtual functions

Prototype: `virtual` *return data type function name* (*parameter list*);

Example:

```
virtual void print(ostream&);
class Templates expression
template <typename identifier>
```

Notes

1. Use constructors and member functions of the base class to assign values to inherited data members.

Debugging Notes

1. Function to overload ≪ operator must return an ostream reference.
2. Function to overload ≫ operator must return an istream reference.
3. Derived class must include a set of constructor functions.
4. Derived classes do not inherit constructor functions from their base class.

Problems

Exam Practice!

True or False
Indicate whether each of the following is true (T) or false (F).

1. A derived class inherits the constructor functions of the base class. T F
2. Overloaded functions must have unique function signatures. T F
3. The function signature of an overridden function must be unique. T F
4. A `virtual` function is called based on the dynamic data type of the calling object. T F
5. A `friend` function of a class has access to all of the public, protected, and private members of the class. T F

Multiple Choice

6. Assume that the following function prototype is provided in the declaration of a class named Myclass:

   ```
   friend void input(istream&, Myclass&);
   ```

   Which of the following is a valid function header for this prototype?
   a. friend void input(istream& in, Myclass C)
   b. friend void Myclass::input(istream& in, Myclass C)
   c. Myclass::input(istream& in, Myclass C)
   d. void input(istream& in, Myclass)
   e. Myclass::friend input(istream& in)

7. Assume that the following function prototype is provided in the declaration of a class named Myclass:

   ```
   virtual void input(istream&);
   ```

   Which of the following is a valid function header for this prototype?
   a. virtual void input(istream& in)
   b. virtual void Myclass::input(istream& in)
   c. void Myclass::input(istream& in)
   d. void input(istream& in)
   e. void Myclass::virtual input(istream& in)

Programming Problems

8. Add a recursive method to the `BinaryTree class` that returns a count of the number of leaf nodes in the tree.
9. Write a program that uses the `BinaryTree class` to order a set of data read from a data file. Your program should open a data file, read the data and store it in your tree, then print the data using the inOrder print method.
10. Download an image from the web and implement a function to "dither" the image by setting every other pixel to black. Do not allow vertical black lines to appear.
11. Download an image, and implement the function to fade an image.

12. Download an image from the Web and implement a function to perform your own creative modification.

13. Define a rational number `class`. A rational number is a number composed of two integers with division indicated, as in 1/2, 2/3, 4/5. A rational number is defined using two integer objects; numerator and denominator. Overload the ≪ and ≫ operators and arithmetic operators to perform the following operations:

```
a/b + c/d = (a*d + b*c) / (b*d) (addition)
a/b - c/d = (a*d - b*c) / (b*d) (subtraction)
(a/b) * (c/d) = (a*c)/(b*d) (multiplication)
(a/b) / (c/d) = (a*d) /(c*b) (division)
```

14. The game of WAR is a simple card game for two players. Each player receives a deck of 52 cards. Each deck is shuffled and placed face down in front of the player. Play then proceeds as a series of rounds. During each round, both players draw the top card from their deck and place it face up. The player with the highest-ranking card wins both cards. If the two cards have the same rank, there is WAR. In the case of WAR, both players draw six cards from their deck and place them face down. A seventh card is drawn and turned face up. The player with the highest-ranking card wins all the cards that have been played. If the two cards have the same rank, there is WAR. The traditional game ends when one player runs out of cards, but you may wish to simplify the game by ending the game when all 52 cards have been played once. The player with the most cards at the end then wins the game. Write a program to simulate the game of WAR, using card class developed in Chapter 8.

15. Write a simulation for a high-tech vending machine. After an initial state is established for the machine (i.e., the items for sale, their costs, and the initial inventory counts), the user can have an interactive dialog with the simulation. In this dialog, the user can view the current state of the machine, deposit money (cents) into the machine, purchase an item in the machine, get the item and any change due in return, and execute a coin return function to get back all deposited money. For simplicity, assume that the vending machine has exactly nine types of item for sale. An item can be defined using three objects:

    string, represent the name of the item
    The cost (in cents) of the item
    The quantity of the item initially available for sale

    The following data can be used to establish the initial state of the machine:

    Tortilla_Chips 60 3
    Pretzels 60 10
    Popcorn 60 5
    Cheese_Crackers 40 2
    Creme_Cookies 65 1
    Mint_Gum 25 5
    Chocolate_Bar 55 3
    Licorice 85 9
    Fruit_Chews 55 7

Conceptually, the items can be organized as a 3-by-3 matrix as follows:

```
A1   A2   A3
B1   B2   B3
C1   C2   C3
```

Define two classes, an item class and a machine class, to implement this simulation.

16. Modify the program `chapter10_9` to allow more than two players to play IPD. This can be considered an IPD tournament, where every player plays every other player in an IPD game. In this case you may want your strategy to vary from opponent to opponent. The winner is the player who accumulates the most points during the tournament.

17. Modify the IPD tournament program to allow players to meet each other more than once during a tournament. In this game you can improve your strategy by "remembering" your opponent's strategy for the next time you meet.

18. Define an `Image class`. An Image has a two-dimensional array of `Pixels` and member functions to support the smoothing and brightening of an `image`.

APPENDIX A ■ C++ Standard Library

This appendix presents a short discussion on the information defined in a few of the many header files in the Standard C++ Library. These brief discussions are not intended to provide all the details necessary to use the functions, but to provide enough information so that you can determine whether the functions may be of use in a particular application; you can then obtain more details from the Web. A good Web resource is http://www.cplusplus.com/ref/.

⟨cassert⟩

The header file ⟨cassert⟩ provides a definition of the assert function that can be used to provide diagnostic information when testing a program. This system-dependent diagnostic information is stored in the standard error file, which can be accessed after a program is completed.

⟨cctype⟩

The header file ⟨cctype⟩ defines several functions for testing and converting characters. The function prototype statements and corresponding discussions use the following definitions:

digit	one of the characters 0123456789
hexadecimal digit	a digit or one of the characters ABCDEFabcdef
uppercase letter	one of the characters ABCDEFGHIJKLMNOPQRSTUVWXYZ
lowercase letter	one of the characters abcdefghijklmnopqrstuvwxyz
alphabetic character	an uppercase or a lowercase letter
alphanumeric character	a digit or an alphabetic character
punctuation character	one of the characters ! "#%&'();<=>?[\]*+,-./:^
graph character	an alphanumeric character or a punctuation character
print character	a graph character or the space character
motion control character	one of the control characters form feed (FF), new line (NL), carriage return (CR), horizontal tab (HT), vertical tab (VT)
whitespace	the space character or one of the motion control characters
control character	one of the motion control characters or bell (BEL) or backspace (BS)

We now list each function prototype and give a brief definition for the corresponding function:

```
int  isalnum(int c);
```
  returns a nonzero (true) value if and only if the input character is a digit or an uppercase or lowercase letter
```
int  isalpha(int c);
```
  returns a nonzero (true) value if and only if the input character is an uppercase or lowercase letter

```
int  iscntrl(int c);
```
returns a nonzero (true) value if and only if the input character is one of the control characters
```
int  isdigit(int c);
```
returns a nonzero (true) value if and only if the input character is a digit
```
int  isgraph(int c);
```
returns a nonzero (true) value if and only if the input character is a graph character
```
int  islower(int c);
```
returns a nonzero (true) value if and only if the input character is a lowercase letter
```
int  isprint(int c);
```
returns a nonzero (true) value if and only if the input character is a printing character
```
int  ispunct(int c);
```
returns a nonzero (true) value if and only if the input character is a punctuation character
```
int  isspace(int c);
```
returns a nonzero (true) value if and only if the input character is a whitespace character
```
int  isupper(int c);
```
returns a nonzero (true) value if and only if the input character is an uppercase character
```
int  isxdigit(int c);
```
returns a nonzero (true) value if and only if the input character is a hexadecimal character
```
int  tolower(int c);
```
converts an uppercase letter to a lowercase letter
```
int  toupper(int c);
```
converts a lowercase letter to an uppercase letter

`<climits>`

The header file `<climits>` provides several macros that give various limits and characteristics for integer values. These macros and their definitions are as follows:

```
int  CHAR_BIT;
```
number of bits for the smallest nonbit value
```
int  CHAR_MIN;
int  CHAR_MAX;
```
minimum and maximum values for type `char`
```
int  INT_MIN;
int  INT_MAX;
```
minimum and maximum values for type `int`
```
int  LONG_MIN;
int  LONG_MAX;
```
minimum and maximum values for type `long int`

```
int   MB_LEN_MAX;
```
maximum number of bytes in a multibyte character
```
int   SCHAR_MIN;
int   SCHAR_MAX;
```
minimum and maximum values for type `signed char`
```
int   SHRT_MIN;
int   SHRT_MAX;
```
minimum and maximum values for type `short int`
```
int   UCHAR_MAX;
```
maximum values for type `unsigned char`
```
int   UINT_MAX;
```
maximum value for type `unsigned int`
```
int   ULONG_MAX;
```
maximum value for type `unsigned long int`
```
int   USHRT_MAX;
```
maximum value for type `unsigned short int`

\<cmath\>

The header file \<cmath\> defines many useful functions for scientific programming.

```
double   acos(double x);
```
computes the arccosine or inverse cosine of x, where x must be in the range $[-1, 1]$; returns an angle in radians in the range $[0, \pi]$
```
double   asin(double x);
```
computes the arcsine or inverse sine of x, where x must be in the range $[-1, 1]$; returns an angle in radians in the range $[\frac{-\pi}{2}, \frac{\pi}{2}]$
```
double   atan(double x);
```
computes the arctangent or inverse tangent of x; returns an angle in radians in the range $[\frac{-\pi}{2}, \frac{\pi}{2}]$
```
double   atan2(double y, double x);
```
computes the arctangent or inverse tangent of the value $\frac{y}{x}$ returns an angle in radians in the range $[-\pi, \pi]$
```
   int   ceil(double x);
```
rounds x to the nearest integer towards ∞ (infinity)
```
double   cos(double x);
```
computes the cosine of x, where x is in radians
```
double   cosh(double x);
```
computes the hyperbolic cosine of x, which is equal to $\frac{e^x + e^{-x}}{2}$
```
double   exp(double x);
```
computes the value of e^x, where e is the base for natural logarithms, or approximately 2.718282
```
double   fabs(double x);
```
computes the absolute value of x
```
   int   floor(double x);
```
rounds x to the nearest integer towards $-\infty$ (negative infinity)

```
double   log(double x);
```
computes ln x, the natural logarithm of x to the base e; errors occur if $x \leq 0$
```
double   log10(double x);
```
computes $\log_{10}x$, the common logarithm of x to the base 10; errors occur if $x \leq 0$
```
double   pow(double x, double y);
```
computes the value of x to the y power, or x^y; errors occur if $x = 0$ and $y \leq 0$, or if $x < 0$ and y is not an integer
```
double   sin(double x);
```
computes the sine of x, where x is in radians
```
double   sinh(double x);
```
computes the hyperbolic sine of x, which is equal to $\frac{e^x - e^{-x}}{2}$
```
double   sqrt(double x);
```
computes the square root of x where $x \geq 0$
```
double   tan(double x);
```
computes the tangent of x, where x is in radians
```
double   tanh(double x);
```
computes the hyperbolic tangent of x, which is equal to $\frac{\sinh x}{\cosh x}$

`<cstdlib>`

The header file `<cstdlib>` defines types, macros, and functions that did not fit in any of the other header files. The types `div_t` and `ldiv_t` are structures for storing a quotient and a remainder. The macros are the following:

```
NULL
```
an integer value of binary zero
```
EXIT_FAILURE
EXIT_SUCCESS
```
integral expressions used to return unsuccessful or successful termination status, respectively, to the host
```
RAND_MAX
```
an integral expression that is the maximum value returned by the RAND function
```
MB_CUR_MAX
```
a positive integer expression whose value is the maximum number of bytes in a multibyte character

The functions that are most likely to be used in engineering application are as follows, with the function prototype statement and a brief description:

```
    void   abort(void);
```
causes an abnormal program termination of the program
```
     int   abs(int k);
long int   labs(long int k);
```
computes the absolute value of the integer k
```
     int   atexit(void (*func)(void));
```
registers the function pointed to by func to be called without arguments at normal program termination

```
    double  atof(const char *s);
       int  atoi(const char *s);
  long int  atol(const char *s);
    double  strtod(const char *s, char **endptr);
  long int  strtol(const char *s, char **endptr, int base);
  unsigned
  long int  strtoul(const char *s, char **endptr, int base);
```
converts the initial portion of the string pointed to by s to a numerical representation

```
    void*  bsearch(const void *key, const void *base, size_t n,
                      size_t
    size,  int(*compar)(const void *,const void *));
```
searches an array of n objects searching for the value pointed to by key

```
    void*  calloc(size_t n, size_t size);
```
allocates space for an array of n objects, each of size size

```
    div_t  div(int numer, int denom);
   ldiv_t  ldiv(long int numer, long int denom);
```
computes the quotient and remainder of the division of numer by denom

```
     void  exit(int status);
```
causes normal program termination to occur

```
     void  free(void *ptr);
```
deallocates the space pointed to by ptr

```
    void*  malloc(size_t size);
```
allocates space for an object of size size

```
     void  qsort(void *base, size_t nmemb, size_t size,
                    int (*compar)(const void*, const void *));
```
sorts an object of n objects into ascending order

```
      int  rand(void);
```
returns a pseudorandom integer in the range of 0 to RAND_MAX

```
    void*  realloc(void *ptr, size_t size);
```
changes the size of the object pointed to by ptr

```
     void  srand(unsigned int seed);
```
uses the seed to initialize a new sequence of values from the RAND function

<cstring>

The header file <cstring> defines the type size_t, which is an unsigned integer, and the macro NULL, which has the value of binary zero. In addition, the header file defines a number of functions for handling strings.

```
    void*  memchr(const void *s, int c, size_t n);
```
returns a pointer to the first occurrence of c in the initial n characters of the object pointed to by s

```
      int  memcmp(const void *s, const void *t, size_t n);
```
returns an integer greater than, equal to, or less than zero, accordingly, as the string pointed to by s is greater than, equal to, or less than the string pointed to by t

`void*`   `memcpy(void *s, const void *t, size_t n);`
copies n characters from the object pointed to by t into the object pointed to by s

`void*`   `memmove(void *s, const void *t, size_t n);`
copies n characters from the object pointed to by t into the object pointed to by s, using a temporary area

`void*`   `memset(void *s, int c, size_t n);`
copies the value of c into the first n characters of the object pointed to by s

`char*`   `strcat(char *s, const char *t);`
concatenates string pointed to by t to the end of string pointed to by s; returns a pointer to string pointed to by s

`char*`   `strchr(const char *s, int c);`
returns a pointer to the first occurrence of the character c in the string pointed to by s

`int`   `strcmp(const char *s, const char *t);`
compares string s to string t in an element-by-element comparison; returns an integer greater than, equal to, or less than zero, depending on whether the string pointed to by s is greater than, equal to, or less than, respectively, the string pointed to by t

`int`   `strcoll(const char *s, const char *t);`
returns an integer greater than, equal to, or less than zero, depending on whether the string pointed to by s is greater than, equal to, or less than, respectively, the string pointed to by t

`char*`   `strcpy(char *s, const char *t);`
copies string pointed to by t to string pointed to by s; returns a pointer to string pointed to by s

`size_t`   `strcspn(const char *s, const char *t);`
returns the length of the initial segment of the string pointed to by s that consists entirely of characters not in the string pointed to by t

`size_t`   `strlen(const char *s);`
returns the length of the string pointed to by s

`char*`   `strncat(char *s, const char *t, size_t n);`
concatenates at most n characters of string t to string s; returns a pointer to string pointed to by s

`int`   `strncmp(const char *s, const char *t, size_t n);`
compares at most n characters of string s to string t in an element-by-element comparison; returns an integer greater than, equal to, or less than zero, depending on whether the string pointed to by s is greater than, equal to, or less than, respectively, the string pointed to by t

`char*`   `strncpy(char *s, const char *t, size_t n);`
copies at most n characters from string pointed to by t to string pointed to by s; if t has fewer characters than s, then s is padded with null characters; returns a pointer to s

`char*`   `strpbrk(const char *s, const char *t);`
returns a pointer to the first occurrence in string pointed to by s of any character of string pointed to by t

```
        char*   strrchr(const char *s, int c);
```
returns a pointer to the last occurrence of the character c in the string pointed to by s

```
        size_t  strspn(const char *s, const char *t);
```
returns the length of the initial segment of the string pointed to by s that consists entirely of characters in the string pointed to by t

```
        char*   strstr(const char *s, const char *t);
```
returns a pointer to the start of the string pointed to by t within the string pointed to by s

<ctime>

The header file <ctime> defines two macros, four types, and several functions for representing and manipulating calendar time and local time. The types clock_t and time_t are arithmetic types capable of representing times, and the structure tm contains a calendar time broken into seconds (tm_sec), minutes (tm_min), hours (tm_hour), day of the month (tm_mday), months since January (tm_mon), years since 1900 (tm_year), days since Sunday (tm_wday), days since January 1 (tm_yday), and a daylight saving time flag (tm_isdst); the order of the values in the structure is system dependent. The related macros are the following:

```
CLOCKS_PER_SEC
```
number per second of the value returned by the clock function
```
NULL
```
an integer representing binary zero

Function prototypes and brief descriptions of their related computations follow:

```
        char*   asctime(const struct tm *timeptr);
```
returns a pointer to the string containing a converted time

```
        clock_t clock(void);
```
returns the current processor time

```
        char*   ctime(const time_t *timer);
```
returns a pointer to a string containing a converted time

```
        double  difftime(time_t time1, time_t time0);
```
computes the difference between two calendar times

```
        struct  tm* gmtime(const time_t *timer);
```
returns a pointer to a time expressed in Coordinated Universal Time

```
        struct  tm* localtime(const time_t *timer);
```
returns a pointer to a time converted from calendar time

```
        time_t  mktime(struct tm *timeptr);
```
converts the broken-down time to a calendar time value

```
        time_t  time(time_t *timer)
```
returns the current calendar time

```
        size_t  strftime(char *s, size_t maxsize, const char
                        *format, const struct tm *timeptr);
```
converts time into a formatted multibyte character sequence

```
<iostream>
```

The header `<iostream>` contains many functions used for standard input and output. We now list a few of them in their most general form:

```
istream functions:
```

```
      istream& operator >>
```
Input (extraction) operation
```
      int gcount();
```
Returns the number of characters extracted by last input operation
```
      int get(char ch);
```
Extract one character from input stream
```
      getline(c_string var, int max, [char delimiter]);
```
read max-1 characters or until delimiter is found. \n is the default delimiter
```
      ignore();
```
Extract and discard a character from the input stream
```
      char peek();
```
Returns the value of next character on the input stream
Leaves the character on the input stream (does not extract)
```
      putback(ch);
```
Put the last character back on the input stream

```
ostream functions:
```

```
      ostream& operator<<
```
Output (insertion) operator
```
      flush();
```
Flush output buffer
```
      put(ch char);
```
Put char in the output stream

APPENDIX B ■ ASCII Character Codes

The following table contains the 128 ASCII characters and their equivalent integer values and binary values. The characters that correspond to the integers 1 through 31 have special significance to the computer system. For example, the character BEL is represented by the integer 7 and causes the bell to sound on the keyboard.

The order of the characters from low to high is the collating sequence and has several interesting characteristics. Note that the digits are less than uppercase letters and that uppercase letters are less than lowercase letters. Also, note that special characters are not grouped together: Some are before digits, some are after digits, and some are between uppercase and lowercase characters.

Character		Integer Equivalent	Binary Equivalent
NUL	(Binary Zero)	0	0000000
SOH	(Start of Header)	1	0000001
STX	(Start of Text)	2	0000010
ETX	(End of Text)	3	0000011
EOT	(End of Transmission)	4	0000100
ENQ	(Enquiry)	5	0000101
ACK	(Acknowledge)	6	0000110
BEL	(Bell)	7	0000111
BS	(Backspace)	8	0001000
HT	(Horizontal Tab)	9	0001001
LF	(Line Feed or New Line)	10	0001010
VT	(Vertical Tabulation)	11	0001011
FF	(Form Feed)	12	0001100
CR	(Carriage Return)	13	0001101
SO	(Shift Out)	14	0001110
SI	(Shift In)	15	0001111
DLE	(Data Link Escape)	16	0010000
DC1	(Device Control 1)	17	0010001
DC2	(Device Control 2)	18	0010010
DC3	(Device Control 3)	19	0010011
DC4	(Device Control 4-Stop)	20	0010100
NAK	(Negative Acknowledge)	21	0010101
SYN	(Synchronization)	22	0010110
ETB	(End of Text Block)	23	0010111
CAN	(Cancel)	24	0011000
EM	(End of Medium)	25	0011001
SUB	(Substitute)	26	0011010

(continued)

Character		**Integer Equivalent**	**Binary Equivalent**
ESC	(Escape)	27	0011011
FS	(File Separator)	28	0011100
GS	(Group Separator)	29	0011101
RS	(Record Separator)	30	0011110
US	(Unit Separator)	31	0011111
SP	(Space)	32	0100000
!		33	0100001
"		34	0100010
#		35	0100011
$		36	0100100
%		37	0100101
&		38	0100110
'	(Closing Single Quote)	39	0100111
(		40	0101000
)		41	0101001
*		42	0101010
+		43	0101011
,	(Comma)	44	0101100
-	(Hyphen)	45	0101101
.	(Period)	46	0101110
/		47	0101111
0		48	0110000
1		49	0110001
2		50	0110010
3		51	0110011
4		52	0110100
5		53	0110101
6		54	0110110
7		55	0110111
8		56	0111000
9		57	0111001
:		58	0111010
;		59	0111011
<		60	0111100
=		61	0111101
>		62	0111110
?		63	0111111
@		64	1000000
A		65	1000001
B		66	1000010
C		67	1000011
D		68	1000100
E		69	1000101
F		70	1000110

(*continued*)

G		71	1000111
H		72	1001000
I		73	1001001
J		74	1001010
K		75	1001011
L		76	1001100
M		77	1001101
N		78	1001110
O		79	1001111
P		80	1010000
Q		81	1010001
R		82	1010010
S		83	1010011
T		84	1010100
U		85	1010101
V		86	1010110
W		87	1010111
X		88	1011000
Y		89	1011001
Z		90	1011010
[		91	1011011
\		92	1011100
]		93	1011101
^	(Circumflex)	94	1011110
_	(Underscore)	95	1011111
'	(Opening Single Quote)	96	1100000
a		97	1100001
b		98	1100010
c		99	1100011
d		100	1100100
e		101	1100101
f		102	1100110
g		103	1100111
h		104	1101000
i		105	1101001
j		106	1101010
k		107	1101011
l		108	1101100
m		109	1101101
n		110	1101110
o		111	1101111
p		112	1110000
q		113	1110001
r		114	1110010
s		115	1110011

(continued)

Character	**Integer Equivalent**	**Binary Equivalent**
t	116	1110100
u	117	1110101
v	118	1110110
w	119	1110111
x	120	1111000
y	121	1111001
z	122	1111010
{	123	1111011
Ω	124	1111100
}	125	1111101
,	126	1111110
DEL (Delete/Rubout)	127	1111111

APPENDIX C ■ Using MATLAB to Plot Data from ASCII Files

To understand engineering problems and engineering solutions to problems, it is important to be able to visualize the numerical information that is involved. Therefore, the ability to easily obtain simple xy-plots from data files is an important capability in solving engineering problems.

In this appendix, we present a simple C++ program that generates a data file, and we then show how to use MATLAB to obtain a plot of the data. We chose MATLAB (MATrix LABoratory) to generate the plots in this appendix and also in the text chapters because it is an extremely powerful software environment for interactive numeric computations, data analysis, and graphics. An extensive discussion on generating different types of plots and on additional options that can be specified within the plots is included in Chapter 7 of *Engineering Problem Solving with MATLAB*, by D. M. Etter, Prentice Hall, 1993.

In the following example, we use a C++ program to generate an ASCII (American Standard Code for Information Interchange) data file, and we then plot the information using MATLAB. An ASCII data file can also be generated using a word processor, and then the same steps can be used to plot the information using MATLAB. If the data file is generated with a word processor, it is important to select the options for saving the file such that it is saved as a text file instead of as a word processor file.

The program that follows generates a data file containing 100 lines of information. Each line contains the corresponding time and function value from the equation for a damped sine function, namely,

$$f(t) = e^{-t} \sin(2\pi t),$$

where $t = 0.0, 0.1, 0.2, \ldots, 9.9$ seconds.

C++ Program to Generate a Data File

```
/*------------------------------------------------------------*/
/*  Program app_c                                             */
/*                                                            */
/*  This program generates a data file of values             */
/*  from a damped sine function.                              */

#include<iostream>
#include <fstream>
#include <cmath>
using namespace std;
const double PI = 3.141593;
```

```
int main()
{
   /*  Define objects.  */
   double t, f;
   ifstream dsine;

   /*  Generate data file.  */
   dsine.open("dsine.dat");
   for (int k=1; k<=100; k++)
   {
      t = 0.1*(k-1);
      f = exp(-t)*sin(2*PI*t);
      dsine << t << f << endl;
   }

   /*  Close data file and exit program. */
   dsine.close();
   return 0;
}
/*-------------------------------------------------------*/
```

ASCII Data File Generated by the C++ Program

The data file generated by this program is an ASCII file that contains two numbers per line. The first few lines of information and the last line of information are

```
0.0   0.000
0.1   0.532
0.2   0.779
...
9.9   0.000
```

Generating a Plot with MATLAB

To generate a plot of this information with MATLAB, we only need two statements. The first statement loads the file into the MATLAB workarea, and the second statement generates the xy-plot:

```
>>load dsine.dat
>>plot(dsine(:,1),dsine(:,2))
```

These steps generate the plot shown in Figure C.1.

Since it is important to label the information in a plot, we could also add the statements to give the plot a title, to label the axes, and to add a background grid:

```
>>load dsine.dat
>>plot(dsine(:,1),dsine(:,2)),
>>title('Damped Sine Function'),
>>xlabel('Time, s'), ylabel('f(t)'), grid
```

The plot with these labels is shown in Figure C.2.

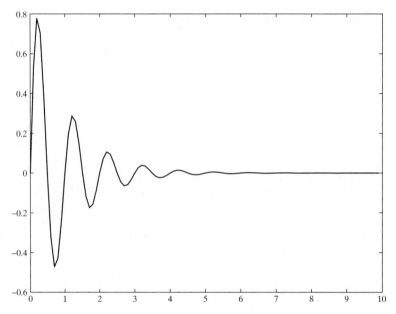

Figure C.1 Plot of a damped sine function.

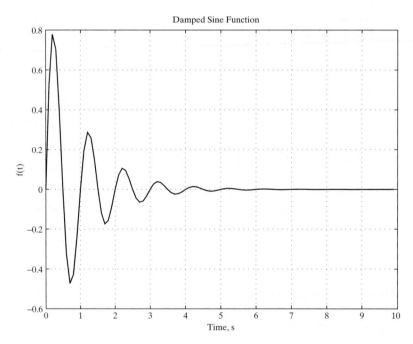

Figure C.2 Enhanced plot of a damped sine function.

APPENDIX D ■ References

[1] "10 Outstanding Achievements, 1964–1989." National Academy of Engineering, Washington, DC, 1989.

[2] Etter, D. M. *Structured FORTRAN 77 for Engineers and Scientists,* 4th ed. Benjamin/Cummings, Redwood City, CA, 1993.

[3] "The Federal High Performance Computing Program." Executive Office of the President, Office of Science and Technology Policy, Washington, DC, September 8, 1989.

[4] Etter, D. M., and J. Bordogna. "Engineering Education for the 21st Century." IEEE International Conference on Acoustics, Speech, and Signal Processing, April 1994.

[5] Fairley, R. *Software Engineering Concepts*. McGraw-Hill, New York, 1985.

[6] Etter, D. M. *Engineering Problem Solving with MATLAB*. Prentice Hall, Englewood Cliffs, NJ, 1993.

[7] Plauger, P. J. *The Standard C Library*. Prentice Hall, Englewood Cliffs, NJ, 1992.

[8] Jones, E. R., and R. L. Childers. *Contemporary College Physics*. Addison-Wesley, Reading, MA, 1990.

[9] Etter, D. M. *FORTRAN 77 with Numerical Methods for Engineers and Scientists*. Benjamin/Cummings, Redwood City, CA, 1992.

[10] Spanier, Jerome and Keith B. Oldham. *An Atlas of Functions*. Hemisphere Publishing Corporation, 1987.

[11] Edwards, Jr., C. H., and D. E. Penney. *Calculus and Analytic Geometry*. 3d ed. Prentice Hall, Englewood Cliffs, NJ, 1990.

[12] Master, G. M. *Introduction to Environmental Engineering and Science*. Prentice Hall, Englewood Cliffs, NJ, 1991.

[13] Gille, J. C., and J. M. Russell, III. "The Limb Infrared Monitor of the Stratosphere; Experiment Description, Performance, and Results," Journal of Geophysical Research, Vol. 89, No. D4, pp. 5125–5140, June 30, 1984.

[14] Roberts, Richard A. *An Introduction to Applied Probability*. Addison-Wesley, Reading, MA, 1992.

[15] Richardson, M. *College Algebra,* 3d ed. Prentice Hall, Englewood Cliffs, NJ, 1966.

[16] Kahaner, D., Cleve Moler, and Stephen Nash. *Numerical Methods and Software*. Prentice Hall, Englewood Cliffs, NJ, 1989.

[17] Rallston Anthony and Edwin D. Reilly, eds. *Encyclopedia of Computer Science,* 3d ed. Van Nostrand Reinhold Publishing Company, New York, NY, 1993.

[18] Kreyszig, E. *Advanced Engineering Mathematics*. John Wiley & Sons, New York, 1979.

[19] Wirth, Niklaus. *Algorithms + Data Structures = Programs*. Prentice Hall, Englewood Cliffs, NJ, 1976.

[20] Stroustrup, Bjarne. *C++ Programming Language*. Addison Wesley, 1997.

[21] Wampler, Bruce E. *The Essence of Object Oriented Programming with Java and UML*. Addison Wesley, 2002.

[22] Kolman, Busby, Ross. *Discrete Mathematical Structures*, Prentice Hall, 2000.

[23] www.wikipedia.com

APPENDIX E ■ PRACTICE! Solutions

Chapter 1

PRACTICE! PAGE 20

1. $921_{10} = 1110011001_2$
2. $8_{10} = 1000_2$
3. $100_{10} = 1100100_2$
4. $100_8 = 64_{10}$
5. $247_8 = 167_{10}$
6. $16_8 = 14_{10}$
7. $100_2 = 4_8$
8. $3716_8 = 011111001110_2$
9. $110100111_2 = 423_{10}$
10. $221_6 = 125_8$

PRACTICE! PAGE 22

1. $921_{10} = 399_{16}$
2. $8_{10} = 8_{16}$
3. $100_{10} = 64_{16}$
4. $1CO_{16} = 448_{10}$
5. $29E_{16} = 670_{10}$
6. $16_6 = 22_{10}$
7. $10010011_2 = 93_{16}$
8. $3A1B_{16} = 0011101000011011_2$
9. $110100111_2 = 423_{10}$
10. $261_8 = B1_{16}$

PRACTICE! PAGE 24

1. 00110001

2. 00000010

3. 10111011

Chapter 2

PRACTICE! PAGE 41

1. valid

2. valid

3. valid

4. valid

5. valid

6. invalid, (special character -)

7. valid

8. invalid, (special character *)

9. valid

10. invalid, (keyword)

11. invalid, (special character #)

12. invalid, (special character $)

13. valid

14. invalid, (keyword)

15. invalid, (special characters (and))

16. valid

17. valid

18. invalid, (special character .)

19. valid

20. valid

21. invalid, (special character /)

PRACTICE! PAGE 42

1. 3.5004×10^1 4 digits

2. 4.2×10^{-4} 1 digit

3. -5.0×10^4 0 digits

4. 3.15723×10^0 5 digits

5. -9.997×10^{-2} 3 digits

6. 1.0000028×10^7 7 digits

7. 0.0000103

8. -105000

9. -3552000

10. 0.000667

11. 0.09

12. -0.022

PRACTICE! PAGE 47

1. const double LightSpeed = 2.99792e08;

2. const double ChargeE = 1.602177e-19;

3. const double N_A = 6.022e23;

4. const double G_mss = 9.8;

5. const double G_ftss = 32;

6. const double EarthMass = 5.98e24;

7. const double MoonRadius = 1.74e6;

8. const char UnitLength = 'm';

9. const char UnitTime = 's';

PRACTICE! PAGE 55

1. 6

2. 4.5

3. 3.1 is computed value, 3 is assigned to integer a

4. 3.0 is computed value

5. p1-> | 0.0 |
        | 0.0 |

6. x-> | 2.0 |

   y-> | 4.3 |

   p1-> | 2.0 |
         | 4.3 |

PRACTICE! PAGE 57

```
const double G_mss = 9.80665;
```

1. `distance = x + v*t + a*t*t;`

2. `tension = (2*m1*m2)/(m1 + m2)*G_mss;`

3. `p2 = p1 + (p*v*(a2*a2 - a1*a1))/(2*a1*a1);`

4. $centripetal = \frac{4\pi^2 r}{T^2}$

5. $potential\ energy = \frac{-GM_E m}{r}$

6. $change = GM_E m(\frac{1}{R_E} - \frac{1}{R_E+h})$

PRACTICE! PAGE 61

1. z $\boxed{8}$ x $\boxed{3}$ y $\boxed{4}$

2. z $\boxed{12}$ x $\boxed{3}$ y $\boxed{4}$

3. x $\boxed{6}$ y $\boxed{4}$ z $\boxed{?}$

4. y $\boxed{0}$ x $\boxed{2}$ z $\boxed{?}$

PRACTICE! PAGE 66

1. Output:
   150 12.368

2. Output:
   15012.368

3. Output:
   150
   12.368

4. Output:
   150
   12

5. Output:
   150,12.4

6. Output:
   150,12.368

7. Output:
   150
   12

8. Output:
   ____12.368
   _____150

PRACTICE! PAGE 78

1. -3

2. -2

3. 0.125

4. 3.16228

5. 25

6. 11

7. -1

8. -32

PRACTICE! PAGE 79

1. velocity = sqrt(pow(v0,2) + 2*a*(x − x0));

2. length = pow(len − pow(v/c,2),1.0/k);

3. center = (38.1972*(pow(r,3) − pow(s,3))*sin(a))/((pow(r,2) − pow(s,2))*a);

4. $Frequency = \frac{1}{\sqrt{2*\pi*\frac{c}{I}}}$

5. $Range = \frac{v_0^2}{g} * \sin(2\theta)$

6. $V = \sqrt{\frac{2gh}{1+\frac{I}{mr^2}}}$

PRACTICE! PAGE 81

1. cothX = cosh(x)/sinh(x);

2. sechX = 1.0/cosh(x);

3. cschX = 1.0/sinh(x);

4. acothX = 0.5*log((1 + 1/x)/(1 − 1/x));

5. acoshX = log(x + sqrt(pow(x,2)−1));

6. acschX = log(1/x + sqrt(1 + pow(x,2))/fabs(x));

Chapter 3

PRACTICE! PAGE 104

1. true

2. true

3. true

4. false

5. true

6. true

7. true

8. false

PRACTICE! PAGE 110

1. ```
if(time > 15.0)
   ++time;
```

2. ```
if(sqrt(poly) < 0.5)
   cout << poly;
```

3. ```
if(abs(volt1 - volt2) > 10.0)
   cout << volt1 << ' ' << volt2;
```

4. ```
if(den < 0.05)
{
   result=0;
}
else
{
   result = num/den;
}
```

5. ```
if(log(x) >= 3)
{
   time=0;
   count--;
}
```

6. ```
if(dist < 50.0 && time > 10.0)
{
   time+=2;
}
else
{
   time+=2.5;
}
```

7. ```
if(dist >= 100.0)
{
   time+=2;
}
else if(dist >=50)
{
   time++;
}
else
{
   time+=0.5;
}
```
```

PRACTICE! PAGE 113

1. 75.92 89.35 111.25 109.92

2. 0.69 1.6 1.71 1.87

3. There are five time values that correspond to 110 degrees, as can be seen from Figure 2.5. These values can be computed to be the following: 1.71 2.84 3.39 4.42 5.33

PRACTICE! PAGE 122

```
switch(rank)
{
  case 1:
  case 2:
   cout << "Lower division" << endl;
   break;
  case 3:
  case 4:
   cout << "Upper division" << endl;
   break;
  case 5:
   cout << "Graduate student" << endl;
   break;
  default:
   cout << "Invalid rank" << endl;
}
```

PRACTICE! PAGE 133

1.

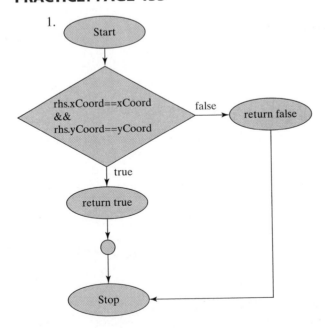

2. Pseudocode:
Set *diffX* to *rhs.xCoord - xCoord*
Set *diffY* to *rhs.yCoord - yCoord*
Set distance to $\sqrt{diffX^2 + diffY^2}$
Return distance

Chapter 4

PRACTICE! PAGE 147

1. 5

2. Infinite Loop

3. -2

4. 3

PRACTICE! PAGE 152

1. 18

2. 18

3. 17

4. 0

5. Infinite loop

6. 15

Chapter 5

PRACTICE! PAGE 208

1. i $\boxed{1}$ j $\boxed{0}$ badbit:0 failbit:1 eofbit:0 goodbit:0

2. x $\boxed{1}$ y $\boxed{0}$ badbit:0 failbit:1 eofbit:0 goodbit:0

3. ch1 $\boxed{1}$ ch2 $\boxed{,}$ badbit:0 failbit:0 eofbit:0 goodbit:1

4. x $\boxed{1}$ ch $\boxed{,}$ y $\boxed{2.3}$ badbit:0 failbit:0 eofbit:0 goodbit:1

Chapter 6

PRACTICE! PAGE 241

1.

Formal Parameters	a	b	c
	25	5	−5
Function Arguments	x	sqrt(x)	x−30
	25	5	−5

2. total = 2

PRACTICE! PAGE 247

1. valid
   before: x [1] y [3]
   after: x [3] y [1]

2. invalid: cannot pass constant to reference parameter

3. invalid: cannot pass expression ($y + 5$) to reference parameter

4. error: Test this on your system.

5. output:
   0
   2

PRACTICE! PAGE 273

1. No.

2. Yes. A default constructor has been defined for the Point class.

3. No. xCoord is private.

4. Yes. getY() is a public method.

5. Yes. The subtraction operator has been overloaded for the Point class and returns the distance between p1 and p2.

6. Method Implementation:

```
void Point::setXY(double xVal, double yVal)
{
    xCoord = xVal;
    yCoord = yVal;
}
```

Chapter 7

PRACTICE! PAGE 315

1. x [−5] [4] [3] [0] [0] [0] [0] [0] [0] [0]

2. letters [a] [b] [c]

3. z [?] [−5.5] [5.5] [5.5]

4. time [−0.4] [−0.3] [−0.2] [−0.1] [0] [0.1] [0.2] [0.3] [0.4]

5. arr[0] is 0
   arr[1] is 3
   arr[2] is 6
   arr[3] is 9
   arr[4] is 12

PRACTICE! PAGE 319

1. output:
   3 8
   15 21
   30 41

2. output:
   8 30

PRACTICE! PAGE 324

1. 9.8

2. 9.8

3. 3.2

4. 1.5

PRACTICE! PAGE 334

1. 9.0

2. 6.0

3. 5.36

4. 2.32

5. 2.5

6. 5.75

PRACTICE! PAGE 354

1. The Cheese

2. The mice, Cheese

3. The mice, Sniff and Scurry, had only simple brains.

Chapter 8

PRACTICE! PAGE 385

1.

1	0
2	0	a
3	0

2.

1	2	3
4	5	6	b
0	0	0

3.

1	2	3	4
0	3	0	6	c
8	3	−6	−1

4.

1	2	3	0
3	0	6	3	d
−6	−1	0	0

PRACTICE! PAGE 388

1.

1
4
6

2.

5	2
−2	3
0	0
0	0
0	0
0	0

3.

0	0	0	0
0	0	0	0
0	0	0	0
0	0	0	0

4.

1	0	0
0	1	0
0	0	1

5.

0	1	2	3	0
1	2	3	4	0
2	3	4	5	0
3	4	5	6	0
4	5	6	7	0

6.

1	−1	1	−1	1
1	−1	1	−1	1
1	−1	1	−1	1
1	−1	1	−1	1
1	−1	1	−1	1

PRACTICE! PAGE 391

    1. 9

    2. 4

    3. −6

    4. 3

PRACTICE! PAGE 395

    1. 13

    2. 2

    3. 18

    4. 22

PRACTICE! PAGE 406

1. r ⬚3⬚ c ⬚5⬚

?	?	?	?	?
?	?	?	?	?
?	?	?	?	?

2. Series

?	?	?	?
?	?	?	?
?	?	?	?
?	?	?	?

3.
```
double maxColumnVal(vector<vector<double> > v, int colNum)
{
    //Preconditions:  The vector v has at least colNum+1
    //                columns of data

    double largeVal = v[0][0];
    int rowSize = v.size();
    for(int i=0; i<rowSize; ++i)
    {
      if(v[i][colNum] > largeVal)
      {
        largeVal = v[i][colNum];
      }
    }
    return largeVal;
}
```

4.
```
double maxRowVal(vector<vector<double> > v, int rowNum)
{
    //Preconditions:  The vector v has at least rowNum+1
    //        rows of data
    double smallVal = v[0][0];
    int colSize = v[rowNum].size();
```

```
      for(int i=0; i<colSize; ++i)
      {
        if(v[rowNum][i] < smallVal)
        {
          smallVal = v[rowNum][i];
        }
      }
      return smallVal;
    }
```

PRACTICE! PAGE 411

1. −8

2.
5	−1	3
3	−3	2

3.
−5	9
1	−5
−6	6

4.
−2	−2	4
7	−9	10

5.
8	−24	32
−12	20	−24
14	−18	20

PRACTICE! PAGE 418

1. $x = 2, y = 1$
2. $x = 3, y = -1, z = 2$

Chapter 9

PRACTICE! PAGE 441

1. a | 1 |
   b | 2 |
      ↑
   prt | | |

2. a | 2 |
   b | 2 |
      ↑
   prt | | |

3. a [1]
   b [5]
   c [1]

   prt [↑]

4. a [2]
   b [2]
   c [2]

   prt [↑]

PRACTICE! PAGE 444

1. x   [15.6]

   prt_2 [↑]

   y   [31.2]

   prt_1 [↑]

2. x   [−8]

   prt_2 [↑]

   w   [10]

3.   ptr_2 [↓]

   x [2|4|6|8|3]

   ptr_3 [↑] ptr_1 [↖]

4.   w [?|?|?|?]

   first_ptr [↑]   [↑] last_ptr

PRACTICE! PAGE 446

g[0] [2] ←[ ] prt1
g[1] [4]
g[2] [5]
g[3] [8] ←[ ] prt2
g[4] [10]
g[5] [32]
g[6] [78]

1. 2
2. 4
3. 3
4. 32
5. 2
6. 8
7. 4
8. 32

PRACTICE! PAGE 453

1. valid

2. not valid (jptr is const)

3. not valid (can't use cptr to modify object)

4. not valid (can't use cptr to modify object)

5. valid

6. valid

PRACTICE! PAGE 467

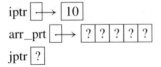

1. 10 10
   two hex address
   two garbage values

2. hex address
   0 1 2 3
   hex address plus 16 (assuming 4-byte integers)
   ???? Explain your output.

3. two hex addresses
   0 2
   two hex addresses? Explain.

Chapter 10

PRACTICE! PAGE 501

1.
```
pixel pixel::operator/(pixel p1)
{
   pixel temp;
   temp.red = red/p1.red;
   temp.green = green/p1.green;
   temp.blue = blue/p1.blue;
   return temp;
}
```

2.
```
bool pixel::operator==(pixel p1)
{
   if( red==p1.red &&
       green==p1.green&&
       blue==p1.blue )
     return true;
   return false;
}
```

PRACTICE! PAGE 502

1.
```
pixel operator*(pixel p1, pixel p2)
{
   pixel temp;
   temp.red = p1.red*p2.red;
   temp.green = p1.green*p2.green;
   temp.blue =p1.blue*p2.blue;
   return temp;
}
```

2.
```
pixel operator/(pixel p1, pixel p2)
{
   pixel temp;
   temp.red = p1.red/p2.red;
   temp.green = p1.green/p2.green;
   temp.blue =p1.blue/p2.blue;
   return temp;
}
```

3.
```
pixel operator-(pixel p1, pixel p2)
{
   pixel temp;
   temp.red = p1.red-p2.red;
   temp.green = p1.green-p2.green;
   temp.blue =p1.blue-p2.blue;
   return temp;
}
```

PRACTICE! PAGE 529

1. 0

2. 0

3. 5

4. 0xbffffb74, 0, 0

PRACTICE! PAGE 553

1. Fixed point at: (1,2)
   Width: 4
   Height: 4
   Depth: 4 Fixed point at: (1,2)
   Width: 4
   Height: 4
   Depth: 4

2. Fixed point at: (1,2)
   Width: 4
   Height: 4

3. Fixed point at: (0,0)
   Width: 5
   Height: 5
   Fixed point at: (0,0)
   Width: 5
   Height: 5

Index

A

Abbreviated assignment operators, 60–61
ABC (Atanasoff Berry Computer), 6
Abstraction, 226, 297. *See also* Data
    abstraction
Accessor methods, 268–269
Accumulator, 11
`acos(x)`, 78
`acosh(x)`, 80
`acsch(x)`, 80
Actual parameters, 239. *See also*
    Function arguments
Ada, 6
Addition, matrix, 409–410
Addresses, 242
    pointers and, 435–436
    space, 16
Address operator &, 436–438
Advanced composite materials design, 8,
    274–279
Aggregate output operations, on arrays,
    317
Aircraft
    center of gravity calculation, 250–254
    turboprops, 34, 81
    unducted fan problem, 81–82, 97, 98
Algorithms, 28
Algorithm development
    advanced composite materials design,
        276–279
    alternative solutions evaluated, 99
    card deck probabilities calculation
        program, 370–373
    center of gravity calculation, 251–253
    color image processing, 516–519
    concordance of text file, 478–482
    electrical circuit analysis, 420–424
    ENSO data, 454–456
    freezing temperature of seawater,
        116–118
    GPS, 154–156
    html file modification, 199–201
    hurricane categories, 326–329
    instrumentation reliability, 262–265
    IPD, 557–562
    ozone measurements, 214–216
    as problem-solving methodology step,
        28–29
    real roots of cubic polynomial,
        286–288
    repetition structures, 139–140

seismic event detection, 463–466
selection structures, 95–97
speech signal analysis, 337–341
straight-line distance between two
    points in a plane, 28–29
terrain navigation, 400–402
top-down design, 95–97
tsunami warning systems, 348–351
velocity computation, 83–84
weather balloons, 164–166
ALU (Arithmetic logic unit), 11–12
American National Standards Institute
    (ANSI), 23, 44–45
Analytical Engine, 3–5, 11, 16
Analyzing data, 10
And, logical operator, 100
ANSI. *See* American National Standards
    Institute
Application satellites, 8
Architectural Desktop, 13
Arguments. *See* Function arguments
Arithmetic logic unit (ALU), 11–12
Arithmetic operators, 54–55
    `Point` class and, 129–130
    precedence, 56–58, 60, 104
Arrays. *See also* One-dimensional arrays;
    Two-dimensional arrays
    defined, 310, 426
    dynamically allocated, 458–460
    elements, pointers to, 444–453
    higher-dimensional, 424–426
    maximum size of, 318
    subarrays, 394–395
Artificial intelligence, 488
`asech(x)`, 80
`asin(x)`, 78
`asinh(x)`, 80
Assembly language, 14
Assignment operators, 52–54, 60–61
Assignment statements, 52, 53
Associativity, 56, 60, 103–104
`atan(x)`, 78
`atan2(y,x)`, 78
Atanasoff Berry Computer (ABC), 6
`atanh(x)`, 80
Atmosphere
    ENSO data, 434, 453–456
    global climate change, 180
    layers around earth, 212
    Martian, 8
    NOAA, 308, 346

ozone measurements, 211–217
weather balloons, 138, 163–168,
    196–198
weather patterns, 434
weather prediction, 9, 180
AutoCAD, 13
Automatic storage class, 248
Average value, 331

B

Babbage, Charles, 3, 4, 5, 6
`back()`, 358
Back substitution, 417
`badbit`, 203, 204
Base ten, 16, 17, 18, 19, 20, 21, 22
Base two, 3, 16, 18, 19, 23
Base type, 438, 542
`begin()`, 358
Binary ANSI representation, 23,
    44–45
Binary codes, 44
Binary language, 14
Binary numbers, 17–18
Binary operators, 54
Binary search, 345–346
Binary search tree, 530–532
`BinaryTree` class, 524–525,
    532–541
Binary trees, 524–535
Bit, 12
Bitmap, 514
Bit masks, 508
Bitwise operators, 510–513
Blanks, 99
Block of code, 37
`bool bad()`, 204
Boolean data type, 44
`bool eof()`, 204
`bool fail()`, 204
`bool good()`, 204
Braces, 105, 109, 233, 384
Brackets, 384
`break` statement, 120, 157–158
Brighten images, 495
Bugs, 15
Buoys, DART, 308
Bus error, 313
Byron, Ada, 5–6
Bytes, 16